Selected Titles in This Series

29 **Doron A. Peled, Vaughan R. Pratt, and Gerard J. Holzmann, Editors,** Partial Order Methods in Verification

28 **Larry Finkelstein and William M. Kantor, Editors,** Groups and Computation II

27 **Richard J. Lipton and Eric B. Baum, Editors,** DNA Based Computers

26 **David S. Johnson and Michael A. Trick, Editors,** Cliques, Coloring, and Satisfiability: Second DIMACS Implementation Challenge

25 **Gilbert Baumslag, David Epstein, Robert Gilman, Hamish Short, and Charles Sims, Editors,** Geometric and Computational Perspectives on Infinite Groups

24 **Louis J. Billera, Curtis Greene, Rodica Simion, and Richard P. Stanley, Editors,** Formal Power Series and Algebraic Combinatorics/Séries formelles et combinatoire algébrique, 1994

23 **Panos M. Pardalos, David I. Shalloway, and Guoliang Xue, Editors,** Global Minimization of Nonconvex Energy Functions: Molecular Conformation and Protein Folding

22 **Panos M. Pardalos, Mauricio G. C. Resende, and K. G. Ramakrishnan, Editors,** Parallel Processing of Discrete Optimization Problems

21 **D. Frank Hsu, Arnold L. Rosenberg, and Dominique Sotteau, Editors,** Interconnection Networks and Mapping and Scheduling Parallel Computations

20 **William Cook, László Lovász, and Paul Seymour, Editors,** Combinatorial Optimization

19 **Ingemar J. Cox, Pierre Hansen, and Bela Julesz, Editors,** Partitioning Data Sets

18 **Guy E. Blelloch, K. Mani Chandy, and Suresh Jagannathan, Editors,** Specification of Parallel Algorithms

17 **Eric Sven Ristad, Editor,** Language Computations

16 **Panos M. Pardalos and Henry Wolkowicz, Editors,** Quadratic Assignment and Related Problems

15 **Nathaniel Dean and Gregory E. Shannon, Editors,** Computational Support for Discrete Mathematics

14 **Robert Calderbank, G. David Forney, Jr., and Nader Moayeri, Editors,** Coding and Quantization: DIMACS/IEEE Workshop

13 **Jin-Yi Cai, Editor,** Advances in Computational Complexity Theory

12 **David S. Johnson and Catherine C. McGeoch, Editors,** Network Flows and Matching: First DIMACS Implementation Challenge

11 **Larry Finkelstein and William M. Kantor, Editors,** Groups and Computation

10 **Joel Friedman, Editor,** Expanding Graphs

9 **William T. Trotter, Editor,** Planar Graphs

8 **Simon Gindikin, Editor,** Mathematical Methods of Analysis of Biopolymer Sequences

7 **Lyle A. McGeoch and Daniel D. Sleator, Editors,** On-Line Algorithms

6 **Jacob E. Goodman, Richard Pollack, and William Steiger, Editors,** Discrete and Computational Geometry: Papers from the DIMACS Special Year

5 **Frank Hwang, Fred Roberts, and Clyde Monma, Editors,** Reliability of Computer and Communication Networks

4 **Peter Gritzmann and Bernd Sturmfels, Editors,** Applied Geometry and Discrete Mathematics, The Victor Klee Festschrift

3 **E. M. Clarke and R. P. Kurshan, Editors,** Computer-Aided Verification '90

2 **Joan Feigenbaum and Michael Merritt, Editors,** Distributed Computing and Cryptography

1 **William Cook and Paul D. Seymour, Editors,** Polyhedral Combinatorics

Partial Order Methods in Verification

DIMACS

Series in Discrete Mathematics
and Theoretical Computer Science

Volume 29

Partial Order Methods in Verification

DIMACS Workshop
July 24–26, 1996

Doron A. Peled
Vaughan R. Pratt
Gerard J. Holzmann
Editors

NSF Science and Technology Center
in Discrete Mathematics and Theoretical Computer Science
A consortium of Rutgers University, Princeton University,
AT&T Labs, Bell Labs, and Bellcore

American Mathematical Society

This DIMACS volume contains papers presented at the Workshop on Partial Order Methods in Verification (POMIV '96) and a lively e-mail debate, which took place between October 21 and November 19, 1990. POMIV '96 was held at DIMACS on July 24–26, 1996.

1991 *Mathematics Subject Classification.* Primary 68Q10, 68Q45, 68Q55, 68Q60.

Library of Congress Cataloging-in-Publication Data

Workshop on Partial Order Methods in Verification (1996 : Princeton University)

Partial order methods in verification : Workshop on Partial Order Methods in Verification, July 24–26, 1996, Princeton University / Doron Peled, Vaughan Pratt, Gerard J. Holzmann, editors.

p. cm. — (DIMACS series in discrete mathematics and theoretical computer science, ISSN 1052-1798 ; v. 29)

Includes bibliographical references.

ISBN 0-8218-0579-7

1. Electronic data processing—Distributed processing—Congresses. 2. Computer software—Verification—Congresses. I. Peled, Doron, 1962– . II. Pratt, Vaughan R. III. Holzmann, Gerard J. IV. Title. V. Series.

QA76.9.D5W665 1996

005.2′76—dc21

96-48739

CIP

---

10 9 8 7 6 5 4 3 2 1   02 01 00 99 98 97

Contents

Foreword

POMIV'96, the Workshop on Partial Order Methods in Verification, was held at DIMACS in July 1996 as part of the DIMACS 1995–1996 Special Year on Logic and Algorithms. We would like to thank the organizers of the Workshop, Doron Peled, Vaughan Pratt, and Gerard Holtzman, for their tireless and fruitful efforts to organize the program and encourage the participation and interaction of researchers with a variety of views and approaches to verification.

The Workshop played an important role in the broader Special Year program which focused on computer aided verification, finite models, and proof complexity. The Special Year encouraged collaborations among very different research communities and this volume records one of many workshops in which this was achieved. We extend our thanks to Eric Allender, Robert Kurshan, and Moshe Vardi for their work over many months as Special Year organizers.

DIMACS gratefully acknowledges the generous support that makes these programs possible. The National Science Foundation, through its Science and Technology Center program, the New Jersey Commission on Science and Technology, DIMACS partners at Rutgers, Princeton, AT&T Labs, Bell Labs, and Bellcore generously supported the Special Year. Additional funding from AT&T, Lucent Technologies, and the Office of Naval Research was essential to this Workshop and allowed broader participation from scientists worldwide.

Fred S. Roberts
Director

Bernard Chazelle
Co-Director for Princeton

Stephen R. Mahaney
Associate Director

DIMACS Series in Discrete Mathematics
and Theoretical Computer Science
Volume **29**, 1997

Preface

Research in the last few decades on the connection between partial order semantics and interleaving semantics has resulted in a class of new verification techniques for distributed systems that are beginning to prove themselves to be of great practical value in routine industrial applications of formal verification techniques.

Much of the new work in this area is being pursued by people from quite distinct fields who rarely have an opportunity to meet and exchange ideas directly. These groups include, for instance, verification tool builders, logicians, semantic researchers, and process algebra specialists. The aim of the Workshop was to bring together researchers from these different disciplines.

The Workshop on Partial Order Methods in Verification, POMIV'96, was held during July 24–26, 1996, in the Computer Science Department of Princeton University, New Jersey.

The organizers invited twenty-five researchers representing different areas, including automata and formal languages, category theory, concurrency theory, logic, process algebra, program semantics, specification and verification, topology and trace theory. The Workshop focused on the following three main themes:

- Experience with the application of verification methods and tools based on partial order semantics and partial order reduction techniques.
- Formal description techniques, logics and algebras, based on partial orders.
- Formal specification methods where partial order semantics are more natural than interleaving semantics.

The talks in the Workshop focused on both the practical and the theoretical aspects of using partial order models.

This proceedings volume includes eighteen papers presented at POMIV'96. It also contains a lively e-mail debate, taking place between October 21 and November 19, 1990, via the concurrency mailing list, moderated at that time by Albert Meyer. It discusses the importance of the partial order dichotomy in modeling concurrency.

Some of the papers in this volume discuss partial order based semantic models such as event structures, pomsets, and traces. These permit expression of the causality relation between the events executed in a concurrent system. Their use allows the phenomena of concurrency and nondeterminism to be distinguished, an important distinction not drawn by interleaved semantics. Various specification formalisms allow the expression of properties based on partial order semantics, e.g., using classical and temporal logics, process algebras, or special automata.

The study of formalisms over partial orders has grown into an interesting research field of its own. Some of the papers presented in the conference focused on formal language research of trace theory, decision algorithms that are beneficial for automatic verification of concurrent programs, and a topological study of families of such languages and their connection with program specification. Such models were studied also with respect to automata theory, category theory and topology.

Various specification languages, such as classical logics (e.g., first and second order monadic logics), are used to express properties over partial order structures. Several papers also focused on new temporal logics designed for partial order models, aimed at specifying the behavior of concurrent programs. Other works study the issues of expressiveness and axiomatizability of such formalisms.

Automated verification tools based on automata theory and partial order reduction techniques are beginning to gain acceptance as effective tools for distributed system design. The success of partial order techniques in the domain of software verification may be compared to the success of BDDs (binary decision diagrams) in the domain of hardware verification. They are used to alleviate the state space explosion in automatically verifying concurrent programs. Unlike many other problem domains, any improvement in our understanding of this area can translate almost immediately into improvements of industrial practice.

Using partial order reduction techniques, it has become possible to analyze larger problem sizes, which did not lend themselves to automatic verification before. The simplicity of the principles behind these methods suggests that they can be integrated into any state-based automatic verification tool. Such practical methods have already been integrated into various model-checking tools, allowing more efficient checking of bigger systems. New results, reported in this volume, show how such methods can preserve specifications given in various formalisms, including linear and branching temporal logic properties and various process algebras.

The talks given in the Workshop included many new results and state-of-the-art techniques. We expect this volume to be an important resource on research done in the area of modeling, specifying, and verifying concurrent systems in general, and the theory of partial orders in formal methods in particular.

The Workshop included two social events: a reception, held in the Prospect Gardens building at Princeton University on July 23rd, and a Workshop dinner, held at the computer science building on July 25th. Pictures taken at the Workshop dinner can be found in the Internet Web page:

http://boole.stanford.edu/pomiv.html

POMIV'96 was sponsored by the ONR (Office of Naval Research), AT&T, and Lucent Technologies. It was run under the Special Year on Logic and Algorithms (SYLA), organized by DIMACS—Center for Discrete Mathematics and Computer Science.

Local arrangements were made by Sandy Barbu of the Computer Science Department, Princeton University, Princeton, New Jersey.

The organizers would like to thank Sandy for her hard work in helping to arrange this event. We would like to thank the invited speakers, the participants, and the sponsors.

Rationale for Concurrent Verification and Partial Orders

The Problem. Enhancing the reliability of concurrent systems is an increasingly important and challenging problem for information technology today. The problem is more serious than for sequential systems for two reasons. First, the possible interactions in a computer network are far more complex than for a traditional stand-alone sequential program. Second, one little bug may ruin the whole day not just of an individual computer user but an entire community, many of whom need not even be directly involved with computers.

With increasing system complexity, whether concurrent or sequential, come increasing costs of system failure. The widespread outage of the telephone system on the U.S. east coast in January 1991 dramatically testified to the expensive havoc that one tiny programming error could wreak, as did the $475 million Pentium chip division bug, and the recent $5 billion crash of the Ariane 5 rocket.

Expectations. It is unreasonable to expect to eliminate all errors, even catastrophic ones, but any improvements in software technology that will reduce their frequency and severity are well worth the effort. If each $100 million invested in enhanced system reliability avoided one billion-dollar catastrophe, the rate of return on this investment would be a thousand percent even without counting the savings from the many lesser bugs that would also have been avoided.

Given the magnitude of the software reliability problem, the software industry should not put all its eggs in one basket, but instead aggressively explore all reasonable alternatives.

The Verification Option. One alternative that has strong support from a large segment of the software engineering community is verification, the application of logic to the efficient search of the entire space of possible behaviors. No tool can hope for perfection, and logic is no exception. What logic accomplishes is not the infallibility popularly attributed to it, but rather the efficient search of combinatorially large or even infinite state spaces for all the known types of bugs in a practical amount of time. No methodology comes near the efficacy of logic in that role, particularly in the case of infinite search spaces where mathematical induction permits seeking out in finite time every nook and cranny that may hide a known type of bug.

One weakness of logic is that it cannot guarantee to recognize bugs of a kind not anticipated by the axioms of the logical system. For this and other reasons logic should be viewed as just one player on a team whose overall goal is improved reliability. Logic has proved a valuable player in this role on many documented occasions, fully justifying its continued support and growth.

Logic works best when understood as a discipline for manipulating not just symbols (proof theory) but also facts about some world (model theory). To the latter end one develops a mathematical model of that world, and evaluates the soundness of the proof system relative to that model. The model must be faithful to the world, yet simple enough to permit the soundness of the logic to be assessed.

What is concurrency? A burning problem in program verification today is how to model the world of concurrent systems. The excellent models of sequential behavior that have evolved during the past thirty years of sequential program verification do not adequately reflect the nature of a concurrent universe. Only when one imagines each and every event in the universe lining up to take its turn can one confidently apply any of the sequential models. A variety of "testing scenarios" reveals situations where sequential models yield a visibly wrong answer and hence an unsound logic. These scenarios have spurred interest in *true concurrency* as it has come to be called; namely, in modeling concurrency in a way that is faithful to all currently understood modes of interaction of system components, particularly those beyond the reach of sequential models.

Two concurrency models. There are two basic approaches to true concurrency: state based and event based. The state-based approach as the standard model for sequential behavior has the advantage of familiarity. In this model, the passage from sequential to concurrent behavior is accompanied by an increase in structural complexity of the transition system. The basic additional structure required is a higher-dimensional filling in of the spaces between the "commuting squares" characteristic of the state diagrams of concurrent systems. While this structure is most simply realized directly by geometric means, a number of more or less equivalent ways of achieving essentially the same effects have been proposed by the concurrency community in the past decade or so.

The event-based approach models behavior in terms of occurrence of events. A system, or any of its components, is modeled as the set of all events the system is capable of performing, usually infinite in practice. Pure concurrency, with no synchronous behavior, interference, or other interaction, is simply the set of events itself with no additional structure. The many ways in which system components can interact, whether cooperating synchronously (communication), competing for shared resources that forbid simultaneous access (mutual exclusion), or inhibiting one another's occurrence altogether (conflict), are modeled by equipping the event set with structure consisting of constraints formally expressing those interactions. Note the change in direction here: with states structure increases with increasing *independence* while with events it increases with increasing *interaction*, the opposite of independence.

Just as physics needs both waves and particles to model the physical universe, so does computer science need both state-based and event-based models of true concurrency.

Partial Orders. The focus of this Workshop is on the concurrent structures supporting the event-based approach, the basic such structure being the partial order. Total order semantics views each execution of a concurrent system as a sequence of events, where actions executed concurrently appear according to some arbitrary order. Partial order semantics allows events to appear either ordered or unordered, disallowing causality cycles, e.g., action A happens before action B, which happens before action C, which happens before A.

Total order semantics, also called *interleaving semantics*, is traditionally considered easier to work with as it lends itself to simple representations, e.g., with finite state machines. Until recently partial order semantics had not been widely applied in practical verification due to a lack of maturity in the methodology of its use and a shortage of suitable tools for verification based on partial orders.

Continuing research into partial order semantics has improved this situation in recent years, and the partial order approach can now reasonably be looked to as a viable extension of total order semantics. Since total orders are a special case of partial orders, the move to the latter has freed verification system builders to employ new methods without having to abandon those sequential methods that have proved useful in concurrent verification. These new methods are now starting to show worthwhile efficiency gains in the exploration of state spaces.

Doron Peled, Vaughan Pratt, Gerard Holzmann
Murray Hill, NJ and Palo Alto, CA.

DIMACS Series in Discrete Mathematics
and Theoretical Computer Science
Volume **29**, 1997

Prefix function view of states and events

Antoni Mazurkiewicz*
Institute of Computer Science of PAS
Ordona 21, 01-237 **Warsaw**, Poland
amaz@ipipan.waw.pl

Abstract

Prefix functions are thought as a unifying concept for different ways of looking at discrete processes. The idea of prefix function consists in establishing relations between events and states; different types of such relations correspond to different ways of understanding states being reached in the course of computation. This concept covers such concurrent systems description tools as finite state automata, trees, Petri Nets, traces, occurring graphs, vector languages, multi-trees and similar. Special attention is paid to operations of contraction and synchronization on prefix functions.

Keywords: events; states; discrete processes; concurrency.

1 Introduction

The purpose of the present paper is to situate trace calculus within a broader context of concurrency description tools. Trace theory turns out to be useful for describing and analysing some concurrency phenomena because of its similarity to the well established and familiar theory of automata and formal languages on one hand and of its ability to capture such properties of concurrent processes as partiality of event occurrences ordering. However, trace theory has succeded only in a limited family of concurrent systems that can roughly be compared with cooperating sequential processes; to find its sound extension suitable for more general models is then of primary interest. To this end, it seems worthwhile to look closier at the basic concepts of trace theory, identify those that can be generalized, and try to adapt them to a broader context.

Traces over an alphabet (consisting of events names) equipped with a dependency relation (a symmetric and reflexive binary relation in it) arise by identification

1991 *Mathematics Subject Classification.* Primary 68Q10, 68Q90, 68Q45.
*partially supported by grant KBN 8T11C 029 08

all strings over the alphabet that differ only by order of two consecutive not dependent symbols; the result of such an identification is a trace, representing an action composed of a number of events, some of them occurring independently of other, or (equivalently) a system state reached after occurring these events. In trace theory dependency relation defining the way of state identification is fixed for the whole modelled system; it causes mentioned above limitations of the trace usage. In this paper the state identification is not restricted to that induced by a dependency relation; instead, it is considered as a tool that can be tailored to current needs of system verification: state equivalence useful for proving some eventualities of system behaviour may be different from that needed for proving some system invariants. In a system specification or verification, some states can be treated as equivalent, restricting in this way the number of cases to be analysed; in case of concurrent systems this restriction may be quite serious.

Labelled graphs, like Pratt's pomsets [9], or labelled posets, indicating causal relationships of (named) events offer another possibility of concurrent process descriptions. They can be related to strings of symbols as follows: for each string w over an alphabet of events, or elementary actions, say A, denote by $\gamma(w)$ the graph defined recursively: $\gamma(\epsilon)$ is the empty graph, $\gamma(wa)$ arises from the graph $\gamma(w)$ by adding to it a new node labelled with symbol a and new arcs leading to it from all vertices of $\gamma(w)$ labelled with symbols that a causally depends on. Thus, for any prefix-closed language L representing sequences of actions of a concurrent process, function defined on L assigning to each $w \in L$ the graph $\gamma(w)$ constructed as explained above can be viewed as a description of the process. In this case states of a process are determined by initial pieces of causally ordered histories.

Yet another view on states of a process takes into account only the 'future' of a process after its partial execution. In this case it does not matter which is the history of the process reaching some point, but only which are the possibilities of its continuation. This approach resembles that of automata theory; number of states in a process is equal to the number of different continuations of the process; it it is finite, then the number of states is finite.

Looking at processes as activities of a number of sequentially acting agents, as in Hoare language [3] with the Shields theoretical background [12], it is quite natural to define concurrent process as a composition of sequential processes. This approach looks very promising for at least two reasons: first, the theory of sequential processes is well elaborated and established, the second, it uses directly compositionality methods that are especially valuable in dealing with multiagent systems. However, composition used in this approach concernes only sequential processes, not accepting cases where single agents can act in nonsequential way; applying basic concepts of this approach one can expect a perfect tool for process descriptions.

Thus, the answer what is the 'real' state of a process depends on questions concerning the process itself. Proving some eventualities that will occur during a process run, the notion of a state may be different from that needed for proving some invariant properties or estimating the time limit of the process duration. Therefore, in this paper the notion of a state is not determined. The nature of states is irrelevant for the present purposes; it is convenient to abstract from their specific properties, but to concentrate only on the way they are reached by the system. It leads to the concept of prefix functions, discussed through the paper.

The standard mathematical notation is used in the paper. The set of all integers is denoted by $\mathbf{Z}$, and the set of all non-negative integers by $\mathbf{N}$. If f is a function, $D(f)$ denotes the domain of f and $R(f)$ the range of f. Symbol $f : A \longrightarrow B$ is used to indicate that f is a function with domain A and range contained in B. If $R(f) = B$, f is said to be *onto* B; a one-to-one function is a bijection. If $f : A \longrightarrow B, g : B \longrightarrow C$, then $fg : A \longrightarrow C$ denotes the composition of f with g defined by $fg(x) = g(f(x))$ for all $x \in A$.

Any finite set (of symbols) is an alphabet; A^* is the set of all strings over A, i.e. finite sequences of symbols in A, including ϵ, the empty string. Any subset of A^* is called a language over A. If w is a string, A is an arbitrary alphabet, then the projection $\pi_A(w)$ of w onto A is a string arising from w by erasing in w all symbols not in A; if L is a language, $\pi_A(L)$ is the set of projections of all strings in L onto A. If $u, v \in A^*$, then uv is the concatenation of strings u, v; string u is a prefix of string w, if there exists string v with $w = uv$. Clearly, relation "to be a prefix of" is a (partial) ordering relation in the set of all strings. Language is prefix closed, if together with a string it contains all prefixes of this string. The *kernel* of language L is the greatest prefix-closed language $\mathrm{ker}(L)$ contained in L; the *prefix closure* of language L is the least prefix closed language $\mathrm{Pref}(L)$ containing L. For any string w and symbol a, the number of occurrences of a in w is denoted by $w(a)$. For any language L and any string w, the *continuation* of w in L is the set $\theta(L, w) = \{u \mid wu \in L\}$.

2 Algebraic tools.

The discrete processes considered here are assumed to be composed of finite or infinite number of event occurrences; the set of events, called here alphabet, is assumed to be finite. In order to build processes of events a number of algebraic means has been applied; below some of them are briefly presented. To make possible their comparison the alphabet A of events is fixed for what follows.

Monoid of strings. Free monoid generated by alphabet A, i.e. the algebra $(A^*, \circ, \epsilon)$ with composition (concatenation) $\circ$ and the empty string ϵ as the neutral element, called the monoid of strings over A, is the basic algebra serving in the sequel for defining others. This monoid will be denoted by $S(A)$ in the sequel.By the definition of freeness, for any other monoid $(X, \circ, \mathbf{1})$ and any mapping $f : A \longrightarrow X$ there exists the unique extension $f^* : A^* \longrightarrow X$ of f such that

$$f^*(\epsilon) = \mathbf{1}, f^*(ua) = f^*(u) \circ f(a).$$

As it has been mentioned above, prefixes of any string are linearly ordered.

Monoid of traces. Let $D \subseteq A^2$ be a symmetric and reflexive relation, called *dependency* relation in A and let $I_D = A^2 - D$; symbols a, b are called *dependent*, if $(a, b) \in D$, and *independent* otherwise. Let $\equiv_D$ be the least congruence in monoid $S(A)$ such that

$$ab \equiv_D ba \Leftrightarrow (a, b) \in I_D.$$

Then the quotient monoid $S(A)/\equiv_D$ denoted by $T(D)$ is called the trace monoid over D and its elements *traces* over D (observe that the relation D, as reflexive, determines alphabet A). By definition of quotient algebras, $T(D)$ arises from $S(A)$ by identifying strings that differ only by swapping over some adjacent occurrences of independent symbols. As usual, $[w]_D$ denotes the equivalence class of string w w.r. to the congruence $\equiv_D$ (the trace determined by w); symbol $[\ ]_D$ denotes also the homomorphism $\phi : S(A) \longrightarrow T(D)$ such that $\phi(w) = [w]_D$. Symbol $T(D)$ will also denote the base set of the monoid of traces over D.

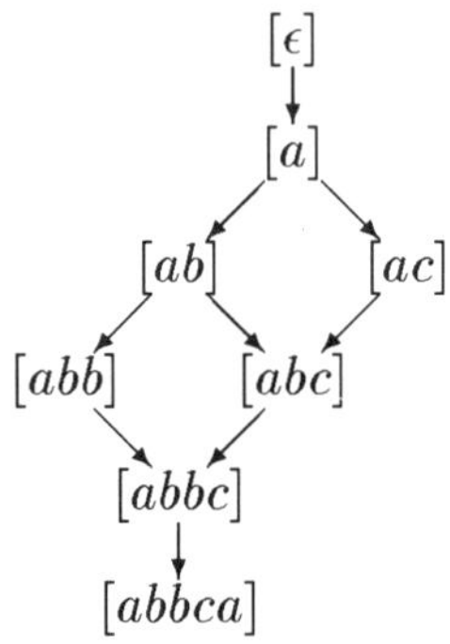

Figure 1: The prefix structure of $[abbca]_D$ for $D = \{a, b\}^2 \cup \{a, c\}^2$.

By definition we have $[u]_D[w]_D = [uw]_D$ for all $u, w \in A^*$; call trace $[u]_D$ a prefix of trace $[w]_D$, if $[u]_D[v]_D = [w]_D$ for some trace $[v]_D$. In contrast to $S(A)$, the set of prefixes of a trace is ordered by the prefix relation only partially, as it is shown in Fig.1.

A subset P of $T(D)$ is *confluent*, if for each traces $t', t'' \in P$ there is a trace $t \in P$ such that t' as well as t'' are prefixes of t.

Shields algebras. Let $\mathbf{A} = (A_1, A_2, \ldots, A_N)$ be a tuple of alphabets such that $A = \bigcup_{i=1}^{N} A_i$ and let $D = \bigcup_{i=1}^{N} A_i^2$; clearly, D is a dependency relation in A. Let

$$P(\mathbf{A}) = \prod_{i=1}^{N} S(A_i)$$

be the product of monoids $S(A_1), S(A_2), \ldots, S(A_N)$, where $S(A_i) = (A_i^*, \circ, \epsilon)$; elements of this monoid, i.e. tuples belonging to

$$A_1^* \times A_2^* \times \cdots \times A_N^*$$

are called *string vectors*. Let π denotes the homomorphism of $S(A)$ to $P(\mathbf{A})$, such that

$$\pi(w) = (\pi_1(w), \pi_2(w), \ldots, \pi_N(w)),$$

where $\pi_i(w)$ denotes the projection of w onto A_i, for each $i = 1, 2, \ldots, N$ and each $w \in A^*$. The Shields algebra over $\mathbf{A}$ is the image of $S(A)$ given by π; this image, denoted here by $V(\mathbf{A})$, is a subalgebra of $P(\mathbf{A})$, generated by the set $\mathbf{A}_0$:

$$\mathbf{A}_0 = \{\pi(a) \mid a \in A\}.$$

Images of prefix-closed languages over A given by π ('prefix-closed' subsets of $S(\mathbf{A})$) are called here Shields languages. String vectors are ordered by the prefix relation defined pointwise: vector $(u_1, u_2, \ldots, u_N)$ is a prefix of vector $(w_1, w_2, \ldots, w_N)$, if u_i is a prefix of w_i for all $i = 1, 2, \ldots, N$.

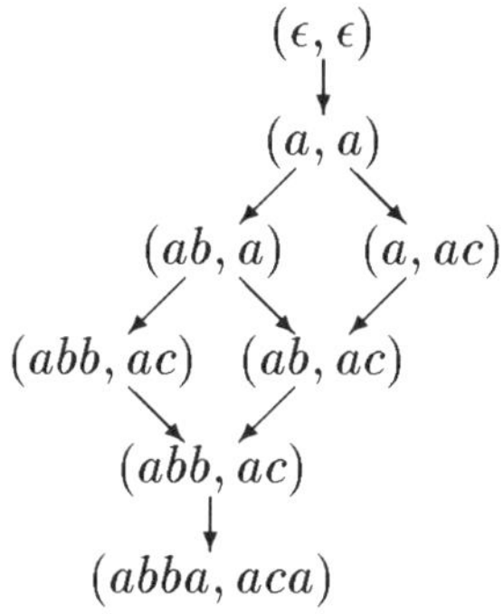

Figure 2: The prefix structure of string vector $(abba, aca)$ for $\mathbf{A} = (\{a, b\}, \{a, c\})$.

The concept of the monoid of string vectors as formulated above originates in papers of M.W. Shields [12]. His main idea was to represent non-sequential processes by a collection of individual histories of concurrently running components; an individual history is a string of events concerning only one component, and the global history is a collection of individual ones. This approach, appealing directly to the intuitive meaning of parallel processing, is particularly well suited to CSP-like systems [3] where individual components run independently of each other, with one exception: an event concerning a number of (in CSP at most two) components can occur only coincidently in all these components ('handshaking' or 'rendez-vous' synchronization principle). The presentation and the terminology used here have been adjusted to the present purposes and differ from those of the author.

Dependence graphs monoid. Let D be a dependency relation in A. Dependence graphs over D (or d-graphs for short) are finite, oriented, acyclic graphs with nodes labelled with symbols from A in such a way that two nodes of a d-graph are connected with an arc if and only if they are different and labelled with dependent symbols. Formally, a graph with the set of nodes V labelled by φ, and with the set of arcs R, is a dependence graph (d-graph) over D, iff

$$(v_1, v_2) \in R \vee (v_2, v_1) \in R \vee v_1 = v_2 \quad \Leftrightarrow \quad (\varphi(v_1), \varphi(v_2)) \in D$$

for all $v_1, v_2 \in V$. Two d-graphs γ', γ'' are isomorphic, $\gamma' \simeq \gamma''$, if there exists a bijection between their nodes preserving labelling and arc connections. As usual, two isomorphic graphs are identified; all inherent properties of d-graphs are formulated up to isomorphism. The empty d-graph $(\emptyset, \emptyset, \emptyset)$ is denoted by λ and the set of all (isomorphism classes of) d-graphs over D by $\Gamma(D)$.

The monoid $G(D)$ of dependence graphs over dependency $D \subseteq A^2$ is the monoid $(\Gamma(D), \circ, \lambda)$ generated by the family $\{g(a) \mid a \in A\}$ of singleton graphs, where

$$g(a) = (\{a\}, \emptyset, \{(a, a)\}),$$

and with the composition $\circ$ defined as follows: the composition $\gamma_1 \circ \gamma_2$ of γ_1 with γ_2 is (isomorphic to) the graph arising from disjoint representations of γ_1, γ_2 by introducing new arcs leading from each node of γ_1 to each node of γ_2, provided they are labelled with dependent symbols. It is easy to prove that the composition of d-graphs is a d-graph again and that the composition operation is associative, with λ as the neutral element. It turns out that the homomorphic extension of the mapping $g_D : A \longrightarrow \Gamma$ to $A^* \longrightarrow \Gamma$ is a homomorphism of $S(A)$ onto $G(D)$.

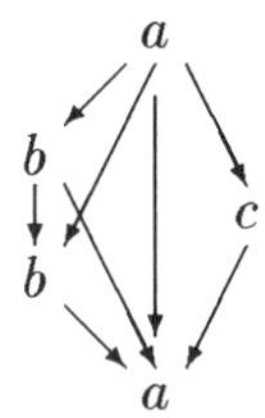

Figure 3: Dependence graph over $D = \{a, b\}^2 \cup \{a, c\}^2$.

For a given dependence graph γ, node v of γ is a prececessor of another node u of γ, if (v, u) is an arc of γ. Clearly, all predecessors of a node labelled with symbol a are labelled with symbols dependent on a. Any full subgraph of γ which, together with a node, contains all its predecessors, is a prefix of γ. It turns out that dependence graphs are partially ordered by the above prefix relation. Dependence graphs are thought as graphical representations of runs of non-sequential processes which make explicit the ordering of action occurrences within compound actions. If the dependency in A reflects the causal relationship among events symbolized by elements of A, then dependence graphs are representations of causal succession of event occurrences in a process run.

It turns out that for a given dependency D and $I_D = A^2 - D$ all the three monoids: of traces, Shields' monoid, and d-graph monoid, can be characterized as images of the monoid of strings $S(A)$ given by homomorphisms ϕ meeting conditions:

$$\phi(w) = \phi(\epsilon) \Rightarrow w = \epsilon,$$
$$(a,b) \in I_D \Rightarrow \phi(ab) = \phi(ba),$$
$$\phi(ua) = \phi(v'av'') \Rightarrow \phi(u) = \phi(v'v''),$$
$$\phi(ua) = \phi(vb) \wedge a \neq b \Rightarrow (a,b) \in I_D,$$

for each $a, b \in A, u, v', w \in A^*, v'' \in (A - \{a\})^*$. From the above condition one can prove all the three monoids to be isomorphic, hence, it is only a matter of taste which objects are chosen for representing concurrent processes: equivalence classes of strings, string vectors, or dependence graphs.

Monoid of multisets. Free commutative monoid $(A^{\oplus}, +, 0)$ generated by A is the *multiset* monoid over A (or the monoid of *linear forms* over A), denoted by $R(A)$. The additive notation is used here because of commutativity of $+$ operation. Let $\mu : A^* \longrightarrow A^{\oplus}$ be a mapping such that $\mu(\epsilon) = 0, \mu(a) = a$ for $a \in A$, and $\mu(uv) = \mu(u) + \mu(v)$ for all $u, v \in A^*$. Clearly, μ is a homomorphism of $S(A)$ onto $R(A)$. Multiset $2a + 2b + c$ is an example of an element of $A^{\oplus}$; it is the value of $\mu(abbca)$. For any multiset r and symbol a the nonnegative integer $r(a)$ is called the *multiplicity* of a in r. For any multiset r we have clearly $r = \sum_{a \in A} r(a)a$. Multisets over an alphabet are pointwise ordered: $r' \leq r''$ iff $r'(a) \leq r''(a)$ for all $a \in A$; if $r' \leq r''$, we say that r' is a prefix of r''.

If r', r'' are multisets over A, then $\max(r', r'')$ is the multiset r over A such that $r(a) = \max(r'(a), r''(a))$ for each $a \in A$. The set R of multisets is *confluent*, if $r', r'' \in R$ implies $\max(r', r'') \in R$; and is *linear*, if for any multisets $r', r'' \in R$ either $r' \leq r''$, or $r'' \leq r'$. The set R of multisets is *connected*, if for each $r \in R$ there exists a string $w \in A^*$ such that $\mu(w) = r$ and $\mu(u) \in R$ for each prefix u of w. Clearly, any prefix-closed set of multisets is connected, but not the other way round. The following condition is necessary and sufficient for connectedness of R:

$$r \in R \Leftrightarrow r = 0 \vee \exists r' \in R, a \in A : r = r' + a.$$

Define the kernel of a set R of multisets over A as the least set $\ker(R)$ of multisets such that

$$0 \in R \Rightarrow 0 \in \ker(R), \qquad r \in \ker(R) \wedge r + a \in R \Rightarrow r + a \in \ker(R),$$

for all $r \in A^{\oplus}, a \in A$. Thus, $\ker(R)$ is the greatest connected subset of R, for each $R \subseteq A^{\oplus}$.

3 Specification tools.

Algebraic tools described in the previous section have been developed in order to capture in a satisfactory way concurrency phenomena that came out while specifying and analysing non-sequential systems. In particular, the partial order of event occurrences during systems runs made necessary to look for non-standard way of describing processes. Historically, the specifications of non-sequential systems became before the rigorous notions of their behaviour has been proposed. Below we briefly describe some formal system specifications that are inherently connected with algebraic tools given in the previous section.

Elementary net systems. Elementary net systems [11, 13] (presented here with some minor changes) are particular cases of Petri nets, well suited for many applications and manageable using some formal means. An elementary net system is any system

$$\mathbf{E} = (P, T, \text{Pre}\,, \text{Post}\,, m^0)$$

where P, T are finite, nonempty sets, of *places* and *transitions*, and

$$\text{Pre}\,: P \longrightarrow 2^T,\ \text{Post}\,: P \longrightarrow 2^T,\ m^0 \subseteq P,$$

are such that $T = \text{Pre}\,(P) \cup \text{Post}\,(P)$ (no isolated transitions) and $\text{Pre}\,(p) \cup \text{Post}\,(p) \neq \emptyset$ for all $p \in P$ (no isolated places).

Functions Pre and Post are extended to $P \cup T$ by setting

$$\text{Pre}\,(t) = \{p \mid t \in \text{Post}\,(p)\}, \text{Post}\,(t) = \{p \mid t \in \text{Pre}\,(p)\}.$$

Partial function $\delta : 2^P \times T \longrightarrow 2^P$ is defined as follows:

$$\delta(m_1, t) = m_2 \Leftrightarrow \text{Pre}\,(t) \subseteq m_1 \wedge \text{Post}\,(t) \subseteq m_2 \wedge m_1 - \text{Pre}\,(t) = m_2 - \text{Post}\,(t).$$

The *sequential behaviour* of $\mathbf{E}$ is then defined as the partial function $\beta_{\mathbf{E}} : T^* \longrightarrow 2^P$ defined recursively:

$$\beta_{\mathbf{E}}(\epsilon) = m^0, \qquad \beta_{\mathbf{E}}(wt) = \delta(\beta_{\mathbf{E}}(w), t)$$

for all $w \in T^*, t \in T$. The domain of $\beta_{\mathbf{E}}$ is the set of *execution sequences* of $\mathbf{E}$ and its range is the set of *reachable markings* of $\mathbf{E}$. Obviously, the domain of $\beta_{\mathbf{E}}$ is a prefix-closed language over T.

Set $\text{Prox}\,(t) = \text{Pre}\,(t) \cup \text{Post}\,(t)$. Define in T dependency relation D by the equivalence $(t', t'') \in D \Leftrightarrow \text{Prox}\,(t') \cap \text{Prox}\,(t'') \neq \emptyset$. It turns out that

$$w' \equiv_D w'' \Rightarrow (w' \in D(\beta_{\mathbf{E}}) \Leftrightarrow w'' \in D(\beta_{\mathbf{E}})) \wedge \beta_{\mathbf{E}}(w') = \beta_{\mathbf{E}}(w'').$$

Therefore, from the point of view of reachable markings, strings of transitions equivalent w.r. to the trace equivalence are also behaviourally equivalent. Moreover, if to each execution sequence $w \in D(\beta_{\mathbf{E}})$ assigns trace $[w]$, the prefix structure of $[w]$ exhibits the expected partial ordering of reachable markings. Thus, it is possible to define the trace behaviour of $\mathbf{E}$ as a partial function $[\beta_{\mathbf{E}}] : [D(\beta_{\mathbf{E}})] \longrightarrow 2^P$, such that $[\beta_{\mathbf{E}}]([w]) = \beta_{\mathbf{E}}(w)$; this definition is correct in view of the implication above. Any confluent subset of the domain $D([\beta_{\mathbf{E}}])$ of $[\beta_{\mathbf{E}}]$ is a *concurrent run* of the elementary net system $\mathbf{E}$.

Cooperating sequential languages. Let $\mathbf{A} = (A_1, A_2, \ldots, A_N)$ be a tuple of alphabets and let $\mathbf{L} = (L_1, L_2, \ldots, L_N)$ be a corresponding tuple of prefix-closed languages, $L_i \subseteq A_i^*$ for each $i = 1, 2, \ldots, N$. The concurrent behaviour of system $\mathbf{L}$ is function $\beta_{\mathbf{L}}$ with

$$D(\beta_{\mathbf{L}}) = \ker\{w \mid \pi(w) \in \prod_{i=1}^{N} L_i\}$$

and $R(\beta_{\mathbf{L}}) \subseteq \prod_{i=1}^{N} L_i$ such that $\beta_{\mathbf{L}}(w) = \pi(w)$ for each $w \in D(\beta_{\mathbf{L}})$.

Place-transition Petri Nets. Any place/transition Petri net (abbreviated as PT-net) is the system N,

$$\mathrm{N} = (P, T, F, m^0),$$

where P, T are finite, non-empty, disjoint sets (of *places* and *transitions*, resp.), $F : P \times T \longrightarrow \mathrm{N}$, and $m^0 : P \longrightarrow \mathrm{N}$ (the *initial* marking). Any function $m : P \longrightarrow \mathrm{N}$ is called a marking of net N; the set of all such markings is denoted by M. The value of marking m for place p is interpreted as the (instantaneous) number of 'tokens' contained in p. Transition execution of N is the partial function $\delta_{\mathrm{N}} : M \times T \longrightarrow M$ defined as follows:

$$\delta_{\mathrm{N}}(m', t) = m'' \Leftrightarrow \forall p \in P : m''(p) = m'(p) + F(p, t) \geq 0$$

for all $m', m'' \in M, t \in T$. This function assigns to marking m' and transition t marking m'' obtained from m' in effect of the execution of t; execution of t is possible, if each place p for which $F(p,t) < 0$ (from which t 'takes' tokens) contains sufficiently many of them $(m' + F(p,t) \geq 0)$ and the resulting number of tokens in any place after execution of t is equal to their previous number minus the number of tokens taken from this place by t (if $F(p,t) < 0$) plus the number of tokens put by t into the place (if $F(p,t) < 0$).

Let N be an arbitrary PT-net. The marking behaviour of N is defined as the partial function $\beta_{\mathrm{N}} : T^* \longrightarrow M$ defined in a similar way as in case of elementary net systems:

$$\beta_{\mathrm{N}}(\epsilon) = m^0, \beta_{\mathrm{N}}(wt) = \delta(\beta_{\mathrm{N}}(w), t)$$

for $w \in T^*, t \in T$. Elements of $D(\beta_{\mathrm{N}})$ are called *firing* or *execution sequences*, those of $R(\beta_{\mathrm{N}})$ the *reachable markings*. It is clear that $D(\beta_{\mathrm{N}})$ is a prefix closed language. The sequential behaviour of N is the domain $D(\beta_{\mathrm{N}})$ of the marking behaviour; for sake of uniformity, it will be considered as the identity function with the domain $D(\beta_{\mathrm{N}})$. However, the sequential behaviour itself is not a sufficient tool to distingush concurrent runs of a net.

A natural aim in exploring partial order behaviour of PT-nets is to establish a sort of independency relation among transition ocurrences and then an equivalence between states reached in effect of such occurrences. However, in contrast to elementary net systems, where independency was fixed once for ever and determined by structructure of the net, independency between transitions in PT-nets may depend on the reached marking. It is even not quite obvious whether independency, as exhibited by PT-nets, leads to a partial order of transition occurrences in a system run. This issue will be discussed further on; for the time being algebra of multisets, as defined above, seems to be a promising tool for describing non-sequential behaviour of PT-nets, as explained below.

Let A be an alphabet, $L \subseteq A^{\oplus}$. Call L *linearly definable*, if there is a function $k : A \cup \{\epsilon\} \longrightarrow \mathbf{Z}$ such that $k(\epsilon) \geq 0$ and

$$L = \{r \in A^{\oplus} \mid \sum_{a \in A} k(a)r(a) + k(\epsilon) \geq 0\}.$$

L is *conjunctive*, if it is an intersection of a finite number of linearly definable sets. The kernel of a conjunctive set is a *multitree* and any confluent subset of a multitree is a *multitrace*. Any maximal linear subset of a multitrace is its (sequential) observation. The multiset behaviour of a PT-net $\mathrm{N} = (P, T, F, m^0)$ is defined by means of homomorphism $\mu : A^* \longrightarrow A^{\oplus}$ applied to the domain of its sequential behaviour, i.e. as function β'_{N} with the domain

$$D(\beta'_{\mathrm{N}}) = \ker\{w \in T^* \mid \bigwedge_{p \in P} (\sum_{t \in T} F(p,t)w(t) + m^0(p) \geq 0)\}$$

such that $\beta'_{\mathrm{N}}(w) = \mu(w)$ for each $w \in D(\beta'_{\mathrm{N}})$. It turns out that $R(\beta'_{\mathrm{N}}) = B$, where

$$B = \ker\{r \in T^{\oplus} \mid \bigwedge_{p \in P} (\sum_{t \in T} F(p,t)u(t) + r^0(p) \geq 0)\} \tag{1}$$

and that B is a multitree (recall that $r(t)$ is the multiplicity of t in multiset r). Maximal multitraces of B can be viewed as runs of N. In this description B is a state space of N and it determines uniquely all reachable markings of the net. Let $r \in B$; then any $r' \in B$ such that $r' \leq r$ is an initial part of a history leading to r; because of the partiality of multiset ordering, this description exhibit partial ordering of initial histories (or states) of the net runs.

Below we give two examples of PT-nets N_1, N_2 together with their state spaces B_1, B_2 defined by the multiset behaviour. Let

$$N_1 = (\{1,2,3,4\}, \{a,b,c\}, F, m^0)$$

where

$$F(1,a) = F(2,b) = F(3,c) = F(4,c) = -1, F(4,a) = F(4,b) = 1,$$
$$m^0(1) = m^0(2) = m^0(3) = 1, m^0(4) = 0.$$

Graphical representation of net N_1 together with its marking is given below:

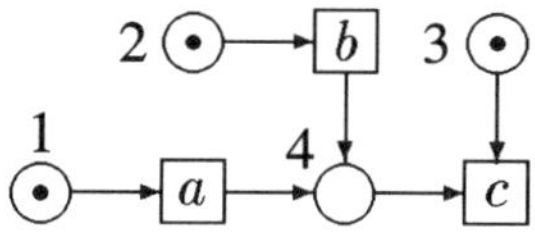

Figure 4: N_1: an example of PT-net.

According to (1) the state space of N_1 is the following set of multisets:

$$B_1 = \ker\{r \mid r(a) \leq 1 \wedge r(b) \leq 1 \wedge r(c) \leq 1 \wedge r(c) \leq r(a) + r(b)\};$$

i.e.

$$B_1 = \{0, a, b, a+b, a+c, b+c, a+b+c\}.$$

This set is confluent, hence it represents the (only one) run of the net. Graphical representation of the ordering of multisets in B_1 is given below:

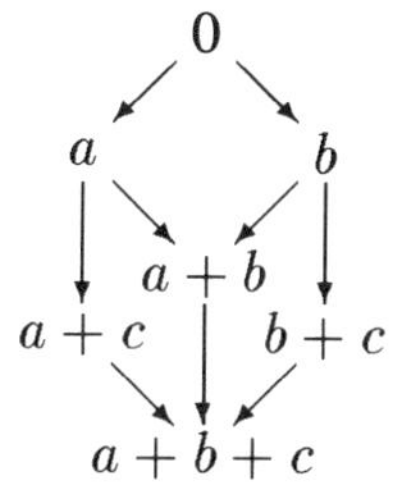

Figure 5: Structure of the state space given by the multiset behaviour of N_1.

Observe that no partial ordering of events can describe the above ordering of reachable markings (any multiset in P determines uniquely a marking of the corresponding net).

The second example is in a sense the revers of the previous one; net N_2 is defined as

$$N_2 = (\{1,2,3,4\}, \{a,b,c\}, F, m^0)$$

where

$$F(1,a) = F(2,b) = F(4,b) = F(3,c) = F(4,c) = -1, F(4,a) = 1,$$
$$m^0(1) = m^0(2) = m^0(3) = m^0(4) = 1$$

which in the graphical form is presented in Figure 6:

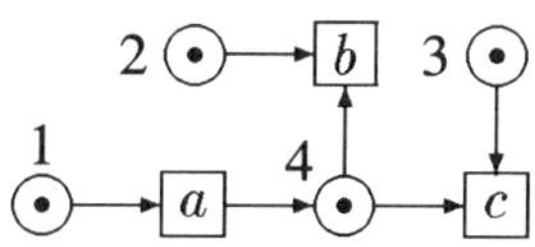

Figure 6: N_2: another example of a PT-net.

The state space of N_2 given by the multiset behaviour is

$$B_2 = \ker\{r \mid r(a) \leq 1 \wedge r(b) \leq 1 \wedge r(c) \leq 1 \wedge r(b) + r(c) \leq r(a) + 1\};$$

hence,

$$B_2 = \{0, a, b, c, a+b, a+c, a+b+c\}.$$

This set is not confluent, since $\{b, c\} \subseteq B_2$, but $\max(b, c) = b + c \notin B_2$. Two maximal confluent subsets of B_2, hence two different runs of N_2, are:

$$R_1 = \{0, a, c, a+c, b+c, a+b+c\}, \quad R_2 = \{0, a, b, a+c, b+c, a+b+c\}.$$

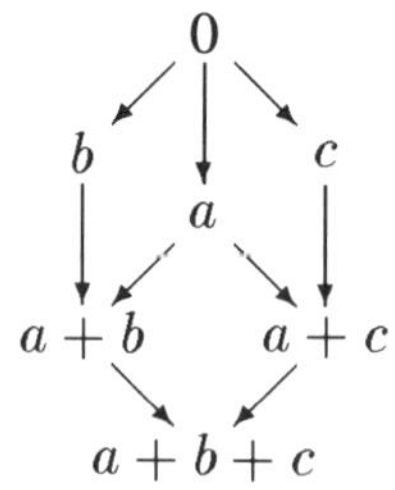

Figure 7: Structure of the state space of N_2 given by the multiset behaviour.

4 Prefix functions

In the previous section some methods of non-sequential systems behaviour description have been given. There is a similarity of all these descriptions: the non-sequential behaviour of a system has been defined as a function defined on a prefix-closed language over the alphabet of (elementary) system actions and with values viewed as the system states reached after executing initial parts of a system run. Thus, in the present approach the most important aspects of the behaviour concern the way of assigning states to sequences of events occurrences rather than the states themselves. In particular, for many reasons it is useful to reduce the number of considered states by assigning the same state to a number of strings, and thus identifying some sequences. It can be then useful to unify all these similar notions and to find some common features of their construction.

Let A be an alphabet. Any function defined on a prefix closed subset of A^* will be called here a *concrete prefix function* over A. For any concrete prefix function σ the alphabet of σ is denoted by $A(\sigma)$. Interpreting concrete prefix functions as descriptions of a discrete processes, elements of their alphabets are considered as events (or actions) of the processes, elements of their domains as all possible execution sequences of the processes, and elements of their ranges as (concrete) states of the processes.

Two concrete prefix functions σ_1, σ_2 are *isomorphic*: $\sigma_1 \simeq \sigma_2$, if $A(\sigma_1) = A(\sigma_2)$, $D(\sigma_1) = D(\sigma_2)$, and there exists a bijection $\phi : R(\sigma_1) \longrightarrow R(\sigma_2)$ such that $\sigma_1\phi = \sigma_2$. Class of all isomorphic concrete prefix functions over A

is an *abstract prefix function* over A, or simply, a *prefix function* over A. Thus, in fact, values of prefix functions are known only up to isomorphisms of their representations (members of isomorphism classes).

There is, however, a *canonical* representation of values of prefix functions, defined in a standard way. Let, for any concrete prefix function σ, $\equiv_\sigma$ be the equivalence relation in $D(\sigma)$ such that $u \equiv_\sigma v \Leftrightarrow \sigma(u) = \sigma(v)$. It is clear that the equivalence $\equiv_\sigma$ is the same for all concrete prefix functions isomorphic to σ; then the concrete prefix function $\hat{\sigma}$ over A assigning to each string w the equivalence class $[w]_\sigma$ of $\equiv_\sigma$ containing w:

$$\hat{\sigma}(w) = [w]_\sigma$$

can serve as a canonical representation of the abstract prefix function determined by σ. On the other hand, for any equivalence relation in a prefix closed subset of A^* there exists precisely one prefix function represented by function assigning to each string the equivalence class containing this string.

Two prefix functions are distinguished for any prefix closed domain: the *identity* prefix function, isomorphic with the identity function, and the *constant* prefix function, isomorphic with a function assigning a constant value for all strings in its domain (notice here that, up to isomorphism, there is only one constant prefix function).

Prefix functions can be viewed as a tool for the discrete systems behaviour description, interpretating their arguments as the system actions sequences and their values as the resulting states. Having in mind the intended interpretation and using prefix functions as models of processes, we avoid then answering the question "what are states", defining only their representations; the nature of states is irrelevant from the point of view of prefix functions. Instead, from this point of view relevant is how execution sequences, or sequences of events, can be identified without losing essential features of a system behaviour. Thus, we are interested in those features of prefix functions that are independent of their interpretations; speaking of abstract prefix functions we always use their concrete representations, remembering however their abstract nature. The function assigning to each (initiated) transition sequence of a Petri net the resulting marking is an example of a prefix function. Another example is related to transition systems with a fixed initial state: a function, assigning to each sequence of transitions its resulting state is a prefix function. Yet another example is the function assigning to each string its trace equivalence class, for a given dependency relation, and the function assigning to each string of symbols the vector of its projections on distinguished subalphabets. A common feature of all these functions is the identification of sequences that are considered as identical from the state space point of view.

For any prefix function σ over A and each $a \in A$ let the *transition* relation of σ be defined as follows:

$$s' \xrightarrow{a}_\sigma s'' \Leftrightarrow \exists u \in A^* : s' = \sigma(u), s'' = \sigma(ua)$$

for each $s', s'' \in R(\sigma)$ and $a \in A$. The *step* relation of σ is the relation $\rightarrow_\sigma$ defined as

$$s' \rightarrow_\sigma s'' \Leftrightarrow \exists a \in A : s' \xrightarrow{a}_\sigma s'';$$

the transitive and reflexive closure $\rightarrow_\sigma^*$ of the step relation is the *progress* relation of σ. Clearly, the progress relation of any prefix function is a quasi-ordering relation. Let σ be a prefix function, $\rightarrow$ be the step relation of σ. Prefix function σ is *strict*, if $s' \rightarrow s'' \Rightarrow s' \neq s''$ for all $s', s'' \in R(\sigma)$; is *monotone*, if $\rightarrow^*$ is an ordering of $R(\sigma)$, and σ is *strictly monotone*, if it is strict and monotone. If σ is monotone and for each $w \in D(\sigma)$ the set $\{s \mid s \rightarrow^* \sigma(w)\}$ is linearly ordered by $\rightarrow^*$, then σ is *sequential*. In particular, the identity prefix function is strictly monotone and sequential.

Prefix function σ is *additive*, if the implication

$$\sigma(w') = \sigma(w'') \Rightarrow w'(a) = w''(a)$$

holds for all strings w and symbols a. Clearly,

1. *Any additive prefix function is strictly monotone.*

Let L be a prefix closed language over A. Prefix function σ is *congruent*, if it preserves continuations, i.e. if for each $w', w'' \in D(\sigma)$

$$\sigma(w') = \sigma(w'') \Rightarrow \theta(D(\sigma), w') = \theta(D(\sigma), w'').$$

Clearly, the identity is congruent. Let L be a prefix closed language; diagram of the transition relation for the prefix function defined by $\sigma(w) = \theta(L, w)$ for each $w \in L$ is the *state diagram* for L; if the state diagram for a language L is finite, L is regular (rational).

2. *Trace behaviour of any elementary net system is a congruent and additive prefix function.*

Some typical prefix functions used for specifying or analysis of concurrent systems are listed below. In these examples A is an alphabet, $L \subseteq A^*$ is a prefix closed language, D is a dependency relation in A.

- $\iota(L) : L \longrightarrow L$ with $\iota(w) = w$ (identity prefix function).
- $\tau_D(L) : L \longrightarrow T(D)$ with $\tau_D(w) = [w]_D$ (trace prefix function);
- $\gamma_D : L \longrightarrow \Gamma(D)$ with $\gamma_D(w) = g_D(w)$ (d-graph prefix function);
- $\pi : L \longrightarrow A_1^* \times A_2^* \times \cdots \times A_N^*$, with $\pi(w) = (\pi_1(w), \pi_2(w), \ldots, \pi_N(w))$ (vector prefix function);
- $\mu_L : L \longrightarrow A^{\oplus}$ (multiset prefix function);

- $\Theta : L \longrightarrow 2^L$ such that $\Theta(w) = \theta(L, w)$ (continuation of w in L) (continuation prefix function);
- $l : L \longrightarrow \mathbf{Z}$, where $l(w)$ is the length of w (the length prefix function);
- For $P \subseteq L$, $\delta : L \longrightarrow \{0, 1\}$ with $\delta(w) = 1 \Leftrightarrow w \in P$ (test prefix function).

<table>
<tr><th rowspan="2">Prefix function</th><th rowspan="2">States</th><th colspan="2">Type of</th></tr>
<tr><th>identification</th><th>ordering</th></tr>
<tr><td>identity</td><td>execution sequences</td><td>none</td><td rowspan="5">monotone</td></tr>
<tr><td>trace</td><td>execution traces</td><td>partial commutation</td></tr>
<tr><td>vector</td><td>string vectors</td><td>equal projections</td></tr>
<tr><td>graph</td><td>dependence graphs</td><td>isomorphic graphs</td></tr>
<tr><td>multiset</td><td>multisets</td><td>all permutations</td></tr>
<tr><td>continuation</td><td>control states</td><td>same continuations</td><td rowspan="3">folding</td></tr>
<tr><td>test</td><td>truth values</td><td>subset</td></tr>
<tr><td>constant</td><td>singleton</td><td>all</td></tr>
</table>

Table 1 A ‘taxonomy’ of prefix functions w.r. to identification properties.

5 Contractions of prefix functions

Let F be a family of prefix functions over a common alphabet with a common domain. Let σ_1, σ_2 be two elements of F; we say that σ_2 is a *contraction* of σ_1 (and write $\sigma_1 \geq \sigma_2$), if there exists a function ψ such that $\sigma_1\psi = \sigma_2$. Such a function is called a contraction of σ_1 to σ_2. Strictly speaking, any contraction is a class of equivalent functions; for prefix functions σ_1, σ_2, contractions ψ', ψ'' of σ_1 to σ_2 are equivalent: $\psi' \equiv \psi''$, if there exists a bijection ϕ with

$$\sigma_1\psi' = \sigma_2\psi''\phi.$$

It is easy to see that any contraction ψ of σ_1 to σ_2 has its canonical form $\hat{\psi}$, which is the contraction of $\hat{\sigma}_1$ to $\hat{\sigma}_2$ defined by the equality

$$\hat{\psi}[w]_{\sigma_1} = [w]_{\sigma_2}$$

for all $w \in D(\sigma_1) = D(\sigma_2)$. From the definition of the canonical representation of prefix functions it follows that the equivalence determined by prefix function σ_1 is a refinement of that determined by prefix function σ_2. Observe that the identity mapping is a particular case of contraction.

Any two prefix functions over the same alphabet and with a common domain will be called *similar*. Since any function determines uniquely an equivalence relation in its domain, and all equivalence relations in any set forms a lattice, we have the following property of prefix functions:

3. *A family of similar prefix functions ordered by contractions is a complete lattice with identity as the greatest and the constant as the least element.*

The above property implies that any prefix function is (isomorphic to) a contraction of identity, and can be contracted to the constant. Observe, as an application of the contraction ordering, that the continuation prefix function is the least congruent prefix function over its domain.

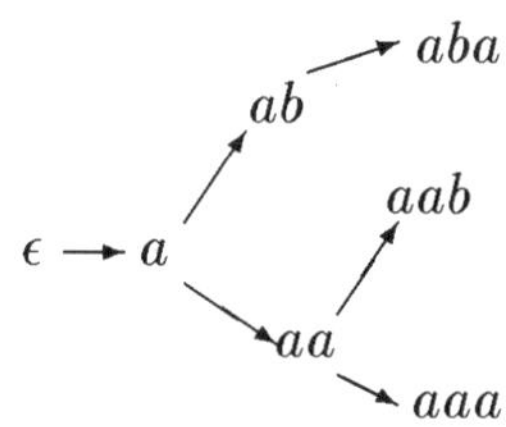

Figure 8: Diagram of an identity prefix function.

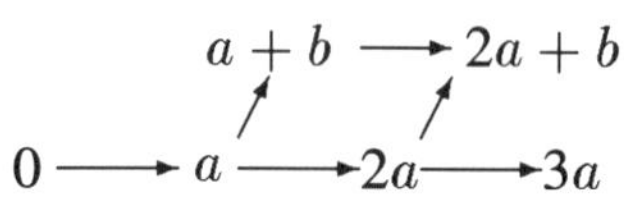

Figure 9: Multiset contraction of the prefix function in Fig. 8.

4. *Contractions preserve progress relation.*

A special part in the whole family of prefix functions over A with domain D play monotone and congruent members of the family; contractions of such prefix functions to their state diagrams are called *foldings*, and the prefix functions themselves *unfoldings* of their own state diagrams.

6 Prefix functions synchronization

One of the most important issues concerning discrete systems is their compositionality. In case of concurrent systems composition makes independently acting systems to communicate with each other and to synchronize some of their actions. On the abstract level, composition of systems is modelled by synchronization of prefix functions. Synchronization operation defined below allows us to build complex prefix functions of simple ones, to introduce an independency relation to the join set of events, and to combine state spaces of components into a single state space. It also enables to apply synchronization in the 'opposite' direction, decomposing complex system into simpler ones and then making analysis and description of these systems easier.

Let J be a set of indices and $(A_i)_{i\in J}$ be a family of alphabets and let $L_i \subseteq A_i^*$ for each $i \in J$. The language

$$\mathop{\&}_{i\in J} L_i = \{w \in (\bigcup_{i\in J} A_i)^* \mid \forall i \in J : \pi_i(w) \in L_i\},$$

is called the *conjunction* of languages L_i. In case of $J = \{1,2\}$ write $L_1 \& L_2$ rather than $\&_{i\in\{1,2\}} L_i$.

5. *Conjunction of any family of prefix-closed languages is a prefix-closed language.*

Let $(\sigma_i)_{i\in J}$ be a family of prefix functions. The *synchronization* of σ_i for $i \in J$ is the prefix function

$$\sigma : \mathop{\&}_{i\in J} D(\sigma_i) \longrightarrow \prod_{i\in J} R(\sigma_i)$$

such that for each $w \in \bigcup_{i\in J} A_i$ and each $i \in J$

$$(\sigma(w))_i = \sigma_i(\pi_i(w)),$$

where $(\sigma(w))_i$ denotes the i-th component of the tuple $\sigma(w)$ being a member of the cartesian product $\prod_{i\in J} R(\sigma_i)$. The synchronization of family $\{\sigma_i\}_{i\in J}$ will be denoted by $\|_{i\in J}\ \sigma_i$. In case of $J = \{1,2\}$ write $\sigma_1 \parallel \sigma_2$ rather than $\|_{i=1,2}\ \sigma_i$.

The idea of the synchronization defined above originates from modular description of Petri nets [5] and from string vectors of Shields [12]. Since the domain of the synchronization defined as above is prefix closed, we have the following:

6. *The synchronization of prefix functions is a prefix function.*

Since for any sets S_1, S_2, S_3 there exist obvious bijections from $S_1 \times S_2$ to $S_2 \times S_1$, from $\{(s,s) \mid s \in S\}$ to S, and from $(S_1 \times S_2) \times S_3$ to $S_1 \times (S_2 \times S_3)$ meeting the required isomorphism conditions, we have the following property of synchronization operation:

7. *The synchronization is idempotent, commutative, and associative, i.e. for all prefix functions* $\sigma, \sigma_1, \sigma_2, \sigma_3$*:*

$$\begin{aligned} \sigma \parallel \sigma &= \sigma, \\ \sigma_1 \parallel \sigma_2 &= \sigma_2 \parallel \sigma_1, \\ (\sigma_1 \parallel \sigma_2) \parallel \sigma_3 &= \sigma_1 \parallel (\sigma_2 \parallel \sigma_3). \end{aligned}$$

If $R_1 \subseteq S_1^2, R_2 \subseteq S_2^2$, then the product of R_1, R_2 is the relation $R_1 \times R_2 \subseteq (S_1 \times S_2)^2$ such that

$$(s_1', s_2')(R_1 \times R_2)(s_1'', s_2'') \Leftrightarrow s_1' R_1 s_1'' \wedge s_2' R_2 s_2''.$$

From the synchronization definition it follows that

8. *Progress relation of the synchronization is the product of progress relations of the synchronization components restricted to the range of the synchronization.*

By the definition of the step relation of prefix functions and of the synchronization operation we have:

9. *Synchronization of (strictly) monotone prefix functions is (strictly) monotone.*

The cartesian product of functions $\phi_1 : D_1 \longrightarrow R_1, \phi_2 : D_2 \longrightarrow R_2$, is the function $\phi_1 \times \phi_2 : D_1 \times D_2 \longrightarrow R_1 \times R_2$ such that

$$(\phi_1 \times \phi_2)(d_1, d_2) = (\phi_1(d_1), \phi_2(d_2)).$$

10. *Synchronization of contracted prefix functions is a contraction of their synchronization; more precisely,*

$$(\sigma_1 \phi_1 \parallel \sigma_2 \phi_2) = (\sigma_1 \parallel \sigma_2)(\phi_1 \times \phi_2)$$

for all prefix functions σ_1, σ_2 *and all contractions* ϕ_1, ϕ_2.

The above fact is crucial for a compositional approach to system description. If systems descriptions are viewed as contractions of their behaviours, then by the above fact the behaviour of composed systems is the composition of their components behaviours; and both: systems and their behaviours can be represented on arbitrary level of abstraction.

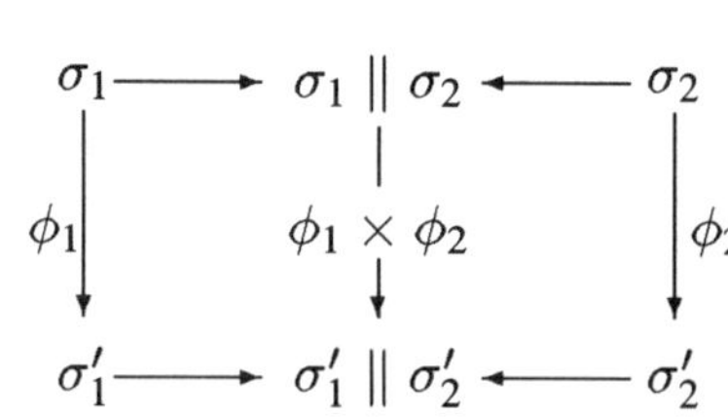

Figure 10: Synchronization and contractions.

According to the above definition of the synchronization operation, synchronization of identity prefix functions is, in general, not sequential. Moreover, it turns out that

11. *Any trace prefix function is the synchronization of a finite number of sequential prefix functions.*

It is worthwhile to compare the synchronization of identity prefix functions with conjunction of their domains. Let A_1, A_2 be alphabets, $L_1 \subseteq A_1^*, L_2 \subseteq A_2^*$ be prefix-closed languages; then relationship between conjunction and synchronization is as shown on the diagram below ($\pi : (A_1 \cup A_2)^* \longrightarrow A_1^* \times A_2^*$ is defined by $\pi(w) = (\pi_1(w), \pi_2(w))$ where π_1, π_2 are projections on A_1, A_2, respectively).

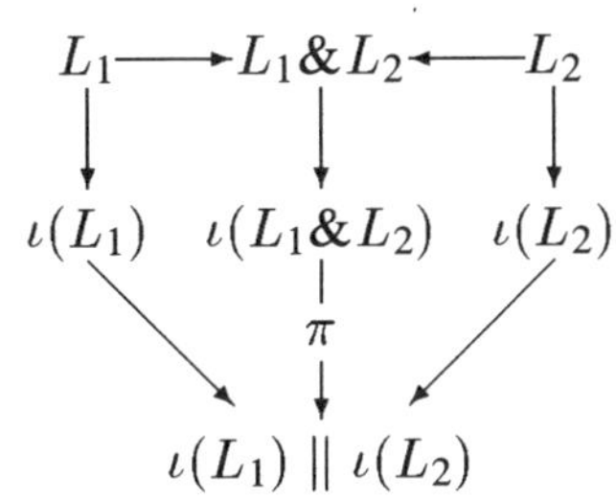

Figure 11: Conjunction and synchronization.

Synchronization of identity prefix functions is, in general, not an identity prefix function and can introduce an independency of some actions (and hence convert linear orderings of components into a partial ordering of the synchronization result); this independency is 'static', i.e. fixed for all possible runs of the described system. By the synchronization defined above it is not possible to introduce a 'context-sensitive' concurrency (depending upon the system history). To be more precise, let us define so-called structural independency. Let σ be a prefix function, a, b be elements of $A(\sigma)$. We say that a, b are *structurally independent* in σ, if there are prefix functions σ', σ'' such that $\sigma = \sigma' \parallel \sigma''$ and $a \in A(\sigma') - A(\sigma''), b \in A(\sigma'') - A(\sigma')$. If a, b are structurally independent, then $a \neq b$, and for each $w \in A(\sigma)^*$

$$wab \in D(\sigma) \Leftrightarrow wba \in D(\sigma) \wedge \sigma(wab) = \sigma(wba).$$

The trace independency is an example of structural independency. There is, however, another type of independency, call it *inner independency*; say a and b are in the inner independency relation, if for all $w \in A^*$

$$wba \in D(\sigma) \Rightarrow wab \in D(\sigma) \wedge \sigma(wba) = \sigma(wab),$$

but for some $w \in A^*$

$$wab \in D(\sigma) \wedge wba \notin D(\sigma).$$

The inner independency of transitions is typical for the behaviour of the place/transition Petri nets.

7 Atomic prefix functions

A prefix function is *atomic*, if it is not the result of synchronization of components with different domains. Thus, any prefix function is either atomic, or it can be obtained by the synchronization of a number of atomic prefix functions. Knowledge of properties of atomic prefix functions of a family can be extended to knowledge of properties of all members of the family. Here, we concentrate on families of prefix functions that are applied for descriptions or specifications of Petri nets. In particular, we shall seek for atomic prefix functions for some descriptive means considered above.

It follows directly from the definition that in atomic prefix functions no two symbols are structurally independent; thus, finding atomic prefix functions allows us to discuss the inner independency. It turns out that even very simple atomic prefix functions exhibit inherent difficulties of adequate description of concurrency.

12. *Every sequential prefix functions is atomic.*

Since in a trace prefix function all independent symbols are structurally independent, and because of isomorphism of trace prefix functions, Shields prefix functions, and d-graph prefix functions, we have the following:

13. *Every atomic trace prefix function is sequential; every atomic Shields prefix function has a single component, and every atomic d-graph prefix function is a graph of linear ordering.*

Let consider behaviour of PT-nets and atomic prefix functions describing their behaviour. First, define the composition of PT-nets [5]. Let

$$N_1 = (P_1, T_1, F_1, m_1), N_2 = (P_2, T_2, F_2, m_2)$$

be PT-nets; their composition is defined as the PT-net

$$N_1 \bowtie N_2 = (P_1 + P_2, T_1 \cup P_2, F, m)$$

where $P_1 + P_2$ is the disjoint union of P_1, P_2 and F, m are defined as follows for all $p \in P_1 + P_2, t \in T_1 \cup T_2$:

$$F(p,t) = \begin{cases} F_1(p,t), \text{ if } p \in P_1 \wedge t \in T_1, \\ F_2(p,t), \text{ if } p \in P_2 \wedge t \in T_2, \\ 0, \text{ if } p \in P_1 \wedge t \notin T_1 \vee p \in P_2 \wedge t \notin T_2, \end{cases}$$

$$m(p) = \begin{cases} m_1(p), \text{ if } p \in P_1, \\ m_2(p), \text{ if } p \in P_2 \end{cases}$$

(notice that T_1 and T_2 need not be disjoint). From the definition it follows at once that the composition operation on PT-nets is associative and commutative (under a suitable isomorphism of nets it can be also made idempotent). This definition can be easily extended for any number of components.

14. *Let $\beta_i^s, \beta_i^m, \beta_i^\oplus$ be the sequential behaviour, marking behaviour, multiset behaviour, respectively, of N_i (i=1,2), and let $\beta^s, \beta^m, \beta^\oplus$ be the sequential behaviour, marking behaviour, multiset behaviour, respectively, of $N_1 \bowtie N_2$. Then*

$$\begin{aligned} \beta^s &= \beta_1^s \parallel \beta_2^s, \\ \beta^m &= \beta_1^m \parallel \beta_2^m, \\ \beta^\oplus &= \beta_1^\oplus \parallel \beta_2^\oplus. \end{aligned}$$

It proves soundness of the prefix functions synchronization definition with respect to the composition of concurrent systems described by PT-nets.

Atomic multiset prefix functions are provided to define the behaviour of the following one-place PT-net and, in contrast to the previous ones, may exhibit inner independency of symbols. The net in Figure 12 is an example of atomic PT-net, or *producer-consumer* system. Any PT-net can be viewed as the synchronization of a number of producer-consumer systems; thus, the behaviour of PT-nets depends upon the understanding of the producer-consumer system activity. In particular, having chosen a state space for such atomic systems, the set of states of all PT-nets is the cartesian product of atomic sets of states.

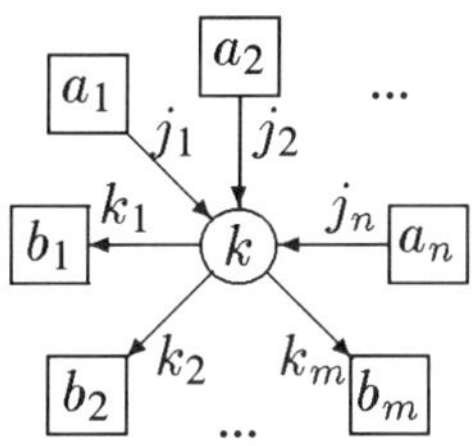

Figure 12: An atomic place/transition net.

The behaviour of the above PT-net, according to the common interpretation, can be described by means of execution sequences and it is given by the identity prefix function with the domain

$$D = \ker\{w \in T^* \mid k + \sum_{i=1}^{n} j_i w(a_i) - \sum_{i=1}^{m} k_i w(b_i) \geq 0\},$$

where $T = \bigcup_{i=1}^n a_i \cup \bigcup_{i=1}^m b_i$ (recall that $w(a)$ denotes the number of occurrences of symbol a in string w). However, this description does not capture the inner independency of transitions in T. The multiset description, introducing as much independency as possible, is given by the contraction of $\iota(D)$ by homomorphism μ from T^* to $T^\oplus$. The choice of multiset prefix function as a mean of description is here natural, since the condition defining the above set of strings depends exclusively on multiplicity of symbols in strings, the same for strings and the corresponding to them multisets.

The behaviour of an arbitrary PT-net is given by the synchronization of atomic prefix functions, constructed for each place of the original net. Let $\mathrm{N} = (P, T, F, m^0)$ be a PT-net and let for each $p \in P$ net $\mathrm{N}_p = (\{p\}, T_p, F_p, m_p^0)$ be the atomic (i.e. one-place) PT-net with functions F_p, m_p^0 arising from F, m^0 by their restriction to $\{p\} \times T$ and $\{p\}$, respectively. By the result quoted above, the behaviour of $N = (P, T, F, m^0)$ can be obtained by the synchronization of the behaviours of all its atomic (one-place) nets, constructed for each $p \in P$:

$$\beta_{\mathrm{N}} = \|_{p \in P}\, \beta_{\mathrm{N}_p}.$$

It is worthwhile to note the simplicity of atomic prefix functions describing the behaviour of one place nets; interpreting them as producer-consumer systems, production and consumption rates are assumed here to be fixed and contribute to the whole production in a linear way. One can imagine a theory of 'cooperating' producer-consumer systems that act acording to a more general principle; such system would be e.g. the synchronization of atomic prefix functions σ_i with domains

$$D(\sigma_i) = \ker\{w \in A_i^* \mid \rho_i(w) \geq 0\},$$

where $\rho_i : A_i^* \longrightarrow \mathbf{Z}$ is a more general 'total productivity' function of unit i, returning for the activity sequence w of agents from A_i the total balance of produced and consumed items.

8 Conclusions

Prefix functions thought as a unifying concept for describing concurrent processes on different levels of accuracy have been presented. Sets of strings built up from elementary actions (events) occurring in processes have been taken as the basis for further transformations. Prefix functions connect strings (called also execution sequences) with some objects that can be called states. States can be chosen depending on actual needs; therefore, in prefix function approach the choice of states is left for the user. From prefix functions point of view states are some abstract entities, determined by sets of event sequences leading to them; interpretation of states lies outside the prefix functions formalism and serves only as a tool for states identification. In the prefix function approach states are nothing but classes of equivalent sequences of event occurrences; different prefix function descriptions of the same system differ only by the degree of such sequences identification.

From examples of applying prefix functions to the behaviour description of known systems, as Petri nets, it follows adequacy of prefix functions as describing tools. The stress has been put upon two main operations on prefix functions that allow to construct new prefix functions of the already defined ones: contraction, 'squeezing' a considered state space, and synchronization, introducing structural concurrency and enlarging the state space.

References

[1] Abadi, M., Lamport, L. (1989) Composing Specifications. *Lecture Notes in Computer Science*, **430**,1-41

[2] Diekert, V., Rozenberg, G. (eds.) (1994) *The book of traces*. World Scientific, Singapore,New Jersey,London,Hong Kong.

[3] Hoare,C.A.R.: *Communicating Sequential Processes*, Communications of the ACM 21 vol.8 (1978)

[4] Mazurkiewicz, A. (1977) Concurrent Program Schemes and Their Interpretation. *Technical Report DAIMI PB-78, Århus University*

[5] Mazurkiewicz, A.(1985) Semantics of Concurrent Systems: A Modular Fixed-Point Trace Approach. *Lecture Notes in Computer Science*, **188**.

[6] Mazurkiewicz, A., Ochmański, E.,Penczek, W. (1989) Concurrent systems and inevitability.*Theoretical Computer Science*, **64**, 281-304.

[7] Mazurkiewicz,A., Rabinovich,A.,Trakhtenbrot B.A. (1991) Connectedness and Synchronization. *Theoretical Computer Science*,**90** 1,171-184

[8] Petri, C.A. (1977) Non-Sequential Processes.*GMD Report ISF-77-05.*

[9] Pratt, V. (1986) Modeling Concurrency with Partial Orders. *International Journal of Parallel Processing*, **15**, 33-71.

[10] Reisig, W. (1985) *Petri Nets: an Introduction*, EATCS Monographs on Comp.Sci.

[11] Rozenberg, G. (1987) Behaviour of Elementary Net Systems. *Lecture Notes in Computer Science*, **254**, 26-59

[12] Shields, M.W. (1979) *Non-sequential behaviour, part I.* Int. Report CSR-120-82, Dept. of Computer Science, University of Edinburgh.

[13] Thiagarajan, P.S. (1987) Elementary Net Systems. *Lecture Notes in Computer Science*, **254**, 26-59.

[14] Winskel, G. (1988) An introduction to event structures. *Lecture Notes in Computer Science*, **354**, 123-172

DIMACS Series in Discrete Mathematics
and Theoretical Computer Science
Volume **29**, 1997

Elements of an Automata Theory Over Partial Orders

Wolfgang Thomas

ABSTRACT. A model of nondeterministic finite automaton over (finite) partial orders is introduced. It captures existential monadic second-order logic in expressive power and generalizes classical word automata and tree automata. Special forms, such as deterministic automata, are discussed, and logical and algorithmic properties are analyzed, like closure under complement and decidability of the nonemptiness problem. These questions are studied in the context of different classes of partial orders, such as trees, Mazurkiewicz traces, or rectangular grids.

1. Introduction

While automata over strings and trees are a well-known, widely used, and robust model, with many applications in the specification and verification of concurrent programs, the area of "finite automata over partial orders" cannot be called an established subject, despite the fact that partial orders are a natural domain for the study of concurrency. A possible reason for this is that many properties of finite automata which are essential in logical or algorithmic applications fail to hold when partial orders are considered as inputs (instead of strings or trees). Such properties are: equivalence between the deterministic and the nondeterministic model, closure under operations like complementation or projection, characterization by natural logical systems (like monadic second-order logic), and decidability of the nonemptiness problem (in logical terms: satisfiability problem). A possible remedy in this situation is to confine oneself to a narrower view of partial orders, for instance by extracting only sets of paths from partial orders, which brings back the framework of classical formal language theory.

In the present paper we stay with proper partial orders as inputs of automata and try to set up connections between such generalized automata and logical systems. We suggest a model of finite automaton which keeps the basic intuitive idea of nondeterministic automata on words: It is a device which scans "local neighbourhoods" in a given partial order while (nondeterministically) assigning states to the points of this partial order. We show that the details of this idea can be fixed in such a way as to allow a clear connection to logical descriptions: A set of (finite and labelled) partial orders is recognizable by such a finite automaton iff it is

1991 *Mathematics Subject Classification.* Primary 54C40, 14E20; Secondary 46E25, 20C20.

definable in existential monadic second-order logic (i.e., by a sentence which begins with a prefix of existential set quantifiers, followed by a first-order formula). If the structures under consideration are even linearly ordered (i.e., words) or if they are labelled trees, this result can be sharpened to the well-known equivalence between automata and (full) monadic second-order logic. So, regarding automata theory in a general context, existential monadic second-order logic can be considered as more basic than unrestricted monadic second-order logic.

In the automata theoretic view, where the notion of "local neighbourhood" is essential, it is useful to identify a (discrete) partial order $\leq$ with an acyclic directed graph, taking as edge relation E the minimal relation which generates by its reflexive transitive closure the partial order $\leq$. (Thus $(u, v) \in E$ holds iff u and v are distinct, $u \leq v$, and there is no w with $u < w < v$.)

We shall confine ourselves to finite acyclic graphs of this form in the present paper. While the basic ideas are easily transferred also to infinite structures, some additional difficulties arise in connection with logic, namely the choice of appropriate acceptance conditions in automata. It is (as yet) not clear whether simple acceptance conditions exist which lead to a characterization of interesting logical systems (as, for example, the model of tree automaton with the Rabin acceptance condition of [**Rab69**] characterizes monadic second-order logic over infinite labelled binary trees).

As it turns out, the properties of automaton definable sets depend on the particular class of partial orders (or acyclic graphs) which are allowed as inputs. Special cases of such classes are: words, trees, Mazurkiewicz trace graphs, and labelled rectangular grids. We investigate two basic questions: Are the automaton recognizable sets closed under complement? When is the nonemptiness problem decidable?

The paper is structured as follows: In the subsequent two sections we introduce the necessary terminology concerning partial orders and acyclic graphs, as well as the logical systems of first-order logic and monadic second-order logic. Some easy propositions are listed which illustrate the expressive power of these logics. In a section on first-order logic we present the key theorem which supplies a bridge to automata theory. It is a classical result of first-order model theory, due to Hanf [**Hnf65**], but not well-known in the community of theoretical computer science. Automata over acyclic graphs are introduced in Section 5. Some special forms are presented, and classes of partial orders are singled out over which these special forms are no restriction (i.e., normal forms of automata). In Section 6 we analyze the possibility of showing complementation lemmas and study the nonemptiness problem. The concluding section offers some directions for further research.

The approach adopted in this paper is based on ideas of [**Th91**]. Further results which serve as background have been shown in [**GRST96**] (mostly concerning labelled rectangular grids) and [**PST94**] (concerning general acyclic graphs). We cannot provide full proofs in this short communication, but try to give enough information to enable the reader to supply the details.

2. Partial Orders and Acyclic Graphs

As indicated in the introduction, we consider partial orders in the form of acyclic vertex-labelled and edge-labelled directed graphs. Usually we take A as label alphabet for vertices and B as label alphabet for edges (both alphabets are finite). As a relational structure, a graph is thus presented in the form

$$G = (V, (P_a)_{a \in A}, (E_b)_{b \in B})$$

where V is the set of vertices, the P_a are disjoint subsets of V whose union is V, and the E_b are disjoint non-reflexive binary relations over V. The edge set is the union $E = \bigcup_{b \in B} E_b$. Thus, we consider a vertex v to be labelled with letter a if $v \in P_a$, and an edge (u, v) to be labelled with letter b if $(u, v) \in E_b$. In the sequel, such graphs are always assumed to be acyclic (which means that no nonempty path exists from a vertex v back to v). Hence one obtains a partial order when forming the reflexive transitive closure E^* of the edge set E. We shall also assume that E is given as minimal edge relation generating a partial order; this means we exclude the existence of an edge (u, v) in the presence of a vertex w with nonempty paths from u to w and from w to v. A vertex u is called *root* of a partial order $\leq$ if $u \leq v$ for all vertices v; in the dual case (when $v \leq u$ holds for all vertices v) we speak of a *co-root*.

A special case of edge labelling is called *indexing*, namely when the label alphabet is a set $\{1, \ldots, k\}$ and either the out-edges of each vertex are numbered by $1, \ldots, i$ for some $i \leq k$, or the corresponding holds for the ingoing edges of each vertex. (We shall speak of out-edge indexing, respectively in-edge indexing.)

Let us consider the possibility of accepting such graphs by finite-state devices. We follow the intuitive idea that acceptance is based on a scanning process which checks all "local neighbourhoods" in the graph G under consideration. This scanning process should associate (generally in a nondeterministic way) states from a finite state-set Q to the vertices of G. Here, a minimal version of neighbourhood is given by a vertex together with its incoming and outgoing edges and their source vertices, respectively target vertices. If the acceptor (or graph automaton) is honestly finite, it can distinguish only a fixed number of different local neighbourhoods. In order to match this assumption on finite-state acceptors, we allow only graphs of bounded degree in a recognizable or definable set, i.e., graphs where for each vertex v the number of vertices u with $(u, v) \in E$ or $(v, u) \in E$ is bounded by a predefined constant d. If such a bound is dropped, non-isomorphic neighbourhoods will be confused. This more general case could also be handled in the framework to be developed below, but it adds complications and distracts from the essential points.

Let us list some basic classes of graphs and associated partial orders which fall under these conventions.

- *Words over an alphabet* A: These are (in our case nonempty) structures $(\{1, \ldots, n\}, (P_a)_{a \in A}, E)$ where n is the length of the word, $1, \ldots, n$ are the letter positions, P_a collects the positions carrying letter a, and E is the successor relation on $\{1, \ldots, n\}$.
- *Ordered labelled trees*: Taking the case of binary trees as a typical example, these are graphs of the form $(V, (P_a)_{a \in A}, E_1, E_2)$, where V is the set of tree nodes, the sets P_a are used as for words, and E_1, E_2 are the two relations of "first successor" and "second successor", respectively. In the usual way, this numbering of the successors induces a "left-to-right ordering" on the set of leaves.
- *Dependency graphs of Mazurkiewicz traces* (cf. **[DR95]**): Here the alphabet A is given together with a reflexive and symmetric dependency relation $D \subseteq A \times A$. The format of dependency graphs is the same as for words,

however E does not necessarily generate a linear order but just a partial one: The edge relation E respects D in the sense that edges connect only vertices with dependent letters and that any two vertices labelled by dependent letters are connected by a path. By reflexivity of D, the size of antichains in dependency graphs (subsets consisting of pairwise unrelated vertices in the associated partial order) is bounded by the size of the alphabet; we say that dependency graphs have *bounded antichains.*

- *Rectangular grids* ("two-dimensional words", "pictures", cf. [**GRST96**]): In this case, the vertices are arranged in a two-dimensional array, connected by a horizontal successor relation E_1 ("to the right") and a vertical successor relation E_2 ("downwards"). Thus the signature coincides with that of binary trees.
- *Mirror tree concatenations*: These are obtained by concatenating tree structures $t_1, s_1, t_2, s_2, \ldots, t_k, s_k$ in the following way (we just consider the case of binary trees): Each t_i is a binary tree as above, each s_i is obtained from a binary tree (with the same number of leaves as in t_i) by inverting the edge directions (which makes leaves into "sources" and the root into a "target"), and concatenation is carried out by identifying the leaves of t_i (left to right) with the sources of s_i (right to left), and identifying the target of s_i with the root of t_{i+1}.
- *(Acyclic) graphs of bounded tree-width k* (cf. e.g. [**Cou89**], [**See92**]): These graphs are associated to trees by the following condition: There is a covering of the vertex set by a collection of vertex sets (called "clusters" here), on which an undirected edge relation R exists such that
  1. for each graph edge (u, v) there is a cluster containing u and v,
  2. the clusters together with R define an undirected tree t,
  3. each cluster C contains at most k vertices,
  4. the clusters in which a given vertex v occurs form a connected subset of the tree t.

In the order of the list above, we denote the respective classes of acyclic graphs by *Words*, *Trees*, *Traces*, *Grids*, *MTreeC*, *BTWGraphs*.

3. Basic Logics

In the sequel, words, trees, traces, grids, and, in general, acyclic graphs, are considered as relational structures of the forms above. This allows to introduce logical definability notions in a uniform way. Here we do this in the framework of monadic second-order logic. Over graphs with the label alphabets A (for vertices) and B (for edges), formulas of monadic second-order logic involve variables $x, y, \ldots$ for vertices and $X, Y, \ldots$ for sets of vertices; they are built up from atomic formulas

$$P_a(x) \text{ (for } a \in A), \ E_b(x, y) \text{ (for } b \in B), \ x = y, \ X(y)$$

by means of the connectives $\neg, \vee, \wedge, \rightarrow, \leftrightarrow$ and the quantifiers $\exists, \forall$ which may be applied to either kind of variable. The notation $\varphi(x_1, \ldots, x_m, X_1, \ldots, X_n)$ indicates that in the formula φ at most the variables $x_1, \ldots, x_m, X_1, \ldots, X_n$ occur free, i.e., not in the scope of a quantifier. If $G = (V, (P_a^G)_{a\in A}, (E_b^G)_{b\in B})$ is a graph, $v_1, \ldots, v_m \in V$, $V_1, \ldots V_n \subseteq V$, the satisfaction relation

$$(G, v_1, \ldots, v_m, V_1, \ldots V_n) \models \varphi(x_1, \ldots x_m, X_1, \ldots, X_n)$$

holds if φ is formed for the signature given by the label alphabets A, B and satisfied in G when interpreting x_i by v_i, X_i by V_i, and of course $=$ by equality, P_a by P_a^G, and E_b by E_b^G. The superscripts G thus distinguish the relations in interpretations from relation symbols in formulas; they will be omitted (as done also above) when no confusion arises.

Let $\mathcal{K}$ be a class of (acyclic) graphs. Relative to $\mathcal{K}$, a sentence φ defines the (graph) language

$$L(\varphi) = \{G \in \mathcal{K} \mid G \models \varphi\}.$$

A language $L \subseteq \mathcal{K}$ is called definable in monadic second-order logic (short: MSO-definable) if some sentence φ with $L = L(\varphi)$ exists.

The significance of monadic second-order logic (MSO-logic) for automata theory rests on the following classical result for the class *Words*:

THEOREM 3.1. (Büchi [**Bü60**], Elgot [**Elg61**])
A language $L \subset A^+$ is recognizable by a finite automaton iff it is MSO-definable.

PROOF. The idea for the step from automata to MSO-formulas is to introduce, for any state q_i of the given automaton, a set variable X_i for the set of those positions in a word where state q_i is assumed in a run. One formalizes the existence of an accepting run of an automaton with n states $q_0, \dots, q_{n-1}$ over a word w by saying that there are sets $X_0, \dots, X_{n-1}$ such that the first letter position belongs to X_0 (assuming q_0 is the initial state), each successor step is compatible with the transition relation of the automaton, and from the state on the last position, one reaches by the last letter a final state. Note that the first and last position are definable by the formulas $\neg\exists y E(y, x)$ and $\neg\exists y E(x, y)$, respectively. The resulting formula is an existential monadic second-order formula, short an EMSO-formula.

The converse direction, from MSO-formulas to automata, is based on standard closure properties of automaton recognizable languages, namely closure under union and complement (which captures propositional logic) and projection (which captures the existential quantifier). For a more detailed proof see e.g. [**Th96**]. □

By applying the second and the first part of the proof in succession, one obtains that an MSO-formula (over word graphs) can be rewritten as an EMSO-formula.

The basis of the proof above is the equivalence between nondeterministic and deterministic finite automata: Nondeterminism serves to show closure of recognizable sets under projection, determinism shows closure under complement. The reduction to deterministic automata was shown also for finite automata over trees (using the "frontier-to-root mode" in tree automata, cf.[**GS84**]), whence an analogue of the theorem above holds also for the class *Trees*, including the reduction of MSO-logic to EMSO-logic. Without treating definitions in detail, let us also mention that over *Traces* a similar development is possible, now invoking Zielonka's construction of deterministic asynchronous automata ([**Zi87**]).

Let us introduce further subsystems of MSO-logic, including first-order logic with different signatures.

In the traditional classification of second-order formulas, the EMSO-formulas are also called monadic Σ_1^1-formulas. The dual formulas, where a prefix of universal set quantifiers precedes a first-order kernel, are called monadic Π_1^1-formulas. The corresponding properties (defined by such formulas) are called monadic Σ_1^1-properties, respectively monadic Π_1^1-properties. A property which is both monadic-Σ_1^1 and monadic-Π_1^1 is called a monadic Δ_1^1-property. In short we speak of monΣ_1^1-, monΠ^1_1-, and monΔ^1_1-properties. By $(\text{mon}\Delta^1_1)_{Words}$ we denote the class of word properties (or: word languages) which are monΔ^1_1-definable; similarly for the other definability notions.

As an example, consider a monadic Σ^1_1-sentence which says that a successful run of a finite automaton over a word exists (see the proof above). For a *deterministic* finite automaton this sentence can also be written as a monadic Π^1_1-sentence, namely as saying: "All state sequences which start in the initial state and which for any two succeeding positions are compatible with the transition relation, have a state on the last letter position from which (by the last letter) a final state is reached." Since finite automata on words can be made deterministic, we thus have the following equalities:

PROPOSITION 3.2.

$$(\text{mon}\Delta^1_1)_{Words} = (\text{mon}\Sigma^1_1)_{Words} = (\text{mon}\Pi^1_1)_{Words} = \text{MSO}_{Words}.$$

The same is true over *Trees*.

First-order logic, short FO-logic (over acyclic graphs) is obtained from MSO-logic as above by dropping set quantifications. Typical quantifications in this logic are of the form $\exists y(E_b(x,y) \wedge \varphi(y))$ and $\forall y(E_b(x,y) \to \varphi(y))$, which express "there is a b-successor of x satisfying φ", respectively "all b-successors of x satisfy φ". Thus FO-logic includes standard process logics, such as the finitary version of "Hennessy-Milner-logic" (cf. [**Mil90**]).

It is well-known that in first-order logic the transitive closure of a given relation is (in general) not definable: In particular, in acyclic graphs the associated partial order is not definable. (A proof will be given in the next section.) Thus we obtain a stronger system of "first-order logic with $\leq$" when to FO-logic as above a symbol $\leq$ for the reflexive transitive closure of the edge relation E is added. We denote this system by FO[$\leq$]-logic. Typically, it allows to express properties of linear or partial orders which are formalizable in systems of propositional temporal logic. Over grids, we obtain an expressively equivalent variant of FO[$\leq$]-logic when for the two edge relations E_1 and E_2 the respective reflexive transitive closures $\leq_1$ and $\leq_2$ are introduced instead of $\leq$. Note that we have $x \leq y$ iff $x \leq_1 z$ and $z \leq_2 y$ for some z. Conversely, each relation $\leq_i$ is first-order definable in terms of the relation E_i and $\leq$: We have $x \leq_i y$ iff $x \leq y$ and (in case x and y are distinct) any z with $x < z \leq y$ is E_i-successor of some z' with $x \leq z' \leq y$.

For a class $\mathcal{K}$ of acyclic graphs, any of the above notions of definability induces a corresponding class of definable graph sets. We denote this class by the logical system with an index for the class $\mathcal{K}$, in the form $\text{FO}_{\mathcal{K}}$, $\text{FO}[\leq]_{\mathcal{K}}$, $(\text{mon}\Sigma^1_1)_{\mathcal{K}}$ ($= \text{EMSO}_{\mathcal{K}}$), etc.

The following statement is trivial.

PROPOSITION 3.3. *For any class $\mathcal{K}$ of acyclic graphs, we have*

$$\text{FO}_{\mathcal{K}} \subseteq (\text{mon}\Delta^1_1)_{\mathcal{K}} \subseteq (\text{mon}\Sigma^1_1)_{\mathcal{K}} \subseteq \text{MSO}_{\mathcal{K}}.$$

Over *Words* and *Trees*, FO[$\leq$]-logic can be placed between FO-logic and EMSO-logic: One notes that $x \leq y$ is defined by the MSO-formula

$$\forall X(X(x) \wedge \forall z \forall z'((X(z) \wedge E(z,z')) \to X(z')) \to X(y)),$$

whence the claim follows by the expressive equivalence of EMSO-logic and MSO-logic over *Words*, respectively *Trees*. In fact, we have a sharper result, establishing the following proper inclusions (indicated by "$\subset$") and equalities:

PROPOSITION 3.4.

$$\mathrm{FO}_{Words} \subset \mathrm{FO}[\leq]_{Words} \subset (\mathrm{mon}\Delta_1^1)_{Words} = (\mathrm{mon}\Sigma_1^1)_{Words} = \mathrm{MSO}_{Words}.$$

PROOF. (Hint.) The language $a^*ba^*ca^*$ is an example of a word set which is definable in FO[$\leq$]-logic by the sentence

$$\exists x \exists y (P_b(x) \wedge x < y \wedge P_c(y) \wedge \forall z(\neg(z = x \vee z = y) \rightarrow P_a(z)))$$

but not in FO-logic (see next section). The next proper inclusion is exemplified by the set of words of even length. It is definable by a monadic Σ_1^1-sentence requiring a set X of positions which contains the first letter position, then every second position (i.e. satisfying $\forall z \forall z'(E(z,z') \rightarrow (X(z) \leftrightarrow \neg X(z')))$, and does not contain the last position. An equivalent Π_1^1-sentence says that all sets which contain the first position and then every second position do not contain the last position. An application of the Ehrenfeucht-Fraissé method shows that the word property of having even length is not expressible in first-order logic with linear ordering (cf. e.g. [**EF95**], [**Th96**]). The last two equalities are clear from Proposition 3.2. □

In Section 6 we shall see that over *Grids*, FO[$\leq$]-logic and EMSO-logic (or (monΣ_1^1)-logic) are incompatible in expressive power, and that the last two equalities of Proposition 3.4 turn into strict inclusions.

4. Hanf's Theorem

In [**Hnf65**], Hanf showed that in the first-order language of graphs only "local properties" can be specified. A property is local if it depends only on the occurrence (or non-occurrence) of certain local neighbourhoods around vertices. More precisely, call (for $r \geq 0$) *r-sphere around vertex v in the graph G* the induced subgraph over those vertices in G which have distance $\leq r$ to v, and with v as designated center. (The distance of u to v is $\leq r$ if there is a path $v_0 v_1 \dots v_k$ with $k \leq r$, $v_0 = v$, $v_k = u$, and $(v_i, v_{i+1}) \in E$ or $(v_{i+1}, v_i) \in E$ for $i < k$.) Clearly, if the graphs under consideration are of bounded degree (and of a fixed signature regarding the labellings), there are only finitely many possible isomorphism types of r-spheres.

It is easy to write down a sentence $\varphi_{\tau,\geq n}$ which says that there are at least n different occurrences of spheres of a given isomorphism type τ. Using conjunctions of such sentences and negations of such sentences, one can specify for finitely many types $\tau_1, \dots, \tau_m$ that the occurrence number of τ_i is $\leq n_i$, or $< n_i$, or $= n_i$. A graph language L defined by a disjunction of such conditions (or equivalently: by a boolean combination of sentences $\varphi_{\tau,\geq n}$) is called *locally threshold testable.*

Equivalently, L is representable in terms of a certain equivalence relation $\sim_{r,t}$ between graphs. Define $G \sim_{r,t} G'$ to hold if for all types τ of r-spheres, the occurrence numbers of τ in G and G' are both $\geq t$ or else coincide. Over graphs of bounded degree, $\sim_{r,t}$ is an equivalence relation of finite index. An easy exercise shows that a set L is locally threshold testable iff L is a union of $\sim_{r,t}$-classes for some radius r and threshold number t.

The main result in the first-order model theory of graphs says that the above mentioned conditions on occurrence numbers already exhaust the expressive power of first-order logic:

THEOREM 4.1. (essentially Hanf [**Hnf65**])
A first-order definable set of graphs (of bounded degree) is locally threshold testable.

In particular, a first-order sentence is equivalent to a boolean combination of sentences of the form "there are $\geq n$ occurrences of r-spheres of type τ".

The proof rests on an application of the Ehrenfeucht-Fraissé-game. We refer the reader to **[EF95]**, **[FSV95]**, or **[Th96]** for details.

Let us sketch three applications. First, we verify that the language $L = a^*ba^*ca^*$ is not in FO_{Words}. Otherwise, we would obtain a contradiction: From an assumed FO-sentence defining L we would obtain r and t such that two words (word models) which are $\sim_{r,t}$-equivalent are both in L or both not in L. But it is easily seen that for sufficiently large n the words $a^nba^nca^n (\in L)$ and $a^nca^nba^n (\notin L)$ have the the same occurrence numbers of r-spheres counted up to threshold t and thus are $\sim_{r,t}$-equivalent.

In a similar way, it is shown in the domain *Grids* that the set of all square grids (of size $n \times n$ for $n \geq 1$, whose vertices are all labelled with a) is not first-order definable.

Finally, as a preparation to the next section, we note the following consequence of Hanf's Theorem:

PROPOSITION 4.2. *The class* $\mathrm{EMSO}_{\mathcal{K}}$ *coincides with the class of projections of locally threshold testable languages* $L \subseteq \mathcal{K}$.

PROOF. As a preparation, consider a graph G with vertex labels in A. An expansion $(G, V_1, \dots, V_m)$ by designated vertex sets V_i, which allows to interpret a formula $\varphi(X_1, \dots, X_m)$, can be represented as a graph H with vertex labels in $A \times \{0,1\}^m$: The i-th additional component has value 1 for vertex v iff $v \in V_i$.

Now a graph G satisfies a sentence $\exists X_1 \dots \exists X_m \varphi(X_1, \dots X_m)$ (with first-order formula φ) iff some graph H, which arises from G by expanding the vertex labels from A to $A \times \{0,1\}^m$, satisfies $\varphi(X_1, \dots, X_m)$. But this is equivalent to the existence of a graph H in $L(\varphi)$ (which by Hanf's Theorem is a locally threshold testable language) such that $h(H) = G$ for the projection $h : A \times \{0,1\}^m \to A$. □

Hanf's Theorem connects first-order logic to local properties and is thus a good starting point for a logically motivated automata theory over graphs.

5. Finite-State Acceptors and Special Forms

We introduce graph acceptors which capture projections of locally threshold testable sets:

A *graph acceptor* over the alphabets A, B has the form $\mathcal{A} = (Q, A, B, \Delta, Occ)$ where

- Q is a finite set (of "states"),
- Δ is, for some $r \geq 0$, a finite set of r-spheres with vertex labels in $A \times Q$ and edge labels in B,
- Occ is a boolean combination of conditions "there are $\geq n$ occurrences of spheres of type τ" (where τ is an r-sphere type over the label alphabets $A \times Q$ and B).

We call Δ the set of *transitions* and Occ the *occurrence constraint*.

The graph acceptor $\mathcal{A}$ *accepts* the graph G if it can be "tiled by transitions" such that a consistent assignment of states to vertices (a "run") is defined and such that the occurrence constraint is satisfied. Formally, there should be a run $\rho : V \to Q$ such that each r-sphere of the expanded graph G_ρ with vertex labels in $A \times Q$ matches a transition from Δ, and the occurrences of these spheres are compatible with the constraint *Occ*. We call this covering of G an "accepting tiling" of G and sometimes speak of transitions as "tiles" and graph acceptors as "tiling systems" (cf. [**Th91**]).

The graph language recognized by $\mathcal{A}$ (relative to the graph class $\mathcal{K}$) is

$$L_{\mathcal{K}}(\mathcal{A}) = \{G \in \mathcal{K} \mid \mathcal{A} \text{ accepts } G\}.$$

We say that $L \subseteq \mathcal{K}$ is *recognizable* iff $L = L_{\mathcal{K}}(\mathcal{A})$ for some graph acceptor $\mathcal{A}$.

By Proposition 4.2, graph acceptors characterize existential monadic second-order logic:

PROPOSITION 5.1. *For any class $\mathcal{K}$ of graphs of bounded degree, a language $L \subseteq \mathcal{K}$ is recognizable iff $L \in \mathrm{EMSO}_{\mathcal{K}}$.*

Similarly, a language L is recognizable by a graph acceptor with only one state iff L is first-order definable.

Usual finite automata over words or trees are simulated by special graph acceptors, in which only 1-spheres are used as transitions and the occurrence constraints are cancelled. The use of initial and final states in the classical model is captured by the use of 1-spheres whose designated center has no predecessor, respectively no successor; such transitions can only be used at the beginning, respectively at the end of a word.

In comparison with classical automata, two features of graph automata seem complicated: the use of r-spheres for $r > 1$, and the use of occurrence constraints. We shall see that both features can be eliminated only with extra restrictions on the input graphs.

In order to see that over acyclic graphs in general the use of r-spheres in transitions can not be eliminated by resorting to 1-spheres only, we consider the following example, suggested by S. Seibert.

PROPOSITION 5.2. *Let L_n be the set of "n-supergrids", which have vertex label "a" throughout and are obtained from standard grids by substituting for any edge an edge sequence of length n (called "superedge"). L_n is recognizable (in the class of partial orders) by a graph acceptor with $2n$-sphere transitions, but not by graph acceptors with 1-sphere transitions.*

PROOF. It is easy to verify recognizability of L_n by a graph acceptor with $2n$-sphere transitions. For contradiction, consider a graph acceptor $\mathcal{A}$ which recognizes L_n (say for $n \geq 4$) with 1-sphere transitions. In an accepting run of a large enough n-supergrid, there will be two occurrences of the same 1-sphere transition at corresponding positions on two superedges, not touching the ends of the superedges and unrelated in the partial order of the supergrid. (One may choose two occurrences of the same 1-sphere transition at the central positions of two superedges in the same row or in the same column of a large enough n-supergrid.) Obtain a new graph by exchanging the targets of the outgoing edges in the two 1-spheres covered by these transitions. The new graph is still acyclic, accepted by $\mathcal{A}$, but not in L_n. □

A similar idea appears in Example 3.2 of [**Th91**]; there it is shown that our graph acceptors are properly more expressive than the dag automata of Kamimura and Slutzki [**KS81**].

In contrast to the proposition above, one verifies that over the classes *Words*, *Trees*, *Traces*, and *Grids*, the use of 1-spheres is sufficient. (The reduction from

r-sphere transitions to 1-sphere transitions involves a blow-up in the number of states.) Moreover, in the domain *Grids* there is a variant of 1-spheres which may seem more natural: In the approach developed in [**GRST96**] over *Grids*, the transitions are just (2×2)-squares of four vertices and edges. In this model, where transitions have no designated center, the corners and borders of grids are no more detectable (i.e., tilable by special transitions only), and thus grids are presented with extra rows and columns of border markers #, also to be covered by transitions.

A precise description of the class of acyclic graphs where in graph acceptors the use of 1-sphere transitions suffices is not known.

Let us turn to the occurrence constraints. In general they can also not be eliminated: We consider the set of acyclic graphs G_n made up of vertices $u_1, \dots, u_n$ and $v_1, \dots, v_n$ as follows: From u_i there are two edges, one to v_i and one to $v_{(i+1) \bmod n}$. One may imagine the u_i and the v_i arranged in two circles (modulo n), with two pointers from each vertex of the first circle to the second circle. Now consider the graph language L consisting of such graphs where at least one u_i is labelled a and the remaining vertices (not labelled a) are labelled b. It is clear that by an occurrence constraint the existence of a vertex with label a can be guaranteed. Now, for a contradiction suppose that L is recognizable without occurrence constraints. Consider the graphs G_n over $u_1, \dots, u_n$ and $v_1, \dots, v_n$ with precisely one label a, say at u_1. For sufficiently large n, there will be an accepting tiling where a transition is repeated, say with centers at u_i and u_j and such that u_1 is not covered by these two copies of the transition. Then the graph with vertices $u_{i+1}, \dots, u_j, v_{i+1}, \dots v_j$ (built up modulo $j - i$), which has no label a, admits also an accepting tiling, a contradiction.

In some situations, however, the occurrence constraints can be eliminated (at the cost of more states in graph acceptors). In particular, this applies to the classes *Words*, *Trees*, and *Grids*. The idea is to implement a threshold counting procedure within the transitions, using the partial order to avoid loops in the counting process. It is essential that the overall counting result can be collected at some special vertex. This motivates the following claim:

PROPOSITION 5.3. *Let $\mathcal{K}$ be a class of acyclic graphs which have indexed out-edges and a co-root (and hence are connected). Then a language $L \subseteq \mathcal{K}$ is recognizable iff it is recognizable by a graph acceptor without occurrence constraints. The same holds if the graphs in $\mathcal{K}$ have indexed in-edges and a root.*

PROOF. Consider a graph acceptor with state set Q, transitions $\tau_1, \dots, \tau_k$ (say of radius r), and occurrence constraint *Occ* in which t is a threshold such that occurrence numbers $\geq t$ are not distinguished in *Occ*. We construct a new graph acceptor whose states are vectors $(q, n_1, \dots, n_k)$ with $n_i \leq t$ for $i = 1, \dots, k$. At vertex v this vector indicates that state $q \in Q$ is assumed and "up to now" the transition τ_i has occurred n_i times. These occurrence numbers are updated following the paths of the partial order of the input graph. The indices of the out-edges serve to avoid double-counting: The accumulated occurrence numbers are transferred only along the outgoing edges with index 1. Thus, for an r-sphere of type τ_i whose center has no incoming edges, only the vector $(n_1, \dots, n_k)$ with $n_i = 1$ and $n_j = 0$ for $j \neq i$ is allowed. Any given r-sphere, say of type τ_i, which has incoming edges, is (in its center) supplied with a vector $(n_1, \dots, n_k)$ where each n_j is the sum of the j-th components of the sources of incoming edges which carry index 1, and where furthermore 1 is added to n_i (to capture that the present type is τ_i). Finally, r-sphere transitions for the co-root (the vertex without outgoing edges) are allowed only for the case that the center vertex is labelled with some vector $(n_1, \ldots, n_k)$ which satisfies Occ.

The proof for the case of indexed in-edges and the existence of a root is analogous. □

It is clear that words, trees, and grids are subsumed by the preceding proposition. Formally, in the case of grids one has to modify the edge labels in order to have indexed out-edges: The vertices of the last column of a grid, which have no (horizontal) E_1-successors in the original convention, should now have vertical out-edges in E_1 (instead of E_2). The elimination of occurrence constraints over grids is treated in detail in [**GRST96**].

Finally, we turn to a special form of acceptor on partial orders which represents a proper restriction: *deterministic acceptors.* Partial orders are a useful assumption for introducing deterministic acceptors; there should be a uniqueness in the construction of runs when proceeding from smaller to greater vertices in the partial order. There seems to be no canonical definition of deterministic graph acceptors; and even over simple acyclic graphs like the rectangular grids there are several possibilities. We suggest here a "determinism by states" (rather than "determinism by transitions"). We call an acceptor (say with r-sphere transitions) over partial orders *deterministic* if for any r-sphere around a vertex v and any state assignment to the vertices $u < v$ in this r-sphere, the assignment of a state to v (by the available transitions) is unique. (Note that a certain "lookahead" is built into this definition because a sphere has to match a whole neighbourhood of the input graph.) So, the state assignment is unique *per se* for vertices which have no predecessors in the partial order. This definition is compatible with determinism over words and trees (using frontier-to-root tree automata, i.e., with the reversed partial order in trees). For a class $\mathcal{K}$ of acyclic graphs, denote by $\mathrm{Det}_{\mathcal{K}}$ the class of languages $L \subseteq \mathcal{K}$ which are recognized by deterministic graph acceptors.

An example of a language in Det_{Grids} is the set of square grids (trivially labelled by a throughout). The assignment of states can be arranged such that a special state is associated to the diagonal starting from the unique vertex without incoming edges (which we assume to be on the top left corner). The square property is verified when in transitions for other border positions this special state is allowed only for the vertex without any outgoing edges (at the bottom right corner).

Let us verify that determinism is a proper restriction. A well-known example is provided by the domain *Trees* when scanned in root-to-frontier mode (cf. [**GS84**]). But also over partial orders which have a co-root (where information of a run can be gathered in a single vertex) this phenomenon occurs:

PROPOSITION 5.4. *There is a grid language which is recognizable by a graph acceptor but not by a deterministic graph acceptor.*

PROOF. A suitable example is provided in [**PST94**]: Consider the set L of square grids which have label b everywhere except for two vertices labelled a on the right border and bottom border, in the same distance δ to the right-bottom corner. (Call this δ the "a-distance".) An appropriate nondeterministic graph acceptor guesses a point on the diagonal (from the top left to the bottom right corner), and from this point sends two "signals" (in the form of special states), one horizontally to the right, one vertically to the bottom. If at the two border points hit in this way letter a occurs, this information can be transmitted to the bottom right corner (where the transitions are defined as to check this). The test that otherwise letter b occurs is easily implemented.

Now suppose that a deterministic graph acceptor recognizing this grid language L exists. Invoking the construction of Proposition 5.3, we can assume that occurrence constraints are eliminated (note that the construction transforms deterministic graph acceptors again into deterministic ones). Suppose the acceptor has r-sphere transitions. Then the states of accepting runs on two grids from L of the same size are identical except for the last r rows and last r columns. The $(r+1)$-st last rows thus coincide except for the last r columns. Because there are only finitely many assignments of transitions to the last r positions of a row, there exist (for sufficiently large size of input squares) two squares $G_1, G_2 \in L$ of same size and with two different a-distances such that in the corresponding accepting runs also the last r transitions on the $(r+1)$-st last row coincide in G_1 and G_2. Then the last r rows from the accepting tiling of G_1 can be exchanged with the last r rows of the accepting tiling of G_2. Hence a grid outside the language L is accepted, a contradiction. □

For deterministic acceptors over *Grids*, the reduction of r-spheres to 1-spheres is no more possible. A simple example is the set of computations of a Turing machine. Such computations are represented in a space-time diagram and hence in grid form. To check a labelled grid for being a computation of a given Turing machine, one can use a deterministic (single-state) acceptor using 2-sphere transitions, but not a deterministic acceptor with 1-sphere transitions.

Determinism corresponds to a restriction of EMSO-logic. As in the case of words (see Proposition 3.2), monadic Σ_1^1-definitions can be put into Π_1^1-form:

PROPOSITION 5.5. *If a language $L \subseteq \mathcal{K}$ of acyclic graphs is recognizable deterministically, then $L \in (\text{mon}\Delta_1^1)_{\mathcal{K}}$.*

6. Some Results on Expressiveness and Decidability

In this section we come back to the question raised in the introduction: Over which classes of acyclic graphs (or generated partial orders) are the recognizable sets closed under complement (i.e., EMSO-logic is as expressive as MSO-logic), and when is the nonemptiness problem decidable? Whereas both questions are solved positively in the domains *Words*, *Trees*, *Traces*, let us see that this fails over *Grids*. In the statement below we also include the relation to deterministic recognizability and Δ_1^1-properties. At the same time, we settle the relation between EMSO-logic and FO[$\leq$]-logic over grids.

THEOREM 6.1. (a) *The following inclusion chain is proper:*

$$\text{Det}_{Grids} \subset (\text{mon}\Delta_1^1)_{Grids} \subset (\text{mon}\Sigma_1^1)_{Grids} \subset \text{MSO}_{Grids}$$

(b) *The classes* $\text{FO}[\leq]_{Grids}$ *and* $(\text{mon}\Sigma_1^1)_{Grids}$ *are incompatible with respect to inclusion.*

(c) *The nonemptiness problem of graph acceptors over grids is undecidable.*

PROOF. (a) The inclusions as such are clear from the preceding remarks. To verify that the first inclusion is strict, take the example set L of Proposition 5.4. To show that L is in $(\text{mon}\Delta_1^1)_{Grids}$, it remains to supply a $(\text{mon}\Pi_1^1)$-definition. Such a sentence can be constructed starting from the following condition: "For each set X of vertices consisting of (1) a prefix of the diagonal up to some vertex u, (2) the vertices to the right of u on the same row, ending with v, and (3) the vertices below u on the same column, ending with w, we have: if v is labelled with a, so is w."

For the strictness of the second inclusion, we identify a grid with its sequence of columns, regarding as column the associated sequence of vertex labels. Following **[GRST96]**, we consider the set N of grids of the form GH where G and H are distinct square grids of the same size over the vertex label alphabet $\{a, b\}$. This set is monadic Σ_1^1, because the existence of a pair (x, y) of vertices (at corresponding positions in G and H) with distinct labels can be formulated using existential set quantifiers. (Namely, there should be a set X_1 containing all points on the same horizontal as x, and furthermore a set X_2 which occupies the diagonal, which starts at the topmost vertex above x, downward to the right. Now y is the unique point above the end of this diagonal which belongs to X_1.) In order to show that N is not monadic Π_1^1, it suffices to show that the set of grids GG, consisting of two identical square grids, is not monadic Σ_1^1. Here we use the characterization of monadic Σ_1^1, i.e. EMSO-logic, by graph acceptors with 1-sphere transitions and without occurrence constraints. Such a graph acceptor can transfer the information from the left square grid to the right square grid only via the two stripes of transitions along the border between the two half grids (of square form). For the given graph acceptor, the number of such stripes is $k^{(r \cdot n)}$ (for some fixed k and r) in the length n of the sides of squares. However the number of possible squares grows by the rate 2^{n^2}. Thus, for sufficiently large n we find distinct squares G and H of side length n such that on accepting tilings over GG and HH the stripes of 1-spheres right and left to the central border are identical. This implies that GH and HG are also accepted, a contradiction.

The set of grids GG where G is square shows that also the last inclusion of the claim is proper.

(b) The set of grids consisting of a single column of even length is (monΣ_1^1)-definable but not FO[$\leq$]-definable (see Proposition 3.4). In order to exhibit a grid language which is FO[$\leq$]-definable but not (monΣ_1^1)-definable (i.e., not recognizable), consider a variant of the set N above: the set M of grids of the form GCH where C is a column labelled by a special letter c and where the sets of different column words occurring in G and H (over the vertex label alphabet $\{a, b\}$) coincide. This set M is definable in FO[$\leq$]-logic, making use of the condition that for all positions x in the first row before the vertex labelled c, there is a position y in the first row after the vertex labelled c such that the columns associated to x and y coincide; similarly for each such y after the c-labelled vertex there is a corresponding x before the c-labelled vertex. The coincidence of the columns below x and y is easily formalizable with the relations $\leq_1$ and $\leq_2$, which in turn are definable in terms of $\leq$ (as shown in Section 3). The proof that M is not (monΣ_1^1)-definable is analogous to part (a) above, using the fact that for any constants k and r, the number of distinct sets of columns of length n exceeds $k^{(r \cdot n)}$ for sufficiently large n.

(c) We show that for any Turing machine $\mathcal{M}$ we can define a graph acceptor $\mathcal{A}_{\mathcal{M}}$ over an appropriate label alphabet which accepts some grid iff $\mathcal{M}$ halts when started on the empty tape. The idea is to let $\mathcal{A}$ accept just those grids which code a halting computation of $\mathcal{M}$ on the empty tape. Such a halting computation is finite in space and time (the two dimensions of the grid). Thus, the first line of such a grid is a sequence of blanks, with one pair (s_0, blank) (where s_0 is the initial state of $\mathcal{M}$). The correct succession of Turing machine configurations can be checked using 2-sphere transitions. That the grid is suffiently large to include all work cells of the computation is guaranteed by excluding transitions for border vertices which code work cells. Finally the last line should include a final state of $\mathcal{M}$. □

It should be noted that over *Words*, *Trees*, and *Traces* all classes of part (a) of the preceding theorem coincide (cf. Proposition 3.2).

An interesting problem is to find classes of partial orders beyond the domains *Words*, *Trees*, and *Traces*, over which EMSO-logic is closed under complement and/or where the nonemptiness problem for recognizable sets (satisfiability of EMSO-logic) is decidable. We discuss three classes: the partial orders with bounded antichains, the mirror tree concatenations, and the acyclic graphs of bounded tree-width.

Partial orders with bounded antichains constitute a generalization of trace graphs, in which the partial order is no more tied to a dependence structure of the vertex label alphabet. By a small modification of parts (a) and (c) of the preceding theorem, one verifies the following:

PROPOSITION 6.2. *Over acyclic graphs with bounded antichains, EMSO-logic is not closed under complement, and the satisfiability problem for EMSO-sentences (and hence the nonemptiness problem for finite-state graph acceptors) is undecidable.*

PROOF. We modify the grids of the preceding theorem (following an idea of I. Schiering): In the definition of the first successor relation (which proceeds horizontally from left to right), add an extra edge from the last vertex of each row (excluding the last two rows) to the first vertex of the second-next row, respectively. The resulting grid structure generates a partial order with antichains of at most two elements. One can now adapt the proofs of claims (a) and (c) above for these modified grids. □

For the class *MTreeC* if mirror tree concatenations we do not know whether a complementation result of EMSO-logic holds. However, it is easy to see that the nonemptiness problem for graph acceptors over the class *MTreeC* is undecidable: We use the undecidability of the nonemptiness problem for intersections of context-free languages. Given two context-free grammars G_1, G_2, one can construct a graph acceptor which accepts a pair (t, s) of mirror-concatenated trees iff t is a derivation tree for G_1, s is an inverted derivation tree for G_2, and the common sequence of leaves for t and s consists of terminal symbols only. Such a pair (t, s) exists iff G_1 and G_2 generate a common terminal word.

A better candidate domain for generalizing the classical closure and decidability results of automata theory seems to be the class of graphs of bounded tree-width. As shown by Courcelle [**Cou89**], the satisfiability of MSO-sentences over *BTWGraphs* is decidable. However, a reduction of MSO-logic to EMSO-logic (or equivalently: a complementation theorem for EMSO-logic) is unknown. In a restricted case, this reduction is possible ([**ST96**]), namely where a tree decomposition exists whose clusters are vertex sets which are connected by the symmetric closure of the graph edge relation.

7. Conclusion

In this paper, some suggestions were developed towards an automata theory over partial orders, and connections to various logical systems were established. We studied EMSO-logic and acceptors over several classes of finite partial orders and investigated the complementation problem and the nonemptiness problem for recognizable sets.

Some open questions have been mentioned already. Let us list some further directions which are unexplored.

(1) A theory of recognizable sets of infinite partial orders. Over which classes of infinite partial orders is it possible to introduce logically meaningful acceptance conditions, and what are these conditions? Over which classes is the nonemptiness problem decidable, possibly such that furthermore nonempty recognizable sets contain "regular" partial orders (where the meaning of "regular" is also open)?

(2) Complexity bounds for transformation algorithms and decision procedures. We did not discuss the complexity issue, e.g. in the conversion of formulas into automata or for the nonemptiness test. Note that already in the domain *Traces*, the available algorithms are of such a high complexity that a practical application seems hard.

(3) Development of other descriptive formalisms. Instead of systems of classical logic, more restrictive systems should be studied, whose expressive power might suffice for interesting applications but with acceptable complexity bounds e.g. for the satisfiability problem. These can be versions of regular expressions (cf. [**BDW95**]), or restrictions of EMSO-logic, or of FO[$\leq$]-logic, over partial orders.

(4) Comparison with the algebraic approach to recognizability. Here we refer to Courcelle's theory of recognizability, which is based on many-sorted and locally finite graph algebras (cf. [**Cou90**]). The class of recognizable graph sets in this setting is closed under boolean operations, and all MSO-definable sets turn out to be recognizable. Over *Grids*, recognizability in the algebraic sense is even strictly stronger than MSO-definability. It is open whether, for instance, the two approaches of recognizability (via tilings and via locally finite algebras) coincide for exactly those classes of partial orders where EMSO-logic is closed under complement.

8. Acknowledgment

I thank Oliver Matz, Ina Schiering, and Sebastian Seibert for their comments and suggestions, which led to corrections and improvements.

References

[BDW95] F. Bossut, M. Dauchet, B. Warin, A Kleene Theorem for a class of planar acyclic graphs, *Inform. and Comput.* **117** (1995), 251-265.

[Bü60] J.R. Büchi, Weak second-order arithmetic and finite automata, *Z. Math. Logik Grundl. Math.* **6** (1960), 66-92.

[Cou89] B. Courcelle, The monadic second-order theory of graphs II: Infinite graphs of bounded width, *Math. Syst. Theory* **21** (1989), 187-221.

[Cou90] B. Courcelle, The monadic second-order logic of graphs I: recognizable sets of finite graphs *Inform. and Comput.* **85** (1990), 12-75.

[DR95] V. Diekert, G. Rozenberg (Eds.), *The Book of Traces*, World Scientific, Singapore 1995.

[EF95] H.D. Ebbinghaus, J. Flum, *Finite Model Theory*, Springer-Verlag, New York 1995.

[Elg61] C.C. Elgot, Decision problems of finite automata design and related arithmetics, *Trans. Amer. Math. Soc.* **98**, (1961), 21-52.

[FSV95] R. Fagin, L.J. Stockmeyer, M.Y. Vardi, On monadic NP versus monadic co-NP, *Information and Computation* **120** (1995), 78-92.

[GRST96] D. Giammarresi, A. Restivo, S. Seibert, W. Thomas, Monadic second-order logic over rectangular pictures and recognizability by tiling systems, *Information and Computation* **125** (1996), 32-45.

[GS84] F. Gécseg, M. Steinby, *Tree Automata*, Akadémiai Kiodó, Budapest 1984.

[Hnf65] W. Hanf, Model-theoretic methods in the study of elementary logic, in: *The Theory of Models* (J. Addison, L. Henkin, P. Suppes, Eds.), North-Holland, Amsterdam 1965, pp. 132-145.

[Mil90] R. Milner, Operational and algebraic semantics of concurrent processes, in: *Handbook of Theoretical Computer Science* (J. v. Leeuwen, Ed.), Vol. B, Elsevier Sci. Publ., Amsterdam 1990.

[KS81] T. Kamimura, G. Slutzki, Parallel and two-way automata on directed ordered acyclic graphs, *Inform. Contr.* **49** (1981), 10-51.

[PST94] A. Potthoff, S. Seibert, W. Thomas, Nondeterminism versus determinism of finite automata over directed acyclic graphs, *Bull. Belg. Math. Soc. Simon Stevin* **1** (1994), 285-298.

[Rab69] M.O. Rabin, Decidability of second-order theories and automata on infinite trees, *Trans. Amer. Math. Soc.* **141** (1969), 1-35.

[See92] D. Seese, Interpretability and tree automata: a simple way to solve algorithmic problems on graphs closely related to trees, in: *Tree Automata and Languages* (M. Nivat, A. Podelski, Eds.), Elsevier Science Publishers, 1992, pp. 83-114.

[ST96] I. Schiering, W. Thomas, work in progress.

[Th91] W. Thomas, On logics, tilings, and automata, in: *Automata, Languages, and Programming* (J. Leach et al., Eds.), Lecture Notes in Computer Science **510** , Springer-Verlag, Berlin 1991, pp. 441-453.

[Th96] W. Thomas, Languages, automata and logic, in: *Handbook of Formal Language Theory*, Vol. III (G. Rozenberg, A. Salomaa, Eds.), Springer-Verlag, New York (to appear).

[TW68] J.W. Thatcher, J.B. Wright, Generalized finite automata with an application to a decision problem of second order logic, *Math. Syst. Theory* **2** (1968), 57-82.

[Zi87] W. Zielonka, Notes on asynchronous automata, *RAIRO Inform. Théor. Appl.* **21** (1987), 99-135.

Institut für Informatik und Praktische Mathematik, Universität Kiel, D-24098 Kiel
E-mail address: wt@informatik.uni-kiel.de

DIMACS Series in Discrete Mathematics
and Theoretical Computer Science
Volume **29**, 1997

Algebraic Manipulations and Vector Languages

M. W. Shields

1. Introduction.

Vector languages [3, 4] stand in relation to Mazurkiewicz trace languages [2] in much the same way as matrices stand in relation to linear transformations. Given a basis, a linear transformation determines a matrix; given an indexed cover, a Mazurkiewicz trace determines an α-vector, a vector of strings. The advantage of the representations in each case is that they are in some sense easier to manipulate. In particular, operations such as concatenation or constructing least upper bound may be performed co-ordinatewise

We illustrate this claim in section 4, in which we prove various order theoretic properties of the monoid of α-vectors. In section 3, we show that this monoid is structurally identical to a monoid of Mazurkiewicz traces. These results are used to establish properties of a partial order semantics for a class of extended automata, the hybrid transition systems. In particular, we show that any system of labelled partial orders which is prefix closed with respect to an ordering interpretable as 'is an initial part of' may, up to isomorphism, be generated by some hybrid transition system from an initial state.

2. Hybrid Transition Systems.

2.1. DEFINITION. A *hybrid transition system* is a 6-tuple $H = (Q, A, \rightarrow, \iota, E, \mu)$, where

- Q is a set of (global) *states,;*
- A is a set of *actions;*
- $\rightarrow \subseteq Q \times A \times Q$ is the *transition relation.* We write $q_1 \rightarrow^a q_2$ to indicate that $(q_1, a, q_2) \in \rightarrow$;
- $\iota \subseteq A \times A$ is an irreflexive, symmetric relation, the *independence relation;*
- E is a set of events;
- $\mu: A \rightarrow \mathcal{B}(E)$, where $\mathcal{B}(E)$ denotes the set of *bags* over E.

satisfying

1991 *Mathematics Subject Classification.* Primary 68Q68, 68Q45, 68Q05.

(1) If $q_1, q_2, q_3 \in Q$ and $a \in A$ such that $q \rightarrow^a q_1$ and $q \rightarrow^a q_2$, then $q_1 = q_2$

(2) If $q_1, q_2, q_3 \in Q$ and $a, b \in A$ such that $q_1 \rightarrow^a q_2 \rightarrow^b q_3$ and $a \iota b$, then there exists $\hat{q}_2 \in Q$ such that $q_1 \rightarrow^b \hat{q}_2 \rightarrow^a q_3$.

Informally, if $q_1 \rightarrow^a q_2$ then at state q_1 it is possible for events belonging to the bag $\mu(a)$ to occur *simultaneously*, sending the system to state q_2. For the purpose of this paper, we shall concentrate on asynchronous systems, and treat μ as a function $\mu: A \rightarrow E$. Thus, if $q_1 \rightarrow^a q_2$ then at state q_1 it is possible for the event $\mu(a)$ to occur sending the system to state q_2. If $a \iota b$, and both $q_1 \rightarrow^a q_2$ and $q_1 \rightarrow^b q_3$ then it is possible for the events $\mu(a)$ and $\mu(b)$ to occur *concurrently* from state q_1. Figure 1 pictures a hybrid transition system in which the states are represented by dots and the transition relation is represented by labelled arrows. For example, there is a transition $q_1 \rightarrow^a q_2$ with $\mu(a) = e$. The shading in the lozenge shape indicates that $a \iota b$

We shall now describe a partial-order semantics for hybrid transition systems; this is built on a means for deriving systems of partial orders from a left-closed trace language as developed in [1, 5, 6].

Let H be a hybrid transition system We define a partial function $\theta_H: Q \times A^* \rightarrow Q$ by

$$\theta_H(q, \Omega) = q$$
$$\theta_H(q, x.a) = q' \Leftrightarrow \theta_H(q, x) \rightarrow^a q'$$

where Ω is the empty sequence, $x \in A^*$ and $a \in A$. If $q_0 \in Q$, then we define

$$L(H, q_0) = \{x \in A^* \mid \theta_H(q_0, x) \text{ is defined}\}$$

and note that $L(H, q_0)$ is a prefix closed, in the sense that

$$x \in L(H, q_0) \wedge y \leq x \Rightarrow y \in L(H, q_0)$$

where $\leq$ is the usual prefix ordering on strings.

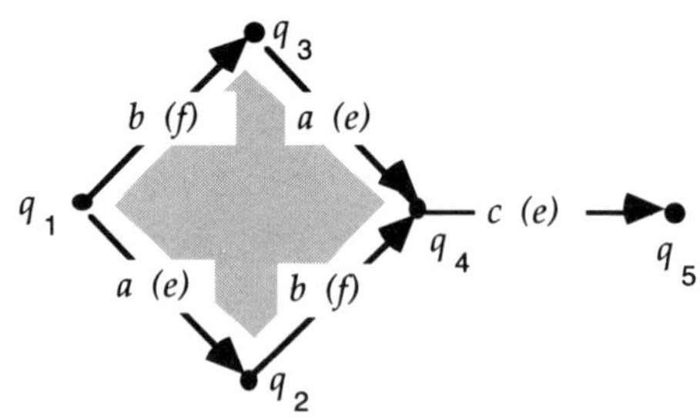

Figure 1

In the example of figure 1, we have $L(H,q_1) = \{\Omega, a, b, ab, ba, abc, bac\}$.

We define $\cong_\iota$ to be the smallest congruence relation on A^* such that if $a \iota b$, then $ab \cong_\iota ba$, A $\cong_\iota$-equivalence class is a *Mazurkiewicz trace*. We shall write x_ι for the $\cong_\iota$-equivalence class of $x \in A^*$. and denote the set of all $\cong_\iota$-equivalence classes of A^* by A_ι^*. A *trace language* is a subset of A_ι^*.

Since $\cong_\iota$ is a congruence relation, we may make A_ι^* into a semigroup by defining

$$x_\iota . y_\iota = (x.y)_\iota \tag{2.1}$$

We may also define what may easily be proved to be a partial order on A_ι^* by

$$x_\iota \leq y_\iota \Leftrightarrow \exists z \in A^* : x_\iota . z_\iota = y_\iota \tag{2.2}$$

Returning to hybrid transition systems, we associate the pair (H, q_0) with the trace language

$$TL(H,q_0) = \{x_\iota \mid x \in L(H,q_0)\}$$

and note that $TL(H,q_0)$ is a prefix closed, in the sense that

$$x_\iota \in TL(H,q_0) \wedge y_\iota \leq x_\iota \Rightarrow y_\iota \in TL(H,q_0)$$

In the example if figure 1, we have

$$TL(H,q_0) = \{\Omega_\iota, a_\iota, b_\iota, (ab)_\iota = (ba)_\iota, (abc)_\iota = (bac)_\iota\}$$

We shall say that an element x_ι of A_ι^* is *prime* if and only if

$$\forall y_1, y_2 \in A^* \, \forall a_1, a_2 \in A : (y_1.a_1)_\iota = x_\iota = (y_2.a_2)_\iota \Rightarrow a_1 = a_2$$

and define $\lambda(x_\iota)$ to be the unique $a \in A$ such that $x_\iota = (y.a)_\iota$, some $y \in A^*$. Thus, for each $x_\iota \in A_\iota^*$, we may define a labelled partial order $PO(x_\iota) = (X, \leq, \mu \circ \lambda)$, where X is the set of primes $\leq x_\iota$. The interpretation is that the elements of X are occurrences, where p_ι is an occurrence of event $\mu(\lambda(p_\iota))$. If $p_\iota \leq p'_\iota$, then p_ι occurs before p'_ι.

Incidentally, it may be shown that these elements are the primes of A_ι^* in the order theoretic sense; if a prime p_ι lies below the least upper bound of a set, then it lies under one of the element of that set.

In the example of figure 1, the primes are the traces a_ι, b_ι and $(abc)_\iota$

Thus, if $H = (Q, A, \rightarrow, \iota, E, \mu)$ is a hybrid transition system and $q_0 \in Q$, then we may associate the pair (H, q_0) with a set of labelled partial orders:

$$PO(H,q_0) = \{PO(x_\iota) \mid x_\iota \in TL(H,q_0)\}$$

$PO(H,q_1)$ for the example of figure 1 is pictured in figure 2.

Let us investigate the sets $PO(H,q_0)$. First, we define a relation on labelled partial orders.

2.2. DEFINITION. $(X_1,\leq_1,\phi_1) \preceq (X_2,\leq_2,\phi_2)$ if and only if:

(1) $X_1 \subseteq X_2$
(2) $\forall x_1, x_2 \in X_2 : x_1 \leq_1 x_2 \Leftrightarrow x_2 \in X_1 \wedge x_1 \leq_2 x_2$
(3) $\forall x \in X_1 : \phi_1(x) = \phi_2(x)$ and $range(\phi_1) = range(\phi_2)$

$\preceq$ is easily seen to be reflexive, antisymmetric and transitive, so restricting it to $PO(H,q_0)$ turns the latter set into a partial order. The ordering relation on $PO(H,q_1)$ for the example of figure 1 is shown in figure 2.

A set of labelled partial orders is *prefix closed* if and only if

$$P_2 \in \mathcal{B} \wedge P_1 \preceq P_2 \Rightarrow P_1 \in \mathcal{B}$$

The following theorem states the main properties of this construction. For convenience, if $U \in A_\iota^*$, then we define $(X_U,\leq_U,\phi_U) = PO(U)$ and if $P = (X,\leq,\phi)$, then we define $X_P = X$, $\leq_P = \leq$ and $\phi_P = \phi$.

2.3. THEOREM . If $H = (Q,A,\rightarrow,\iota,E,\mu)$ is a hybrid transition system and $q_0 \in Q$, then

(1) $PO : TL(H,q_0) \rightarrow PO(H,q_0)$ is a poset isomorphism;
(2) $PO(H,q_0)$ is a prefix closed set of finite labelled partial orders.

PROOF. (1) Let $U,V \in A_\iota^*$. It is immediate that if $U \leq V$, then $X_U \subseteq X_V$ and that if $p \in X_U$, then $\phi_U(p) = \lambda(p) = \phi_V(p)$ and $range(\phi_U) = E = range(\phi_V)$. If $p_1,p_2 \in X_V$, then

$$p_1 \leq_U p_2 \Leftrightarrow p_1 \leq p_2 \wedge p_1,p_2 \in X_U \Leftrightarrow p_1 \leq p_2 \wedge p_2 \in X_U \Leftrightarrow p_1 \leq_V p_2 \wedge p_2 \in X_U$$

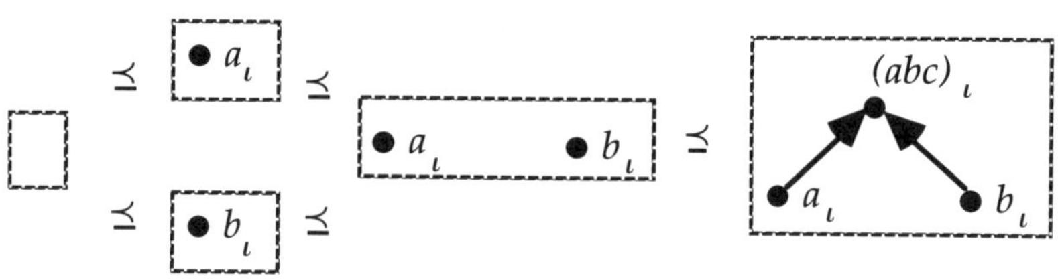

Figure 2.

and we have established that $PO(U) \preceq PO(V)$. It is now clear that PO is monotonic and onto. To complete the proof of (1) we need the following order theoretic property, which we establish in section 4.

$$U \in A_\iota^* \Rightarrow \sqcup X_U = U \tag{2.3}$$

where $\sqcup X_U$ denotes the least upper bound of the set X_U. From this, we obtain

$$PO(U) \preceq PO(V) \Rightarrow X_U \subseteq X_V \Rightarrow U = \sqcup X_U \leq \sqcup X_V = V$$

which entails that PO is injective, and hence bijective, and that PO^{-1} is monotonic.

(2) It is clear that the posets in $PO(H, q_0)$ are finite. Suppose that $U \in TL(H, q_0)$ and $P \preceq PO(U)$. We need another order theoretic property, which we also establish in section 4:

$$(\exists W \in A_\iota^* \; \forall Z \in P: Z \leq W) \Rightarrow \sqcup P \in A_\iota^* \tag{2.4}$$

It then follows that $V = \sqcup P \in A_\iota^*$ and that $V \leq U$. Since $TL(H, q_0)$ is prefix closed, $V \in TL(H, q_0)$. We conclude the proof by showing that $P = PO(V)$ and in view of the definition of PO, it suffices to prove that $X_P = X_V$. But if W is prime then $W \in X_P \Leftrightarrow W \leq V \Leftrightarrow W \in V_P$.

QED

Our next theorem shows that up to isomorphism, every prefix-closed system of labelled partial orders is determined by an initialised hybrid transition system. This means that our automata model is in some sense capable of describing any discrete, discrete system.

2.4. DEFINITION. Labelled partial orders $(X_1, \leq_1, \phi_1)$ and $(X_2, \leq_2, \phi_2)$ are *isomorphic* if and only if there is a bijective function $f: X_1 \to X_2$ satisfying

(1) $\forall x, x' \in X_1: x \leq_1 x' \Leftrightarrow f(x) \leq_2 f(x')$;

(2) $\forall x \in X_1: \phi_1(x) = \phi_2(f(x))$

We write $(X_1, \leq_1, \phi_1) \equiv (X_2, \leq_2, \phi_2)$ to indicate that $(X_1, \leq_1, \phi_1)$ and $(X_2, \leq_2, \phi_2)$ are isomorphic.

2.5 DEFINITION. Two sets of labelled partial orders $\mathcal{B}_1$ and $\mathcal{B}_2$ are *isomorphic* if and only if there exists a bijective function $\Phi: \mathcal{B}_1 \to \mathcal{B}_2$ such that

(1) $\forall P, P' \in \mathcal{B}_1: P \preceq P' \Leftrightarrow \Phi(P) \preceq \Phi(P')$;

(2) $\forall P \in \mathcal{B}_1: P \equiv \Phi(P)$.

We write $\mathcal{B}_1 \equiv \mathcal{B}_2$ to indicate that $\mathcal{B}_1$ and $\mathcal{B}_2$ are isomorphic.

2.6 THEOREM . Suppose that $\mathcal{B}$ is a prefix closed set of finite labelled partial orders, then there exists a hybrid transition system $H = (Q, A, \rightarrow, \iota, E, \mu)$ and $q_0 \in Q$ such that $\mathcal{B} \equiv PO(H, q_0)$.

The proof of this theorem uses a result about systems of partial orders. So as not to introduce too long a break in this exposition, we have consigned both to an appendix.

3. Vector Languages.

Let A be a set. An *indexed cover* for A is a function $\alpha: I \rightarrow \hat{}\ (A)$ satisfying

$$\bigcup_{i \in I} \alpha(i) = A$$

It is clear that the relation $\iota_\alpha \subseteq A \times A$ given by

$$a\, \iota_\alpha\, b \Leftrightarrow (\forall i \in I: \{a, b\} \not\subseteq \alpha(i)) \tag{3.1}$$

is an independence relation. On the other hand, if ι is an independence relation, then there exists an indexed cover α such that $\iota = \iota_\alpha$. For example, define

$$I = \{\{a, b\} \subseteq A \mid a \not\iota\, b\}$$

and let α be the identity function.

3.1. EXAMPLE. If $A = \{a, b, c\}$ and $\iota = \{(a, b), (b, a)\}$, and $\alpha: \{1, 2\} \rightarrow \hat{}\ (A)$ is defined by $\alpha(1) = \{a, c\}$ and $\alpha(2) = \{b, c\}$, then $\iota = \iota_\alpha$.

3.2. DEFINITION. We define M_α to be the set of all functions $\underline{x}: I \rightarrow \hat{}\ (A^*)$ satisfying

$$\forall i \in I: \underline{x}(i) \in \alpha(i)^*.$$

If $I = \{1, \cdots, n\}$, then we may represent $\underline{x} \in M_\alpha$ as a tuple $(\underline{x}(1), \cdots, \underline{x}(n))$. We refer to the elements of M_α as *string vectors*.

We may make M_α into a semigroup and partially ordered set by defining

$$\forall i \in I: (\underline{x}.\underline{y})(i) = \underline{x}(i).\underline{y}(i) \tag{3.2}$$

$$\underline{x} \leq \underline{y} \Leftrightarrow (\forall i \in I: \underline{x}(i) \leq \underline{y}(i)) \tag{3.3}$$

M_α has as semigroup identity and poset bottom element the string vector $\underline{\Omega}_\alpha$ which satisfies $\forall i \in I: \underline{\Omega}_\alpha(i) = \Omega$.

3.3. DEFINITION. If $a \in A$, then we define the string vector $\underline{a}_\alpha$ by

$$\underline{a}_\alpha(i) = \begin{cases} a \text{ if } a \in \alpha(i) \\ \Omega \text{ otherwise} \end{cases} \tag{3.4}$$

We define the set $A_\alpha{}^*$ of *α-vectors* to be the submonoid of M_α generated by the set $A_\alpha = \{\underline{a}_\alpha \mid a \in A\}$. $A_\alpha{}^*$ inherits the partial order structure, including the bottom element, from M_α. An *α-vector language* is a subset of $A_\alpha{}^*$.

In example 3.1 above, we have $\underline{a}_\alpha = (a, \Omega)$, $\underline{b}_\alpha = (\Omega, b)$ and $\underline{c}_\alpha = (c, c)$.

We shall occasionally need to argue by induction on the length of a vector. If $\underline{x} \in A_\alpha{}^*$ and $a \in \alpha(i) \cap \alpha(j)$, then it is easy to see that $\#_a \underline{x}(i) = \#_a \underline{x}(j)$, where $\#_a x$ denotes the number of occurrences of a in x. We may therefore unambiguously define $\#_a \underline{x} = \#_a \underline{x}(i)$ where $a \in \alpha(i)$ and the length of $\underline{x}$ by

$$|\underline{x}| = \sum_{a \in A} \#_a \underline{x}$$

It is not hard to show that $|\underline{\Omega}_\alpha| = 0$, that $|\underline{a}_\alpha| = 1$ if $a \in A$ and $|\underline{x}.\underline{y}| = |\underline{x}| + |\underline{y}|$, if $\underline{x}, \underline{y} \in A_\alpha{}^*$.

We also define

$$\underline{x} \; ind_\alpha \; \underline{y} \Leftrightarrow (\forall i \in I: \underline{x}(i) > \Omega \Rightarrow \underline{y}(i) = \Omega)$$

and observe that ind_α is an independence relation which satisfies

$$\underline{x} \; ind_\alpha \; \underline{y} \Rightarrow \underline{x}.\underline{y} = \underline{y}.\underline{x} \tag{3.5}$$

Our first result relates the order structure of $A_\alpha{}^*$ to its monoid structure

3.4. PROPOSITION. $\underline{x}, \underline{y} \in A_\alpha{}^*$, then

$$\underline{x} \le \underline{y} \Leftrightarrow \exists \underline{z} \in A_\alpha{}^*: \underline{y} = \underline{x}.\underline{z}$$

PROOF. The $\Leftarrow$ implication is trivial. For the $\Rightarrow$ implication, we argue by induction on then length of $\underline{x}$. The base case, where $\underline{x} = \underline{\Omega}_\alpha$, is also trivial. For the induction step, we have $\underline{a}_\alpha \le \underline{x}$, some $a \in A$. We argue that there exists $\underline{x}' \in A_\alpha{}^*$ such that $\underline{x} = \underline{a}_\alpha.\underline{x}'$.

Indeed, since $\underline{a}_\alpha \le \underline{x}$, we may write $\underline{x} = \underline{x}_1.\underline{a}_\alpha.\underline{x}_2$ where $\#_a \underline{x}_1 = 0$. If $a \in \alpha(i)$, then $a \le \underline{x}_1(i).a.\underline{x}_2(i)$ and so $\underline{x}_1(i) = \Omega$. Therefore $\underline{a}_\alpha \; ind \; \underline{x}_1$ and by (3.5) $\underline{x} = \underline{x}_1.\underline{a}_\alpha.\underline{x}_2 = \underline{a}_\alpha.\underline{x}_1.\underline{x}_2$. Thus our claim holds if we define $\underline{x}' = \underline{x}_1.\underline{x}_2$. Likewise, since $\underline{a}_\alpha \le \underline{x} \le \underline{y}$, there exists $\underline{y}' \in A_\alpha{}^*$ such that $\underline{y} = \underline{a}_\alpha.\underline{y}'$. But now, since

$\underline{a}_\alpha(i).\underline{x}'(i) \le \underline{a}_\alpha(i).\underline{y}'(i)$, it follows that $\underline{x}'(i) \le \underline{y}'(i)$, each i. that is, $\underline{x}' \le \underline{y}'$. By induction, there exists $\underline{z} \in A_\alpha^*$ such that $\underline{y}' = \underline{x}'.\underline{z}$ and $\underline{y} = \underline{a}_\alpha.\underline{y}' = \underline{a}_\alpha.\underline{x}'.\underline{z} = \underline{x}.\underline{z}$.

QED

If $\underline{x}.\underline{z}_1 = \underline{x}.\underline{z}_2$, then $\underline{x}(i).\underline{z}_1(i) = \underline{x}(i).\underline{z}_2(i)$ each i. and so $\underline{z}_1(i) = \underline{z}_2(i)$ each i and so $\underline{z}_1 = \underline{z}_2$. Hence, the vector $\underline{z}$ of proposition 3.4 is unique; we denote it by $\underline{y}/\underline{x}$. We shall use the same notation for sequences; if $x \le y$, then y/x is defined to be the unique string such that $x.(y/x) = y$.

By (3.1), (3.2) and (3.4)

$$a\, \iota_\alpha\, b \Leftrightarrow \underline{a}\ ind_\alpha\ \underline{b} \tag{3.6}$$
$$a\, \iota_\alpha\, b \Leftrightarrow a \ne b \wedge \underline{a}.\underline{b} = \underline{b}.\underline{a} \tag{3.7}$$

from which it follows that if $\iota = \iota_{\alpha'}$, then the monoid epimorphism $f_\alpha : A^* \to A_\alpha^*$ given by $f_\alpha(a^1 \cdots a^n) = \underline{a}^1{}_\alpha \cdots \underline{a}^n{}_\alpha$ satisfies

$$\forall x, y \in A^* : x \cong_\iota y \Rightarrow f_\alpha(x) = f_\alpha(y)$$

so that there exists a monoid epimorphism $\varphi_\alpha : A_\iota^* \to A_\alpha^*$ given by $\varphi_\alpha(x_\iota) = f_\alpha(x)$. In fact:

3.5. THEOREM. The function $\varphi_\alpha : A_\iota^* \to A_\alpha^*$ satisfying $\varphi_\alpha(x_\iota) = f_\alpha(x)$, all $x \in A^*$, is both a monoid and poset isomorphism.

PROOF. We first show that φ_α is injective. Since we know that φ_α is a monoid epimorphism, this shows that φ_α is a monoid isomorphism.

Suppose that $X, Y \in A_\iota^*$ such that $\varphi_\alpha(X) = \varphi_\alpha(Y)$ and let $x \in X$ and $y \in Y$ be such that if $x' \in X$ and $y' \in Y$, then $|x \wedge y| \ge |x' \wedge y'|$. Here $x \wedge y$ denotes the longest common prefix of x and y and $|x|$ denotes the length of x. We prove that $x = y$, from which it follows that $X = Y$.

Suppose $x \ne y$, then since $\varphi_\alpha(X) = \varphi_\alpha(Y)$, we may write $x = u.a.v$ and $y = u.b^1 \cdots b^r.a.w$ such that $a \ne b^n$, $n = 1, \cdots, r$. Now, $\varphi_\alpha(X) = \varphi_\alpha(Y)$ means that

$$f_\alpha(u).\underline{a}_\alpha.f_\alpha(v) = f_\alpha(u).\underline{b}^1{}_\alpha \cdots \underline{b}^r{}_\alpha.\underline{a}_\alpha.f_\alpha(w)$$

and so if $\underline{a}_\alpha(i) > \Omega$, then $a \le \underline{b}^1{}_\alpha(i) \cdots \underline{b}^r{}_\alpha(i).a.f_\alpha(w)$, and since $a \ne b^n$, $n = 1, \cdots, r$, we must have $\underline{b}^n{}_\alpha(i) = \Omega$. Thus, for all $n = 1, \cdots, r$, $\underline{a}_\alpha\ ind_\alpha\ \underline{b}^n{}_\alpha$. and hence $a\, \iota_\alpha\, b^n$, by (3.6) and (3.7), so if we define $y' = u.a.b^1 \cdots b^r.w$, then $y' \cong_{\iota_\alpha} y$, so that $y' \in Y$. But, $|x \wedge y| < |x \wedge y'|$, the desired contradiction.

Finally, suppose that $x, y \in A$, then

$$x_\iota \le y_\iota \Leftrightarrow \exists z_\iota \in A_\iota^* : x_\iota.z_\iota = y_\iota, \text{ by (2.1) and (2.2)}$$
$$\Leftrightarrow \exists z_\iota \in A_\iota^* : \varphi_\alpha(x_\iota).\varphi_\alpha(z_\iota) = \varphi_\alpha(y_\iota), \text{ by the first part of the proof}$$

$\Leftrightarrow \exists \underline{z} \in A_\alpha{}^*: \varphi_\alpha(x_\iota).\underline{z} = \varphi_\alpha(y_\iota)$
$\Leftrightarrow \varphi_\alpha(x_\iota) \leq \varphi_\alpha(y_\iota)$, by proposition 3.4.

QED

4. Operations with Vectors.

Consider the following proof that every non-empty set of strings has a greatest lower bound.

Suppose that $\varnothing \subset X \subseteq A^*$. If for no $a \in A$, is it the case that $a \leq x$, all $x \in X$, then the greatest lower bound of X, denoted by $\sqcap X$, exists and equals Ω. Otherwise, we may form the set $X/a = \{x/a \mid x \in X\}$, which is non-empty By induction (on the length of the shortest string in X), $\sqcap(X/a)$ exists, and for all $u \neq \Omega$

$$u \leq a.(\sqcap(X/a)) \Leftrightarrow u/a \leq \sqcap(X/a) \Leftrightarrow \forall x \in X: u/a \leq x/a \Leftrightarrow \forall x \in X: u \leq x$$

so $\sqcap X$, exists and equals $a.(\sqcap(X/a))$.

In the above chain of equivalences we are making an implicit use of certain properties of strings. For example, the first equivalence uses the fact that the set $\downarrow x$ of prefixes of a sequence x is totally ordered, so that if $u \leq a.v$ and $u \neq \Omega$, then $a \leq u$ and so u/a is defined and $u/a \leq v$. This argument cannot be generalised directly to vectors. For instance, in example 3.1, we have and $(a,\Omega),(\Omega,b) \leq (a,b)$ but neither $(a,\Omega) \leq (\Omega,b)$ nor $(\Omega,b) \leq (a,\Omega)$. However:

4.1. LEMMA. Suppose $\underline{x},\underline{y} \in A_\alpha{}^*$ and $a \in A$, then

(1) $\underline{a}_\alpha, \underline{x} \leq \underline{y} \wedge \underline{a}_\alpha \not\leq \underline{x} \Rightarrow \underline{a}_\alpha \; ind_\alpha \; \underline{x}$;

(2) $\underline{x} \leq \underline{a}_\alpha.\underline{y} \wedge \underline{a}_\alpha \; ind_\alpha \; \underline{x} \Rightarrow \underline{x} \leq \underline{y}$.

PROOF. (1) If it is not the case that, $\underline{a}_\alpha \; ind_\alpha \; \underline{x}$ then for some $i \in I$, $\underline{a}_\alpha(i) > \Omega$ and $\underline{x}(i) > \Omega$, so that $a, \underline{x}(i) \leq \underline{y}(i)$ and so $a \leq \underline{x}(i)$, which means that $\#_a \underline{x} > 0$ Hence, for all $i \in I$, if $\underline{a}_\alpha(i) > \Omega$ then $\underline{x}(i) > \Omega$ and so $a \leq \underline{x}(i)$. But then $\underline{a}_\alpha \leq \underline{x}$.
(2) If $\underline{a}_\alpha(i) = \Omega$, then $\underline{x}(i) \leq (\underline{a}_\alpha.\underline{y})(i) = \underline{y}(i)$, whereas if $\underline{a}_\alpha(i) > \Omega$, then $\underline{x}(i) = \Omega \leq \underline{y}(i)$.

QED

Taking these additional complications into account, we can generalise the above argument from A^* to $A_\alpha{}^*$.

4.2. PROPOSITION. If $\varnothing \subset X \subseteq A_\alpha{}^*$, then X has a greatest lower bound.

PROOF. Suppose that $\varnothing \subset X \subseteq A^*$. If for no $a \in A$, is it the case that $\underline{a}_\alpha \le \underline{x}$, all $\underline{x} \in X$, then $\sqcap X$, exists and equals $\underline{\Omega}_\alpha$. Otherwise, we may form the set $X/\underline{a}_\alpha = \{\underline{x}/\underline{a}_\alpha \mid \underline{x} \in X\}$, which is non-empty. By induction (on the length of the shortest vector in X), $\sqcap(X/\underline{a}_\alpha)$ exists, Suppose that $\underline{u} \in A_\alpha{}^*$. If $\underline{a}_\alpha \le \underline{u}$, then

$$\underline{u} \le \underline{a}_\alpha.(\sqcap(X/\underline{a}_\alpha)) \Leftrightarrow \underline{u}/\underline{a}_\alpha \le \sqcap(X/\underline{a}_\alpha) \Leftrightarrow \forall \underline{x} \in X: \underline{u}/\underline{a}_\alpha \le \underline{x}/\underline{a}_\alpha \Leftrightarrow \forall \underline{x} \in X: \underline{u} \le \underline{x}$$

whereas if $\underline{a}_\alpha \not\le \underline{u}$, then by lemma 4.1.

$$\begin{aligned} \underline{u} \le \underline{a}_\alpha.(\sqcap(X/\underline{a}_\alpha)) &\Leftrightarrow (\underline{a}_\alpha \; ind_\alpha \; \underline{u} \wedge \underline{u} \le \sqcap(X/\underline{a}_\alpha) \\ &\Leftrightarrow (\underline{a}_\alpha \; ind_\alpha \; \underline{u} \wedge \forall \underline{x} \in X: \underline{u} \le \underline{x}/\underline{a}_\alpha) \Leftrightarrow \forall \underline{x} \in X: \underline{u} \le \underline{x} \end{aligned}$$

so $\sqcap X$, exists and equals $\underline{a}_\alpha.(\sqcap(X/\underline{a}_\alpha))$.

QED

The advantage of a vector representation is well demonstrated in the computation of least upper bounds; both the existence and the value of a least upper bound may be determined co-ordinatewise, as we shall show in proposition 4.4. First, if $\underline{x}, \underline{y} \in A_\alpha{}^*$, then define

$$\underline{x} \leftrightarrow \underline{y} \Leftrightarrow \forall i \in I: \underline{x}(i) \le \underline{y}(i) \vee \underline{y}(i) \le \underline{x}(i) \tag{4.1}$$

and if $\underline{x} \leftrightarrow \underline{y}$, then define $\underline{x} \vee \underline{y} \in M_\alpha$

$$(\underline{x} \vee \underline{y})(i) = max(\underline{x}(i), \underline{y}(i)) \tag{4.2}$$

We prove an extension of lemma 4.1 (1).

4.3 LEMMA. If $\underline{x}, \underline{y} \in A_\alpha{}^*$, then

$$\underline{x} \leftrightarrow \underline{y} \wedge \underline{a}_\alpha \le \underline{x} \wedge \underline{a}_\alpha \not\le \underline{y} \Rightarrow \underline{a}_\alpha \; ind_\alpha \; \underline{y}.$$

PROOF. If it is not the case that $\underline{a}_\alpha \; ind_\alpha \; \underline{y}$, then there exists $i \in I$, such that $\underline{a}_\alpha(i) > \Omega$ and $\underline{y}(i) > \Omega$. As $\underline{a}_\alpha \le \underline{x}$, $a \le \underline{x}(i)$, and as either $\underline{x}(i) \le \underline{y}(i)$ or $\underline{y}(i) \le \underline{x}(i)$, we must have $a \le \underline{y}(i)$. Arguing as in lemma 4.1, we conclude that $\underline{a}_\alpha \le \underline{y}$.

QED

If $\underline{x}, \underline{y} \in A_\alpha{}^*$, then we denote the least upper bound of $\underline{x}$ and $\underline{y}$, if it exists, by $\underline{x} \sqcup \underline{y}$.

4.4. PROPOSITION. If $\underline{x}, \underline{y} \in A_\alpha{}^*$, then

(1) If $\underline{x} \sqcup \underline{y}$. exists, then $\underline{x} \leftrightarrow \underline{y}$;

(2) If $\underline{x} \leftrightarrow \underline{y}$, then $\underline{x} \sqcup \underline{y}$ exists and equals $\underline{x} \vee \underline{y}$.

PROOF. (1) If $\underline{z} = \underline{x} \sqcup \underline{y}$, then for all $i \in I$, $\underline{x}(i), \underline{y}(i) \leq \underline{z}(i)$ and so $\underline{x} \leftrightarrow \underline{y}$ as $\downarrow \underline{z}(i)$ is totally ordered.

(2) It is clear that for all $i \in I$, $(\underline{x} \vee \underline{y})(i) \leq \underline{u}(i) \Leftrightarrow \underline{x}(i) \leq \underline{u}(i) \wedge \underline{y}(i) \leq \underline{u}(i)$ and so it remains to be shown that $\underline{x} \vee \underline{y} \in A_\alpha{}^*$. We argue by induction on the length of $\underline{x}$. The base case, $\underline{x} = \underline{\Omega}_\alpha$ is trivial. For the induction step, suppose that $\underline{a}_\alpha \leq \underline{x}$.

If $\underline{a}_\alpha \leq \underline{y}$, then a co-ordinatewise argument gives $\underline{x}/\underline{a}_\alpha \leftrightarrow \underline{y}/\underline{a}_\alpha$; for example, if $\underline{x}(i) \leq \underline{y}(i)$, then $\underline{x}(i)/\underline{a}_\alpha(i) \leq \underline{y}(i)/\underline{a}_\alpha(i)$. By induction $(\underline{x}/\underline{a}_\alpha) \vee (\underline{y}/\underline{a}_\alpha) \in A_\alpha{}^*$ so, $\underline{x} \vee \underline{y} = \underline{a}_\alpha.((\underline{x}/\underline{a}_\alpha) \vee (\underline{y}/\underline{a}_\alpha)) \in A_\alpha{}^*$, as

$$\forall i \in I: max(\underline{x}(i), \underline{y}(i) = \underline{a}_\alpha(i).max((\underline{x}(i)/\underline{a}_\alpha(i)), (\underline{y}(i)/\underline{a}_\alpha(i)))$$

Otherwise $\underline{a}_\alpha \not\leq \underline{y}$ and so by lemma 4.3 $\underline{a}_\alpha \; ind_\alpha \; \underline{y}$. Again, a co-ordinatewise argument gives $\underline{x}/\underline{a}_\alpha \leftrightarrow \underline{y}$. Indeed, if $\underline{a}_\alpha(i) > \Omega$, then $\underline{y}(i) = \Omega \leq \underline{x}(i)$, while otherwise, $(\underline{x}/\underline{a}_\alpha)(i) = \underline{x}(i)$. By induction $(\underline{x}/\underline{a}_\alpha) \vee \underline{y} \in A_\alpha{}^*$. If $\underline{a}_\alpha(i) > \Omega$, then $\underline{y}(i) = \Omega$ and so

$$(\underline{a}_\alpha.((\underline{x}/\underline{a}_\alpha) \vee \underline{y}))(i) = a.max(\underline{x}(i)/a, \Omega) = \underline{x}(i) = max(\underline{x}(i), \underline{y}(i)) = (\underline{x} \vee \underline{y})(i)$$

Otherwise $\underline{a}_\alpha(i) = \Omega$ and so $(\underline{a}_\alpha.((\underline{x}/\underline{a}_\alpha) \vee \underline{y}))(i) = max(\underline{x}(i), \underline{y}(i)) = (\underline{x} \vee \underline{y})(i)$ and we have established that $\underline{x} \vee \underline{y} = \underline{a}_\alpha.((\underline{x}/\underline{a}_\alpha) \vee \underline{y}) \in A_\alpha{}^*$.

QED

The following corollary, together with theorem 3.5, establishes (2.4) which we used in the proof of theorem 2.3.

4.5. COROLLARY. If $X \subseteq A_\alpha{}^*$ and $\sqcup X$ exists if and only if X is bounded above and then

$$\forall i \in I: (\sqcup X)(i) = \sqcup \{\underline{x}(i) \mid \underline{x} \in X\}.$$

PROOF. If $\sqcup X$ then X is bounded above, by $\sqcup X$. Conversely, suppose that X is bounded above by $\underline{y}$, say, then X must be finite, as every vector may have only a finite number of distinct prefixes. If X is empty, then $\sqcup X = \underline{\Omega}_\alpha$, or $X = \{\underline{x}_1, \cdots, \underline{x}_n\}$, $n > 0$, $X' = \{\underline{x}_2, \cdots, \underline{x}_n\}$ is bounded above, by $\underline{y}$ so by induction, $\underline{x'} = \sqcup X'$ exists and $\forall i \in I: (\sqcup X')(i) = \sqcup \{\underline{x}(i) \mid \underline{x} \in X'\}$. Both $\underline{x}_1$ and $\underline{x'}$ are bounded above by $\underline{y}$, so $\underline{x}_1 \leftrightarrow \underline{x'}$, so $\underline{x}_1 \sqcup \underline{x'}$ exists and consequently $\underline{x}_1 \sqcup \underline{x'} = \sqcup X$. Furthermore,

$$\forall i \in I: (\sqcup X)(i) = \underline{x}_1 \sqcup \sqcup\{\underline{x}(i) \mid \underline{x} \in X'\} = \sqcup\{\underline{x}(i) \mid \underline{x} \in X\}.$$

QED

We now establish a vector version of (2.3), thereby completing the proof of theorem 2.3. We shall say that $\underline{p} \in A_\alpha{}^*$ is *prime* if and only if:

$$\forall \underline{u}, \underline{v} \in A_\alpha{}^* \ \forall a, b \in A: \underline{u}.\underline{a}_\alpha = \underline{p} = \underline{v}.\underline{b}_\alpha \Rightarrow a = b \tag{4.3}$$

and note that by theorem 3.5, if $p \in A^*$, then p_{ι_α} is prime if and only if $\varphi_\alpha(p_{\iota_\alpha})$ is prime. We write Pr_α for the set of primes and for all $\underline{x} \in A_\alpha{}^*$ define $X_{\underline{x}} = \{\underline{p} \in Pr_\alpha \mid \underline{p} \leq \underline{x}\}$.

4.6. PROPOSITION. For all $\underline{x} \in A_\alpha{}^*$, $\sqcup X_{\underline{x}}$. exists and $\underline{x} = \sqcup X_{\underline{x}}$.

PROOF. Since $X_{\underline{x}}$ is bounded above by $\underline{x}$, $\sqcup X_{\underline{x}}$ exists by corollary 4.5 and $\sqcup X_{\underline{x}} \leq \underline{x}$. To complete the proof, we show that for each $i \in I$, there exists $\underline{p} \in X_{\underline{x}}$ such that $\underline{p}(i) = \underline{x}(i)$ and appeal to corollary 4.5.

Let $Y = \{\underline{y} \in A_\alpha{}^* \mid \underline{y} \leq \underline{x} \wedge \underline{y}(i) = \underline{x}(i)\}$, then Y is non-empty, since it contains $\underline{x}$. Let $\underline{p} \in Y$ have minimal length. If $\underline{p}$ is not prime, then there exists $\underline{u}, \underline{v} \in A_\alpha{}^*$ and $a, b \in A$ such that $\underline{u}.\underline{a}_\alpha = \underline{p} = \underline{v}.\underline{b}_\alpha$ and $a \neq b$. So $\underline{u}(i).\underline{a}_\alpha(i) = \underline{v}(i).\underline{b}_\alpha(i)$ and since $a \neq b$, we cannot have $\underline{a}_\alpha(i), \underline{b}_\alpha(i) > \Omega$. Without loss of generality, $\underline{a}_\alpha(i) = \Omega$, and now we have $\underline{u} < \underline{p} \leq \underline{x}$ and $\underline{u}(i) = (\underline{u}.\underline{a}_\alpha)(i) = \underline{p}(i) = \underline{x}(i)$, so that $\underline{u} \in Y$ and has shorter length than $\underline{p}$, a contradiction.

QED

The construction of primes in the proof of proposition 4.6 may be generalised. as follows. Suppose that $\underline{x} \in A_\alpha{}^*$ and $a \in \alpha(i)$, then an element of the shortest length from the set $Y_i = \{\underline{y} \in A_\alpha{}^* \mid \underline{y} \leq \underline{x}.\underline{a}_\alpha \wedge \underline{y}(i) = \underline{x}(i).a\}$ is prime, and furthermore, if we apply this construction to Y_j, where $a \in \alpha(j)$, then we obtain exactly the same vector. We denote it by $pr_\alpha(\underline{x}, a)$.

The following proposition will be needed in the proof of theorem 2.6, which we present in the appendix.

4.7. PROPOSITION. $\underline{x} = \underline{a}^1{}_\alpha \cdots \underline{a}^r{}_\alpha$, then $X_{\underline{x}} = \{pr(\underline{a}^1{}_\alpha \cdots \underline{a}^k{}_\alpha, a^{k+1}) \mid 0 \leq k < r\}$.

PROOF. Certainly, $\{pr(\underline{a}^1{}_\alpha \cdots \underline{a}^k{}_\alpha, a^{k+1}) \mid 0 \leq k < r\} \subseteq X_{\underline{x}}$, while if $\underline{u}.\underline{a}_\alpha \in X_{\underline{x}}$, then $\underline{u}.\underline{a}_\alpha = pr(\underline{a}^1{}_\alpha \cdots \underline{a}^i{}_\alpha, a^{i+1})$ where $a = a^{i+1}$ and $\#_a \underline{u} = \#_a \underline{a}^1{}_\alpha \cdots \underline{a}^i{}_\alpha$.

QED

We conclude this section with a useful result which allows us to factorise the prefix of the concatenation of two vectors as a concatenation of their prefixes.

4.8. PROPOSITION. If $\underline{x}, \underline{y}, \underline{z} \in A_\alpha^*$, then

$$\underline{x} \le \underline{y}.\underline{z} \Rightarrow \exists \underline{u}, \underline{v} \in A_\alpha^*: \underline{u}.\underline{v} = \underline{x} \wedge \underline{u} \le \underline{y} \wedge \underline{v} \le \underline{z} \wedge \underline{v}\ ind_\alpha\ (\underline{y}/\underline{u})$$

Consequently, $\underline{y}.\underline{z} = \underline{x}.(\underline{y}/\underline{u}).(\underline{z}/\underline{v})$.

PROOF. Let $\underline{u} = \underline{x} \sqcap \underline{y}$, then $\underline{u} \le \underline{x}$ and so we may define $\underline{v} = \underline{x}/\underline{u}$. It immediately follows that $\underline{x} = \underline{u}.\underline{v}$ and that $\underline{u} \le \underline{y}$.

Now, $\underline{v} \le (\underline{y}/\underline{u}).\underline{z}$ and $\underline{y}/\underline{u} \le (\underline{y}/\underline{u}).\underline{z}$. So

$$\underline{v} \sqcap (\underline{y}/\underline{u}) = (\underline{x}/\underline{u}) \sqcap (\underline{y}/\underline{u}) = (\underline{x} \sqcap \underline{y})/\underline{u} = (\underline{x} \sqcap \underline{y})/(\underline{x} \sqcap \underline{y}) = \underline{\Omega}_\alpha$$

and a repeated application on lemma 4.1 establishes that $\underline{v}\ ind_\alpha\ (\underline{y}/\underline{u})$. Finally, from $\underline{u} \le \underline{y}$ and a coordinatewise argument, we may conclude that $(\underline{y}.\underline{z})/\underline{u} = (\underline{y}/\underline{u}).\underline{z}$, so $\underline{v} = \underline{x}/\underline{u} \le (\underline{y}.\underline{z})/\underline{u} = (\underline{y}/\underline{u}).\underline{z}$. This, together with $\underline{v}\ ind_\alpha\ (\underline{y}/\underline{u})$, entails that $\underline{v} \le \underline{z}$.

QED

5. Conclusions and Related Work.

We have demonstrated the use of vectors as representations of traces which simplify certain relations and constructions. The work reported here is actually part of a larger study [7] in which, among other things:

- Hybrid transition systems are labelled by bags of events and behaviours are modelled by labelled pre-orders; the induced equivalence relation on occurrences is that of simultaneity.

- The use of vectors is otherwise illustrated in establishing structure theorems for important subclasses of the class of vector languages

- Hybrid transition systems are used to provide a non-interleaving semantic s for a variety of specification notations, from Net theory to CCS.

- The machinery of category theory is used to related the expressive power of the specification notations on the basis of the above common semantic domain.

Appendix: Proof of Theorem 2.6.

Before we prove the theorem, we need the following property of sets of finite labelled partial orders.

PROPOSITION. If $\mathcal{B}$ is a prefix closed set of finite labelled partial orders, then there exists a prefix closed set of finite labelled partial orders $\mathcal{B}'$ such that $\mathcal{B} \equiv \mathcal{B}'$ and that for all $P_1, P_2 \in \mathcal{B}'$,

$$P_1 \preceq P_2 \Leftrightarrow X_{P_1} \subseteq X_{P_2} \tag{A.1}$$

PROOF. Let $M_{\mathcal{B}}$ denote the set of all $P \in \mathcal{B}$ having a unique maximal element $\lambda(P)$. If $P \in \mathcal{B}$, then define $\Phi(P) = (\hat{X}_P, \hat{\leq}_P, \hat{\phi}_P)$, where

- $\hat{X}_P = \{\hat{P} \in M_{\mathcal{B}} \mid \hat{P} \preceq P\}$
- $\hat{P}_1 \leq_P \hat{P}_2 \Leftrightarrow \hat{P}_1 \preceq \hat{P}_2$
- $\hat{\phi}_P(\hat{P}) = \phi_P(\lambda(\hat{P}))$

and let $\mathcal{B}' = \{\Phi(P) \mid P \in \mathcal{B}\}$.

To prove (A.1), it suffices to show that if $P_1, P_2 \in \mathcal{B}$, then $\hat{X}_{P_1} \subseteq \hat{X}_{P_2} \Rightarrow \Phi(P_1) \preceq \Phi(P_2)$, and in view of the definition of Φ, we need only establish (2) of definition 2.2. But if $\hat{P}_1, \hat{P}_2 \in X_{P_2}$, then

$$\hat{P}_1 \leq_{\Phi(P_2)} \hat{P}_2 \wedge \hat{P}_2 \in X_{P_1} \Rightarrow \hat{P}_1 \preceq \hat{P}_2 \preceq P_1 \Rightarrow \hat{P}_1 \in X_{P_1}$$

and so

$$\hat{P}_1 \leq_{\Phi(P_1)} \hat{P}_2 \Leftrightarrow \hat{P}_1 \preceq \hat{P}_2 \wedge \hat{P}_1, \hat{P}_2 \in X_{P_1} \Leftrightarrow \hat{P}_1 \leq_{\Phi(P_2)} \hat{P}_2 \wedge \hat{P}_2 \in X_{P_1}$$

Since (A.1) holds, to show that $\Phi{:}\mathcal{B} \to \mathcal{B}'$ satisfies (1) of definition 2.5 we need only show that if $P_1, P_2 \in \mathcal{B}$, then $P_1 \preceq P_2 \Leftrightarrow \hat{X}_{P_1} \subseteq \hat{X}_{P_2}$. If $P_1 \preceq P_2$, then $\hat{P} \in \hat{X}_{P_1} \Rightarrow \hat{P} \preceq P_1 \Rightarrow \hat{P} \preceq P_2 \Rightarrow \hat{P} \in \hat{X}_{P_2}$. Conversely, suppose that $\hat{X}_{P_1} \subseteq \hat{X}_{P_2}$. If $x \in X_{P_1}$, then define $\downarrow_{P_1} x = (X, \leq, \phi)$, where

$X = \{y \in X_{P_1} \mid y \leq_{P_1} x\}$
$\forall y, y' \in X{:}\, y \leq y' \Leftrightarrow y \leq_{P_1} y'$
$\forall y \in X{:}\, \phi(y) = \phi_P(y)$.

We note that $\downarrow_{P_1} x \in \hat{X}_{P_1}$ with $\lambda(\downarrow_{P_1} x) = x$. Hence $\downarrow_{P_1} x \in \hat{X}_{P_2}$, and in particular, $\downarrow_{P_1} x \preceq P_2$, so $x \in X_{P_2}$ and we have proved that $X_{P_1} \subseteq X_{P_2}$. Since $\downarrow_{P_1} x \preceq P_2$, we also have $\phi_{P_1}(x) = \phi_{\downarrow_{P_1} x}(x) = \phi_{P_2}(x)$ and

$$y \leq_{P_1} x \Leftrightarrow y \leq_{\downarrow_{P_1} x} x \Leftrightarrow y \leq_{P_2} x \wedge x \in X_{\downarrow_{P_1} x} \Leftrightarrow y \leq_{P_2} x \wedge x \in X_{P_1}$$

Finally, suppose that $P \in \mathcal{B}$, then it is straightforward to check that the function $\varphi: P \to \Phi(P)$ given by $\varphi(x) = (X, \leq, \phi)$ is an isomorphism, where

$$X = \{\downarrow_P y \mid y \leq_P x\}$$
$$\downarrow_P y_1 \leq \downarrow_P y_2 \Leftrightarrow y_1 \leq_P y_2$$
$$\phi(\downarrow_P x) = \phi_P(x).$$

QED

If P is a labelled partial order and $X \subseteq X_P$ then we define

$$P|X = (X, \leq_P \cap (X \times X), \phi_P | X)$$

We sketch the proof of theorem 2.6. By the proposition, we may assume that $\mathcal{B}$ satisfies $P_1 \preceq P_2 \Leftrightarrow X_{P_1} \subseteq X_{P_2}$. Define $H = (Q, A, \to, \iota, E, \mu)$, where

- $Q = \mathcal{B}$;
- $A = \bigcup_{P \in \mathcal{B}} X_P$
- $P_1 \to^x P_2 \Leftrightarrow X_{P_1} \subseteq X_{P_2} \wedge X_{P_2} - X_{P_1} = \{x\}$
- $x_1 \,\iota\, x_2 \Leftrightarrow x_1 \not\leq x_2 \wedge x_2 \not\leq x_1 \wedge (\exists P \in \mathcal{B}: x_1, x_2 \in P)$
- $E = \bigcup_{P \in \mathcal{B}} range(\phi_P)$
- $\mu(x) = e \Leftrightarrow \exists P \in \mathcal{B}: x \in X_P \wedge \phi_P(x) = e.$

If $P \to^x P_1$ and $P \to^x P_2$, then $X_{P_1} = X_P \cup \{x\} = X_{P_2}$ and so, by the assumption $P_1 \preceq P_2 \Leftrightarrow X_{P_1} \subseteq X_{P_2}$, we must have $P_1 = P_2$. Suppose that $P \to^x P_1$ and $P_1 \to^y P_2$ with $x \,\iota\, y$ and define $\hat{P}_1 = P_2|(X_{P_2} - \{x\})$, It is not hard to check that $\hat{P}_1 \preceq P_2$, giving $\hat{P}_1 \in \mathcal{B}$, by left-closure. And now, $P \to^y \hat{P}_1$ and $\hat{P}_1 \to^x P_2$. We have shown that H is a hybrid transition system

Define q_0 to be the empty labelled partial order, with label set E. We now define a function Φ, which we shall show to be an isomorphism from $\mathcal{B}$ to $PO(H, q_0)$ is given as follows. Suppose $P \in \mathcal{B}$, and let $X_P = \{x_1, \cdots, x_n\}$, where the numbering is such that $x_i <_P x_j \Rightarrow i < j$; $x_1 \cdots x_n$ is a linear ordering of P. It may be shown that $u = x_1 \cdots x_n \in L(H, q_0)$ and that $\Phi(P) = PO(u_\iota)$ does not depend on the particular linear ordering chosen.

Indeed, it is not hard to show that if we define $P_i = P|\{x_1, \cdots, x_i\}$, each i, then $P_1 \preceq P_2 \cdots P_{n-1} \preceq P$ and so $P_i \in \mathcal{B}$ each i, by left closure. We also have $q_0 \to^{x_1} P_1$ and $P_i \to^{x_i} P_{i+1}$, each i, and so $u = x_1 \cdots x_n \in L(H, q_0)$. If $x_i \,\iota\, x_{i+1}$, then $x_1 \cdots x_{i+1} \cdot x_i \cdots x_n$ is also a linear ordering of P and that any other linear ordering of P may be obtained from $x_1 \cdots x_n$ by permuting adjacent, unordered elements. Hence, the linear ordering of P form a $\cong_\iota$-class and Φ is well-defined.

If $P_1 \preceq P_2$, then any linear ordering u of P_1 may be extended to a linear ordering v of P_2, so that $u_\iota \leq v_\iota$ and consequently $PO(u_\iota) \preceq PO(v_\iota)$, as was established in the proof of theorem 2.3. Thus, Φ is monotonic. If $u \in L(H, q_0)$, then $\Phi(P) = PO(u_\iota)$, where $P = \theta_H(q_0, u)$ and so Φ is onto. If $PO(u_\iota) \preceq PO(v_\iota)$, then $u_\iota \leq v_\iota$ as was also established in the proof of theorem 2.3, so $X_{P_1} \subseteq X_{P_2}$ and hence $P_1 \preceq P_2$, by (A.1). Thus, Φ is injective and Φ^{-1} is monotonic.

The isomorphism from P to $\Phi(P)$ will be defined by

$$\varphi(x_i) = pr((x_1 \cdots x_{i-1})_\iota, x_i)$$

By proposition 4.7, φ maps X_P onto $X_{\Phi(P)}$ and so φ is bijective. If $x_i < x_j$ then $i < j$ and $x_i \not\iota\, x_j$, and so $pr((x_1 \cdots x_{i-1})_\iota, x_i) < pr((x_1 \cdots x_{j-1})_\iota, x_j)$. Conversely, if $pr((x_1 \cdots x_{i-1})_\iota, x_i) < pr((x_1 \cdots x_{j-1})_\iota, x_j)$, then $x_i \in \{x_1 \cdots x_{j-1}\}$ and $x_i \not\iota\, x_j$.so $x_i < x_j$. Thus, φ is a poset isomorphism. Finally:

$$\phi_{u_\iota}(\varphi(x_i)) = \phi_{u_\iota}(pr((x_1 \cdots x_{i-1})_\iota, x_i)) = \mu(x_i) = \phi_P(x_i)$$

QED

References

[1] Bednarcztk, M. A.: Categories of Asynchronous Systems, Ph.D. Thesis, University of Sussex, October 1987

[2] Mazurkiewicz, A.: Concurrent Program Schema and their Interpretations, Proceedings Aarhus Workshop on Verification of Parallel Programs, 1977

[3] Shields, M. W.: Adequate Path Expressions, Proceedings, Symposium on the Semantics of Concurrent Computation, Lecture Notes in Computer Science, volume 70, pp. 249-265, Springer Verlag, 1979

[4] Shields, M. W.: Non-sequential Behaviours I, Technical Report CRS-119-82, Computer Science Department, University of Edinburgh, June, 1982

[5] Shields, M.W.: Concurrent Machines, Computer Journal, volume 28, pp. 449-465, 1985

[6] Shields, M. W.: Behavioural Presentations, Proceedings REX Workshop on Linear Time, Branching Time and Partial Order in Logics and Models for Concurrency, Lecture Notes in Computer Science, volume 354, Springer Verlag, 1989

[7] Shields, M. W.: Semantics of Parallelism, a Non-Interleaving Approach, Springer Verlag, to appear.

Department of Mathematical and Computing Sciences
The University of Surrey
Guildford
Surrey GU2 5XH
United Kingdom

DIMACS Series in Discrete Mathematics
and Theoretical Computer Science
Volume **29**, 1997

Refinement With Global Equivalence Proofs In Temporal Logic

Shmuel Katz*
Computer Science Department
The Technion, Haifa, Israel
email: katz@cs.technion.ac.il

Abstract

Refinement of abstract atomic operations is considered. The temporal logic $ISTL^*$ is used to demonstrate a two-stage approach to verification of such refinements for distributed systems. In each refinement, convenient lower level computations are first shown to implement upper level operations, and then in the second stage, all other computations are shown to be equivalent to one of the convenient ones. The equivalence maintains the ordering of all causally dependent events, but allows independent events to occur in different orders. The advantage of this separation is that different kinds of reasoning and induction can be used for the two aspects. A proof rule with well-founded sets is proposed for the proofs of equivalence. The approach is demonstrated for a refinement that adds output queues between processors and a main memory.

1 Introduction

In refinements of distributed systems high level atomic operations are replaced by collections of lower level operations that loosen the synchrony among distributed processors, but still maintain some key properties. In the approach to justifying the correctness presented here, each refinement proof is divided into two independent stages. The first stage shows that convenient executions of operations from the next lower level are a simple refinement of executions from the upper level, and can be demonstrated correct using standard refinement mappings. The convenient executions are precisely those where the lower level operations that implement a higher level one appear as a subsequence, with no other lower level operations interspersed. These are legal lower level executions, even if they are unlikely to occur in practice because the operations are distributed in a collection of asynchronously executing processors. A mapping function from each convenient execution to some abstract computation is generally simple and iterative. After this first stage, we have only shown that every convenient execution sequence is a refinement of some higher level abstract execution.

1991 *Mathematics Subject Classification.* Primary 68Q60, 03B45.

*This research was supported by the Fund for the Promotion of Research in the Technion.

Then we show that every additional execution sequence at the lower level is equivalent to one of the convenient ones. This stage could be considered as a 'loosening' of the ordering imposed by the convenient executions.

The two-step reasoning at each level saves having to directly relate each lower level sequence through a mapping to an upper level one, as is done in other proof methods. Although such a mapping exists, the use of history and prophecy variables may be required. The mapping may be extremely difficult to express and justify because the collection of lower level operations that can be considered the 'implementation' of an upper level one is interleaved with an arbitrary number of operations that implement other higher level operations. Thus it is difficult to obtain an iterative proof that is uniform for all the computations when a direct mapping is required. Note that the difficulty is not in the proof obligations once appropriate mappings and invariants are found, but in the conceptual complexity in suggesting appropriate candidates for mappings and intermediate assertions. In contrast, here we claim that the reasoning used is not far from that used intuitively by designers of such systems.

The refinement we consider here could be one step in a derivation and verification of a cache consistency protocol. In this example, we will require that the refinement maintain what is known as *sequential consistency*. Intuitively, this means that the projection of local events of each processor is consistent with use of a serial memory, even if a version with queues and local caches is used instead. Although this is natural in the context of cache consistency protocols, note that there are other applications of the refinement verification technique that have no such requirement.

The temporal logic $ISTL^*$ is used to express the properties of computations. It is based on the idea of a *partial order computation* which is simply a maximal set of occurrences of operations (called events) of a distributed system that have some partial ordering among them. The ordering includes any causality required among events, and may have additional restrictions. Events which are ordered are called *dependent*, and the others are *independent*. A program or system defines a collection of such partial order computations. As shown previously in [KP90, KP92b, KP92a], the collection of all linearizations of the events that are consistent with the partial order can be considered in a temporal logic framework. Each linearization generates an execution sequence, which is a sequence of alternating events and global states. All such execution sequences generated from a given partial order computation define an *interleaving set* and are considered equivalent. Intuitively, two execution sequences will be equivalent if they differ only in that strictly independent events are executed in a different order in the two sequences.

In $ISTL^*$, a branching time assertion is interpreted as *true* for a distributed system, if it is true for every interleaving set of the system. This is analogous to the standard interpretation of a linear temporal logic assertion being true of a system if it holds for every execution sequence. Then it is easy to express that each equivalence class has some execution sequence satisfying a property p, simply as Ep, using the existential modality E. This allows easy expression of the claim that every equivalence class has a convenient execution. Such properties are often natural for distributed systems and allow expressing specifications for problems such as database serializability, distributed snapshots, and sequential consistency of cache-based shared memory systems.

The logic also is natural for a proof of equivalence which is global, using temporal logic assertions about the entire computation, along with formulas that encode which operations are independent of each other.

In previous proofs of assertions with Ep [KP92b, PP90], the two stages suggested here were mixed together. The motivation for showing both properties at once is to allow a classic iterative proof on the computation, maintaining compositionality and modularity in the proof. At each step we can assume both that p is true for (some extension of) the parts of the computations considered so far, and that sufficient computations are being included so that every computation is equivalent to one of those explicitly considered. This allows compositional proofs and proof rules to be used, but has the price of complicated proof rules. In the inductive step, it is necessary to show that the states reached so far all have a possible next state that will both maintain p and extend the existing computations to sufficient representatives. Here, different kinds of reasoning can be used for the two subproofs.

The rest of this paper is structured as follows. In Section 2, the idea of (convenient) interleaving sequences and the dependency relation is explained in greater detail. The implications for independence of queue operations are also examined. The temporal logic $ISTL^*$ is then briefly described in Section 3. In Section 4, a precise definition of sequential consistency in terms of $ISTL^*$ is given. In this framework the needed restrictions on the independence relation are defined, as is the implementation of a collection of execution sequences by another collection. Then the correctness requirements are defined for any refinement that maintains sequential consistency, using convenient executions and equivalence. A proof method based on well founded sets is presented to show that each execution sequence is equivalent to some convenient one.

Section 5 treats the replacement of an abstract sequential global memory by a less synchronized version with queues between the processors and the global memory. In the abstract version, each processor can execute atomic read and write operations directly from the memory. In the lower level version, a processor can only write to a local queue, while later the head of the queue is written to the memory internally. This is one basic step in a series of refinements that can be used to derive a caching protocol. The proof obligations are presented as temporal logic implications. Using the properties of queues, it is easy to define convenient executions for them and show that these implement the more abstract level, and maintain sequential consistency.

The next crucial step involves showing that each lower level execution sequence is equivalent to some convenient sequence, through a proof involving well-founded sets. To guarantee this equivalence, reading from memory is restricted on the implementation level. Care must be taken in defining which events are dependent, in order to obtain the appropriate equivalence relation for sequential consistency. Section 6 summarizes the approach.

2 Defining dependencies and convenient executions

Definition 1 (Execution sequence) *An* execution sequence ρ *is an alternating* *sequence of states and events (occurrences of operations) denoted* $\sigma_0\alpha_0\sigma_1\alpha_1\ldots$ *For each state* σ_i *in the sequence,* $\sigma_{i+1} = \alpha_i(\sigma_i)$. *The subsequence of states is denoted by* σ, *and the subsequence of events is denoted by* α.

The terms 'execution sequence' and 'computation' are used interchangeably in the continuation. To apply the methodology, the independence of operations must be made explicit in a relation among events, and equivalence among execution sequences under the independence relation must be defined. Knowledge of the independence relation is essential for the loosening stage, which involves precise reasoning about which operations are independent in which states. Each operation is viewed as a guard c (i.e., a condition for applicability on the state s) followed by a command f that is simply a function of s (with the operation written $c \rightarrow f$), as in [ABM93]. Note that such an interpretation of an event is reasonable only when a state is assumed as a semantic object, as part of the definition of an execution sequence.

Definition 2 (Conditional independence) *Two operations,* $op1$ *and* $op2$ *of the form* $c1 \rightarrow f1$ *and* $c2 \rightarrow f2$, *respectively, are* independent *in a state* s, *denoted* $s \Rightarrow I(op1, op2)$, *if beginning in state* s *neither affects the truth of the other's guard, and the result of executing them in either order is the same, i.e.,*

$$c1(s) \Rightarrow (c2(f1(s)) \Leftrightarrow c2(s))$$

$$c2(s) \Rightarrow (c1(f2(s)) \Leftrightarrow c1(s))$$

$$(c1(s) \wedge c2(s)) \Rightarrow (f1(f2(s)) = f2(f1(s))).$$

The definition above is known as *conditional independence*[KP92a] because a pair of operations may be dependent in some states, and independent in others. The states in which two operations are independent are defined by a state predicate. Two execution sequences are considered equivalent if they differ only in that independent operations appear in a different order, but all dependent operations appear in the same order. More formally,

Definition 3 (Equivalence) *Two execution sequences* ρ_0 *and* ρ_n *are* equivalent under independence relation I *(denoted* $\rho_0 \equiv_I \rho_n$*) if they are the first and last elements in a sequence of execution sequences that each contain the same collection of operation occurrences and for each adjacent pair, if* ρ_i *has the form* $us\alpha t_1\beta v$ *then* ρ_{i+1} *has the form* $us\beta t_2\alpha v$ *where* $s \rightarrow I(\alpha, \beta)$.

This definition means that the operation occurrences of one are a permutation of those in the other, and one can be reached from the other by repeated interchanging of events from states in which they are independent.

As a particularly relevant example, we consider the dependencies for a queue q with operations $empty_q()$, $put_q(e)$, and $get_q(e)$, where e is a data element. When the queue is nonempty, then $put_q(e)$ is independent of $get_q(f)$:

$$(\neg empty_q()) \Rightarrow I(put_q, get_q) \tag{1}$$

When the queue is empty, a put_q and a get_q operation will be dependent:

$$empty_q() \Rightarrow \neg I(put_q, get_q) \tag{2}$$

All adjacent pairs of put_q's are dependent:

$$\neg(I(put_q, put_q)) \tag{3}$$

All adjacent pairs of get_q's are dependent:

$$\neg(I(get_q, get_q)) \tag{4}$$

The first rule is intuitively true because a put_q and a get_q by different processors on a nonempty queue are done at opposite ends of the queue, and never involve the same item. This is not so when the queue is initially empty, as seen in rule (2). In that case the get_q operation must follow a put_q. Note that if only complete independence of operations were expressible, we would not be able to exploit the above independence in those states when the queue is nonempty.

Rules (3) and (4) follow from the fact that the contents of the queue differ according to the order of put_q's, while the states of the rest of the system differ if get_q's are done in a different order. Therefore those operations are *not* independent because the final state differs according to the order in which they are executed.

Here the independence relations above are viewed as given assumptions that are part of the definition of a queue. Alternatively, an algebraic specification of the queue operations can be defined as in [GH93] to express that the value at the head of the queue is the oldest one put in that has not yet been removed. Then the independence relations (1) – (4) can be derived from the algebraic queue axioms and the definition of conditional independence. In Section 5, a temporal logic version of the queue axioms is introduced.

3 The logic

The version of temporal logic used in this paper is an adaptation of the logic $ISTL^*$ introduced in [KP90], with additions to facilitate showing equivalence of execution sequences. Most of the operators are those of CTL^* [EH86], but interpreted as true for a system if they hold for each interleaving set. The semantics of a system, denoted M, is thus the collection of interleaving sets– each a set of equivalent execution sequences– that are possible from each state. An interleaving set is defined as an equivalence class of execution sequences for an independence relation I. The syntax is thus standard, and the semantics (implicitly) universally quantifies over the interleaving sets. In other temporal logics, the assertions are interpreted over sequences of states. Here, we consider them over the derived sequence of states from an execution sequence of alternating states and events. Arbitrary atomic predicates are assumed, where each predicate is *true* for a subset of the states, and *false* for the complement. Thus for a predicate without temporal modalities, if an individual state is considered, $s \models p$ is equivalent to $p(s)$. For a sequence, we evaluate a predicate in the first state:
$\sigma \models p$ – is $\sigma_0 \models p$, when p has no temporal modalities

There are two kinds of temporal modalities in the logic. The modalities E and A are known as *state* modalities because they deal with all of the possible continuations from a given global state. The other modalities (F, G, X, and U) are known as *path* modalities since they deal with restrictions on a given execution path.

For the path modalities, their semantics is given for a subsequence of states σ derived from an execution sequence ρ. We have:
$\sigma \models Fp$ – for some state in σ, p is true, $\exists i.\sigma_i \models p$
$\sigma \models Gp$ – for every state in σ, p is true, $\forall i.\sigma_i \models p$
$\sigma \models Xp$ – for the next state in σ, p is true, $\sigma_1 \models p$
$\sigma \models pUq$ – p is true in states of σ until q becomes true (and q does become true), $\exists i.\forall j.(0 \leq j < i \Rightarrow \sigma_j \models p) \wedge \sigma_i \models q$

On the other hand, an assertion beginning with a state modality is true if it is true for every interleaving set of executions beginning from that state. Since the system M is now a set of interleaving sets of execution sequences, we will quantify over these sets also. In particular:
$(M, s) \models Ap$ – for every computation in each interleaving set of M from s, p is true, $\forall L \in M.\forall \sigma \in L.s = \sigma_0 \Rightarrow (\sigma \models p)$
$(M, s) \models Ep$ – for some computation in each interleaving set of M from s, p is true, $\forall L \in M.\exists \sigma \in L.s = \sigma_0 \Rightarrow (\sigma \models p)$

Such assertions are said to be true of a system if they are true in the initial state of the system. To facilitate reasoning about sequences of operations, we add some conventions. First, an operation name also serves as a state predicate that is true precisely when that operation was executed in the transition from the previous state. (An alternative temporal logic that treats operations more directly can be seen in Lamport's TLA [Lam94]). Then sequences of operations (or other predicates) can be denoted using

Definition 4 (Sequencing) *"$s;t$" is a concise notation for the temporal logic assertion $X(s \wedge Xt)$ (in the next state s holds, followed by a state with t).*

Sequencing relates to a single execution sequence and can be preceded by E or A. A longer sequence is written "$s;t;u;...$" and is the obvious generalization.

The notation "$\langle s_i | i = 1, n\rangle$" is used to denote a sequence executing an s_i operation on each processor i in turn, i.e., "$s_1; s_2; ...; s_n$" Note that all such sequences are simply temporal logic assertions using the next operator X.

An expression $EFEGp$ means that in each interleaving set there is a computation such that eventually, there is a state such that for each interleaving set there is a computation such that along the computation, p is true in all states from that point. In the starred version of the logic, $ISTL^*$, there is no restriction on which combinations of the temporal operators are allowed. When temporal logics are used in model checking of finite state programs, as is done for CTL, it is common to restrict the combinations to facilitate efficient checking. In particular, the state modalities E and A are required to alternate with the other (path) modalities. Although many aspects of the specification below can be treated in $ISTL$ with alternating state and path modalities, here we do not treat whether such restrictions allow sufficient expressibility, since in any case, model checking techniques are not used.

Additional information on I within the temporal descriptions of computations means that more execution sequences can be proven equivalent. In some sense the equivalence classes are demonstrably larger and fewer convenient executions are required to guarantee that each equivalence class contains a convenient execution.

4 Expressing independence and allowed computations

As noted in the Introduction, the refinement here will maintain sequential consistency among a group of processors. The definition of sequential consistency given in [ABM93] is:

> A memory M is sequentially consistent with respect to a serial memory M_{serial}, iff
>
> $$\forall\sigma \in Beh(M)\exists\tau \in Beh(M_{serial})\forall i = 1 \ldots n \ \ \sigma|i = \tau|i$$

$Beh(M)$ is the set of execution sequences associated with M, and $Beh(M_{serial})$ is the set where *read* and *write* operations are atomically done on the global memory. The above asserts that the projections of a general execution on each processor are the same as those in some execution using a serial memory, even though the general execution may have extra internal steps associated with the memory, so that a *write* operation may not affect the memory directly. Note that in that formulation, there are no abstract operations: all *read* and *write* operations are considered the same, even though there is a great difference between a *write* that directly affects a central memory atomically, and one to a queue that eventually will have its value transferred elsewhere. To express this in a context with refinement, the behavior of the serial memory is viewed as a sequence of abstract atomic *read* and *write* operations that satisfy the usual memory consistency requirements (to be defined below). In a refinement, these are shown to correspond to lower level convenient sequences, where each abstract operation is implemented as a series of lower level operations, and where an abstract *write* will only be associated with a single lower level *write* in the sequence, and the same for a *read*.

In order to define the requirements within the suggested framework, at each level of refinement a formula Gen_i (standing for *general*) is used to describe the collection of general execution sequences at that level, as those satisfying the restrictions seen in the formula. For each level except the first, an additional assertion, called Con_i (for *convenient*), is used to describe additional restrictions that define a subset of the computations satisfying Gen_i.

The highest level abstract *read* and *write* operations will be described by a formula Gen_0. To capture the intuition of reading and writing into memory, we express that the value returned for a variable or memory location x in an action $read(c, x)$ (meaning, read the value c in the variable x) is the last value written into it by a $write(d, x)$ (that is, write the value d in variable x) action, in the assertion:

$$AG((write(d, v) \wedge X(\forall b(\neg write(b, v))U read(c, v))) \Rightarrow c = d) \tag{5}$$

This is known as *read/write consistency* and is a fundamental assumption when truly atomic reads and writes are being used. It states that if $write(d, x)$ has just been executed, and from the next state, there is no *write* action to x with any value until a $read(c, x)$ action is executed, then the value read is the one previously written. Note that if there is an intermediate *write* with the same value as d, then the left side of the implication does not hold in the state after the first occurrence of $write(d, x)$, but instead the assertion must hold from the later $write(d, x)$, where the left side of the implication is true, and thus $c = d$ still must be true. This requirement does not seem to appear explicitly in [ABM93]. However, the operations there are defined using a *Memory* data structure (an array representing the contents of memory), and the effects of the atomic operations are defined so that a value can be returned for a variable only if it is the latest value written to that variable. Thus the same consistency requirement is simply given implicitly.

Read/write consistency says nothing about a *read* operation on a variable never written to. Among the common default assumptions are that a fixed initial value is then read, that the value read is arbitrary, or that such an operation is illegal. In the continuation, we do not treat this issue, since whatever assumption is made on the abstract level can be easily implemented in the refinements. If a fixed initial value is assumed, dummy initialization operations can be assumed at the beginning of every computation. The simplest assumption for verification is that such a *read* operation of an undefined variable is never attempted on the abstract level, and thus the issue will also not arise in refinements.

As part of the specification of sequential consistency, the operations are augmented with subscripts that identify the processor in which they are executed (e.g., $write_3$ is associated with processor 3). Since the operations are atomic and global in effect, this association has no other significance, but does establish a local ordering for each execution sequence that must be maintained by subsequent refinements in order to show sequential consistency. Thus Gen_0 is the above equation with all possible combinations of subscripts added, for every possible state, namely:

For all processors i and k (where j also quantifies over processors),

$$AG((write_i(d, v) \wedge X(\forall j \forall b(\neg write_j(b, v))U read_k(c, v))) \Rightarrow c = d) \qquad (6)$$

The execution sequences defined by Gen_0 can be identified with M_{serial}.

At the next level, where queues and delayed memory writes are defined, another temporal logic formula Gen_1 will define all legal computations, and the additional properties true of those computations that trivially implement the abstract ones will be described in Con_1. The computations defined by Con_1 also need to be shown not to effect the ordering of local operations seen in the serial memory.

As part of the proof requirements of a refinement, it is necessary to express as a formula in the logic which adjacent operations in an execution are independent and which are not. This is used in proving that each execution sequence of the system is equivalent to a convenient one within the logic.

The independence relation must be defined so that it reflects sequential consistency. That is, the local operations of each processor must be unchanged for any two computations that are to be considered equivalent. Thus we assume a total order (i.e., non-independence) among local operations of a single processor. Since this order must be maintained for all equivalent execution sequences, we obtain the identity of local projections for every two equivalent execution sequences, as required in the definition of sequential consistency.

Before stating the requirements for a correct refinement, some definitions and properties of the needed independence relation are summarized.

Definition 5 *An independence relation I is known as* s.c. independent *if for any two operations a_i and b_i, local to processor i,*

$$\neg I(a_i, b_i) \tag{7}$$

Lemma 1 *If two sequences differ by one exchange that occurs in a state that satisfies the s.c. independence condition I, and one of the sequences is sequentially consistent, then so is the other.*

Proof: by requirement 7 two local operations from a single processor do not satisfy I, and thus these could not be the operations exchanged. Therefore the exchange does not change the order of the operations for any single processor, and the projections for each processor are identical in the two sequences. Since the definition of sequential consistency only relates to these projections, if one sequence satisfies the definition, so does the other. □

Lemma 2 *If two sequences are equivalent under an s.c. independence relation I, and one is sequentially consistent, then so is the other.*

Proof: Since the two execution sequences are equivalent under I, there is a sequence of sequences that each differ by one exchange. The lemma follows by repeated application of Lemma 1. □

Lemma 3 *If $Gen \Rightarrow E\ Con$ for an s.c. independence relation I and Con defines computations that are sequentially consistent, then all sequences in Gen are sequentially consistent.*

Proof: Computations defined by Con are sequentially consistent by assumption. $E\ Con$ means that every equivalence class of Gen has at least one such computation. The result follows by Lemma 2. □

In showing a refinement to a lower level, the legal computations of the implementation are described as temporal logic predicates. This in fact encodes the essential properties of the implementation, including, for cache consistency, restrictions on when a read action is possible.

Moreover, predicates are needed that make the independence of adjacent operations explicit. These can be justified from the underlying semantics of the model, or by properties of the data structures used. In the case of sequential consistency, the independence is further restricted by the problem specification, namely that there is a total ordering among local processor *write*'s and *read*'s. These properties can often be shown once for a large collection of related problems. The most important independence relations, that allow exploiting the essential nature of distributed systems, state that local operations of different processors are independent. That is, local operations a_i and b_j of *different* processors are independent:

$$i \neq j \Rightarrow I(a_i, b_j) \tag{8}$$

The independence relations define what exchanges of operations can be made, and thus which computations are equivalent. This needs to be introduced into the logic explicitly, through the formula

$$AG(\ I(a,b) \ \Rightarrow \ ((E\text{``}a;b\text{''}) \Leftrightarrow (E\text{``}b;a\text{''}))) \tag{9}$$

In words, if $I(a,b)$ holds in a state, then for every interleaving set there is a sequence that begins in that state and then has "$a; b$" iff there is one with "$b; a$" at that point.

The convenient executions, also described by a temporal logic formula, need to be shown to correctly implement the general computations from the next higher level, using the following definition:

Definition 6 *A collection of execution sequences S* implements *a collection T if there is a mapping function between the states of S and those of T such that for each sequence in S the mapping yields a sequence in T, and each sequence in T has at least one sequence in S that maps into it.*

Note that it is not sufficient to show that the mapping of the lower level computations are a subset of the higher level ones. As is pointed out in the refinement calculus of Z [MV94] and elsewhere [BS90], there must be a lower level computation that implements each higher level one, i.e., we are not allowed to "refuse" to implement a legal higher level sequence of *read*'s and *write*'s. Although the mapping appears to be unrestricted in the definition, the result must satisfy the higher level temporal assertion that defines the collection of abstract computations, and thus only intuitively reasonable mappings will prove acceptable.

Now the correctness requirements for a refinement may be summarized:

Definition 7 *For general computations Gen_i and a lower level defined by general computations Gen_{i+1} and additional properties that define a convenient computation Con_{i+1}, under the equivalence defined by I, the lower level is a* correct refinement for sequential consistency *if*

- *The relation I in Gen_{i+1} is s.c. independent.*
- $(Gen_{i+1} \ \wedge \ A\ Con_{i+1})$ *implements* Gen_i
- *If Gen_i is sequentially consistent, so is $Gen_{i+1} \wedge A\ Con_{i+1}$.*
- $Gen_{i+1} \Rightarrow E\ Con_{i+1}$

The independence relations will be constructed with s.c. independence built in (because local operations will not be independent), and so this aspect will generally be trivially satisfied. The correctness of the implementation for convenient sequences requires defining the mapping function, and then showing by induction on any lower level convenient execution sequence that it maps to a higher level execution sequence, if the mapping is applied to each state. As noted, we also need to show that each higher level computation has a lower-level convenient one that maps into it. Because the correspondence between the levels seen here involves a simple substitution, both directions can be shown at once.

The proof of the third requirement, that the lower level convenient computations are sequentially consistent if the higher level general ones are, is also structural in nature, and is shown by a simple induction. Since the lower level convenient executions are obtained by substituting a sequence of operations in place of one, it is enough to show that in the sequence, local *read* and *write* operations are done in the same order and from the same local state as before the substitution. Since the upper level computation is given as sequentially consistent, the lower level one is also.

The remaining requirement, that every lower level computation is equivalent to some convenient one, can be shown in several ways. One promising approach applies model checking techniques to this problem, especially techniques modifying known approaches that exploit partial order. Here we will not pursue that direction, and instead present semantic proofs of equivalence based on a well-founded function. That is, for each sequence a measure into a well-founded set is shown. The base values of the measure are shown to be the result of applying the measure function to the convenient execution sequences, and every other sequence is shown to be equivalent to one with a smaller measure.

Theorem 1 *Given a temporal predicate P describing a collection of execution sequences and independence conditions that define a relation $\equiv_I$, and another temporal predicate Q describing an additional restriction, then $P \Rightarrow\ E\ Q$ if there is a well-founded set with an ordering relation $(W, >)$, and a function f from sequences such that*

- $P(\sigma) \Rightarrow\ f(\sigma) \in W$
- $(P(\sigma) \Rightarrow (Q(\sigma) \Leftrightarrow\ f(\sigma)$ *is a minimal element of* $W)$
- $(P \wedge \neg Q)(\sigma) \Rightarrow \exists \tau\ .\ P(\tau)\ \wedge\ f(\sigma) > f(\tau)\ \wedge\ \sigma \equiv_I \tau$

The proof of the soundness of the proof rule seen in the above theorem is identical to soundness proofs of termination of programs using well-founded sets. Each minimal element is the result of a mapping from a sequence satisfying Q (that will correspond to a convenient sequence). Since the domain of the measures is well-founded, by the definition of well-foundedness, each decreasing chain of values is finite. Each nonconvenient sequence is shown equivalent under I to one with a smaller function value, and so both map to values that are part of a decreasing chain. Since these chains are finite, each sequence is equivalent to one of minimal measure, i.e., to a convenient sequence.

The definition of the measure is, of course, non-automatic. However, for the example here a standard measure can be used involving the number of operations that are interspersed among the sequential subsequences that correspond to the implementations of upper level operations seen in the convenient execution sequences. This will be illustrated in the proof presented later. A drop in the value of the mapping for two equivalent computations can be shown by using the information on which operations are independent of which other ones. This checking of equivalence can be automated, and a project is presently underway to implement this.

Theorem 2 *If a series of refinements Gen_0, Gen_1, ..., Gen_n (with convenient executions Con_1, ...,Con_n) are shown to be correct refinements for sequential consistency, then the computations defined by Gen_n are sequentially consistent.*

Proof: By induction on the levels. Gen_0 is sequentially consistent by definition. For each pair of levels, the lower convenient executions are a correct implementation of the upper level operations, as seen through the mapping function (the second condition for correctness in Definition 7). In addition, if the upper level is sequentially consistent, then the convenient executions at the next lower level are also (the third condition). Since the independence relation is s.c. independent (the first condition), and every equivalence class contains one of the convenient execution sequences (the fourth condition), it follows, using Lemma 3, that every computation at this level is equivalent to a correct implementation and is sequentially consistent, as required. □

5 Introducing Out queues

We consider how to refine abstract *read* and *write* actions. An abstract *write* action can be implemented by adding to the end of a queue the pair consisting of the value to be written and the memory address, later removing that pair from the head of the queue, and then writing it in the memory. If we denote the action of putting the value-address pair in the queue by $W(d, v)$, and the action of removing the pair from the head of the queue and writing to the memory by $MW(d, v)$ (standing for *Memory Write*), such a pair is the implementation of the abstract *write*. Thus W is associated with a *put* operation, and MW combines a *get* with writing to memory.

Similarly, an abstract *read* could be implemented by reading from the memory, adding the value-location pair to another queue, and later reading the value-address pair from the head of that queue into the local processor. However, this is not done here, and we assume a direct atomic action denoted $R(d, v)$, meaning that value d is read from address (or variable) v.

If we now replace the abstract *read* and *write* actions of the serial memory by the lower level actions above, we arrive at a situation that can be viewed as the addition of abstract *write* queues to the serial memory. Since we have a collection of such queues, the "lower" level involves operations on an Out_i queue between the processor i and the central memory, for each processor. Since there now is a queue for each processor, we denote writing to the end of the ith queue by W_i, and removing an element from the head of that queue plus writing to the memory by MW_i. Reading by processor i is denoted by R_i. All of these have the same parameters as previously, namely the value and the address (or variable name). The events that are considered local to a processor i are not independent, and these include all occurrences of W_i and R_i, but not MW_i. On this level, only the MW_i and R_i operations directly involve the memory and are required to satisfy read/write consistency. Thus we have:

For all processors i, j, and k,

$$AG((MW_i(d, v) \wedge X(\forall j \forall b(\neg MW_j(b, v))U R_k(c, v))) \Rightarrow c = d) \tag{10}$$

Now we shall define a collection of convenient executions that are guaranteed to satisfy the requirements from M_{serial} (i.e., from the abstract computations defined by Gen_0). In the convenient executions, items are inserted by the processor i using W_i operations into the corresponding Out_i queue and immediately removed and copied to the central memory by the MW_i action. In these very particular computations, every W_i is immediately followed by writing into the memory using MW_i, with no intervening operations anywhere in the system. The queues are thus always empty except when a single item has just been put in and has not yet been written to the memory in the next step. In temporal logic we can state the requirement for a convenient computation (beyond those for any general computation) as simply

$$G(W_i(c,x) \Leftrightarrow XMW_i(c,x)) \tag{11}$$

That is, throughout the computation, if a W_i has occurred, it is immediately followed by the corresponding MW_i, and every MW_i is preceded by a W_i with the same parameters. Note that only the W_i and R_i operations are local to processor i. The MW_i operations involve only the head of the i-th queue and the main memory, and are considered nonlocal to processor i. Every adjacent $W_i; MW_i$ pair is clearly a trivial implementation of the direct write on the abstract level. In order to prove this precisely, we have the lemma:

Lemma 4 *For each computation with atomic read and write operations, there is a computation where each write is replaced by a $W_i; MW_i$ pair, and those are a correct implementation of the abstract computations.*

Proof: By induction on the two sequences, using the identity function from the lower level central memory to the higher level one, and ignoring the contents of the queues. The initial states are the same. Assuming the sequences correspond up to a state where a *write* occurs in the abstract sequence, then the next lower state (after the W_i) still is mapped to the present upper one. The state after the MW_i is mapped (and is identical) to the next abstract state. The *read* commands correspond identically. Thus the concrete sequence implements the abstract one. □

Lemma 5 *The convenient sequences defined by memory consistency and the formula*

$$AG(W_i(c,x) \Leftrightarrow XMW_i(c,x))$$

are sequentially consistent.

Proof: The upper level executions have atomic *read*'s and *write*'s that are by definition sequentially consistent. There is a one-to-one correspondence between the atomic *write*'s and the W_i's, in the same order, and the lower level R_i operations are still atomic. The R_i operations have unchanged values relative to the upper level, because the needed MW_i occurs immediately after the W_i. Thus the lower level executions are also sequentially consistent. □

Then we need to claim that every execution of the lower level satisfying the queue axioms and the memory consistency assumptions is equivalent under the s.c. independence relation I to one of the convenient executions defined above. This is almost true, but we need to restrict the R_i operations of the lower level to maintain the total order among local actions of a single processor. Consider a situation where a processor has written a pair (d, x) to its *Out* queue, then reads the value of x (implemented as an R), and only then is a MW executed on that queue, changing the memory. The value read is clearly whatever was in the memory before the last MW. This implies that there is a linearization consisting of

$$W_i(d,x); R_i(c,x); MW_i(d,x)$$

with $d \neq c$. But such a computation is not consistent with the dependency requirements, because we claim that it is not equivalent to any convenient computation.

If we wish to find a convenient execution to which this one is equivalent, we must show that the R operation can be exchanged, either with the following MW or the preceding W. The former exchange would lead to

$$W_i(d,x); MW_i(d,x); R_i(c,x)$$

This is not a convenient execution, since it violates the restrictions on the value read being the last one written in the memory location (read/write consistency). Exchanging the R_i and W_i operations would lead to

$$R_i(c,x); W_i(d,x); MW_i(d,x)$$

This is a convenient sequence, but is not equivalent to the original one, because it does not have the same total order of the local operations in processor i.

This difficulty is inherent to any implementation that must maintain sequential consistency (although explained here in terms of equivalent sequences) and is solved, for example, in [ABM93] by simply requiring that the lower level operations be restricted: any R_i, is 'delayed' until the Out_i queue is empty, i.e., until all of the 'pending' MW_i operations have been done. In that case the problematic computation described above is simply declared impossible. Of course, there is no such restriction for reading and writing from *different* processors (when the subscripts are different). The restriction on the implementation is again a temporal logic formula and can be expressed in several ways. One approach treats the actions directly, using a # symbol to denote the number of times an operation has occurred:

$$AG(R_i \Rightarrow (\#W_i = \#MW_i))$$

That is, no R_i is between a W_i and an MW_i, because every W_i before R_i has a corresponding MW_i that also appears in the execution sequence before R_i. Another way to express this is to define a predicate *empty* that is true when the queue is empty and simply state that

$$AG(R_i \Rightarrow empty(Out_i)). \tag{12}$$

Such a predicate is expressed using temporal formulas derived from well-known algebraic axioms. A predicate *number* is defined recursively in terms of each operation (incrementing when an item is inserted and decrementing when one is removed) and *empty* can be seen as a derived predicate true when $number = 0$. We shall assume that expressions defining such predicates have been defined, and use the second alternative.

Now we need to express the properties of a queue within our formalism. The independence relations for queues (1–4) will have W_i corresponding to *put* and MW_i to *get* for each queue Out_i. A temporal logic queue axiom will be added to fix the value at the head of the queue when a single item is inserted into an empty queue:

$$(empty(Out_i) \wedge \text{``}W_i(c,x); MW_i(d,y)\text{''}) \;\Rightarrow\; c = d \wedge x = y \tag{13}$$

Along with the independence of W_i and MW_i when the queue is nonempty, assertion (13) corresponds to the usual recursive algebraic axiom that a *get* is independent of a *put* when the queue is initially nonempty, and otherwise the value returned by the *get* is the one just inserted by the *put* operation. Using this axiom along with the other independence axioms about queues, we can deduce the expected behavior of a queue. For example, starting from an empty queue, if the sequence of actions

$$W_i(a,x); W_i(b,y); MW_i(c,z)$$

is done, then the pair (c,z) must be exactly (a,x) (because the last two operations are independent by the adaptation of assertion (1), and in the resultant equivalent execution sequence the assertion (13) can be used).

In addition to the axioms given above, a *progress property* [MP92] on queues is needed. It is essential that every element put in the queue will eventually be removed (with the other axioms fixing the order). Otherwise, a scheduler in which elements accumulate forever in one of the queues could lead to an incorrect implementation. This property will be expressed as

$$AG(W_i(c,x) \Rightarrow AF\ MW_i(c,x)) \tag{14}$$

Note that this assertion by itself could be satisfied by a computation where two $W_i(c,x)$ are followed by only one $MW_i(c,x)$. By the assertions that define the queue, however, such a computation is equivalent to one where the second $W_i(c,x)$ is exchanged with the $MW_i(c,x)$ (because the queue is nonempty at that point). In that equivalent computation there must be a second $MW_i(c,x)$ by the above assertion. Since all equivalent computations have the same collection of events, it follows that the original computation also had a second $MW_i(c,x)$, i.e., every *put* is followed by a matching *get*.

The properties of the general lower level computations can be obtained by summarizing the discussion so far in temporal logic, with the assertions seen in Figure 1. The queue axioms above are of course essential. We also have the independence and dependence relations on all local actions in each processor (7–8). To these we add the read/write consistency rules for simple memory locations (10), the delay condition on reads (12), and the formula connecting I and equivalence (9). Gen_1 is the assertion beginning AG over the conjunction of the assertions in Figure 1, defining the legal computations in the first level of refinement that adds Out queues. Note that some independence relations are not given explicitly in Gen_1, but can be derived from the relations among the operations that are given. For example, read/write consistency on this level implies that in some states MW_i and R_j are not independent since their order affects the value read.

The higher level, Gen_0, is defined by the assertion (6). The added restriction on the computations satisfying Gen_1 that defines the convenient computations, i.e., Con_1, is the assertion (11). Considering the proof obligations, it is clear that I is s.c. independent, by definition. Lemma 4 is a proof that $Gen_1 \wedge ACon_1$ implements Gen_0 while Lemma 5 shows that if Gen_0 is sequentially consistent, so is $Gen_1 \wedge ACon_1$.

It remains to show that an execution sequence satisfying these dependencies must be equivalent (under the relations I) to one where all $W - MW$ pairs from the same queue are adjacent (11), i.e., to one of the convenient sequences. In terms of $ISTL^*$, the temporal logic formula Gen_1 must imply $ECon_1$. Below the lemma is proven by applying the well founded set technique seen in Theorem 1.

Lemma 6 $Gen_1 \;\Rightarrow\; E\ Con_1$.

queues, for processor i:

$$(\neg empty(Out_i)) \Rightarrow I(W_i, MW_i)$$

$$empty(Out_i) \Rightarrow \neg I(W_i, MW_i)$$

$$(empty(Out_i) \wedge \text{“}W_i(c,x); MW_i(d,y)\text{”}) \;\Rightarrow\; c = d \wedge x = y$$

$$\neg I(MW_i, MW_i)$$

$$W_i(c,x) \Rightarrow AF\ MW_i(c,x)$$

locality, for a, b operations W or R in processors i, j:

$$\neg I(a_i, b_i)$$

$$i \neq j \Rightarrow I(a_i, b_j)$$

read/write memory consistency, for all processors i, j, and k:

$$AG(\ (MW_i(d,v) \wedge X(\forall j \forall b(\neg MW_j(b,v)) U R_k(c,v))) \Rightarrow c = d\ )$$

delay of reads, for processor i:

$$AG(R_i \Rightarrow empty(Out_i)).$$

independence and equivalence, for operations a and b:

$$AG(\ I(a,b) \;\Rightarrow\; (\ (E\text{“}a;b\text{”}) \Leftrightarrow (E\text{“}b;a\text{”})\ ))$$

Figure 1: Conjuncts in the formula Gen_1 describing lower level computations

Proof: The formula Gen_1 is AG (universal quantification over the states) of the conjunction of the formulas in Figure 1. Assuming this formula, we must show

$$EG(W_i(c,x) \Leftrightarrow XMW_i(c,x)).$$

As noted previously, the queue axioms in Gen_1 imply that each $W_i(d,x)$ is eventually followed by a matching $MW_i(d,x)$. Each matching $W_i(d,x)$ — $MW_i(d,x)$ pair defines an *interval*: the subsequence of states between the pair. The *distance* of the interval is the number of states in it. An adjacent pair has an empty interval and a distance of zero. The *measure* of a finite computation sequence is the sum of the distances of all intervals in it. For all convenient sequences, the measure is zero, and every sequence with a measure of zero is a convenient one.

The measure thus is the function needed to apply Theorem 1, and it remains to show that each sequence with a nonzero measure is equivalent to one with a smaller measure. Consider any nonconvenient sequence σ (which thus has a nonzero measure), and a matching pair in it (denoted $W_i(d,x) - -MW_i(d,x)$) with the smallest positive distance. Call the interval of that matching pair the *interval of interest*. We will show that the sequence σ is equivalent to one with a smaller measure by showing that there is a one-to-one correspondence among intervals in the two sequences where all other intervals have a distance no larger than the corresponding one in σ, and the interval in the new sequence corresponding to the interval of interest is strictly smaller.

In practice, either an operation at the beginning of the interval of interest can be moved to before the preceding $W_i(d,x)$ without affecting other intervals, or one can be moved from the end of the interval past the following $MW_i(d,x)$. If the first state in the interval of interest satisfies $MW_j(c,y)$ for any j, c, and y (including $j = i$), the independence relations show that there is an equivalent computation with the MW_j before the $W_i(d,x)$ ($j = i$ is included because the queue is nonempty at that point). The same is true of any R_j where $j \neq i$ (and R_i cannot appear by equation 12). In each of these cases, the measure of the equivalent sequence is smaller because all other intervals are unaffected or are made smaller.

If in the first state of the interval of interest there is a $W_j(c,y)$ followed immediately by a matching $MW_j(c,y)$ (thus defining an empty interval) there is an equivalent computation with that pair before the $W_i(d,x)$ and thus with a smaller measure. The equivalence must be shown in two stages: after the first exchange the empty interval corresponds to one with a distance of one, but after the second, it returns to zero. Note that in this case j must be different from i since otherwise the queue axioms for Out_i would be violated: two items are inserted into the queue in one order and then removed in the opposite order, which contradicts the definition of a queue.

The only other possibility at the beginning of the interval of interest is of a $W_j(c,v)$ not followed by a corresponding MW_j until after the interval of interest (otherwise the interval of interest would not define the smallest positive distance). In this case we must consider how to move an operation past the *end* of the interval of interest. The last such W_j before the $MW_i(c,x)$ at the end of the interval of interest also cannot have its corresponding MW_j within the interval of interest, since otherwise the queue axioms for the Out_j queue would be violated. There also cannot be a R_j in the interval. Thus the independence relations on the remaining

	W_j	MW_j	R_j	W_i	MW_i	R_i
W_i	+	+	+	-	(1)	-
MW_i	+	(2)	(2)	(1)	(2)	(2)
R_i	+	(2)	+	-	(2)	-

(1) '+' if $\neg empty(Out_i)$, '-' if $empty(Out_i)$
(2) '-', but could extend to '+' for different variables.

Table 1: Summary of independence relations for Gen_1.

operations guarantee that there is an equivalent computation like the one being considered except with that last W_j exchanged with all possible operations between it and the end of interval of interest and finally with the $MW_i(d, x)$ after the interval of interest. This again yields a computation with a smaller measure. □

The proof here systematically analyzes which pairs of operations are independent under what conditions, to show that any computation is equivalent to a convenient one. We show exchanges that bring a general computation 'closer' according to some measure to a convenient one.

An aid to following (and generating) the argument above can be given in table form. In Table 1 the independence relations are given for a matching pair W_i and MW_i, and for R_i, relative to all of the other operations, both for other processors $j \neq i$ and within i, assuming that they relate to the same variable. The relations explained previously are the justifications for the symbols, where "+" means that the operations are independent, while "–" means that they are not. Note that a conservative approach is taken where sometimes operations are considered dependent even if in some cases (e.g., reading and writing to different variables in the memory) they may be independent. This only means that some execution sequences cannot be proven equivalent even though otherwise they could be, and thus each must be shown equivalent to a different representative execution.

Note that R_i is not independent of either W_i (because they both are local to i) nor to MW_i (because they both relate to the central memory and must maintain memory consistency). This again reinforces the implementation decision to forbid such a read operation between writing to the local output queue and writing from the head of the queue to the central memory. The need to 'shorten' the distances in intervals of interest, along with the independence relations, dictates which equivalent sequences must be investigated, and can be used for automatic generation of the cases to be treated.

Theorem 3 *Gen_1 is sequentially consistent.*

Proof: By Theorem 2, using Lemmas 4–6 and the fact that I is s.c. independent. □

Further top-down development of a caching algorithm could similarly be divided into a series of refinements, with each described first by a convenient sequence, followed by a loosening stage to the rest of the computations at that level. Note that the convenient executions are lower level implementations of *any* computation from the upper level, and not just the convenient upper level ones. In such a series of refinements we might first define a level where In queues and local caches are used, and then afterwards consider the introduction of cache misses in a separate refinement level.

6 Concluding remarks

In this paper we proved the correctness of a refinement introducing queues, starting from the definition of serial and sequentially consistent memory. Reasoning in terms of convenient sequences and their equivalence classes is well-suited for this purpose. At each refinement, a two-stage proof is used, first showing that the convenient sequences are a simple refinement using usual mapping functions, and then separately showing every lower level execution sequence equivalent to one of the convenient ones, using well-founded sets.

Although the formulas of temporal logic require familiarization, this should not obscure the fact that the convenient execution sequences are intuitively natural and are easily devised. Moreover, in those sequences the lower level state is only examined when the system is in a stable (quiescent) state, so the mapping functions are also simple.

The independence relations and restrictions on possible implementations are also intuitively clear to the designer, once the appropriate questions are asked.

In order to prove a refinement stage, the possible computations of the upper level must be described by an $ISTL^*$ formula. The lower level computations also will have a formula defining them, including conjuncts that make the independence of adjacent operations explicit. These can be justified from the underlying semantics of the model, or by properties of the data structures used. In the case of sequential consistency, the independence is further restricted by the problem specification, namely that there is a total ordering among local processor writes and reads. These properties can often be shown once for a large collection of related problems. The lower level legal computations also are derived from a description of the implementation (either lower level code or a less formal description). In the example given here, these include restrictions on when a read action is possible. Next, the convenient computations of the lower level are described, also using the temporal logic.

At each refinement stage, four correctness claims must be shown: that the independence relation is appropriate for sequential consistency, that the lower level convenient executions implement the general computations of the upper level, that the lower level convenient executions are sequentially consistent if the upper level executions were, and that every computation on the lower level is equivalent to a convenient one.

The proof that every equivalence class has a convenient execution in it is done using a mapping into a well-founded set. In effect, this is an induction showing that each computation is equivalent to one that is 'closer' to a convenient one. This is the more difficult part of the proof, mainly because there are a large number of cases to consider ($O(n^2)$ if there are n kinds of operations). A systematic examination of which operations can be exchanged is done using the independence information. This aspect seems particularly amenable to automation, since it involves a large number of very simple assertions. Specific tools for integrating such proofs into automatic theorem proving systems or to model checking techniques for finite state programs are not yet available, but work has begun in this direction. Such a tool could be expected to query the user on whether certain pairs of operations are independent in various states, helping to cover all of the possibilities. Since the answers on which pairs are independent are generally clear to the designer, the goal of such a tool is to ensure that all cases are examined.

References

[ABM93] Y. Afek, G. Brown, and M. Merritt. Lazy caching. *ACM Transactions on Programming Languages and Systems*, 15(1):182–206, 1993.

[BS90] R.J.R. Back and K. Sere. Stepwise refinement of parallel algorithms. *Science of Computer Programming*, 13:133–180, 1990.

[EH86] E.A. Emerson and J.Y. Halpern. Sometimes and not never revisited: on branching versus linear time temporal logic. *Journal of the ACM*, 33:151–178, 1986.

[GH93] J.V. Guttag and J.J. Horning, editors. *Larch: Languages and Tools for Formal Specification.* Springer-Verlag, 1993.

[KP90] S. Katz and D. Peled. Interleaving set temporal logic. *Theoretical Computer Science*, 75:263–287, 1990.

[KP92a] S. Katz and D. Peled. Defining conditional independence using collapses. *Theoretical Computer Science*, 101:337–359, 1992.

[KP92b] S. Katz and D. Peled. Verification of distributed programs using representative interleaving sequences. *Distributed Computing*, 6:107–120, 1992.

[Lam94] L. Lamport. The temporal logic of actions. *ACM Transactions on Programming Languages and Systems*, 16(3):872–923, 1994.

[MP92] Z. Manna and A. Pnueli. *The Temporal Logic of Reactive and Concurrent Systems: Specification.* Springer-Verlag, 1992.

[MV94] C. C. Morgan and T. Vickers, editors. *On the Refinement Calculus.* Formal Approaches to Computing and Information Technology series (FACIT). Springer-Verlag, 1994.

[PP90] D. Peled and A. Pnueli. Proving partial order liveness properties. In *Proc. of 17th ICALP*, pages 553–571. Springer-Verlag, LNCS 443, 1990.

DIMACS Series in Discrete Mathematics
and Theoretical Computer Science
Volume 29, 1997

A complete axiomatization of a first-order temporal logic over trace systems*

Wojciech Penczek and Marian Srebrny

Institute of Computer Science
Polish Academy of Sciences
Ordona 21, Warszawa, Poland
{penczek, marians}@ipipan.waw.pl

Abstract

A complete axiomatization of a first-order temporal logic over trace systems is introduced. The proof system contains infinitary rules for temporal operators. In order to show how these rules work, a toy concurrent program is considered, for which a temporal semantics is provided, and the correctness of the program is formally proved within our logic.

1 Introduction

Temporal logic is an important tool for program verification. Depending on the notion of model, three kinds of temporal logic can be distinguished: temporal logic of linear time (LTL) [15, 10], temporal logic of branching time (BTL) [7], and partial order temporal logic [21].

Mazurkiewicz traces and trace systems [13] are partial order structures frequently used to give semantics to concurrent programs and interpreting propositional temporal logics ([12, 6], ISTL [11], TrPTL [26], TSL [22], TLC [1]). The first-order versions of temporal logics are intended for specifying and proving properties of infinite-state concurrent programs [23]. The process of program verification requires either a relatively complete program proof rules or a complete proof system of the pure logic usually extended by the temporal semantics axioms of a given program.

Program proof rules were defined for first-order versions of the following logics: LTL [14], fair CTL [9], and ISTL [23]. However, a complete proof system is known only for the first-order LTL [25, 16], propositional versions of CTL [8], TSL,

1991 *Mathematics Subject Classification.* Primary 68Q60, 03B45, 03B48.

*Partially supported by The State Committee for Scientific Research under two grants No. 8 T11C 029 08 and No. 2 P301 007 04.

and ISTL [22]. The logics TSL and TrPTL have not yet been extended to their first order versions.

In the present paper we partialy fill this "gap". We define a first-order version of the logic TSL (FTSL, for short), interpreted over Mazurkiewicz trace systems. The modalities allow universal and existential quantification over forward and backward paths of the models. This makes most of the branching and partial order properties expressible in our temporal language. The first-order language is two-sorted; it has static and dynamic variables and terms. Dynamic variables correspond to variables declared in the programs. They can change their values during a program execution. The values of the static variables do not depend on the time points. Quantification is allowed only over the static variables.

We provide a proof system of the logic and prove its completeness by the Rasiowa–Sikorski method [24]. The proof system contains infinitary rules for temporal operators. In order to show how these rules work, we consider a toy concurrent program for which the corresponding models are exhibited, the temporal semantics axioms are defined and the correctness of the program is formally proved within our logic.

The rest of the paper is organized as follows. In Section 2 the trace transition systems are defined. In Section 3 we introduce the syntax and semantics of the First-order Trace System Logic. Its proof system is given in Section 4. The completeness is shown in Section 5. An example of formal verification of the Concurrent Factorial program is given in Section 6. In Section 7 we extend the FTSL by allowing quantification over the points of time. Section 8 contains some general remarks.

2 Trace Transition Systems

The trace systems were introduced by Mazurkiewicz [13] as semantics of Elementary Net Systems. The trace systems are isomorphic to the trace transition systems [22, 6], which form a subclass of the occurrence transition systems [17, 6]. The trace transition systems enjoy a nice structural characterization, which is taken as their definition here. The concept of a trace transition system captures the main features of transition relation $w \stackrel{a}{\rightarrow} w'$ from state w to w' by performing action a.

Definition 2.1 *A* trace transition system *is a 4-tuple* $\mathcal{F} = (W, \Sigma, \rightarrow, w_{init})$, *where* W *is a set of states,* Σ *is a finite set of action labels,* $\rightarrow \subseteq W \times \Sigma \times W$ *is a labelled successor relation, and* $w_{init} \in W$ *is the initial state, satisfying the following conditions:*

C1. $W = \{w \mid w_{init} \rightarrow'^{*} w\}$, *where* $\rightarrow' = \{(v, v') \mid (\exists a \in \Sigma)\ v \stackrel{a}{\rightarrow} v'\}$ *and* $\rightarrow'^{*}$ *denotes the reflexive and transitive closure of* $\rightarrow'$ (reachability from w_{init}),

C2. $(\forall w \in W)\{v \mid w \rightarrow' v\} \neq \emptyset$ ($\rightarrow'$ is total),

C3. $\{w \mid w \rightarrow' w_{init}\} = \emptyset$ (beginning),

C4. $(\forall a \in \Sigma)(\forall w, w', w'' \in W)\ w \xrightarrow{a} w'$ *and* $w \xrightarrow{a} w''$ *implies* $w' = w''$ (determinism),

C5. $(\forall a \in \Sigma)(\forall w, w', w'' \in W)\ w' \xrightarrow{a} w$ *and* $w'' \xrightarrow{a} w$ *implies* $w' = w''$ (no auto-concurrency),

C6. $(\forall a, b \in \Sigma)(\forall w, w', w'' \in W)(\exists v \in W)$: *if* $w' \xrightarrow{a} w$ *and* $w'' \xrightarrow{b} w$ *and* $a \neq b$, *then* $v \xrightarrow{a} w''$ *and* $v \xrightarrow{b} w'$ (backward-diamond property),

C7. Let $I = \{(a, b) \in \Sigma^2 \mid (\exists w, w', w'' \in W) :\ w' \xrightarrow{a} w,\ w'' \xrightarrow{b} w$ *and* $a \neq b\}$,

$(\forall a, b \in \Sigma)(\forall w, w', w'' \in W)(\exists v \in W)$: *if* $w \xrightarrow{a} w'$, $w \xrightarrow{b} w''$, *and* $(a, b) \in I$, *then* $w' \xrightarrow{b} v$ *and* $w'' \xrightarrow{a} v$ (forward-diamond property),

C8. $(\forall a, b \in \Sigma)(\forall w, w', w'' \in W)(\exists v \in W)$: *if* $w \xrightarrow{a} w' \xrightarrow{b} w''$ *and* $(a, b) \in I$, *then* $w \xrightarrow{b} v \xrightarrow{a} w''$ (concurrency closure property).

Condition C2 is an inessential restriction of the class of the trace transition systems, which allows to consider only infinite paths and enables a simpler axiomatization.

The forward and backward paths are defined as follows. Let $w_0 \in W$. A *forward path* x starting at w_0 is a maximal sequence of states and actions $x = w_0 a_0 w_1 a_1 \ldots$ such that $w_i \xrightarrow{a_i} w_{i+1}$, for all $i \geq 0$. A *backward path* x starting at w_0 is a sequence of states and actions $x = w_0 a_0 w_1 a_1 \ldots w_k$ such that $w_{i+1} \xrightarrow{a_i} w_i$, for all $i < k$, and $w_k = w_{init}$.

3 First-order TSL

Syntax

The logic is formalized in the usual first-order language with identity, equipped with the symbols for temporal operators treated as logical connectives to be used in building formulas. We distinguish two sorts of variables: $v_i \in SV$ (called static variables) and $z_j \in DV$ (called dynamic, program, or local variables), for natural numbers i and j. That is, we have a two-sorted language. Its predicate and function symbols act within their sorts, although the identity is assumed to allow comparison of all the objects (variables, terms) of whatever sorts they come from. We assume there are no function or predicate symbols on the sort of dynamic variables except for the equality just mentioned. The formulas are built up as usual in a many-sorted language except that quantification over the dynamic variables is not allowed.

Formally, the sets of terms and formulas are defined as follows.

Definition 3.1 *The set of static terms* T_s *is the least set satisfying the following conditions:*

- *all static variables are in* T_s,

- *all individual constants are in* T_s,
- *whenever* f *is an* n*-ary function symbol and* $t_1, \ldots, t_n \in T_s$, *then* $f(t_1, \ldots, t_n) \in T_s$.

The set of all terms T *is the extension of* T_s *by the dynamic variables; i.e.,* $T = T_s \cup DV$.

Definition 3.2 *The set of temporal formulas* TF *is the least set satisfying the following conditions:*

- *if* $t_1, t_2 \in T_s$ *and* $z \in DV$, *then* $(t_1 = t_2), (z = t_1) \in TF$,
- *if* p *is an* m*-ary predicate symbol and* $t_1, \ldots, t_n \in T_s$ *are static terms of the appriopriate sorts, then* $p(t_1, \ldots, t_n) \in TF$,
- *if* $\psi, \varphi \in TF$ *and* $v \in SV$, *then* $\neg\psi, \psi \wedge \varphi, \forall v\psi, \exists v\psi$, $E(\varphi U \psi)$, $EG\varphi$ *and* $EX_a\varphi$ *(for* $a \in \Sigma$*)*, $E(\varphi S \psi)$, $EH\varphi$ *and* $EY_a\varphi$ *(for* $a \in \Sigma$*) are in* TF.

Thus the language has EG, EX_a, EH and EY_a as unary connestives (operators) and $E(.U.)$ and $E(.S.)$ as two binary connectives (operators) on formulas. The notation with prefix E is meant to indicate the interpretation in the sense *there exists a path suth that....* Otherwise this is the usual notation for modalities *always*, *next step* and *until*, together with their past counterparts. The intended interpretation of the future temporal formulas is as follows: $EG\varphi$ - there is a forward path s.t. φ holds along it; $E(\varphi U \psi)$ - there is a forward path s.t. eventually ψ holds and always before φ holds; $EX_a\varphi$ - φ holds in the next moment in the future after executing a. For the past formulas the interpretation is the same but with backward paths replacing the forward ones.

Semantics

Definition 3.3 *The language is interpreted in the* relational structures (models) *of the form* $\mathcal{M} = (\mathcal{F}, A, \mathcal{I}, S)$, *where*

- $\mathcal{F} = (W, \Sigma, \rightarrow, w_{init})$ *is a trace transition system,*
- A *is a carrier set,*
- $\mathcal{I}$ *is an interpretation of the function and the predicate symbols (i.e.,* $(A, \mathcal{I})$ *is a first-order) relational structure as usual in model theory, possibly many-sorted),*
- $S : W \times DV \longrightarrow A$ *is a valuation of the dynamic variables.*

We write $W^{\mathcal{M}}$ *to denote the set* W *of* $\mathcal{F}$ *in* $\mathcal{M}$. *By a valuation of the static variables we mean a function* $V : SV \longrightarrow A$. *The valuation functions are extended to* T_s *in the standard way,* $V_s : T_s \longrightarrow A$.

The satisfaction relation of a formula φ to be satisfied by a valuation V in a model $\mathcal{M}$ at a state w_0, $(\mathcal{M}, V, w_0) \models \varphi$, is defined by induction on the complexity of the formula:

- $(\mathcal{M}, V, w_0) \models (t_1 = t_2)$ iff $V_s(t_1) = V_s(t_2)$, for $t_1, t_2 \in T_s$,
- $(\mathcal{M}, V, w_0) \models (z = t)$ iff $S(w_0, z) = V_s(t)$, for $z \in DV, t \in T_s$,
- $(\mathcal{M}, V, w_0) \models p(t_1, \ldots, t_m)$ iff $\mathcal{I}p(V_s(t_1), \ldots, V_s(t_m))$, where $p \in P$ is an m-ary predicate symbol and $t_1, \ldots, t_m \in T_s$,
- $(\mathcal{M}, V, w_0) \models \neg\varphi$ iff $(\mathcal{M}, V, w_0) \not\models \varphi$,
- $(\mathcal{M}, V, w_0) \models \varphi \wedge \psi$ iff $(\mathcal{M}, V, w_0) \models \varphi$ and $(\mathcal{M}, V, w_0) \models \psi$,
- $(\mathcal{M}, V, w_0) \models \forall v\varphi$ iff for every $a \in A$, $(\mathcal{M}, V', w_0) \models \varphi$, where $V'(v') = V(v')$ for $v' \in SV \setminus \{v\}$ and $V'(v) = a$,
- $(\mathcal{M}, V, w_0) \models \exists v\varphi$ iff there exists $a \in A$ such that $(\mathcal{M}, V', w_0) \models \varphi$, where $V'(v') = V(v')$ for $v' \in SV \setminus \{v\}$ and $V'(v) = a$,
- $(\mathcal{M}, V, w_0) \models E(\varphi U \psi)$ iff there is a forward path $x = w_0 a_0 w_1 a_1 \ldots$ and $k \geq 0$ with $(\mathcal{M}, V, w_k) \models \psi$, and for all $0 \leq i < k$: $(\mathcal{M}, V, w_i) \models \varphi$,
- $(\mathcal{M}, V, w_0) \models EG\varphi$ iff there is a forward path $x = w_0 a_0 w_1 a_1 \ldots$ s.t. for all $i \geq 0$: $(\mathcal{M}, V, w_i) \models \varphi$,
- $(\mathcal{M}, V, w_0) \models EX_a\varphi$ iff $(\exists w \in W)(w_0 \xrightarrow{a} w$ and $(\mathcal{M}, V, w) \models \varphi)$,
- $(\mathcal{M}, V, w_0) \models E(\varphi S \psi)$ iff there is a backward path $x = w_0 a_0 w_1 a_1 \ldots w_k$ and $k \geq 0$ with $(\mathcal{M}, V, w_k) \models \psi$, and for all $0 \leq i < k$: $(\mathcal{M}, V, w_i) \models \varphi$,
- $(\mathcal{M}, V, w_0) \models EH\varphi$ iff there is a backward path $x = w_0 a_0 w_1 a_1 \ldots w_k$ s.t. for all $0 \leq i \leq k$: $(\mathcal{M}, V, w_i) \models \varphi$,
- $(\mathcal{M}, V, w_0) \models EY_a\varphi$ iff $(\exists w \in W)(w \xrightarrow{a} w_0$ and $(\mathcal{M}, V, w) \models \varphi)$.

We also need the following definitions:

- $(\mathcal{M}, V) \models \varphi \stackrel{\text{def}}{\equiv} (\mathcal{M}, V, w) \models \varphi$ for each $w \in W$,
- $(\mathcal{M}, w) \models \varphi \stackrel{\text{def}}{\equiv} (\mathcal{M}, V, w) \models \varphi$ for each valuation V,
- $\mathcal{M} \models \varphi \stackrel{\text{def}}{\equiv} (\mathcal{M}, V) \models \varphi$ for each valuation V.

4 Proof system

We shall need the following abbreviations:

- $\varphi \vee \psi \stackrel{def}{=} \neg(\neg\varphi \wedge \neg\psi)$, $\varphi \Rightarrow \psi \stackrel{def}{=} \neg\varphi \vee \psi$,
- $true \stackrel{def}{=} \varphi \vee \neg\varphi$, $false \stackrel{def}{=} \neg true$, $\varphi \equiv \psi \stackrel{def}{=} (\varphi \Rightarrow \psi) \wedge (\psi \Rightarrow \varphi)$,
- $AF\varphi \stackrel{def}{=} \neg EG\neg\varphi$, $EF\varphi \stackrel{def}{=} E(trueU\varphi)$, $AG\varphi \stackrel{def}{=} \neg EF\neg\varphi$,
- $EP\varphi \stackrel{def}{=} E(trueS\varphi)$, $AH\varphi \stackrel{def}{=} \neg EP\neg\varphi$,
- $AX_a\varphi \stackrel{def}{=} \neg EX_a\neg\varphi$, $AY_a\varphi \stackrel{def}{=} \neg EY_a\neg\varphi$, $EX\varphi \stackrel{def}{=} \bigvee_{a\in\Sigma} EX_a\varphi$,
- $EY\varphi \stackrel{def}{=} \bigvee_{a\in\Sigma} EY_a\varphi$, $AX\varphi \stackrel{def}{=} \neg EX\neg\varphi$, $AY\varphi \stackrel{def}{=} \neg EY\neg\varphi$.
- $EX^i(\varphi) \stackrel{def}{=} \varphi \wedge EX(\varphi \wedge EX(\varphi \wedge ...EX(\varphi)...))$
  (the operator EX occurs i times, for $i \geq 0$),
- $EX^0(\varphi, \psi) \stackrel{def}{=} \psi$, $EX^i(\varphi, \psi) \stackrel{def}{=} \varphi \wedge EX(\varphi \wedge EX(\varphi \wedge ...EX(\psi)...))$,
  $AX^0(\varphi, \psi) \stackrel{def}{=} \psi$, $AX^i(\varphi, \psi) \stackrel{def}{=} \varphi \wedge AX(\varphi \wedge AX(\varphi \wedge ...AX(\psi)...))$,
  (the operator $EX(AX)$ occurs i times, for $i \geq 0$),
- $EX_{a_1\ldots a_n}\varphi \stackrel{def}{=} EX_{a_1}\ldots EX_{a_n}\varphi$, for $a_1 \ldots a_n \in \Sigma^*$,
- $I(a,b) \stackrel{def}{=} EPEF(EY_a true \wedge EY_b true)$, for $a, b \in \Sigma$,

Axioms

A0. all formulas in the form of the tautologies of the classical propositional calculus

A1. $v_j = v_j$ and $z_j = z_j$, for each natural j

A2. $EX_a(\varphi \wedge \psi) \equiv EX_a(\varphi) \wedge EX_a(\psi)$, for $a \in \Sigma$ (determinism)

A3. $EG\varphi \equiv \varphi \wedge EX(EG\varphi)$

A4. $E(\varphi U \psi) \equiv \psi \vee (\varphi \wedge EX(E(\varphi U \psi)))$

A5. $EY_a(\varphi \wedge \psi) \equiv EY_a(\varphi) \wedge EY_a(\psi)$, for $a \in \Sigma$ (no auto-concurrency)

A6. $EH\varphi \equiv \varphi \wedge (AY false \vee EY(EH\varphi))$

A7. $E(\varphi S \psi) \equiv \psi \vee (\varphi \wedge EY(E(\varphi S \psi)))$

A8. $\varphi \Rightarrow AX_a EY_a\varphi$ for $a \in \Sigma$ (relating past and future)

A9. $\varphi \Rightarrow AY_a EX_a \varphi$ for $a \in \Sigma$ (relating past and future)

A10. $EXtrue$ (infiniteness of paths)

A11. $EP(AYfalse)$ (beginning)

A12. $EY_a AY_b \varphi \Rightarrow AY_b EY_a \varphi$, for $a \neq b$ (backward-diamond property)

A13. $(I(a,b) \wedge EX_a AX_b \varphi) \Rightarrow AX_b EX_a \varphi$, for $a \neq b$ (forward-diamond property)

A14. $(I(a,b) \wedge EX_a EX_b \varphi) \Rightarrow EX_b EX_a \varphi$ (concurrency closure property)

A15. $\forall v \varphi(v) \Rightarrow \varphi(t)$, $t \in T_s$

A16. $\exists v EX_a \varphi(v) \equiv EX_a \exists v \varphi(v)$ (Barcan formula)

A17. $\forall v EX_a \varphi(v) \equiv EX_a \forall v \varphi(v)$ (Barcan formula)

A18. $\exists v \varphi \equiv \neg \forall v \neg \varphi$

A19. $(AYfalse \wedge EX_u true) \Rightarrow \exists v EX_u(z_j = v)$, for $j \in \omega$ and $u \in \Sigma^*$

A20. $(t_1 = t_2) \equiv (AG(t_1 = t_2) \wedge AH(t_1 = t_2))$, for $t_1, t_2 \in T_s$,

A21. $p(t_1, \ldots, t_m) \equiv (AG(p(t_1, \ldots, t_m)) \wedge AH(p(t_1, \ldots, t_m)))$, where p is any m- argument predicate symbol

A22. $(v_1 = v_1' \wedge \ldots \wedge v_n = v_n') \Rightarrow (f(v_1, \ldots, v_n) = f(v_1', \ldots, v_n'))$, where f is any n-argument function symbol

A23. $(v_1 = v_1' \wedge \ldots \wedge v_m = v_m') \Rightarrow (p(v_1, \ldots, v_n) \equiv p(v_1', \ldots, v_n'))$, where p is any m-argument predicate symbol.

Proof rules

MP. $\varphi,\ \varphi \Rightarrow \psi \ \vdash \ \psi$

R1. $\varphi \Rightarrow \psi \ \vdash \ EX_a \varphi \Rightarrow EX_a \psi$

R2. $\varphi \Rightarrow \psi \ \vdash \ EY_a \varphi \Rightarrow EY_a \psi$

R3. $\{\phi \Rightarrow EX_u EX^i(\varphi)\}_{i \in \omega} \ \vdash \ \phi \Rightarrow EX_u EG\varphi$, for $u \in \Sigma^*$

R4. $\{EX_u EX^i(\varphi, \psi) \Rightarrow \phi\}_{i \in \omega} \ \vdash \ EX_u E(\varphi U \psi) \Rightarrow \phi$, for $u \in \Sigma^*$

R5. $AYfalse \Rightarrow AG\varphi \ \vdash \ \varphi$

R6. $\varphi \Rightarrow \psi \ \vdash \ \varphi \Rightarrow \forall v \psi(v)$, v not free in φ

5 Completeness

In this section we show that the proof system is sound and complete.

Lemma 5.1 ([22]) *For every model $\mathcal{M}$ and $w \in W^{\mathcal{M}}$,*

(a) $(\mathcal{M}, w) \models EG\varphi$ *iff* $(\mathcal{M}, w) \models EX^i(\varphi)$ *for each* $i \in \omega$,

(b) $(\mathcal{M}, w) \models E(\varphi U \psi)$ *iff* $(\mathcal{M}, w) \models EX^i(\varphi, \psi)$, *for some* $i \in \omega$.

Theorem 5.1 *The proof system is sound and complete.*

Proof. Soundness is straightforward, so we are only concerned here with proving completeness. To this end let σ be a sentence that is not provable in our proof system from a given set Ax of axioms, i.e., $Ax \nvdash \sigma$. We build a model for Ax and $\neg\sigma$. That is, we construct a model $\mathcal{M} = (\mathcal{F}, A, \mathcal{I}, S)$ with $\mathcal{M} \models Ax$ and $(\mathcal{M}, w) \models \neg\sigma$, for some $w \in W^{\mathcal{M}}$.

We follow the idea of Rasiowa and Sikorski for constructing models on ultrafilters in the Lindenbaum-Tarski algebra of a given theory. (See, e.g., [24] or [2].) By axiom A15 and the generalization rule R6, the quantifiers correspond to certain sups and infs in Lindenbaum–Tarski algebra:

- $[\forall v\varphi] = inf\{[\varphi(t)] : t \in T_s\}$,
- $[\exists v\varphi] = sup\{[\varphi(t)] : t \in T_s\}$.

By a *temporal ultrafilter* we mean a maximal proper filter U in the Lindenbaum-Tarski algebra of Ax preserving the sups and infs corresponding to the existential and universal quantifiers and to the following infinite operations:

- $[EX_u EG\varphi] = inf_{i\in\omega}\{[EX_u EX^i(\varphi)]\}$, for $u \in \Sigma^*$,
- $[EX_u E(\varphi U \psi)] = sup_{i\in\omega}\{[EX_u EX^i(\varphi, \psi)]\}$, for $u \in \Sigma^*$.

That is,

- if $[EX_u E(\varphi U \psi)] \in U$, then there is $i \in \omega$ s.t. $[EX_u EX^i(\varphi, \psi)] \in U$, for $u \in \Sigma^*$,
- if $[EX_u EG\varphi] \notin U$, then there is $i \in \omega$ s.t. $[EX_u EX^i\varphi] \notin U$, for $u \in \Sigma^*$.

We construct the time frame $\mathcal{F}$ of $\mathcal{M}$ consisting of temporal ultrafilters. Let w_{init} of $\mathcal{M}$ be an arbitrary temporal ultrafilter containing the equivalence class of the formula $AY false \wedge EF(\neg\sigma)$. Such an ultrafilter exists by the Rasiowa-Sikorski lemma: if a collection Q of infinite operations in a Boolean algebra is at most denumerable, then every non-zero element of the Boolean algebra belongs to an ultrafilter preserving all the operations of Q. It follows from proof rule R5 that the equivalence class $[AY false \wedge EF(\neg\sigma)]$ is non-zero. That is, Ax does not prove $\neg(AY false \wedge EF(\neg\sigma))$. Otherwise, $Ax \vdash (AY false \Rightarrow AG(\sigma))$ would give

$Ax \vdash \sigma$, by R5, contradicting our assumption. For all the temporal ultrafilters U and U', we define

$$U \xrightarrow{a} U' \stackrel{\text{def}}{\equiv} [EX_a\varphi] \in U \ \mathit{implies} \ [\varphi] \in U'.$$

Now, the universe of $\mathcal{F}$ is defined by

$$W \stackrel{\text{def}}{=} \{U \mid \exists n \geq 0 \ \exists a_1, \ldots, a_n \exists U_1, \ldots, U_{n-1} \ \ w_{init} \xrightarrow{a_1} U_1 \xrightarrow{a_2} \ldots U_{n-1} \xrightarrow{a_n} U\}.$$

The definition of W is unambigous since one can show that there is at most one U for each $n \geq 0$ and each sequence $a_1, \ldots, a_n$.

Slightly abusing the notation we define the relation $\rightarrow$ of $\mathcal{F}$ as the restriction of $\rightarrow$ introduced above to $W \times \Sigma \times W$. It is easy to check that the conditions C1–C8 hold (see [22]).

To make sure the above construction of W is not void, we show the existence of the appropriate ultrafilter for the next step. That is, the induction clause for the statement that for each $n \geq 0$, the appropriate U exists, whenever the sequence $u = a_1 \ldots a_n$ is such that $[EX_u true] \in w_{init}$. The immediate a-successor of a temporal ultrafilter U, denoted EX_aU, can be constructed as follows:

$$EX_aU \stackrel{\text{def}}{=} \{[\varphi] \mid [EX_a\varphi] \in U\}.$$

One can show that EX_aU is a proper non-principal temporal ultrafilter using the argument of Lemma 4.9 in [18] and Lemma 5.6 in [22]. Let us now show that EX_aU preserves the infs corresponding to the universal quantifier.

Assume that $[\varphi(t)] \in EX_aU$, for each term t. Then $[EX_a\varphi(t)] \in U$, for each t, by the definition of EX_aU. Since U is an utrafilter preserving the infs corresponding to the universal quantifiers, $[\forall v EX_a\varphi(v)] \in U$. Therefore $[EX_a\forall v\varphi(v)] \in U$ by axiom A17. Thus $[\forall v\varphi(v)] \in EX_aU$ by the definition of EX_aU.

Similarly, we can use axiom A16 to show that EX_aU preserves the sups corresponding to the existential quantifier. Suppose that $[\exists v\varphi(v)] \in EX_aU$. Then $[EX_a\exists v\varphi(v)] \in U$ by the definition of EX_aU. Thus $[\exists v EX_a\varphi(v)] \in U$, by A16. Hence $[EX_a\varphi(t)] \in U$ for some term t, since U preserves the sups corresponding to the existential quantifiers. Thus $[\varphi(t)] \in EX_aU$ for some term t, once more by the definition of EX_aU.

Now, we define the other components of $\mathcal{M} = (\mathcal{F}, A, \mathcal{I}, S)$. For any $t \in T_s$ let $[t]_= = \{t' \in T_s \mid [t = t'] \in w_{init}\}$. These are the equivalence classes of the identity relation according to w_{init} on the static terms. It follows from A20 that if $[t = t'] \in w_{init}$, then $[t = t'] \in w$ for all $w \in W^{\mathcal{M}}$. Let

- $A = \{[t]_= \mid t \in T_s\}$,
- $(\mathcal{I})(t_1 = t_2)$ iff $[t_1]_= = [t_2]_=$,

- $\mathcal{I}(f)([t_1]_=, \ldots, [t_n]_=) = [f(t_1, \ldots, t_n)]_=$, for every n-placed function symbol f and $t_1, \ldots, t_n \in T_s$,
- $\mathcal{I}(p)([t_1]_=, \ldots, [t_m]_=)$ iff $[p(t_1, \ldots, t_m)] \in w_{init}$, for every m-placed predicate symbol p and $t_1, \ldots, t_m \in T_s$,
- $S(w, z) = [t]_=$ iff $[z = t] \in w$, for $w \in W$, $z \in DV$, and $t \in T_s$.

Notice that these definitions are unambiguous. To this end, observe that for each $w \in W^{\mathcal{M}}$,

- $[p(t_1, \ldots, t_m)] \in w_{init}$ iff $[p(t_1, \ldots, t_m)] \in w$, and
- $[f(t_1, \ldots, t_n) = t] \in w_{init}$ iff $[f(t_1, \ldots, t_n) = t] \in w$,

for any p, f, $t_1, \ldots, t_m, \ldots, t_n$, t, z. It follows from A19 that there is $t \in T_s$ such that $[z = t] \in w$. It follows from the transitivity and symmetry of $=$ that for all $t_1, t_2 \in T_s$ if $[z = t_1], [z = t_2] \in w$, then $[t_1 = t_2] \in w$.

Lemma 5.2 *For each formula $\varphi(v_0, \ldots, v_n)$ of FTSL, whose free (static) variables are among $v_0, \ldots, v_n$,*

(*) for all valuations $V : SV \longrightarrow A$, and all $w \in W^{\mathcal{M}}$,

$$(\mathcal{M}, V, w) \models \varphi \text{ iff } [\varphi(v_0/t_0, \ldots, v_n/t_n)] \in w,$$

where $t_0 \in V(v_0), \ldots, t_n \in V(v_n)$ are any representatives (members) of the equivalence classes $V(v_0), \ldots, V(v_n)$.

Proof. By induction on the complexity of φ according to a well-founded ordering on the set TF of temporal formulas respecting Lemma 5.1. That is, $EG\varphi$ must be greater in this ordering than $EX^i(\varphi)$, for each $i \in \omega$, and $E(\varphi U \psi)$ greater than $EX^i(\varphi, \psi)$, for each $i \in \omega$.

In the case of primitive formulas $t = t'$, $p(t_1, ..., t_n)$, and $z = t$ the proof follows immediately from the definitions of A, $\mathcal{I}$, and S. In the case of negation and conjunction the proof follows by the ultrafilter properties.

The quantifier step follows by axiom A15 and the generalization rule R6. To this end, suppose $(\mathcal{M}, V, w) \models \forall v \phi(v)$. Then, $\phi(t) \in w$ for each term t by the quantifier clause, the definition of the satisfaction relation, and by the inductive hypothesis. Thus also $inf\{[\phi(t)] : t \in T_s\} \in w$, since w is closed under this inf. Hence $[\forall v \phi(v)] \in w$, because we have $[\forall v \phi(v)] = inf\{[\phi(t)] : t \in T_s\}$ in the algebra. For the converse implication, suppose $[\forall v \phi(v)] \in w$. Then $[\phi(t)] \in w$, for each term t, since $[\forall v \phi(v)] \leq [\phi(t)]$. By the induction hypothesis this means $(\mathcal{M}, V, w) \models \phi(t)$ for each term t. Hence by the definition of the satisfaction relation, we get $(\mathcal{M}, V, w) \models \forall v \phi(v)$.

The cases of the temporal operators are similar to those in [22]. We give details for two of them.

Assume ϕ is of the form $EG\psi$, where ψ is a formula whose free variables are among $v_0, ..., v_n$. Then $(\mathcal{M}, V, w) \models \phi$ iff $(\mathcal{M}, V, w) \models EX^i(\psi)$, for each $i \in \omega$, by Lemma 5.1. The induction hypothesis $(*)$ holds for all the formulas $EX^i(\psi)$, for each $i \in \omega$. Thus, $(\mathcal{M}, V, w) \models EX^i(\psi)$ iff for each $i \in \omega$, $[EX^i(\psi(v_0/t_0, \ldots, v_n/t_n))] \in w$, with $t_0 \in V(v_0), \ldots, t_n \in V(v_n)$. Since w preserves all the infs of this form the latter holds iff $[EG\psi(v_0/t_0, \ldots, v_n/t_n)] \in w$, with $t_0 \in V(v_0), \ldots, t_n \in V(v_n)$. That is $(\mathcal{M}, V, w) \models \phi$ iff $\phi(v_0/t_0, \ldots, v_n/t_n)] \in w$, with $t_0 \in V(v_0), \ldots, t_n \in V(v_n)$.

Now, assume $\phi = E(\chi U \psi)$, where χ and ψ are formulas whose free variables are among $v_0, \ldots, v_n$. Then $(\mathcal{M}, V, w) \models \phi$ iff $(\mathcal{M}, V, w) \models EX^i(\chi, \psi)$, for some $i \in \omega$, by Lemma 5.1. The induction hypothesis, (*) holds for all the formulas $EX^i(\chi, \psi)$, for each $i \in \omega$. Thus, $(\mathcal{M}, V, w) \models EX^i(\chi, \psi)$ iff for some $i \in \omega$, $[EX^i(\chi(v_0/t_0, \ldots, v_n/t_n), \psi(v_0/t_0, \ldots, v_n/t_n))] \in w$ with $t_0 \in V(v_0), \ldots, t_n \in V(v_n)$. Since w preserves the sups of this form the latter holds iff $E(\chi(v_0/t_0, \ldots, v_n/t_n) U \psi(v_0/t_0, \ldots, v_n/t_n))] \in w$ with $t_0 \in V(v_0), \ldots, t_n \in V(v_n)$. That is, $(\mathcal{M}, V, w) \models \phi$ iff $phi(v_0/t_0, \ldots, v_n/t_n)] \in w$, with $t_0 \in V(v_0), \ldots, t_n \in V(v_n)$. This completes the proof.

Clearly, $\mathcal{M}$ is a model with $\mathcal{M} \models Ax$ and $(\mathcal{M}, w) \models \neg\sigma$, for some $w \in W^{\mathcal{M}}$, which completes the proof of the Theorem 5.1.

6 Toy example: Concurrent Factorial

Consider the concurrent program CONFAC, shown in Figure 1, for computing the factorial $n!$, for each nonnegative integer input n.

The program has one input variable x of type Nat, one local variable y of type Nat assumed to be preset to 0, and one output variable z of type Nat assumed to be preset to 1. CONFAC is composed of two processes (marked by the dotted lines) synchronizing on the action $b : \ y := x$. There are two control variables l_1 and l_2 pointing to locations in these processes, respectively. The initial states of the processes are marked with 1 and 4, while the terminal states with 6 and 4, respectively.

The variables x, y, z, l_1, and l_2 are dynamic variables according to our terminology.

The data domain on which the program operates is described in the FTSL language with 0, successor, addition and multiplication, as the specific symbols, by Peano axioms with the induction scheme for all the formulas of the FTSL language. Alternatively, one can admit the ω–rule. The latter is not a big deal here, since we already have infinitary proof rules anyway.

The frame $\mathcal{F}$ for CONFAC on input $x = 1$ is shown in Figure 2. The number of actions executed by CONFAC depends on the input (see Figure 3). Therefore, there are different frames for different inputs.

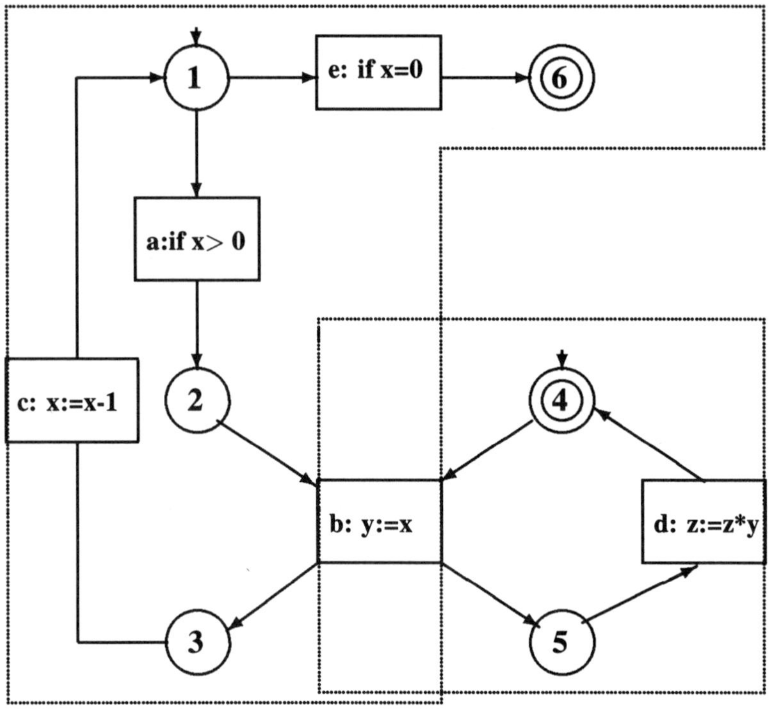

Figure 1: Program Concurrent Factorial

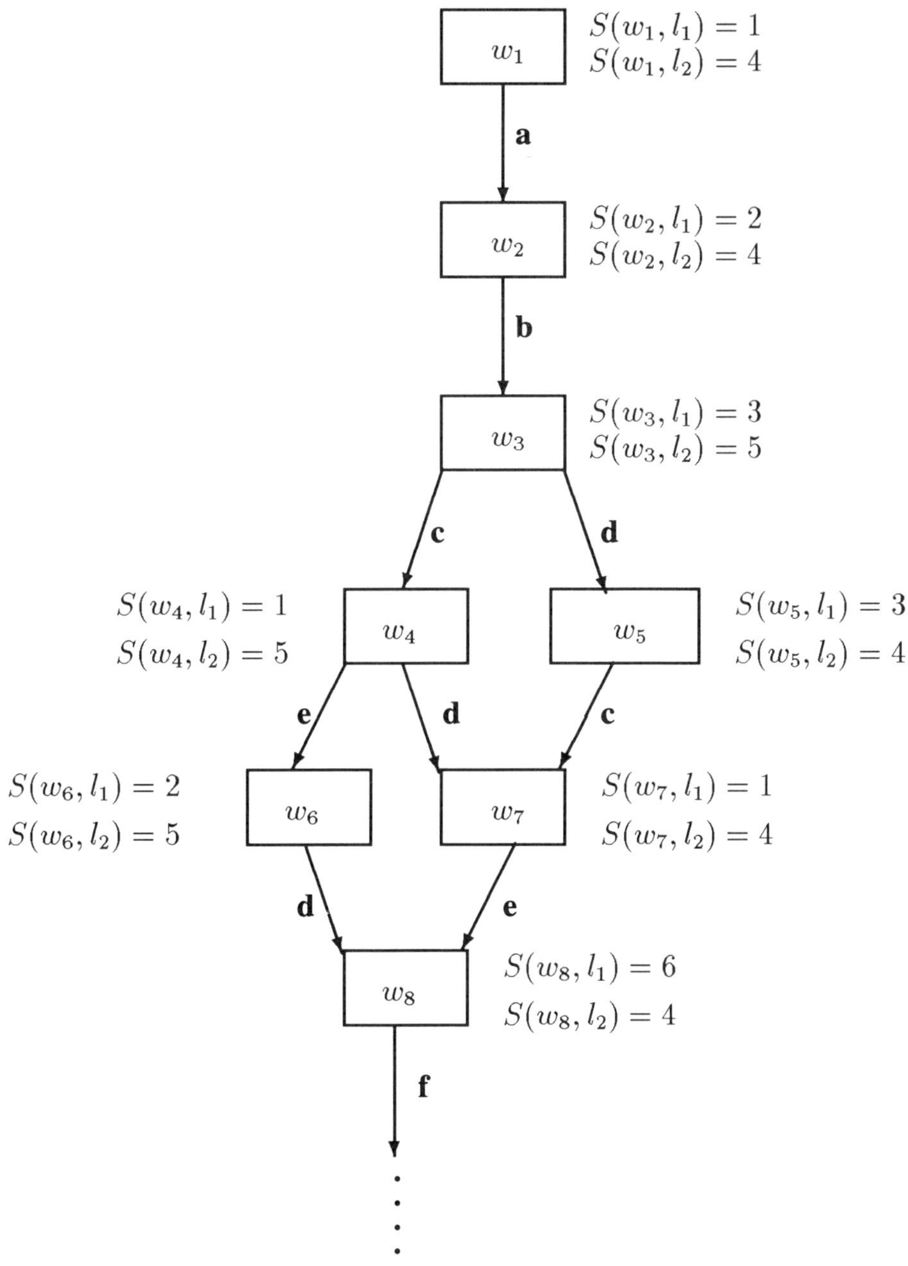

Figure 2: The frame for CONFAC on input $x = 1$

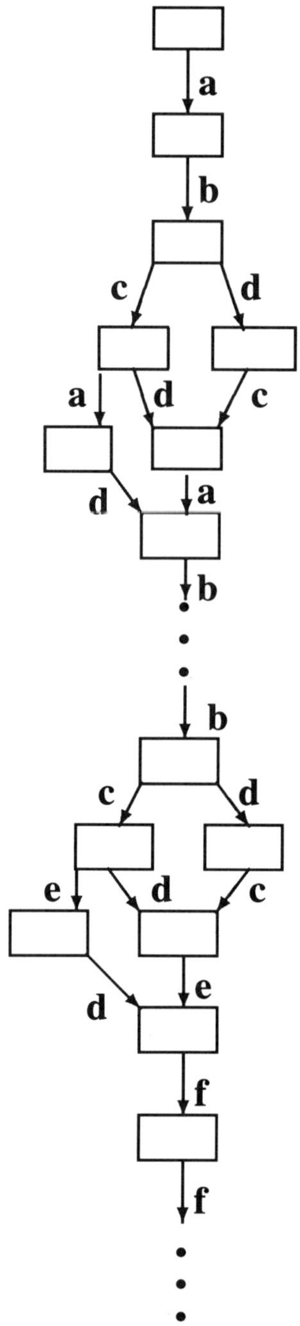

Figure 3: The frames for CONFAC

As the FTSL temporal semantics for CONFAC we take the conjunction of the requirements listed below. It restricts the class of the FTSL models to the ones corresponding to trace transition systems representing the computations of CONFAC on all possible inputs. One of such models is shown in Figure 2. In order to satisfy the restriction C2 (infiniteness of paths) for the trace transition systems representing the computations of CONFAC, we adopt the convention that the final state of CONFAC is repeated infinitely often by executing an additional "dummy" action f. This is reflected in $S7$. Let $\Sigma_C = \{a, b, c, d, e, f\}$ be the set of actions of CONFAC.

- The initial state:

  IS $\exists v_0(AY false \Rightarrow l_1 = 1 \wedge l_2 = 4 \wedge x = v_0 \wedge y = 0 \wedge z = 1)$,

- The successor states:

  S1 $\forall n_1, n_2, n_3(l_1 = 1 \wedge l_2 = 4 \wedge x = n_1 \wedge y = n_2 \wedge z = n_3 \wedge n_1 > 0 \Rightarrow (EX_a(l_1 = 2 \wedge l_2 = 4 \wedge x = n_1 \wedge y = n_2 \wedge z = n_3) \wedge AX(l_1 = 2 \wedge l_2 = 4 \wedge x = n_1 \wedge y = n_2 \wedge z = n_3)) \wedge \bigwedge_{g \in \Sigma_C \setminus \{a\}} \neg EX_g true)$

  S2 $\forall n_1, n_2, n_3(l_1 = 1 \wedge l_2 = 4 \wedge x = n_1 \wedge y = n_2 \wedge z = n_3 \wedge x = 0 \Rightarrow (EX_e(l_1 = 6 \wedge l_2 = 4 \wedge x = n_1 \wedge y = n_2 \wedge z = n_3) \wedge AX(l_1 = 6 \wedge l_2 = 4 \wedge x = n_1 \wedge y = n_2 \wedge z = n_3) \wedge \bigwedge_{g \in \Sigma_C \setminus \{e\}} \neg EX_g true)$

  S3 $\forall n_1, n_2, n_3(l_1 = 2 \wedge l_2 = 4 \wedge x = n_1 \wedge y = n_2 \wedge z = n_3 \Rightarrow (EX_b(l_1 = 3 \wedge l_2 = 5 \wedge x = n_1 \wedge y = n_1 \wedge z = n_3) \wedge AX(l_1 = 3 \wedge l_2 = 5 \wedge x = n_1 \wedge y = n_2 \wedge z = n_3)) \wedge \bigwedge_{g \in \Sigma_C \setminus \{b\}} \neg EX_g true)$

  S4 $\forall n_1, n_2, n_3(l_1 = 3 \wedge l_2 = 5 \wedge x = n_1 \wedge y = n_2 \wedge z = n_3 \Rightarrow (EX_c(l_1 = 1 \wedge l_2 = 5 \wedge x = n_1 - 1 \wedge y = n_2 \wedge z = n_3) \wedge EX_d(l_1 = 3 \wedge l_2 = 4 \wedge x = n_1 \wedge y = n_2 \wedge z = n_3 * n_2) \wedge AX((l_1 = 1 \wedge l_2 = 5 \wedge x = n_1 - 1 \wedge y = n_2 \wedge z = n_3) \vee (l_1 = 3 \wedge l_2 = 4 \wedge x = n_1 \wedge y = n_2 \wedge z = n_3 * n_2)) \wedge \bigwedge_{g \in \Sigma_C \setminus \{c,d\}} \neg EX_g true)$

  S5 $\forall n_1, n_2, n_3(l_1 = 1 \wedge l_2 = 5 \wedge x = n_1 \wedge y = n_2 \wedge z = n_3 \Rightarrow (EX_d(l_1 = 1 \wedge l_2 = 4 \wedge x = n_1 \wedge y = n_2 \wedge z = n_3 * n_2) \wedge EX_a(l_1 = 2 \wedge l_2 = 5 \wedge x = n_1 \wedge y = n_2 \wedge z = n_3) \wedge AX((l_1 = 3 \wedge l_2 = 4 \wedge x = n_1 \wedge y = n_2 \wedge z = n_3 * n_2) \vee l_1 = 2 \wedge l_2 = 5 \wedge x = n_1 \wedge y = n_2 \wedge z = n_3) \wedge \bigwedge_{g \in \Sigma_C \setminus \{d\}} \neg EX_g true)$

  S6 $\forall n_1, n_2, n_3(l_1 = 3 \wedge l_2 = 4 \wedge x = n_1 \wedge y = n_2 \wedge z = n_3 \Rightarrow (EX_c(l_1 = 1 \wedge l_2 = 5 \wedge x = n_1 - 1 \wedge y = n_2 \wedge z = n_3) \wedge AX((l_1 = 1 \wedge l_2 = 5 \wedge x = n_1 - 1 \wedge y = n_2 \wedge z = n_3)) \wedge \bigwedge_{g \in \Sigma_C \setminus \{c\}} \neg EX_g true)$

  S7 $\forall n_1, n_2, n_3(l_1 = 6 \wedge l_2 = 4 \wedge x = n_1 \wedge y = n_2 \wedge z = n_3 \Rightarrow (EX_f(l_1 = 6 \wedge l_2 = 4 \wedge x = n_1 \wedge y = n_2 \wedge z = n_3) \wedge AX(l_1 = 6 \wedge l_2 = 4 \wedge x = n_1 \wedge y = n_2 \wedge z = n_3)) \wedge \bigwedge_{g \in \Sigma_C \setminus \{a\}} \neg EX_g true)$

  S8 $\forall n_1, n_2, n_3(l_1 = 2 \wedge l_2 = 5 \wedge x = n_1 \wedge y = n_2 \wedge z = n_3 \Rightarrow (EX_d(l_1 = 2 \wedge l_2 = 4 \wedge x = n_1 \wedge y = n_2 \wedge z = n_3 * n_2) \wedge AX(l_1 = 3 \wedge l_2 = 4 \wedge x = n_1 \wedge y = n_2 \wedge z = n_3 * n_2) \wedge \bigwedge_{g \in \Sigma_C \setminus \{d\}} \neg EX_g true)$

The program is correct iff for each natural number n, whenever the program starts with input $x = n$, it eventually reaches the state with $l_1 = 6, l_2 = 4$ and output $z = n!$. This property can be expressed in our formal language by the formula:

$$Spec = \forall n(AY\,false \wedge x = n \Rightarrow AF(l_1 = 6 \wedge l_2 = 4 \wedge z = 1 * 2 * \ldots * n).$$

Next, we show that the formula $Spec$ can be derived from our temporal semantics $TSem = IS \wedge S1 \wedge \ldots \wedge S8$ using the proof system, i.e., $TSem \vdash Spec$.

We show only the major steps of the derivation. First, decompose $Spec$ to the formulas 1) and 2), from which $Spec$ can be easily derived using first order calculus rules.

1) $TSem \vdash \forall n_1(AY\,false \wedge x = n_1 \Rightarrow EF(l_1 = 6 \wedge l_2 = 4 \wedge z = 1 * 2 * \ldots * n_1)$.

2) $TSem \vdash \forall n(EF(l_1 = 6 \wedge l_2 = 4 \wedge z = n) \Rightarrow AF(l_1 = 6 \wedge l_2 = 4 \wedge z = n))$

Now in order to prove 2), we derive from the specification $Spec$:

- $TSem \vdash \forall n(EX^i(true, l_1 = 6 \wedge l_2 = 4 \wedge z = n) \Rightarrow AX^i(true, l_1 = 6 \wedge l_2 = 4 \wedge z = n))$, for each $i \in \omega$,

  then using axiom $A3$ we derive:

- $TSem \vdash \forall n(EX^i(true, l_1 = 6 \wedge l_2 = 4 \wedge z = n) \Rightarrow AF(l_1 = 6 \wedge l_2 = 4 \wedge z = n))$, for each $i \in \omega$,

  and then using rule $R4$ we get:

- $TSem \vdash \forall n(EF(l_1 = 6 \wedge l_2 = 4 \wedge z = n) \Rightarrow AF(l_1 = 6 \wedge l_2 = 4 \wedge z = n))$

Now in order to prove 1), we use axiom $A4$ to derive from $TSem$:

- $TSem \vdash \forall n_1(AY\,false \wedge x = n_1 \wedge n_1 > 0 \Rightarrow EF(l_1 = 1 \wedge l_2 = 4 \wedge x = n_1 - 1 \wedge z = n_1))$,

- $TSem \vdash \forall n_1, n_3(l_1 = 1 \wedge l_2 = 4 \wedge x = n_1 \wedge x > 0 \wedge z = n_3 \Rightarrow EF(l_1 = 1 \wedge l_2 = 4 \wedge x = n_1 - 1 \wedge z = n_3 * n_1))$,

  then, using induction on n_1, we derive

- $TSem \vdash \forall n_1(AY\,false \wedge x = n_1 \wedge n_1 > 0 \Rightarrow EF(l_1 = 1 \wedge l_2 = 4 \wedge x = 0 \wedge z = 1 * 2 * \ldots * n_1))$

  and using axiom $S2$ and axiom $A4$, we get:

- $TSem \vdash \forall n_1(AY\,false \wedge x = n_1 \Rightarrow EF(l_1 = 6 \wedge l_2 = 4 \wedge z = 1 * 2 * \ldots * n_1))$

7 Quantifying over the time points

In this section we consider FTSL with variables ranging over the points of time. For an interesting account of the debate whether such an approach is justified we refer the reader to [3], especially section 2.4.2. With no intention to even enter that discussion we just announce the technical result of a complete axiomatization of such logic, within the same mathematical framework as above.

The syntax of this new logic is the same as in Section 3 above but with one more sort of variables x_k called the temporal variables (TV, for short); the same sort as that of a new temporal constant C for the time beginning. We allow the existential and universal quantification over the temporal variables. We interpret this language in the structures of the same form as above. Here by valuations we mean mappings $V = V_s \cup V_t$ such that $V_s : SV \longrightarrow A$ and $V_t : TV \longrightarrow W$. The satisfaction relation is defined as above with the obvious alterations. We include C2–C8 in the set of axioms now. C1 can be handled by taking the reachable (initial segment) substructure of the time frame.

The same argument as above gives the soundness and completeness theorems.

8 Conclusions

We have given a complete proof system of the first-order version of TSL. This is the first known axiomatization of a first-order temporal logic interpreted over trace (transition) systems. Our proof system can be easily adapted to ISTL [23] (with modalities ranging over maximal paths) by removing the formula $I(a, b)$ from axiom A13. The new axiom restricts the frames to conflict-free ones.

It follows from the completeness theorem that the set of all theorems of FTSL is at most Π^1_1. Since the validity problem for TSL is Π^1_1-hard [20], it is Π^1_1-hard for FTSL. Therefore, the validity problem for FTSL is Π^1_1-complete. Identifying interesting fragments of FTSL with low complexity is left out as an important open problem.

We believe that FTSL might turn useful for proving most of interesting branching–time and partial-order properties of the real life concurrent programs (not only the academic toy examples) in an (human aided) axiomatic way.

References

[1] R. Alur, D. Peled, and W. Penczek, Model-Checking of Causality Properties, *Proc. of LICS'95*.

[2] J.L. Bell and A.B. Slomson, *Models and Ultraproducts*, North-Holland, 1971.

[3] J. van Benthem, Time, logic and computation, in: J.W. de Bakker, W.P. de Roever, G. Rozenberg, eds., *Linear Time, Branching Time and Partial Order in Logics and Models for Concurrency*, Lecture Notes in Computer Science, volume 354, Springer–Verlag, 1989, pp. 1–49.

[4] L. Bolc, A. Szalas, eds., *Time and Logic: A Computational Approach*, UCL Press Ltd., London, 1995.

[5] E. M. Clarke, E. A. Emerson, and A. P. Sistla. Automatic verification of finite state concurrent systems using temporal logic specifications: A practical approach. *ACM Transactions on Programming Languages and Systems*, 8(2):244–263, 1986.

[6] V. Diekert and G. Rozenberg, editors. *The Book of Traces*. World Scientific, Singapore. 1995.

[7] E.A. Emerson. Temporal and Modal Logic. In J.V.Leuven, editor, *Formal Models and Semantics*, Volume B, The MIT Press Elsevier, 1990, pp. 995–1067.

[8] E.A. Emerson, and J.Y. Halpern, Decision Procedures and Expressiveness in the Temporal Logic of Branching Time, *Proc. of 14th Annual ACM Symp. on Theory of Computing*, San Francisco, pp. 169-180, 1982, also appeared in *Journal of Computer and System Sciences*, vol. 30 (1), pp. 1-24, 1985.

[9] L. Fix, O. Grumberg. Verification of temporal properties, CS Cornell Univ. Ithaca NY, TR 93-1368 Aug. 1993.

[10] F. Kröger, On temporal program verification rules, TCS 19(3), 1985, pp. 261–280.

[11] S. Katz and D. Peled. Interleaving set temporal logic, *Theoretical Computer Science*, 75(3):21–43, 1991.

[12] K. Lodaya, R. Parikh, R. Ramanujam and P.S. Thiagarajan, A logical study of distributed transition systems, Report IMSC.92.07, The Institute of Mathematical Sciences, Madras, India, 1992, and to appear in Information and Control.

[13] A. Mazurkiewicz, Trace theory, In W. Brauer et al., editors, *Petri Nets, Applications and Relationship to other Models of Concurrency*, number 255 in Lecture Notes in Computer Science, pages 279–324, Springer-Verlag, 1987.

[14] Z. Manna, A. Pnueli, Verification of concurrent programs: temporal proof principles, in: D. Boyer and J.S. Moore, eds., *The Correctness Problem in Computer Science*, Academic Press, New York, 1981, pp. 215–273.

[15] Z. Manna, A. Pnueli, *Linear Time Temporal Logic*, Springer Verlag, 1991.

[16] H. Andreka, V. Goranko, S. Mikulas, I. Nemeti, and I. Sain, Effective temporal logics of programs, chapter 2 in [4].

[17] M. Nielsen, G. Rozenberg, and P.S. Thiagarajan, Transition systems, event structures and unfoldings, *Information and Computation* 118, 1995.

[18] W. Penczek, A temporal logic for event structures, *Fundamenta Informaticae* XI, pp. 297–326, 1988.

[19] W. Penczek, On undecidability of temporal logics on trace systems, *Information Processing Letters* 43, pp. 147–153, 1992.

[20] W. Penczek, Temporal logics on trace systems: on automated verification, *International Journal of Foundations of Computer Science*, Vol. 4 No. 1, pp. 31–67, 1993.

[21] W. Penczek, Branching time and partial order in temporal logics, chapter 4 in [4].

[22] W. Penczek, Axiomatizations of temporal logics on trace systems, *Fundamenta Informaticae* 25, pp. 183-200, 1996.

[23] D. Peled, A. Pnueli, Proving partial order properties, Theoretical Computer Science 126, pp. 143–182, 1994.

[24] H. Rasiowa and R. Sikorski, *The mathematics of metamathematics*, North-Holland, 1970.

[25] A. Szalas, A Complete Axiomatic Characterization of first-order temporal logic of linear time, *Theoretical Computer Science* 54, pp. 199–214, 1987.

[26] P.S. Thiagarajan, A trace based extension of Linear Time Temporal Logic, Proceedings of LICS'94.

DIMACS Series in Discrete Mathematics
and Theoretical Computer Science
Volume **29**, 1997

INTERLEAVED PROGRESS CONCURRENT PROGRESS AND LOCAL PROGRESS

W. REISIG
HUMBOLDT UNIVERSITY OF BERLIN, GERMANY

1. Introduction

The relevant properties of distributed algorithms can be classified as *safety* and *liveness* properties, as suggested e.g. in [1, 3, 7]. Such properties can adequately be represented and proven by help of *Temporal Logic* [5].

We consider particular safety- and liveness properties in the sequel, called *state-* and *progress* properties. They are sufficient to describe the decisive properties of a large class of distributed algorithms. Furthermore, there exist powerful proof rules for such properties.

Intuitively formulated, a state property p characterizes a subset of system states (*p-states*). A state property p is said to *hold in a system* Σ iff each reachable state of Σ is a p-state. Correspondingly, a progress property is based on *two* state properties, and characterizes a subset of *runs*: A progress property (p, q) *holds in a run* w iff each p-state in w is followed by a q-state in w. In the setting of linear time temporal logic, which we assume exclusively in the sequel, a progress property (p, q) *holds in a system* Σ iff (p, q) holds in each reachable run of Σ.

This informal characterization of progress properties is far from unique. We will discuss and mutually relate three versions of progress properties, called *interleaved*, *concurrent* and *local* progress. Each of which has its own merits.

We concentrate on properties that also are considered in the logic ISTL of [8]. We suggest proof techniques that reveal simpler proofs in many cases.

2. Elementary System Nets

The description of an algorithm usually goes with the implicit assumption of *progress*. As an example, each execution of a PASCAL program is assumed to continue as long as the program counter points at some executable statement. The situation is more involved for *distributed* algorithms: Progress is usually assumed for *most*, but not necessarily all actions.

As an example, Fig. 2.1 shows a quite simple producer/consumer system, Σ_1. One may intend Σ_1 not to terminate in a state with *deliver* enabled. Likewise one may want *receive* and *consume* not to remain enabled infinitely. Not enforcing *produce* may however be adequate; this action may depend on the environment of Σ_1, not represented in Fig. 2.1. The action *produce* is said to be *quiescent* in this case (and inscribed with "q"), whereas all other actions are *progressing*. Consequently, each acceptable run of Σ_1 turns out to be either infinite or terminates

1991 *Mathematics Subject Classification.* Primary 68Q10, 68Q55, 68Q90.
Date: September 10, 1996.

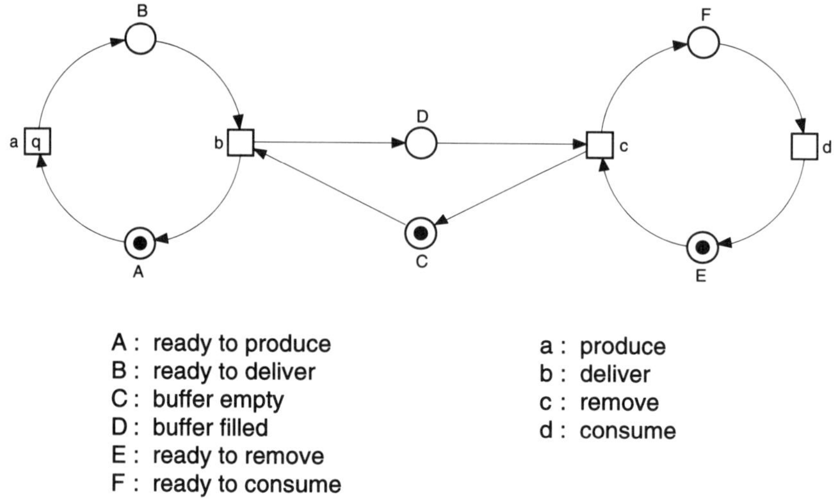

FIGURE 2.1. es-net Σ_1: producer/consumer with *quiescent* produce

in the initial state. Distributed Algorithms frequently assume *fairness* for some progressing actions. This issue is not covered here; we refer to [11–13] instead. Finally, loops are frequently convenient.

This leads to a class of Petri Nets that have not been identified in the literature so far: One-safe place/transition nets with quiescent and fair transitions. This class is worth being named by its own, and we have chosen the term *elementary system nets*, in accordance with *advanced system nets*, considered elsewhere.

As usual we write a net N as $N = (P, T, F)$. We employ standard notations such as ${}^\bullet x$ and $x^\bullet$, denoting the *pre-set* and the *post-set* of $x \in P \cup T$ or $x \subseteq P \cup T$, respectively. Due to the intended use of nets, the elements of P and T will frequently be called *local states* and *actions*, respectively. We employ the usual graphical representation of nets, depicting elements of P, T and F as circles, squares and arcs, respectively. P_N, T_N and F_N will denote P, T and F, respectively.

Enabledness and occurrence of actions are defined as follows:

Definition 2.1. *Let N be a net.*

(1) *Any subset $a \subseteq P_N$ of local states is called a (global)* state *of N.*
(2) *An action $t \in T_N$ is* enabled *in $a \subseteq P_N$ iff ${}^\bullet t \subseteq a$ and $(t^\bullet \setminus {}^\bullet t) \cap a = \emptyset$.*
(3) *Let $a \subseteq P_N$ and $t \in T_N$. Then $\text{eff}(a,t) := (a \setminus {}^\bullet t) \cup t^\bullet$ is the* effect of *t's* occurrence on *a.*
(4) *Let $t \in T_N$ be enabled at $a \subseteq P_N$. Then $(a, t, \text{eff}(a,t))$ is a* step of *N, written $a \xrightarrow{t} \text{eff}(a,t)$.*
(5) *Any finite or infinite sequence $a_0 \xrightarrow{t_1} a_1 \xrightarrow{t_2} a_2 \dots$ of steps $a_{i-1} \xrightarrow{t_i} a_i$ $(i = 1, 2, \dots)$ of N is an N-*based interleaved run. *a_0 is its* initial state.
(6) *Let $t \in T_N$ and let $w = a_0 \xrightarrow{t_1} a_1 \xrightarrow{t_2} \dots$ be a N-based interleaved run. w is said to* respect progress of *t iff to each state a_i that enables t there exists an index $j \geq i$, with $t_j \in ({}^\bullet t)^\bullet$.*

An *elementary system net* has an initial state and declares each action either as *progressing* or as *quiescent*.

Definition 2.2. *A net Σ is called an* elementary system net *(es-net, for short) iff*

(1) *a state $a_\Sigma \subseteq P_\Sigma$ is distinguished, called the* initial state *of Σ,*
(2) *each action in T_Σ is denoted as either* progressing *or* quiescent.

The initial state a_Σ is graphically depicted by a dot in the corresponding circle, and each quiescent action is inscribed with "q". Reachable states and runs of elementary system nets are defined as follows:

Definition 2.3. *Let Σ be an elementary system net.*

(1) *A state $a \subseteq P_\Sigma$ is* reachable in Σ *iff there exists a Σ-based run $w = a_0 \xrightarrow{t_1} a_1 \dots \xrightarrow{t_n} a_n$ with $a_0 = a_\Sigma$ and $a_n = a$.*
(2) *A Σ-based interleaved run $w = a_0 \xrightarrow{t_1} a_1 \xrightarrow{t_2} \dots$ is an* interleaved, reachable run of Σ *iff w respects progress of each progressing action of Σ and a_0 is a reachable state of Σ.*

In the sequel we also employ concurrent runs of es-nets. They can be defined as usual for en-systems, and are based on *occurrence nets*:

Definition 2.4. *A net K is called an* occurrence net *iff*

(1) *for each $p \in P_K$, $|{}^\bullet p| \leq 1$ and $|p^\bullet| \leq 1$,*
(2) *for each $t \in T_K$, $|{}^\bullet t| \geq 1$ and $|t^\bullet| \geq 1$,*
(3) *the transitive closure F_K^+ of F_K, frequently written $<_K$, is irreflexive (i.e. $x_1 F_K x_2 F_K \dots F_K x_n$ implies $x_1 \neq x_n$),*
(4) *for each $x \in P_K \cup T_K$, $\{y \mid y <_K x\}$ is finite.*

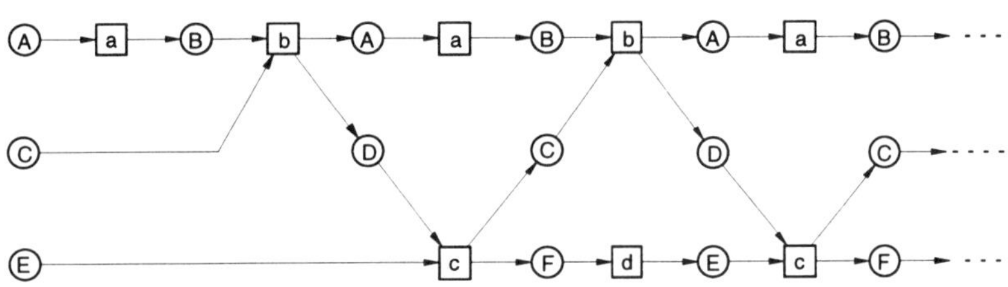

FIGURE 2.2. The unique infinite concurrent run of Σ_1 starting at a_{Σ_1}

Fig. 2.2 shows an element labelled occurrence net. $<_K$ is a strict partial order in each occurrence net K. In fact, $x <_K y$ iff there exists an arrow sequence from x to y.

We are particularly interested in states consisting of pairwise unordered places and consider each occurrence net canonically as an es-net, with the minimal local states constituting the initial state:

Definition 2.5. *Let K be an occurrence net.*

(1) *K is* element labelled *iff a set M and a mapping $l : P_K \cup T_K \to M$ is assumed.*
(2) *Two elements $p, q \in P_K \cup T_K$ are* concurrent *iff neither $p <_K q$ nor $q <_K p$.*
(3) *A state $a \subseteq P_K$ is* concurrent *iff its elements are pairwise concurrent.*
(4) *A state $a \subseteq P_K$ is* maximally concurrent *iff a is concurrent and for all $p \in P_K \setminus a$ holds: $a \cup \{p\}$ is not concurrent.*
(5) *Let ${}^\circ K := \{k \in K \mid {}^\bullet k = \emptyset\}$ and let $K^\circ := \{k \in K \mid k^\bullet = \emptyset\}$.*

(6) *A state* $a \subseteq P_K$ *is* reachable in K *iff* a *is reachable from the initial state* ${}^\circ K$.

The above definitions immediately imply:

Lemma 2.6. *Let* K *be an occurrence net and let* $a \xrightarrow{t} b$ *be a step of* K.

(1) *If* a *is concurrent, then* b *is concurrent, too;*
(2) *If* a *is maximal concurrent, then* b *is maximal concurrent, too.*
(3) *Each reachable state* $a \subseteq P_K$ *is maximally concurrent.*

According to the (above described) intended use of an occurrence net K to describe a run of a net Σ, each reachable state a of K represents a state of Σ that might have been observed during the course of K. Two a-enabled actions of K represent concurrent (independent) occurrences of the corresponding actions of Σ.

Definition 2.7. *Let* Σ *be a net and let* K *be an element labelled occurrence net.* K *is a* Σ*-based* concurrent run *iff*

(1) *in each concurrent state* a *of* K, *different elements of* a *are differently labelled,*
(2) *for each* $t \in T_K$, $l(t) \in T_\Sigma$, $l({}^\bullet t) = {}^\bullet l(t)$ *and* $l(t^\bullet) = l(t)^\bullet$.

According to this definition, Fig. 2.2 in fact shows a concurrent run that is based on the producer/consumer system in Fig. 2.1. The notion of progress, above already defined for interleaved runs, is even more intuitive for concurrent runs:

Definition 2.8. *Let* Σ *be an es-net, let* $t \in T_\Sigma$ *and let* K *be a* Σ*-based concurrent run with labeling* l.

(1) K *is said to* respect progress of t *iff* t *is not enabled at* $l(K^\circ)$.
(2) K *is a* reachable concurrent run of Σ *iff* $l({}^\circ K)$ *is reachable in* Σ *and* K *respects progress of each progressing action of* Σ.

Fig. 2.2 outlines a reachable concurrent run of Σ_1. There is in fact exactly one infinite concurrent run of Σ_1 that starts in the initial state of Σ_1. As a further example, the es-net Σ_2 as given in Fig. 2.3 evolves exactly two concurrent runs starting at the initial state of Σ_2. They are shown in Fig. 2.4.

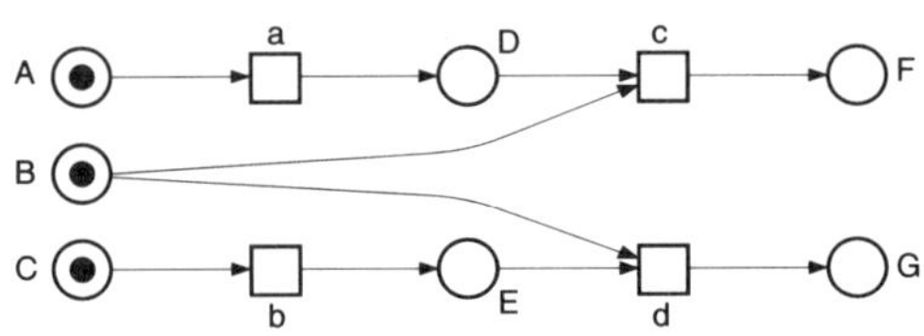

FIGURE 2.3. es-net Σ_2

3. STATE PROPERTIES

Technically, a state property of an es-net Σ is a subset of states of Σ. We describe state properties by help of propositional formulas, taking the local states of Σ as propositional axioms:

Definition 3.1. *Let* P *be a set of symbols. Then*

(1) *each local state* $p \in P$ *is a state formula over* P, *and*

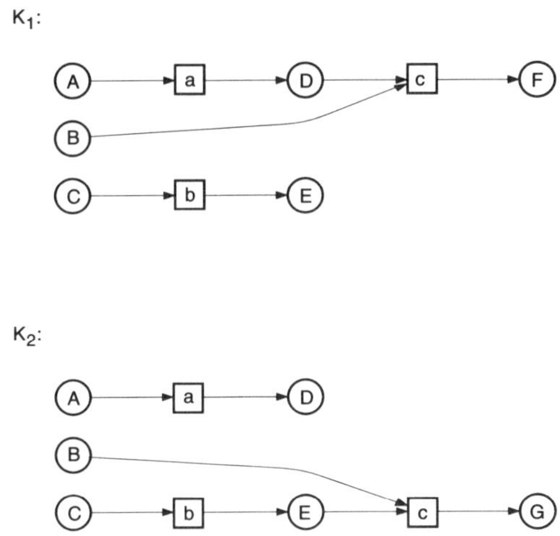

FIGURE 2.4. The concurrent runs of Σ_2

(2) *if p and q are state formulas over P, then $\neg p$ and $p \wedge q$ are state formulas over P.*

Let $\mathrm{sf}(P)$ denote the set of state formulas over P. Validity of state formulas is defined as can be expected:

Definition 3.2. *Let Σ be an es-net, let p, q be state formulas over P_Σ and let $a \subseteq P_\Sigma$ be a state. Then $a \models p$ ("a is a p-state") is inductively defined as follows:*
$a \models p$ iff $p \in a$, for $p \in P_\Sigma$,
$a \models \neg p$ iff not $a \models p$,
$a \models p \wedge q$ iff $a \models p$ and $a \models q$.
Furthermore $\Sigma \models p$ ("p holds in Σ") iff each reachable state of Σ is a p-state.

Of course, we apply the usual propositional conventions such as $p \vee q$, $p \to q$ etc.

$\Sigma \models p$ can frequently be proven by help of *assertional reasoning*: One proves that p holds initially and for each transition t of N one shows, considering p and t only, that each step $a \xrightarrow{t} b$ preserves p. The well known techniques of *place invariants* and *traps* are examples for assertional reasoning.

The following notations turn out useful in the sequel:

Definition 3.3. *Let Σ be an es-net.*

(1) *With $P = \{p_1, \ldots, p_n\} \subseteq P_\Sigma$, the formula $p_1 \wedge \cdots \wedge p_n$ is frequently written $p_1 \ldots p_n$ or just P.*
(2) *Let K be a Σ-based concurrent run, let $p \in \mathrm{sf}(P_\Sigma)$ and let $L \subseteq P_K$. Then L is said to* have a reachable p-state *iff there exists a set $M \subseteq P_K$, reachable from L, such that $l(M)$ is a p-state .*

For example, let K be the run of Fig. 2.2 and let $L = \{s_1, s_2\} \subseteq P_K$ be concurrent with $l(s_1) = B$ and $l(s_2) = C$. Then L has a reachable $A \wedge D$-state as well as a reachable $B \wedge D$-state, but no reachable $A \wedge C$-state.

4. Interleaved Progress

In accordance with other formalisms such as UNITY, interleaved progress is described by help of formulas formed $p \mapsto q$ ("p leads to q"). Validity of such a formula in an es-net Σ is based on its validity in all interleaved runs of Σ:

Definition 4.1. *Let Σ be an es-net and let $p, q \in \mathrm{sf}(P_\Sigma)$.*

(1) *For any Σ-based interleaved run w let $w \models p \mapsto q$ iff w has a q-state provided its initial state is a p-state.*

(2) *$\Sigma \models p \mapsto q$ iff for each reachable interleaved run w of Σ holds: $w \models p \mapsto q$.*

For example, in the producer/consumer system Σ_1 holds $B \mapsto A$ but not $A \mapsto B$. Likewise, in Σ_2 holds $ABC \mapsto F \vee G$, and in Σ_3 holds $AB \mapsto E$ and $A \mapsto E$, but not $AB \mapsto AD$.

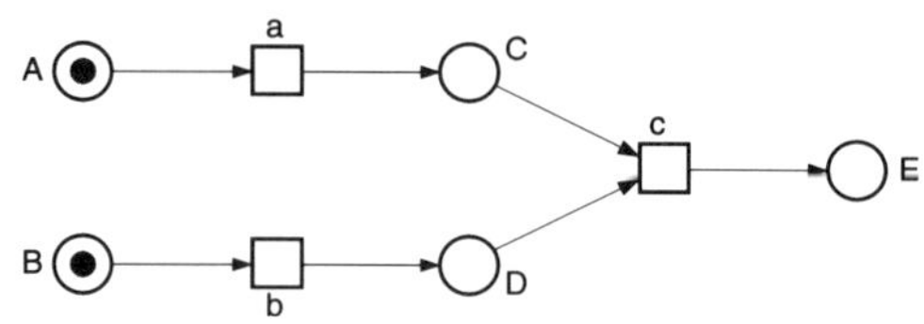

FIGURE 4.1. A technical example, Σ_3

Elementary *leads-to* properties can be *picked up* from the static structure of an es-net. To this end we define:

Definition 4.2. *Let Σ be an es-net and let $Q = \{q_1, \ldots, q_n\} \subseteq P_\Sigma$.*

(1) *Q is* progress prone *iff Q enables at least one progressing action of Σ.*

(2) *Q* prevents an action *$t \in T$ iff for ${}^\bullet t = \{p_1, \ldots, p_m\}$ holds: The state formula $(q_1 \wedge \cdots \wedge q_n) \rightarrow \neg(p_1 \wedge \cdots \wedge p_m)$ holds in Σ.*

(3) *$U \subseteq T$ is a* change set *of Q iff $U \neq \emptyset$ and Q prevents each $t \in Q^\bullet \setminus U$.*

The pick-up rule for progress is now captured in a Theorem:

Theorem 4.3. *Let Σ be an es-net, let $Q \subseteq P_\Sigma$ be progress prone and let $U \subseteq T_\Sigma$ be a change set of Q. Then*

$$\Sigma \models Q \mapsto \bigvee_{u \in U} \mathrm{eff}(Q, u).$$

Proof. Let $w = a_0 \xrightarrow{t_1} a_1 \xrightarrow{t_2} \ldots$ be a reachable interleaved run of Σ and let a_0 be a Q-state. Then a_0 enables a progressing action u with ${}^\bullet u \subseteq Q$ (as Q is assumed to be progress prone). Furthermore, ${}^\bullet u \subseteq a_0$ (by Definition 3.2). Then there exists an index $j \geq 1$ with $t_j \in ({}^\bullet u)^\bullet$ (by Definition 2.3(2) and Definition 2.1(6)). Then there exists an index $l \leq j$ with $t_l \in Q^\bullet$. Let k be the smallest such index. Then $a_k \models \mathrm{eff}(Q, t_k)$. Furthermore, $t_k \in U$ (as U is assumed to be a change set of Q), hence $a_k \models \bigvee_{u \in U} \mathrm{eff}(Q, u)$. Then $w \models Q \mapsto \bigvee_{u \in U} \mathrm{eff}(Q, u)$ with Definition 4.1(1) and the proposition follows with Definition 4.1(2). □

This Theorem in fact allows to pick up $\Sigma_1 \models BC \mapsto AD$ with $Q = BC$ and $U = \{b\}$ but not $\Sigma_1 \models A \mapsto B$ because A is not progress prone. Furthermore, $\Sigma_2 \models DBE \mapsto DG \vee EF$ with $Q = DBE$ and $U = \{c, d\}$; even more, $\Sigma_2 \models BD \mapsto DG \vee F$ with $Q = BD$ and $U = \{c, d\}$.

Not all valid leads-to properties can be picked up this way. But many such properties can be gained as the result of *combining* picked up properties by help of the following Lemma:

Lemma 4.4. *Let Σ be an es-net, and let p and q be state formulas of Σ.*
(1) *If $\Sigma \models p \to q$ then $\Sigma \models p \mapsto q$.*
(2) *If $\Sigma \models p \mapsto q$ and $\Sigma \models q \mapsto r$ then $\Sigma \models p \mapsto r$.*
(3) *If $\Sigma \models p \mapsto r$ and $\Sigma \models q \mapsto r$ then $\Sigma \models (p \vee q) \mapsto r$.*

Proof of this Lemma just applies Definition 4.1 and is left to the reader. The transitivity of $\mapsto$ can graphically be depicted by $p \mapsto q \mapsto r$, and a disjunctive formula $p \mapsto (q_1 \vee \cdots \vee q_n)$ by

(4.1)

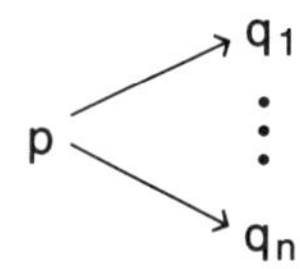

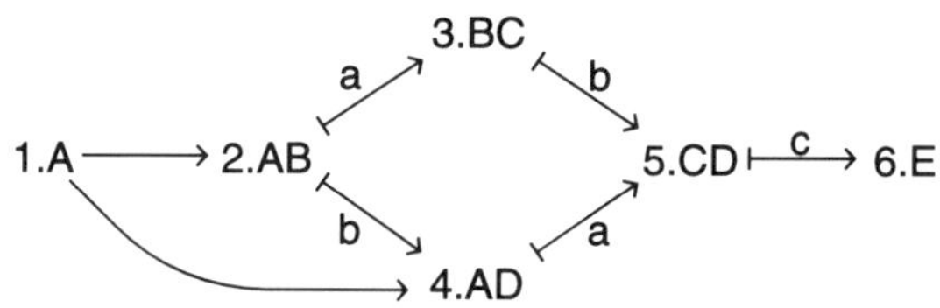

FIGURE 4.2. Proof graph for $\Sigma_3 \models A \mapsto E$

Proofs of *leads-to* properties can thus nicely be presented as *proof graphs* (in [7] called proof lattices). As an example, the proof graph of Fig. 4.2 proves $\Sigma_3 \models A \mapsto E$. With the invariants $i_1 = A + C - B - D = 0$, $i_2 = A + C + E = 1$ and $i_3 = B + D + E = 1$ its nodes are justified as follows:

Node 1: i_1 implies $A \to B \vee D$;
node 2: trivial;
node 3: B prevents c by i_3;
node 4: A prevents c by i_2;
node 5: trivial.

As a further example, the proof graph of Fig. 4.3 proves $\Sigma_2 \models AB \mapsto F \vee DG$. The question mark at arc inscriptions indicates that enabledness of action d was not guaranteed.

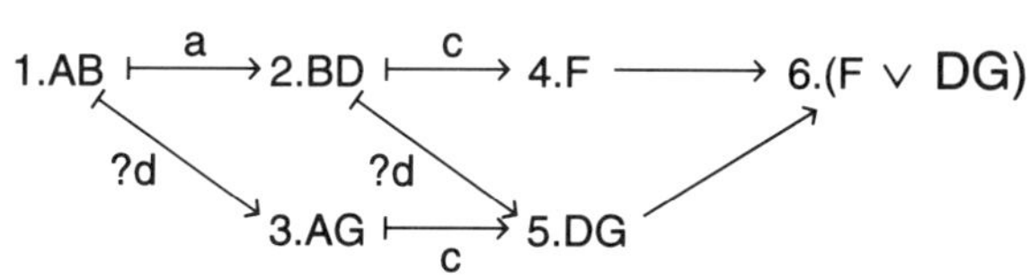

FIGURE 4.3. Proof graph for $\Sigma_2 \models AB \mapsto (F \vee DG)$

5. Concurrent Progress

Concurrent progress is described by help of formulas formed $p \hookrightarrow q$ ("*p causes q*"). Validity of such a formula in an es-net Σ is based on its validity in all concurrent runs of Σ.

Concurrent progress is *weaker* than interleaved progress: $\Sigma \models p \mapsto q$ implies $\Sigma \models p \hookrightarrow q$. Vice versa, $\Sigma \models p \hookrightarrow q$ implies $\Sigma \models p \mapsto q$ in case q is a disjunction $\bigvee Q$ of a set $Q \subseteq P_\Sigma$ of atomic state formulas. In this case, *causes* formulas can be employed for proving *leads-to* formulas. As the pick-up rule for *causes* formulas is more expressive than the pick-up rule for *leads-to* formulas, concurrent progress frequently reduces the size of proof graphs for *leads-to* properties.

Definition 5.1. *Let Σ be an es-net and let $p, q \in \mathrm{sf}(P_\Sigma)$.*

(1) *For any Σ-based concurrent run K let $K \models p \hookrightarrow q$ iff K has a reachable q-state in K, provided ${}^\circ K$ is a p-state.*
(2) *$\Sigma \models p \hookrightarrow q$ iff for each reachable concurrent run K of Σ holds: $K \models p \hookrightarrow q$.*

Examples for valid *causes* formulas $p \hookrightarrow q$ are $\Sigma_1 \vdash B \hookrightarrow ACE$, $\Sigma_2 \models ABC \hookrightarrow ABE$ and $\Sigma_3 \models AB \hookrightarrow CB$. The corresponding leads-to formulas $p \mapsto q$ are not valid in the respective es-nets.

The causes operator allows for proof graphs:

Lemma 5.2. *Let Σ be an es-net and let $p, q, r \in \mathrm{sf}(P_\Sigma)$.*

(1) $\Sigma \models p \hookrightarrow p$
(2) *If $\Sigma \models p \hookrightarrow q$ and $\Sigma \models q \hookrightarrow r$ then $\Sigma \models p \hookrightarrow r$.*
(3) *If $\Sigma \models p \hookrightarrow r$ and $\Sigma \models q \hookrightarrow r$ then $\Sigma \models (p \vee q) \hookrightarrow r$.*

Proof of this Lemma just applies Definition 5.1 and is left to the reader. It is likewise easy to show that *causes* is in fact weaker than *leads-to*:

Lemma 5.3. *Let Σ be an es-net and let $p \in \mathrm{sf}(P_\Sigma)$.*

(1) *Let $q \in \mathrm{sf}(P_\Sigma)$. If $\Sigma \models p \mapsto q$ then $\Sigma \models p \hookrightarrow q$.*
(2) *Let $Q \subseteq P_\Sigma$ and let $q := \bigvee Q$. If $\Sigma \models p \hookrightarrow q$ then $\Sigma \models p \mapsto q$.*

The concurrent pick-up rule again is based on change sets of progress prone sets of states:

Theorem 5.4. *Let Σ be an es-net, let $R \subseteq Q \subseteq P_\Sigma$, let R be progress prone and let U be a change set of R such that ${}^\bullet U \subseteq R$. Then $\Sigma \models Q \hookrightarrow (Q \backslash R) \wedge (\bigvee_{u \in U} \mathrm{eff}(R, u))$.*

Proof. Let K be a reachable concurrent run of Σ and let ${}^\circ K$ be a Q-state. Let $S_R \subseteq S_Q \subseteq {}^\circ K$ with $l(S_R) = R$ and $l(S_Q) = Q$. Then $l(S_R)$ enables at least one progress prone action $u \in T_\Sigma$ (by construction of R). Then $S_R \not\subseteq K^\circ$ (by Definition 2.8(2)). Then there exists some $t \in S_R{}^\bullet$ with $l(t) \in U$ (as U is a change set of R). Even more, ${}^\bullet t \subseteq S_R$ (as ${}^\bullet U \subseteq R$ and Definition 2.7(2)). Then $({}^\circ K \backslash {}^\bullet t) \cup t^\bullet$ is a $(Q \setminus R) \wedge \mathrm{eff}(R, l(t))$-state. Hence the Lemma. □

$$1.BCE \xhookrightarrow{b} 2.ADE \xhookrightarrow{c} 3.ACF \xhookrightarrow{d} 4.ACE$$

FIGURE 5.1. Proof graph for $\Sigma_1 \models BCE \hookrightarrow ACE$

As an example, Fig. 5.1 shows a proof graph for $\Sigma_1 \models BCE \hookrightarrow ACE$. Each node is justified by immediate application of the pick-up rule.

FIGURE 5.2. Proof graph for $\Sigma_3 \models A \hookrightarrow E$

Likewise, Fig. 5.2 shows a proof graph for $\Sigma_3 \models A \hookrightarrow E$. The first node is justified by the place invariant $A + C - B - D = 1$ which implies $A \to (B \vee D)$. All other nodes are gained by immediate application of the pick-up rule. Together with Lemma 5.3(2), this proof graph coincidently proves $\Sigma_3 \models A \mapsto E$. This graph is smaller than the direct proof graph of Fig. 4.2.

As a further example,

$$\Sigma_2 \models ABC \hookrightarrow AG \vee CF \tag{5.1}$$

is certainly valid, as with respect to the two concurrent runs of Σ_2, given in Fig. 2.4, holds $K_1 \models ABC \hookrightarrow CF$ and $K_2 \models ABC \hookrightarrow AG$. But the pick-up rule of Theorem 5.4 does not suffice to show (5.1). Intuitively formulated, Theorem 5.4 does not squeeze sufficient information out of Σ_2. Proof of (5.1) in fact requires a further operator, *yields*, and is postponed to Chapter 7.

6. ROUND BASED ALGORITHMS

Distributed Algorithms are frequently *round based*. Intuitively formulated, each concurrent run of a round based algorithm Σ can be considered as a sequence of *rounds*. Each round is an instance of a Σ-based run that begins and ends at the same global state a of Σ (in fact, mostly the initial state). Hence, an a-state will be reached from *any* reachable state of any concurrent run of Σ, formally: $\Sigma \models true \hookrightarrow a$. This implies that each finite concurrent run ends in an a-state and each infinite concurrent run has infinitely many a-states.

We will refrain from a precise characterization of rounds and consider the more general notion of *ground formulas*:

Definition 6.1. *Let Σ be an es-net and let $p \in \mathrm{sf}(P_\Sigma)$ be a state formula. p is a* ground formula *of Σ iff $\Sigma \models true \hookrightarrow p$.*

Examples for ground formulas are ACE for Σ_1 and $ACEG$ for Σ_4 in Fig. 6.1. There is an operational characterization of ground formulas. It is based on the notion of *change sets* as introduced in Definition 4.2(3).

Theorem 6.2. *Let Σ be an es-net, let $p \subseteq P_\Sigma$ and let U be a change set of p. Then p is a* ground formula *of Σ iff $\Sigma \models a_\Sigma \hookrightarrow p$ and for each $u \in U$ holds: $\Sigma \models \mathrm{eff}(p, u) \hookrightarrow p$.*

Proof. "$\Rightarrow$" is trivial. To show "$\Leftarrow$", let K be a reachable concurrent run of Σ and let C be a reachable state of K. For each reachable state $B \subseteq P_K$ of K, let $\delta(B) = \{t \in T_K \mid b <_K t <_K c$ for some $b \in B$ and some $c \in C\}$. Then holds:

(1) For each reachable state $B \subseteq P_K$, $\delta(B)$ is finite (by Definition 2.4(4)).
(2) B is reachable from C iff $\delta(B) = \emptyset$.
(3) If A is reachable from B then $\delta(A) \subseteq \delta(B)$.

The Theorem's assumption of $\Sigma \models a_\Sigma \hookrightarrow p$ implies there exists a reachable p-state, D. If $\delta(D) = \emptyset$ then D is reachable from C (by (2)) and we are done. Otherwise, with (1) there exists a reachable p-state E of K with minimal, nonempty $\delta(E)$, i.e.

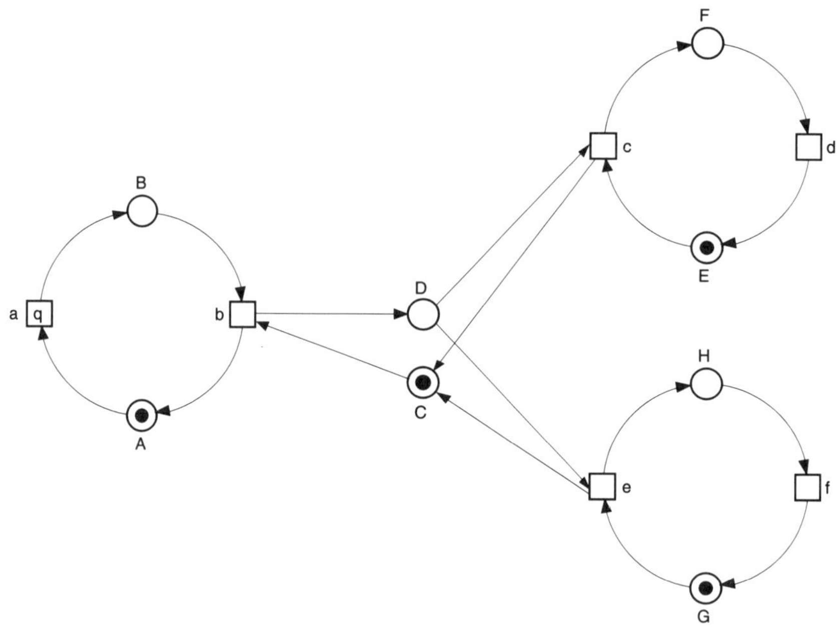

FIGURE 6.1. es-net Σ_4

(4) for no reachable p-state E' holds: $\emptyset \neq \delta(E') \subsetneqq \delta(E)$. Let $t \in \delta(E)$ be a minimal element w.r.t. $<_K$ (which exists according to (1)). Then ${}^{\bullet}t \subseteq E$ (by definition of $\delta(E)$). Then $F := (E \setminus {}^{\bullet}t) \cup t^{\bullet}$ is reachable from E and $\delta(F) = \delta(E) \setminus \{t\}$, hence

(5) $\delta(F) \subsetneqq \delta(E)$.

Now we distinguish two cases, and first assume that F is a p-state. Then $\delta(F) = \emptyset$ (by (5) and (4)), hence F is reachable from C (by (2)) and we are done.

Otherwise, F is no p-state. Then $u := l(t) \in p^{\bullet}$. Even more, $u \in U$ (as U is assumed a change set of p). Then F is an eff(p, u)-state. Then K has a p-state, G, that is reachable from F (by the Theorem's assumption of $\Sigma \models \text{eff}(p, u) \hookrightarrow p$). Then $\delta(G) \subseteq \delta(F)$ (by (3)) $\subsetneqq \delta(E)$ (by (5)), hence $\delta(G) = \emptyset$ (by (4)), hence G is reachable from E (by (2)) and we are done also in this case. □

As an example, we prove that the initial state ACE is a ground formula of Σ_1 by help of Theorem 6.2. The first condition, $\Sigma_1 \models a_\Sigma \hookrightarrow ACE$, is trivially fullfilled. For the second condition of Theorem 6.2 we choose $q = \{A\}$ and $U = \{a\}$. Hence we have to show: $\Sigma_1 \models BCE \hookrightarrow ACE$. The proof graph

$$1.BCE \overset{b}{\hookrightarrow} 2.ADE \overset{c}{\hookrightarrow} 3.ACF \overset{d}{\hookrightarrow} 4.ACE \tag{6.1}$$

shows this property . Its nodes are justified as follows:

Node 1: context E;
node 2: context A;
node 3: context A.

Hence (6.1) proves that ACE will eventually be reached from *any* reachable state, though (6.1) does not argue about all reachable states of Σ_1, e.g. not about BDE or BDF. This advantage of the causes operator is even more evident in the proof of the ground formula $ACEG$ of Σ_4: It is sufficient to prove $\Sigma_4 \models BCEG \hookrightarrow ACEG$, which in turn is gained by help of the proof graph

$$
\text{(6.2)} \qquad
\begin{array}{ccccc}
 & & & 3.\ ACFG & \\
 & & {}^{c}\nearrow & & \searrow^{d} \\
1.\ BCEG & \overset{b}{\hookrightarrow} & 2.\ ADEG & & 5.\ ACEG \\
 & & {}_{e}\searrow & & \nearrow_{f} \\
 & & & 4.\ ACHE &
\end{array}
$$

This proof graph concisely argues about 16 reachable states and infinitely many concurrent runs of Σ_4! Generally, n consumers yield 2^n states and a proof graph with $n+3$ nodes.

Ground formulas support the proof of any causes formulas: In Theorem 5.4, the requirement of R to be progress prone may be replaced by the requirement to imply $\neg p$ for some ground formula p:

Theorem 6.3. *Let Σ be an es-net, let $R \subseteq Q \subseteq P_\Sigma$, let p be a ground formula of Σ with $\Sigma \models R \to \neg p$ and let U be a change set of R such that ${}^\bullet U \subseteq R$. Then $\Sigma \models Q \hookrightarrow (Q \setminus R) \wedge (\bigvee_{u \in U} \mathrm{eff}(R,u))$.*

Proof. Let K be a reachable concurrent run of Σ and let C be a R-state of K. Then C has a reachable p-state D (as p is a ground formula) and $C \neq D$ (as $\Sigma \models R \to \neg p$). Then there exists a transition $t \in C^\bullet$ with $l(t) \in U$. Hence the proposition. □

7. Local Progress

Here we consider a progress operator $\triangleright$ ("yields") that again is defined over concurrent runs. It squeezes more information out of an es-net's structure than the above described *causes* operator does. Hence $\Sigma \models p \triangleright q$ implies $\Sigma \models p \hookrightarrow q$, for each es-net Σ and all state formulas $p, q \in \mathrm{sf}(P_\Sigma)$. In addition to a pick-up rule (in the line of Theorems 4.3 and 5.4), there are rules to *embed yields* formulas into a concurrent context and to *compose* such formulas. Those rules are sharp enough to prove (among other properties) the validity of the above described property $\Sigma_2 \models ABC \hookrightarrow AG \vee CF$.

It is the *disjunctive composition* of *yields* formulas $p \triangleright q$ that fully exploits the power of the *yields* operator. Hence we define:

Definition 7.1. *Let P be a set and let $p_1, \ldots, p_n, q_1, \ldots, q_n \in \mathrm{sf}(P)$ be state formulas over P. Then $p := (p_1 \triangleright q_1) \vee \cdots \vee (p_n \triangleright q_n)$ is a* yields formula *over P. Let $\mathrm{Yf}(P)$ denote the set of all yields formulas over P.*

yields formulas over an es-net's local states are interpreted over its concurrent runs:

Definition 7.2. *Let Σ be an es-net, let $p := (p_1 \triangleright q_1) \vee \cdots \vee (p_n \triangleright q_n) \in \mathrm{Yf}(P_\Sigma)$ be a yields formula over P_Σ and let K be a Σ-based run.*

(1) *For $1 \leq i \leq n$, $K \models p_i \triangleright q_i$ iff each p_i-state $L \subseteq {}^\circ K$ has a reachable q_i-state.*
(2) *$K \models p$ iff for some $1 \leq i \leq n$ holds: $K \models p_i \triangleright q_i$.*
(3) *$\Sigma \models p$ iff for each reachable concurrent run K of Σ holds: $K \models p$.*

yields is in fact stronger than *causes*:

Lemma 7.3. *Let Σ be an es-net and let $p, q \in \mathrm{sf}(P_\Sigma)$. If $\Sigma \models p \triangleright q$ then $\Sigma \models p \hookrightarrow q$.*

Proof. Let $\Sigma \models p \triangleright q$. Then for each reachable run K holds: Each p-state $L \subseteq {}^\circ K$ has a reachable q-state. Hence ${}^\circ K$ is no p-state or has a reachable q-state. Hence $K \models p \hookrightarrow q$. □

The operator $\triangleright$ essentially differs from $\mapsto$ and $\hookrightarrow$ with respect to implication: $\Sigma \models p \to q$ does in general *not* imply $\Sigma \models p \triangleright q$. Hence $\Sigma \models p \mapsto q$ does in general not imply $\Sigma \models p \triangleright q$. As an example, $\Sigma_3 \models C \mapsto E$ but not $\Sigma_3 \models C \triangleright E$.

The *yields* operator allows of proof graphs, too:

Lemma 7.4. (1) *If $\Sigma \models p \triangleright q$ and $\Sigma \models q \triangleright r$ then $\Sigma \models p \triangleright r$.*
(2) *If $\Sigma \models p \triangleright r$ and $\Sigma \models q \triangleright r$ then $\Sigma \models (p \vee q) \triangleright r$.*
(3) *If $\Sigma \models (p \triangleright q) \vee (p \triangleright r)$ then $\Sigma \models p \triangleright (q \vee r)$.*

Proof of this Lemma just applies Definition 7.2 and is left to the reader.

We stick to *standard* yields formulas in the sequel: Each state formula p_i in each component $p_i \triangleright q_i$ is just a conjunction (written as a subset according to Definition 3.3(1)) of local states:

Definition 7.5. *Let P be a set of symbols and let $p = (p_1 \triangleright q_1) \vee \cdots \vee (p_n \triangleright q_n) \in$ $\mathrm{Yf}(P)$ be a* yields *formula over P. Then P is said to be* standard *iff $p_1, \ldots, p_n \subseteq P$. In this case,* $\mathrm{pre}(p) := p_1 \cup \cdots \cup p_n$ *is the* precondition of p.

The validity of standard *yields* formulas can be characterized as follows:

Lemma 7.6. *Let Σ be an es-net, let $p \triangleright q \in \mathrm{Yf}(P_\Sigma)$ be standard and let K be a Σ-based run. Then $K \models p \triangleright q$ iff either $p \not\subseteq l({}^\circ K)$ or $L := \{k \in {}^\circ K \mid l(k) \in p\}$ has a reachable q-state.*

Proof. For $p \subseteq P_\Sigma$, $L \subseteq {}^\circ K$ is a p-state iff $p \subseteq l(L)$. □

Local progress can be picked up from the structure of an es-net:

Theorem 7.7. *Let Σ be an es-net, let $Q \subseteq P_\Sigma$ be progress prone and let U be a change set of Q with $Q = {}^\bullet U$. Then $\Sigma \models \bigvee_{u \in U} {}^\bullet u \triangleright u^\bullet$.*

Proof. Let K be a reachable run of Σ. According to Definition 7.2 we have to show:

(1) $K \models {}^\bullet u \triangleright u^\bullet$ for some $u \in U$.

The formula $\bigvee_{u \in U} {}^\bullet u \triangleright u^\bullet$ is apparently standard. In case ${}^\bullet U \not\subseteq l({}^\circ K)$, there exists an action $u \in U$ with ${}^\bullet u \not\subseteq l({}^\circ K)$ and we are done with Lemma 7.6 and Definition 7.2. Otherwise ${}^\bullet U \subseteq l({}^\circ K)$, hence $Q \subseteq l({}^\circ K)$ (as $Q \subseteq {}^\bullet U$), hence $l({}^\circ K)$ enables at least one progressing action $u \in Q^\bullet$ (as Q is progress prone). Hence for $L := \{k \in {}^\circ K \mid l(k) \in Q\}$ holds: $L \not\subseteq K^\circ$ (by Definition 2.8). Hence there exists a transition $t_0 \in L^\bullet$. Before continuing the proof's main stream we show

(2) If there exists some $t \in L^\bullet$ then there exists some $r \in T_K$ with ${}^\bullet r \subseteq L$.

by induction on the *height* $h(t)$ of t: Inductively let $h(t) := 0$ if ${}^\bullet t \subseteq L$ and $h(t) = \max\{h(r) \mid r^\bullet \cap {}^\bullet t \neq \emptyset\} + 1$ if ${}^\bullet t \not\subseteq L$. Fig. 7.1 outlines the forthcoming arguments. If $h(t) = 0$, then (2) holds with $r = t$. Now for $n \geq 1$ assume (2) for all t' with $h(t') < n$ and let $t \in L^\bullet$ with $h(t) = n$. Then there exists some $s \in {}^\bullet t \setminus L$. Furthermore, $l(t) \in U$ (as U is a change set of Q). Then $l(s) \in Q$ (as ${}^\bullet U = Q$ by the Theorem's assumption). Then there exists some $s' \in L$ with $l(s') = l(s)$ (by

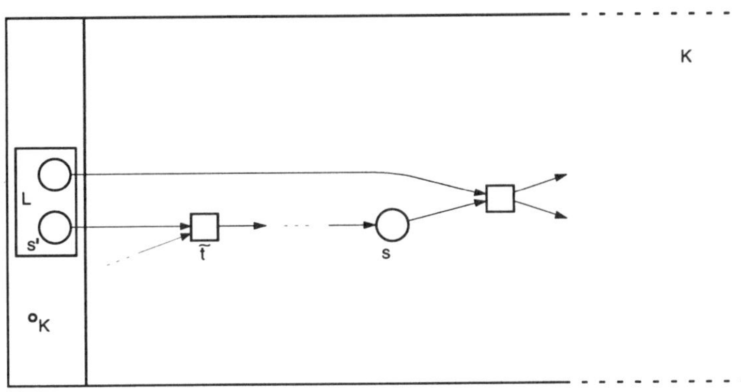

FIGURE 7.1. Outline of the proof of (2)

construction of L). Then s and s' are not concurrent (by Definition 2.7(1)). Then $s' <_K s$ (as $s' \in {}^\circ K$). Then there exists some $\tilde{t} \in T_K$ with $s' F_K \tilde{t} F_K^* s F_K t$. Then $h(\tilde{t}) < h(t)$ (by construction of h). Then there exists some $r \in T_K$ with ${}^\bullet r \subseteq L$ (by the inductive assumption). Hence the proposition (2).

Turning back to the proof's mainstream, $t_0 \in L^\bullet$ implies some $r \in T_K$ with ${}^\bullet r \subseteq L$ (by (2)). Then $l(r) \in U$ (by construction of L and U). In order to show (1) we more concretely show

(3) $K \models {}^\bullet l(r) \rhd l(r)^\bullet$

by help of Lemma 7.6 as follows:
$\{k \in {}^\circ K \mid l(k) \in {}^\bullet l(r)\} = \{k \in {}^\circ K \mid l(k) \in l({}^\bullet r)\}$ (by Definition 2.7(2)) $= \{k \in {}^\circ K \mid k \in {}^\bullet r\}$ (by Definition 2.7(1)) $= {}^\bullet r$. Obviously, $r^\bullet$ is reachable from ${}^\bullet r$ in K, and $r^\bullet$ is a $l(r^\bullet)$-state (by construction), i.e. a $l(r)^\bullet$-state (by Definition 2.7(2)). Hence (3) by Lemma 7.6. □

Components of *yields* formulas can be *embedded* into a concurrent context:

Theorem 7.8. *Let Σ be an es-net, let $p, q, r \subseteq P_\Sigma$ with $p \cap r = \emptyset$ and let $u \in \mathrm{Yf}(P_\Sigma)$. If $\Sigma \models (p \rhd q) \vee u$ then $\Sigma \models ((p \cup r) \rhd (q \cup r)) \vee u$.*

Proof. Let K be a reachable concurrent run of Σ. According to Definition 7.2(3) we have to show:

(1) $K \models ((p \cup r) \rhd (q \cup r)) \vee u$.

In case $K \models u$ we are done by Definition 7.2(2). Otherwise holds $K \models p \rhd q$, by the Theorem's assumption $\Sigma \models (p \rhd q) \vee u$ and Definition 7.2. Then either $p \not\subseteq l({}^\circ K)$ or $L_p := \{k \in {}^\circ K \mid l(k) \in p\}$ has a reachable q-state, M (by Lemma 7.6). Then either $p \cup r \not\subseteq l({}^\circ K)$ or for $L_r := \{k \in {}^\circ K \mid l(k) \in r\}$ holds: $M \cup L_r$ is reachable from $L_p \cup L_r$, hence $L_p \cup L_r$ has a reachable $q \cup r$-state, hence $K \models (p \cup r) \rhd (q \cup r)$ (again by Lemma 7.6, and by construction of M and L_r). This implies (1) by Definition 7.2(2). □

Yields formulas can quite generally be composed, provided some of the involved components are standard and their preconditions are sufficiently disjoint:

Theorem 7.9. *Let Σ be an es-net, let $p, q, r, s \subseteq P_\Sigma$ with $(p \cap r) \subseteq q$, let $u \in \mathrm{Yf}(P_\Sigma)$ and let v be a standard* yields *formula with $\mathrm{pre}(v) \cap p = \emptyset$. Furthermore assume $\Sigma \models (p \rhd q) \vee u$ and $\Sigma \models (r \rhd s) \vee v$. Then $\Sigma \models (p \cup (r \setminus q) \rhd s \cup (q \setminus r)) \vee u \vee v$.*

Proof. According to Definition 7.2(3) we have to show for each reachable concurrent run K of Σ: $K \models (p \cup (r \setminus q) \triangleright s \cup (q \setminus r)) \vee u \vee v$. Hence assume a reachable concurrent run K of Σ.

If $K \models u$ or $K \models v$, we are done (by Definition 7.2(2)). Otherwise holds

(1) $K \not\models v$ and

(2) $K \models (p \triangleright q)$,

by the Theorem's assumptions and Definition 7.2, and we have to show $K \models p \cup (r \setminus q) \triangleright s \cup (q \setminus r)$. In case $p \cup (r \setminus q) \not\subseteq l(°K)$, we are done. Otherwise let $L \subseteq °K$ with $L = \{k \in °K \mid l(k) \in p \cup (r \setminus q)\}$. By Lemma 7.6 we have to show that

(3) L has a reachable $(s \cup (q \setminus r))$-state.

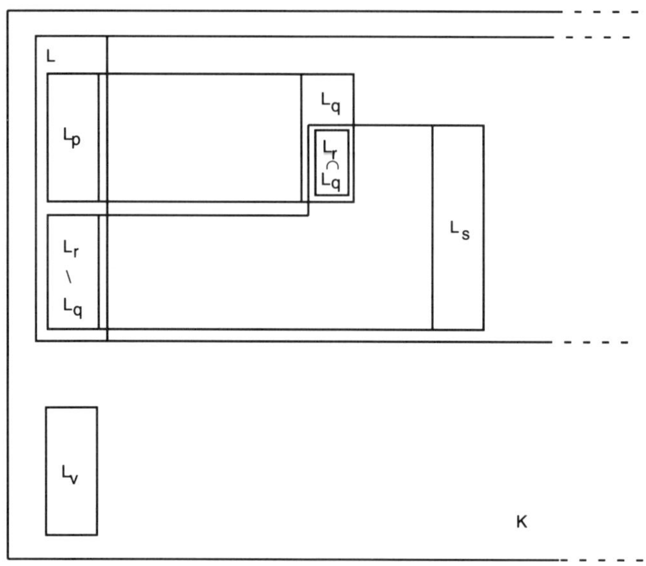

FIGURE 7.2. Outline of the proof of Theorem 7.9

Fig. 7.2 outlines the forthcoming arguments.

• There exists a subset $L_p \subseteq L$ with $l(L_p) = p$ (by construction of L). Then L_p has a reachable q-state L_q (by (2) and Lemma 7.6). Then $L' := (L \setminus L_p) \cup L_q$ is reachable from L and L' is a $((p \cup (r \setminus q)) \setminus p) \cup q$-state (by construction) and even a $(r \cup q)$-state (by the Theorem's assumption $(r \cap p) \subseteq q$). Hence there exists a subset $L_r \subseteq L'$ with $l(L_r) = r$.

• Let $\tilde{L} := (°K \setminus L_p) \cup L_q$. $\tilde{L}$ is reachable in K and hence

(4) $l(\tilde{L})$ is reachable in Σ, and

(5) $L_r \subseteq \tilde{L}$

because $L_r \subseteq L' \subseteq \tilde{L}$ by construction of L_r, L' and $\tilde{L}$.

• Let K' be the *largest subnet of* K such that $^\bullet K' = \tilde{L}$ (i.e. K' coincides with the elements of K that are reachable from $(°K \setminus L_p) \cup L_q$).

• Let $v = (p_1 \triangleright q_1 \vee \cdots \vee p_n \triangleright q_n)$. Then for all $1 \leq i \leq n$ holds: $K \not\models p_i \triangleright q_i$ (by (1) and Definition 7.2(2)), hence there exists a subset $L_i \subseteq °K$ with $l(L_i) = p_i$ and L_i has no reachable q_i-state (by Lemma 7.6). Furthermore, $L_i \cap L_p = \emptyset$ (by the

Theorem's assumption $\text{pre}(v) \cap p = \emptyset$), hence $L_i \subseteq {}^\circ K'$ (by construction of K'), hence $K' \not\models p_i \rhd q_i$.
Then $K' \not\models v$ (by Definition 7.2(2)). Then $K' \models r \rhd s$ (by the Theorem's assumption $\Sigma \models (r \rhd s) \vee v$, Definition 7.2(2) and Definition 7.2(3)). Then L_r has a reachable s-state, L_s (by (5), construction of K, and Lemma 7.6). Then $L'_s := (L' \setminus L_r) \cup L_s$ is reachable from L' and L'_s is a $((r \cup q) \setminus r) \cup s$-state, hence a $s \cup (q \setminus r)$-state. Furthermore, L'_s is reachable from L (by construction of L' and Lemma 7.4(1)). This implies (3). □

Theorems 7.7, 7.8 and 7.9 provide rules to pick up, to embed and to compose *yields* formulas, sufficient to prove $\Sigma_2 \models ABC \hookrightarrow AG \vee CF$, as discussed in (5.1). The proof gives a formal basis for an intuitive justification of (5.1):

1. $A \rhd D$, picked up: $\{a\}$ is a change set of A.
2. $C \rhd E$, picked up: $\{b\}$ is a change set of C.
3. $(BD \rhd F) \vee (BE \rhd G)$, picked up: $\{c, d\}$ is a change set of BDE.
4. $(AB \rhd F) \vee (BE \rhd G)$ composed, with 1. and 3.
5. $(AB \rhd F) \vee (BC \rhd G)$ composed, with 2. and 4.
6. $(ABC \rhd FC) \vee (BC \rhd G)$ embedded, with 5.
7. $(ABC \rhd FC) \vee (ABC \rhd AG)$ embedded, with 6.
8. $ABC \rhd (FC \vee AG)$ Lemma 7.4(3).
9. $ABC \hookrightarrow (FC \vee AG)$ Lemma 7.3.

We consider the corresponding proof in [8] less oriented at intuition. As a variant, assume quiescence for the action a of Σ_2. Then the above discussed property (5.1) remains valid. But the above proof fails, because $A \rhd D$ cannot be picked up anymore: $\{a\}$ is no change set of A because a change set must contain at least one progressing action. Proof of (5.1) can nevertheless be conducted by help of the change set $\{a, d\}$ of ABE (the action c is excluded by the place invariant $A + D + F = 1$). Employing 2., 3., 5.–9. of the above proof we now argue as follows:

10. $(A \rhd D) \vee (BE \rhd G)$, picked up: $\{a, d\}$ is a change set of ABE.
11. $(AB \rhd F) \vee (BE \rhd G) \vee (BE \rhd G)$, composed, with 3. and 10. From 11. now follows 4. by propositional logic, and 5.–9. as above.

8. Conclusion

This paper reports some aspects of sustained effort to set an adequate basis for Distributed Algorithms. One of the outcomes of this effort is the notion of *elementary system nets* as introduced in Chapter 2, and particularly the notions of *quiescence*, *progress* and *fairness*, as required for many real life algorithms, [10–14]. The notion of fairness, as well as the high level formalism of *system nets* have not played any role in this paper.

Three versions of temporal logic have been studied in this paper. They are examples of *linear time temporal logic*, because for each of them a formula p is said to hold in a system Σ if and only if p holds in each reachable run of Σ. The three versions of logic differ however with respect to the considered runs (interleaved runs for *leads-to* and concurrent runs for *yields* and *causes*), and with respect to the granularity of information that is squeezed out of a concurrent run (*yields* with finer granularity than *causes*).

Properties of distributed algorithms that are usually considered essential, can mostly be formulated by help of *leads-to* formulas $p \mapsto q$, where q is a disjunction $q = \bigvee Q$ of a set Q of atoms. We have shown that *yields* and *causes* can be used to prove such *leads-to* properties more elegantly.

The deepening understanding of distributed algorithms reveals that there are also crucial properties that are not captured by leads-to properties. Examples include the property (5.1) and *rounds*: A variant of Σ_2 with property (5.1) has been introduced in [8] as a description of serializability of distributed database transactions. The concept of *rounds* allows to simply structure the behaviour of many distributed algorithms, in particular algorithms on networks of communicating agents. The behaviour of many such algorithms Σ can be described by help of "regular" operators over a finite set of finite, cyclic, Σ-based concurrent runs (more precisely, as a regular Mazurkiewicz trace language, c.f. [6]). *Causes* formulas $p \hookrightarrow q$ are an adequate means to represent such properties. Their proof can occasionally be simplified by help of *yields* formulas $p \rhd q$ (as in the proof given in Chapter 6 for (5.1)).

Properties described by *causes* formulas $p \hookrightarrow q$ are intuitively obvious. But examples of corresponding essential properties of real-life distributed algorithms remain to be found.

Acknowledgments

This paper advocates a blend of concepts and operators, developed during many years by help of many people. It started in 1988 in the framework of the "Sonderforschungsbereich 342" at the Technical University of Munich, together with the EC-based projects DEMON and CALIBAN. It is still going on at the Humboldt University of Berlin [2, 10–14] now supported by the projects "Distributed Algorithms" and "Consensus Algorithms" and the "Forschergruppe Petri Net Technology", all granted by the "Deutsche Forschungsgemeinschaft".

People involved include, among others, Jörg Desel, Dominik Gomm, Ekkart Kindler, Sibylle Peuker, Tobias Vesper, Hagen Völzer and Rolf Walter.

Amir Pnueli drew my attention to Σ_2 (Fig. 2.3) and property (5.1) a couple of years ago. This provided a sustained challenge to me and my research group's several attempts to design an adequate logic for concurrency, and strongly influenced the design of the *causes* and *yields* operators given in this paper. Many thanks to Amir and all colleagues mentioned above.

References

[1] B. Alpern and F. B. Schneider. Defining Liveness. In *Information Processing Letters*, volume 21, pages 181–185, 1985.

[2] E. Kindler. *Modularer Entwurf verteilter Systeme mit Petrinetzen.* PhD thesis, Technische Universität München. Edition Versal vol. 1. Bertz Verlag Berlin, December 1995.

[3] L. Lamport. Proving the Correctness of Multiprocess Programs. In *IEEE Trans. on Software Engineering*, volume 3, pages 125–143, 1977.

[4] Z. Manna and A. Pnueli. How to Cook a Temporal Proof System for Your Pet Language. In *Proceedings of the Symposium on Principles of Programming Languages (POPL)*, 1983.

[5] Z. Manna and A. Pnueli. The Temporal Logic of Reactive and Concurrent Systems. Springer-Verlag, 1992.

[6] A. Mazurkiewicz. Basic Notions of Trace Theory. In de Bakker, de Roever, and Rozenberg, editors, *Linear Time, Branching Time and Partial Orders in Logics and Models for Concurrency*, volume 938 of *LNCS*, pages 285–263. Springer-Verlag, 1988.

[7] S. Owicki and L. Lamport. Proving Liveness Properties of Concurrent Programs. In *ACM Transact. on Programming Languages and Systems*, volume 4(3), pages 455–495, July 1982.
[8] D. Peled and A. Pnueli. Proving Partial Order Properties. In *Theoretical Computer Science*, volume 126, pages 143–182, 1994.
[9] V. R. Pratt. Modelling Concurrency with Partial Orders. In *Int. J. on Parallel Programming*, volume 15, pages 33–71, 1986.
[10] W. Reisig. Distributed Algorithms: Modelling and Analysis with Petri Nets. Monography (to appear).
[11] W. Reisig. Correctness Proofs of Distributed Algorithms. In K. P. Birman, editor, *Theory and Practice in Distributed Systems*, volume 938 of *LNCS*, pages 164–177. Springer-Verlag, 1995.
[12] W. Reisig. Petri Net Models of Distributed Algorithms. In J. van Leeuwen, editor, *Computer Science Today: Recent Trends and Developments*, volume 1000 of *LNCS*, pages 441–454. Springer-Verlag, 1995.
[13] W. Reisig. Modelling and Verification of Distributed Algorithms. In *CONCUR 96*, LNCS. Springer-Verlag, 1996.
[14] R. Walter. *Petrinetzmodelle verteilter Algorithmen.* PhD thesis, Humboldt-Universität zu Berlin, Institut für Informatik. Edition Versal vol. 2. Bertz Verlag Berlin, December 1995.

HUMBOLDT UNIVERSITY OF BERLIN, GERMANY
E-mail address, W. Reisig: `reisig@informatik.hu-berlin.de`

DIMACS Series in Discrete Mathematics
and Theoretical Computer Science
Volume **29**, 1997

Teams Can See Pomsets (Preliminary Version)

Gordon Plotkin and Vaughan Pratt*
University of Edinburgh and Stanford University
gdp@dcs.edinburgh.ac.uk, pratt@cs.stanford.edu

Abstract

The sequentiality postulate assumes that events occur in a definite order. We explore some of the boundary of applicability of this postulate for the case of sequential observers, varying number of observers, duration of events, and variability of events. When there is one observer or events are atomic, the sequentiality postulate holds, making linear orders a fully abstract model of concurrent behavior. With more than one observer and with structured events it fails. We show that unlimited observers and variable events make pomsets a fully abstract model. Putting duration in place of variability yields an intermediate situation in which the sequentiality postulate does not hold but pomsets are not a fully abstract model.

1 Overview

It is widely believed that trace or interleaving semantics, which assigns a definite order of occurrence to every pair of events, is sufficient for all practical purposes. In support of this belief, Jonsson [Jon89] and Russell [Rus89] show that trace semantics is fully abstract for parallel computation, at least of the kind represented by Kahn networks.

However these full abstractness results suffer from an overly constrained notion of observer. In this paper we consider a wider range of observational behaviors or *testing scenarios*, and give a detailed picture of just where full abstractness for trace semantics becomes unsound for the eight scenarios obtained by varying three basic parameters of computation, namely duration D, variability V, and multiplicity M of observers ("teams").

Duration expresses the notion of an ongoing action, one that can be analyzed as a sequence of subactions. Duration is naturally modeled as a string. An

1991 *Mathematics Subject Classification.* Primary 68Q55.
*This work was supported by ONR under grant number N00014-92-J-1974.

action a may be analyzed as say the string a_1a_2 indicating that a decomposes into two consecutively performed actions, a_1 then a_2.

Variability expresses choice, naturally modeled as a set of alternatives. An action a may be analyzed as say the set $\{a_1, a_2\}$ indicating that for a to occur means that exactly one of a_1 or a_2 occurs.

Multiplicity expresses the notion of two or more observers both observing the same run of a computation, but from different vantage points. We shall assume that when two observers see the same events from different viewpoints, they agree on all choices that have been made, including those associated with variability, but may disagree on the relative order of events. We understand choice as absolute, in that it is unambiguous which of two alternatives has been chosen. However we view time as relative in that two events not occurring in each other's light cone do not have a well-defined order of occurrence. This asymmetry of choice and time, while certainly questionable, is consistent with physics as standardly taught.

Our results in the case of computational behaviors consisting of single pomsets (labeled partial orders) is summarized by the following cube.

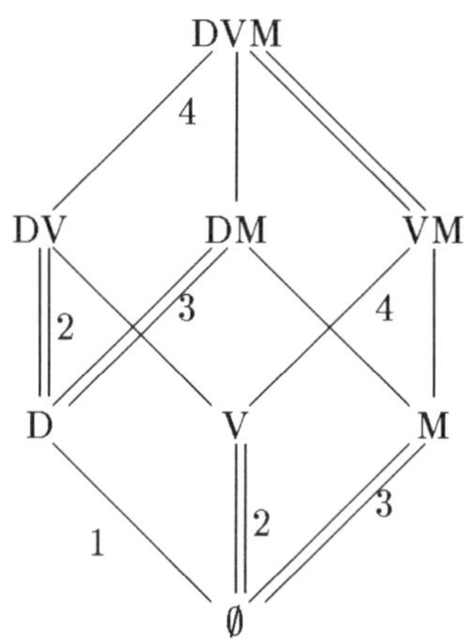

Figure 1. Eight testing scenarios

Edges are labeled with the number of the relevant proposition, while the double lines indicate equivalence, with respect to distinguishing power, of two kinds of observational behavior, with the remaining lines then indicating strict inequalities. Thus Proposition 1 shows that Duration on its own makes a difference while Propositions 2 and 3 show that neither Variability nor Multiplicity make any difference, neither on their own nor as an addition to Duration. Proposition 4 shows that in the presence of Variability, Multiplicity does make a difference. Moreover an unlimited supply of observers leads to full abstractness for pomsets even at VM, whence DVM cannot be any bigger and so must equal VM. This then has the side effect of removing Duration as a contributing factor.

The identifications reduce the classes to three, namely $\emptyset = V = M$, $D = DV = DM$, and $VM = DVM$, while Propositions 1 and 4 show that these three classes are distinct.

As a refinement of these all-or-nothing results, Proposition 5 extends Proposition 4 to a hierarchy theorem: $n+1$ observers can observe distinctions invisible to n observers.

We also consider processes as *sets* of pomsets, and show that the identifications of VM with DVM, and of $\emptyset$ with V, continue to hold. (Rob van Glabbeek has pointed out to us that this cannot be improved, via examples separating D from DV and from DM, and $\emptyset$ from M.)

2 Background

Linearly ordered multisets (labelled chains up to isomorphism) are strings. Pomsets as partially ordered multisets therefore constitute a generalization of strings to partial orders. This model as an extension of formal language theory is due to Grabowski [Gra81] who called it a partial word, the characterization as a partially ordered multiset being due to the second author [Pra82]. Pomsets with a conflict relation are called event structures, introduced by Nielsen, Plotkin, and Winskel [NPW81]. Prior related notions are Mazurkiewicz's partial monoids [Maz77, Maz84] and Greif's treatment of actors [Gre75]. A list of more recent papers on the topic [MS80, Gis88, Pra86, AH87, Win88] would be bound to be incomplete.

We shall identify observation with linearization. That is, at least in the case of atomic events, an observer of a pomset sees its events in some linear order consistent with the order of the pomset.

To a zeroth order approximation, two pomsets should be observationally equivalent when they have the same set of linearizations.

The familiar theorem that (the graph of) a poset is the intersection of the set of (graphs of) its linearizations is due to Szpilrajn [Szp30]. In our framework posets are pomsets with no repeated elements, i.e. the function assigning labels to poset elements is injective. Thus in our application Szpilrajn's theorem states that distinct posets are not observationally equivalent.

At the other extreme from posets are pomsets over a one-letter alphabet, say the alphabet $\{a\}$. In our framework these amount to posets up to isomorphism. (So pomsets span a spectrum from posets-up-to-isomorphism to posets.) There are just two two-element pomsets over $\{a\}$, which we write as aa (linearly ordered) and $a|a$ (discretely ordered). These have the same set of linearizations and hence are observationally equivalent. So whereas Szpilrajn's theorem applies to posets this example shows that it does not apply to posets up to isomorphism.

The meaning of $a|a$ is that we have two copies of an activity a that are running in parallel. If a is an instantaneous event, as we have been assuming up to now, and the possibility of exact simultaneity is neglected, then there would seem to be no basis for distinguishing between aa and $a|a$ in either theory or practice.

If however a has duration we have the possibility of overlap for the case $a|a$, but not for aa. We may represent duration by taking a to be a pomset of size two or more, e.g. the string 01. Then the only linearization of aa is 0101, whereas $a|a$ has for its linearizations both 0101 and 0011. Hence in the presence of events with duration it becomes possible to observe a difference between aa and $a|a$. A similar difference is observable if we take a to be $0|1$. In this case the linearizations of aa are 0101, 0110, 1001, and 1010, while those of $a|a$ are those four together with 0011 and 1100.

Gischer [Gis88] shows that any two pomsets that are observationally equivalent for strings of length two are observationally equivalent for strings of any length, whence there is no duration hierarchy for strings. Gischer conjectured, and Tschantz has shown [Tsc94], that duration suffices to distinguish any two series-parallel (N-free) pomsets. (A series-parallel pomset is a pomset constructible using only the operations of concatenation ab and concurrence $a|b$.) Hence series-parallel pomsets are extensional in the presence of duration. (Another striking corollary of this result is that the equational theory of concatenation and interleaving of languages is completely axiomatized by the equations for commutativity of interleaving and associativity of both.)

Gischer gives as an example of pomsets indistinguishable even with duration the two pomsets $N(a,a,b,b)$ and $ab|ab$, where $N(1,2,3,4)$ is the 4-vertex pomset ordered so that $1 < 3$, $2 < 4$, and $1 < 4$, these constraints constituting respectively the two verticals and the diagonal of the letter N, so that $N(a,a,b,b)$ is $ab|ab$ plus the diagonal. If they could be distinguished it would have to be by a string of $ab|ab$ not allowed by $N(a,a,b,b)$, possible only by violating the diagonal $1 < 4$ of the N. Hence 1 and 4 overlap; where they do, 2 cannot have started but 3 must have finished, so the other diagonal $2 < 3$ is satisfied. But that diagonal belongs to an isomorphic copy of $N(a,a,b,b)$, whence that string must be allowed after all.

We may further take a to be not just a single string but a set of strings, that is, a language. This provides a notion of variety for a: we have a variety of choices of behaviors of a. When all strings of a are of unit length we have variety without duration. Variety provides those little unpredictable hints that can allow observers to reach consensus as to the identities of entities without them being a part of the observation language. In some observations the observers may be unlucky and not get enough such hints; it only matters that there exist observations that do provide sufficient hints.

Gischer's argument above remains valid in the presence of variety, giving a pair of pomsets which variety does not help distinguish.

Two minor results concerning refinements of observational equivalence in this setting are as follows.

(i) For a single observer, duration helps but variety does not.

(ii) For multiple observers to make a difference, variety without duration helps but duration without variety does not.

Our main result is:

(iii) With enough variety and observers any two finite pomsets can be distinguished, even without duration.

Results (i) and (ii) assign very different roles to duration and variety. Duration is a loner that can help, though not always, as evidenced by Gischer's example above of $N(a, a, b, b) = ab|ab$. Variety on the other hand is useless by itself but in collaboration with multiple observers is able not only to outperform duration but, as (iii) shows, to make pomsets fully visible, i.e. extensional. The proof of (iii) is via a straightforward reduction to the poset case, allowing us to apply Szpilrajn's theorem.

A refinement of (iii) is that with enough variety, the number of observers needed to distinguish two pomsets is at most the larger of the dimensions of their underlying posets.[1] This shows that the hierarchy of observational equivalences with n observers is strict: $n + 1$ observers can resolve more detail than n. Although our proof of this result is not long, neither is it at all obvious!

3 Definitions

The following notions are essentially as in [Gis84]. We start out by defining labelled partial orders and their maps.

Definition 1. A *labelled partial order* or *lpo* over a set Σ is a structure $(V, \leq, \sigma, \Sigma)$ where $\leq$ partially orders V and $\sigma : V \to \Sigma$ assigns to each element of V an element of Σ. When necessary we write the components of lpo p as $(V_p, \leq_p, \sigma_p, \Sigma_p)$.

We think of Σ as an alphabet of *actions* and V as instances of that alphabet, or *events* forming a word, with the order of occurrences of letters in the word given by $\leq$. The usual formal language theoretic notion of a word obtains for $\leq$ linear. An atomic lpo is one with $|V| = 1$.

Definition 2. A *map* of lpo's $(f, t) : (V, \leq, \sigma, \Sigma) \to (V', \leq', \sigma', \Sigma')$ consists of a monotone map $f : (V, \leq) \to (V', \leq')$ of posets together with an alphabet map (function) $t : \Sigma \to \Sigma'$ such that for all v in V, $\sigma'(f(v)) = t(\sigma(v))$.

Certain maps of lpo's are of special interest here. An *isomorphism* of lpo's is a map (f, t) for which f is an isomorphism of posets and t is the identity map on Σ (so isomorphic lpo's have a common alphabet). An *augmentation* of lpo's is a map (f, t) for which t is the identity function and f is the identity function on the elements of the poset (but not necessarily an isomorphism of posets, i.e. the

[1] The dimension of a poset is the least number of linearizations of that poset whose intersection is that poset. The notion is due to Dushnik and Miller [DM41], see Kelly and Trotter [KT82] for a survey.

order may increase); an augmentation yields an *augment* of its argument. We write $p\alpha q$ to indicate that q is an augment of p; this is the converse of Gischer's *subsumption* relation $q \succ p$ [Gis84].

Definition 3. A *pomset* is the isomorphism class of an lpo.

More intuitively a pomset is an lpo in which we pay no attention to the choice of the set V, other than its cardinality, but retain all other details. Thus if we replace $V = \{0,1,2\}$ by $V = \{5,6,7\}$ without otherwise disturbing either $\leq$ or σ the pomset does not change. With our definition of observation, isomorphic lpo's will be seen to be observationally equivalent, whence the most we can hope to resolve even with multiple observers is pomsets.

We shall understand a map between two pomsets to be a map between representative lpo's of the respective pomsets.

Definition 4. A *process* P is a set of finite pomsets. A process is *augment closed* when for all $p\alpha q$, $p \in P$ implies $q \in P$. The *augment closure* $\alpha(P)$ of P is the least augment closed process containing P.

We wish to define observation in terms of the notions of *linearization* and *substitution*, which we now define.

Definition 5. A *linearization* of a pomset p is a linear augment of p. We write $\lambda(p)$ for the set of all linearizations of p. This extends to $\lambda(P)$ for P a set of pomsets, namely as $\lambda(P) = \bigcup_{p \in P} \lambda(p)$.

Formal language theory has the notions of homomorphism and substitution [HU79]. These both generalize immediately from strings to pomsets. (This notion of homomorphism is quite different from that of map between two pomsets: the former goes between sets of pomsets, the latter between single pomsets.)

Definition 6. A *pomset homomorphism* is a function mapping pomsets on Σ to pomsets on Σ'. It is determined by a function f assigning a pomset on Σ' to each letter of Σ. It maps p to the pomset whose set of events is the disjoint sum of the events of the $f(\sigma(u))$'s over all $u \in V_p$, definable as $\{(u,v) | u \in V_p, v \in V_{f(\sigma(u))}\}$. Each (u,v) is labelled with $\sigma_{f(\sigma(u))}(v)$, i.e. just as v was labelled in $f(\sigma(u))$, and ordered so that $(u,v) \leq (u',v')$ just when $u <_p u'$ (i.e. $u \leq_p u'$ and $u \neq u'$) or ($u = u'$ and $v \leq_{f(u)} v'$), that is, lexicographic ordering.

Intuitively this is what is obtained by substituting a pomset for each label of p and flattening the resulting nested structure in the obvious way. For example the homomorphism taking a to bc takes aa to $bcbc$ and $a|a$ to $bc|bc$, while the homomorphism taking a to $b|c$ takes aa to $(b|c)(b|c)$ and $a|a$ to $b|b|c|c$.

This generalizes to *substitutions* of sets of pomsets exactly analogously to the generalization of homomorphisms of strings to substitutions of sets of strings [HU79], in which the result of substituting a set of strings for a letter is the set of all strings obtainable by choosing any string from each substitution instance of such a set. In lieu of a formal definition we offer the example of substituting the set $\{b,c\}$ for a in $a|a$, having two substitution instances of $\{b,c\}$ and so yielding the set of three pomsets $b|b$, $b|c$, $c|c$ ($c|b$ being isomorphic to $b|c$ as an lpo and hence equal as a pomset). Just as for formal languages, a homomorphism can be viewed as the special case of a substitution of singletons.

We may now regard pomsets as expressions, with the labels acting as variables. Evaluation is then just substitution: values for the variables determine the value of the expression. Thus the pomset aba is an expression with variables a and b, and if the value of a is cd and that of b is $\{e, f\}$ then the value of aba is $\{cdecd, cdfcd\}$. With this interpretation of substitution in mind we write $p(s)$ for the value of p under the substitution s. By $P(s)$ for a set P of pomsets we understand the union over the elements $p \in P$ of $p(s)$.

We might say that two pomsets are equivalent when their values are the same for all substitutions. But merely taking the value of each variable to be itself already suffices to distinguish distinct pomsets, so this equivalence is trivially the identity relation.

The notion of observation as linearization, reflecting the sequential life of an individual observer, leads to more interesting equivalences. We tentatively define an observation of a pomset to be a linearization of it. Thus the set of all observations of p is $\lambda(p)$, and the set of all observations of a set P of pomsets is $\lambda(P)$. Pomsets p and q are *equivalent* when $\lambda(p(s)) = \lambda(q(s))$ for all substitutions s.

We now extend this notion of observation to multiple observers. The idea is that n observers see n possibly different linearizations of the one observed pomset.

Definition 7. An *n-observation* of a pomset p is an n-tuple of linearizations of p. We write $\lambda_n(p)$ for the set consisting of all n-observations of p, a set of n-tuples of strings. For a process P we take $\lambda_n(P) = \bigcup_{p \in P} \lambda_n(p)$.

Definition 8. Pomsets p and q are *n-equivalent*, written $p \equiv_n q$, when $\lambda_n(p) = \lambda_n(q)$. Likewise for processes, $P \equiv_n Q$ when $\lambda_n(P) = \lambda_n(P)$.

Our tentative definitions of observation and equivalence are now subsumed as 1-observation and 1-equivalence.

Implicit in our definition of n-equivalence is a consensus between the observers as to which pomset of P to linearize, when constructing an n-observation in $\lambda_n(P)$. This reflects our intuition that the observers agreed on what happened but not when.

Finally we need the notion of dimension [KT82] in order to show the strictness of the hierarchy of n-equivalence in the presence of variety.

Definition 9. The *dimension* of a poset is the minimum number of its linearizations such that the intersection of those linearizations is that poset. We take the dimension of a pomset p to be the dimension of the underlying poset of a representative lpo of p.

4 Observation of Single Pomsets

In order to capture duration, variety, etc. we need a parametrized notion of n-equivalence, parametrized by the permitted substitutions. If substitutions are restricted so that the assignment to any variable must come from a class C of sets of pomsets, e.g. singletons, sets of one-element pomsets, languages (sets of linear pomsets), we say that two pomsets are n-equivalent for C when they have the same n-observations of their values for all substitutions where the assignments to the variables are drawn from C.

In the following we are interested in substitutions that have variety without duration, and duration without variety. We denote these respective classes of substitutions by **Var** and **Dur** respectively. A substitution from **Var** can replace each label by a set of labels. A substitution from **Dur** can replace each label by a pomset. The class of substitutions permitting neither duration nor variety, corresponding to mere renamings of labels, we call **Atm** for atomic substitutions.

None of our results make essential use of nonlinearity in the substructure of events. For example if **Dur** is taken instead to consist of those substitutions that replace labels by strings rather than pomsets, no modifications are required to either the following propositions or their proofs.

The first two propositions are simple, but give some insight into the respective roles played by duration and variety.

We first show that for a single observer, duration without variety helps but variety without duration does not.

Proposition 1. 1-equivalence for **Dur** is strictly finer than 1-equivalence for **Atm**.

Proof. It is finer because **Dur** includes **Atm**. The example of aa and $a|a$ shows strictness. ∎

Proposition 2. 1-equivalence for **Var** coincides with 1-equivalence for **Atm**.

Proof. This follows from $\lambda(p(s)) = (\lambda(p))(s)$. That is, we can substitute sets for variables in p and then linearize, or linearize p first (yielding a language) and then substitute, with the same result in either case. Hence $\lambda(p(s)) = (\lambda(p))(s) = (\lambda(q))(s) = \lambda(q(s))$. ∎

Proposition 3. For all $n \geq 1$, 1-equivalence for **Dur** coincides with n-equivalence for **Dur**.

Proof. In this case $p(s)$ is a singleton, substitutions being homomorphisms, for which $\lambda_n(p(s))$ is the set of all n-tuples of linearizations of the pomset $p(s)$. Hence $\lambda_n(p(s))$ can be computed from $\lambda(p(s))$. Thus if $\lambda(p(s)) = \lambda(q(s))$, we must have $\lambda_n(p(s)) = \lambda_n(q(s))$ as well. ∎

Corollary. For all $n \geq 1$, 1-equivalence for **Atm** coincides with n-equivalence for **Atm**.

We now come to the main results. The next two propositions show that for multiple observers to make a difference, variety without duration helps but duration without variety does not. The former, proposition 3, is the main result in that it shows that any two pomsets can be distinguished by n observers for sufficiently large n. It is noteworthy that duration plays no role in this result! Since our first explorations in this area focused on the role of duration in distinguishing pomsets we did not at first expect such a result. In retrospect it is not so surprising, nor particularly deep, being a straightforward reduction to Szpilrajn's theorem..

Proposition 4. For any pomset p there exists n such that p is not n-equivalent for **Var** to any other pomset.

Proof. We use variety to distinguish the otherwise indistinguishable events of a pomset. Let m be the size of p. We take n to be $m!$. Consider the substitution s mapping each letter a of Σ to the m-element set $\{(a,i)|0 \leq i < m\}$. This is enough variety for $p(s)$ to include at least one poset, call it q. Then $\lambda(q)$ has at most $m!$ members, whence some $m!$-tuple of $\lambda_{m!}(q)$ will contain all of them. This gives us a procedure for recovering p from $\lambda_{m!}(p(s))$. Discard $m!$-tuples of $\lambda_{m!}(q)$ not corresponding to posets (repeated letters). From the remainder select any $m!$-tuple with a maximum number of different components, an $m!$-observation of some poset q. Use Szpilrajn's theorem to infer q from the $m!$-observation. Replace each label (a,i) by a in q, to yield p. This construction shows that the p so recovered will be independent of the choice of poset from $p(s)$. ∎

The argument for proposition 4 can be extended to show that, for any class including **Var**, n-equivalence for increasing n forms a strict hierarchy. Our particular witnesses to this hierarchy are independent of the class of substitutions.

Proposition 5. For every $n > 1$ there exist pomsets p and q such that for any class C of substitutions including **Var**, p and q are n-1-equivalent for C but not n-equivalent for C.

Proof. It suffices to consider pomsets over a one-letter alphabet, i.e. posets up to isomorphism. (Note that Szpilrajn's theorem separates even isomorphic posets, and cannot be applied directly here.) Given n we take for our counterexample a certain pair p, q of posets of dimension n. Using essentially the same argument as in Proposition 4 we show that as one-letter pomsets p and q cannot be n-equivalent for **Var**, and hence for any larger class. We then show that they are n-1-equivalent for any class.

We take p to be the *standard* poset S_n [KT82], having $2n$ elements $\{a_0, \ldots, a_{n-1}, b_0, \ldots, b_{n-1}\}$, ordered so that $a_i \leq b_j$ just when $i \neq j$. An equivalent description of S_n is as the lattice of atoms and coatoms of an n-atom Boolean algebra. S_n is known to have dimension n [KT82]. We take q to be S_n augmented with $a_0 \leq b_0$. (As pomsets, p and q are determined only up to isomorphism, so augmenting p with $a_i \leq b_i$ for any i yields the same pomset q.) Since q has $2n$ elements it is of dimension at most n [KT82]. Hence p and q are not n-equivalent for **Var**. The role of **Var** here is as for Proposition 4, namely allowing us to treat pomsets as posets.

For n-1-equivalence, suppose some linearization of an element of $p(s)$ violates $a_i \leq b_i$ for some i, necessary if we are to distinguish p and q. Then there is a point in that string where a_i has not yet finished (a_i could have duration in the general case) yet b_i has started. The constraints of p require that at that point all the other a_j's are done (for b_i to start) and none of the other b_j's have started (since a_i is not yet done). Hence for every $j \neq i$, $a_j \leq b_j$, that is, there can be at most one violation of $a_i \leq b_i$ for any i in any one linearization. But then any n-1-observation of $p(s)$ can collectively violate at most $n-1$ of the constraints of the form $a_i \leq b_i$. This always leaves one such constraint unviolated, which is consistent with observing q. Hence the n-1-observations of $p(s)$ must coincide with those of $q(s)$ for all s. ∎

5 Observation of Processes

A process is a set of pomsets, as per Definition 4. All our definitions of linearization, n-equivalence, etc. have been formulated to hold for processes in general, with single pomsets identified with singleton processes.

The following shows a basic limitation of all the testing scenarios considered in this paper when applied to processes.

Proposition 6. Observationally equivalent processes have equal augment closures.

Proof. Any pomset p of a process P must be visible to a team of size $\dim(P)$. If Q is observationally equivalent to P the same team must be able to observe p as an apparent behavior of Q. Hence Q must contain a behavior q of which p is an augment, whence $P \subseteq \alpha(Q)$. By symmetry of equivalence $Q \subseteq \alpha(P)$, whence $\alpha(P) = \alpha(Q)$.

Lemma 7. Let p be a pomset. Then there exists n such that for any family $\langle q_i \rangle_i$ of pomsets for which $\lambda_n(p) \subseteq \lambda_n(\bigcup_i q_i)$, there must exist q_j in the family such that p is an augment of q.

Proof. The only q_i's that can contribute to $\lambda_n(p)$ have the same number of vertices as p. Since each n-tuple in $\lambda_n(\bigcup_i q_i)$ arises from a choice of a particular q_i, and since $\lambda_n(p)$ includes a single n-tuple completely encoding p, it follows that some q_i must yield that n-tuple. But this is only possible for a q_i of which p is an augment. ∎

Proposition 8. For any two augment-closed processes P and Q there exists n such that P is not n-equivalent for **Var** to Q.

Proof. Assume without loss of generality that P contains a pomset p absent from Q. Then p is not an augment of any pomset of Q. Let n be the number associated to p by Lemma 7. Then $\lambda_n(p)$ cannot belong to $\lambda_n(Q)$, whence $\lambda_n(P)$ contains n-tuples not in $\lambda_n(Q)$. ∎

This generalizes Proposition 4 to full abstraction for processes. Hence VM for processes makes all possible distinctions between processes, whence DVM can only make the same distinctions. Thus for processes we retain the $VM = DVM$ edge of Figure 1.

Proposition 2 showed that variability alone makes no difference for single pomsets. But that proposition applies equally to pomsets and processes, whence variability also makes no difference for processes and we retain the $\emptyset = V$ edge of Figure 1.

References

[AH87] S. Anderson and P. Hudak. Pomset interpretations of parallel functional programs. In *Proc. 3rd International Conf. on Functional Programming Languages and Computer Architecture*, Portland, OR, September 1987.

[DM41] B. Dushnik and E.W. Miller. Partially ordered sets. *Amer. J. Math.*, 63:600–610, 1941.

[Gis84] J.L. Gischer. *Partial Orders and the Axiomatic Theory of Shuffle.* PhD thesis, Computer Science Dept., Stanford University, December 1984.

[Gis88] J.L. Gischer. The equational theory of pomsets. *Theoretical Computer Science*, 61:199–224, 1988.

[Gra81] J. Grabowski. On partial languages. *Fundamenta Informaticae*, IV.2:427–498, 1981.

[Gre75] I. Greif. *Semantics of Communicating Parallel Processes.* PhD thesis, Project MAC report TR-154, MIT, 1975.

[HU79] J.E. Hopcroft and J.D. Ullman. *Introduction to Automata Theory, Languages, and Computation.* Addison-Wesley, 1979.

[Jon89] B. Jonsson. A fully abstract trace model for dataflow networks. In *Proc. 16th Annual ACM Symposium on Principles of Programming Languages*, pages 155–165, January 1989.

[KT82] D. Kelly and W.T. Trotter. Dimension theory for ordered sets. In I. Rival, editor, *Ordered Sets*, pages 171–211. D. Reidel, 1982.

[Maz77] A. Mazurkiewicz. Concurrent program schemas and their interpretation. In *Proc. Aarhus Workshop on Verification of Parallel Programs*, 1977.

[Maz84] A. Mazurkiewicz. Traces, histories, graphs: Instances of a process monoid. In *Proc. Conf. on Mathematical Foundations of Computer Science*, volume 176 of *Lecture Notes in Computer Science.* Springer-Verlag, 1984.

[MS80] U. Montanari and C. Simonelli. On distinguishing between concurrency and nondeterminism. In *Proc. Ecole de Printemps on Concurrency and Petri Nets*, Colleville, 1980.

[NPW81] M. Nielsen, G. Plotkin, and G. Winskel. Petri nets, event structures, and domains, part I. *Theoretical Computer Science*, 13:85–108, 1981.

[Pra82] V.R. Pratt. On the composition of processes. In *Proceedings of the Ninth Annual ACM Symposium on Principles of Programming Languages*, January 1982.

[Pra86] V.R. Pratt. Modeling concurrency with partial orders. *Int. J. of Parallel Programming*, 15(1):33–71, February 1986.

[Rus89] J. Russell. Full abstraction for nondeterministic dataflow networks. In *Proc. 30th IEEE Symposium on Foundations of Computer Science*, October 1989.

[Szp30] E. Szpilrajn. Sur l'extension de l'ordre partiel. *Fund. Math.*, 16:386–389, 1930.

[Tsc94] S.T. Tschantz. Languages under concatenation and shuffling. December 1994.

[Win88] G. Winskel. An introduction to event structures. In *Linear Time, Branching Time and Partial Order in Logics and Models for Concurrency, REX'88*, volume 354 of *Lecture Notes in Computer Science*, Noordwijkerhout, June 1988. Springer-Verlag.

DIMACS Series in Discrete Mathematics
and Theoretical Computer Science
Volume 29, 1997

PRESHEAVES AS TRANSITION SYSTEMS

GLYNN WINSKEL AND MOGENS NIELSEN

BRICS[1]
Department of Computer Science, University of Aarhus, Denmark

1. Introduction

Recall, as background, the content of the handbook chapter [22]. There, a model for process calculi is presented as a class of objects (like transition systems, or Petri nets), equipped with a notion of morphism, so that it forms a category. The morphisms represent a form of simulation between processes, and arise naturally in relating the behaviour of a construction on processes to that of its components. Basic operations of process calculi may now be understood as universal constructions (like product and coproduct) of the category, and so are characterised abstractly, up to isomorphism. Categorical notions also come into play in relating different models, for instance, in relating the model of transition systems to that of Petri nets. Adjunctions, especially coreflections, provide a way to translate between one model and another. The understanding of the operations of process calculi as universal constructions guides definitions away from the *ad hoc*, while the preservation properties of adjoints help relate semantics in one model to a semantics in another.

The richness of the morphisms in the categories of models, a richness which is essential in yielding the universal constructions, means that many objects with strikingly different behaviours are connected by morphisms; in particular, morphisms of transition systems relate transition systems which are far from strongly, or weakly, bisimilar. The categories do not immediately yield useful abstract equivalences between processes. However, in [8] it is shown how a general concept of bisimulation arises from the definition of open map. The definition of open map, applicable to all the categories of models, picks out those morphisms which, roughly speaking, reflect as well as preserve behaviour. It is then sensible to take two processes to be bisimilar, in a generalised sense, if they are connected by open maps.

The definition of open map relies not just on a categorical presentation of a model (for example, as a category rather than just a class of transition systems) but also on an acceptance of a notion of computation path and what it means to extend a computation path by another. For the interleaving model of transition systems a reasonable idea is to take a computation path (or run) as a sequence of consecutive transitions, which we can think of as picked out by a morphism from a string of action labels; here it is hard to escape from the idea that extending a computation path is associated with extending the string of action labels. For an independence model like event structures a reasonable idea is to take a computation path as a configuration, or more generally as a morphism from a pomset to the event structure; this time several ideas suggest themselves as to how we might extend a computation path shaped like a pomset, because, roughly, we can extend a pomset in

1991 *Mathematics Subject Classification.* Primary 68Q55; Secondary 18B20. 68Q70.

[1]**B**asic **R**esearch **I**n **C**omputer **S**cience, Centre of the Danish National Research Foundation

"width" (adding concurrent events) as well as "height" (adding later, causally dependent events).

In the case of familiar models like transition systems or event structures the general definition of bisimulation specialises to familiar concepts; in particular, on transition systems with strings of actions as paths we obtain Park and Milner's strong bisimulation.

Presheaves offer a method to derive a model directly from a path category whose objects are path shapes and whose morphisms describe the extension of one path by another. Forming the category of presheaves over a path category has the effect of freely closing the path category under small colimits. More intuitively, a presheaf represents the effect of gluing together a set of computation paths to form a nondeterministic computation; the category of presheaves can be thought of as a category of nondeterministic computations. This intuition is backed up by canonical embeddings of traditional models into categories of presheaves over appropriately chosen path categories (*cf.* Theorem 4). Because the original path category embeds via the Yoneda functor into the category of its presheaves, we automatically obtain a notion of open map and bisimulation on presheaves.

A range of models and their notion of bisimulation can be understood in a uniform way via their represention as presheaves. Here we emphasise the view that presheaves can be profitably looked upon as transition systems, in which the labels are morphisms of path extension. This yields transition-system characterisations of open maps and bisimulation on presheaves, and through these to generalisations of Hennessy-Milner logic and games, providing a more operational characterisation. In particular, bisimulation on presheaves coincides with back-and-forth bisimulation between their associated transition systems.

In a way, by regarding presheaves as transition systems we can repay a debt to the foundational influence transitions systems have had in the theory of concurrent computation. Many original motivations and intuitions were formed around the model of transition systems. Through the medium of presheaves, we are able to cope uniformly with a range of models and their equivalences, from interleaving to independence models, and at the same time, by altering our view a little, see the approach as only a slight adjustment in the perspective that motivated Park and Milner's definition of strong bisimulation.

2. Models, Morphisms and Computation Paths

We quickly describe the models and notions of computation paths we shall use as running examples.

Transition systems consist of a set of states, with an initial state, together with transitions between states which are labelled to specify the kind of events they represent. Formally, a *transition system* is a structure

$$(S, i, L, tran)$$

where

- S is a set of *states* with *initial state* i,
- L is a set of *labels*, and
- $tran \subseteq S \times L \times S$ is the *transition relation*. As usual, we write

$$s \xrightarrow{a} s'$$

to indicate that $(s, a, s') \in tran$.

A state s is said to be *reachable* when $i \xrightarrow{a_1} \cdots \xrightarrow{a_n} s$ for some, possibly empty, string $a_1 \cdots a_n$.

As morphisms on transition systems we take functions on states which preserve initial states and transitions. Let

$$T_0 = (S_0, i_0, L_0, \mathit{tran}_0) \text{ and}$$
$$T_1 = (S_1, i_1, L_1, \mathit{tran}_1)$$

be transition systems. A *morphism* $f : T_0 \to T_1$ is a function $\sigma : S_0 \to S_1$ such that $\sigma(i_0) = i_1$ and

$$(s, a, s') \in \mathit{tran}_0 \Rightarrow (\sigma(s), a, \sigma(s')) \in \mathit{tran}_1 .$$

Morphisms on transition systems compose as functions. For the concerns of [22], morphisms on transitions systems were more general. They could change labels and even send labels to undefined. This is necessary in relating the behaviour of compound processes to that of their components in languages like Milner's CCS, and in obtaining a repertoire of universal constructions, rich enough to yield a general process language. Here we concentrate on bisimulation for which we can take the simpler label-preserving morphisms as our starting point—such label preserving morphisms play an important role in the categorical account of [22], for example, in understanding restriction and relabelling operations of CCS-like languages as universal constructions.

We shall call transition systems which look like trees *synchronisation trees*. More precisely, synchronisation trees are those transition systems with no loops, no distinct transitions *to* the same state, in which all states are reachable. Synchronisation trees inherit morphisms from transition systems, and themselves form a category. The inclusion of synchronisation trees in transition systems is a left adjoint to the functor unfolding a transition systems to a synchronisation tree.

Special synchronisation trees will play a role in our treatment of bisimulation. Consider a (finite) computation (or run) in a transition system T. It is a sequence of transitions

$$i = s_0 \xrightarrow{a_1} s_1 \xrightarrow{a_2} \cdots \xrightarrow{a_n} s_n$$

—the sequence might possibly be empty. Let us identify strings like $s = a_1 a_2 \cdots a_n$ in L^* with "path shapes", rather special synchronisation trees consisting of a single branch of transitions

$$\bullet \xrightarrow{a_1} \bullet \xrightarrow{a_2} \cdots \xrightarrow{a_n} \bullet .$$

Then the computation path in T is identified with the morphism

$$p : s \to T$$

picking out the chain of transitions in T. Morphisms between such path shapes, consisting of a single-branch synchronisation trees, inherited from transition systems correspond to extensions of the associated strings. So we can identify the category of such path shapes with the (partial-order) category of strings L^*; a morphism from string s to string t corresponds to s being an initial prefix of t.

We focus on event structures as our primary example of an independence model—other independence models like Petri nets and Mazurkiewicz trace languages are related to event structures via adjunctions in [22] in such a way that they inherit a common notion of bisimulation (see [8, 15]).

Define a *(labelled) event structure* to be a structure $(E, \leq, Con, l)$ consisting of a set E, of *events* which are partially ordered by $\leq$, the *causal dependency relation*, a *consistency relation* Con consisting of finite subsets of events, and a *labelling function* $l : E \to L$, which satisfy

$$\{e' \mid e' \leq e\} \text{ is finite,}$$
$$\{e\} \in Con,$$
$$Y \subseteq X \in Con \Rightarrow Y \in Con,$$
$$X \in Con \;\&\; e \leq e' \in X \Rightarrow X \cup \{e\} \in Con,$$

for all events e, e' and their subsets X, Y.

Two events $e, e' \in E$ are said to be *concurrent* (causally independent) iff

$$(e \not\leq e' \;\&\; e' \not\leq e \;\&\; \{e, e'\} \in Con).$$

Define a *configuration* (or state) of E to be a subset $x \subseteq E$ which is

downwards-closed: $\forall e, e'.\ e' \leq e \in x \Rightarrow e' \in x$, and
consistent: $\forall X.\ X$ finite & $X \subseteq x \Rightarrow X \in Con$.

As before, we restrict attention to label-preserving morphisms on event structures over a common labelling set L. Let $E = (E, \leq, Con, l), E' = (E', \leq', Con', l')$ be event structures over L. A *morphism* from E to E' consists of a function $\eta : E \to E'$ on events which preserves labels (*i.e.* $l = l' \circ \eta$) such that

if x is a configuration of E, then ηx is a configuration of E' and if for $e_1, e_2 \in x$ their images are equal, *i.e.* $\eta(e_1) = \eta(e_2)$, then $e_1 = e_2$.

In the category of event structures, morphisms are composed componentwise. The definition of morphism on event structures is rather abrupt—see [22] for motivation.

In the case of an independence model like event structures a computation path carries more structure than simply a string of actions. This time we take path shapes to be finite pomsets. Pomsets are special event structures where all finite subsets of events are consistent. They are essentially labelled partial orders, and morphisms between them, got by restricting those of event structures, are injective functions which send downwards-closed sets to downwards-closed sets. Thus a morphism from pomset P to pomset Q may not just extend P by extra events but also relax the causal dependency relation; two events causally related in P may have images no longer causally related in Q. We separate the forms of morphism corresponding to the different ways one pomset can extend another.

Definition: Let L be a labelling set. Define $\mathbf{Pom}_L$ to be the full subcategory of event structures with finite pomsets with labels in L as objects.

Say a morphism $m : P \to Q$ in $\mathbf{Pom}_L$ is a *prefix* morphism iff m preserves and reflects the causally dependency order. Define $\mathbf{Pom}_L^p$ to be the subcategory of $\mathbf{Pom}_L$ where all morphisms are prefix morphisms.

Say a morphism $m : P \to Q$ in $\mathbf{Pom}_L$ is an *augmentation* morphism iff m is epimorphic. Define $\mathbf{Pom}_L^a$ to be the subcategory of $\mathbf{Pom}_L$ where all morphisms are augmentation morphisms.

Proposition 1. *Any morphism $m : P \to Q$ factors uniquely to within isomorphism as a composition $m = P \xrightarrow{a} Q_0 \xrightarrow{j} Q$ where a is an augmentation and j is a prefix morphism.*

3. Open-Maps and Bisimulation

Assume a category of models $\mathbf{M}$—this could be any one of the categories of models with label preserving morphisms of the previous section. Assume also a choice of path category, a subcategory $\mathbf{P} \hookrightarrow \mathbf{M}$ consisting of path objects (these could be branches, or pomsets) together with morphisms expressing how they can be extended.

Define a *path* in an object X of $\mathbf{M}$ to be a morphism

$$p : P \to X,$$

in $\mathbf{M}$, where P is an object in $\mathbf{P}$. A morphism $f : X \to Y$ in $\mathbf{M}$ takes such a path p in X to the path $f \circ p : P \to Y$ in Y. The morphism f expresses the sense in which Y simulates X; any computation path in X is matched by the computation path $f \circ p$ in Y.

We might demand a stronger condition of a morphism $f : X \to Y$ expressed succinctly in the following *path-lifting condition* which when satisfied picks out the *open* morphisms. For our purposes later, it is convenient to define open morphisms with respect to a subclass of morphisms $\mathbf{P}_0$ of $\mathbf{P}$—of course $\mathbf{P}_0$ could consist of all the morphisms of the whole category $\mathbf{P}$, when we shall identify the class of morphisms with $\mathbf{P}$ itself.

Whenever, for $m : P \to Q$ a morphism in $\mathbf{P}_0$, a "square"

$$\begin{array}{ccc} P & \xrightarrow{p} & X \\ {\scriptstyle m}\downarrow & & \downarrow{\scriptstyle f} \\ Q & \xrightarrow{q} & Y \end{array}$$

in $\mathbf{M}$ commutes, *i.e.* $q \circ m = f \circ p$, meaning the path $f \circ p$ in Y can be extended via m to a path q in Y, then there is a morphism p' such that in the diagram

$$\begin{array}{ccc} P & \xrightarrow{p} & X \\ {\scriptstyle m}\downarrow & \overset{p'}{\nearrow} & \downarrow{\scriptstyle f} \\ Q & \xrightarrow{q} & Y \end{array}$$

the two "triangles" commute, *i.e.* $p' \circ m = p$ and $f \circ p' = q$, meaning the path p can be extended via m to a path p' in X which matches q. When the morphism f satisfies this condition we shall say it is $\mathbf{P}_0$-*open*.

Say two objects X_1, X_2 of $\mathbf{M}$ are $\mathbf{P}_0$-*bisimilar* iff there is a *span* of $\mathbf{P}_0$-open morphisms f_1, f_2:

$$\begin{array}{ccccc} & & X & & \\ & {\scriptstyle f_1}\swarrow & & \searrow{\scriptstyle f_2} & \\ X_1 & & & & X_2 \end{array}$$

For the well-known model of transition systems open morphisms and the bisimulation induced by them are already familiar:

Proposition 2. *With respect to a labelling set L, the L^*-open morphisms of the category of transition systems with labelling set L are the "zig-zag morphisms" of* [20] *(the "p-morphism" of* [18]*, the "abstraction homomorphisms" of* [4]*, and the "pure morphisms" of* [3]*) i.e. those label-preserving morphisms $(\sigma, 1_L) : T \to T'$ on transition systems over labelling set L with the property that for all reachable states s of T*

if $\sigma(s) \xrightarrow{a} s'$ in T' then $s \xrightarrow{a} u$ in T and $\sigma(u) = s'$,
for some state u of T.

Two transition systems (and so synchronisation trees), over the same labelling set L, are L^*-bisimilar iff they are strongly bisimilar in the sense of [12].

In the case of event structures with $\mathbf{Pom}_L$ as the path category we obtain the equivalence of strong history preserving bisimulation on event structures (see [8] or [15]).

In checking whether a morphism is $\mathbf{P}$-open or for $\mathbf{P}$-bisimulation, for a path category $\mathbf{P}$, it suffices to consider a restricted class of morphisms, sufficient to generate the category $\mathbf{P}$.

Definition: Let $\mathbf{P}$ be a category. Let $\mathbf{P}_0$ consist of a subclass of morphisms of $\mathbf{P}$. Say $\mathbf{P}_0$ *generates* $\mathbf{P}$ iff the only subcategory of $\mathbf{P}$ which includes $\mathbf{P}_0$ and all isomorphisms of $\mathbf{P}$ is $\mathbf{P}$ itself.

In particular, if $\mathbf{P}_0$ is a skeletal subcategory of $\mathbf{P}$, then $\mathbf{P}_0$ generates $\mathbf{P}$.

Example: The category L^* is generated by the set of morphisms representing the extension of a string by a single label.

The category $\mathbf{Pom}_L$ is generated by the class of "atomic" morphisms of two kinds:

prefix: morphisms $m : P \to Q$ in $\mathbf{Pom}_L$ expressing that pomset P is a prefix of pomset Q where Q contains one more event than P; so m expresses that pomset Q consists of a copy of P with one additional event adjoined on top;

augmentation: morphisms $m : P \to Q$ in $\mathbf{Pom}_L$ expressing that pomset P is an augmentation of pomset Q but where the graph of the causal dependency relation in P contains one more pair than that of Q; so the pomset P consists of a copy of Q with one extra link of causal dependency between previously concurrent events.

To see that this class of morphisms generates $\mathbf{Pom}_L$, note that any morphism $m : P \to Q$ in $\mathbf{Pom}_L$ factors uniquely (to within isomophism) as a composition $m = j \circ a$ where

$$a : P \to Q_0$$

expresses that P is an augmentation of Q_0 and

$$j : Q_0 \to Q$$

expresses that Q_0 is a prefix of Q. Then, clearly any augmentation, or prefix, breaks down into a composition of basic augmentations, or prefixes, respectively, as above.

Clearly $\mathbf{Pom}_L^p$ is generated by the atomic prefix morphisms while $\mathbf{Pom}_L^a$ is generated by the atomic augmentation morphisms described above.

Proposition 3. *Suppose* $\mathbf{P}$ *is generated by a subclass of morphisms* $\mathbf{P}_0$.

1. *Letting* f *be a morphism of* $\mathbf{M}$, f *is* $\mathbf{P}$*-open iff* f *is* $\mathbf{P}_0$*-open.*
2. *Let* X_1, X_2 *be objects of* $\mathbf{M}$. *Then,* X_1, X_2 *are* $\mathbf{P}$*-bisimilar iff* X_1, X_2 *are* $\mathbf{P}_0$*-bisimilar.*

4. Presheaf Models

Given a path category $\mathbf{P}$ we can build the category $\widehat{\mathbf{P}}$ of presheaves over $\mathbf{P}$.[2] The objects of $\widehat{\mathbf{P}}$ consist of functors $\mathbf{P}^{op} \to \mathbf{Set}$, to the category of sets. The morphisms of $\widehat{\mathbf{P}}$ are natural transformations between functors. Intuitively a presheaf $F : \mathbf{P}^{op} \to \mathbf{Set}$ can be thought of as specifying for a typical path object P the set $F(P)$ of paths from P. It acts on a morphism $m : P \to Q$ in $\mathbf{P}$ to give a function $F(m) : F(Q) \to F(P)$ saying how Q-paths restrict to P-paths.

Let us see how a model, like a transition system or a labelled event structure, gives rise to a presheaf. Consider a category of models $\mathbf{M}$ and a choice of path category forming a subcategory $\mathbf{P} \hookrightarrow \mathbf{M}$. There is a *canonical functor* from the category of models $\mathbf{M}$ to the category of presheaves $\widehat{\mathbf{P}}$. It takes an object X of $\mathbf{M}$ to the presheaf $\mathbf{M}(-, X)$—more intuitively, it takes the model X to the to the presheaf which for each path object P

[2] Proofs for presheaf models can be found in [8]. A good introduction to presheaves can be found in Chapter 1 of [10].

yields the set of paths $\mathbf{M}(P, X)$ from P into X. The canonical functor takes a morphism $f : X \to Y$ in $\mathbf{M}$ to the natural transformation

$$\mathbf{M}(-, f) : \mathbf{M}(-, X) \to \mathbf{M}(-, Y)$$

whose component at an object P of $\mathbf{P}$ is the function $\mathbf{M}(P, X) \to \mathbf{M}(P, Y)$ taking p to $f \circ p$—intuitively, a path $p : P \to X$ in X is taken to a path $f \circ p : P \to Y$ in Y.

Theorem 4.

(i) *The canonical functor synchronisation trees, all with labelling set* L, *to* $\widehat{L^*}$ *is full, faithful and dense.*

(ii) *The canonical functor from event structures, all with labelling set* L, *to* $\widehat{\mathbf{Pom}_L}$ *is full, faithful and dense.*

The embeddings of Theorem 4 extend the Yoneda embedding of $\mathbf{P} \to \widehat{\mathbf{P}}$, regarding a path object P as the presheaf $\mathbf{P}(-, P) = \mathbf{M}(-, P)$ because, in these cases, the subcategory $\mathbf{P} \hookrightarrow \mathbf{M}$ is full. Now, if we regard presheaves as the model $\mathbf{M}'$ and the image of $\mathbf{P}$ under the Yoneda embedding as its path category $\mathbf{P}'$, we can apply the general definition of Section 3, to obtain the class of $\mathbf{P}'$-open morphisms of the presheaf category. They form a category of *open maps* of the topos $\widehat{\mathbf{P}}$, in the sense of Joyal and Moerdijk.[3] The two notions of $\mathbf{P}$-open and open map agree for the models of synchronisation trees and event structures, because generally:

Proposition 5. *Let* $\mathbf{P}$ *be a dense, full subcategory of* $\mathbf{M}$. *A morphism* $f : X \to Y$ *of* $\mathbf{M}$ *is* $\mathbf{P}$*-open iff the morphism* $\mathbf{M}(-, f) : \mathbf{M}(-, X) \to \mathbf{M}(-, Y)$ *is an open map of presheaves.*

When it comes to relating notions of bisimilarity, we must be a little careful. It is not the case that two synchronisation trees are L^*-bisimilar iff their associated presheaves are related by a span of open maps in $\widehat{L^*}$. But this is only because there are presheaves which correspond to processes without an initial state; in particular, there is always a span of open maps between any two presheaves subtended from the initial (always empty) presheaf.

A way to get a correspondence is to restrict the objects in the presheaf category.

Definition: In the situation where the path category $\mathbf{P}$ of a model $\mathbf{M}$ has an initial object I, a *rooted presheaf* is a presheaf F in which $F(I)$ is a singleton.

Remark: Another way to get a correspondence is to define bisimilarity in the entire presheaf category via spans of *surjective* open maps. This is the more robust definition, and indeed the one used in [8]; it applies even when the path category does not have an initial object, and open maps between rooted presheaves are necessarily surjective (see *e.g.* [23]).

Proposition 6. (i) *Two synchronisation trees, over labelling set* L, *are* L^**-bisimilar (i.e. strong bisimilar) iff their corresponding presheaves, under the canonical embedding, are related by a span of open maps in the full subcategory of rooted presheaves of* $\widehat{L^*}$.

(ii) *Two event structures, over labelling set* L, *are* $\mathbf{Pom}_L$*-bisimilar (i.e. strong history-preserving bisimilar) iff their corresponding presheaves, under the canonical embedding, are related by a span of open maps in the full subcategory of rooted presheaves of* $\widehat{\mathbf{Pom}_L}$.

[3] See [7], Example 1.1, though there the definition is expressed in terms of the existence of certain quasi-pullbacks; its equivalence with $\mathbf{P}'$-openness, expressed as a path-lifting property, follows by the Yoneda Lemma.

5. Presheafs as Transition Systems

Assume that a path category $\mathbf{P}$ has an initial object I, and that $\mathbf{P}_0$ is a subclass of morphisms of $\mathbf{P}$.

It will be helpful to think of a rooted presheaf over $\mathbf{P}$ as a transition system with labels taken from morphisms of $\mathbf{P}_0$:

Definition: Let X be a rooted presheaf over $\mathbf{P}$. Define its $\mathbf{P}_0$-*transition system*, denoted by $\mathcal{E}l_{\mathbf{P}_0}(X)$ to consist of:

> *states:* (P, p) where P is an object of $\mathbf{P}$ and $p \in X(P)$; take the unique member of $X(I)$ as the initial state;
> *labelling set:* $\mathbf{P}_0$;
> *transitions:* $(P, p) \xrightarrow{m} (Q, q)$ whenever $m : P \to Q$ in $\mathbf{P}_0$ and $(Xm)(q) = p$.

Remark: The construction $\mathcal{E}l_{\mathbf{P}_0}(X)$ on a presheaf X is a slight generalisation of a well-known construction of a *category of elements* of a presheaf (see *e.g.* [10]).

Notice what the construction does on a presheaf X: it forms a transition system with "states" $p \in X(P)$ which by the Yoneda Lemma correspond 1-1 with the computation paths from P (or strictly its image under the Yoneda embedding) into X.

Given a morphism of presheaves, *i.e.* a natural transformation between them, we obtain a morphism of transition systems; $\mathcal{E}l_{\mathbf{P}_0}$ extends to a functor on presheaves.

Definition: Suppose $f : X \to Y$ is a natural transformation between presheaves X and Y. Define $\mathcal{E}l_{\mathbf{P}_0}(f)$ to be the morphism of transition systems σ which acts on states so that $(P, p) \mapsto (P, f_P(p))$; thus the transition $(P, p) \xrightarrow{m} (Q, q)$ is sent to the transition $(P, f_P(p)) \xrightarrow{m} (Q, f_Q(q))$.
(It takes a little checking that $\mathcal{E}l_{\mathbf{P}_0}(f)$ is indeed a morphism of transition sytems.)

So, thinking of categories of elements as transition systems, the associated functor is a label-preserving morphism of transition systems. More than this, provided $\mathbf{P}_0$ generates $\mathbf{P}$, a natural transformation f between presheaves is open iff $\mathcal{E}l_{\mathbf{P}_0}(f)$ is a zig-zag morphism between the associated transition systems (*cf.* Proposition 2).

Proposition 7. *Assume $\mathbf{P}_0$ generates $\mathbf{P}$. A morphism $f : X \to Y$ between rooted presheaves in $\widehat{\mathbf{P}}$ is open iff $\mathcal{E}l_{\mathbf{P}_0}(f) : \mathcal{E}l_{\mathbf{P}_0}(X) \to \mathcal{E}l_{\mathbf{P}_0}(Y)$ is a zig-zag morphism between transition systems with labelling sets $\mathbf{P}_0$.*

We can go further and characterise bisimulation on presheaves as a form of bisimulation on transition systems with labels in a generating class of morphisms $\mathbf{P}_0$.

Definition: Say two transition systems T_1, T_2 with a common label set are *back-and-forth bisimilar* iff there is a relation R between their states such that $i_1 R i_2$, so their initial states are related, and whenever $s_1 R s_2$, then

> if $s_1 \xrightarrow{a} s_1'$ then $s_2 \xrightarrow{a} s_2'$ and $s_1' R s_2'$, for some state s_2' of T_2,
> if $s_2 \xrightarrow{a} s_2'$ then $s_1 \xrightarrow{a} s_1'$ and $s_1' R s_2'$, for some state s_1' of T_1,
> if $s_1' \xrightarrow{a} s_1$ then $s_2' \xrightarrow{a} s_2$ and $s_1' R s_2'$, for some state s_2' of T_2, and
> if $s_2' \xrightarrow{a} s_2$ then $s_1' \xrightarrow{a} s_1$ and $s_1' R s_2'$, for some state s_1' of T_1.

Proposition 8. *Let X_1, X_2 be presheaves over $\mathbf{P}$. Assume $\mathbf{P}_0$ is a subclass of morphisms generating $\mathbf{P}$. The presheaves X_1, X_2 are $\mathbf{P}$-bisimilar iff their transition systems $\mathcal{E}l_{\mathbf{P}_0}(X_1), \mathcal{E}l_{\mathbf{P}_0}(X_2)$ are back-and-forth bisimilar.*

Remark: Though this result is presented in a different guise it consists essentially of Lemma 17 in [8] characterising bisimulation between rooted presheaves as strong path bisimulation.

Warning: This result should *not* be interpreted in the broader sense that we advocate back-and-forth bisimulation as the appropriate bisimulation on transition systems. In fact, the presheaves in $\widehat{L^*}$ of transition systems with labelling set L, obtained by the canonical functor from transition system to presheaves, will be bisimilar iff the original transition systems are strongly bisimilar in the sense of Park and Milner.

Example:

Paths as strings: When we specialise to the (partial order) category of strings L^*, the subcategory of rooted presheaves in $\widehat{L^*}$ is equivalent to the category of synchronisation trees. Bisimulation between rooted presheaves in $\widehat{L^*}$ is reduced to back-and-forth bisimulation based on extensions of strings by a single label. Thus bisimulation between rooted presheaves coincides with back-and-forth bisimulation on synchronisation trees, and as is well-known [13] this coincides with Park and Milner's strong bisimulation. As remarked above, the bisimulation on transition systems induced by the canonical functor to $\widehat{L^*}$ is strong bisimulation.

Paths as pomsets: Two subcategories of rooted presheaves are of interest, those over path categories $\mathbf{Pom}_L$ and $\mathbf{Pom}_L^s$.

In the case of bisimulation between presheaves over $\mathbf{Pom}_L$ it suffices to consider "atomic" prefix and augmentation morphisms. Presheaves of event structures under the canonical embedding are bisimilar iff the event structures are strong history-preserving bisimilar (see [8] for the proof).

Just for the moment, consider the full subcategory of event structures, over labelling set L, where morphisms $\eta : E \to E'$ are further constrained to satisfy:

> if x is a configuration of E, then ηx is a configuration of E', and the restriction of η from x to ηx is an isomorphism of pomsets.
> ((–Here we identify a configuration of an event structure E with its pomset structure induced by E.–))

We call such morphisms *prefix* morphisms because they generalise their namesakes on pomsets. The canonical functor from the category of event structures with prefix morphisms, to rooted presheaves in $\widehat{\mathbf{Pom}_L^s}$ is full and faithful (because the category of pomsets with prefix morphisms is dense in the category of event structures with prefix morphisms). Under it two event structures give rise to bisimilar presheaves iff they are strong history-preserving bisimilar. This is essentially because if we look at the transition system of the presheaf obtained from an event structure, its states will correspond to configurations of the event structure.

Thus, strong history-preserving bisimulation of event structures coincides with bisimulation of the canonical presheaves (obtained by the canonical embedding) in the presheaves $\mathbf{Pom}_L$, and also with bisimulation between the canonical presheaves over just $\mathbf{Pom}_L^p$, where we restrict to simply prefix morphisms of pomsets and event structures. In investigating the bisimilarity of event structures it suffices to consider just "atomic" prefix morphisms in $\mathbf{Pom}_L^s$ where a single new event is adjoined.

6. Logic and Game Corollaries

By characterising bisimulation on presheaves as back-and-forth bisimulation on their associated transition systems we can connect with logic and game characterisations of bisimulation of the kind discussed in [12] (for logic) and [19] (for games and logic).

6.1. **A specification logic.** Assume the path category $\mathbf{P}$ is a small subcategory with initial object I. Let $\mathbf{P}_0$ be a subclass of morphisms of $\mathbf{P}$.

Define $\mathbf{P}_0$-*assertions* by:

$$A ::= \overline{\langle m \rangle} A \mid \langle m \rangle A \mid \neg A \mid \bigwedge_{j \in J} A_j$$

where m is a morphism in $\mathbf{P}_0$, and J is an indexing set, possibly empty and *not* restricted to being finite. The modality $\overline{\langle m \rangle}$ is a "backwards" modality, while $\langle m \rangle$ is a "forwards" modality. We define the semantics with respect to a transition system with labelling set $\mathbf{P}_0$:

- $s \models \langle m \rangle A$ iff $\exists s'.\ s \xrightarrow{m} s'$ and $s' \models A$
- $s \models \overline{\langle m \rangle} A$ iff $\exists s'.\ s' \xrightarrow{m} s$ and $s' \models A$
- the boolean operations receive their expected meanings.

The logic is but a step away from Hennessy-Milner logic, well-known to be characteristic for strong bisimulation, and the proof is virtually the same (see [12, 8]).

Theorem 9. *Let $\mathbf{P}_0$ generate $\mathbf{P}$. Two rooted presheaves in $\widehat{\mathbf{P}}$ are bisimilar iff their $\mathbf{P}_0$-transition systems satisfy the same assertions.*

Example: We determine a satisfaction relation for synchronisation trees and event structures via their canonical embeddings in presheaf categories $\widehat{L^*}$, $\widehat{\mathbf{Pom}_L}$ and $\widehat{\mathbf{Pom}^s_L}$; for a more direct definition of the satisfaction relation for these concrete models, based on their paths—see [8].

Paths as strings: Traditional Hennessy-Milner logic arises by reducing the seemingly richer logic based on all extension morphisms in L^*. Firstly, as remarked earlier we can restrict to just the forwards modalities; for synchronisation trees back-and-forth bisimulation amounts to strong bisimulation. Because extensions by a single symbol are enough to generate the category of strings L^*, it suffices in getting a logic characteristic for bisimulation on synchronisation trees to restrict to forward modal assertions of the form $\langle b \rangle A$ where b is a single label; specifying the label b together with the domain of the morphism is enough to determine the morphism in the path category.

Paths as pomsets: Bisimulation between rooted presheaves over $\mathbf{Pom}_L$ or $\mathbf{Pom}^s_L$ is characterised by satisfaction of assertions with modalities labelled by "atomic" morphisms. The category of event structures, with labelling set L, with prefix morphisms embeds canonically in $\widehat{\mathbf{Pom}^s_L}$. So strong history-preserving bisimulation of event structures is characterised by logic with forwards and backwards modalities labelled by "atomic" prefix morphisms. In the case where the event structures have no autoconcurrency (*i.e.* no concurrent events with the same label) the labels associated with the modalities can be simplified to single labels—see [14].

6.2. **Games on presheaves.** Assume again that the path category $\mathbf{P}$ is a small subcategory with initial object I, and that $\mathbf{P}_0$ be a subclass of morphisms of $\mathbf{P}$.

Viewing presheaves as transition systems, we may also lift existing notions of games for transition systems to presheaves. As an example we adopt here a back-and-forth version of the games for transition systems defined by e.g. [19], well known to be characteristic for strong bisimulation.

Let $T_0 = (S_0, i_0, L_0, \mathit{tran}_0)$ and $T_1 = (S_1, i_1, L_1, \mathit{tran}_1)$ be two transition systems. The game $G(T_0, T_1)$ played by two players (I and II) is defined as follows. The configurations of the game consist of pairs of states $(s_0 \in S_0, s_1 \in S_1)$ with (i_0, i_1) as the starting configuration. A *play* consists of a sequence of alternating moves by the two players (Player I making the first move), where a move consists of a choice of a transition from one of the systems, according to the following game rules:

At configuration (s_0, s_1)

- either Player I chooses a transition $s_0 \xrightarrow{a} s_0'$, after which Player II chooses a transition $s_1 \xrightarrow{a} s_1'$, and the game continues at configuration (s_0', s_1'),
- or Player I chooses a transition $s_1 \xrightarrow{a} s_1'$, after which Player II chooses a transition $s_0 \xrightarrow{a} s_0'$, and the game continues at configuration (s_0', s_1'),
- or Player I chooses a transition $s_0' \xrightarrow{a} s_0$, after which Player II chooses a transistion $s_1' \xrightarrow{a} s_1$, and the game continues at configuration (s_0', s_1'),
- or Player I chooses a transition $s_1' \xrightarrow{a} s_1$, after which Player II chooses a transition $s_0' \xrightarrow{a} s_0$, and the game continues at configuration (s_0', s_1').

Player I wins a play if Player II gets stuck, *i.e.* at some point cannot match a move by Player I according to the rules of the game. All other plays are won by Player II, *i.e.* all infinite plays, and plays where Player I at some point cannot make a move. A (history-free) *strategy* for a player is a set of rules which for each configuration tells the player how to proceed, *i.e.* for Player II a rule will associate to each configuration and a choice of back or forth transition in one of the systems by Player I, a set of matching transitions in the other system. A strategy is *winning* for a player, if he or she wins every play played according to the strategy.

Intuitively, the two players have different goals in game $G(T_0, T_1)$: Player I wants to show that the two transition systems are distinguishable, Player II that they are not. Viewing presheaves as transition systems notion of distinguishablity is determined by:

Theorem 10. *Let* $\mathbf{P}_0$ *generate* $\mathbf{P}$. *Two rooted presheaves in* $\widehat{\mathbf{P}}$ *are bisimilar iff Player II has a winning strategy in the game defined by their two* $\mathbf{P}_0$*-transition systems.*

This theorem follows from Theorem 8 by essentially the proof of the corresponding theorem for transition systems from [19].

Example: Games for synchronization trees and event structures are obtained from their canonical embeddings in presheaf categories.

Paths as strings: We obtain the original Stirling games characteristic for synchronization trees in the same way we obtained the original Hennessy-Milner logic above. First of all, from [13] we can restrict the games to only forwards moves, *i.e.* transitions labelled by extension morphisms. Secondly, from the theorem above we may restrict games to allow only moves involving extension with a single symbol, and finally such a morphism in the path category is determined by its domain and the label of the extended single symbol.

Paths as pomsets: Bisimulation between rooted presheaves over $\mathbf{Pom}_L$ or $\mathbf{Pom}_L^s$ is characterised by games with moves restricted to transitions labeled by "atomic" morphisms. We may obtain games for event structures via their canonical embedding in $\widehat{\mathbf{Pom}_L^s}$, and hence we get that games with moves restricted to forwards and backwards transitions labelled by "atomic" prefix morphisms are characteristic for strong history-preserving bisimulation of event structures.

7. Concluding Remarks

So are presheaves *just* transition systems? No, they are really much more. While it can provide helpful intuition to think of presheaves as transition systems, presheaves possess a great deal of mathematical structure, which has already proved useful, or is potentially useful. For instance, there are results like that of [5] showing that constructions obtained from certain left Kan extensions automatically preserve open maps, and observations like that of [23], that moving to the category of *profunctors*, essentially presheaves acting as morphisms, we can begin to tackle higher-order features like process-passing; in recent work there appear to be technical advantages in viewing profunctors as transition systems. More speculatively, we can hope that the fact that presheaves form a topos will become helpful.

REFERENCES

[1] Barr, M., and Wells, C., *Category theory for Computer Science*. Prentice Hall, 1990.
[2] Bednarczyk, M., Hereditary history preserving bisimulation or what is the power of the future perfect in program logics. Technical report, Polish Academy of Sciences, Gdansk, 1991.
[3] Benson, D.B., and Ben-Shachar, O., Bisimulation of automata. *Information and Computation*, 79, pp. 60–83, 1988.
[4] Castellani, I., Bisimulation and abstraction homomorphisms. Proc. of CAAP 85, *Springer Lecture Notes in Computer Science*, 1985.
[5] Cattani, G.-L. and Winskel, G., Presheaf models for concurrency. To appear in the proc. of CSL'96, Utrecht, August 1996.
[6] Van Glabeek, R.J., and Goltz, U., Equivalence notions for concurrent systems and refinement of actions. Proc of MFCS'89, *Springer Lecture Notes in Computer Science* 379, pp. 237-248, 1989.
[7] Joyal, A., and Moerdijk, I., A completeness theorem for open maps. In *Annals of Pure and Applied Logic* 70, pp. 51–86, 1994.
[8] Joyal, A., Nielsen, M. and Winskel, G., Bisimulation from Open Maps. *Information and Computation*, 127, no. 2, pp. 164–185, 1996.
[9] MacLane, S., *Categories for the Working Mathematician*. Graduate Texts in Mathematics, Springer Verlag, 1971.
[10] MacLane, S., and Moerdijk, I., *Sheaves in geometry and logic: a first introduction to topos theory*, Springer Verlag, 1992.
[11] Milner, A.J.R.G., *Calculus of communicating systems*. Springer Lecture Notes in Computer Science 92, 1980.
[12] Milner, A.J.R.G., *Communication and concurrency*. Prentice Hall, 1989.
[13] De Nicola, R., Montanari, U., and Vaandrager, F., Back and Forth Bisimulations. Proceedings of CONCUR'90, *Springer Lecture Notes in Computer Science* 458, pp. 152–165, 1990.
[14] Nielsen, M., and Clausen, C., Bisimulations, Games, and Logic. Proceedings of CONCUR'94, *Springer Lecture Notes in Computer Science* 836, pp. 385–400, 1994.
[15] Nielsen, M., and Winskel, G., Petri nets and bisimulations. *Theoretical Computer Science*, vol. 153, pp. 211-244, 1996.
[16] Pratt, V.R., Modelling concurrency with partial orders, *International Journal of Parallel Programming*, 15, 1, pp. 33–71, 1986.
[17] Rabinovitch, A., and Trakhtenbrot, B., Behaviour structures and nets. *Fundamenta Informatica*, 11(4), pp. 357–404, 1988.
[18] Segerberg, K., Decidability of S4.1, *Theoria* 34, pp. 7–20, 1968.
[19] Stirling, C., Model Checking and Other Games. Notes for Mathfit Workshop on Finite Model Theory, University of Wales, Swansea, 1996.
[20] Van Benthem, J., Correspondence theory. In the *Handbook of Philosophical Logic*, Vol. II, eds. Gabbay and Guenther, Reidel, pp. 167–247, 1984.
[21] Winskel,G., Event structures. *Springer Lecture Notes in Computer Science* 255, pp. 325-392, 1987.
[22] Winskel, G., and Nielsen, M., Models for concurrency. In the *Handbook of Logic in Computer Science*, vol. IV, eds. Abramsky, Gabbay and Maibaum, Oxford University Press, 1995.
[23] Winskel, G., A presheaf semantics of value-passing processes. CONCUR'96, *Springer Lecture Notes in Computer Science* 1119, pp. 98-114, 1996.

BRICS, DEPARTMENT OF COMPUTER SCIENCE, UNIVERSITY OF AARHUS, DENMARK

DIMACS Series in Discrete Mathematics
and Theoretical Computer Science
Volume **29**, 1997

On topological hierarchies of temporal properties

Christel Baier and Marta Kwiatkowska

ABSTRACT. The classification of properties of concurrent programs into safety and liveness was first proposed by Lamport [**20**]. Since then several characterizations of hierarchies of properties have been given, see e.g. [**3, 18, 7, 19**]; this includes *syntactic* characterizations (in terms classes of formulas of logics such as the linear temporal logic) as well as *extensional* (as sets of computations in some abstract domain). The latter often admits a *topological* characterization with respect to the natural topologies of the domain of computations. We introduce a general notion of a linear time model of computation which consists of partial and completed computations satisfying certain axioms. The model is endowed with a natural topology. We show that the usual topologies on strings, Mazurkiewicz traces and pomsets arise as special cases. We then introduce a hierarchy of properties including safety, liveness, guarantee, response and persistence properties, and show that our definition subsumes the hierarchies of: Alpern & Schneider [**3**]; Chang, Manna & Pnueli [**7**]; and Kwiatkowska, Peled & Penczek [**19**]. Syntactic characterizations of the properties in the hierarchy in terms of temporal logic are also studied.

1. Introduction

The classification of properties of concurrent programs into *safety* and *liveness* was first proposed by Lamport [**20**]. According to the informal intuition introduced there, safety properties assert that "nothing bad happens", whereas liveness properties ensure that "something good will happen". Thus, a safety property is satisfied in a program if and only if at no point during its execution something "bad" happens. Examples of safety properties are: mutual exclusion (where the bad thing is two processes being in their critical sections at the same time), deadlock freedom (the bad thing is deadlock, i.e. a state in which no progress can be made) or partial correctness (where the bad thing is violating the postcondition assuming the execution started in a state satisfying the precondition). Safety properties are proved by means of arguments involving invariants; such arguments are usually too weak to guarantee that something will happen at all (e.g. partial correctness is no guarantee of termination).

In contrast to safety, proofs of liveness properties often employ well-founded induction. A liveness property states that at some point during the execution the program enters a desirable state. Termination is a typical liveness property; in the

1991 *Mathematics Subject Classification.* Subject Classification. Primary (68Q05, 68Q60); Secondary (03B70).

The second author was in part supported by EPSRC grant GR/K42028.

context of a mutual exclusion protocol it is the statement that a process trying to enter its critical section will *eventually* be allowed to enter. Some authors include also starvation freedom (every process ready to make progress infinitely often is allowed to do so infinitely often) within the class of liveness properties; here the desirable state (the process making progress) has to be entered *infinitely often*.

Apart from the underlying proof methodology, the distinction between safety and liveness can be made at other levels as well. This includes *syntactic* characterizations, i.e. classes of formulas that denote the given properties (e.g. safety is stated in terms of the 'always' modality in temporal logics, whereas liveness in terms of 'eventually'), see e.g. [**23, 7, 19**]; *automata-theoretic* characterizations (i.e. classes of automata which accept precisely the properties of a given class), see e.g. [**4, 23, 7**]; and *extensional* characterizations as certain sets of computations in some domain, see e.g. [**3, 18, 15, 23, 7, 19**]. The latter often admit the corresponding *topological* characterization for some topology on the domain of computations.

While all concerned agree that safety properties are the closed sets, disagreement between what precisely constitutes a liveness property in an abstract domain of computations persists. For example, Alpern & Schneider [**3**], working with the Cantor topology in the domain of infinite sequences of states, define liveness as the dense sets. In contrast, Chang, Manna & Pnueli [**7**], see also [**23, 8**], who work with the same domain but focus on the syntactic classes of properties expressed in Linear Time Temporal Logic (LTL), formulate a finer-grain hierarchy of four classes of properties (*safety*, *guarantee*, *response* and *persistence*) and show that they correspond to the two lower levels of the Borel hierarchy; they also show that the Alpern & Schneider characterization is orthogonal to their hierarchy. When considering a partial order semantic domain of computations, e.g. Mazurkiewicz traces, pomsets, etc, together with a partial order temporal logic, the picture complicates further, as the natural topologies of such domains (the relativised Scott topology) are coarser than, and need not coincide with, their metric topologies[1]; only certain aspects of the hierarchy of [**7**] generalise to this case. For example, in [**18, 15**], where the domain of Mazurkiewicz traces is used, liveness is defined as a G_δ-set, and fairness as a dense G_δ-set. In [**19**] this is developed further to a hierarchy of properties which reduces to the Chang, Manna & Pnueli hierarchy by considering a syntactic classification in the partial order temporal logic GISTL, together with a corresponding topological characterization in terms of the relativised Scott topology. While several aspects of [**7**] generalise to the partial order case, the automata-theoretic characterization does not, and only a subset of formulas of GISTL is considered.

This paper aims to define hierarchies of properties in terms of an abstract, axiomatically given, semantic domain of computations, which is a common generalisation of domains such as Mazurkiewicz traces [**24**], pomsets [**29**] or partial order executions [**13**]. The starting point is a linear time model $\overline{A}$, i.e. a semantic domain $\overline{A}$ subdivided into the 'finite elements' (the set $\mathcal{K}(A)$ of *partial* computations) and 'infinite elements' (the set A of *complete* computations). Partial computations can be thought of as finite execution fragments of complete computations; we suppose the existence of a mapping $x \mapsto \mathcal{K}(x)$ which assigns to each computation $x \in \overline{A}$

[1]This problem does not arise in the Cantor topology: it is simultaneously Hausdorff and the Scott topology of the finite and infinite sequences relativised to the maximal (infinite) sequences.

the set of its partial computations. The behaviour of a program is denoted by the set of its (complete) computations. A (complete) computation of a program P denotes a possible behaviour of P which arises by resolving all the non-deterministic choices in advance. If there is a non-deterministic choice in a program then exactly one computation will record the specific choice made in that execution (i.e. computations do not contain branches). For convenience, we assume that all terminating computations are modelled by the complete (infinite) elements of $\overline{A}$; this can be achieved by extending each terminating computation with infinitely many occurrences of a special action which does not affect the state of the system.

Observe that $\overline{A}$ admits both interleaving and partial order (i.e. 'true concurrency') models, but does not faithfully represent branching behaviour. In interleaving models – where parallelism is reduced to non-determinism and sequential composition – no distinction is made between non-determinism arising from parallelism and that arising from explicit choice. In contrast to this, such distinctions can be made in true concurrency models; there, the execution of concurrent events can happen in any order or in parallel. Synchronization among processes is treated in the same way as explicit non-determinism. Hence, in interleaving models the linearization of a computation is uniquely determined, whereas in true concurrency models there may exist more than one linearization of a computation (which differ in the order of concurrent events).

For a fixed model $\overline{A}$ a *property* is any subset of 2^A (consisting of those programs which are assumed to have this property). We suppose that the decision as to which of the possible computations is executed is made by the environment, and not by the program itself. Hence, in order to prove the correctness of a program one has to show that all computations behave well. For this reason we suppose that the properties under consideration are of the form $E_T = \{ P \in 2^A : P \subseteq T \}$ where T is a subset of A which consists of those computations which behave well. In the sequel we refer to any subset T of A as a property.

In an abstract model $\overline{A}$, following [**7, 19**], we define a hierarchy of four types of properties which can be verified by observing finite execution fragments: safety, guarantee, response and persistence properties. This is achieved by means of operators $\mathcal{A}$, $\mathcal{E}$, $\mathcal{R}$ and $\mathcal{P}$ that assign to each finitary property F (i.e. $F \subseteq \mathcal{K}(A)$) a subset of A. For example, a safety property asserts that *all* finite approximations fulfill a certain finitary property F (i.e. a safety property consists of those computations x such that $\mathcal{K}(x) \subseteq F$), while a guarantee property states that all executions may pass a state which satisfies a certain finitary property F (i.e. a guarantee property consists of those computations x where $\mathcal{K}(x) \cap F \neq \emptyset$.). Recurrence $\mathcal{R}$ and persistence $\mathcal{P}$ are defined similarly. Furthermore, we endow the model with natural topologies (order-theoretic and, in the presence of the length function, a metric) and give the corresponding, topological, characterizations of the classes of properties as described above. Finally, we compare our results with existing hierarchies defined for the domains of strings and Mazurkiewicz traces. We show that the result of [**3**] that safety, resp. liveness, properties are the closed, resp. dense, subsets carries over to arbitrary linear time models $\overline{A}$. In addition, the hierarchy of [**7**] corresponds to ours, while that of [**19**] does not w.r.t. the operators $\mathcal{R}$ and $\mathcal{P}$ unless the definition of response in [**19**] is appropriately strengthened.

Our definitions are general enough to admit the transfer of our results to other interleaving, as well as the partial order, models, e.g. pomsets.

The paper is organized as follows. Section 2 presents the axiomatization of our model $\overline{A}$, and in Section 2.1 we show that the semantic domains of strings, Mazurkiewicz traces and pomsets are linear time models in our sense. Later we show that linear time models as defined here are closely related to algebraic dcpo's (directed-complete partial orders) and metric spaces (section 2.2 and 2.3). In section 3 we define the properties of: safety, liveness, guarantee, response and persistence, and give a topological characterization of each class of properties. In section 4 we show how temporal logic can be used to describe properties in any linear time model. We intrepret the linear time logic LTL [**7**] over the 'interleaving models' (where the next step of a computation in a given state is uniquely determined, see section 4.2) and the partial order temporal logic $ISTL^*$ [**13**] over 'true concurrency models' (where there might be several alternatives – arising from the way in which concurrent events are executed – to proceed in a given state, see section 4.3).

2. Linear time models

In this section we define the notion of an abstract linear time model. We then show (Section 2.2) that linear time models in our sense can be endowed with a natural ordering and that (under additional assumptions) they form algebraic dcpo's. Furthermore, in Section 2.3 we consider the class of models equipped with a length function (which counts the number of atomic steps that a partial computation has to perform) and show that they can be endowed with a distance. We assume that the reader is familiar with the basic notions of domain theory, see e.g. [**2**], and metric spaces, see e.g. [**10**].

DEFINITION 2.1. A *linear time model* is a set $\overline{A}$ which is divided into disjoint subsets $\mathcal{K}(A)$ and A, together with a mapping $x \mapsto \mathcal{K}(x)$ which assigns to each $x \in \overline{A}$ a subset $\mathcal{K}(x)$ of $\mathcal{K}(A)$ such that:

(1) If $\xi \in \mathcal{K}(x)$ then $\mathcal{K}(\xi) \subseteq \mathcal{K}(x)$.
(2) For each $\xi \in \mathcal{K}(A)$ there is some $x \in A$ with $\xi \in \mathcal{K}(x)$.
(3) $\xi \in \mathcal{K}(\xi)$ for each $\xi \in \mathcal{K}(A)$.
(4) If $\mathcal{K}(x) = \mathcal{K}(y)$ then $x = y$.
(5) For each $x \in A$ there exists an *x-path*, i.e. a sequence $(\xi_n)_{n\geq 0}$ in $\mathcal{K}(x)$ such that

$$\mathcal{K}(\xi_0) \subset \mathcal{K}(\xi_1) \subset \mathcal{K}(\xi_2) \subset \ldots \quad \text{and} \quad \mathcal{K}(x) = \bigcup_{n\geq 0} \mathcal{K}(\xi_n).$$

The elements of $\mathcal{K}(A)$ should be thought of as *partial* computations (the 'finite' elements), and the elements of A as *complete* computations, or briefly computations (the 'infinite', or 'maximal' elements). The set $\mathcal{K}(x)$ is the set of all partial computations of x. Condition (1) states that if ξ is a partial computation of some computation x then all partial computations of ξ are partial computations of x. (2) ensures that only those partial computations are considered which are execution fragments of complete computations, or, in other words, which can be extended to a complete computation. (3) says that each partial computation approximates itself. (4) ensures that different computations can be distinguished by their partial computations. By condition (5) each complete computation can be approximated by its partial computations.

Each x-path should be viewed as a fragment of a possible execution (linearization) of x: if $\xi_0, \xi_1, \xi_2, \ldots$ is an x-path we think of ξ_i as an intermediate state which the execution reaches after performing the partial computation described by ξ_i. It might be the case that there are additional intermediate states which are not represented by an element of the x-path. When considering the next step relation as in Section 4, which determines the possible next steps in an intermediate state, the *executions* of a computation x are defined to be those x-paths which obey the next step relation. In this case the x-paths are exactly the subsequences of the executions of x. The criterion for an x-path to approximate x (in the sense that $\bigcup \mathcal{K}(\xi_n) = \mathcal{K}(x)$) imposes a fairness (or maximal progress) constraint, since every partial computation must be subsumed by a partial computation of the x-path, i.e. each action which is performed in some execution is executed in every execution. This corresponds to the notion of an 'acceptable path' as in [**13**], 'maximality' of [**18**], or 'justice' in the sense of [**30**]. We extend the notion of an x-path to partial computations as follows. If $\xi \in \mathcal{K}(A)$ then a ξ-path is a sequence $(\xi_n)_{n\geq 0}$ in $\mathcal{K}(A)$ such that

$$\mathcal{K}(\xi_0) \subset \mathcal{K}(\xi_1) \subset \mathcal{K}(\xi_2) \subset \ldots \subset \mathcal{K}(\xi_n) = \mathcal{K}(\xi_{n+1}) = \ldots = \mathcal{K}(\xi).$$

DEFINITION 2.2. A linear time model *with an initial state* is a linear time model $\overline{A}$ satisfying:

(6) There exists $\perp \in \mathcal{K}(A)$ with $\mathcal{K}(\perp) = \{\perp\}$ and $\perp \in \mathcal{K}(x)$ for all $x \in \overline{A}$.

Because of conditions (3) and (4), the element $\perp$ in condition (6) is unique if it exists. $\perp$ can be interpreted as the partial computation which represents the state in which no action has been performed. By our intrepretation of the partial computations as the intermediate states of executions the element $\perp$ can be considered as the (common) initial state. (This explains the notion 'linear time models with an initial state').

2.1. Concrete examples of linear time models. Throughout the paper we illustrate the use of our framework by means of examples defined for the linear time models of *strings*, *Mazurkiewicz traces* and *pomsets*. In this section we recall basic definitions.

We suppose Σ to be a countable set of atomic actions including special symbols $\surd$ and δ which model termination and deadlock. Both $\surd$ and δ are assumed not to affect the state of the system, and which cannot be performed except when the system has reached its final state.

2.1.1. *The domain of strings.* By a string over the alphabet Σ we mean a (finite or infinite) sequence $s = \alpha_0\alpha_1\alpha_2\ldots$ of elements in Σ such that either the actions $\surd$ and δ do not occur in s or there is some $k \geq 0$ such that $\alpha_i \neq \surd, \delta$, for all $0 \leq i < k$ and either $\alpha_i = \surd$ for all $i \geq k$ or $\alpha_i = \delta$ for all $i \geq k$. Infinite strings containing $\surd$ represent successfully terminating computations, those containing δ model deadlocked computations, while those not containing any occurrence of $\surd$ and δ non-terminating computations. Finite prefices of a string represent its partial computations. Σ^* denotes the set of finite strings over Σ, Σ^ω the set of infinite strings over Σ. $\overline{A} = \Sigma^\infty$ is a linear time model in our sense; take $\mathcal{K}(A) = \Sigma^*$, $A = \Sigma^\omega$, and define $\mathcal{K}(x)$ to be the set of all finite prefices of x.

If $x \in \Sigma^\infty$ then $x[n]$ denotes the n-th prefix of x. (If the length of x is $\leq n$ put $x[n] = x$.) We assume Σ^∞ to be endowed with the usual distance

$$d(s,t) = \inf \left\{ \frac{1}{2^n} : s[n] = t[n] \right\}$$

and the usual prefix order (denoted by $\sqsubseteq$). Then Σ^∞ is a complete ultrametric space and and an algebraic dcpo. The finite strings are the compact elements in Σ^∞ viewed as an algebraic dcpo. Σ^* is a dense subset of isolated elements in Σ^∞ when viewed as a metric space.

2.1.2. *Mazurkiewicz traces.* An independency relation on alphabet Σ is an irreflexive and symmetric binary relation $\iota \subseteq \Sigma \times \Sigma$ such that $\surd$ and δ are dependent on every action, i.e. $\neg(\alpha \,\iota\, \surd) \wedge \neg(\alpha \,\iota\, \delta)$ for all $\alpha \in \Sigma$. The pair (Σ, ι) is called a concurent alphabet. The independency relation ι identifies those actions in the system which can happen concurrently; thus, if $\alpha \,\iota\, \beta$ then α, β are independent actions of two concurrent processes P and Q, i.e. P and Q cannot communicate via α and β. Let $\equiv$ [**24, 17**] be the smallest equivalence relation on Σ^∞ such that

$$\text{whenever } s \in \Sigma^*,\ t \in \Sigma^\infty,\ \alpha, \beta \in \Sigma,\ \alpha \,\iota\, \beta \text{ then } s\alpha\beta t \ \equiv\ s\beta\alpha t.$$

A *trace* is an equivalence class $[s]$ of a string $s \in \Sigma^\infty$. If s is (in)finite then $[s]$ is called (in)finite. The length of a trace is the length of one of its representatives. $[\Sigma^*]$ denotes the set of finite traces, while $[\Sigma^\omega]$ the set of infinite traces. Clearly, $[\Sigma^\infty] = [\Sigma^*] \cup [\Sigma^\omega]$ forms a linear time model in our sense; to see this take the finite traces as partial computations, the infinite traces as complete computations, and define the set $\mathcal{K}(x)$ of partial computations of x as consisting of all those finite traces $[s]$ where s is a prefix of some representative of x.

If x is a trace then $x^{(n)}$ denotes the set of finite traces $[s]$ where s is a prefix of some representative $t \in \Sigma^\infty$ of x and where the length of s is at most n. As in [**17, 16**], we consider the linear time model $[\Sigma^\infty]$ of traces in the following sense. We suppose $[\Sigma^\infty]$ to be equipped with the prefix order:

$$x \sqsubseteq y \quad \Longleftrightarrow \quad \exists\, s, t \in \Sigma^\infty \ \ s \sqsubseteq t,\ x = [s],\ y = [t]$$

Then $[\Sigma^\infty]$ is an algebraic dcpo (see e.g. [**17**]), with finite traces being the compact elements. Moreover, $[\Sigma^\infty]$ also has an associated metric d given by:

$$d(x,y) \ = \ \inf \left\{ \frac{1}{2^n} \ : \ x^{(n)} = y^{(n)} \right\}.$$

Then $[\Sigma^\infty]$ is a complete ultrametric space and $[\Sigma^*]$ is a dense subset of isolated elements (see [**16**]).

2.1.3. *Pomsets.* Pomsets (partially ordered multisets) were first introduced in [**29**]. Several variants of pomsets are known from the literature; here we use the notion of a pomset as a labelled prime event structure without conflicts in the sense of [**33**]. The underlying partial order is that of [**33**] restricted to pomsets, and the underlying metric is due to [**5**].

A *pomset* is a partially ordered set $(S, \leq)$ which is endowed with a labelling function $l : S \to \Sigma$ that maps the elements of S (called events) to an action and such that either all events are labelled with actions $\alpha \neq \surd, \delta$, or there exists an event $e \in S$ labelled by $\surd$ or δ such that:

- $e\uparrow = \{e' \in S : e \leq e'\}$ is totally ordered and $l(e) = l(e')$ for all events $e' \in e\uparrow$.
- No event $e' \in S$, $e' < e$, is labelled by $\surd$ or δ.

By a finite pomset we mean a pomset where the underlying partially ordered set is finite. Pomsets represent computations in the following sense. The execution of an event $e \in E$ means the execution of the associated action $l(e)$. If $e < e'$ (i.e. $e \leq e'$ and $e \neq e'$) then e must be executed before e'. If e, e' are independent events (i.e. neither $e \le e'$ nor $e' \le e$) then e and e' may be executed in parallel. In addition, we require that each event is reachable, i.e. for each $e \in E$ the set of predecessors of e is finite. Infinite (non-terminating) computations are represented by infinite pomsets where no event is labelled by $\surd$ or δ. Terminating computations correspond to infinite pomsets where some (and hence almost all) events are labelled by $\surd$. Deadlocked computations are modelled by those infinite pomsets in which almost all events are labelled by δ. Partial computations are denoted by finite pomsets.

If $x = (S, \le, l)$ is a pomset and $e \in S$ then the depth of e in x is given by:

$$depth_x(e) \;=\; \sup\;\{\; n \;:\; \exists e_1, \ldots, e_n \in S \;\; e_1 < \ldots < e_n = e \;\}$$

If $S' \subseteq S$ is left-closed (i.e. whenever $e \in S'$ and $e' \le e$ then $e' \in S'$) then we define

$$x\lceil S' \;=\; (\; S',\; \le \cap\, S' \times S',\; l|S' \;).$$

We put $x[n] \;=\; x \lceil S[n]$, where $S[n] = \{e \in S : depth_x(e) \le n\}$. Pom^∞ denotes the set of all (finite and infinite) pomsets, and Pom^* the subset of finite pomsets. For convenience we assume that the set of events is contained in a fixed countable set *Events*[2]. Clearly, Pom^∞ forms a linear time model in our sense. To see this take Pom^* as the set of partial computations and $Pom^\omega \;=\; Pom^\infty \setminus Pom^*$ as the set of complete computations. If $x = (S, \le, l)$ is a pomset then define $\mathcal{K}(x)$ to be all the pomsets $x\lceil S'$ where S' is a finite and left-closed subset of S. Pom^∞ can be endowed with the distance

$$d(x,y) \;=\; \inf\; \left\{ \frac{1}{2^n} \;:\; x[n] = y[n] \right\}$$

and the partial order $x \sqsubseteq y \iff \exists S \;\; x = y\lceil S$. Then Pom^∞ is a complete ultrametric space (see e.g. **[5]**) and an algebraic dcpo. The compact elements in Pom^∞, when viewed as an algebraic dcpo, are the finite pomsets. Since the underlying set *Events* is countable, the set S of events of a pomset is also countable. Hence, for each pomset x the set of finite pomsets ξ with $\xi \sqsubseteq x$ is countable (since the set of finite subsets of a countable set is countable). Pom^* is a dense subspace of isolated elements in Pom^∞ as a metric space.

2.2. Linear time models and algebraic dcpo's. The relation of 'being a partial computation of' on linear time models induces a partial order in the following sense. Let $\overline{A}$ be a linear time model and define

$$x \sqsubseteq y \quad\iff\quad \mathcal{K}(x) \subseteq \mathcal{K}(y)$$

Then $\sqsubseteq$ is a partial order on $\overline{A}$ (called the *natural order* on $\overline{A}$). The partial computations of $\overline{A}$ are the compact elements. Conditions (1) and (5) of Definition 2.1 ensure that for each $x \in \overline{A}$ the set $\mathcal{K}(x)$ is an ideal (i.e. left-closed and directed), and x is the least upper bound of $\mathcal{K}(x)$. In linear time models with an initial state the unique element $\bot$ with $\bot \in \mathcal{K}(x)$ for all $x \in \overline{A}$ is the bottom element.

DEFINITION 2.3. An *order-enriched* linear time model is a linear time model $\overline{A}$ with an initial state and which satisfies:

(7) For each directed subset X of $\mathcal{K}(A)$ there exists $z \in \overline{A}$ with

$$\mathcal{K}(z) \;=\; \bigcup_{\xi \in X} \mathcal{K}(\xi).$$

[2]This assumption is essential to ensure that Pom^∞ is a set.

The following two theorems show that order-enriched linear time models correspond to the algebraic dcpo's satisfying the condition that the set of compact elements below any element is countable.

THEOREM 2.4. *Each order-enriched linear time model $\overline{A}$ is an algebraic dcpo. $\mathcal{K}(A)$ is the set of compact elements and $\perp$ the bottom element. $\mathcal{K}(x)$ is the set of compact elements $\xi \sqsubseteq x$. Whenever $X \subseteq \overline{A}$ is directed then the (unique) element $z \in \overline{A}$ with*

$$\mathcal{K}(z) = \bigcup_{x \in X} \mathcal{K}(x)$$

is the least upper bound of X.

PROOF. We only show that for each directed subset X of $\overline{A}$ the least upper bound $\bigsqcup X$ exists. The remaining statements are easy verifications. Let X be a directed subset of X and let $K = \bigcup_{x \in X} \mathcal{K}(x)$. Then K is a directed subset of $\mathcal{K}(A)$ (this is because X and the sets $\mathcal{K}(x)$ are directed). By condition (7) there exists $z \in \overline{A}$ with $\mathcal{K}(z) = \bigcup_{\xi \in K} \mathcal{K}(\xi)$. It is easy to see that then $\mathcal{K}(z) = K$. Hence, $\mathcal{K}(x) \subseteq \mathcal{K}(z)$ for all $x \in X$, i.e. z is an upper bound of X. If $y \in \overline{A}$ is also an upper bound of X then $\mathcal{K}(x) \subseteq \mathcal{K}(y)$ for all $x \in X$. Thus, $\mathcal{K}(z) = K \subseteq \mathcal{K}(y)$ and therefore $z \sqsubseteq y$. Hence, $z = \bigsqcup X$. □

THEOREM 2.5. *If $\overline{D}$ is an algebraic dcpo such that*

(i) *For every $x \in \overline{D}$ the set of compact elements ξ with $\xi \sqsubseteq x$ is countable.*
(ii) *For every compact element ξ there exists a non-compact element $x \in \overline{D}$ with $\xi \sqsubseteq x$.*

Then $\overline{D}$ is an order-enriched linear time model where the natural order on $\overline{D}$ as a linear time model agrees with the original partial order on $\overline{D}$. The finite elements are the compact elements in $\overline{D}$. The set $\mathcal{K}(x)$ is the set of compact elements $\xi \sqsubseteq x$.

PROOF. We define $\mathcal{K}(D)$ to be the set of compact elements of $\overline{D}$ and $D = \overline{D} \backslash \mathcal{K}(D)$. Then it is easy to see that conditions (1), (3), (4), (6) and (7) are satisfied. Condition (2) follows by (ii), condition (5) by (i) and the fact that $\bigsqcup \mathcal{K}(x) = x$. □

EXAMPLE 2.6. The algebraic dcpo's Σ^∞, $[\Sigma^\infty]$ and Pom^∞ satisfy the conditions (i) and (ii) of Theorem 2.5, and hence all are order-enriched linear time models.

If $\overline{D}$ is an algebraic dcpo satisfying condition (i) of Theorem 2.5 then $\overline{D}$ can be embedded into an order-enriched linear time model $\overline{A}$ such that for each $x \in \overline{D}$ the set $\mathcal{K}(x)$ is the set of compact elements $\xi \in \overline{D}$ with $\xi \sqsubseteq x$. Notice that in $\overline{D}$ condition (2) might be violated. In order to fulfill condition (2), for each compact element $\xi \in \overline{D}$ which does not have a non-compact upper bound in $\overline{D}$ we create new elements (ξ, n) where $n \in \mathbb{N}_0 \cup \{\infty\}$, and we extend the original partial order $\sqsubseteq$ on $\overline{D}$ as follows: $\sqsubseteq'$ is the smallest partial order on $\overline{A}$ (which contains $\overline{D}$ and the new elements (ξ, n)) which satisfies

$$\xi \sqsubset' (\xi, 0) \sqsubset' (\xi, 1) \sqsubset' \dots \sqsubset' (\xi, \infty).$$

Then the elements (ξ, n), $n \in \mathbb{N}_0$, are compact in $\overline{A}$ and (ξ, ∞) is a non-compact upper bound of ξ in $\overline{A}$.

COROLLARY 2.7. Each ω-algebraic cpo $\overline{D}$ can be embedded into an order-enriched linear time model $\overline{A}$ such that for each $x \in \overline{D}$ the set $\mathcal{K}(x)$ is the set of compact elements $\xi \in \overline{D}$, $\xi \sqsubseteq x$.

2.3. Linear time models and metric spaces. If partial computations consist of executions of finitely many atomic actions then we have a natural notion of a length on $\mathcal{K}(A)$: the length of a partial computation ξ is the maximum number of atomic steps which an execution of ξ needs. This notion is similar to that defined for a partial order in [**22**]. We show that linear time models with a suitable length function are metric spaces.

DEFINITION 2.8. A *length function* on a linear time model $\overline{A}$ with initial state $\perp$ is a function

$$|\cdot| : \mathcal{K}(A) \to \mathbb{N}_0$$

such that:

(8) $|\perp| = 0$ and $\xi \in \mathcal{K}(\eta)$ implies $|\xi| \le |\eta|$.
(9) For each $x \in \overline{A}$ there exists an x-path $(\xi_n)_{n\geq 0}$ with $|\xi_n| = \min\{ |x|, n \}$ for all $n \geq 0$. Here we put $|x| = \infty$ if $x \in A$.

Condition (8) ensures that partial computations of η do not require more steps than η itself. Condition (9) asserts that each computation x can be approximated by a length-increasing sequence (ξ_n) of partial computations of x, where the length of ξ_n is exactly n or $|x|$. Given a length function on a linear time model $\overline{A}$ we put

$$\mathcal{K}_n(A) = \{ \xi \in \mathcal{K}(A) : |\xi| \le n \}$$

and $\mathcal{K}_n(x) = \mathcal{K}_n(A) \cap \mathcal{K}(x)$. Then

$$d(x,y) = \inf \left\{ \frac{1}{2^n} : \mathcal{K}_n(x) = \mathcal{K}_n(y) \right\}$$

is an ultrametric on $\overline{A}$. Note that condition (4) ensures that $d(x,y) = 0$ implies $x = y$.

NOTATION 2.9. If (M,d) is a metric space, $x \in M$ and $r > 0$ then $B(x,r)$ denotes the open ball with centre x and radius r. $\overline{B}(x,r)$ denotes the closure of $B(x,r)$, i.e.

$$\overline{B}(x,r) = \{ y \in M : d(x,y) \le r \}.$$

Since the induced distance can only be given values 0 or $1/2^n$ for some natural number n, for all elements x of a linear time model with a length function we have that $B(x,r) = \overline{B}(x,1/2^n)$ where $n = 0$ if $r \geq 1$ and n is the unique natural number satisfying $1/2^n < r \le 1/2^{n-1}$ otherwise.

LEMMA 2.10. *Let $\overline{A}$ be a linear time model with a length function. Then $\mathcal{K}(A)$ is a dense subset of $\overline{A}$ and all elements of $\mathcal{K}(A)$ are isolated in $\overline{A}$.*

In general, the induced metric space of a linear time model with a length function is not complete. In order to ensure completeness the following condition is needed:

(10) *If $(x_n)_{n\geq 0}$ is a sequence in $\overline{A}$ with $\mathcal{K}_n(x_n) = \mathcal{K}_n(x_{n+1})$ for all $n \geq 0$ then there exists $x \in \overline{A}$ with $\mathcal{K}(x) = \mathcal{K}_n(x_n)$ for all $n \geq 0$.*

EXAMPLE 2.11. The linear time models Σ^∞ and $[\Sigma^\infty]$ can be endowed with the length function which assigns to each finite string/trace its usual length. On Pom^∞ the function

$$|\cdot| : Pom^* \to \mathbb{N}_0, \quad |\xi| = \max \{ \, depth_\xi(e) \; : \; e \text{ is an event in } \xi \, \}$$

is a length function. In all three cases the ultrametric induced by the underlying length function coincides with the usual metric (cf. Section 2.1).

THEOREM 2.12. *Let $\overline{M}$ be an ultrametric space, M_0 a subspace of $\overline{M}$ and $|\cdot| : M_0 \to \mathbb{N}_0$ a function such that:*

(i) *For all $\xi \in M_0$, $|\xi| = n$, there exists $x \in \overline{M} \setminus M_0$ with $d(\xi, x) \leq 1/2^n$.*
(ii) *For each $x \in \overline{M}$ with either $x \notin M_0$ or $|x| \geq n$ there exists a unique element $x[n] \in M_0$ with*

$$|x[n]| = n \quad \text{and} \quad d(\, x[n], \, x) \leq \frac{1}{2^n}.$$

We put $\xi[n] = \xi$ if $\xi \in M_0$, $|\xi| < n$ and $|x| = \infty$ if $x \in \overline{M} \setminus M_0$. Then $\overline{M}$ is a linear time model with $\mathcal{K}(M) = M_0$ and

$$\mathcal{K}(x) = \{ \, x[n] \; : \; n \geq 0 \, \}.$$

In addition, we have for all $x, y \in \overline{M}$:

(a) *$x[n]$ is the unique element $\xi \in \mathcal{K}(x)$ with $|\xi| = \min\{|x|, n\}$.*
(b) *$d(x, y) \leq 1/2^n$ iff $x[n] = y[n]$*
(c) *$(x[m])[n] = (x[n])[m] = x[n]$ for all $0 \leq n \leq m$*
(d) *$|x| = \sup \{ \, |\xi| \; : \; \xi \in \mathcal{K}(x) \, \}$*

PROOF. Let $M = \overline{M} \setminus M_0$. (a), (b), (c) and (d) are easy verifications. Conditions (1) and (3) are satisfied because of (c). Condition (2) follows by (i), conditions (5) and (9) by (ii), condition (8) by (d).

To see that (4) holds, let x, y be such that $\mathcal{K}(x) = \mathcal{K}(y)$, then $x[n] = y[n]$ for all $n \geq 0$. This is because of (a). Hence, $x = \lim x[n] = \lim y[n] = y$. □

DEFINITION 2.13. A linear time model with a length function satisfying the conditions (i) and (ii) of Theorem 2.12 is called *metric-enriched.*

EXAMPLE 2.14. The linear time model Σ^∞ and the linear time model of pomsets $x \in Pom^\infty$ such that $x[n] \in Pom^*$ for all $n \geq 0$ are metric-enriched.

In Example 2.14 it is essential that we deal with pomsets whose n-cuts $x[n]$ are finite ('finitely approximable' pomsets in the sense of [**12**]), as otherwise condition (ii) of Theorem 2.12 would be violated since if x is a pomset where $x[n]$ is infinite then there is no pomset $\xi \in Pom^*$ with $|\xi| = n$ and $d(x, \xi) \leq 1/2^n$. Condition (ii) of Theorem 2.12 is also violated when we deal with the linear time model of Mazurkiewicz traces with a non-empty independency relation. For instance, for the trace x induced by the string $s = \alpha\beta\gamma\gamma\gamma\ldots$ with $\alpha \, \iota \, \beta$ there does not exist a finite trace ξ of length 1 with $d(x, \xi) = 1/2$. This is because $\mathcal{K}_1(x)$ contains the traces $[\alpha]$ and $[\beta]$, and the distance $d(x, [\alpha]) = d(x, [\beta]) = 1$. An alternative length function for traces can be found by embedding traces into pomsets; with this length function traces form a metric-enriched model.

3. Defining properties on linear time models

In this section we give general definitions of *safety*, *guarantee*, *response*, *persistence* and *liveness* properties. Following [**3**] we define liveness properties to be those properties $T \subseteq A$ such that each partial computation $\xi \in \mathcal{K}(A)$ has a complete computation $x \in T$ which is above it in the ordering. As in [**7, 19**], we define safety, guarantee, response and persistence properties by operators $\mathcal{A}$, $\mathcal{E}$, $\mathcal{R}$ and $\mathcal{P}$ acting on sets of partial computations (the *finitary* properties). When applied to the linear time model Σ^∞, our definitions agree with those of [**3, 7**]; some early work due to Landweber, see e.g. [**32**], introduces a similar topological hierarchy for accepting conditions of automata on infinite sequences. We show that the hierarchy and the topological characterizations stated in [**3, 7**] carry over to arbitrary linear time models.

For simplicity assume from now on that $\overline{A}$ is a fixed linear time model. If $F \subseteq \mathcal{K}(A)$ then F is called a *finitary property*. Following [**7**] we put:

$$\begin{aligned}
\mathcal{A}(F) &= \{\, x \in A \;:\; \mathcal{K}(x) \subseteq F \,\}\\
\mathcal{E}(F) &= \{\, x \in A \;:\; \mathcal{K}(x) \cap F \neq \emptyset \,\}\\
\mathcal{R}(F) &= \{\, x \in A \;:\; \text{there exists an } x\text{-path } (\xi_n) \text{ with } \xi_n \in F \text{ for all } n \,\}\\
\mathcal{P}(F) &= \{\, x \in A \;:\; \text{if } (\xi_n) \text{ is an } x\text{-path then } \xi_n \in F \text{ for almost all } n \,\}
\end{aligned}$$

and

$$\mathcal{A}_{\text{fin}}(F) = \{\xi \in \mathcal{K}(A) : \mathcal{K}(\xi) \subseteq F\}, \quad \mathcal{E}_{\text{fin}}(F) = \{\xi \in \mathcal{K}(A) : \mathcal{K}(\xi) \cap F \neq \emptyset\}.$$

$\mathcal{A}(F)$, $\mathcal{E}(F)$, $\mathcal{P}(F)$ and $\mathcal{R}(F)$ respectively denote the sets of all the complete computations x such that: *all* partial computations of x are contained in F; *some* partial computation of x belongs to F; whenever (ξ_n) is an x-path then *almost all* (ξ_n) belong to F; and there exists an x-path (ξ_n) such that *infinitely many* (ξ_n) belong to F.

The above definitions of $\mathcal{A}$, $\mathcal{E}$, $\mathcal{R}$ and $\mathcal{P}$ correspond precisely to those of [**7**] when applied to the linear time model of strings. In the linear time model of traces, our definitions of the operators $\mathcal{A}$ and $\mathcal{E}$ coincide with those of [**19**], but the definitions of $\mathcal{R}$ and $\mathcal{P}$ do not. In [**19**], where a partial order temporal logic is used, $\mathcal{R}(F)$ is defined as the set of all the infinite traces whose infinitely many prefices belong to F, and $\mathcal{P}(F)$ as the set of all the infinite traces whose almost all prefices belong to F. This is not compatible with our definition since we require an x-path to approximate x (in the sense that x is the least upper bound of a x-path w.r.t. the natural order). For instance, let F be the set of all finite traces

$$\underbrace{\alpha\alpha\ldots\alpha}_{n}, \quad n \geq 0.$$

Let $\alpha \;\iota\; \beta$ and let $x = [\beta\alpha\alpha\alpha\ldots]$. Then x belongs to $\mathcal{R}(F)$ in the sense of [**19**], but $x \notin \mathcal{R}(F)$ according to the definition in this paper. The operators $\mathcal{R}$ and $\mathcal{P}$ as defined above admit an alternative definition shown below.

LEMMA 3.1. *Let* $F \subseteq \mathcal{K}(A)$. *Then:*

(a) $x \in \mathcal{R}(F)$ *iff for every* $\xi \in \mathcal{K}(x)$ *there exists* $\xi' \in \mathcal{K}(x) \cap F$ *with* $\xi \in \mathcal{K}(\xi')$.
(b) $x \in \mathcal{P}(F)$ *iff there exists* $\xi \in \mathcal{K}(x)$ *such that* $\xi' \in \mathcal{K}(x)$, $\xi \in \mathcal{K}(\xi')$ *implies* $\xi' \in F$.

PROOF. (a) If $x \in \mathcal{R}(F)$ then there exists an x-path (ξ_n) in F. Let $\xi \in \mathcal{K}(x)$. Then $\xi \in \mathcal{K}(x) = \bigcup_{n\geq 0} \mathcal{K}(\xi_n)$. Hence, there exists $n \geq 0$ such that $\xi \in \mathcal{K}(\xi_n)$.

Assume that the condition on the right hand side of (a) is fulfilled. Let (η_n) be an x-path. For each $n \geq 0$ there exists $\xi_n \in \mathcal{K}(x) \cap F$ with $\eta_n \in \mathcal{K}(\xi_n)$. Then a suitable subsequence of (ξ_n) is an x-path in F.

(b) Follows by the duality of $\mathcal{R}$ and $\mathcal{P}$ and part (a).

□

DEFINITION 3.2. A *safety, guarantee, response*, resp. *persistence* property is any property of the form $\mathcal{A}(F)$, $\mathcal{E}(F)$, $\mathcal{R}(F)$, resp. $\mathcal{P}(F)$, where F is a finitary property. A subset T of A is called a *liveness property* iff for each $\xi \in \mathcal{K}(A)$ there exists $x \in T$ such that $\xi \in \mathcal{K}(x)$. An *obligation property* is a property of the form

$$T = \bigcap_{1\leq i\leq m} (S_i \cup G_i)$$

where $S_1, \ldots, S_m$ are safety properties and $G_1, \ldots, G_m$ are guarantee properties. A *reactivity property* is a property of the form

$$T = \bigcap_{1\leq i\leq m} (R_i \cap P_i)$$

where $R_1, \ldots, R_m$ are response properties and $P_1, \ldots, P_m$ are persistence properties.

The hierarchy of safety, guarantee, response, persistence, obligation and reactivity properties, and the duality of $\mathcal{A}$ and $\mathcal{E}$, resp. $\mathcal{R}$ and $\mathcal{P}$, as stated in [**7**] carry over to our general framework:

THEOREM 3.3. *Persistence properties subsume safety properties, guarantee properties are special kinds of response properties.*

$$\mathcal{A}(F) = \mathcal{P}(\ \mathcal{A}_{\text{fin}}(F)\ ),\quad \mathcal{E}(F) = \mathcal{R}(\ \mathcal{E}_{\text{fin}}(F)\ )$$

Guarantee properties are complements of safety properties, while response properties complements of persistence properties.

$$A \setminus \mathcal{A}(F) = \mathcal{E}(\ \mathcal{K}(A) \setminus F\ ),\quad A \setminus \mathcal{P}(F) = \mathcal{R}(\ \mathcal{K}(A) \setminus F\ )$$

Obligation properties are special kinds of response and persistence properties.

$$\bigcap_{1\leq i\leq m} (\mathcal{A}(F_i) \cup \mathcal{E}(F_i')) = \mathcal{R}\left(\bigcap_{1\leq i\leq m} H_i\right) = \mathcal{P}\left(\bigcap_{1\leq i\leq m} H_i\right)$$

where

$$H_i = \mathcal{A}_{\text{fin}}(F_i) \cup \mathcal{E}_{\text{fin}}(F_i').$$

Reactivity properties subsume response and persistence properties, obligation properties subsume safety and guarantee properties.

PROOF. The duality of $\mathcal{A}$ and $\mathcal{E}$ resp. $\mathcal{R}$ and $\mathcal{P}$ is an easy verification. It is clear that each safety or guarantee property is an obligation property since:

$$\mathcal{A}(F) = \mathcal{A}(F) \cup \mathcal{E}(\emptyset),\quad \mathcal{E}(F') = \mathcal{A}(\emptyset) \cup \mathcal{E}(F')$$

and that each response or persistence property is a reactivity property:

$$\mathcal{R}(F) = \mathcal{R}(F) \cup \mathcal{P}(\emptyset),\quad \mathcal{P}(F') = \mathcal{R}(\emptyset) \cup \mathcal{P}(F')$$

The equation $\mathcal{E}(F) = \mathcal{R}(\mathcal{E}_{\text{fin}}(F))$ follows by $\mathcal{A}(F) = \mathcal{P}(\mathcal{A}_{\text{fin}}(F))$ and the duality of $\mathcal{A}$ and $\mathcal{E}$, resp. $\mathcal{R}$ and $\mathcal{P}$.

(1) We show $\mathcal{A}(F) = \mathcal{P}(\mathcal{A}_{\text{fin}}(F))$. If $x \in \mathcal{A}(F)$ then $\mathcal{K}(x) \subseteq F$. Hence, for all $\xi \in \mathcal{K}(x)$, $\mathcal{K}(\xi) \subseteq \mathcal{K}(x) \subseteq F$. Therefore, $\xi \in \mathcal{A}_{\text{fin}}(F)$. We conclude that $\mathcal{K}(x) \subseteq \mathcal{A}_{\text{fin}}(F)$, and hence $x \in \mathcal{P}(\mathcal{A}_{\text{fin}}(F))$.

If $x \in \mathcal{P}(\mathcal{A}_{\text{fin}}(F))$ then (by Lemma 3.1(b)) there exists $\xi \in \mathcal{K}(x)$ such that whenever $\xi' \in \mathcal{K}(x)$, $\xi \in \mathcal{K}(\xi')$, then $\xi' \in \mathcal{A}_{\text{fin}}(F)$. Let $\eta \in \mathcal{K}(x)$. There exists $\xi' \in \mathcal{K}(x)$ with $\xi, \eta \in \mathcal{K}(\xi')$. Then $\xi' \in \mathcal{A}_{\text{fin}}(F)$ and therefore $\eta \in \mathcal{K}(\xi') \subseteq F$. It follows that $x \in \mathcal{A}(F)$.

(2) Next we prove that if $F, F' \subseteq \mathcal{K}(A)$ then $\mathcal{A}(F) \cup \mathcal{E}(F') = \mathcal{R}(H) = \mathcal{P}(H)$ where $H = \mathcal{A}_{\text{fin}}(F) \cup \mathcal{E}_{\text{fin}}(F')$.

If $x \in \mathcal{A}(F)$ then by part (1) of this proof $x \in \mathcal{P}(\mathcal{A}_{\text{fin}}(F)) \subseteq \mathcal{R}(\mathcal{A}_{\text{fin}}(F))$. Hence, $x \in \mathcal{P}(\mathcal{A}_{\text{fin}}(F)) \subseteq \mathcal{P}(H)$ and $x \in \mathcal{R}(\mathcal{A}_{\text{fin}}(F)) \subseteq \mathcal{R}(H)$. If $x \in \mathcal{E}(F')$ then there is some $\xi \in \mathcal{K}(x) \cap F'$. Let (ξ_n) be an x-path. Then $\xi \in \mathcal{K}(\xi_{n_0})$ for some n_0. Then $\xi \in \mathcal{K}(\xi_n)$ for all $n \geq n_0$. Hence, $\xi_n \in \mathcal{E}_{\text{fin}}(F')$ for almost all n. Therefore, $x \in \mathcal{P}(\mathcal{E}_{\text{fin}}(F'))$. We conclude $x \in \mathcal{R}(\mathcal{E}_{\text{fin}}(F')) \subseteq \mathcal{R}(H)$ and $x \in \mathcal{P}(H)$.

Let $x \in \mathcal{R}(H)$. (Since $\mathcal{P}(H) \subseteq \mathcal{R}(H)$ this includes the case $x \in \mathcal{P}(H)$.) Then there is an x-path (ξ_n) in H.

- If there exists $n \geq 0$ such that $\xi_n \in \mathcal{E}_{\text{fin}}(F')$ then $\mathcal{K}(\xi_n) \cap F' \neq \emptyset$. Since $\mathcal{K}(\xi_n) \subseteq \mathcal{K}(x)$, $\mathcal{K}(x) \cap F' \neq \emptyset$. Thus $x \in \mathcal{E}(F')$.
- If $\xi_n \notin \mathcal{E}_{\text{fin}}(F')$ for all n then $\xi_n \in \mathcal{A}_{\text{fin}}(F)$ for all n. Hence, $\mathcal{K}(\xi_n) \subseteq F$ for all n. Therefore, $\mathcal{K}(x) = \bigcup_{n \geq 0} \mathcal{K}(\xi_n) \subseteq F$. It follows that $x \in \mathcal{A}(F)$.

(3) To show $\mathcal{P}\left(\bigcap_{1 \leq i \leq m} F_i\right) = \bigcap_{1 \leq i \leq m} \mathcal{P}(F_i)$ observe that $\subseteq$ is clear. If $x \in \bigcap \mathcal{P}(F_i)$ then there exists $\xi_i \in \mathcal{K}(x)$ such that, for all $\xi \in \mathcal{K}(x)$, $\xi_i \in \mathcal{K}(\xi)$ implies $\xi \in F_i$. Since $\mathcal{K}(x)$ is directed there is some $\eta \in \mathcal{K}(x)$ with $\xi_1, \ldots, \xi_m \in \mathcal{K}(\eta)$. Hence, whenever $\xi \in \mathcal{K}(x)$, $\eta \in \mathcal{K}(\xi)$ then $\xi_i \in \mathcal{K}(\xi)$, and therefore $\xi \in \bigcap F_i$. We conclude $x \in \mathcal{P}\left(\bigcap F_i\right)$.

(4) $\bigcap_{1 \leq i \leq m} (\mathcal{A}(F_i) \cup \mathcal{E}(F_i')) = \mathcal{R}\left(\bigcap_{1 \leq i \leq m} H_i\right) = \mathcal{P}\left(\bigcap_{1 \leq i \leq m} H_i\right)$ where $H_i = \mathcal{A}_{\text{fin}}(F_i) \cup \mathcal{E}_{\text{fin}}(F_i')$.

By part (2) of this proof, $\mathcal{A}(F_i) \cup \mathcal{E}(F_i') = \mathcal{R}(H_i) = \mathcal{P}(H_i)$. and part (3) we have that

$$\bigcap (\mathcal{A}(F_i) \cup \mathcal{E}(F_i')) = \bigcap \mathcal{P}(H_i) = \mathcal{P}\left(\bigcap H_i\right)$$

and

$$\bigcap \mathcal{R}(H_i) = \bigcap \mathcal{P}(H_i) = \mathcal{P}\left(\bigcap H_i\right) \subseteq \mathcal{R}\left(\bigcap H_i\right) \subseteq \bigcap \mathcal{R}(H_i).$$

Therefore

$$\mathcal{R}\left(\bigcap H_i\right) = \bigcap \mathcal{R}(H_i) = \bigcap \mathcal{P}(H_i) = \bigcap (\mathcal{A}(F_i) \cup \mathcal{E}(F_i')).$$

□

It is an open question whether liveness properties are special kinds of reactivity properties.

Liveness does not subsume safety or guarantee properties. This is because $\emptyset$ is a safety and a guarantee property, but not a liveness property. In general, neither response nor persistence properties subsume liveness properties, as can be seen from the example below.

EXAMPLE 3.4. In the linear time model Σ^∞ the set

$$T_1 = \{ x \in \Sigma^\omega : \alpha^\omega \text{ is a suffix of } x \}$$

is a liveness property (eventually always α), but not a response property. The set

$$T_2 = \{ x \in \Sigma^\omega : \alpha^\omega \text{ is not a suffix of } x \}$$

is a liveness property (always eventually not α), but not a persistence property. (Here α^ω stands for the infinite string $\alpha\alpha\alpha\ldots$.)

PROOF. It is clear that T_1 and T_2 are liveness properties. Suppose $T_1 = \mathcal{R}(F)$ for some $F \subseteq \Sigma^*$. Then $x_1 = \beta\alpha^\omega \in T_1$. Hence, there exists $n_1 \geq 1$ such that $\xi_1 = \beta\alpha^{n_1} \in F$. Then $x_2 = \beta\alpha^{n_1}\beta\alpha^\omega \in T_1$. Thus, there exists $n_2 \geq 1$ with $\xi_2 = \beta\alpha^{n_1}\beta\alpha^{n_2} \in F$. Proceeding in this way we get a sequence of natural numbers $n_k \geq 1$ such that

$$\xi_k = \beta\alpha^{n_1}\beta\alpha^{n_2}\ldots\beta\alpha^{n_k} \in F.$$

Let $x = \lim \xi_k$ (i.e. x is the unique infinite string where ξ_k are prefices of x). Then $x \in \mathcal{R}(F)$ (since (ξ_k) is an x-path in F), but $x \notin T_1$. Contradiction.

The argument for T_2 is similar. □

Part (a) of the following lemma shows that our definition of safety properties is a generalization of the definition of safety properties in the sense of [**3**].

LEMMA 3.5. *Let $T \subseteq A$. Then:*

(a) *T is safety property iff for each $x \in A \setminus T$ there exists some $\xi \in \mathcal{K}(x)$ such that whenever $y \in A$, $\xi \in \mathcal{K}(y)$ then $y \notin T$.*
(b) *T is a guarantee property iff for each $x \in T$ there exists some $\xi \in \mathcal{K}(x)$ such that whenever $y \in A$, $\xi \in \mathcal{K}(y)$, then $y \in T$.*

NOTATION 3.6. If $\xi \in \mathcal{K}(A)$ we put $U(\xi) = \{x \in \overline{A} : \xi \in \mathcal{K}(x) \}$.

It is easy to see that, because of condition (5), whenever $\zeta, \eta \in \mathcal{K}(x)$ for some $x \in \overline{A}$ then there exists $\xi \in \mathcal{K}(x)$ with $\zeta, \eta \in \mathcal{K}(\xi)$. In particular, whenever $x \in U(\zeta) \cap U(\eta)$ then $x \in U(\xi) \subseteq \mathcal{U}(\zeta) \cap U(\eta)$ for some $\xi \in \mathcal{K}(A)$. Hence, the sets $U(\xi)$, $\xi \in \mathcal{K}(A)$, form a topological basis. In what follows we assume $\overline{A}$ to be equipped with the topology induced by the basis $U(\xi)$, $\xi \in \mathcal{K}(A)$, and that A is endowed with the subspace topology. In part (b) of Lemma 3.7 we show that in order-enriched linear time models the topology induced by the basis $U(\xi)$, $\xi \in \mathcal{K}(A)$, is the Scott-topology on $\overline{A}$ considered as an algebraic dcpo. In general, the topology on $\overline{A}$ is not T_2. This is because whenever $\mathcal{K}(x) \subseteq \mathcal{K}(y)$ then each neighbourhood of x contains y. In particular, a converging sequence might have more than one limit. We write $x = \lim x_n$ to denote that x is one of the limits of the sequence (x_n). Since the topology on $\overline{A}$ is not T_2, we cannot expect that in the case where a linear time model $\overline{A}$ is equipped with a length function the metric on $\overline{A}$ induces the topology on $\overline{A}$. In part (c) of Lemma 3.7 we show that if $\overline{A}$ is metric-enriched the metric on A induces the (subspace-)topology on A. Part (c) of Lemma 3.7 can be applied to the metric-enriched linear time model Σ^∞ or the metric-enriched linear time model of pomsets $x \in Pom^\infty$ where $x[n]$ is finite for all n.

LEMMA 3.7. *Let $\overline{A}$ be a linear time model.*

(a) *Whenever $(x_n)_{n\geq 0}$ is a sequence in $\overline{A}$ such that there exists an x-path $(\xi_n)_{n\geq 0}$ with $\xi_n \in \mathcal{K}(x_n)$ for all $n \geq 0$ then $x = \lim x_n$. In particular, each x-path converges to x.*

(b) *If $\overline{A}$ is order-enriched then the topology on $\overline{A}$ agrees with the Scott topology on $\overline{A}$ as an algebraic dcpo.*

(c) *If $\overline{A}$ is metric-enriched in the sense of Definition 2.13 then the metric on A induces the topology on A.*

PROOF. (b) is an easy verification using the fact that $U(\xi) = \xi\uparrow$.

(a) Let (x_n) be a sequence in $\overline{A}$ and (ξ_n) an x-path with $\xi_n \in \mathcal{K}(x_n)$. Let U be an open neighbourhood of x. Then there exists $\eta_1, \ldots, \eta_n \in \mathcal{K}(A)$ such that

$$x \in \bigcup_{1\leq j\leq n} U(\eta_j) \subseteq U.$$

Then $\eta_j \in \mathcal{K}(x) = \bigcup \mathcal{K}(\xi_i)$. Since $\mathcal{K}(\xi_i) \subset \mathcal{K}(\xi_{i+1})$ there exists $k \geq 0$ such that $\eta_j \in \mathcal{K}(\xi_k)$, $j = 1, \ldots, n$. Then for all $i \geq k$ and $j = 1, \ldots, n$: $\eta_j \in \mathcal{K}(\xi_k) \subseteq \mathcal{K}(\xi_i) \subseteq \mathcal{K}(x_i)$. Hence, for all $i \geq k$:

$$x_i \in \bigcup_{1\leq j\leq n} U(\eta_j) \subseteq U.$$

Thus, we conclude that $x = \lim x_i$.

(c) We first show that if $\xi \in \mathcal{K}(A)$, $|\xi| = n$, then $U(\xi) = B(\xi, 1/2^{n-1})$. Let $x \in U(\xi)$. Then $\xi \in \mathcal{K}(x)$ and, by Theorem 2.12(a) and (c), $\xi[n] = \xi = x[n]$ and hence $d(x,\xi) \leq 1/2^n$. Therefore: $x \in \overline{B}(\xi, 1/2^n) = B(\xi, 1/2^{n-1})$. If $x \in B(\xi, 1/2^{n-1})$ then $d(x,\xi) \leq 1/2^n$. Hence, $\xi \in \mathcal{K}(\xi) = \mathcal{K}_n(\xi) = \mathcal{K}_n(x) \subseteq \mathcal{K}(x)$. and $x \in U(\xi)$ follows as required.

Next we show that if $x \in A$ and $r > 0$ then $B(x,r) = U(x[n])$ where n is the natural number with $n = 0$ if $r \geq 1$ and $1/2^n < r \leq 1/2^{n-1}$ otherwise. If $y \in B(x,r)$ then $d(x,y) < r \leq 1/2^{n-1}$. Hence, $d(x,y) \leq 1/2^n$. Then $\mathcal{K}_n(x) = \mathcal{K}_n(y)$, and thus $x[n] = y[n] \in \mathcal{K}(y)$, from which we immediately obtain $y \in U(x[n])$.

If $y \in U(x[n])$ then $x[n] \in \mathcal{K}(y)$. Since $x \in A$ we have $|x[n]| = n$. Hence $x[n] = y[n]$ and therefore $d(x,y) \leq \frac{1}{2^n} < r$. Thus, $y \in B(x,r)$ as required. □

COROLLARY 3.8.
- The topology on $\overline{A}$ is coarser than the topology on $\overline{A}$ induced by the metric. This is because every basis open $U(\xi)$ can be written as $B(x, 1/2^{n-1})$ where $\xi = x[n]$, $x \in A$. Note that $B(x[n], 1/2^{n-1}) = B(x, 1/2^{n-1})$ and that all elements $\xi \in \mathcal{K}(A)$ are of the form $\xi = x[n]$ for some $x \in A$ and $n \geq 0$.
- For order-enriched models the topology on A is the relative Scott topology. A is the subspace of maximal (and also non-compact) elements of $\overline{A}$.

The following theorem generalizes the topological characterizations of safety, guarantee and liveness properties as established in [**3, 7, 19**].

THEOREM 3.9. *Let $\overline{A}$ be a linear time model and $T \subseteq A$. Then:*

(a) *T is a safety property iff T is closed.*

(b) *T is a guarantee property iff T is open.*

(c) *T is a liveness property iff T is dense.*

PROOF. (a) Let T be closed. Then we show $T = \mathcal{A}(F)$ where $F = \bigcup_{x \in T} \mathcal{K}(x)$. If $x \in T$ then $\mathcal{K}(x) \subseteq F$. Hence, $x \in \mathcal{A}(F)$. Let $x \in \mathcal{A}(F)$, then $\mathcal{K}(x) \subseteq F$. Let (ξ_n) be a x-path. Since $\xi_n \in F$ and, by definition of F, there exists a sequence (x_n) in T with $\xi_n \in \mathcal{K}(x_n)$ we have by Lemma 3.7(a) that $x = \lim x_n$. Since T is closed and since $x_n \in T$ for all $n \geq 0$ we conclude $x \in T$.

Let $T = \mathcal{A}(F)$, $x \in A$ and (x_n) a sequence in T such that x is a limit of (x_n). We have to show that $x \in T$. Let $\xi \in \mathcal{K}(x)$. We have to show that $\xi \in F$. Since $U(\xi)$ is an open neighbourhood of x, and since (x_n) converges to x, there exists $m \geq 0$ such that $x_m \in U(\xi)$. Thus, $\xi \in \mathcal{K}(x_m)$, and since $x_m \in T = \mathcal{A}(F)$ we obtain $\xi \in F$.

(b) follows by (a) and the duality of $\mathcal{A}$ and $\mathcal{E}$.

(c) Let T be a liveness property. We have to show that whenever U is an open subset of $\overline{A}$ with $U \cap A \neq \emptyset$ then $U \cap T \neq \emptyset$. It is sufficient to consider the case that U is basic open, i.e. $U = \bigcap_{1 \leq i \leq n} U(\xi_i)$ for some $\xi, \ldots, \xi_n \in \mathcal{K}(A)$. Since $U \cap A \neq \emptyset$ there exists $x \in U \cap A$. Then there exists $\xi \in \mathcal{K}(x)$ with $\xi_i \in \mathcal{K}(\xi)$, $i = 1, \ldots, n$. Hence, $U(\xi) \subseteq U$. Since T is a liveness property there exists $y \in T$ with $\xi \in \mathcal{K}(y)$. Then $y \in U(\xi)$, and thus $y \in T \cap U$.

Let T be dense in A. If $\xi \in \mathcal{K}(A)$ then $U(\xi)$ is open, and because of condition (3) there exists $x \in A \cap U(\xi)$. Hence, $A \cap U(\xi) \neq \emptyset$. Since T is dense in A there is some $y \in T \cap U(\xi)$, from which it follows that $y \in T$ and $\xi \in \mathcal{K}(y)$.

□

In general, we do not obtain the results of [**7**, **19**] which characterize response and persistence properties as the G_δ, resp. F_σ-sets, unless the model satisfies stronger conditions (see Theorem 3.10); in the latter case the hierarchy as in [**7**] can be obtained. It is worth noting that the additional conditions are satisfied by the linear model of strings, but not by traces and pomsets. As a counter-example, consider $\alpha\iota\beta$ and the trace $x = [(\alpha\beta)^\infty]$, then there exists an infinite subset $[\alpha^*]$ of $K(x)$ which does not contain an infinite x-path. The case for pomsets is similar, except that a partial solution can be obtained by modifying the definition of the map $\mathcal{K}(x)$ to assign to an infinite pomset x the set of its n-cuts $x[n]$, instead of assigning all finite prefices of x. The results of [**19**] are more problematic as the definitions of $\mathcal{R}(F)$ and $\mathcal{P}(F)$ differ from ours.

Recall that F_σ-sets are countable unions of closed sets, G_δ-sets countable intersection of open sets.

THEOREM 3.10. *Let $\overline{A}$ be a linear time model such that:*

(i) *If $x \in A$ and X is an infinite subset of $\mathcal{K}(x)$ then X contains an x-path.*
(ii) *For each $\xi \in \mathcal{K}(A)$ the set $\mathcal{K}(\xi)$ is finite.*

Then for each subset T of A:

(a) *T is a response property iff T is a G_δ-set.*
(b) *T is a persistence property iff T is a F_σ-set.*

PROOF. (b) follows by (a) and the duality of $\mathcal{R}$ and $\mathcal{P}$. We show (a). Let $T = \mathcal{R}(F)$. We define F_k to be the set consisting of all $\xi \in F$ such that there exist

$\xi_1, \ldots, \xi_k \in F \cap \mathcal{K}(\xi)$ with

$$\mathcal{K}(\xi_1) \subset \mathcal{K}(\xi_2) \subset \ldots \subset \mathcal{K}(\xi_k) \subseteq \mathcal{K}(\xi).$$

We prove that $T = \bigcap \mathcal{E}(F_k)$. Note that because of Theorem 3.9 (b) the sets $\mathcal{E}(F_k)$ are open, hence $\bigcap \mathcal{E}(F_k)$ is a G_δ-set.

- If $x \in T$ then there exists an x-path $(\xi_k)_{k\geq 1}$ such that $\xi_k \in F$ for all k. Then $\xi_k \in F_k$ and therefore $x \in \mathcal{E}(F_k)$.
- If $x \in \bigcap \mathcal{E}(F_k)$ then for each $k \geq 1$ there exists $\xi_k \in F_k \cap \mathcal{K}(x)$. By definition of F_k the cardinality of $\mathcal{K}(\xi_k)$ is at least k. Since by assumption (ii) the cardinality of $\mathcal{K}(\xi_k)$ is finite, the set $\{\xi_i : i \geq 1\}$ is infinite. By assumption (i) there exists an x-path in $\{\xi_i : i \geq 1\}$. Since $\xi_k \in F_k \subseteq F$ all elements of the x-path belong to F. Therefore, $x \in \mathcal{R}(F)$.

If $T = \bigcap G_k$, where G_k are open sets in A, we may assume that $G_1 \supseteq G_2 \supseteq \ldots$. Otherwise we deal with $G'_k = G_1 \cap \ldots \cap G_k$. Because of Theorem 3.9 (b) there exists subsets F_k of $\mathcal{K}(A)$ such that $G_k = \mathcal{E}(F_k)$. W.l.o.g. $F_1 \supseteq F_2 \supseteq \ldots$ (otherwise we deal with $F'_k = \bigcup_{i\geq k} F_i$). Let H_k be the set consisting of all $\xi \in F_k$ such that:

$$\text{whenever } \xi' \in \mathcal{K}(\xi),\ \xi' \neq \xi, \text{ then } \xi' \notin F_k.$$

Let $H = \bigcup H_k$ and $F = \bigcap F_k$. We show $T = \mathcal{E}(F) \cup \mathcal{R}(H)$ Note that $\mathcal{E}(F) = \mathcal{R}(\mathcal{E}_{\text{fin}}(F))$ and hence $\mathcal{E}(F) \cup \mathcal{R}(H) = \mathcal{R}(F')$ where $F' = \mathcal{E}_{\text{fin}}(F) \cup H$.

- If $x \in T$ then for each $k \geq 1$ there exists $\xi_k \in F_k$. Since $\mathcal{K}(\xi_k)$ is finite (by assumption (i)) we may assume that ξ_k is minimal, i.e. whenever $\xi \in \mathcal{K}(\xi_k)$, $\xi_k \neq \xi'$, then $\xi' \notin F_k$.

  Case 1: The set $\{\xi_k : k \geq 1\}$ is finite.

  Then there exists $\xi \in \{\xi_k : k \geq 1\}$ with $\xi = \xi_k$ for infinitely many k. Hence, $\xi \in F_k$ for infinitely many k. Since $F_1 \supseteq F_2 \supseteq \ldots$ we get $\xi \in F_k$ for all k, i.e. $\xi \in F$ and $x \in \mathcal{E}(F)$.

  Case 2: The set $\{\xi_k : k \geq 1\}$ is infinite.

  Because of the minimality of ξ_k we have that $\xi_k \in H_k \subseteq H$. Let (η_k) be an x-path in $\{\xi_k : k \geq 1\}$ (which exists because of assumption (i)). Then $\eta_k \in H$ for all k, and thus $x \in \mathcal{R}(H)$.
- If $x \in \mathcal{E}(F)$ then $\xi \in F$ for some $\xi \in \mathcal{K}(x)$. Hence, $\xi \in F_k$ for all k and therefore $x \in \bigcup \mathcal{E}(F_k) = T$. If $x \in \mathcal{R}(H)$ then there exists an x-path (ξ_k) in H. Then $\xi_k \in H_{m_k}$ for some $m_k \geq 1$. Since $\mathcal{K}(\xi_k) \subset \mathcal{K}(\xi_{k+1})$ we have:

  $$\xi_k \in \mathcal{K}(\xi_{k+1}) \quad \text{and} \quad \xi_k \neq \xi_{k+1}$$

  By definition of H_{m_k} we get:

  $$\xi_{k+1} \in F_{m_{k+1}} \quad \text{and} \quad \xi_k \notin F_{m_{k+1}}$$

  Since $F_1 \supseteq F_2 \supseteq \ldots$ we get: $m_1 < m_2 < \ldots$ and therefore $m_k \geq k$. Hence, $\xi_k \in F_{m_k} \subseteq F_k$ for all k. Therefore, $x \in \bigcup \mathcal{E}(F_k) = T$.

□

In [**19**] the respective definitions of $\mathcal{R}$ and $\mathcal{P}$ differ from ours, i.e.

$$\mathcal{R}(F) = \{x \in A : \exists(\xi_n) : \mathcal{K}(\xi_1) \subset \mathcal{K}(\xi_2) \subset \ldots \mathcal{K}(x) \text{ and } \xi_n \in F\ \}.$$

One can show that under the assumptions (ii) and

(i') Each infinite subset of $\mathcal{K}(x)$ contains an increasing sequence the proof of Theorem 3.10 carries over to the modified definitions of $\mathcal{R}$ and $\mathcal{P}$ if we work with increasing sequences in $\mathcal{K}(x)$ instead of x-paths. Note that under the above conditions the domain of Mazurkiewicz traces becomes finitely concurrent.

LEMMA 3.11. *Let F_1, F_2 be finitary properties. Then:*

(a) $\mathcal{A}(F_1) \cap \mathcal{A}(F_2) = \mathcal{A}(F_1 \cap F_2)$ *and* $\mathcal{A}(F_1) \cup \mathcal{A}(F_2) = \mathcal{A}\left(\mathcal{A}_{\text{fin}}(F_1) \cup \mathcal{A}_{\text{fin}}(F_2)\right)$
(b) $\mathcal{E}(F_1) \cup \mathcal{E}(F_2) = \mathcal{E}(F_1 \cup F_2)$ *and* $\mathcal{E}(F_1) \cap \mathcal{E}(F_2) = \mathcal{E}\left(\mathcal{E}_{\text{fin}}(F_1) \cap \mathcal{E}_{\text{fin}}(F_2)\right)$
(c) $\mathcal{R}(F_1 \cup F_2) = \mathcal{R}(F_1 \cup F_2)$
(d) $\mathcal{P}(F_1 \cap F_2) = \mathcal{P}(F_1) \cap \mathcal{P}(F_2)$

It is an open question whether $\mathcal{R}$ and $\mathcal{P}$ are closed under intersection and union respectively. However, under the assumptions (i) and (ii) of Theorem 3.10 we obtain that $\mathcal{R}(F_1 \cap F_2) = \mathcal{R}(F)$, where F is the set of $\eta \in F_2$ such that there exists $\xi \in F_1 \cap K(\eta)$ satisfying: whenever $\eta' \in F_2 \cap \mathcal{K}(\eta)$ and $\xi \in \mathcal{K}(\eta')$ then $\eta' = \eta$. The duality of $\mathcal{R}$ and $\mathcal{P}$ then yields the closedness of $\mathcal{P}$ under union.

4. Temporal logic and linear time models

In this section we show how linear or branching time temporal formulas can be interpreted over arbitrary linear time models with an initial state $\bot$ and a next step relation $\rightarrow$. If $x \in A$ then we interpret the elements of $\mathcal{K}(x)$ as possible intermediate states which an execution of x may pass. If an execution of x reaches the intermediate state ξ then the possible next steps are those which lead to an intermediate state $\xi' \in \mathcal{K}(x)$ such that $\xi \rightarrow \xi'$. We associate $\rightarrow$ with a mapping which assigns to each step $\xi \rightarrow \xi'$ a multiset $act(\xi, \xi')$ of all those actions which are executed in the step from ξ to ξ'. If $act(\xi, \xi')$ contains more than one action then the actions in $act(\xi, \xi')$ are executed in parallel. An execution (called ***observation***) of a (complete) computation is a sequence $(\xi_n)_{n \geq 0}$ which

- starts in the initial state $\xi_0 = \bot$
- successively performs $\rightarrow$-steps, i.e. $\xi_n \rightarrow \xi_{n+1}$
- approximates x, i.e. (ξ_n) is an x-path.

Observe that the next step relation allows the simultanous execution of independent actions; this should be compared with maximal progress.

In the case where the next step relation ensures the existence of a unique execution, i.e. where the next step of a computation x in an intermediate state ξ is uniquely determined, we consider the linear time logic LTL which is closely related to the linear time logic of [**21, 7**]. When the next step relation allows more than one possible next steps, we use a partial order logic $ISTL^*$.

In section 4.1 we formalize the conditions which a suitable next step relation on a linear time model has to fulfill. Section 4.2 introduces our interpretation of the linear time logic LTL over linear time models with a determinisitic next step relation. We show that our interpretation of LTL over Σ^∞ and a suitable next step relation coincides with those of [**21, 23**]. In section 4.3 we extend the interpretation of the logic $ISTL^*$ [**13, 27**] to arbitrary linear time models with a next step relation. The reader is cautioned to note that our intepretation of $ISTL^*$ is non-standar.

Our approach applied to the model $[\Sigma^\infty]$ of traces differs from that of [**19**] as we require an execution of a computation x to approximate x. This imposes fairness in the sense of maximality, see e.g. [**14, 18**]. If we consider the linear time model of partial order executions we get the interpretation of $ISTL$ à la [**13**].

4.1. Linear time models with a next step relation. Let Σ be a countable set of atomic actions. In what follows $\overline{A}$ is a linear time model with an initial state $\bot$. By a multiset of atomic actions we mean a function $\kappa : \Sigma \to I\!N_0$. If $\kappa(\alpha) = n \geq 1$ then n copies of α are contained in κ. If $\kappa(\alpha) = 0$ then α does not occur in κ. We write $\alpha \in \kappa$ to denote that α appears at least once in κ, i.e. $\kappa(\alpha) \geq 1$. Union of multisets is defined to be addition.

DEFINITION 4.1. A *next step relation* on $\overline{A}$ is a pair $(\to, act)$ consisting of a binary relation $\to$ on $\mathcal{K}(A)$ and a mapping *act* which assigns to each pair (ξ, ξ') of finite elements with $\xi \to \xi'$ a multiset $act(\xi, \xi')$ of atomic actions such that the following conditions (i) - (iv) are fulfilled:

(i) If $\xi \to \eta$ then $\xi \sqsubset \eta$.
(ii) If $\xi_1 \to \xi_2$ and $\xi_1 \sqsubset \eta \sqsubset \xi_2$ then $\xi_1 \to \eta$ and $\eta \to \xi_2$.
(iii) If $\xi \sqsubset \eta$ then there exists $k \geq 2$ and $\xi_1, \xi_2, \ldots, \xi_k \in \mathcal{K}(A)$ such that

$$\xi = \xi_1 \ \to \ \xi_2 \ \to \ \ldots \ \to \ \xi_{k-1} \ \to \ \xi_k = \eta.$$

(iv) Whenever $\xi = \xi_1 \to \xi_2 \to \ldots \to \xi_k = \eta$ and $\xi = \xi_1 \to \xi_2' \to \ldots \to \xi_n' = \eta$ then

$$\bigcup_{1 \leq i < k} act(\xi_i, \xi_{i+1}) \ = \ \bigcup_{1 \leq j < n} act(\xi_j, \xi_{j+1}).$$

Conditions (i) and (iii) assert that the next step relation is compatible with the natural order. By condition (i), whenever η is a possible next step of ξ then η respresents a partial computation of ξ, and by (iii), whenever ξ is a partial computation of η then the intermediate state η can be reached from ξ by performing finitely many steps. Condition (ii) states that whenever ξ_2 can be reached from ξ_1 in one step then each partial computation η which lies between ξ_1 and ξ_2 can be reached from ξ_1 in one step, and there is a step leading from η to ξ_2. Condition (ii) (together with (iv)) reflects the assumption that, whenever the parallel execution of a multiset κ of actions leads from a state ξ_1 to ξ_2 and η is a state between ξ_1 and ξ_2, then κ can be divided into multisets κ_1 and κ_2 such that first performing the actions in κ_1 in parallel, and then the actions in κ_2 leads from ξ_1 to ξ_2 via η. Note that it might be the case that $\xi_1 \to \xi_2$ is a step such that $act(\xi_1, \xi_2)$ consists of more than one action, and that $\xi_1 \to \xi_2$ cannot be broken down into a sequence of steps where in each step only a single action is performed. This is due to the fact that a step might stand for the synchronized execution of atomic steps which we represent by the multiset of all actions which participate in the synchronization. Condition (iv) asserts that each state η is associated with a unique multiset of actions which lead from a previous state ξ to η. In other words, we suppose each state to be associated with its 'history': the multiset of actions (more precisely, the partially ordered set of events) which must be performed to reach η from the initial state $\bot$.

DEFINITION 4.2. If $(\to, act)$ is a next step relation on $\overline{A}$ we say $(\overline{A}, \to, act)$ is a *linear time model with next step relation.* We say $(\overline{A}, \to, act)$ is an *interleaving model* iff for each $x \in A$ there exists an enumeration $\xi_0, \xi_1, \xi_2, \ldots$ of the elements of $\mathcal{K}(x)$ such that

$$\xi_0 = \bot \ \to \ \xi_1 \ \to \ \xi_2 \ \to \ \ldots$$

Otherwise we say $(\overline{A}, \to, act)$ is a *true concurrency model.*

In interleaving models the sets $\mathcal{K}(x)$ are totally ordered w.r.t. the natural order on $\overline{A}$ and the x-paths are exactly the subsequences of the unique sequence (ξ_n) in

$\mathcal{K}(x)$ with $\xi_0 = \bot$ and $\xi_n \to \xi_{n+1}$ for all $n \geq 0$. We say (ξ_n) is the *full x-path.* We refer to the n-th element ξ_n of the (unique) full x-path as the *n-cut* of x and denote it by $x[n]$. In interleaving models, the next step of a computation x is uniquely determined. Because of this, for the case of interleaving models we choose a linear time logic. In contrast, in true concurrency models, where the partial computations does not specify the order in which concurrent events are executed, there might exist several predecessors for a given intermediate state ξ. For this reason, for the true concurrency approach we use a branching time logic, where the predecessors of an intermediate state arise from parallelism, and not from an explicit non-deterministic choice operator.

Each metric-enriched linear time model $\overline{A}$, together with a next step relation of the form $(\to, act)$ where

$$\xi \to \eta \quad \Longleftrightarrow \quad \exists x \in A \; \exists n \in I\!N_0 \;\; (\; \xi = x[n] \;\; \wedge \;\; \eta = x[n+1] \;)$$

is an interleaving model. Vice versa, if there is a next step relation $\to$ on A then a length function on $\overline{A}$ can be defined which turns $\overline{A}$ into a metric-enriched linear time model.

4.2. Linear time logic and interleaving models. We consider a linear time logic LTL which is essentially that of [**23, 7**]. The syntax of LTL is given by:

$$\phi \;::=\; tt \;\mid\; a \;\mid\; \phi_1 \wedge \phi_2 \;\mid\; \neg\phi \;\mid\; X_\alpha\, \phi \;\mid\; Y_\alpha\, \phi \;\mid\; \phi_1\, \mathcal{U}\, \phi_2 \;\mid\; \phi_1\, \mathcal{S}\, \phi_2$$

where $a \in AP$ (AP denotes a set of atomic propositions) and $\alpha \in \Sigma$.

We interpret LTL over arbitrary interleaving models $\overline{A}$ as follows.

DEFINITION 4.3. A *LTL structure* is a 4-tuple $(\overline{A}, \to, act, L)$ consisting of an interleaving model $(\overline{A}, \to, act)$ and an interpretation L of the atomic propositions, i.e. L assigns to each atomic proposition a subset $L(a)$ of $\mathcal{K}(A)$.

Let $(\overline{A}, \to, act, L)$ be a LTL-structure. The elements of $L(a)$ fulfill the condition represented by the atomic proposition a. We identify each computation $x \in A$ with the execution which successively enters the states $x[0], x[1], x[2] \ldots$. In the n-th state $x[n]$, the unique step leading to $x[n+1]$ is performed. A formula ϕ is interpreted over the states of computations which are represented by pairs (x, n) where $x \in A$ is a computation and n a natural number. $(x, n) \models \phi$ means that in the n-th step of the computation x the condition specified by ϕ is fulfilled. An element $x \in A$ satisfies a formula ϕ (denoted by $x \models \phi$) iff ϕ is fulfilled in the initial state, i.e. $(x, 0) \models \phi$. The relation $(x, n) \models \phi$ is defined by structural induction.

$$(x,n) \models tt$$

$$(x,n) \models a \iff x[n] \in L(a)$$

$$(x,n) \models \phi_1 \wedge \phi_2 \iff (x,n) \models \phi_i,\ i=1,2$$

$$(x,n) \models \neg\phi \iff (x,n) \not\models \phi$$

$$(x,n) \models X_\alpha\, \phi \iff (x,n+1) \models \phi \text{ and } \alpha \in act(x[n], x[n+1])$$

$$(x,n) \models Y_\alpha\, \phi \iff n \geq 1,\ (x,n-1) \models \phi,\ \alpha \in act(x[n-1], x[n])$$

$$(x,n) \models \phi_1\, \mathcal{U}\, \phi_2 \iff \text{there exists } k \geq n \text{ s.t. } (x,k) \models \phi_2 \text{ and } (x,j) \models \phi_1,\ j = n, n+1, \ldots, k-1$$

$$(x,n) \models \phi_1\, \mathcal{S}\, \phi_2 \iff \text{there exists } k \leq n \text{ s.t. } (x,k) \models \phi_2 \text{ and } (x,j) \models \phi_1,\ j = k+1, \ldots, n-1, n$$

$Sat(\phi)$ denotes the elements $x \in A$ which satisfy ϕ. X_α and $\mathcal{U}$ are called future operators, Y_α and $\mathcal{S}$ past operators. A *past formula* is any formula which does not contain any occurrence of a future operator. A *future formula* is any formula which does not contain any occurrence of a past operator. For Φ to be a past formula and $\xi \in \mathcal{K}(A)$, there exists $x \in A$ and $n \geq 0$ with $x[n] = \xi$ and $(x,n) \models \Phi$ if and only if $(x,n) \models \Phi$ for all $x \in A$ and $n \geq 0$ with $x[n] = \xi$. We put:

$$F_\Phi = \{\ x[n]\ :\ x \in A,\ n \geq 0,\ (x,n) \models \Phi\ \}$$

We use the following abbreviations. We put:

$$ff = \neg tt, \quad \phi_1 \vee \phi_2 = \neg(\neg\phi_1 \wedge \neg\phi_2), \quad \phi_1 \rightarrow \phi_2 = \neg\phi_1 \vee \phi_2$$

and

$$X\phi = \bigvee_{\alpha\in\Sigma} X_\alpha\phi, \qquad Y\phi = \bigvee_{\alpha\in\Sigma} Y_\alpha\phi,$$

$$\Diamond\phi = tt\, \mathcal{U}\, \phi, \qquad \Box\phi = \neg\Diamond\neg\phi$$

As in [7], we define safety, guarantee, response and persistence formulas to be formulas of the form $\Box\Phi$, $\Diamond\Phi$, $\Box\Diamond\Phi$ and $\Diamond\Box\Phi$ respectively, where Φ is a past formula. A *liveness* formula is an LTL formula of the form

$$\Diamond\left(\bigvee_{i=1}^{n} (\ \Phi_i\ \wedge\ \Diamond\Lambda_i\ )\right)$$

where Φ_i are past formulas and Λ_i are future formulas such that:

- $\Box(\ \bigvee_{i=1}^{n}\ \Phi_i\ )$ is valid.
- The formulas Λ_i are everywhere eventually satisfiable, i.e. for all $1 \leq i \leq n$, $y \in A$ and $N \geq 0$ there exists $x \in A$ and $k \geq N$ such that $x[N] = y[N]$ and $(x,k) \models \Lambda_i$.

Instead of the second condition [7] require that the future formulas Λ_i are satisfiable. In the case of the linear time model Σ^∞ satisfiability is equivalent to our second condition, which can be seen as follows. Let Λ is a satisfiable future formula (satisfiability w.r.t. Σ^∞) and $s \in \Sigma^\infty$, $l \geq 0$ such that $(s,l) \models \Lambda$. Then, for each

$t \in \Lambda^\infty$ and $N \geq 0$, let u be the string $s[N]t$. Then $u[N] = t[N]$ and $(u,k) \models \Lambda$ where $k = N + l$. In order to see that $(u,k) \models \Lambda$ it is essential that Λ does not contain past operators.

LEMMA 4.4. *Let Φ be a past formula.*

(a) $Sat(\ \Box\Phi\ ) = \mathcal{A}(F_\Phi)$ *(a safety property)*
(b) $Sat(\ \Diamond\Phi\ ) = \mathcal{E}(F_\Phi)$ *(a guarantee property)*
(c) $Sat(\ \Box\Diamond\Phi\ ) \setminus \mathcal{K}(M) = \mathcal{R}(F_\Phi)$ *(a response property)*
(d) $Sat(\ \Diamond\Box\Phi\ ) \setminus \mathcal{K}(M) = \mathcal{P}(F_\Phi)$ *(a persistence property)*
(e) *If Λ is a liveness formula then $Sat(\Lambda)$ is a liveness property.*

PROOF. (a) $x \in Sat(\ \Box\Phi\ )$ iff $(x,\perp) \models \Box\Phi$ iff $(x,n) \models \Phi$ for all $n \geq 0$ iff $x[n] \in F_\Phi$ for all $n \geq 0$ iff $x \in \mathcal{A}(F_\Phi)$.
(b) $x \in Sat(\ \Diamond\Phi\ )$ iff $(x,\perp) \models \Diamond\Phi$ iff $(x,n) \models \Phi$ for some $n \geq 0$ iff $x[n] \in F_\Phi$ for some $n \geq 0$ iff $x \in \mathcal{E}(F_\Phi)$.
(c) $x \in Sat(\Box\Diamond\Phi)$ iff $(x,n) \models \Phi$ for infinitely many n iff $x[n] \in F_\Phi$ for infinitely many n iff $x \in \mathcal{R}(F_\Phi)$.
(d) $x \in Sat(\Diamond\Box\Phi)$ iff $(x,n) \models \Phi$ for almost all n iff $x[n] \in F_\Phi$ for almost all n iff $x \in \mathcal{R}(F_\Phi)$.
(e) Let $\xi \in \mathcal{K}(A)$. Then $\xi = y[N]$ for some $y \in A$ and $N \geq 0$. We have to show that there exists $x \in Sat(\Lambda)$ with $x[N] = \xi$. Let

$$\Lambda = \Diamond\left(\bigvee_{i=1}^{n} (\ \Phi_i \wedge \Diamond\Lambda_i\ )\right)$$

Since $\Box(\bigvee \Phi_i)$ is valid, $(y,N) \models \Phi_i$ for some i. Because Λ_i is everywhere eventually satisfiable, there exists $x \in A$ and $k \geq N$ such that $x[N] = \xi$ and $(x,k) \models \Lambda_i$. Since Φ_i is a past formula we get $(x,N) \models \Phi_i$. Since $k \geq N$ we have $(x,N) \models \Diamond\Lambda_i$, and hence

$$(x,N) \models \Phi_i \wedge \Diamond\Lambda_i$$

and therefore $x \models \Lambda$.

□

4.3. Partial order logic and true concurrency models. In this section we briefly introduce the logic $ISTL^*$ [**13, 27**] and show how its formulas can be interpreted over order-enriched linear time models. The reader is cautioned to note that our interpretation of $ISTL^*$ is over more general, non-standard models, but coincides with that of [**27**] for a suitably chosen next step relation. In [**13**] and [**27**] $ISTL^*$ formulas are interpreted over *interleaving sequences* of partial order executions (i.e. linearizations of pomsets of a certain kind), and Mazurkiewicz traces respectively, whereas we give semantics (for syntactically the same formulas) in arbitrary order-enriched linear time models.

A *state formula* of $ISTL^*$ is a formula ϕ given by the grammar:

$$\phi ::= tt \mid a \mid \phi_1 \wedge \phi_2 \mid \neg\phi \mid A\psi$$

where $a \in AP$ is an atomic formula and ψ is a *path formula* built from the following production system:

$$\psi := \phi \mid \psi_1 \wedge \psi_2 \mid \neg\psi \mid X_\alpha\,\psi \mid Y_\alpha\,\psi \mid [\psi_1\,\mathcal{U}\,\psi_2] \mid [\psi_2\,\mathcal{S}\,\psi_2]$$

where ϕ is a state formula and $\alpha \in \Sigma$.

We use the following abbreviations:

$$ff = \neg tt, \quad f_1 \vee f_2 = \neg(\neg f_1 \wedge \neg f_2), \quad f_1 \rightarrow f_2 = \neg f_1 \vee f_2$$

for all state or path formulas f_1, f_2. If ψ, ψ' are path formulas then

$$E\psi = \neg A(\neg\psi), \qquad F\psi = [tt\,\mathcal{U}\,\psi], \qquad G\psi = \neg[tt\,\mathcal{U}\,(\neg\psi)],$$

$$P\psi = [tt\,\mathcal{S}\,\psi], \qquad H\psi = \neg[tt\,\mathcal{S}\,(\neg\psi)],$$

$$X\psi = \bigvee_{p\in\Gamma} X_p\psi, \qquad Y\psi = \bigvee_{p\in\Gamma} Y_p\psi.$$

DEFINITION 4.5. A $ISTL^*$ *structure* is a 4-tuple $(\overline{A}, \rightarrow, act, L)$ where $(\overline{A}, \rightarrow, act)$ is a linear time model with next step relation and L an interpretation of the atomic propositions, i.e. a function which assigns to each atomic proposition a subset $L(a)$ of $\mathcal{K}(A)$ consisting of those states ξ which are supposed to satisfy the condition a.

Let $(\overline{A}, \rightarrow, act, L)$ be a $ISTL^*$ structure. State formulas are interpreted over intermediate states of computations which we represent by pairs (x, ξ) where $x \in A$ and $\xi \in \mathcal{K}(x)$. Path formulas are interpreted over states of observations.

DEFINITION 4.6. Let $(\overline{A}, \rightarrow, act)$ be a linear time model with next step relation. An *observation* on $\overline{A}$ is a sequence $\pi = (\xi_n)_{n\geq 0}$ in $\mathcal{K}(A)$ such that:

- either $\xi_i \rightarrow \xi_{i+1}$ for all $i \geq 0$, or
- there is some $k \geq 0$ such that

$$\xi_0 \rightarrow \xi_1 \rightarrow \xi_2 \rightarrow \dots \rightarrow \xi_k = \xi_{k+1} = \xi_{k+2} = \dots$$

We write $\pi(i)$ to denote the i-th element of π, i.e. if $\pi = (\xi_0, \xi_1, \dots)$ then $\pi(i) = \xi_i$. π is called a *x-observation* iff in addition $\bigsqcup \xi_i = x$. An *initial x-observation* is an x-observation $\pi = (\xi_0, \xi_1, \dots)$ with $\xi_0 = \perp$.

The path quantifiers A and E of $ISTL^*$ range over x-observations. The set of all such observations is an 'Abramhamson structure', i.e. suffix-closed and fusion-closed (cf. [**1, 9, 13**]). Suffix-closedness means that if $(\xi_n)_{n\geq 0}$ is an x-observation then also $(\xi_n)_{n\geq k}$ is an x-observation for arbitrary $k \geq 0$. Fusion-closedness means that if $(\xi_n)_{n\geq 0}$ and $(\eta_n)_{n\geq 0}$ are x-observations such that $\xi_n = \eta_k$ for some $n \geq 0$ and $k \geq 0$ then the sequence

$$\xi_0,\ \xi_1,\ \dots,\ \xi_n = \eta_k,\ \eta_{k+1},\ \eta_{k+2},\ \dots$$

is an x-observation.

A computation x is said to satisfy a state formula ϕ (denoted by $x \models \phi$) iff x satisfies ϕ in its initial state $\perp$, i.e. iff $(x, \perp) \models \phi$. Here $(x, \xi) \models \phi$ where $x \in A$, $\xi \in \mathcal{K}(x)$, is defined by structural induction:

$$(x, \xi) \models tt$$

$$(x, \xi) \models a \iff \xi \in L(a)$$

$$(x, \xi) \models \phi_1 \wedge \phi_2 \iff (x, \xi) \models \phi_i,\ i = 1, 2$$

$$(x, \xi) \models \neg\phi \iff (x, \xi) \not\models \phi$$

$$(x, \xi) \models A\psi \iff (\pi, i) \models \psi \text{ for each } x\text{-observation } \pi \text{ with } \pi(i) = \xi$$

and for each observation $\pi = (\xi_0, \xi_1, \xi_2, \dots)$ and $i \geq 0$:

$$\begin{array}{lcl}
(\pi, i) \models \phi & \iff & (x, \xi_i) \models \phi \text{ where } x = \bigsqcup \xi_n \\
(\pi, i) \models \psi_1 \wedge \psi_2 & \iff & (\pi, i) \models \psi_i,\ i = 1, 2 \\
(\pi, i) \models \neg\psi & \iff & (\pi, i) \not\models \psi \\
(\pi, i) \models X_\alpha\, \psi & \iff & (\pi, i+1) \models \psi,\quad \alpha \in act(\xi_i, \xi_{i+1}) \\
(\pi, i) \models Y_\alpha\, \psi & \iff & i \geq 1 \text{ and } (\pi, i-1) \models \psi,\quad \alpha \in act(\xi_{i-1}, \xi_i) \\
(\pi, i) \models [\psi_1\, \mathcal{U}\, \psi_2] & \iff & \text{there exists } k \geq i \text{ s.t. } (\pi, k) \models \psi_2 \\
 & & \text{and } (\pi, j) \models \psi_1,\ j = i, i+1, \dots, k-1 \\
(\pi, i) \models [\psi_1\, \mathcal{S}\, \psi_2] & \iff & \text{there exists } k \leq i \text{ with } (\pi, k) \models \psi_2 \\
 & & \text{and } (\pi, j) \models \psi_1,\ j = k+1, \dots, i-1, i
\end{array}$$

REMARK 4.7. If $ISTL^*$ formulas are interpreted over a LTL structure $(\overline{A}, \rightarrow, act, L)$ then the quantifiers E and A have the same interpretation. This is because $x[0], x[1], \dots$ is the unique x-observation. In this case the logic $ISTL^*$ reduces to the linear time logic. Let $\widehat{\phi}$ be the LTL formula which arises from a state formula ϕ by removing the quantifiers A and E. Then $x \models_{IST} \phi$ if and only if $x \models_{LT} \widehat{\phi}$. (The index LT, resp. IST, denotes whether $(\overline{A}, \rightarrow, act, L)$ is assumed to be a LTL structure or a $ISTL^*$ structure.)

Let $Sat(\phi)$ be the set of all $x \in D$ which satisfies ϕ:

$$Sat(\phi) \;=\; \{\, x \in D \;:\; x \models \phi \,\}$$

The operators $\mathcal{U}$ and X are called future operators, $\mathcal{S}$ and Y past opertors. A *past formula* is a formula which does not contain any future operators. A future formula is a formula without past operators. Let Φ be a past state formula and $\xi \in \mathcal{K}(A)$. Then $(x, \xi) \models \Phi$ for some $x \in A$ with $\xi \sqsubseteq x$ if and only if $(x, \xi) \models \Phi$ for all $x \in A$ with $\xi \sqsubseteq x$. We define:

$$F_\Phi \;=\; \{\xi \in \mathcal{K}(A) \;:\; (x, \xi) \models \Phi \text{ for some } x \in A\,\}$$

Safety, guarantee, response and persistence properties are given by the forms $AG\Phi$, $EF\Phi$, $EGF\Phi$ and $AFG\Phi$ respectively, where Φ is a past state formula. A *liveness* formula is a state formula of the form

$$EF\left(\bigvee_{i=1}^{n} (\Phi_i \;\wedge\; F\Lambda_i)\right)$$

where Φ_i are past state formulas and Λ_i future state formulas such that

- $AG(\bigvee\ \Phi_i)$ is valid
- Λ_i is everywhere eventually satisfiable, i.e. for each $\xi \in \mathcal{K}(A)$ there exists $x \in A$ and $\eta \in \mathcal{K}(x)$ with:

$$\xi \sqsubseteq \eta \sqsubset x, \quad (x, \eta) \models \Lambda_i$$

LEMMA 4.8. *Let Φ be a past formula. Then:*

(a) $Sat(\ AG\Phi\ ) \;=\; \mathcal{A}(\ F_\Phi\ )$

(b) $Sat(\ EF\Phi\ ) \ = \ \mathcal{E}(\ F_\Phi\ )$
(c) $Sat(\ EGF\Phi\ ) \setminus \mathcal{K}(D) \ = \ \mathcal{R}(\ F_\Phi\ )$
(d) $Sat(\ AFG\Phi\ ) \setminus \mathcal{K}(D) \ = \ \mathcal{P}(\ F_\Phi\ )$
(e) *If Λ is a liveness formula then $Sat(\Lambda)$ is a liveness property.*

PROOF. (a)-(d) The proof is similar to Lemma 4.4.
(e) Let $\Lambda \ = \ EF(\ \bigvee(\Phi_i \wedge F\Lambda_i)\ )$ be a liveness formula. Let $\xi \in \mathcal{K}(A)$. Since Φ_i are past formulas and since $AG(\bigvee \Phi_i)$ is valid, there is some i with $\xi \in F_{\Phi_i}$. Since Λ_i is everywhere eventually satisfiable there exists $x \in A$ and $\eta \in \mathcal{K}(x)$ such that $\xi \sqsubseteq \eta \sqsubset x$ and $(x, \eta) \models \Lambda_i$. Let π be an initial x-observation such that $\pi(j) = \xi$ and $\pi(k) = \eta$ for some $0 \leq j \leq k$. Then $(\pi, k) \models \Lambda_i$ and $(\pi, j) \models \Phi_i$. Hence, $(\pi, j) \models \Phi_i \wedge F\Lambda_i$ and therefore

$$(\pi, 0) \models F(\bigvee(\Phi_i \wedge F\Lambda_i)).$$

Thus, $x \models \Lambda$, i.e. $x \in Sat(\Lambda)$.

□

We have not been able to find syntactic descriptions of obligation and reactivity properties, and also progress properties in the sense of [**7**]. It is an open problem whether it can be shown that each of these classes of formulas is characteristic in the sense that each extensional property corresponds to a syntactic property.

The following lemma shows that our requirement that an x-observations approximates x ensures that each action α which is enabled in some state ξ during some execution of x is actually performed in every linearization of x at a state subsuming (above) ξ, cf maximality [**14**]. If $\alpha \in \Sigma$ then we put:

$$en_\alpha \ = \ EX_\alpha tt, \quad ex_\alpha \ = \ AFX_\alpha tt$$

Then $(x, \xi) \models en(\alpha)$ iff the action α is enabled (i.e. can be performed) in the state ξ. $(x, \xi) \models ex_\alpha$ iff in each execution of x the action α will be performed at some state subsuming ξ.

LEMMA 4.9. *The formula $AG(\ en_\alpha \ \rightarrow \ ex_\alpha)$ holds for all $x \in A$.*

4.4. Examples.

4.4.1. *Interpreting LTL over strings.* The temporal logic used in [**28, 23, 7**] is essentially the same as our logic LTL, the only difference being that our next/previous step operators X_α, Y_α are labelled with actions α. Our interpretation of LTL formulas (using X, Y instead of X_α, Y_α) over the metric-enriched linear time model Σ^∞ coincides with that of [**7**].

The language LTL also includes Lamport's linear time logic (called TL) [**21, 26**]. TL formulas are built from the atomic propositions using the ordinary logical operators $\vee$, $\wedge$ and $\neg$, and the temporal operators $\Box$ and $\Diamond$. The interpretation of [**21**] of TL-formulas over sequences of system states corresponds to our interpretation of TL for the case of the interleaving model $\Theta^\infty \ = \ \Theta^* \ \cup \ \Theta^\omega$. Here Θ denotes a set of (possible) system states, typically mappings from program and control variables to values. Θ^* denotes the set of finite sequences over Θ and Θ^ω the set of infinite sequences. Terminating computations are represented by infinite strings where the final state is repeated infinitely often.

[**26**] defines safety properties as those which are induced by formulas of the form $a \rightarrow \Box b$ where a and b are atomic propositions. Liveness formulas in the sense of [**26**] have the form $\Box(a \rightarrow \Diamond b)$.

4.4.2. *Interpreting ISTL over traces.* The logic $ISTL^*$ of [**27**] is interpreted over Mazurkiewicz traces. We now consider its relationship with our linear model framework.

In [**27**], the starting point is a program described by a tuple $(\Sigma, \iota, \Theta, \overline{y})$ where (Σ, ι) is a concurrent alphabet, Θ a satisfiable predicate (the initial condition) and $\overline{y}$ a finite sequence of program variables. An assignment for $\overline{y}$ is a function J which assigns to each program variable y a value $J(y)$ of the domain of y. The assignments can be viewed as states of the program. Each $\alpha \in \Sigma$ is associated with a pair $< en_\alpha, f_\alpha >$ where en_α is an enabling condition and f_α a transformation that describes the effect of α applied in a state where en_α holds, i.e. f_α is a function which assigns to each assignment J for $\overline{y}$ with $J \models en_\alpha$ an assignment $f_\alpha(J)$. (Here a satisfaction relation $\models$ for the enabling conditions and the assignments for $\overline{y}$ is supposed such that $J \models en_\alpha$ iff α is enabled in J.) Moreover, the commutativity of independent actions and the fact that independent actions can neither disable nor enable each other is required. Formally, for all actions α, β with $\alpha\iota\beta$ and all assignments J for $\overline{y}$:

- If $J \models en_\alpha \wedge en_\beta$ then $f_\alpha(f_\beta(J)) = f_\beta(f_\alpha(J))$.
- If $J \models en_\alpha$ then $J \models en_\beta$ if and only if $f_\alpha(J) \models en_\beta$.

For simplicity, we assume a fixed initial state (an assignment J_{init} for $\overline{y}$). (J_{init} might be either an assignment where the initial condition Θ holds or an 'accessible' assignment, i.e. an assignment J which is reachable from an assignment where the initial condition holds.) We define Σ^*_{init} to be the set of finite strings $s = \alpha_0\alpha_1 \dots \alpha_n$ over Σ such that $J_i \models en_{\alpha_i}$, $i = 0, 1, \dots, n$ where $J_0 = J_{init}$ and $J_{i+1} = f_{\alpha_i}(J_i)$. The interpretation J_{n+1} is called the 'final interpretation' of s and is denoted by fin_s. The commutativity of independent actions implies that if $s \equiv t$ then $fin_s = fin_t$. Hence, we may define $fin_\xi = fin_s$ for each finite trace $\xi = [s]$ where $s \in \Sigma^*_{init}$. Let x be an infinite trace such that $x = [s]$ for some infinite string s over Σ where all prefices of s belong to Σ^*_{init}. x can be viewed as a 'run' in the sense of [**27**] (which is defined as a maximal subset of $[\Sigma^*_{init}]$ consisting of pairwise consistent traces where the consistency of two finite traces ξ_1, ξ_2 means that ξ_1, $\xi_2 \sqsubseteq \xi$ for some finite trace ξ). An 'observation' of x in the sence of [**27**] is a sequence of traces $\xi_0, \xi_1, \dots$ such that ξ_0 is the empty trace, $\xi_{i+1} = \xi_i[\alpha_i]$ for some $\alpha_i \in \Sigma$, and whenever $\xi \sqsubseteq x$ then $\xi \sqsubseteq \xi_i$ for some i. Hence, the observations of x in the sense of [**27**] are exactly the x-observations in the linear time model $[\Sigma^\infty]$, together with the next step relation $\rightarrow$ defined by:

$$x \rightarrow y \iff \exists s \in \Sigma^*, \alpha \in \Sigma x = [s] \wedge y = [s\alpha]$$

where $act([s], [s\alpha]) = \{\alpha\}$ is the multiset containing α.

We assume that there is a satisfaction relation $\models$ for the atomic propositions and the interpretations J for the program variables $\overline{y}$ such that $J \models a$ iff a is true in the state J. This yields an interpretation L for the atomic propositions which assigns to each atomic proposition a a set $L(a)$ of finite traces $\xi \in [\Sigma^*_{init}]$:

$$\xi \in L(a) \text{ iff } fin_\xi \models a.$$

[**27**] associates each run x with an $ISTL^*$-structure and obtains a satisfaction relation $\models_x$ for each run x. This satisfaction relation agrees with ours (in the sense that $\perp \models_x \varphi$ iff $x \models \varphi$) when we deal with the linear time model of traces, the next step relation $\rightarrow$ and the interpretation L as above. Here we replace the next step

operator X in **[27]** by the labelled next step operators X_α, and similarly their first order (state) formulas are substituted by atomic propositions.

Instead of x-observations, which are maximal in the order-theoretic sense, **[19]** use arbitrary observations (ξ_n) in $\mathcal{K}(x)$ as executions of x; for example, the latter admits non-maximal Mazurkiewicz traces. In **[19]** a computation x in a state ξ satisfies a formula of the form $E\phi$ iff there exists an observation π in $\mathcal{K}(x)$ starting in ξ with $(\pi, 0) \models \phi$. Notice that it is not required that π approximates x, i.e. the case $\bigsqcup \pi(i) \sqsubset x$ is allowed. For instance, the formula

$$\Phi = EGX_\alpha tt$$

is satisfied in the approach of **[19]** by the trace $[s]$, $s = \beta\alpha\alpha\alpha\ldots$, where $\alpha \,\iota\, \beta$, but not in our framework. This is because

$$[\alpha] \to [\alpha\alpha] \to [\alpha\alpha\alpha] \to \ldots$$

is considered an execution of $[s]$ in **[19]**, but not in this paper.

Another useful next step relation on $[\Sigma^\infty]$ is given by:

$$x \Rightarrow y$$

iff there exists pairwise independent actions $\alpha_1, \ldots, \alpha_n \in \Sigma$ such that $x[\alpha_1 \ldots \alpha_n] = y$. The associated multiset of actions is

$$act(\ x,\ x[\alpha_1, \ldots, \alpha_n]\ ) = \text{multiset consisting of } \alpha_1, \ldots, \alpha_n.$$

This next step relation allows the parallel execution of pairwise independent actions in one step. The interpretation of $ISTL^*$ formulas over the $ISTL^*$ structure

$$([\Sigma^\infty], \Rightarrow, act, L)$$

differs from the interpretation over $([\Sigma^\infty], \to, act, L)$ in the next (resp. previous) step operators X_α (resp. Y_α).

LEMMA 4.10. *If ϕ is a formula which does not contain the operators X_α and Y_α then an infinite trace x satisfies ϕ w.r.t. the next step relation $\to$ if and only if ϕ is satisfied by x using the interpretation based on the next step relation $\Rightarrow$.*

If $ISTL^*$ is used to formulate real-time constraints such as 'a process responds to a request within 3 time units', and if we suppose that each atomic action can be executed in a single time unit, the next step relation $\to$ is not helpful since it ignores the fact that the parallel execution of pairwise independent actions $\alpha_1, \ldots, \alpha_n$ can be performed within a single time unit. Consider the formula

$$\phi = EG(Y_\beta tt \to XX_\alpha tt)$$

where β stands for an (input-)action which is performed by a handshake mechanism and where α is an (output-)action representing the acknowledge for the receipt of the message transmitted by β. Then ϕ ensures the existence of an execution which satisfies the following: whenever the system receives a message it acknowledges the receipt after two time units. Let $s = \beta\gamma\alpha t$ where $\beta \,\iota\, \gamma$, $\neg(\ \alpha \,\iota\, \beta\ )$ and $\neg(\ \alpha \,\iota\, \gamma\ )$ and where $t = \surd\surd\surd\ldots$. One might think of γ as an input-action where the message is transmitted on a channel different from that which is used for β (hence β and γ can be performed in parallel) and the acknowledge sent by α consists of a message that uses an information which is given by γ (hence α and γ are dependent). Using the next step relation $\Rightarrow$ we get that the trace $[s]$ satisfies ϕ. By means of $\to$ the trace $[s]$ does not satisfy ϕ.

4.4.3. *Interpreting $ISTL$ over pomsets.* When considering the order-enriched linear time model Pom^{∞} there are two natural ways to define the next step relation.

The first possibility is to define the step relation $x \to y$ iff $x \sqsubset y$ and whenever $x \sqsubseteq z \sqsubseteq y$ then either $x = z$ or $z = y$. Then $x \to y$ iff $x = y\lceil S$ where S arises from the event set of y by removing a single event e of maximal depth. If α is the label of this event e in y then we put $act(x, y) = \{\alpha\}$.

[**13**] proposes an interpretation of $ISTL^*$ over pomsets of a certain kind, called 'partial order executions'. In the approach of [**13**] the actions α are associated with an operation which explains how the variables of a system are modified when α is executed. A partial order execution is then a pomset together with an initial 'snapshot' (i.e. a partial function from variables to values) such that each pair of events e, e' which affect the same variables are ordered, i.e. either $e \leq e'$ or $e' \leq e$. In the approach of [**13**] intermediate states of a computation represented by a partial order execution x are 'slices', i.e. a left-closed finite set S' of the event set of x. Hence, a slice of a pomset x can be identified with a finite pomset $\xi \in \mathcal{K}(x)$ which is an intermediate state in our approach. [**13**] interpret path formulas over 'acceptable paths': if x is a partial order execution then an acceptable path of x is a sequence (S_n) of x-slices such that $S_n = S_{n+1} \setminus \{e\}$ for some maximal event e in S_{n+1} and such that each event e of x is contained in some slice S_n. Hence, an acceptable path is an x-observation w.r.t. the next step relation $\to$. Identifying partial order executions and pomsets we obtain that the interpretation of $ISTL$ in the sense of [**13**] agrees with our interpretation using the linear time model of pomsets and the next step relation $\to$.

Secondly, we consider the next step relation $\Rightarrow$ defined as follows. Let $y = (S, \leq, l)$ and $x = y\lceil S'$ where $S' \subset S$ is left-closed. Then $x \Rightarrow y$ iff, for all $e, e' \in S \in S'$, either $e = e'$ or $\neg(e \leq e') \wedge (e' \leq e)$. I.e. $x \Rightarrow y$ iff the events in $S \setminus S'$ are pairwise independent. In this case the step from x to y stands for the parallel execution of the events $S \setminus S'$. We define $act(x, y)$ to be multiset of all actions $l(e)$, $e \in S \setminus S'$.

5. Conclusion and Further Work

We have formulated an abstract, axiomatically given notion of a *linear time* model, and considered classes of behavioural properties in such models. Our framework admits the interleaving models, as well as some 'true concurrency' models such as Mazurkiewicz traces and pomsets as special cases, but it does not handle full non-determinism. In this general framework we have been able to obtain extensional, topological and temporal characterizations of classes of properties including safety and liveness, generalising many of the results of [**3, 7, 19**]. As yet, we do not know how to admit the automata-theoretic characterization of [**7**] into our framework, and how to syntactically characterize properties such as reactivity. This is the subject of future study.

References

[1] K. Abrahamson, *Decidability and expressiveness of logics of programs*, Ph.D. Thesis, University of Washington at Seattle, 1980.

[2] S. Abramsky, A. Jung, *Domain Theory*, In S. Abramsky, D.M. Gabbay and T.S.E. Maibaum, editors, Handbook of Logic in Computer Science, vol. 3, Clarendon Press, 1994.

[3] B. Alpern, F. Schneider, *Defining liveness*, Information Processing Letters **21**, 1985, 181–185.

[4] B. Alpern, F. Schneider, *Recognizing safety and liveness*, Distributed Computing **2**, 1987, 117–126.

[5] J.W. de Bakker, J.H.A. Warmerdam, *Metric pomset semantics for a concurrent language with recursion*, In I. Guessarian, editor, Semantics of Systems of Concurrent Processes, LNCS vol. 469, Springer-Verlag, 1990, 21–49.

[6] E.M. Clarke, E.A. Emerson, *Design and Synthesis of Synchronization Skeletons using Branching Time Temporal Logic*, In Proc. Workshop on Logics of Programs, LNCS vol. 131, Springer-Verlag, 1981.

[7] E. Chang, Z. Manna, A. Pnueli, *The Safety-Progress Classification*, In Proc. Computer and System Science, NATO Advanced Science Institute Series, Springer-Verlag, 1992.

[8] E. Chang, Z. Manna, A. Pnueli, *Characterization of Temporal Property Classes*, In W. Kuich, editor, Proc. ICALP92, LNCS vol. 623, Springer-Verlag, 1992, 474–486.

[9] C. Courcoubetis, M. Vardi, P. Wolper, *Reasoning about fair concurrent programs*, In Proc. 18th ACM Symposium on Theory of Computing, Berkeley, ACM Press, 1986.

[10] R. Engelking, *General Topology*, Sigma Series in Pure Mathematics, vol. 6, Heldermann Verlag, Berlin, 1989.

[11] G. Gierz, H. Hofmann, K. Keimel, J. Lawson, M. Mislove, D. Scott, *A Compendium of Continuous Lattices*, Springer-Verlag, 1980.

[12] U. Goltz, R. Loogen, *Modelling Nondeterministic Concurrent Processes with Event Structures*, Fundamenta Informaticae **14** 1 (1991) 39–74.

[13] S. Katz, D. Peled, *Interleaving Set Temporal Logic*, Theoretical Computer Science **75** 3 (1990) 21–43.

[14] M. Kwiatkowska, *Event Fairness and Non-Interleaving Concurrency*, Formal Aspects of Computing **1** 3 (1989) 213–228.

[15] M. Kwiatkowska, *Defining Process Fairness for Non-Interleaving Concurrency.* In Proc. Foundations of Software Technology and Theoretical Computer Science, LNCS vol. 472, Springer-Verlag, 1990, 286–300.

[16] M. Kwiatkowska, *A metric for traces*, Information Processing Letters **35** (1990) 129–135.

[17] M. Kwiatkowska. *On the domain of traces and sequential composition.* In S. Abramsky and T.S.E.. Maibaum, editors, Proc. 16th Coll. on Trees in Algebra and Programming (CAAP'91), LNCS vol. 493, Springer-Verlag, 1991, 42–56.

[18] M. Kwiatkowska. *On topological characterization of behavioural properties.* In G. Reed, A. Roscoe, and R. Wachter, editors, Topology and Category Theory in Computer Science, Oxford University Press, 1991, 153–177.

[19] M. Kwiatkowska, D. Peled, W. Penczek, *A Hierarchy of Partial Order Temporal Properties.* In Proc. Temporal Logic, LNCS vol. 827, Springer-Verlag, 1994, 398–414.

[20] L. Lamport, *Proving the Correctness of Multiprocess Programs*, IEEE Trans. Software Engineering **SE-3** 2, (1977) 125–143.

[21] L. Lamport, *Specifying Concurrent Program Modules*, ACM Transactions on Programming Languages and Systems **5** 2 (1983).

[22] M. Majster-Cederbaum, C. Baier, *Metric Completion versus Ideal Completion.* To appear in Theoretical Computer Science.

[23] Z. Manna, A. Pnueli, *A Hierarchy of Temporal Properties.* In Proc. 9th ACM Symposium on Principles of Distributed Computing, ACM Press, 1990, 377–408.

[24] A. Mazurkiewicz, *Basic notions of trace theory.* In Linear Time, Branching Time and Partial Order in Logics and Models for Concurrency, LNCS vol. 354, Springer-Verlag, 1988, 25–34.

[25] R. Milner, *Communication and Concurrency*, Prentice Hall, 1989.

[26] S. Owicki, L. Lamport, *Proving Liveness Properties of Concurrent Programs*, ACM Transactions on Programming Languages and Systems, **4** 3 (1982) 455–495.

[27] D. Peled, A. Pnueli, *Proving Partial Order Liveness Properties.* In Proc. ICALP'90, Warwick, LNCS vol. 443, Springer-Verlag, 553–571.

[28] A. Pnueli, *The Temporal Logic of Programs*, Proc. 18th Ann. Symp. on Foundations of Computer Science, Providence, IEEE Press, 1977.

[29] V. Pratt, *The Pomset Model of Parallel Processes: Unifying the Temporal and the Spatial.* In Proc. Seminar on Concurrency, LNCS vol. 197, Springer-Verlag, 1984.

[30] W. Reisig, *Partial Order Semantics versus Interleaving Semantics for CSP-like Languages and its Impact on Fairness.* In Proc. ICALP'84, LNCS vol. 172, Springer-Verlag, 1984, 403–413.

[31] W. Reisig, *Elements of a Temporal Logic Coping with Concurrency*, SFB-Bericht 342/23, 92A, Techn. Universität München, 1992.

[32] W. Thomas, *Automata on Infinite Objects.* In J. van Leeuwen, editor, Handbook of Theoretical Computer Science vol. B, North-Holland, 1990, 135–191.

[33] G. Winskel, *An introduction to event structures.* In Linear Time, Branching Time and Partial Order in Models and Logics for Concurrency, LNCS vol. 354, Springer-Verlag, 1988, 364–397.

Fakultät für Mathematik & Informatik, Universität Mannheim, 68131 Mannheim, Germany

E-mail address: baier@informatik.uni-mannheim.de

School of Computer Science, University of Birmingham, Edgbaston, Birmingham B15 2TT, UK

E-mail address: M.Z.Kwiatkowska@cs.bham.ac.uk

DIMACS Series in Discrete Mathematics
and Theoretical Computer Science
Volume **29**, 1997

Linear Time Temporal Logics over Mazurkiewicz Traces*

Madhavan Mukund and P.S. Thiagarajan
School of Mathematics, SPIC Science Foundation,
92 G N Chetty Rd, Madras 600 017, India
E-mail: {madhavan,pst}@ssf.ernet.in

Abstract

Temporal logics are a well-established tool for specifying and reasoning about the computations performed by distributed systems. Although temporal logics are interpreted over sequences, it is often the case that such sequences can be gathered together into equivalence classes where all members of an equivalence class represent the same partially ordered stretch of behaviour of the system. This appears to have important implications for improving the practical efficiency of automated verification methods based on temporal logics. With this as motivation, we study logics that are directly interpreted over partial orders. We survey a number of linear time temporal logics whose underlying frames are Mazurkiewicz traces. We describe automata theoretic methods for solving the satisfiability and model checking problems for these logics. It turns out that we still do not know what the "canonical" linear time temporal logic over Mazurkiewicz traces looks like. We identify here the criteria that should be met by this elusive logic.

Introduction

Propositional Linear time Temporal Logic (LTL) proposed by Pnueli [Pnu] has become a well established tool for specifying and reasoning about complex distributed behaviours [MP]. A central feature of LTL is that its formulas are interpreted over infinite sequences. In applications of LTL, the infinite sequences consist of the runs of a distributed system with each run being an infinite sequence of states assumed by the system or an infinite sequence of actions executed by the system during the course of a computation. Interesting distributed systems consist of a number of autonomous sequential agents that coordinate their behaviour with the help of some communication mechanism. In such systems, substantial portions of a computation will consist of causally independent tasks performed by different agents at separate locations. Consequently a single partially ordered stretch of behaviour of the system will be modelled by many different runs that differ from each other only

1991 *Mathematics Subject Classification.* Primary 68Q60, 68Q05, 68Q45, 03B45.

*This paper originally appeared in W. Penczek (Ed.), *Mathematical Foundations of Computer Science (MFCS) 1996, Proceedings*, Lecture Notes in Computer Science, Vol 1113, Springer-Verlag (1996) 62–92.

in the order in which they record causally independent occurrences of actions. This kind of run-based view is often referred to as an interleaved semantics of distributed systems.

The interleaved view of the behaviour of distributed systems has proved to be very successful and popular. However it has been known for some time that the practical effectiveness of LTL and related formalisms can be often enhanced by modelling and analyzing the concerned behaviours in terms of partial orders rather than sequences.

In typical applications, an LTL formula constitutes the specification of the system behaviour and the verification problem consists of checking whether every run of the system is a model of the formula and therefore whether the system meets the specification. The property expressed by the specification is very often of the kind where either *all* the interleaved runs corresponding to a single partially ordered computation have the property or *none* of the interleavings have the property. A typical example of such a property is freedom from deadlock, as pointed out by Valmari [Val]. As a result, it suffices to verify the desired property for just one representative run of each partially ordered computation. The resulting saving in running time and memory usage can be substantial in practice [GW]. This is the background and motivation underlying the so called partial order based verification methods which are a subject of active research [GW, KP, Val].

There is an alternative way to exploit non-sequential behaviours and the attendant partial order based verification methods. It consists of developing temporal logics and related techniques that can be *directly* applied to specify and reason about the properties of partial order based runs of a distributed system. In this paper we survey linear time temporal logics that have arisen from this approach.

In going from sequences to partial orders it is easy to go overboard because so many possibilities are available. Fortunately, in the context of distributed behaviours, Mazurkiewicz has formulated a tractable and yet very fruitful way of passing from sequences to partial orders [Maz]. The resulting restricted partial orders are known as Mazurkiewicz traces, often called—as we shall do here—just traces. The theory of traces is well developed [Die, DR] and is strongly related to the theory of other well known formalisms such as Petri nets and event structures. Further, the classical theory of ω-regular (word) languages in terms of its logical, algebraic and automata-theoretic aspects has been successfully extended to ω-regular trace languages [EM, GP]. Finally, the structures that underlie the partial order based verification methods being developed recently can be almost always be viewed as traces.

Hence there is a good deal of motivation for formulating linear time temporal logics that are to be directly interpreted over traces. Many such logics are now available. In the present survey, we will mainly concentrate on the ones that fulfill two criteria:

(i) The logic should be expressible within the first order theory of traces.

(ii) The satisfiability problem for the logic should admit a treatment in terms of asynchronous Büchi automata.

This seemingly arbitrary choice of criteria can be justified as follows. LTL is *the* linear time temporal logic over sequences in that it is equivalent in expressive power to the first order theory of sequences [Zuc]. We consider the task of identifying the counterpart of LTL for traces to be an important one both from a theoretical and practical standpoint (see the last portion of Section 4). At present we do not know what this counterpart of LTL looks like. However, it seems a good starting point to concentrate on those linear time temporal logics that are at least no more expressive than the first order theory of traces.

As for the second criterion, an appealing feature of LTL is that its satisfiability and model checking problems can be transparently solved using Büchi automata [VW]. This has led to a clean separation of the logical and combinatorial aspects of these problems, thus contributing to the development of automated verification methods and related optimization techniques. The evidence available at present suggests that asynchronous Büchi automata are an appropriate machine model for dealing with ω-regular trace languages. Hence it seems worthwhile to lift the interplay between LTL and Büchi automata to the level of traces.

In the next section we review the basic aspects of traces. In Section 2 we describe asynchronous Büchi automata and present our version of these automata called, for want of a better name, A2-automata. In Section 3, the heart of the paper, we present the logic TrPTL (Trace based Propositional Temporal logic of Linear time) and two of its sublogics $\mathrm{TrPTL}^{\mathrm{con}}$ and $\mathrm{TrPTL}^{\otimes}$. The logic TrPTL is directly interpreted over traces. We show that the satisfiability and model checking problems for TrPTL can be solved using A2-automata. We then show that the syntactic restrictions imposed to obtain $\mathrm{TrPTL}^{\mathrm{con}}$ and $\mathrm{TrPTL}^{\otimes}$ lead to corresponding simplifications in the world of automata. After presenting these results we survey a number of other temporal logics that use traces as their underlying frames. In Section 4 we show that TrPTL is expressible within the first order theory of traces. The final section contains concluding remarks.

Most of the results will be presented without proofs. The proofs are either available in the literature or can be easily manufactured using the results available in the literature.

1 Traces

The starting point for trace theory is a trace alphabet (Σ, I), where Σ, the alphabet, is a finite set and $I \subseteq \Sigma\times\Sigma$ is an irreflexive and symmetric independence relation. In most applications, Σ consists of the actions performed by a distributed system while I captures a strong static notion of causal independence between actions. The idea is that contiguous independent actions occur with no causal order between them. Thus, every sequence of actions from Σ corresponds to an interleaved observation of a partially-ordered stretch of system behaviour. This leads to a natural equivalence relation over execution sequences: two sequences are equated iff they correspond to different interleavings of the same partially-ordered stretch of behaviour.

To formulate this equivalence relation precisely, we need some terminology. For the rest of the section we fix a trace alphabet (Σ, I) and let a, b range over Σ. $D = (\Sigma \times \Sigma) - I$ is called the dependency relation. Note that D is reflexive and symmetric. A set $p \subseteq \Sigma$ is called a D-clique iff $p \times p \subseteq D$. We set $\Sigma^{\infty} = \Sigma^* \cup \Sigma^{\omega}$ where Σ^* is the set of finite words over Σ and Σ^{ω} is the set of infinite words over Σ. We let σ, σ' with or without subscripts range over Σ^{∞} and τ, τ' with or without subscripts range over Σ^*. The equivalence relation $\sim_I \subseteq \Sigma^\infty \times \Sigma^\infty$ induced by I is given by:

$$\sigma \sim_I \sigma' \text{ iff } \sigma \restriction p = \sigma' \restriction p \text{ for every } D\text{-clique } p.$$

Here and elsewhere, if A is a finite set, $\rho \in A^\infty$ and $B \subseteq A$ then $\rho \restriction B$ is the sequence obtained by erasing from ρ all occurrences of letters in $A - B$.

Clearly $\sim_I$ is an equivalence relation. Notice that if $\sigma = \tau ab\sigma_1$ and $\sigma' = \tau ba\sigma_1$ with $(a, b) \in I$ then $\sigma \sim_I \sigma'$. Thus σ and σ' are identified if they differ only in the order of appearance of a pair of adjacent independent actions. In fact, for finite words, an alternative way to characterize $\sim_I$ is to say that $\sigma \sim_I \sigma'$ iff σ' can be obtained from σ by a finite sequence of permutations of adjacent independent actions. Unfortunately, the definition of $\sim_I$ in terms of permutations is too naïve to be transported to infinite words, which is why we work with the less intuitive definition presented here.

The equivalence classes generated by $\sim_I$ are called *(Mazurkiewicz) traces*. The theory of traces is well developed and documented—see [Die, DR] for basic material as well as a substantial number of references to related work.

Traces have many equivalent representations. We shall view traces as special kinds of labelled partial orders. Since sequences can be viewed as labelled *total* orders, this representation emphasizes that traces are an elegant and non-trivial generalization of sequences.

Recall that a Σ-labelled poset is a structure $F = (E, \leq, \lambda)$ where $\leq$ is a partial order on the set E and $\lambda : E \to \Sigma$ is a labelling function. The *covering relation* $\lessdot \subseteq E \times E$ is given by: $e \lessdot e'$ iff $e < e'$ (i.e., $e \leq e'$ and $e \neq e'$) and for every $e'' \in E$, $e \leq e'' \leq e'$ implies $e = e''$ or $e'' = e'$.

For $X \subseteq E$ we define $\downarrow X$ to be the set $\{y \mid y \leq x \text{ for some } x \in X\}$. If X is a singleton $\{x\}$, we write $\downarrow x$ instead of $\downarrow\{x\}$.

We can now formulate traces in terms of labelled partial orders. A *trace* over (Σ, I) is a Σ-labelled poset $F = (E, \leq, \lambda)$ which satisfies the following conditions.

- E is a countable set.
- For each $e \in E$, $\downarrow e$ is a finite set.
- For all $e, e' \in E$, if $e \lessdot e'$ then $(\lambda(e), \lambda(e')) \in D$.
- For all $e, e' \in E$, if $(\lambda(e), \lambda(e')) \in D$ then $e \leq e'$ or $e' \leq e$.

Let $TR(\Sigma, I)$ denote the set of Σ-labelled posets that satisfy the definition above. We now sketch briefly the proof that $\Sigma^\infty/{\sim_I}$ and $TR(\Sigma, I)$ represent the same class of objects. We construct representation maps $\mathsf{str} : \Sigma^\infty \to TR(\Sigma, I)$ and $\mathsf{trs} : TR(\Sigma, I) \to \Sigma^\infty/\sim_I$ and state some results which show that these maps are "inverses" of each other. We shall not prove these results. The details can be easily obtained using the constructions developed in [WN] for relating traces and event structures.

Henceforth, we will not distinguish between isomorphic elements in $TR(\Sigma, I)$. In other words, whenever we write $F = F'$ for traces $F = (E, \leq, \lambda)$ and $F' = (E', \leq', \lambda')$, we mean that there is a label-preserving isomorphism between F and F'.

For $\sigma \in \Sigma^\infty$, $[\sigma]$ stands for the $\sim_I$-equivalence class containing σ. We use $\preceq$ to describe the usual prefix ordering over sequences. Let $\mathrm{prf}(\sigma)$ denote the set of finite prefixes of σ.

We now define $\mathsf{str} : \Sigma^\infty \to TR(\Sigma, I)$. Let $\sigma \in \Sigma^\infty$. Then $\mathsf{str}(\sigma) = (E, \leq, \lambda)$ where:

- $E = \{\tau a \mid \tau a \in \mathrm{prf}(\sigma)\}$. Recall that $\tau \in \Sigma^*$ and $a \in \Sigma$. Thus $E = \mathrm{prf}(\sigma) - \{\varepsilon\}$, where ε is the null string.
- $\leq \subseteq E \times E$ is the least partial order which satisfies:
  For all $\tau a, \tau' b \in E$, if $\tau a \preceq \tau' b$ and $(a, b) \in D$ then $\tau a \leq \tau' b$.
- For $\tau a \in E$, $\lambda(\tau a) = a$.

The map str induces a natural map str' from $\Sigma^\infty / \sim_I$ to $TR(\Sigma, I)$ defined by $\mathsf{str}'([\sigma]) = \mathsf{str}(\sigma)$. One can show that if $\sigma, \sigma' \in \Sigma^\infty$, then $\sigma \sim_I \sigma'$ iff $\mathsf{str}(\sigma) = \mathsf{str}(\sigma')$. This observation guarantees that str' is well defined. In fact, henceforth we shall write str to denote both str and str'.

To go in the other direction let $F = (E, \leq, \lambda)$ be a trace over (Σ, I). Then $\rho \in E^\infty$ is called a linearization of F iff every $e \in E$ appears exactly once in ρ and, moreover, whenever $e, e' \in E$ and $e < e'$, e appears before e' in ρ.

As usual, we can extend the labelling function $\lambda : E \to \Sigma$ to words over E in a canonical way. If $\rho = e_0 e_1 \ldots$ is a word in E^∞ then $\lambda(\rho)$ denotes the corresponding word $\lambda(e_0)\lambda(e_1)\ldots$ in Σ^∞. We can now define the map $\mathsf{trs} : TR(\Sigma, I) \to \Sigma^\infty / \sim_I$ as follows:

$$\mathsf{trs}(F) = \{\lambda(\rho) \mid \rho \text{ is a linearization of } F\}.$$

Proposition 1.1

(i) *For every* $\sigma \in \Sigma^\infty$, $\mathsf{trs}(\mathsf{str}(\sigma)) = [\sigma]$.

(ii) *For every* $F \in TR(\Sigma, I)$, $\mathsf{str}(\mathsf{trs}(F)) = F$.

This result justifies our claim that $\Sigma^\infty / \sim_I$ and $TR(\Sigma, I)$ are indeed two equivalent ways of talking about the same class of objects.

In the poset representation of traces, finite configurations play the same role that finite prefixes do in sequences. Let $F = (E, \leq, \lambda)$ be a trace over (Σ, I). Then $c \subseteq E$ is a *configuration* iff c is finite and $\downarrow c = c$. We let $\mathcal{C}_F$ denote the set of configurations of F. Notice that $\emptyset$, the empty set, is a configuration. It is the least configuration under set inclusion. More importantly, $\downarrow e$ is a configuration for every event e. These "pointed" configurations associated with the events are also called *prime configurations*. They constitute the building blocks for the Scott domains induced by traces [NPW]. We shall see that they also play a fundamental role in defining linear time temporal logics over traces.

We now turn our attention to distributed alphabets. Distributed alphabets can be viewed as "implementations" of trace alphabets. They form the basis for defining machine models with a built-in notion of independence which recognize trace languages.

Let $\mathcal{P}$ be a finite set of sequential agents called *processes*. A distributed alphabet is a family $\{\Sigma_p\}_{p \in \mathcal{P}}$ where Σ_p is a finite non-empty alphabet for each $p \in \mathcal{P}$. The idea is that whenever an action from Σ_p occurs, the agent p must participate in it. Hence the agents can constrain each other's behaviour, both directly *and* indirectly.

Trace alphabets and distributed alphabets are closely related to each other. Let $\widetilde{\Sigma} = \{\Sigma_p\}_{p\in\mathcal{P}}$ be a distributed alphabet. Then $\Sigma_\mathcal{P}$, the global alphabet associated with $\widetilde{\Sigma}$, is the collection $\bigcup_{p\in\mathcal{P}} \Sigma_p$. The distribution of $\Sigma_\mathcal{P}$ over $\mathcal{P}$ can be described using a *location function* $loc_{\widetilde{\Sigma}} : \Sigma_\mathcal{P} \to 2^\mathcal{P}$ defined as follows:

$$loc_{\widetilde{\Sigma}}(a) = \{p \mid a \in \Sigma_p\}.$$

This in turn induces the relation $I_{\widetilde{\Sigma}} \subseteq \Sigma_\mathcal{P} \times \Sigma_\mathcal{P}$ given by:

$$(a, b) \in I_{\widetilde{\Sigma}} \text{ iff } loc_{\widetilde{\Sigma}}(a) \cap loc_{\widetilde{\Sigma}}(b) = \emptyset.$$

Clearly $I_{\widetilde{\Sigma}}$ is irreflexive and symmetric and hence $(\Sigma_\mathcal{P}, I_{\widetilde{\Sigma}})$ is a trace alphabet. Thus every distributed alphabet canonically induces a trace alphabet. Two actions are independent according to $\widetilde{\Sigma}$ if they are executed by disjoint sets of processes. Henceforth, we write loc for $loc_{\widetilde{\Sigma}}$ whenever $\widetilde{\Sigma}$ is clear from the context.

Going in the other direction there are, in general, many different ways to implement a trace alphabet as a distributed alphabet. A standard approach is to create a separate agent for each maximal D-clique generated by (Σ, I). Recall that a D-clique of (Σ, I) is a non-empty subset $p \subseteq \Sigma$ such that $p \times p \subseteq D$. Let $\mathcal{P}$ be the set of maximal D-cliques of (Σ, I). This set of processes induces the distributed alphabet $\widetilde{\Sigma} = \{\Sigma_p\}_{p\in\mathcal{P}}$ where $\Sigma_p = p$ for every process p. The alphabet $\widetilde{\Sigma}$ implements (Σ, I) in the sense that the canonical trace alphabet induced by it is exactly (Σ, I). In other words, $\Sigma_\mathcal{P} = \Sigma$ and $I_{\widetilde{\Sigma}} = I$.

For example, consider the trace alphabet (Σ, I) where $\Sigma = \{a, b, d\}$ and $I = \{(a, b), (b, a)\}$. The canonical D-clique implementation of (Σ, I) yields the distributed alphabet $\widetilde{\Sigma} = \{\{a, d\}, \{d, b\}\}$.

As mentioned earlier, distributed alphabets play a crucial role in the automata-theoretic aspects of trace theory. The fundamental result of Zielonka [Zie] says that every regular trace language over (Σ, I) can be recognized by an asynchronous automaton over a distributed alphabet $\widetilde{\Sigma}$ which implements (Σ, I). This result has been extended to ω-regular trace languages in terms of asynchronous Büchi automata by Gastin and Petit [GP].

Distributed alphabets arise naturally in a variety of models of distributed systems. In particular they are associated with the restricted but very useful model of a distributed system consisting of a network of sequential agents that coordinate their behaviour by performing common actions together. The linear time temporal logics that we consider in this paper will be based on distributed alphabets.

We conclude this section with a technical remark. Most of the theory of traces presented in this paper, including the automata-theoretic and logical aspects, constitutes a natural and conservative extension of the existing theory in the sequential setting. The sequential theory can almost always be recovered by setting $I = \emptyset$ when dealing with trace alphabets. Correspondingly, when dealing with distributed alphabets, the sequential case corresponds to having just one agent—i.e., $|\mathcal{P}| = 1$.

2 Automata over Infinite Traces

From now on we shall focus on infinite traces. With a little additional work most of the material we shall present on automata and logics can be extended to handle finite traces as well. Through the rest of this section we fix a distributed alphabet $\widetilde{\Sigma} = \{\Sigma_p\}_{p\in\mathcal{P}}$ with the induced trace alphabet (Σ, I), where $\Sigma = \bigcup_{p\in\mathcal{P}} \Sigma_p$ and $I = \{(a,b) \mid \mathrm{loc}(a) \cap \mathrm{loc}(b) = \emptyset\}$.

The terminology and notational conventions developed in the previous section are assumed here as well. We will be dealing with many $\mathcal{P}$-indexed families. For convenience we shall often write $\{X_p\}$ to denote the $\mathcal{P}$-indexed family $\{X_p\}_{p\in\mathcal{P}}$. A similar convention will be followed in dealing with Σ-indexed families: $\{Y_a\}$ will denote the family $\{Y_a\}_{a\in\Sigma}$.

Asynchronous Büchi automata, due to Gastin and Petit [GP], are the basic class of automata operating over infinite traces. They constitute a common generalization of the asynchronous automata of Zielonka [Zie] operating over finite traces and a mild variant of the classical Büchi automata operating over infinite sequences. We shall consider here a number of variants of asynchronous Büchi automata, each with a slightly different acceptance condition.

We begin with a brief and slightly non-standard presentation of Büchi automata. A word ω-automaton over Σ is a pair $\mathcal{B} = (TS, \mathcal{T})$ where

- $TS = (S, \{\rightarrow_a\}, S_{in})$ is a finite state transition system over Σ. In other words, S is a finite set of states, $\rightarrow_a \subseteq S \times S$ is an a-labelled transition relation for each $a \in \Sigma$ and $S_{in} \subseteq S$ is a set of initial states.
- $\mathcal{T}$ is an acceptance table accompanied by an acceptance condition.

Before considering a number of possibilities for $\mathcal{T}$, let us define the notion of a run. The Σ-indexed family of transition relations $\{\rightarrow_a\}$ induces a global transition relation $\rightarrow_\mathcal{B} \subseteq S \times \Sigma \times S$ given by $s \xrightarrow{a}_\mathcal{B} s'$ iff $(s, s') \in \rightarrow_a$. Where $\mathcal{B}$ is clear from the context $\rightarrow_\mathcal{B}$ will be written as $\rightarrow$.

Let $\sigma \in \Sigma^\omega$ (i.e., $\sigma : \omega \rightarrow \Sigma$ where, as usual, $\omega = \{0, 1, 2, \ldots\}$ is the set of natural numbers). A *run* of TS over σ is a map $\rho : \omega \rightarrow S$ such that $\rho(0) \in S_{in}$ and $\rho(i) \xrightarrow{\sigma(i)} \rho(i{+}1)$ for every $i \geq 0$.

The set of states encountered infinitely often along the run ρ is denoted $\inf(\rho)$: $\inf(\rho) = \{s \mid \text{ for infinitely many } i, \rho(i) = s\}$.

Let us now consider just two of the various possibilities for $\mathcal{T}$.

(B0) $\mathcal{T} = F \subseteq S$.

A run ρ over σ is accepting with respect to B0 iff $\inf(\rho) \cap F \neq \emptyset$. We shall say that $\mathcal{B}$ is a B0-automaton if it uses B0 as its acceptance criterion. Of course, we shall also refer to these by their standard name; Büchi automata.

$L(\mathcal{B})$, the language accepted (recognized) by $\mathcal{B}$, is the set of infinite words σ such that there is an accepting run of $\mathcal{B}$ on σ. A language $L \subseteq \Sigma^\omega$ is said to be ω-regular iff there exists a Büchi automaton $\mathcal{B}$ over Σ such that $L(\mathcal{B}) = L$. As is well known, ω-regular languages have equivalent algebraic and logical presentations, as detailed in the excellent survey [Tho].

A second possibility for $\mathcal{T}$ is:

(B1) $\mathcal{T} \subseteq 2^S$.

A run ρ over σ is accepting with respect to B1 iff there exists $F \in \mathcal{T}$ such that $\inf(\rho) \supseteq F$. It is easy to show that $L \subseteq \Sigma^\omega$ is ω-regular iff there exists a B1-automaton $\mathcal{B}$ (i.e., an automaton $\mathcal{B}$ that uses B1 as its acceptance criterion) such that $L = L(\mathcal{B})$. Thus at the level of sequences there is no difference in expressive power between Büchi automata and B1-automata. As we shall see, at the level of traces, B0 is weaker than B1.

For defining automata on infinite traces we need to develop some notation. Let $F = (E, \leq, \lambda) \in TR(\Sigma, I)$. Then F is an infinite trace iff E is an infinite set. Let $TR^\omega(\Sigma, I)$ denote the subclass of infinite traces over (Σ, I). Often, we shall write TR^ω instead of $TR^\omega(\Sigma, I)$.

Let $F \in TR^\omega$ with $F = (E, \leq, \lambda)$ and let $p \in \mathcal{P}$. Then $e \in E$ is a p-event iff $\lambda(e) \in \Sigma_p$. Similarly, e is an a-event iff $\lambda(e) = a$. We let E_p denote the set of p-events and E_a denote the set of a-events.

There are two natural transition relations that one can associate with F. The event based transition relation $\Rightarrow_F \subseteq \mathcal{C}_F \times E \times \mathcal{C}_F$ is defined as $c \stackrel{e}{\Longrightarrow}_F c'$ iff $e \notin c$ and $c \cup \{e\} = c'$. The action-based transition relation $\rightarrow_F \subseteq \mathcal{C}_F \times \Sigma \times \mathcal{C}_F$ is defined as $c \stackrel{a}{\longrightarrow}_F c'$ iff there exists $e \in E$ such that $\lambda(e) = a$ and $c \stackrel{e}{\Longrightarrow}_F c'$.

To define automata on infinite traces, we have to first define a distributed version of transition systems. The distributed transition systems we work with here are essentially the *asynchronous automata* of Zielonka [Zie]. We begin with some notation involving local and global states.

Let $\mathcal{P}$ be a set of processes. We equip each process $p \in \mathcal{P}$ with a finite non-empty set of local p-states, denoted S_p. We set $S = \bigcup_{p \in \mathcal{P}} S_p$ and call S the set of *local states.*

We let P, Q range over non-empty subsets of $\mathcal{P}$ and let p, q range over $\mathcal{P}$. A Q-state is a map $s : Q \rightarrow S$ such that $s(q) \in S_q$ for every $q \in Q$. We let S_Q denote the set Q-states. We call $S_\mathcal{P}$ the set of *global states.*

If $Q' \subseteq Q$ and $s \in S_Q$ then $s_{Q'}$ is s restricted to Q'. In other words $s_{Q'}$ is the Q'-state s' which satisfies $s'(q') = s(q')$ for every q' in Q'. We use a to abbreviate $\text{loc}(a)$ when talking about states (recall that $\text{loc}(a) = \{p \mid a \in \Sigma_p\}$). Thus an a-state is just a $\text{loc}(a)$-state and S_a denotes the set of all $\text{loc}(a)$-states. If $\text{loc}(a) \subseteq Q$ and s is a Q-state we shall write s_a to mean $s_{\text{loc}(a)}$.

A *distributed transition system* TS over $\widetilde{\Sigma}$ is a structure $(\{S_p\}, \{\rightarrow_a\}, S_{in})$ where

- S_p is a finite non-empty set of p-states for each process p.
- For $a \in \Sigma$, $\rightarrow_a \subseteq S_a \times S_a$ is a transition relation between a-states.
- $S_{in} \subseteq S_\mathcal{P}$ is a set of initial global states.

The idea is that an a-move by TS involves only the local states of the agents which participate in the execution a. This is reflected in the global transition relation $\rightarrow_{TS} \subseteq S_\mathcal{P} \times \Sigma \times S_\mathcal{P}$ which is defined as:

$$s \stackrel{a}{\longrightarrow}_{TS} s' \text{ iff } (s_a, s'_a) \in \rightarrow_a \text{ and } s_{\mathcal{P}-\text{loc}(a)} = s'_{\mathcal{P}-\text{loc}(a)}.$$

From the definition of $\rightarrow_{TS}$, it is clear that actions which are executed by disjoint sets of agents are processed independently by TS.

A trace ω-automaton over $\widetilde{\Sigma} = \{\Sigma_p\}$ is a pair $\mathcal{A} = (TS, \mathcal{T})$ where $TS = (\{S_p\}, \{\rightarrow_a\}, S_{in})$ is a distributed transition system over $\widetilde{\Sigma}$ and $\mathcal{T}$ is an acceptance table (which we will elaborate on later).

A *trace run* of TS over $F \in TR^\omega$ is a map $\rho : \mathcal{C}_F \rightarrow S_\mathcal{P}$ such that $\rho(\emptyset) \in S_{in}$ and for every $(c, a, c') \in \rightarrow_F$, $\rho(c) \xrightarrow{a}_{TS} \rho(c')$.

To define acceptance we must now compute $\inf_p(\rho)$, the set of p-states that are encountered infinitely often along ρ. The obvious definition, namely $\inf_p(\rho) = \{s_p \mid \rho(c)(p) = s_p \text{ for infinitely many } c \in \mathcal{C}_F\}$, will not work. The complication arises because some processes may make only finitely many moves, even though the overall trace consists of an infinite number of events.

For instance, consider the distributed alphabet $\widetilde{\Sigma}_0 = \{\{a\}, \{b\}\}$. In the corresponding distributed transition system, there are two processes p and q which execute a's and b's completely independently. Consider the trace $F = (E, \leq, \lambda)$ where $|E_p| = 1$ and E_q is infinite—i.e., all the infinite words in $\mathsf{trs}(F)$ contain one a and infinitely many b's. Let s_p be the state of p after executing a. Then, there will be infinitely many configurations whose p-state is s_p, even though p only moves a finite number of times.

Continuing with the same example, consider another infinite trace $F' = (E', \leq', \lambda')$ over the same alphabet where both E_p and E_q are infinite. Once again, let s_p be the local state of p after reading one a. Further, let us suppose that after reading the second a, p never returns to the state s_p. It will still be the case that there are infinitely many configurations whose p-state is s_p: consider the configurations $c_0, c_1, c_2, \ldots$ where c_j is the finite configuration after one a and j b's have occurred.

So, we have to define $\inf_p(\rho)$ carefully in order to be able to distinguish whether or not process p is making progress. The appropriate formulation is as follows:

Case 1 *E_p is finite:* $\inf_p(\rho) = \{s_p\}$, where $\rho(\downarrow E_p) = s$ and $s_p = s(p)$.
Case 2 *E_p is an infinite set:*

$$\inf_p(\rho) = \{s_p \mid \text{for infinitely many } e \in E_p, s_e(p) = s_p, \text{ where } \rho(\downarrow e) = s_e\}.$$

We can now begin to consider various acceptance tables.

(A0) $\mathcal{T} = \{F_p\}$ with $F_p \subseteq S_p$ for each p.

A run ρ over F is accepting with respect to A0 iff $\inf_p(\rho) \cap F_p \neq \emptyset$ for every p. The trace language accepted by the A0-automaton $\mathcal{A}$ (i.e., where $\mathcal{T}$ is of the form A0) is the set $L_{Tr}(\mathcal{A}) = \{F \mid \exists \text{ an accepting run of } TS \text{ over } F\}$. A0-automata are the obvious common generalization of asynchronous automata and Büchi automata. It turns out that A0-automata are not expressive enough: the acceptance criterion cannot distinguish whether or not an agent executes infinitely many actions.

To bring this out and to motivate the acceptance condition we are after, we will put down a crude definition of ω-regular trace languages.

A trace language over $\widetilde{\Sigma}$ is just a subset of TR^ω. To define ω-regular trace languages, we exploit the result from the previous section linking $\Sigma^\infty/\sim_I$ and $TR(\Sigma, I)$ which permits us to associate a language of infinite words with each trace language. We can then transport the definition of ω-regularity from subsets of Σ^ω to infinite traces.

Let $L \subseteq \Sigma^\omega$. Then L is I-consistent iff for every $\sigma \in \Sigma^\omega$, if $\sigma \in L$ then $[\sigma] \subseteq L$. Thus if L is I-consistent either all members of the $\sim_I$-equivalence class $[\sigma]$ are in L or none of them are in L.

Let $L' \subseteq TR^\omega$. We say that L' is an ω-regular trace language iff there exists an I-consistent ω-regular language $L \subseteq \Sigma^\omega$ such that $L' = \{\mathsf{str}(\sigma) \mid \sigma \in L\}$. Stated differently, $L' \subseteq TR^\omega$ is a ω-regular trace language iff $L = \bigcup\{\mathsf{trs}(F) \mid F \in L'\}$ is a ω-regular subset of Σ^ω. As in the word case, algebraic and logical presentations of ω-regular trace languages have been worked out [EM, GP]. These presentations have a flavour which is pleasingly similar to the classical algebraic and logical characterisations of ω-regular subsets of Σ^ω.

Returning to the distributed alphabet $\widetilde{\Sigma}_0 = (\{a\}, \{b\})$, let (Σ_0, I_0) denote the corresponding trace alphabet. Consider $L \subseteq TR^\omega(\Sigma_0, I_0)$ consisting of the single trace $F = (E, \leq, \lambda)$ such that E_a and E_b are both infinite sets. It is easy to check that L is a ω-regular trace language but, as argued in [GP], no A0-automaton over $\widetilde{\Sigma}$ can recognize L.

It is worth noting that having multiple entries in the acceptance table does not help. In other words, one might consider the following acceptance criterion.

(A0′) $\mathcal{T} = \{\mathcal{T}_0, \mathcal{T}_1, \ldots, \mathcal{T}_n\}$ with $\mathcal{T}_i = \{F_p^i\}_{p \in \mathcal{P}}$ and $F_p^i \subseteq S_p$ for each $i \in \{1, 2, \ldots, n\}$ and each $p \in \mathcal{P}$. A run ρ of TS over $F \in TR^\omega$ is accepting with respect to A0′ iff there exists i such that $\mathrm{inf}_p(\rho) \cap F_p^i \neq \emptyset$ for each p.

The reason why A0′ does not help is that the class of languages accepted by A0-automata is closed under union, thanks to the presence of multiple global initial states. We can construct an A0-automaton $\mathcal{A}_i = (TS, \mathcal{T}_i)$ for each entry $\mathcal{T}_i$ from the table of an A0′-automaton $\mathcal{A} = (TS, \mathcal{T})$. If $\mathcal{T} = \{\mathcal{T}_0, \mathcal{T}_1, \ldots, \mathcal{T}_n\}$, it is clear that $L(\mathcal{A}) = \bigcup_{i \in \{1,2,\ldots,n\}} L(\mathcal{A}_i)$. Thus, every A0′-automaton can be simulated by an A0-automaton.

Gastin and Petit showed that the following acceptance condition provides a suitable generalization of classical Büchi automata to the setting of infinite traces.

(A1) $\mathcal{T} = \{\mathcal{T}_1, \mathcal{T}_2, \ldots, \mathcal{T}_n\}$ with $\mathcal{T}_i = \{F_p^i\}_{p \in \mathcal{P}}$ and $F_p^i \subseteq S_p$ for each $i \in \{1, 2, \ldots, n\}$ and each $p \in \mathcal{P}$. A run ρ of TS over $F \in TR^\omega$ is accepting with respect to A1 iff there exists i such that $\mathrm{inf}_p(\rho) \supseteq F_p^i$ for each p.

The condition A1 is an extension of the sequential condition B1 in a distributed setting. Notice that A1 "couples" together final sets of the components in each entry $\mathcal{T}_i \in \mathcal{T}$.

Theorem 2.1 ([GP]) *$L \subseteq TR^\omega$ is a ω-regular trace language iff there exists an A1-automaton $\mathcal{A}$ such that $L_{Tr}(\mathcal{A}) = L$.*

Subsequently, Niebert has shown that the A1 condition can be modified to avoid coupling final sets across processes [Nie]. In effect, it is possible to have a local B1 table for each process and define a run ρ to be accepting if for each process p, $\mathrm{inf}_p(\rho)$ satisfies p's B1 table. Going one step further, we arrive at the acceptance criterion A2, which is the one we will use in connection with the logics to be studied in the next section.

(A2) $\mathcal{T} = \{(F_p^\omega, F_p)\}_{p\in\mathcal{P}}$ with F_p^ω, $F_p \subseteq S_p$ for each p.

A run ρ over $F = (E, \leq, \lambda)$ is accepting with respect to A2 iff for each process p the following conditions are met.

Case 1 *E_p is finite*: Then $\inf_p(\rho) \cap F_p \neq \emptyset$.

Case 2 *E_p is an infinite set*: Then $\inf_p(\rho) \cap F_p^\omega \neq \emptyset$.

Thus, on an input F, the decision as to whether a process p uses F_p or F_p^ω to determine acceptance depends on whether or not p executes infinitely many actions in F.

Theorem 2.2

(i) *The class of languages accepted by A2-automata is closed under union.*

(ii) *The class of languages accepted by A1-automata is identical to the class of languages accepted by A2-automata.*

Proof Sketch.

(i) Suppose $\mathcal{A}_1$ and $\mathcal{A}_2$ are two A2-automata. Then we construct an A2-automaton $\mathcal{A}$ which is the *disjoint* union of $\mathcal{A}_1$ and $\mathcal{A}_2$. The global initial states of $\mathcal{A}$ will determine for each run whether $\mathcal{A}_1$ or $\mathcal{A}_2$ (but not both!) is going to be explored. It is easy to check that $L(\mathcal{A}) = L(\mathcal{A}_1) \cup L(\mathcal{A}_2)$.

(ii) Let $\mathcal{A} = (TS, \mathcal{T})$ be an A1-automaton. From part (i), it suffices to consider the case where $\mathcal{T}$ has just one entry. So assume that $\mathcal{T} = \{\mathcal{T}_1\}$ and $\mathcal{T}_1 = \{F_p\}$. Let $TS = (\{S_p\}, \{\rightarrow_a\}, S_{in})$. Define the A2-automaton $\mathcal{A}' = (TS', \mathcal{T}')$ as follows. $TS' = (\{S'_p\}, \{\Rightarrow_a\}, S'_{in})$ where:

- $S'_p = S_p \times 2^{F_p} \times \{\mathsf{on}, \mathsf{off}\}$ for each p.
- Let s'_a, t'_a be a-states in TS' such that $s'_a(p) = (s_p, X_p, u_p)$ and $t'_a(p) = (t_p, Y_p, v_p)$ for each $p \in \mathcal{P}$. Then $(s'_a, t'_a) \in \Rightarrow_a$ iff there exists $(s_a, t_a) \in \rightarrow_a$ such that the following conditions are satisfied for each $p \in \mathrm{loc}(a)$.
  (1) $u_p = \mathsf{on}$, $s_p = s_a(p)$ and $t_p = t_a(p)$.
  (2) If $X_p = \emptyset$ then $Y_p = F_p$. Otherwise, $Y_p = X_p - \{t_p\}$.
- $S'_{in} = \{s' \in S'_{\mathcal{P}} \mid \exists s \in S_{in}.\ \forall p \in \mathcal{P}.\ \exists u_p \in \{\mathsf{on}, \mathsf{off}\}.\ s'(p) = (s(p), \emptyset, u_p)\}$
- $\mathcal{T}' = \{(G_p^\omega, G_p)\}$ where for each p,

$$\begin{aligned} G_p^\omega &= S_p \times \{\emptyset\} \times \{\mathsf{on}\} \\ G_p &= F_p \times 2^{F_p} \times \{\mathsf{off}\} \end{aligned}$$

It is easy to check that $L_{Tr}(\mathcal{A}) = L_{Tr}(\mathcal{A}')$.

Conversely, let $\mathcal{A} = (TS, \mathcal{T})$ be an A2-automaton with $TS = (\{S_p\}, \{\rightarrow_a\}, S_{in})$ and $\mathcal{T} = \{(F_p^\omega, F_p)\}$. We say that $\mathcal{A}$ is in standard form if it satisfies:

- $F_p^\omega \cap F_p = \emptyset$ for each p.
- If $(s_a, t_a) \in \rightarrow_a$ and $p \in \mathrm{loc}(a)$, then $s_a(p) \notin F_p$.

Thus, if $\mathcal{A}$ is in standard form, the p-states in F_p are "dead" and are disjoint from F_p^ω. It is a simple exercise to verify that every A2-automaton $\mathcal{A}$ can be converted to an A2-automaton $\mathcal{A}'$ in standard form such that $L_{Tr}(\mathcal{A}) = L_{Tr}(\mathcal{A}')$.

So, let $\mathcal{A} = (TS, \mathcal{T})$ be an A2-automaton in standard form with $TS = (\{S_p\}, \{\rightarrow_a\}, S_{in})$ and $\mathcal{T} = \{(F_p^\omega, F_p)\}$. Let G be the set of functions of the form $g : \mathcal{P} \rightarrow S$ such that $g(p) \in F_p^\omega \cup F_p$ for each p. Define the A1-automaton $\mathcal{A}' = (TS', \mathcal{T}')$ where $TS' = TS$ and $\mathcal{T}' = \{\mathcal{T}_g'\}_{g\in G}$, such that for each $g \in G$, $\mathcal{T}_g' = \{\{g(p)\}\}_{p\in\mathcal{P}}$. It is easy to verify that $L_{Tr}(\mathcal{A}) = L_{Tr}(\mathcal{A}')$. □

We now argue that the emptiness problem for A2-automata is decidable. This will be required to settle the satisfiability problem for the logics considered in the next section. Let $\mathcal{A} = (TS, \mathcal{T})$ be an A2-automaton with $TS = (\{S_p\}, \{\rightarrow_a\}, S_{in})$ and $\mathcal{T} = \{(F_p^\omega, F_p)\}$. Though it is not strictly necessary, it will be illuminating to first associate a language of infinite words with $\mathcal{A}$.

Let $\sigma \in \Sigma^\omega$. Then a (word) run of TS over σ is a map $\rho : \omega \rightarrow S_\mathcal{P}$ such that $\rho(0) \in S_{in}$ and $\rho(i) \xrightarrow{\sigma(i)}_{TS} \rho(i{+}1)$ for each $i \geq 0$. The run ρ over σ is accepting iff the following conditions are satisfied for each p.

(i) If $i \in \omega$ such that $\sigma(j) \notin \Sigma_p$ for every $j \geq i$ then $s_i(p) \in F_p$, where $s_i = \rho(i)$.

(ii) If $\sigma(j) \in \Sigma_p$ for infinitely many j then for infinitely many i it is the case that $s_i(p) \in F_p^\omega$, where $s_i = \rho(i)$.

We define $L_{seq}(\mathcal{A})$, the language of infinite words accepted by $\mathcal{A}$ to be the set of all words σ such that there exists an accepting run of $\mathcal{A}$ over σ. The distributed nature of TS together with the basic properties of the maps str and trs defined earlier lead to the next result.

Theorem 2.3 *For any A2-automaton $\mathcal{A}$, $L_{Tr}(\mathcal{A}) = \{\mathsf{str}(\sigma) \mid \sigma \in L_{seq}(\mathcal{A})\}$. Consequently $L_{Tr}(\mathcal{A}) \neq \emptyset$ iff $L_{seq}(\mathcal{A}) \neq \emptyset$.*

Similar statements hold, of course, for A0-automata and A1-automata.

All the A2-automata that we construct in the next section will be in standard form. So assume that $\mathcal{A} = (TS, \mathcal{T})$ is an A2-automaton in standard form with $TS = (\{S_p\}, \{\rightarrow_a\}, S_{in})$ and $\mathcal{T} = \{(F_p^\omega, F_p)\}$. Construct the directed graph $G_\mathcal{A} = (S_\mathcal{P}, E_\mathcal{A})$ where $S_\mathcal{P}$ is the set of global states of TS and $(s, s') \in E_\mathcal{A}$ if there exists $a \in \Sigma$ such that $s \xrightarrow{a}_{TS} s'$. We also label each edge in $G_\mathcal{A}$ with a set of processes. Let $\pi : E_\mathcal{A} \rightarrow 2^\mathcal{P}$ be given by $\pi((s, s')) = \bigcup\{\mathrm{loc}(a) \mid s \xrightarrow{a}_{TS} s'\}$.

We call $X \subseteq S_\mathcal{P}$ a *good component* iff X is a maximal strongly connected component in $G_\mathcal{A}$ which meets one the following conditions for each p.

(i) There exists $s \in X$ such that $s(p) \in F_p$. (Because $\mathcal{A}$ is in standard form this implies that $s'(p) = s''(p) \in F_p$ for every $s', s'' \in X$).

(ii) There exists $s \in X$ such that $s(p) \in F_p^\omega$ and for some $s' \in X$, $(s', s) \in E_\mathcal{A}$ and $p \in \pi((s', s))$.

From Theorem 2.3 we know that $L_{Tr}(\mathcal{A})$ is non-empty iff $L_{seq}(\mathcal{A})$ is. It is not difficult to prove that $L_{seq}(\mathcal{A})$ is non-empty iff $G_\mathcal{A}$ has a good component. It is known that the maximal strongly connected components of a digraph can be computed in time which is linear in the size of the digraph [AHU]. Clearly, the size of $G_{\mathcal{A}}$ is bounded by the number of global states of $\mathcal{A}$. As a consequence it is easy to derive the next result.

Theorem 2.4 *Let $\mathcal{A}$ be an A2-automaton in standard form. Then $L_{Tr}(\mathcal{A}) \neq \emptyset$ iff $G_{\mathcal{A}}$ has a good component. For $p \in \mathcal{P}$, let $n_p = |S_p|$ denote the number of p-states. Let $n = \max\{n_p\}_{p\in\mathcal{P}}$ and $m = |\mathcal{P}|$. Then checking that $G_{\mathcal{A}}$ has a good component can be done in time $O(n^{2m})$.*

We conclude this section with a few remarks on deterministic automata over infinite traces. As with automata on infinite words, non-deterministic A2-automata on infinite traces are strictly more expressive than deterministic A2-automata. In the absence of determinacy, complementation is difficult. When applying these automata to settle questions in logic, complementation is often required to handle negation in formulas. (Fortunately, the automata-theoretic treatment of linear time temporal logic on traces which we will describe here does *not* require complementation.)

To obtain determinacy without loss of expressive power one must use a more sophisticated acceptance criterion corresponding to the Muller, Rabin or Streett acceptance conditions for infinite words. Here, we will look only at the Muller acceptance condition.

(M) $\mathcal{T} = \{\mathcal{T}_1, \ldots, \mathcal{T}_n\}$ with $\mathcal{T}_i = \{F_p^i\}$ and $F_p^i \subseteq S_p$ for each i and each p. A run ρ over $F \in TR^\omega$ is accepting with respect to M iff there exists $\mathcal{T}_i \in \mathcal{T}$ such that $\mathrm{inf}_p(\rho) = F_p^i$ for each p.

Diekert and Muscholl [DM] showed that *deterministic* M-automata are as expressive as non-deterministic A1-automata. Their proof however does not lead to a determinization construction for A1-automata.

There are two independent solutions available in the literature for the difficult problem of complementing A1-automata. Muscholl first showed how to directly construct a non-deterministic A1-automaton which is the complement of the given automaton [Mus]—this approach does not yield a determinization construction for A1-automata. In [Mus] the complementation is carried out for asynchronous *cellular* Büchi automata, in which there is one agent for each letter. To transport this complementation result to A1-automata, one has to resort to a simulation which carries non-trivial overheads in the size of the alphabet. The second solution due to Klarlund, Mukund and Sohoni [KMS] is a direct determinization construction for A1-automata which then easily leads to the complementation result. In both cases, the blow-up in the local state space of each process is exponential in the global state space of the original automaton, which is essentially optimal. Surprisingly in both [Mus] and [KMS], the A1 acceptance condition must be first transformed into an equivalent one which describes in considerable detail the communication patterns established by the infinite trace that is being examined for acceptance.

3 Linear Time Temporal Logics over Traces

A variety of linear time temporal logics to be interpreted over traces have been proposed in the literature. As mentioned in the Introduction, our focus here will be on those logics which meet the following criteria:

(i) The logic should be expressible within the first order theory of traces.

(ii) The logic should admit a treatment in terms of asynchronous Büchi automata of one kind or the other.

We begin with the logic TrPTL (Trace based Propositional Temporal logic of Linear time). This is the earliest and—to date—the most expressive linear time logic of the chosen kind. For a detailed treatment of this logic the reader is referred to [Thi1]. After presenting TrPTL we will consider two subsystems denoted $\text{TrPTL}^{\text{con}}$ (connected TrPTL) and $\text{TrPTL}^{\otimes}$ (product TrPTL). These subsystems are obtained by placing suitable syntactic restrictions on the formulas. The interesting point is that these restrictions result in proportionate simplification of the automata theoretic constructions associated with the logics. Towards the end of the section we will take a quick look at other temporal logics that have been proposed with traces as the underlying frames.

Henceforth, it will be notationally convenient to deal with distributed alphabets in which the names of the processes are positive integers. Through this section and the next, we fix a distributed alphabet $\widetilde{\Sigma} = \{\Sigma_i\}_{i\in\mathcal{P}}$ with $\mathcal{P} = \{1, 2, \ldots, K\}$ and $K \geq 1$. We let i, j and k range over $\mathcal{P}$. As before, let P, Q range over non-empty subsets of $\mathcal{P}$. The trace alphabet induced by $\widetilde{\Sigma}$ is denoted (Σ, I). We assume the terminology and notations developed in the previous sections. In particular when dealing with a $\mathcal{P}$-indexed family $\{X_i\}_{i\in\mathcal{P}}$, we will often write just $\{X_i\}$.

The logic TrPTL is parameterized by the class of distributed alphabets. Having fixed $\widetilde{\Sigma}$ we shall often almost always write TrPTL to mean $\text{TrPTL}(\widetilde{\Sigma})$, the logic associated with $\widetilde{\Sigma}$. Fix a set of atomic propositions AP with p, q ranging over AP. Then $\Phi_{\text{TrPTL}(\widetilde{\Sigma})}$, the set of formulas of $\text{TrPTL}(\widetilde{\Sigma})$, is defined inductively via:

- For $p \in AP$ and $i \in \mathcal{P}$, $p(i)$ is a formula (which is to be read "p at i").
- If α and β are formulas, so are $\neg\alpha$ and $\alpha \vee \beta$.
- If α is a formula and $a \in \Sigma_i$ then $\langle a\rangle_i\alpha$ is a formula.
- If α and β are formulas so is $\alpha\, \mathcal{U}_i \beta$.

From now on, we denote $\Phi_{\text{TrPTL}(\widetilde{\Sigma})}$ as just Φ. In the semantics of the logic which will be based on infinite traces, the i-view of a configuration will play a crucial role. Let $F \in TR^\omega$ with $F = (E, \leq, \lambda)$. Recall that $E_i = \{e \mid e \in E \text{ and } \lambda(e) \in \Sigma_i\}$. Let $c \in \mathcal{C}_F$ and $i \in \mathcal{P}$. Then $\downarrow^i(c)$ is the i-view of c and it is defined as:

$$\downarrow^i(c) = \downarrow(c \cap E_i).$$

We note that $\downarrow^i(c)$ is also a configuration. It is the "best" configuration that the agent i is aware of at c. We say that $\downarrow^i(c)$ is an *i-local configuration.* Let $\mathcal{C}_F^i = \{\downarrow^i(c) \mid c \in \mathcal{C}_F\}$ be the set of i-local configurations. For $Q \subseteq \mathcal{P}$ and $c \in \mathcal{C}_F$, we let $\downarrow^Q(c)$ denote the set $\bigcup\{\downarrow^i(c) \mid i \in Q\}$. Once again, $\downarrow^Q(c)$ is a configuration. It represents the collective knowledge of the processes in Q about the configuration c.

The following basic properties of traces follow directly from the definitions.

Proposition 3.1 *Let $F = (E, \leq, \lambda)$ be an infinite trace. The following statements hold.*

(i) *Let $\leq_i = \leq \cap (E_i \times E_i)$. Then $(E_i, \leq_i)$ is a linear order isomorphic to ω if E_i is infinite and isomorphic to a finite initial segment of ω if E_i is finite.*

(ii) *$(\mathcal{C}_F^i, \subseteq)$ is a linear order. In fact $(\mathcal{C}_F^i - \{\emptyset\}, \subseteq)$ is isomorphic to $(E_i, \leq_i)$.*

(iii) *Suppose $\downarrow^i(c) \neq \emptyset$ where $c \in \mathcal{C}_F$. Then there exists $e \in E_i$ such that $\downarrow^i(c) = \downarrow e$. In fact e is the $\leq_i$-maximum event in $(c \cap E_i)$.*

(iv) *Suppose $Q \subseteq Q' \subseteq \mathcal{P}$ and $c \in \mathcal{C}_F$. Then $\downarrow^Q(c) = \downarrow^Q(\downarrow^{Q'}(c))$. In particular, for a single process i, $\downarrow^i(c) = \downarrow^i(\downarrow^i(c))$.*

We can now present the semantics of TrPTL. A model is a pair $M = (F, \{V_i\}_{i \in \mathcal{P}})$ where $F = (E, \leq, \lambda) \in TR^\omega$ and $V_i : \mathcal{C}_F^i \to 2^{AP}$ is a valuation function which assigns a set of atomic propositions to i-local configurations for each process i. Let $c \in \mathcal{C}_F$ and $\alpha \in \Phi$. Then $M, c \models \alpha$ denotes that α is satisfied at c in M and it is defined inductively as follows:

- $M, c \models p(i)$ for $p \in AP$ iff $p \in V_i\ (\downarrow^i(c))$.
- $M, c \models \neg\alpha$ iff $M, c \not\models \alpha$.
- $M, c \models \alpha \vee \beta$ iff $M, c \models \alpha$ or $M, c \models \beta$
- $M, c \models \langle a \rangle_i \alpha$ iff there exists $e \in E_i - c$ such that $\lambda(e) = a$ and $M, \downarrow e \models \alpha$. Moreover, for every $e' \in E_i$, $e' < e$ iff $e' \in c$.
- $M, c \models \alpha\ \mathcal{U}_i \beta$ iff there exists $c' \in \mathcal{C}_F$ such that $c \subseteq c'$ and $M, \downarrow^i(c') \models \beta$. Moreover, for every $c'' \in \mathcal{C}_F$, if $\downarrow^i(c) \subseteq \downarrow^i(c'') \subset \downarrow^i(c')$ then $M, \downarrow^i(c'') \models \alpha$.

Thus TrPTL is an action based agent-wise generalization of LTL. Indeed both in terms of its syntax and semantics, LTL corresponds to the case where there is only one agent and where this agent can execute only one action at any time. With $\mathcal{P} = \{1\}$ and $\Sigma_1 = \{a_0\}$ one then writes p instead of $p(1)$, $O\alpha$ instead of $\langle a_0 \rangle \alpha$ and $\alpha\ \mathcal{U}\beta$ instead of $\alpha\ \mathcal{U}_i\beta$. The semantics of TrPTL when specialized down to this case yields the usual LTL semantics. In the next section we will say more about the relationship between TrPTL and LTL.

Returning to TrPTL, the assertion $p(i)$ says that the i-view of c satisfies the atomic proposition p. Observe that we could well have $p(i)$ satisfied at c but not $p(j)$ (with $i \neq j$). It is interesting to note that all atomic assertions (that we know of) concerning distributed behaviours are local in nature. Indeed, it is well-known that global atomic propositions will at once lead to an undecidable logic in the current setting [LPRT, Pen].

Suppose $M = (F, \{V_i\})$ is a model and $c \xrightarrow{a}_F c'$ with $j \notin \text{loc}(a)$. Then $M, c \models p(j)$ iff $M, c' \models p(j)$. In this sense the valuation functions are local. There are, of course, a number of equivalent ways of formulating this idea which we will not get into here.

The assertion $\langle a \rangle_i \alpha$ says that the agent i will next participate in an a-event. Moreover, at the resulting i-view, the assertion α will hold. The assertion $\alpha\ \mathcal{U}_i\beta$

says that there is a future i-view (including the present i-view) at which β will hold and for all the intermediate i-views (if any) starting from the current i-view, the assertion α will hold.

Before considering examples of TrPTL specifications, we will introduce some notation. We let α, β with or without subscripts range over Φ. Abusing notation, we will use loc to denote the map which associates a set of locations with each formula.

- $\text{loc}(p(i)) = \text{loc}(\langle a\rangle_i\alpha) = \text{loc}(\alpha\, \mathcal{U}_i \beta) = \{i\}$.
- $\text{loc}(\neg\alpha) = \text{loc}(\alpha)$.
- $\text{loc}(\alpha \vee \beta) = \text{loc}(\alpha) \cup \text{loc}(\beta)$.

In what follows, $\Phi^i = \{\alpha \mid \text{loc}(\alpha) = \{i\}\}$ is the set of i-type formulas. A basic observation concerning the semantics of TrPTL can be phrased as follows:

Proposition 3.2 *Let $M = (F, \{V_i\})$ be a model, $c \in \mathcal{C}_F$ and α a formula such that* $\text{loc}(\alpha) \subseteq Q$. *Then $M, c \models \alpha$ iff $M, \downarrow^Q(c) \models \alpha$.*

A corollary to this result is that in case $\alpha \in \Phi^i$ then $M, c \models \alpha$ iff $M, \downarrow^i(c) \models \alpha$. As a result, the formulas in Φ^i can be used in exactly the same manner as one would use LTL (in the setting of sequences) to express properties of the agent i. Boolean combinations of such local assertions can be used to capture various interaction patterns between the agents implied by the logical connectives as well as the coordination enforced by the distributed alphabet $\tilde{\Sigma}$.

For writing specifications, apart from the usual derived connectives of propositional calculus such as $\wedge$, $\Rightarrow$ and $\equiv$, the following operators are also available

- $\top \triangleq p_1(1) \vee \neg p_1(1)$ denotes the constant "True", where $AP = \{p_1, p_2, \ldots\}$. We use $\bot = \neg\top$ to denote "False". .
- $\Diamond_i\alpha \triangleq \top\, \mathcal{U}_i\alpha$ is a local version of the $\Diamond$ modality of LTL.
- $\Box_i\alpha \triangleq \neg\Diamond_i\neg\alpha$ is a local version of the $\Box$ modality of LTL..
- Let $X \subseteq \Sigma_i$ and $\overline{X} = \Sigma_i - X$. Then $\alpha\, \mathcal{U}_i^X \beta \triangleq (\alpha \wedge \bigwedge_{a\in\overline{X}}[a]_i\bot)\, \mathcal{U}_i\beta$. In other words $\alpha\, \mathcal{U}_i^X\beta$ is fulfilled using (at most) actions taken from X. We set $\Diamond_i^X\alpha \triangleq \top\, \mathcal{U}_i^X\alpha$ and $\Box_i^X\alpha \triangleq \neg\Diamond_i^X\neg\alpha$.
- $\alpha(i) \triangleq \alpha\, \mathcal{U}_i\alpha$ (or equivalently $\bot\, \mathcal{U}_i\alpha$). $\alpha(i)$ is to be read as "α at i". If $M = (F, \{V_i\})$ is a model and $c \in \mathcal{C}_F$ then $M, c \models \alpha(i)$ iff $M, \downarrow^i(c) \models \alpha$. It could of course be the case that $\text{loc}(\alpha) \neq \{i\}$.

A simple but important observation is that every formula is a boolean combination of formulas taken from $\bigcup_{i\in\mathcal{P}}\Phi^i$. In TrPTL we can say that a specific global configuration is reachable from the initial configuration. Let $\{\alpha_i\}_{i\in\mathcal{P}}$ be a family with $\alpha_i \in \Phi^i$ for each i. Then we can define a derived connective $\Diamond(\alpha_1, \alpha_2, \ldots, \alpha_K)$ which has the following semantics at the empty configuration. Let $M = (F, \{V_i\})$ be a model. Then $M, \emptyset \models \Diamond(\alpha_1, \alpha_2, \ldots, \alpha_k)$ iff there exists $c \in \mathcal{C}_F$ such that $M, c \models \alpha_1 \wedge \alpha_2 \wedge \cdots \wedge \alpha_K$.

To define this derived connective set $\Sigma'_1 = \Sigma_1$ and, for $1 < i \leq K$, set $\Sigma'_i = \Sigma_i - \cup\{\Sigma_j \mid 1 \leq j < i\}$. Then $\Diamond(\alpha_1, \alpha_2, \ldots, \alpha_K)$ is the formula:

$$\Diamond_1^{\Sigma'_1}(\alpha_1 \wedge \Diamond_2^{\Sigma'_2}(\alpha_2 \wedge \Diamond_3^{\Sigma'_3}(\alpha_3 \wedge \cdots \Diamond_K^{\Sigma'_K}\alpha_K))\cdots).$$

The idea is that the sequence of actions leading up to the required configuration can be reordered so that one first performs all the actions in Σ_1, then all the actions in $\Sigma_2 - \Sigma_1$ etc. Hence, if now is an atomic proposition, the formula $\Diamond(\mathsf{now}(1), \mathsf{now}(2), \ldots, \mathsf{now}(K))$ is satisfied at the empty configuration iff there is a reachable configuration at which all the agents assert now.

Dually, safety properties that hold at the initial configuration can also be expressed. For example, let $\mathsf{crt}(i)$ be the atomic assertion declaring that the agent i is currently in its critical section. Then it is possible to write a formula φ_{ME} which asserts that at all reachable configurations at most one agent is in its critical section, thereby guaranteeing that the system satisfies the mutual exclusion property. We omit the details of how to specify φ_{ME}.

On the other hand, it seems difficult to express nested global and safety properties in TrPTL. This is mainly due to the local nature of the modalities which results in information about the past sneaking into the semantics even though there are no explicit past operators in the logic. In particular, TrPTL admits formulas that are satisfiable but not root-satisfiable.

A formula α is said to be root-satisfiable iff there exists a model M such that $M, \emptyset \models \alpha$. On the other hand, α is said to be satisfiable iff there exists a model $M = (F, \{V_i\})$ and $c \in \mathcal{C}_F$ such that $M, c \models \alpha$. It turns out that these two notions are not equivalent. Consider the distributed alphabet $\widetilde{\Sigma}_0 = \{\Sigma_1, \Sigma_2\}$ with $\Sigma_1 = \{a, d\}$ and $\Sigma_2 = \{b, d\}$. Then it is not difficult to verify that the formula $p(2)(1) \wedge \Box_2 \neg p(2)$ is satisfiable but not root-satisfiable. (Recall that $p(2)(1)$ abbreviates $\bot\, \mathcal{U}_1 p(2)$). One can however transform every formula α into a formula α' such that α is satisfiable iff α' is root satisfiable.

This follows from the observation that every α can be expressed as a boolean combination of formulas taken from the set $\bigcup_{i \in \mathcal{P}} \Phi^i$. Hence the given formula α can be assumed to be of the form $\alpha = \bigvee_{j=1}^{m}(\alpha_{j1} \wedge \alpha_{j2} \wedge \cdots \wedge \alpha_{jK})$ where $\alpha_{ji} \in \Phi^i$ for each $j \in \{1, 2, \ldots, m\}$ and each $i \in \mathcal{P}$. Now convert α to the formula α' where $\alpha' = \bigvee_{j=1}^{m} \Diamond(\alpha_{j1}, \alpha_{j2}, \cdots, \alpha_{jK})$. (Recall the derived modality $\Diamond(\alpha_1, \alpha_2, \ldots, \alpha_K)$ introduced earlier.) From the semantics of $\Diamond(\alpha_1, \alpha_2, \ldots, \alpha_K)$ it follows that α is satisfiable iff α' is root-satisfiable.

Hence, in principle, it suffices to consider only root-satisfiability in developing a decision procedure for TrPTL. There is of course a blow-up involved in converting satisfiable formulas to root-satisfiable formulas. If one wants to avoid this blow-up then the decision procedure for checking root-satisfiability can be suitably modified to yield a direct decision procedure for checking satisfiability as is done in [Thi1]. In any case, it is root satisfiability which is of importance from the standpoint of model checking. Hence here we shall only develop a procedure for deciding if a given formula of TrPTL is root-satisfiable.

As a first step we augment the syntax of our logic by one more construct.

- If α is a formula, so is $O_i\alpha$. In the model $M = (F, \{V_i\})$, at the configuration $c \in \mathcal{C}_F$, $M, c \models O_i\alpha$ iff $M, c \models \langle a \rangle_i \alpha$ for some $a \in \Sigma_i$. We also define $\mathrm{loc}(O_i\alpha) = \{i\}$.

Thus $O_i\alpha \equiv \bigvee_{a\in\Sigma_i} \langle a\rangle_i\alpha$ is a valid formula and O_i is expressible in the former syntax. It will be however more efficient to admit O_i as a first class modality.

Fix a formula α_0. Our aim is to effectively associate an A2-automaton $\mathcal{A}_{\alpha_0}$ with α_0 such that α_0 is root-satisfiable iff $L_{Tr}(\mathcal{A}_{\alpha_0}) \neq \emptyset$. Since the emptiness problem for A2-automata is decidable (Theorem 2.4), this will yield the desired decision procedure. Let $CL'(\alpha_0)$ be the least set of formulas containing α_0 which satisfies:

- $\neg\beta \in CL'(\alpha_0)$ implies $\beta \in CL'(\alpha_0)$.
- $\alpha \vee \beta \in CL'(\alpha_0)$ implies $\alpha, \beta \in CL'(\alpha_0)$.
- $\langle a\rangle_i\alpha \in CL'(\alpha_0)$ implies $\alpha \in CL'(\alpha_0)$.
- $O_i\alpha \in CL'(\alpha_0)$ implies $\alpha \in CL'(\alpha_0)$.
- $\alpha\, \mathcal{U}_i\beta \in CL'(\alpha_0)$ implies $\alpha, \beta \in CL'(\alpha_0)$. In addition, $O_i(\alpha\, \mathcal{U}_i\beta) \in CL'(\alpha_0)$.

We then define $CL(\alpha_0)$ to be the set $CL'(\alpha_0) \cup \{\neg\beta \mid \beta \in CL'(\alpha_0)\}$.

Thus $CL(\alpha_0)$, sometimes called the Fisher-Ladner closure of α_0, is closed under negation with the convention that $\neg\neg\beta$ is identified with β. From now we shall write CL instead of $CL(\alpha_0)$.

$A \subseteq CL$ is called an *i-type atom* iff it satisfies:

- $\forall\alpha \in CL.\ \alpha \in A$ iff $\neg\alpha \notin A$.
- $\forall\alpha \vee \beta \in CL.\ \alpha \vee \beta \in A$ iff $\alpha \in A$ or $\beta \in A$.
- $\forall\alpha\, \mathcal{U}_i\beta \in CL.\ \alpha\, \mathcal{U}_i\beta \in A$ iff $\beta \in A$ or ($\alpha \in A$ and $O_i(\alpha\, \mathcal{U}_i\beta) \in A$).
- If $\langle a\rangle_i\alpha$, $\langle b\rangle_i\beta \in A$ then $a = b$.

AT_i denotes the set of i-type atoms. We now need to define the notion of a formula in CL being a member of a collection of atoms. Let $\alpha \in CL$ and $\{A_i\}_{i\in Q}$ be a family of atoms with $\text{loc}(\alpha) \subseteq Q$ and $A_i \in AT_i$ for each $i \in Q$. Then the predicate $\alpha \in \{A_i\}_{i\in Q}$ is defined inductively as:

- If $\text{loc}(\alpha) = \{j\}$ then $\alpha \in \{A_i\}_{i\in Q}$ iff $\alpha \in A_j$.
- If $\alpha = \neg\beta$ then $\alpha \in \{A_i\}_{i\in Q}$ iff $\beta \notin \{A_i\}_{i\in Q}$.
- If $\alpha = \alpha_1 \vee \alpha_2$ then $\alpha_1 \vee \alpha_2 \in \{A_i\}_{i\in Q}$ iff $\alpha_1 \in \{A_i\}_{i\in Q}$ or $\alpha_2 \in \{A_i\}_{i\in Q}$.

The construction of the A2-automaton $\mathcal{A}_{\alpha_0}$ is guided by the construction due to Vardi and Wolper for LTL [VW]. However in the much richer setting of traces it turns out that one must make crucial use of the latest information that the agents have about each other when defining the transitions of $\mathcal{A}_{\alpha_0}$. It has been shown by Mukund and Sohoni [MS] that this information can be kept track of by a deterministic A2-automaton whose size depends only on $\widetilde{\Sigma}$. (Actually the automaton described in [MS] operates over finite traces but it is a trivial task to convert it into A2-automaton having the desired properties). To bring out the relevant properties of this automaton, let $F \in TR^\omega$ with $F = (E, \leq, \lambda)$. For each subset Q of processes, the function $\mathsf{latest}_{F,Q} : \mathcal{C}_F \times \mathcal{P} \to Q$ is given by $\mathsf{latest}_{F,Q}(c, j) = \ell$ iff ℓ is the least member of Q (under the usual ordering over the integers) with the property $\downarrow^j(\downarrow^q(c)) \subseteq \downarrow^j(\downarrow^\ell(c))$ for every $q \in Q$. In other words, among the agents in Q, ℓ has the best information about j at c, with ties being broken by the usual ordering over integers.

Theorem 3.3 (**[MS]**) *There exists an effectively constructible deterministic A2-automaton $\mathcal{A}_\Gamma = (TS, \mathcal{T})$ with $TS = (\{\Gamma_i\}, \{\Rightarrow_a\}, \Gamma_{in})$ such that:*

(i) $L_{Tr}(\mathcal{A}_\Gamma) = TR^\omega$.

(ii) *For each $Q = \{i_1, i_2, \ldots, i_n\}$, there exists an effectively computable function $\mathsf{gossip}_Q : \Gamma_{i_1} \times \Gamma_{i_2} \times \cdots \times \Gamma_{i_n} \times \mathcal{P} \to Q$ such that for every $F \in TR^\omega$, every $c \in \mathcal{C}_F$ and every $j \in \mathcal{P}$, $\mathsf{latest}_{F,Q}(c, j) = \mathsf{gossip}_Q(\gamma(i_1), \ldots, \gamma(i_n), j)$ where $\rho_F(c) = \gamma$ and ρ_F is the unique (accepting) run of $\mathcal{A}_\Gamma$ over F.*

Henceforth, we refer to $\mathcal{A}_\Gamma$ as the *gossip automaton*. Each process in the gossip automaton has $2^{O(K^2 \log K)}$ local states, where $K = |\mathcal{P}|$. Moreover the function gossip_Q can be computed in time which is polynomial in the size of K.

Each i-state of the automaton $\mathcal{A}_{\alpha_0}$ will consist of an i-type atom together with an appropriate i-state of the gossip automaton. Two additional component will be used to check for liveness requirements. One component will take values from the set $N_i = \{0, 1, 2, \ldots, |U_i|\}$ where $U_i = \{\alpha\, \mathcal{U}_i \beta \mid \alpha\, \mathcal{U}_i \beta \in CL\}$. This component will be used to ensure that all "until" requirements are met. The other component will take values from the set {on,off}. This will be used to detect when an agent has quit.

The automaton $\mathcal{A}_{\alpha_0}$ can now be defined.

Definition 3.4 *$\mathcal{A}_{\alpha_0} = (TS, \mathcal{T})$, where $TS = (\{S_i\}, \{\to_a\}, S_{in})$ and $\mathcal{T} = \{(F_i^\omega, F_i)\}$ are defined as follows:*

(i) *For each i, $S_i = AT_i \times \Gamma_i \times N_i \times$ {on,off}. Recall that Γ_i is the set of i-states of the gossip automaton and $N_i = \{0, 1, 2, \ldots, |U_i|\}$ with $U_i = \{\alpha\, \mathcal{U}_i \beta \mid \alpha\, \mathcal{U}_i \beta \in CL\}$.*

(ii) *Let $s_a, s'_a \in S_a$ with $s_a(i) = (A_i, \gamma_i, u_i, v_i)$ and $s'_a(i) = (A'_i, \gamma'_i, u'_i, v'_i)$ for each $i \in \mathrm{loc}(a)$. Then $(s_a, s'_a) \in \to_a$ iff the following conditions are met.*

  (1) *$(\gamma_a, \gamma'_a) \in \Rightarrow_a$ (recall that $\{\Rightarrow_a\}$ is the family of transition relations of the gossip automaton) where $\gamma_a, \gamma'_a \in \Gamma_a$ such that $\gamma_a(i) = \gamma_i$ and $\gamma'_a(i) = \gamma'_i$ for each $i \in \mathrm{loc}(a)$.*

  (2) *$\forall i, j \in \mathrm{loc}(a)$, $A'_i = A'_j$.*

  (3) *$\forall i \in \mathrm{loc}(a)\ \forall \langle a \rangle_i \alpha \in CL$. $\langle a \rangle_i \alpha \in A_i$ iff $\alpha \in A'_i$.*

  (4) *$\forall i \in \mathrm{loc}(a)\ \forall O_i \alpha \in CL$. $O_i \alpha \in A_i$ iff $\alpha \in A'_i$.*

  (5) *$\forall i \in \mathrm{loc}(a) \forall \langle b \rangle_i \beta \in CL$. If $\langle b \rangle_i \beta \in A_i$ then $b = a$.*

  (6) *Suppose $j \notin \mathrm{loc}(a)$ and $\beta \in CL$ with $\mathrm{loc}(\beta) = \{j\}$. Further suppose that $\mathrm{loc}(a) = \{i_1, i_2, \ldots, i_n\}$. Then $\beta \in A'_i$ iff $\beta \in A_\ell$ where $\ell = \mathsf{gossip}_{\mathrm{loc}(a)}(\gamma_{i_1}, \gamma_{i_2}, \ldots, \gamma_{i_n}, j)$.*

(7) *Let* $i \in \text{loc}(a)$, $U_i = \{\alpha_1\, \mathcal{U}_i\beta_1, \alpha_2\, \mathcal{U}_i\beta_2, \ldots, \alpha_{n_i}\, \mathcal{U}_i\beta_{n_i}\}$. *Then* u'_i *and* u_i *are related to each other via:*

$$u'_i = \begin{cases} (u_i{+}1) \bmod (n_i{+}1), & \text{if } u_i = 0 \text{ or } \beta_{u_i} \in A_i \text{ or } \alpha_{u_i}\, \mathcal{U}_i\beta_{u_i} \notin A_i \\ u_i, & \text{otherwise} \end{cases}$$

(8) *For each* $i \in \text{loc}(a)$, $v_i = \mathsf{on}$. *Moreover, if* $v'_i = \mathsf{off}$ *then* $\langle a\rangle_i\alpha \notin A'_i$ *for every* $i \in \text{loc}(a)$ *and every* $\langle a\rangle_i\alpha \in CL$.

(iii) *Let* $s \in S_{\mathcal{P}}$ *with* $s(i) = (A_i, \gamma_i, u_i, v_i)$ *for every* i. *Then* $s \in S_{in}$ *iff* $\alpha_0 \in \{A_i\}_{i\in\mathcal{P}}$ *and* $\gamma \in \Gamma_{in}$ *where* $\gamma \in \Gamma_{\mathcal{P}}$ *satisfies* $\gamma(i) = \gamma_i$ *for every* i. *Furthermore,* $u_i = 0$ *for every* i. *Finally, for every* i, $v_i = \mathsf{off}$ *implies that* $\langle a\rangle_i\alpha \notin A_i$ *for every* $\langle a\rangle_i\alpha \in CL$.

(iv) *For each* i, $F_i^\omega \subseteq S_i$ *is given by* $F_i^\omega = \{(A_i, \gamma_i, u_i, v_i) \mid u_i = 0 \text{ and } v_i = \mathsf{on}\}$ *and* $F_i \subseteq S_i$ *is given by* $F_i = \{(A_i, \gamma_i, u_i, v_i) \mid v_i = \mathsf{off}\}$.

The automaton $\mathcal{A}_{\alpha_0}$ extends the automata theoretic construction for LTL described in [VW] to the setting of TrPTL. The main new feature is the use of the gossip automaton in step (ii)(6) when dealing with formulas located at agents not taking part in the current action. A detailed explanation of $\mathcal{A}_{\alpha_0}$ can be found in [Thi1].

This construction differs from the original construction for TrPTL presented in [Thi1] in a number of ways. Each S_i in [Thi1] was defined to be $AT_1 \times AT_2 \times \cdots \times AT_K \times \widetilde{U}_i \times \{\mathsf{act}_i^+, \mathsf{act}_i^-, \mathsf{stop}_i\}$ with $\widetilde{U}_i$ as the set of subsets of U_i. The acceptance condition used was $A1$. Using A2, we need just two elements $\{\mathsf{on}, \mathsf{off}\}$ to record when an agent has quit. Using the counter N_i instead of $\widetilde{U}_i$ leads to a more compact description of $\mathcal{A}_{\alpha_0}$. The significant improvement, namely, replacing $AT_1 \times AT_2 \times \cdots \times AT_K$ by just AT_i is due to Narayan Kumar [Nar]. The arguments described in [Thi1] go through in the present setting with minor modifications. These arguments lead to the next set of results.

Theorem 3.5

(i) α_0 *is root-satisfiable iff* $L_{Tr}(\mathcal{A}_{\alpha_0}) \neq \emptyset$.

(ii) *The number of local states of* $\mathcal{A}_{\alpha_0}$ *is bounded by* $2^{O(\max(n, m^2 \log m))}$ *where* $n = |\alpha_0|$ *and* m *is the number of agents mentioned in* α_0. *Clearly,* $m \leq n$. *It follows that the root-satisfiability problem (and in fact the satisfiability problem) for TrPTL is solvable in time* $2^{O(\max(n, m^2 \log m)\cdot m)}$.

The number of local states of each process in $\mathcal{A}_{\alpha_0}$ is determined by two quantities: the length of α_0 and the size of the gossip automaton $\mathcal{A}_\Gamma$. As far as the size of $\mathcal{A}_\Gamma$ is concerned, it is easy to verify that we need to consider only those agents in $\mathcal{P}$ that are mentioned in $\text{loc}(\alpha_0)$, rather than all agents in the system.

The model checking problem for TrPTL can be phrased as follows. A finite state distributed program over $\widetilde{\Sigma}$ is a pair $Pr = (\mathcal{A}_{Pr}, V_{Pr})$ where $\mathcal{A}_{Pr} = ((\{S_i^{Pr}\}, \{\Rightarrow_a^{Pr}\}, S_{in}^{Pr}), \{(S_i^{Pr}, S_i^{Pr})\})$ is an A2-automaton modelling the state space of Pr and $V_{Pr} : S \to 2^{AP}$ is an interpretation of the atomic propositions over the local states of the program. (In this context, one assumes AP to be a finite set.)

Let ρ be a run of $\mathcal{A}_{Pr}$ over $F = (E, \leq, \lambda)$. Then ρ induces the model M_ρ via V_{Pr} as follows: $M_\rho = (F, \{V_i^\rho\})$ where for each i and each $c \in \mathcal{C}_F$, $V_i^\rho(\downarrow^i(c)) = V_{Pr}(s_i) \cap P$, where $s = \rho(c)$ and $s_i = s(i)$. Viewing a formula α_0 as a specification, we say that Pr meets the specification α_0—denoted $Pr \models \alpha_0$—if for every $F \in TR^\omega$ and for every run ρ of $\mathcal{A}_{Pr}$ over F, it is the case that $M_\rho, \emptyset \models \alpha_0$.

The *model checking problem* is to determine whether $Pr \models \alpha_0$. This problem can be solved by "intersecting" the program automaton $\mathcal{A}_{Pr}$ with the formula automaton $\mathcal{A}_{\neg\alpha_0}$ to yield an automaton $\mathcal{A}$ such that $L_{Tr}(\mathcal{A}) = L_{Tr}(\mathcal{A}_{Pr}) \cap L_{Tr}(\mathcal{A}_{\neg\alpha_0})$. It turns out that $L_{Tr}(\mathcal{A}) = \emptyset$ iff $Pr \models \alpha_0$. It is easy to construct $\mathcal{A}$. The only point to care of is that the i-local states of $\mathcal{A}$ should consist of only those pairs (s_i, s_i') (where s_i is an i-local state of $\mathcal{A}_{Pr}$ and $s_i' = (A_i', \gamma_i', n_i', v_i')$ is an i-local state of $\mathcal{A}_{\neg\alpha_0}$) such that $V_{Pr}(s_i) \cap AP = A_i \cap AP$. The details can be found in [Thi1].

It turns out that this model checking problem has time complexity $O(|\mathcal{A}_{Pr}| \cdot 2^{O(\max(n, m^2 \log m) \cdot m)})$ where $|\mathcal{A}_{Pr}|$ is the size of the global state space of the A2-automaton modelling the behaviour of the given program Pr and, as before, $n = |\alpha_0|$ and m is the number of agents mentioned in α_0, where α_0 is the specification formula.

We now turn to two interesting sublogics of TrPTL. The first is the sublogic TrPTL^{con}, which consists of the so called connected formulas of TrPTL. We define $\Phi^{\text{con}}_{\text{TrPTL}}$ (from now on written as Φ^{con}) to be the least subset of Φ satisfying the following conditions:

(i) $p(i) \in \Phi^{\text{con}}$ for every $p \in P$ and every $i \in \mathcal{P}$.

(ii) If $\alpha, \beta \in \Phi^{\text{con}}$, so are $\neg\alpha$ and $\alpha \vee \beta$.

(iii) If $\alpha \in \Phi^{\text{con}}$ and $a \in \Sigma_i$ such that $\text{loc}(\alpha) \subseteq \text{loc}(a)$ then $\langle a \rangle_i \alpha \in \Phi^{\text{con}}$.

(iv) If $\alpha, \beta \in \Phi^{\text{con}}$ with $\text{loc}(\alpha) = \text{loc}(\beta) = \{i\}$ then $\alpha\, \mathcal{U}_i \beta \in \Phi^{\text{con}}$. Actually one need only demand that $\text{loc}(\alpha), \text{loc}(\beta) \subseteq \bigcap\{\text{loc}(a) \mid a \in \Sigma_i\}$ but this leads to notational complications that we wish to avoid here.

(v) If $\alpha \in \Phi^{\text{con}}$ and $\text{loc}(\alpha) = \{i\}$ then $O_i\alpha \in \Phi^{\text{con}}$. (Once again one needs to just demand that $\alpha \subseteq \bigcap\{\text{loc}(a) \mid a \in \Sigma_i\}$.)

Connected formulas were first identified by Niebert and used by Huhn [Huh]. They have also been independently identified by Ramanujam [Ram]. Thanks to the syntactic restrictions imposed on the next state and until formulas, past information is not allowed to creep in. Indeed one can prove the following:

Proposition 3.6 *Let $\alpha \in \Phi^{\text{con}}$. Then α is satisfiable iff α is root-satisfiable.*

Yet another pleasing feature of TrPTL^{con} is that the gossip automaton can be eliminated in the construction of the automaton $\mathcal{A}_{\alpha_0}$ whenever $\alpha_0 \in \Phi^{\text{con}}$. In fact one can do a bit more.

Let $\alpha_0 \in \Phi^{\text{con}}$ and let $CL_i = CL \cap \Phi^i$ for each i (recall that CL is an abbreviation for $CL(\alpha_0)$). We redefine an i-type atom to be a subset A of CL_i such that:

- $\forall \beta \in CL_i\ \beta \in A$ iff $\neg\beta \notin A$.
- $\forall \alpha \vee \beta \in CL_i.\ \alpha \vee \beta \in A$ iff $\alpha \in A$ or $\beta \in A$.
- $\forall \alpha\, \mathcal{U}_i \beta \in CL_i\ \alpha\, \mathcal{U}_i \beta \in A$ iff $\beta \in A$ or $\alpha \in A$ and $O_i(\alpha\, \mathcal{U}_i \beta) \in A$.

As before (but with the new definition in operation!), AT_i is the set of i-type atoms.

Let $\alpha \in CL$ with $\text{loc}(\alpha) \subseteq Q$. The notion of α belonging to a family of atoms $\{A_i\}_{i \in Q}$, with $A_i \in AT_i$ for each $i \in Q$, is defined inductively in the obvious way—if $\text{loc}(\alpha) = \{i\}$ then $\alpha \in \{A_i\}_{i\in Q}$ iff $\alpha \in A_i$ etc. etc. The construction of $\mathcal{A}_{\alpha_0}$ is as specified in Definition 3.4 with the following modifications:

(i) $S_i = AT_i \times N_i \times$ {on,off} for each $i \in \mathcal{P}$. Thus the gossip automaton is eliminated and AT_i is the set of i-type atoms of the new kind.

(ii) (1) This condition is obviously dropped.

(2) Interestingly enough, this condition is also dropped.

(3) This condition is modified to $\forall \langle a \rangle_i \alpha \in CL_i . \langle a \rangle_i \alpha \in A_i$ iff $\alpha \in \{A'_j\}_{j \in \text{loc}(a)}$.

In addition, condition (ii)(6) is dropped, while conditions (ii)(4), (ii)(5), (ii)(7) and (ii)(8) remain unchanged. Parts (iii) and (iv) are modified to eliminate all references to the gossip automaton. After these alterations, it is not difficult to prove the following result.

Theorem 3.7 *Let $\alpha_0 \in \Phi^{\text{con}}$ and $\mathcal{A}_{\alpha_0}$ be constructed as detailed above.*

(i) *α_0 is satisfiable iff $L_{Tr}(\mathcal{A}_{\alpha_0}) \neq \emptyset$.*

(ii) *The satisfiability problem for* TrPTL^{con} *is solvable in time $2^{O(|\alpha_0|)}$.*

Once again, a suitably modified statement can be made about the associated model checking problem. At present we do not know whether or not TrPTL is strictly more expressive than TrPTL^{con}. We shall formulate this question more rigorously in the next section.

Yet another sublogic of TrPTL is called product TrPTL and is denoted as TrPTL$^{\otimes}$. Let $\Phi^{\otimes}$, the set of formulas of TrPTL$^{\otimes}$, be the least subset of Φ which satisfies:

(i) $p(i) \in \Phi^{\otimes}$ for every $p \in P$ and every $i \in \mathcal{P}$.

(ii) If $\alpha, \beta \in \Phi^{\otimes}$ then so are $\neg\alpha$ and $\alpha \vee \beta$.

(iii) If $\alpha \in \Phi^{\otimes}$ with $\text{loc}(\alpha) = \{i\}$ and $a \in \Sigma_i$ then $\langle a \rangle_i \alpha \in \Phi^{\otimes}$.

(iv) If $\alpha, \beta \in \Phi^{\otimes}$ with $\text{loc}(\alpha) = \text{loc}(\beta) = \{i\}$ then $\alpha\, \mathcal{U}_i \beta \in \Phi^{\otimes}$.

Clearly $\Phi^{\otimes} \subseteq \Phi^{\text{con}} \subseteq \Phi$. In case $\alpha_0 \in \Phi^{\otimes}$, the automaton $\mathcal{A}_{\alpha_0}$ can be simplified even further (than the case when $\alpha_0 \in \Phi^{\text{con}}$). $\mathcal{A}_{\alpha_0}$ essentially consists of a synchronized product of Büchi automata. A detailed treatment of TrPTL$^{\otimes}$ is provided in [Thi2]. The interest in this subsystem lies in the fact that the accompanying program model is particularly simple and commonplace. Namely, it consists of a fixed set of finite state transition systems that coordinate their behaviour by performing common actions together. Here we shall just sketch the construction for $\mathcal{A}_{\alpha_0}$.

A product Büchi automaton over $\widetilde{\Sigma}$ is a structure $\mathcal{A} = (\{TS_i\}_{i\in\mathcal{P}}, S_{in}, \mathcal{T})$ where $TS_i = (S_i, \rightarrow_i)$ for each i with $\rightarrow_i \subseteq S_i \times \Sigma_i \times S_i$ as the local transition relation of the agent i. Everything else is as in the definition of an A2-automaton. Thus the key difference is that each agent comes with its own local transition relation. From these agent transition relations, one can derive the action indexed transition relations $\{\rightarrow_a\}$ as follows: $(s_a, s'_a) \in \rightarrow_a$ iff $s_a(i) \xrightarrow{a} s'_a(i)$ for every $i \in \mathrm{loc}(a)$. Thus product Büchi automata are a (strict) subclass of the class of A2-automata.

Given $\alpha_0 \in \Phi^{\otimes}$, the construction of $\mathcal{A}_{\alpha_0}$ proceeds as in the case where $\alpha_0 \in \Phi^{\mathrm{con}}$. The only difference is, we must define the transition relations $\{\rightarrow_i\}_{i\in\mathcal{P}}$ instead of the transition relations $\{\rightarrow_a\}_{a\in\Sigma}$. This can be done as follows:

Let $s_i, s'_i \in S_i$ with $s_i = (A_i, u_i, v_i)$ and $s'_i = (A'_i, u'_i, v'_i)$. Let $a \in \Sigma_i$. Then $s_i \xrightarrow{a_i} s'_i$ iff the following conditions are satisfied:

(i) $\forall \langle a\rangle_i \alpha \in CL.\ \langle a\rangle_i \alpha \in A_i$ iff $\alpha \in A'_i$.

(ii) $\forall O_i \alpha \in CL.\ O_i \alpha \in A_i$ iff $\alpha \in A'_i$.

(iii) If $\langle b\rangle_i \alpha \in A_i$ then $b = a$.

(iv) u_i and u'_i are related to each other just as in part (ii)(7) of Definition 3.4.

(v) v_i and v'_i satisfy part (ii)(8) of Definition 3.4.

As shown in [Thi2] one can establish the following result for TrPTL$^{\otimes}$.

Theorem 3.8 *Let $\alpha_0 \in \Phi^{\otimes}$ and $\mathcal{A}_{\alpha_0}$ be constructed as above.*

(i) *α_0 is satisfiable iff $L_{Tr}(\mathcal{A}_{\alpha_0}) \neq \emptyset$.*

(ii) *The satisfiability problem for TrPTL$^{\otimes}$ can be solved in time $2^{O(|\alpha_0|)}$.*

Once again, one can make suitably modified statements about the accompanying model checking problem. As mentioned earlier, the program model in this setting consists of a fixed set (one for each i) of finite state transition systems.

We conclude this section with a quick look at some related logics. Katz and Peled introduced the logic ISTL [KP] which can be easily viewed as a temporal logic over traces. However, it has branching time modalities which permit quantification over the so called observations of a trace. ISTL uses global atomic propositions rather than local atomic propositions. Penczek has also studied a number of temporal logics (including a version of ISTL) with branching time modalities and global atomic propositions [Pen]. His logics are interpreted directly over the space of configurations of a trace resulting in a variety of axiomatizations and undecidability results. We feel that local atomic propositions (as used in TrPTL) are crucial for obtaining tractable partial order based temporal logics. Niebert has considered a μ-calculus version of TrPTL [Nie] and has obtained a decidability result using a variant of asynchronous Büchi automata. Since this logic uses "local" fixed points, it is not clear at present what is the expressive power of this logic. The four linear time temporal logics studied by Ramanujam in a closely related setting [Ram] can be easily captured as four sublogics of TrPTL through purely syntactic restrictions. Two of the resulting sublogics are TrPTL$^{\otimes}$ and TrPTL^{con}. It is not clear at present whether the other two logics admit a simpler treatment in terms of asynchronous Büchi automata (than the one for TrPTL).

The temporal logic of causality (TLC) proposed by Alur, Peled and Penczek is basically a temporal logic over traces [APP]. The concurrent structures used in [APP] as frames for TLC can be easily represented as traces over an appropriately chosen trace alphabet. The interesting feature of TLC is that its branching time modalities are interpreted over causal paths. In a trace $(E, \leq, \lambda)$, the sequence $e_0 e_1 \cdots \in E^{\infty}$ is a causal path if $e_0 \lessdot e_1 \lessdot e_2 \cdots$. This logic is almost certainly not expressible within the first order theory of traces although it admits an elementary time (in fact essentially exponential time) decision procedure.

Finally, Ebinger has also proposed a linear time temporal logic to be interpreted over traces [Ebi]. An interesting property of this logic is that when its frames are restricted to be *finite* traces then it is exactly equivalent to the first order theory of *finite* traces. Unfortunately the decidability of this logic is settled using a translation into the first order theory of infinite traces. Hence the decision procedure has non-elementary time complexity.

4 Expressiveness Issues

Our main aim here is to show that TrPTL is expressible within the first order theory of traces. In order to simplify the presentation, we shall eliminate atomic propositions and instead use the single constant $\top$ standing for "True" (and $\bot = \neg\top$ standing for "False"). The resulting logic will also be called TrPTL accompanied by the notations and terminology developed in the previous section. The function loc which assigns a set of processes to a formula works exactly as before except that we start with $\mathrm{loc}(\top) = \emptyset$. As will be seen later, this will entail minor changes in the definition of the syntax of TrPTL^{con} and TrPTL$^{\otimes}$. For now, we repeat that the syntax of Φ, the set of formulas of TrPTL is now given by:

$$\Phi ::= \top \mid \neg\alpha \mid \alpha \vee \beta \mid \langle a \rangle_i \alpha \mid \alpha\, \mathcal{U}_i \beta.$$

As before, for $\langle a \rangle_i \alpha$ to be a formula we require $a \in \Sigma_i$. Local atomic propositions can be coded up into the actions and hence their elimination does not result in loss of expressive power.

A model is just an infinite trace $F \in TR^{\omega}$. We set $F, c \models \top$ for every $c \in \mathcal{C}_F$. The rest of the semantics is as before. L_α, the ω-trace language defined by the formula α is given by, $L_\alpha = \{F \mid F \in TR^{\omega} \text{ and } F, \emptyset \models \alpha\}$. We say that $L \subseteq TR^{\omega}$ is TrPTL-definable iff there exists $\alpha \in \Phi$ such that $L = L_\alpha$.

First we shall compare the expressive powers of TrPTL, TrPTL^{con} and TrPTL$^{\otimes}$. In order to do so, we must define the syntax of the two sublogics in the present setting. For TrPTL^{con} the only changes that are required are:

- $\top \in \Phi^{\mathrm{con}}$.
- If $\alpha, \beta \in \Phi^{\mathrm{con}}$ such that $\mathrm{loc}(\alpha), \mathrm{loc}(\beta) \subseteq \{i\}$ then $\alpha\, \mathcal{U}_i \beta \in \Phi^{\mathrm{con}}$.

For TrPTL$^{\otimes}$, the only changes that are required are

- $\top \in \Phi^{\otimes}$.
- If $\alpha \in \Phi^{\otimes}$ such that $\mathrm{loc}(\alpha) \subseteq \{i\}$ and if $a \in \Sigma_i$ then $\langle a \rangle_i \alpha \in \Phi^{\otimes}$.
- If $\alpha, \beta \in \Phi^{\otimes}$ with $\mathrm{loc}(\alpha), \mathrm{loc}(\beta) \subseteq \{i\}$ then $\alpha\, \mathcal{U}_i \beta \in \Phi^{\otimes}$.

The notion of $L \subseteq TR^{\omega}$ being TrPTL^{con}-definable or TrPTL$^{\otimes}$-definable is formulated in the obvious way. Since $\Phi^{\otimes} \subseteq \Phi^{\mathrm{con}} \subseteq \Phi$ it is clear that TrPTL is at least as expressive as TrPTL^{con} which in turn is at least as expressive as TrPTL$^{\otimes}$. As mentioned earlier we do not know at present if TrPTL is strictly more expressive than TrPTL^{con}, though we conjecture that this the case.

We do know however that TrPTL^{con} is strictly more expressive than TrPTL$^{\otimes}$. To illustrate this it will be convenient to extend the notion of definability to subsets of Σ^{ω}. We say that $L \subseteq \Sigma^{\omega}$ is TrPTL-definable iff L is I-consistent and $\{\mathsf{str}(\sigma) \mid \sigma \in L\}$ is TrPTL-definable. This notion is defined for TrPTL^{con} and TrPTL$^{\otimes}$ in the obvious way. Hence in order to show that TrPTL^{con} is more expressive than TrPTL$^{\otimes}$ it suffices to exhibit some $L \subseteq \Sigma^{\omega}$ which is I-consistent and is TrPTL^{con}-definable but not TrPTL$^{\otimes}$-definable.

Let $\widetilde{\Gamma} = \{\Gamma_1, \Gamma_2\}$ with $\Gamma_1 = \{a, a', d\}$ and $\Gamma_2 = \{b, b', d\}$. Let $\Gamma = \{a, a', b, b', d\}$. Consider $L \subseteq \Gamma^{\omega}$ given by:

$$L = (d(ab + ba + a'b' + b'a'))^{\omega}.$$

It turns out that L is *not* TrPTL$^{\otimes}$-definable. Clearly L is I-consistent. As shown in [Thi2], for L to be TrPTL$^{\otimes}$-definable, it must be a so-called (synchronized) product language. As a result, it would have to possess the following property:

(PR) Suppose $\sigma \in \Gamma^{\omega}$. Then $\sigma \in L$ iff there exist $\sigma_1, \sigma_2 \in L$ such that $\sigma \restriction \Gamma_1 = \sigma_1 \restriction \Gamma_1$ and $\sigma \restriction \Gamma_2 = \sigma_2 \restriction \Gamma_2$.

Now let $\sigma = (dab')^{\omega}$, $\sigma_1 = (dab)^{\omega}$ and $\sigma_2 = (da'b')^{\omega}$. Clearly $\sigma \restriction \Gamma_1 = \sigma_1 \restriction \Gamma_1$ and $\sigma \restriction \Gamma_2 = \sigma_2 \restriction \Gamma_2$. Since $\sigma_1, \sigma_2 \in L$, this implies that $\sigma \in L$ which it is not. Hence L cannot be a product language and therefore is not TrPTL$^{\otimes}$-definable. On the other hand, it is a simple exercise to come up with a formula $\alpha \in \Phi^{\mathrm{con}}$ such that $\{\mathsf{str}(\sigma) \mid \sigma \in L\} = L_{\alpha}$.

We now turn to $FO(\widetilde{\Sigma})$, the first order theory of infinite traces over $\widetilde{\Sigma}$. One starts with a countable set of individual variables $X = \{x_0, x_1, \ldots\}$ with x, y, z with or without subscripts ranging over X. For each $a \in \Sigma$ there is a unary predicate symbol R_a. There is also a binary predicate symbol $\leq$.

$R_a(x)$ and $x \leq y$ are atomic formulas. If φ and φ' are formulas, so are $\neg\varphi$, $\varphi \vee \varphi'$ and $(\exists x)\varphi$. The structures for this first order theory are elements of TR^{ω}. Let $F \in TR^{\omega}$ with $F = (E, \leq, \lambda)$ and let $\mathcal{I} : X \to E$ be an interpretation. Then $F \models_{\mathcal{I}}^{FO} R_a(x)$ iff $\lambda(\mathcal{I}(x)) = a$ and $F \models_{\mathcal{I}}^{FO} x \leq y$ iff $\mathcal{I}(x) \leq \mathcal{I}(y)$. The remaining semantic definitions go along the expected lines. Each sentence φ (i.e., a formula with no free occurrences of variables) defines the ω-trace language $L_{\varphi} = \{F \mid F \models^{FO} \varphi\}$.

We say that $L \subseteq TR^{\omega}$ is FO-definable iff there exists a sentence φ in $FO(\widetilde{\Sigma})$ such that $L = L_{\varphi}$. As before we will say that $L \subseteq \Sigma^{\omega}$ is FO-definable iff L is I-consistent and $\{\mathsf{str}(\sigma) \mid \sigma \in L\}$ is FO-definable.

Using the fact that LTL has the same expressive power as the first order theory of sequences, one can show that $L \subseteq \Sigma^\omega$ is FO-definable iff it is I-consistent and LTL-definable [EM]. It will be worthwhile to pin down the notion of LTL-definability. In the current setting, remembering that (Σ, I) is the trace alphabet induced by $\widetilde{\Sigma}$, we define the syntax of the logic LTL(Σ) as follows:

$$\mathrm{LTL}(\Sigma) ::= \top \mid \neg\alpha \mid \alpha \vee \beta \mid \langle a \rangle \alpha \mid \alpha \,\mathcal{U} \beta.$$

A model is a infinite word σ. For $\sigma \in \Sigma^\omega$ and $n \in \omega$, the notion of $\alpha \in \mathrm{LTL}(\Sigma)$ being satisfied at stage n is denoted by $\sigma, n \models \alpha$. This satisfaction relation is defined in the usual manner. The only point of interest might be that $\sigma, n \models \langle a \rangle \alpha$ iff $\sigma(n{+}1) = a$ and $\sigma, n{+}1 \models \alpha$. We say that $L \subseteq \Sigma^\omega$ is LTL-definable iff there exists $\alpha \in \mathrm{LTL}(\Sigma)$ such $L = L_\alpha$ where $L_\alpha = \{\sigma \in \Sigma^\omega \mid \sigma, 0 \models \alpha\}$.

The result in [EM] relating FO-definable subsets of TR^ω and LTL-definable subsets of Σ^ω can now be phrased as follows.

Proposition 4.1 *Let $L \subseteq \Sigma^\omega$. Then, the following statements are equivalent.*

(i) *L is I-consistent and LTL-definable.*

(ii) *$\{\mathsf{str}(\sigma) \mid \sigma \in L\}$ is an FO-definable subset of TR^ω.*

We now wish to concentrate on showing that TrPTL is expressible within the first order theory of infinite traces.

To show this, we will freely use the standard derived connectives of Propositional Calculus, together with universal quantification and abbreviations such as $x = y$ for $(x \leq y) \wedge (y \leq x)$, $x \leq y \leq z$ for $(x \leq y) \wedge (y \leq z)$ etc.

An event e is an i-event iff $\lambda(e) \in \Sigma_i$. With this in mind, we let $x \in E_i$ stand for the formula $\bigvee_{a \in \Sigma_i} R_a(x)$. The key to the result we are after is the observation that configurations of a trace can be described using predicates of *bounded* dimension. In what follows we let Q, Q', Q'' range over the non-empty subsets of $\mathcal{P}$. For $Q = \{i_1, i_2, \ldots, i_n\}$, the formula $\mathsf{config}(\{x_i\}_{i \in Q})$ is defined as:

$$\begin{aligned}
\mathsf{config}(\{x_i\}_{i \in Q}) &= (\varphi_1 \wedge \varphi_2 \wedge \varphi_3), \text{ where} \\
\varphi_1 &= \textstyle\bigwedge_{i \in Q} x_i \in E_i, \\
\varphi_2 &= \textstyle\bigwedge_{i,j} \bigwedge_a (R_a(x_i) \wedge R_a(x_j)) \Rightarrow x_i = x_j, \\
\varphi_3 &= \textstyle\bigwedge_{i,j} (\forall y)\ (y \in E_j \wedge y \leq x_i) \Rightarrow y \leq x_j.
\end{aligned}$$

We can now write down a formula describing prime configurations—recall that a prime configuration is one of the form $\downarrow e$, where $e \in E$. Let $\mathrm{loc}(a) \subseteq Q$. Then the formula $\mathsf{prime}_a(\{x_i\}_{i \in Q})$ is defined as

$$\mathsf{config}(\{x_i\}_{i \in Q}) \wedge \bigwedge_{i \in \mathrm{loc}(a)} \bigwedge_{j \in Q - \mathrm{loc}(a)} R_a(x_i) \wedge (x_j \leq x_i).$$

A careful examination of this formula along with the basic properties of traces at once leads to the next result.

Proposition 4.2 *Let $F = (E, \leq, \lambda) \in TR^\omega$ and let $\mathcal{I} : X \to E$ be an interpretation. Then $F \models_{\mathcal{I}}^{FO} \mathsf{prime}_a(\{x_i\}_{i \in Q})$ iff there exists an a-event e such that for each $j \in Q$, $\mathcal{I}(x_j)$ is the $\leq_j$-maximum event in $\downarrow e \cap E_j$ and for each $j \notin Q$, $\downarrow e \cap E_j = \emptyset$.*

For each $\alpha \in \Phi$ we now define the sentence $\textsc{Sat}(\emptyset, \alpha)$ and the set of formulas $\{\textsc{Sat}(\{x_i\}_{i \in Q}, \alpha) \mid \{x_i\}_{i \in Q} \subseteq X \text{ and } \emptyset \neq Q \subseteq \mathcal{P}\}$ through simultaneous induction as follows:

- $\textsc{Sat}(\emptyset, \top) = \textsc{Sat}(\{x_i\}_{i \in Q}, \top) = (\exists x)\ x = x.$

- $\textsc{Sat}(\emptyset, \neg\alpha) = \neg\textsc{Sat}(\emptyset, \alpha).$
  $\textsc{Sat}(\{x_i\}_{i \in Q}, \neg\alpha) = \neg\textsc{Sat}(\{x_i\}_{i \in Q}, \alpha).$

- $\textsc{Sat}(\emptyset, \alpha \vee \beta) = \textsc{Sat}(\emptyset, \alpha) \vee \textsc{Sat}(\emptyset, \beta).$
  $\textsc{Sat}(\{x_i\}_{i \in Q}, \alpha \vee \beta) = \textsc{Sat}(\{x_i\}_{i \in Q}, \alpha) \vee \textsc{Sat}(\{x_i\}_{i \in Q}, \beta).$

- $\textsc{Sat}(\emptyset, \langle a \rangle_j \alpha) = \bigvee_{Q \supseteq \mathrm{loc}(a)} (\exists x_{i_1}, \exists x_{i_2}, \ldots, \exists x_{i_n})\ \varphi_1 \wedge \varphi_2 \wedge \varphi_3$
  where $Q = \{i_1, i_2, \ldots, i_n\}$ and

$$\begin{aligned} \varphi_1 &= \mathsf{prime}_a(\{x_i\}_{i \in Q}), \\ \varphi_2 &= \textsc{Sat}(\{x_i\}_{i \in Q}, \alpha), \\ \varphi_3 &= (\forall y)\ (y \in E_j \wedge y \leq x_j) \Rightarrow y = x_j. \end{aligned}$$

  $\textsc{Sat}(\{x_i\}_{i \in Q}, \langle a \rangle_j \alpha)$ is defined according to two cases.

  Case 1 $j \notin Q$: $\textsc{Sat}(\{x_i\}_{i \in Q}, \langle a \rangle_j \alpha) = \textsc{Sat}(\emptyset, \langle a \rangle_j \alpha).$

  Case 2 $j \in Q$
  $\textsc{Sat}(\{x_i\}_{i \in Q}, \langle a \rangle_j \alpha) = \bigvee_{Q' \supseteq \mathrm{loc}(a)} (\exists y_{k_1}, \exists y_{k_2}, \ldots \exists y_{k_n})\ \varphi_1 \wedge \varphi_2 \wedge \varphi_3$
  where $Q' = \{k_1, k_2, \ldots, k_n\}$ and $\{y_k\}_{k \in Q'}$ is disjoint from $\{x_i\}_{i \in Q}$ and

$$\begin{aligned} \varphi_1 &= \mathsf{prime}_a(\{y_k\}_{k \in Q'}), \\ \varphi_2 &= \textsc{Sat}(\{y_k\}_{k \in Q'}, \alpha), \\ \varphi_3 &= \forall y\ (y \in E_j \Rightarrow (y < y_j \Leftrightarrow y \leq x_j)). \end{aligned}$$

- $\textsc{Sat}(\emptyset, \alpha\, \mathcal{U}_j \beta) = \textsc{Sat}(\emptyset, \beta) \vee (\textsc{Sat}(\emptyset, \alpha) \wedge \textsc{Sat}(\emptyset, \bigvee_{a \in \Sigma_j} \langle a \rangle_j \alpha\, \mathcal{U}_j \beta)).$

  $\textsc{Sat}(\{x_i\}_{i \in Q}, \alpha\, \mathcal{U}_j \beta)$ is defined according to two cases.

  Case 1 $j \notin Q$: $\textsc{Sat}(\{x_i\}_{i \in Q}, \alpha\, \mathcal{U}_j \beta) = \textsc{Sat}(\emptyset, \alpha\, \mathcal{U}_j \beta).$

  Case 2 $j \in Q$:
  $\textsc{Sat}(\{x_i\}_{i \in Q}, \alpha\, \mathcal{U}_j \beta) = \bigvee_{a \in \Sigma_j} \bigvee_{Q' \supseteq \mathrm{loc}(a)} (\exists y_{k_1}, \exists y_{k_2}, \ldots \exists y_{k_n})\ \varphi_1 \wedge \varphi_2 \wedge \varphi_3 \wedge \varphi_4$
  where $Q' = \{k_1, k_2, \ldots, k_n\}$ and $\{y_k\}_{k \in Q'}$ is disjoint from $\{x_i\}_{i \in Q}$ and

$$\begin{aligned} \varphi_1 &= \mathsf{prime}_a(\{y_k\}_{k \in Q'}), \\ \varphi_2 &= x_j \leq y_j, \\ \varphi_3 &= \textsc{Sat}(\{y_k\}_{k \in Q'}, \beta), \\ \varphi_4 &= \forall z (z \in E_j \wedge x_j \leq z < y_j) \Rightarrow \varphi_4'. \end{aligned}$$

where $\varphi'_4 = \bigvee_{a\in\Sigma_j} \bigvee_{Q''\supseteq \text{loc}(a)} (\exists z_{\ell_1}, \exists z_{\ell_2}, \ldots, \exists z_{\ell_m})\ \varphi'_{41} \wedge \varphi'_{42} \wedge \varphi'_{43}$ with $Q'' = \{\ell_1, \ell_2, \ldots, \ell_m\}$ and $\{z_\ell\}_{\ell\in Q''}$ disjoint from both $\{x_i\}_{i\in Q}$ and $\{y_k\}_{k\in Q'}$ and

$$\begin{aligned}\varphi'_{41} &= \mathsf{prime}_a(\{z_\ell\}_{\ell\in Q''}),\\ \varphi'_{42} &= (z = z_j),\\ \varphi'_{43} &= \textsc{Sat}(\{z_\ell\}_{\ell\in Q''}, \alpha).\end{aligned}$$

Let f be the map which sends each formula in Φ to a sentence in $FO(\widetilde{\Sigma})$ via $f(\alpha) = \textsc{Sat}(\emptyset, \alpha)$. Using the previous proposition and the semantics of TrPTL, it is not difficult to prove the following:

Theorem 4.3

(i) *For every $F \in TR^\omega$, $F, \emptyset \models \alpha$ iff $F \models^{FO} f(\alpha)$.*

(ii) *If $L \subseteq TR^\omega$ is TrPTL definable then it is also $FO(\widetilde{\Sigma})$-definable.*

As mentioned earlier we do not know at present if TrPTL is expressively complete — i.e., whether every $L \subseteq TR^\omega$ which is $\text{FO}(\widetilde{\Sigma})$-definable is also TrPTL-definable. Clearly from Proposition 4.1 it follows that the expressive completeness of TrPTL can be characterized as follows:

Corollary 4.4 *The following statements are equivalent:*

(i) *TrPTL is expressively complete.*

(ii) *For every $L \subseteq \Sigma^\omega$, if L is I-consistent and L is LTL-definable then L is TrPTL definable.*

We believe that TrPTL is *not* expressively complete. This leads to the following question: What is *the* linear time temporal logic of infinite traces? Such a logic should possess the following properties:

(TR1) It should be expressively complete.

(TR2) It should admit a decision procedure (preferably in terms of asynchronous Büchi automata) whose time complexity is $2^{p(n,m)}$ where n is the size of the input formula, $m = |\Sigma|$ and p is a (low degree) polynomial in n and m.

(TR3) It should be possible to *transparently* express global liveness and safety properties in the logic.

It is worth noting that TrPTL and most of the decidable temporal logics over traces mentioned earlier such as [Nie] and [APP] cannot express all global invariant properties. The somewhat awkward semantics of the logic in [Ebi] also makes it event-based and hence not suitable for expressing invariant properties. However we believe that it should be possible to define a logic with a variant of the until operator defined in [Ebi] which will be able to capture global liveness and safety properties in a straightforward manner.

Any linear time temporal logic over traces which fulfills the properties (TR1)–(TR3) will be a very useful specification tool. In particular it will exactly capture properties that are expressible by I-consistent formulas in LTL—($\alpha \in \text{LTL}(\Sigma)$ is I-consistent iff L_α is I-consistent). This is important because it is such properties which can be verified efficiently using partial order based verification methods [GW, Val].

5 Conclusion

In this paper we have considered linear time temporal logics over traces. Our emphasis has been on TrPTL and its two sublogics $\text{TrPTL}^{\text{con}}$, $\text{TrPTL}^{\otimes}$. The choice of these logics has been mainly motivated by the fact that they are expressible within the first order theory of traces and the fact that they can be studied using asynchronous Büchi automata.

Our formulation of asynchronous Büchi automata in terms of the acceptance condition A2 appears to be particularly suited for logical studies. The present constructions are much more compact and transparent than the ones in [Thi1] which used A1 as the acceptance condition. We feel that, in the future, alternating versions of our automata will play an important role in the study of temporal logics over traces.

As we have mentioned a number of times, an important open problem is to pin down a linear time temporal logic for traces (assuming it exists!) which will fulfill the properties set out in the previous section. A solution to this problem will at once open up the possibility of investigating branching time temporal logics where path quantification is over traces.

References

[AHU] A.V. Aho, J.E. Hopcroft and J.D. Ullman: *The Design and Analysis of Algorithms*, Addison-Wesley, Reading (1974).

[APP] R. Alur, D. Peled and W. Penczek: Model-Checking of Causality Properties, *Proc. 10th IEEE LICS* (1994).

[Die] V. Diekert: *Combinatorics on traces, LNCS* **454** (1990).

[DM] V. Diekert and A. Muscholl: Deterministic Asynchronous Automata for Infinite Traces, *Acta Inf.*, **31** (1993) 379-397.

[DR] V. Diekert, G. Rozenberg (Eds.): *The Book of Traces*, World Scientific, Singapore (1995).

[Ebi] W. Ebinger: *Charakterisierung von Sprachklassen unendlicher Spuren durch Logiken*, Ph.D. Thesis, Institut für Informatik, Universität Stuttgart, Stuttgart, Germany (1994).

[EM] W. Ebinger and A. Muscholl: Logical Definability on Infinite Traces, *Theor. Comput. Sci.*, **154** (1996) 67–84.

[GP] P. GASTIN AND A. PETIT: Asynchronous Cellular Automata for Infinite Traces, *Proc. ICALP '92, LNCS* **623** (1992) 583–594.

[GW] P. GODEFROID AND P. WOLPER: A Partial Approach to Model Checking, *Inform. and Comput.*, **110** (1994) 305–326.

[Huh] M. HUHN: On Semantic and Logical Refinement of Actions, Technical Report, Institut für Informatik, Universität Hildesheim, Germany (1996).

[KP] S. KATZ AND D. PELED: Interleaving Set Temporal Logic, *Theor. Comput. Sci.*, **75** (3) (1992) 21–43.

[KMS] N. KLARLUND, M. MUKUND AND M. SOHONI: Determinizing Büchi asynchronous automata, *Proc. FST&TCS 1995, LNCS* **1026** (1995) 456–470.

[LPRT] K. LODAYA, R. PARIKH, R. RAMANUJAM AND P.S. THIAGARAJAN: A logical study of distributed transition systems, *Inform. and Comput.*, **119** (1995) 91–118.

[MP] Z. MANNA AND A. PNUELI: *The Temporal Logic of Reactive and Concurrent Systems (Specification)*, Springer-Verlag, Berlin (1991).

[Maz] A. MAZURKIEWICZ: Concurrent Program Schemes and their Interpretations, *Report DAIMI-PB-78*, Computer Science Department, Aarhus University, Denmark (1978).

[MS] M. MUKUND AND M. SOHONI: Keeping track of the latest gossip: Bounded time-stamps suffice, *Proc. FST&TCS '93, LNCS* **761** (1993) 388–399.

[Mus] A. MUSCHOLL: On the complementation of Büchi asynchronous cellular automata, *Proc. ICALP '94, LNCS* **820** (1994) 142–153.

[Nar] K. NARAYAN KUMAR: An Improved Decision Procedure for TrPTL, Unpublished Manuscript, Tata Institute of Fundamental Research, Bombay, India (1994).

[Nie] P. NIEBERT: A ν-Calculus with Local Views for Systems of Sequential Agents, *Proc. MFCS'95, LNCS* **969** (1995) 563–573.

[NPW] M. NIELSEN, G.D. PLOTKIN AND G. WINSKEL: Petri Nets, Event Structures and Domains I, *Theor. Comput. Sci.*, **13** (1980) 86–108.

[Pen] W. PENCZEK: Temporal Logics for Trace Systems: On Automated Verification, *Int. J. Found. of Comput. Sci.*, **4**(1) (1993) 31-68.

[Pnu] A. PNUELI: The Temporal Logic of Programs, *Proc. 18th IEEE FOCS* (1977) 46–57.

[Ram] R. RAMANUJAM: Locally Linear Time Temporal Logic, To appear in *Proc. 11th IEEE LICS* (1996).

[Thi1] P.S. THIAGARAJAN: A Trace Based Extension of Linear Time Temporal Logic, *Proc. 9th IEEE LICS* (1994) 438–447. Full version available as: TrPTL: A Trace Based Extension of Linear Time Temporal Logic, *Report TCS-93-6*, School of Mathematics, SPIC Science Foundation, Madras, India (1993).

[Thi2] P.S. THIAGARAJAN: A Trace Consistent Subset of PTL, *Proc. CONCUR'95, LNCS* **962** (1995) 438-452. Full version available as: PTL over Product State Spaces, *Report TCS-95-4*, School of Mathematics, SPIC Science Foundation, Madras, India (1995).

[Tho] W. THOMAS: Automata on infinite objects, in J. van Leeuwen (ed.), *Handbook of Theoretical Computer Science, Volume B*, North-Holland, Amsterdam (1990) 133–191.

[Val] A. VALMARI: Stubborn Sets for Reduced State Space Generation, *LNCS* **483** (1990) 491–515.

[VW] M. VARDI, P. WOLPER: An automata theoretic approach to automatic program verification, *Proc. 1st IEEE LICS* (1986) 332–345.

[WN] G. WINSKEL AND M. NIELSEN: Models for Concurrency, In: S. Abramsky and D. Gabbay (Eds.), *Handbook of Logic in Computer Science*, Vol 3, Oxford University Press, Oxford (1994).

[Zie] W. ZIELONKA: Notes on finite asynchronous automata, *R.A.I.R.O.—Inf. Théor. et Appl.*, **21** (1987) 99–135.

[Zuc] L. ZUCK: *Past Temporal Logic*, Ph.D. Thesis, Weizmann Institute, Rehovot, Israel (1986).

DIMACS Series in Discrete Mathematics
and Theoretical Computer Science
Volume **29**, 1997

A solution of an interleaving decision problem by a partial order technique

Albert R. Meyer* Alexander Rabinovich†

1 Introduction

1.1 Interleaving versus partial order semantics

Approaches to the semantics of concurrent systems may be divided into two main groups: interleaving and partial order. In the interleaving approach, only the temporal behavior of the events of a run is observable; in the partial order approach, 'causal dependency' between events are considered.

The supporters of the interleaving approach argue that

1. Specifications of concurrent systems always refer only to the temporal behavior and ignore causal behavior.

2. Interleaving semantics are technically much simpler than partial order semantics.

Supporters of the partial order approach argue that this approach gives a better account of the activity of a concurrent system. However, in view of (1), it is difficult to convince a researcher of interleaving semantics that casual aspects are important.

Another argument in favor of partial order semantics appeals to partial order heuristics for verification of interleaving behavior. Recently a number of such heuristics were suggested and in several case studies it was empirically demonstrated that these heuristics were efficient (see recent Proceedings of CONCUR and CAV). However, the partial order heuristics do not improve the complexity of verification.

In our paper another argument in favor of partial order semantics is provided. We consider a decision problem which is formulated in terms of interleaving semantics. The decision algorithm will be given in interleaving terms. However, we developed and proved the correctness of the algorithm by appealing to a partial order semantics.

1991 *Mathematics Subject Classification.* Primary 68Q45, 68Q68, 68Q05.

*MIT Laboratory for Computer Science Cambridge, MA 02139, USA

†Department of Computer Science, The Sackler School of Exact Sciences, Tel Aviv University, Israel 69978

This situation is similar with a situation which often occur in mathematics. For example, to find real valued functions that solve a linear differential equation we solve it over the complex numbers. Similarly, if one believes that only interleaving behavior is real he may gain by considering casual semantics.

1.2 Summary of our results

In this paper we consider the following
Decision problem: Given expressions E_1 and E_2 constructed from variables by the regular operations and shuffle. Is identity $E_1 = E_2$ true for all instantiation of its variables by formal languages?

For example, the identity $(X^*Y^*)^* = (X+Y)^*$ is true because for all languages L_1 and L_2, the languages $(L_1^*L_2^*)^*$ and $(L_1 + L_2)^*$ are the same.

The above identity contains only regular operations: concatenation, union and iteration. An easy 'folk' theorem [3] shows that the validity of an identity over regular operations can be verified by instantiating the language variables as single letters. For example, in order to check the validity of $(X^*Y^*)^* = (X+Y)^*$ we instantiate the variables X and Y by a single letters a and b and verify that $(a^*b^*)^* = (a+b)^*$. Checking this variable-free identity is a routine matter of checking equivalence of finite state automata.

In concurrency a very important role is played by parallel composition operators. The simplest of these operator is non-communicating parallel connective $||$, corresponding to shuffle of languages. The above folk theorem fails for the expressions containing shuffle. For, example for single letters a and b, the languages $a||b$ and $ab + ba$ are the same. However, the identity $X||Y = XY + YX$ is not true (indeed, instantiate X by a and Y by bc).

An algorithm for the valid identity problem is provided in this paper. In order to check the validity of an identity $E_1(X_1, \ldots, X_k) = E_2(X_1, \ldots, X_k)$ we will specify (see Theorem 3) finite languages $L_1, \ldots, L_k$ (the languages depends on E_1 and E_2) such that the identity is valid iff the variable-free identity obtained through instantiation of $X_1, \ldots, X_k$ by $L_1, \ldots, L_k$ is true. Checking this last variable-free identity is reduced to the checking of language equivalence of finite state automata.

2 Shuffle Regular Expressions

We presuppose two fixed infinite sets

$$\begin{array}{ll} Act = \{a,\ a_1, \ldots b,\ b_1, \ldots\} & \text{the actions} \\ Var = \{X,\ X_1, \ldots Y,\ Y_1, \ldots\} & \text{the variable symbols.} \end{array}$$

Shuffle regular expressions are defined by the following grammar:

$E ::= x \mid c \mid E + E \mid E; E \mid E||E \mid E^*$, where x ranges over alphabet Var of variable symbols and, c ranges over alphabet Act of constant symbols.

$[\![a]\!]\sigma = \{a\}$
$[\![x]\!]\sigma = \sigma(x)$
$[\![E_1 + E_2]\!]\sigma =$ Union of $[\![E_1]\!]\sigma$ and $[\![E_2]\!]\sigma^{pom}$
$[\![E_1; E_2]\!]\sigma =$ Concatenation of $[\![E_1]\!]\sigma$ and $[\![E_2]\!]\sigma^{pom}$
$[\![E_1 || E_2]\!]\sigma =$ Shuffle of $[\![E_1]\!]\sigma$ and $[\![E_2]\!]\sigma$
$[\![E_1^*]\!]\sigma = ([\![E]\!]\sigma)^*$

Figure 1: Definition of $[\![E]\!]\sigma$

We denote by $FVar(E)$ the set of variables which occur in E.

We say that E is a variable free expression if $FVar(E) = \emptyset$.

We use notation $E\{E_1/X_1 \ldots E_n/X_n\}$ for the expression obtained from E by simultaneous substitution of E_i for X_i. We use $\sum_{i=1}^{n} E_i$ as an abbreviation for for $E_1 + E_2 + \ldots + E_n$.

A string is a finite sequence of actions; we use w, u to range over strings. A string language is a set of strings; we use L to range over string languages.

The operations sum, concatenation, iteration and shuffle are defined in a standard way on the string languages.

We recall that a string w belongs to the shuffle of languages L_1 and L_2 if $w = w_1 u_1 v_2 u_2 \ldots w_k u_k$ where $w_1 w_2 \ldots w_k \in L_1$ and $u_1 u_2 \ldots u_k \in L_2$.

A string language environment for $\{X_1 \ldots X_n\}$ is a function which assigns to X_i a string language. For an expression E and a string language environment σ for a set that contains the free variables of E, the string language $[\![E]\!]\sigma$ is assigned in a standard way by structural induction on the expressions (see Fig. 1).

It is clear that if $\sigma(x) = \sigma'(x)$ for every $x \in Fvar(E)$ then $[\![E]\!]\sigma = [\![E]\!]\sigma'$

3 The Valid Identity Problem

We will consider the following decision problem
Valid Identity Problem:
Input: A pair of shuffle regular expressions E_1 and E_2.
Question: Is the identity $E_1 = E_2$ valid, i.e., are the languages $[\![E_1]\!]\sigma$ and $[\![E_2]\!]\sigma$ equal for every string language environment σ for $Fvar(E_1) \cup FVar(E_2)$.

The main technical result of our paper is

Theorem 1 *The valid identity problem for shuffle regular expressions is decidable.*

Theorem 1 follows from the next two theorems.

Theorem 2 *The valid identity problem for variable free shuffle regular expressions is decidable.*

$sn(X) = sn(a) = 0$
$sn(E_1 + E_2) = sn(E_1; E_2) = max(sn(E_1), sn(E_2))$
$sn(E_1 || E_2) = sn(E_1) + sn(E_2) + 1$
$sn(E^*) = sn(E)$

Figure 2: Shuffle nesting of Expressions

Proof: The problem is easily reduced to the problem of equivalence of finite state automata. □

Notation: The shuffle nesting of an expression E is denoted by $sn(E)$ and is defined in Fig. 2.

Theorem 3 *Let E_1 and E_2 be shuffle expressions over variables $X_1, \ldots, X_n$ such that the shuffle nesting of E_1 and E_2 is bounded by k.*
Let $\{a_{i,j}, \overline{a}_{i,j} : i = 1, \ldots, n;\ j = 1, \ldots, k\}$ be distinct actions which do not occur in the expressions E_1, E_2. Let $SPLIT_k^i$ be the expression $\sum_{j=1}^{k} a_{i,j}; \overline{a}_{i,j}$. Identity $E_1 = E_2$ is valid if and only if the variable free identity
$E_1\{SPLIT_k^1/X_1 \ldots SPLIT_k^n/X_n\} = E_2\{SPLIT_k^1/X_1 \ldots SPLIT_k^n/X_n\}$ is valid.

Proof: In order to proof this theorem we appeal to the notions which were developed in the casual approach to concurrency. Theorem 3 follows from Theorem 7 and Theorem 9, part 2, below. □

4 Pomsets

Definition 1 *(Pratt [6]) A concrete pomset P over set Σ of labels consists of a set of events $Events_P$ which are partially ordered by a relation $\leq_P$ and a function lab_P from $Events_P$ into Σ. A function f is an isomorphism between concrete pomsets P_1 and P_2 if it is label preserving isomorphism between the partial orders of P_1 and P_2. An (abstract) pomset is an isomorphism class of concrete pomsets.*

Throughout the paper we provide some definitions and constructions for concrete pomsets. All these definition/constructions are extended in a natural way to the abstract pomsets.

Definition 2 *Events e_1 and e_2 of a pomset P are* **concurrent** *(notation $e_1\ co_P\ e_2$) if neither $e_1 \leq_P e_2$ nor $e_2 \leq_P e_1$.*

Definition 3 *The* **width** *of a pomset P is the maximal number of mutually concurrent events in the P.*

Definition 4 *A* **pomset language** *over Σ is a set of pomsets over Σ. We say that a pomset language PL has width at most n if all pomsets in PL have width less or equal than n.*

Definition 5 *A concrete pomset P is an* **augmentation** *of a concrete pomset Q if $Events_P = Events_Q$, $lab_P = lab_Q$ and $e_1 \leq_Q e_2$ implies $e_1 \leq_P e_2$ for all $e_1, e_2 \in Events_P$.*

Definition 6 *A concrete pomset P is a* **linearly ordered pomset** *if $\leq_P$ is a linear order over $Events_P$.*

We will identify a linearly ordered pomset over a label set Σ with the corresponding string over alphabet Σ. Also every string language is considered as a pomset language.

Definition 7 *The* **linearization** *of a pomset language PL (notation $Lin(PL)$) is the string language L such that $w \in L$ iff w is a linearly ordered augmentation of a pomset $P \in PL$.*

Notations: A pomset containing only one event labeled by l will be denoted by l. The pomset language containing only one pomset P will be denoted by $\{P\}$; in particular, the language containing only the one element pomset labeled by l will be denoted by $\{l\}$.

5 Refinement

Let P be a pomset and f be a function which assigns a pomset to every event of P.

The **f-expansion** of P is a pomset Q obtained by replacing every event of P by its image. Formally,

$Events_Q = \{(e, e') \ : e \in P,\ e' \in f(e)\}$;

$(e_1, e_2) \leq_Q (e_3, e_4)$ if either $e_1 \leq_P e_3$ or $e_1 = e_3$ and $e_2 \leq_{f(e_1)} e_4$.

$lab_Q((e, e')) = lab_{f(e)}(e')$.

We use the notation $Expan(P, f)$ for the f expansion of pomset P.

Definition 8 *A pomset language environment for a set of labels Σ is a function which assigns a pomset language to every label in Σ.*

Notations We use the notation $[l_1 \rightarrow PL_1,\ l_2 \rightarrow PL_2, \ldots, l_n \rightarrow PL_n]$ for the pomset environment which maps l_i to PL_i, $i = 1, \ldots, n$. We denote by $PLE(\Sigma)$ the set of pomset language environment for Σ. We use α, β to range over pomset language environments. We denote by $SLE(\Sigma)$ the set of string language environments for Σ. We use σ, τ to range over string language environments.

Definition 9 *Let P be a pomset. Let f be a function which assigns a pomset to every event of P and let α be a pomset language environment for Σ. The function f is* **consistent** *with α if for every event e*

1. $f(e) \in \alpha(lab_P(e))$ *if* $lab_p(e) \in \Sigma$,

2. $f(e) = \{lab_P(e)\}$ *otherwise.*

Definition 10 *Let α be a pomset language environment for Σ. The* **α-refinement** *$REF(PL, \alpha)$ of a pomset language PL is $\{Expan(P, f) \colon P \in PL$ and f is consistent with $\alpha\}$.*

The refinement operation has properties similar to substitution operation:

Lemma 4 *Let PL be a pomset language over an alphabet Σ and α be a pomset language environment for an alphabet Σ'. If $\Sigma \cap \Sigma' \subseteq \{l_1, \ldots, l_k\}$ then*
$REF((REF(PL, [l_1 \to PL_1, \ldots, l_k \to PL_k]), \alpha) =$
$= REF(PL, [l_1 \to REF(PL_1, \alpha), \ldots, l_k \to REF(PL_k, \alpha)])$.

The next lemma state how linearization operator interacts with refinement.

Lemma 5 $Lin(REF(PL, [l_1 \to PL_1, \ldots, l_k \to PL_k]) = Lin(REF(PL, [l_1 \to Lin(PL_1), \ldots, l_k \to Lin(PL_k)]$

6 Operations definable by pomset languages

Definition 11 *The* **application of a pomset language** *PL to a string language environment τ (notation $PL \bullet \tau$) is the string language defined as $Lin(REF(PL, \tau))$.*

Definition 12 *Let F be a function from string language environments for Σ into string languages. We say that F is* **definable by a pomset language** *PL if $F\tau = PL \bullet \tau$ for all $\tau \in SLE(\Sigma)$.*

Observation 6 *The regular operations and shuffle are pomset language definable, namely*

1. *Let $PAR(X, Y)$ be the pomset consisting of two unordered events labeled by X and Y. It is easy to see that $[\![X || Y]\!]$ defines the same operation as $\{PAR(X, Y)\}$ over the string environments for $\{X, Y\}$.*

2. *Let $SEQ(X, Y)$ be a pomset with two events labeled by X and Y such that the event X precedes the event Y. It is easy to see that $[\![X; Y]\!]$ defines the same operation as $\{SEQ(X, Y)\}$ over the string environments for $\{X, Y\}$.*

3. *Let $SUM(X, Y)$ be the pomset language consisting of two one element pomsets X and Y. It is easy to see that $[\![X + Y]\!]$ defines the same operation as $SUM(X, Y)$ over the string environments for $\{X, Y\}$.*

4. *Let $ITER(X)$ be the pomset language which consists of all finite strings over symbol X. It is easy to see that $[\![X^*]\!]$ defines the same operation as $ITER(X)$ over the string environments for $\{X\}$.*

$[\![a]\!]^{pom} = \{a\}$
$[\![x]\!]^{pom} = \{x\}$
$[\![E_1 + E_2]\!]^{pom} = REF(SUM(X,Y),\ [X \to [\![E_1]\!]^{pom},\ Y \to [\![E_2]\!]^{pom}])$
$[\![E_1; E_2]\!]^{pom} = REF(SEQ(X,Y),\ [X \to [\![E_1]\!]^{pom},\ Y \to [\![E_2]\!]^{pom}])$
$[\![E_1 || E_2]\!]^{pom} = REF(PAR(X,Y),\ [X \to [\![E_1]\!]^{pom},\ Y \to [\![E_2]\!]^{pom}])$
$[\![E_1^*]\!]^{pom} = REF(ITER(X),\ [X \to [\![E]\!]^{pom}])$

Figure 3: Pomset Semantics

Theorem 7 *For every shuffle regular expression E, the operation $\lambda\sigma.\ [\![E]\!]\sigma$ is definable by a pomset language with width bounded by the shuffle nesting of E.*

Proof: By structural induction on the expressions the pomset language $[\![E]\!]^{pom}$ is assigned to every shuffle regular expression (see Fig. 3). Relying on Lemma 4, Lemma 5 and Observation 6, it can be shown that $[\![E]\!]\sigma = [\![E]\!]^{pom} \bullet \sigma$, where σ is any language environment σ for the $Fvar(E)$. □

Definition 13 *A string language environment $[l_1 \to L_1, \ldots l_n \to L_n]$, is called a split-choice environment for $\{l_1 \ldots l_n\}$ if every L_i contains only strings of length two.*

Lemma 8 *$PL \bullet \tau = PL' \bullet \tau$ for every string language environment τ for Σ iff $PL \bullet \tau = PL' \bullet \tau$ for every split-choice environment τ for Σ.*

This lemma can be strengthened as follows:

Theorem 9 *Let PL and PL' be pomset languages over an alphabet Σ and let $\{a_{i,j},\ \overline{a}_{i,j}\ :\ i = 1, \ldots, n\ ,\ j \in Nat\}$ be distinct labels not in Σ. Let $L_i^{(\infty)}$ be string language $\{a_{i,j}; \overline{a}_{i,j}\ :\ j \in Nat\}$ and let $L_i^{(k)}$ be string language $\{a_{i,j}; \overline{a}_{i,j}\ :\ j = 1, 2, \ldots, k\}$.*

1. *$PL \bullet \tau = PL' \bullet \tau$ for every string language environment τ for $\{m_1, \ldots, m_n\}$ iff $PL \bullet [m_1 \to L_1^{(\infty)}, \ldots, m_n \to L_n^{(\infty)}] = PL' \bullet [m_1 \to L_1^{(\infty)}, \ldots, m_n \to L_n^{(\infty)}]$.*

2. *Let PL and PL' be pomset languages of width at most k. Then $PL \bullet \tau = PL' \bullet \tau$ for every string language environment τ for $\{m_1, \ldots, m_n\}$ if and only if $PL \bullet [m_1 \to L_1^{(k)}, \ldots, m_n \to L_n^{(k)}] = PL' \bullet [m_1 \to L_1^{(k)}, \ldots, m_n \to L_n^{(k)}]$.*

Remarks (1) The above theorem can be strengthened as follows: Let k_i be the bound on the number of mutual concurrent events labeled by m_i in the pomset languages PL and PL'. Then $PL \bullet \tau = PL' \bullet \tau$ for every string language environment τ for $\{m_1, \ldots, m_n\}$ if and only if
$PL \bullet [m_1 \to L_1^{(k_1)}, \ldots, m_n \to L_n^{(k_n)}] = PL' \bullet [m_1 \to L_1^{(k_1)}, \ldots, m_n \to L_n^{(k_n)}]$.
(2) Weaker versions of the above theorem have appeared in the literature.

Gischer [1] considered the operations definable by pomsets. One of his results can be stated as follows: For pomsets P and P' with less than k events, $\{P\} \bullet \tau = \{P'\} \bullet \tau$ for every string language environment τ for $\{m_1, \ldots, m_n\}$ if and only if $\{P\} \bullet [m_1 \to L_1^{(k)}, \ldots, m_n \to L_n^{(k)}] = \{P'\} \bullet [m_1 \to L_1^{(k)}, \ldots, m_n \to L_n^{(k)}]$.

In [5] the special pomsets which are called semi-words are considered. A pomset is a semi-word if no events with the same label are concurrent. It was proved in [5] that for semi-word languages SWL and SWL' the following theorem holds: $SWL \bullet \tau = SWL' \bullet \tau$ for for every string language environment τ for $\{m_1, \ldots, m_n\}$ if and only if
$SWL \bullet [m_1 \to L_1^{(1)}, \ldots, m_n \to L_n^{(1)}] = SWL' \bullet [m_1 \to L_1^{(1)}, \ldots, m_n \to L_n^{(1)}]$.

(3) The proof of Theorem 9 can be extracted from the proofs of these two weaker versions.

7 Further Results

7.1 Complexity of the valid identity problem

An exponential space algorithm can be provided for the valid identity problem. Mayer and Stockmeyer [2] provided EXPSPACE lower bound for the valid identity problem of the variable free shuffle regular expression. These results give a tight lower and upper bound for the valid identity problem.

7.2 Extension by other pomset language definable operations

Let OP be an n-ary operation on string languages. We say that OP is effective on regular languages if there exists an algorithm which constructs a finite automaton for the language $OP(L_1, \ldots, L_n)$ from finite automata for $L_1, \ldots, L_n$.

We say that OP is definable by (finite width) pomset language if there exists a (finite width) pomset language PL such that $PL \bullet [1 \to L_1, \ldots, n \to L_n] = OP(L_1, \ldots, L_n)$ for any languages $L_1, \ldots, L_n$.

Note that the operations definable by finite pomset languages are effective on regular languages. Among such operations are operations which are not definable by any shuffle regular expressions.

The valid identity problem is decidable for the expressions constructed over any set of operations which are effective on regular languages and are definable by finite width pomset languages.

7.3 Extension by Intersection

Micciancio [4] proved the decidability of the valid identity problem for constant free shuffle-intersection regular expressions. These expressions are defined by the following grammar: $E ::= x \mid E \cap E \mid E + E \mid E; E \mid E || E \mid E^*$, where x ranges over variable symbols.

Note that the intersection is not a pomset language definable operation. Micciancio's very interesting proof is given in terms of interleaving semantics and does not use explicitly pomsets. It is an open problem whether his results and techniques can be extended to other pomset language definable operations and in particular to the expressions which contain constants.

Acknowledgments

We would like to thank Yoram Hirshfeld and Boris Trakhtenbrot for stimulating discussions and many constructive suggestions.

References

[1] J. Gischer. Partial Orders and Theory of Shuffle. PhD thesis, Stanford University, 1984.

[2] A. Mayer and L. Stockmeyer. The complexity of word problem - this time with interleaving. Information and Computation, pages 293-311, Vol 115, 1994.

[3] A. R. Meyer. Concurrent Process Equivalences: Some decision problems. In STAC 95, volume 900 of *Lect. Notes in Computer Science*, Springer Verlag, 1995.

[4] D. Micciancio. The Validity problem for Extended regular Expressions. M SC thesis, MIT, 1996.

[5] M.. Nielsen, U. Engberg, and K. Larsen. A Simple Process Language with Refinement. In *REX Workshop on Linear Time, Branching time and Partial Order in Logics and Models for Concurrency* , volume 354 of *Lect. Notes in Computer Science*, pages 523-548, Springer Verlag, 1990.

[6] V. R. Pratt, On the composition of Processes. In *Proc. of the Ninth Annual ACM Symposium on Principles of Programming Languages*, 1982.

DIMACS Series in Discrete Mathematics
and Theoretical Computer Science
Volume **29**, 1997

Stubborn Set Methods for Process Algebras

Antti Valmari

ABSTRACT. The construction of reduced state spaces of concurrent process-algebraic systems using the stubborn set or related methods is discussed. The goal is to avoid altogether the construction of the big ordinary state space of the system, and construct a smaller, but equivalent, state space instead. Five equivalence notions are covered: "deadlock equivalence" (the reduced and full state spaces have exactly the same deadlock states), trace equivalence, CSP-equivalence, CFFD-equivalence and branching bisimilarity. Most of the methods are similar to stubborn set or related methods in other application areas. However, because of the absence of the notion of "structural deterministic transition" (such as the Petri net transition) in process algebras, earlier definitions and proofs were not applicable, and the theory behind the methods had to be re-developed from the beginning.

1. Introduction

The fact that the total effect of a set of concurrent transitions (or operations or actions) is independent of execution order has been utilised in computer-aided verification methods in many ways. One main approach is to generate only a subset of the interleaved executions of the system under verification (see e.g. [God96, Pel93, Val94]). The subset is represented as an ordinary interleaved state space, called *reduced* state space. It is chosen in such a way that from the point of view of the verification task at hand, it can represent all executions. That is, the answer to the verification question is guaranteed to be the same for both the full and the reduced state space.

The reduced state space is obtained by using only a subset of enabled transitions when constructing the immediate successor states of a state. It has turned out that the selection of a "sufficient" subset depends on the verification question. Furthermore, it may be necessary to ensure that certain conditions that depend on more than one state hold in the reduced state space. Even for a fixed verification question, the construction of the sufficient subset depends on the formalism in which the system has been represented — the techniques that are good for Petri nets do not necessarily work for parallel labelled transition systems. Moreover, the subset is not completely defined by the requirement that it has to be "sufficient". Some algorithms are capable of finding smaller sufficient subsets than others, at the price of consuming more time.

As a consequence, different authors have investigated the reduced state space construction problem with different goals and formal frameworks, and have developed a vari-

1991 *Mathematics Subject Classification.* Primary 68Q60; Secondary 03B35, 68Q90.

ety of different algorithms and methods with names such as *persistent sets*, *ample sets* and *stubborn sets*. Despite of the differences, these approaches have quite a lot in common. Many ideas that have been originally developed in the context of, say, ample sets, can be used with, say, stubborn sets. To be consistent with terminology within this article, the stubborn set vocabulary is used. It is emphasized, however, that from the point of view of the subject matter this is a somewhat arbitrary choice; this article could have been written in the ample set or persistent set language.

The generic term "partial-order methods" is often used of the stubborn set method and its relatives. But it covers also methods that are not based on choosing representative interleavings and presenting them in the form of an ordinary (but reduced) state space, such as the *unfolding* method [McM93, Esp94]. So it is too general for the present article. Furthermore, in the opinion of the present author, the term "partial-order methods" is misleading. The term refers to semantic models of concurrency where the ordering of the occurrences of mutually independent transitions is partial. The stubborn set and related methods take advantage of commutativity properties that resemble the "independency" relation of partial-order models, but is slightly different, and has sometimes different consequences. (This difference will not be obvious in the context of the present article, but it has proven important in the case of Petri nets, for instance.)

This article is devoted to the application of the stubborn set approach (or its relatives) to process-algebraic verification. Compared to other applications of stubborn set methods, the biggest difference is in the notion of "transition". Stubborn set methods usually rely on "deterministic" "structural" transitions, such as the transitions of a Petri net. Transitions are responsible of state changes. That they are "deterministic" means that the occurrence of a transition in a state produces always the same immediate successor state. The word "structural" indicates that it is meaningful to talk about the same transition in different states. In process algebras, the word "transition" denotes what would be the *occurrence* of a transition in Petri net terminology. No individual "performer" of the occurrence can be distinguished; the responsibility of (the execution of) the transition is distributed over several processes of the system. Deterministic structural transitions do not exist. The set of processes that participate (the execution of) a transition is determined by the concept of *action*. In some sense, an action is the name of several transitions. Actions are structural, but they are not deterministic.

The absence of deterministic structural transitions affects the development of the theory. It is not any more possible to utilise the assumption that if two transitions occur in both orders, the end result is the same. This is because the end result is no more unique, so the two orderings may choose different members from the set of possible end results. The use of actions has also some effects on the construction of stubborn sets. In other respects, the stubborn set methods and algorithms for process-algebraic verification are pretty much the same as in other stubborn set or related methods.

The goal of the methods described in this article is to produce a reduced state space that is *equivalent* to the full one in the sense of some process-algebraic equivalence. Literally hundreds of different equivalences have been defined in the process algebra literature. The majority of them is, however, based on few main ideas. In this article we discuss some well-known and one less well known equivalence that together cover most of the important ideas.

The earliest explicit application of the stubborn set or related methods to process algebras was [VaC91]. In it, transitions were deterministic, but not structural. As a consequence, the mathematics became complicated, and it was almost impossible to describe how stubborn sets may be constructed. These problems were solved in [Val92b] by using actions as transitions and re-working the theory to allow non-deterministic transitions. The goal of [Val92b] was to produce reduced state spaces that are *CSP*- [BrR85, Hoa85] or *CFFD-equivalent* [VaT91, VaT95] with the full ones. The method was closely related to the linear temporal logic -preserving stubborn set method presented in [Val92a]. A method that preserves *branching bisimilarity* [vGW89, vGl90] was first presented in [GK+95]. Because branching bisimilarity implies *weak bisimilarity* (known also as *observation equivalence*) [Mil89], the [GK+95] method preserves also the latter.

This article is organised as follows. The necessary process-algebraic concepts including the above-mentioned equivalences are introduced in Section 2. To simplify the development of the stubborn set theory, the definitions are presented in a somewhat non-standard form, although the concepts they define are standard. Section 3 presents the basic facts about the stubborn sets of process-algebraic concurrent systems. A method preserving trace equivalence is described in Section 4. This method is a reasonably straightforward application of the results in [Val91] and [Val92b]. The CSP- and CFFD-preserving methods from [Val92b] are repeated in Section 5. Section 6 is devoted to a translation of the [GK+95] branching bisimilarity method to the present framework with non-deterministic actions. The conclusions are in Section 7.

Throughout this article, small improvements are made to the methods presented. For instance, the assumption that the reduced state space is finite, is mostly eliminated. This may become important in the future, if the stubborn set method is combined with methods that represent infinite state spaces by finite data structures.

2. Processes, Parallel Composition, and Equivalences

In process algebras, the behaviour of a system consists of executions of *actions*. There are two kinds of actions: *visible* and *invisible*. Each system has a fixed set of visible actions it may execute, and the environment of the system can observe or even synchronise with the execution of a visible action. Executions of invisible actions cannot be directly observed. It is customary to use the one symbol "τ" to denote all of them. An invisible action may represent a hidden internal action that is participated by several component processes of the system. Knowledge of the set of the component processes that participate the internal action is important for the stubborn set method. Therefore, in this article, invisible actions are not denoted by τ, but it is assumed that each process has its own sets of visible and invisible actions. As was described in [Val92b], a system with τ-transitions can be easily converted to the form required in this article by re-naming the τ-transitions in a suitable way.

In process-algebraic computer-aided verification, the behaviour of a system is usually represented by a *labelled transition system* (*LTS*). An LTS is a directed graph whose vertices correspond to states, one of the vertices is distinguished as the initial state, and edges correspond to transitions and are labelled by actions.

Definition 2.1 A *labelled transition system* (*LTS*) is a five-tuple $(S, \Sigma_V, \Sigma_I, \Delta, is)$, where S is the set of *states*, Σ_V is the set of *visible actions*, Σ_I is the set of *invisible actions*, $\Sigma_V \cap \Sigma_I = \emptyset$, $\Delta \subseteq S \times (\Sigma_V \cup \Sigma_I) \times S$ is the set of *transitions*, and $is \in S$ is the *initial state*. The *action alphabet* is $\Sigma = \Sigma_V \cup \Sigma_I$. □

The following notation is useful for talking about action sequences and enabled actions.

Definition 2.2 Let $L = (S, \Sigma_V, \Sigma_I, \Delta, is)$ be an LTS, s, s' and $s_0, \ldots, s_n \in S$, and a and $a_1, \ldots, a_n \in \Sigma$.

- $s -a\rightarrow s'$ if and only if $(s, a, s') \in \Delta$.
- $s_0 -a_1\rightarrow s_1 -a_2\rightarrow \ldots -a_n\rightarrow s_n$ if and only if $s_0 -a_1\rightarrow s_1$ and $\ldots$ and $s_{n-1} -a_n\rightarrow s_n$.
- $s -a_1a_2\ldots a_n\rightarrow s'$ if and only if there are $s_0, \ldots, s_n \in S$ such that $s_0 = s$, $s_n = s'$, and $s_0 -a_1\rightarrow s_1 -a_2\rightarrow \ldots -a_n\rightarrow s_n$.
- $s \rightarrow^* s'$ if and only if there are $a_1, \ldots, a_n \in \Sigma$ such that $s -a_1a_2\ldots a_n\rightarrow s'$. In particular, $s \rightarrow^* s$.
- $s -a_1a_2\ldots a_n\rightarrow$ if and only if there is s' such that $s -a_1a_2\ldots a_n\rightarrow s'$.
- $s \not\!-a_1a_2\ldots a_n\not\rightarrow s'$ if and only if $\neg(s -a_1a_2\ldots a_n\rightarrow s')$, and similarly with $s \not\!-a_1a_2\ldots a_n\not\rightarrow$ and $s \not\rightarrow^* s'$.
- $next(s) = \{ a \in \Sigma \mid s -a\rightarrow \}$. □

The *parallel composition* of LTSs is defined below. A parallel composition may execute action a if and only if all component processes that have a in their alphabets are ready to execute a. The execution of a forces all those component processes to execute an a-transition, and does not affect the remaining component processes. Synchronisation is thus determined by the alphabets of the component processes.

Definition 2.3 Let $L_1 = (S_1, \Sigma_{V1}, \Sigma_{I1}, \Delta_1, is_1), \ldots, L_n = (S_n, \Sigma_{Vn}, \Sigma_{In}, \Delta_n, is_n)$ be LTSs such that $(\Sigma_{V1} \cup \ldots \cup \Sigma_{Vn}) \cap (\Sigma_{I1} \cup \ldots \cup \Sigma_{In}) = \emptyset$. Their *parallel composition* is the LTS $L_1 \parallel \ldots \parallel L_n = (S, \Sigma_V, \Sigma_I, \Delta, is)$ defined as follows:

- $S = S_1 \times \ldots \times S_n$, $\Sigma_V = \Sigma_{V1} \cup \ldots \cup \Sigma_{Vn}$, $\Sigma_I = \Sigma_{I1} \cup \ldots \cup \Sigma_{In}$, and $is = (is_1, \ldots, is_n)$.
- Let $(s_1, \ldots, s_n) \in S$ and $a \in \Sigma_V \cup \Sigma_I$. We have $((s_1, \ldots, s_n), a, (s'_1, \ldots, s'_n)) \in \Delta$ if and only if for every $1 \le i \le n$, either $a \in \Sigma_{Vi} \cup \Sigma_{Ii}$ and $(s_i, a, s'_i) \in \Delta_i$, or $a \notin \Sigma_{Vi} \cup \Sigma_{Ii}$ and $s'_i = s_i$. □

We use the following notation for sequences.

Definition 2.4

- The empty sequence is denoted by ε.
- X^* and X^ω are the sets of finite and infinite sequences of symbols from X.
- If σ and $\sigma' \in X^* \cup X^\omega$, then $\sigma' < \sigma$ denotes that σ' is a proper prefix of σ, and $\sigma' \le \sigma$ holds if and only if $\sigma' < \sigma$ or $\sigma' = \sigma$. □

The main goal of process-algebraic equivalences is to abstract away from invisible actions. The following notation and concepts are useful for that purpose.

Definition 2.5 Let $L = (S, \Sigma_V, \Sigma_I, \Delta, is)$ be an LTS, s and $s' \in S$, $\rho \in \Sigma^*$, and $\sigma \in \Sigma_V^*$.

- $vis(\rho)$ is the result of the removal of all actions in Σ_I from ρ.
- $s =\sigma\Rightarrow s'$ if and only if there is $\rho \in \Sigma^*$ such that $s -\rho\rightarrow s'$ and $\sigma = vis(\rho)$.
- $s =\sigma\Rightarrow$ if and only if there is an s' such that $s =\sigma\Rightarrow s'$.
- $s \ne\sigma\not\Rightarrow s'$ if and only if $\neg(s =\sigma\Rightarrow s')$, and similarly with $s \ne\sigma\not\Rightarrow$. □

Three of the equivalences that we will discuss can be defined in terms of the following sets. *Stability* of a state means that if a process is in a stable state, then its next action cannot be invisible. A process is stable if its initial state is. The ordinary and infinite *traces* of a process are the finite and infinite sequences of visible actions generated by the (not necessarily complete) executions of the process. A *divergence trace* is a trace after which the process can execute an infinite sequence of invisible actions. A divergence trace is *minimal*, if none of its proper prefixes is a divergence trace. A *stable failure* consists of a trace and a set of visible actions such that after executing the trace, the process may be in a stable state where it cannot execute any action from the set. In the CSP theory [BrR85, Hoa85] divergence is considered catastrophic. The catastrophic nature of divergence can be represented in the present framework by declaring that a process may do just anything after executing a divergence trace. Therefore, any sequence of visible actions that has a "real" divergence trace as its prefix is considered a CSP-divergence trace, and it may be paired with just any set of visible actions to form a CSP-failure.

Definition 2.6 Let $L = (S, \Sigma_V, \Sigma_I, \Delta, is)$ be an LTS.

- $s \in S$ is *stable*, if and only if $s \not\text{-}a\not\to$ for every $a \in \Sigma_I$. Furthermore, L is stable if and only if its initial state *is* is stable. The predicate *stable*(L) is "**true**" if and only if L is stable.
- The set of *traces* of L is $tr(L) = \{ \sigma \in \Sigma_V^* \mid is = \sigma \Rightarrow \}$.
- The set of *stable failures* of L is
  $sfail(L) = \{ (\sigma, A) \in \Sigma_V^* \times 2^{\Sigma_V} \mid \exists s \in S \colon is = \sigma \Rightarrow s \wedge next(s) \subseteq \Sigma_V - A \}$.
- The set of *infinite traces* of L is
  $inftr(L) = \{ \zeta \in \Sigma_V^\omega \mid \exists \omega \in \Sigma^\omega \colon \zeta = vis(\omega) \wedge is -\omega\to \}$.
- The set of *divergence traces* of L is
  $divtr(L) = \{ \sigma \in \Sigma_V^* \mid \exists \omega \in \Sigma^\omega \colon \sigma = vis(\omega) \wedge is -\omega\to \}$.
- The set of *minimal divergence traces* of L is
  $mindiv(L) = \{ \sigma \in divtr(L) \mid \forall \sigma' < \sigma \colon \sigma' \notin divtr(L) \}$.
- The set of *CSP-divergence traces* of L is
  $CSPdiv(L) = \{ \sigma \in \Sigma_V^* \mid \exists \sigma' \in divtr(L) \colon \sigma' \leq \sigma \}$.
- The set of *CSP-failures* of L is
  $CSPfail(L) = sfail(L) \cup (CSPdiv(L) \times 2^{\Sigma_V})$. □

The *trace equivalence*, *CSP-equivalence* [BrR85, Hoa85] and *CFFD-equivalence* [VaT91, VaT95] can be defined as follows. The trace equivalence simply compares the sets of traces of two systems. CSP-equivalence compares the CSP variants of the failures and divergence traces. CFFD-equivalence uses stable failures and "real" divergence traces. In order to maintain the *compositionality* property that is often required from process-algebraic equivalences, CFFD-equivalence compares also the infinite traces and initial stability. CFFD-equivalence is strictly stronger than CSP-equivalence in the sense that CFFD-equivalence makes more distinctions between systems. Unlike CSP-equivalence, CFFD-equivalence preserves meaningful information of the behaviour of a process even after it has executed a divergence trace. The motivation behind the definition of CFFD-equivalence is explained in detail and CFFD-equivalence is compared to CSP-equivalence in [VaT95].

Definition 2.7 Let L_1 and L_2 be two LTSs such that their sets of visible actions are the same, i.e. $\Sigma_{V1} = \Sigma_{V2}$.

- $L_1 =_{tr} L_2$ if and only if $tr(L_1) = tr(L_2)$.
- $L_1 =_{CSP} L_2$ if and only if $CSPfail(L_1) = CSPfail(L_2)$ and $CSPdiv(L_1) = CSPdiv(L_2)$.
- $L_1 =_{CFFD} L_2$ if and only if $stable(L_1) = stable(L_2)$, $sfail(L_1) = sfail(L_2)$, $divtr(L_1) = divtr(L_2)$, and $inftr(L_1) = inftr(L_2)$. □

The last two equivalences discussed in this article are *weak bisimilarity* [Mil89] and *branching bisimilarity* [vGW89, vGl90]. They are both based on a notion of *simulation* between LTSs. Two systems are equivalent, if they can simulate each other starting at their initial states. In weak bisimilarity, an invisible transition may be simulated by a sequence of invisible transitions of any length, and a transition labelled by a visible action a may be simulated by a sequence consisting of an a-transition surrounded by any number of invisible transitions. In branching bisimilarity, invisible transitions may be simulated by doing nothing. Furthermore, any a-transition may be simulated by first executing zero or more invisible transitions in such a way that this sequence may be simulated by doing nothing; and then executing an a-transition if a is visible, or an invisible transition if a is invisible. The simulation relations are traditionally defined on the states of a single LTS.

Definition 2.8 Let $L = (S, \Sigma_V, \Sigma_I, \Delta, is)$ be an LTS. A binary relation "$\sim$" $\subseteq S \times S$ over the states of L is a *weak bisimulation*, if and only if for every $a \in \Sigma$ and every s_1, s_2 and $s \in S$ such that $s_1 \sim s_2$ the following hold:

- If $s_1 -a\rightarrow s$, then there is $s' \in S$ such that $s \sim s'$ and $s_2 = vis(a) \Rightarrow s'$.
- If $s_2 -a\rightarrow s$, then there is $s' \in S$ such that $s' \sim s$ and $s_1 = vis(a) \Rightarrow s'$.

The relation "$\sim$" is a *branching bisimulation*, if and only if for every $a \in \Sigma$ and every s_1, s_2 and $s \in S$ such that $s_1 \sim s_2$ the following hold:

- If $s_1 -a\rightarrow s$, then either $a \in \Sigma_I$ and $s \sim s_2$, or there are s_0 and $s' \in S$ and $b \in \Sigma$ such that $s_1 \sim s_0$, $s \sim s'$, $s_2 =\varepsilon\Rightarrow s_0 -b\rightarrow s'$, and $vis(a) = vis(b)$.
- If $s_2 -a\rightarrow s$, then either $a \in \Sigma_I$ and $s_1 \sim s$, or there are s_0 and $s' \in S$ and $b \in \Sigma$ such that $s_0 \sim s_2$, $s' \sim s$, $s_1 =\varepsilon\Rightarrow s_0 -b\rightarrow s'$, and $vis(a) = vis(b)$.

Furthermore,

- The states $s_1, s_2 \in S$ of L are *weakly / branching bisimilar*, if and only if there is a weak / branching bisimulation "$\sim$" such that $s_1 \sim s_2$.
- Let $L_1 = (S_1, \Sigma_V, \Sigma_I, \Delta_1, is_1)$ and $L_2 = (S_2, \Sigma_V, \Sigma_I, \Delta_2, is_2)$ be two LTSs such that their alphabets are the same and, furthermore, $S_1 \cap S_2 = \emptyset$. They are *weakly / branching bisimilar*, if and only if their initial states is_1 and is_2 are weakly / branching bisimilar in their joint LTS $(S_1 \cup S_2, \Sigma_V, \Sigma_I, \Delta_1 \cup \Delta_2, is_1)$. □

Because any branching bisimulation is also a weak bisimulation, branching bisimilarity is strictly stronger than weak bisimilarity.

3. Stubborn Sets and Reduced State Spaces

The number of states of a parallel composition tends to grow exponentially in the numbers of states of its component processes. The goal of the stubborn set method is to construct a reduced LTS for the parallel composition in such a way that it is equivalent with the full LTS, but contains significantly less states and transitions. This is achieved by investigating at any state of the parallel composition only a subset of enabled actions and thus constructing only a subset of the immediate successors of the state. For the development of the theory, it is handy to talk about a larger set that may also contain disabled actions. This larger set is called *stubborn*.

The construction of stubborn sets for a parallel composition will be discussed soon, but before that the fundamental properties that stubborn sets guarantee are listed. The main theorems of this article will be proven from these properties, without relying on any particular construction of stubborn sets. This makes the theory more modular, and — hopefully — the fundamental ideas clearer.

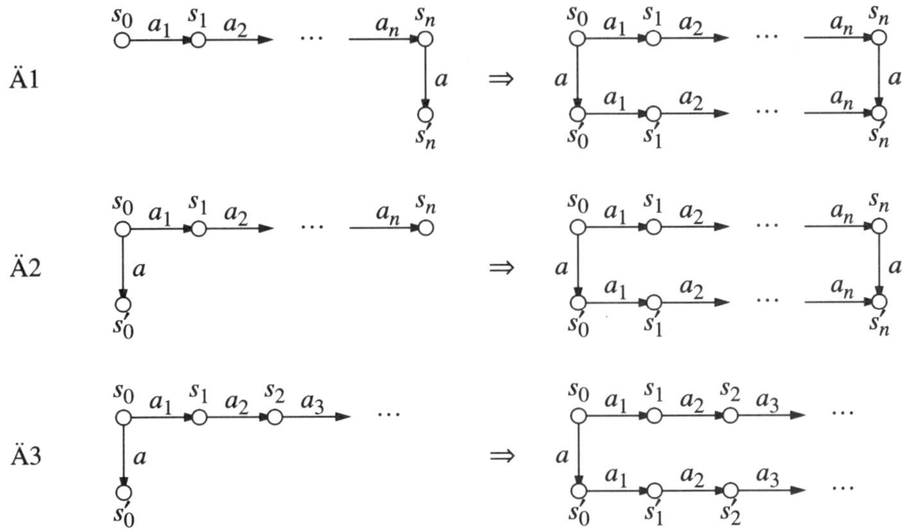

Figure 1 Illustrations of conditions Ä1, Ä2 and Ä3

Because we will not always need both Ä2 and Ä3 in our proofs, we require only one of them in the below definition.

Definition 3.1 Let $L = (S, \Sigma_V, \Sigma_I, \Delta, is)$ be an LTS. A *stubborn set generator* is a function $\ddot{A}: S \to 2^{\Sigma}$ such that for every s'_0, s'_n, and $s_0, s_1, \ldots \in S$, $a \in \ddot{A}(s_0)$, and $a_1, a_2, \ldots \in \Sigma - \ddot{A}(s_0)$, it is true that Ä0, Ä1, and at least one of Ä2 and Ä3 from the below list hold.

(Ä0) If $next(s_0) \neq \emptyset$ then $\ddot{A}(s_0) \cap next(s_0) \neq \emptyset$.

(Ä1) If $s_0 -a_1\to \ldots -a_n\to s_n$ and $s_n -a\to s'_n$, then there are $s'_0, \ldots, s'_{n-1} \in S$ such that $s'_0 -a_1\to \ldots -a_n\to s'_n$ and $s_0 -a\to s'_0$.

(Ä2) If $s_0 -a_1\to \ldots -a_n\to s_n$ and $s_0 -a\to s'_0$, then there are $s'_1, \ldots, s'_n \in S$ such that $s'_0 -a_1\to \ldots -a_n\to s'_n$ and $s_n -a\to s'_n$.

(Ä3) If $s_0 -a_1\to s_1 -a_2\to \ldots$ and $s_0 -a\to s'_0$, then there are $s'_1, s'_2, \ldots \in S$ such that $s'_0 -a_1\to s'_1 -a_2\to \ldots$. □

The set $\ddot{A}(s)$ is called a *stubborn set*. The condition Ä0 requires that a stubborn set should contain an enabled action if there are any. Ä1 guarantees that a disabled action belonging to a stubborn set remains disabled at least until an action belonging to the set occurs. Furthermore, it allows in any execution to "move to the front" the first occurrence of an action in the stubborn set. Ä2 claims that any enabled action within the stubborn set commutes with all finite sequences of outside actions, and Ä3 extends Ä2 to infinite sequences.[1] The conditions Ä1, Ä2 and Ä3 are illustrated in Figure 1. In the illustration, vertical and horizontal transitions correspond to actions inside and outside the stubborn set, respectively.

The following theorem gives a sufficient condition for a stubborn set of a parallel composition $L = L_1 \parallel \ldots \parallel L_n$. The proof of the theorem is dull and omitted, but it can be

[1]Although it might seem that Ä3 follows from Ä2, this is not the case. The possibility has not been ruled out that $s'_1, \ldots, s'_n$ obtain different values for each n, so that $s'_0 -a_1 \ldots a_n\to$ for every n, but $s'_0 \not- a_1 a_2 \ldots \not\to$.

found in [Val92b]. In order to avoid confusion, we use the notation "$-a\rightarrow_j$" and "$next_j(\ldots)$" when talking about the transitions and enabled actions of L_j, while the absence of the subscript refers to L.

Theorem 3.2 Let $L = L_1 \parallel \ldots \parallel L_n$ be the parallel composition of the LTSs $L_1 = (S_1, \Sigma_{V1}, \Sigma_{I1}, \Delta_1, is_1), \ldots, L_n = (S_n, \Sigma_{Vn}, \Sigma_{In}, \Delta_n, is_n)$, and $\ddot{A}: S \rightarrow 2^{\Sigma}$. If $\ddot{A}(s)$ satisfies the following three conditions in the state $s = (s_1, \ldots, s_n)$ of L, then Ä0, Ä1, Ä2 and Ä3 hold in s.

- If $a \in \ddot{A}(s)$ and $s \not{-}a\not\rightarrow$, then there is $1 \leq j \leq n$ such that $a \in \Sigma_j$, $s_j \not{-}a\not\rightarrow_j$, and $next_j(s_j) \subseteq \ddot{A}(s)$.
- If $a \in \ddot{A}(s)$ and $s -a\rightarrow$, then for every $1 \leq j \leq n$, either $a \notin \Sigma_j$, or $next_j(s_j) \subseteq \ddot{A}(s)$.
- If there is $a \in \Sigma$ such that $s -a\rightarrow$, then there is $a \in \ddot{A}(s)$ such that $s -a\rightarrow$. □

Unlike Ä1, Ä2 and Ä3, the conditions in Theorem 3.2 concern only one state. Therefore, it is possible to design algorithms that investigate only that state and construct a stubborn set satisfying the conditions. Many such algorithms have been presented in the literature, for instance in [Val88, Val92a, God96]. Although the algorithms have been expressed mostly in other frameworks than the present one, they can be applied to the context of Theorem 3.2 without much difficulties. Therefore, it is not reasonable to repeat them here. [Val92b] describes some of them in the present framework.

The sets of states and transitions of the reduced LTS are subsets of the sets of states and transitions of the LTS representing the full parallel composition. To facilitate convenient discussion of the same states and transitions as members of the full and reduced LTS, a double-dot notation is introduced.

Definition 3.3 Let $L = (S, \Sigma_V, \Sigma_I, \Delta, is)$ be an LTS and $\ddot{A}: S \rightarrow 2^{\Sigma}$ a stubborn set generator. The *reduced LTS* of L induced by $\ddot{A}$ is $\ddot{L} = (\ddot{S}, \Sigma_V, \Sigma_I, \ddot{\Delta}, is)$, where $\ddot{S}$ is the smallest subset of S and $\ddot{\Delta}$ is the smallest subset of Δ such that

- $is \in \ddot{S}$,
- if $s \in \ddot{S}$, $s -a\rightarrow s'$, and $a \in \ddot{A}(s)$, then $s' \in \ddot{S}$ and $(s, a, s') \in \ddot{\Delta}$.

Furthermore, if s and $s' \in S$, $a \in \Sigma$, and $\rho \in \Sigma^*$, then

- $s \ddot{-}a\ddot{\rightarrow} s'$ if and only if $s -a\rightarrow s'$ and $a \in \ddot{A}(s)$.
- $s \ddot{-}\rho\ddot{\rightarrow} s'$ etc. are defined from $s \ddot{-}a\ddot{\rightarrow} s'$ analogously to Definition 2.2.
- $\ddot{n}ext(s) = \{ a \in \Sigma \mid s \ddot{-}a\ddot{\rightarrow} \} = next(s) \cap \ddot{A}(s)$. □

As developed so far, the stubborn set method guarantees that the reduced and full LTS have the same deadlocks. (It is assumed that the full LTS does not contain unreachable states.) Furthermore, the reduced LTS has an infinite execution if and only if the full LTS has.

Theorem 3.4 Let $L = (S, \Sigma_V, \Sigma_I, \Delta, is)$ be an LTS such that $is \rightarrow^* s$ for every $s \in S$. Let $\ddot{L} = (\ddot{S}, \Sigma_V, \Sigma_I, \ddot{\Delta}, is)$ be a reduced LTS obtained from L with the stubborn set generator $\ddot{A}$.

(a) Assume that Ä0, Ä1 and Ä2 hold. Then $s \in S$ and $next(s) = \emptyset$ if and only if $s \in \ddot{S}$ and $\ddot{n}ext(s) = \emptyset$.

(b) Assume that Ä0, Ä1 and Ä3 hold. There are $a_1, a_2, \ldots$ such that $is -a_1a_2\ldots\rightarrow$ if and only if there are $a_1', a_2', \ldots$ such that $is \ddot{-}a_1'a_2'\ldots\ddot{\rightarrow}$.

Proof (a) If $s \in \ddot{S}$ and $\ddot{n}ext(s) = \emptyset$, then $s \in S$ by $\ddot{S} \subseteq S$, and $next(s) = \emptyset$ by Ä0. If $s \in \ddot{S}$ and $next(s) = \emptyset$, then $\ddot{n}ext(s) = next(s) \cap \ddot{A}(s) = \emptyset$. It remains to be shown that if $s \in S$

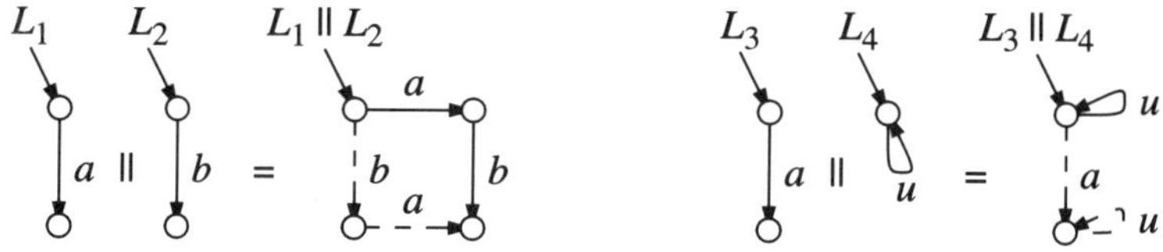

Figure 2 Two parallel compositions with possible reduced LTSs

and $next(s) = \emptyset$, then $s \in \ddot{S}$. We will show that if $next(s) = \emptyset$, $\ddot{s} \in \ddot{S}$, and $\ddot{s} -a_1 \ldots a_n \rightarrow s$ where $n > 0$, then there are $\ddot{s}'$, a, and $a'_1, \ldots, a'_{n-1}$ such that $\ddot{s} \ddot{-}a\ddot{\rightarrow} \ddot{s}'$ and $\ddot{s}' -a'_1 \ldots a'_{n-1} \rightarrow s$. The claim $s \in \ddot{S}$ follows from this and the fact that $is \in \ddot{S}$ by "reversed" induction on n.

If $\ddot{s} -a_1 \ldots a_n \rightarrow s$, then there are $s_0, \ldots, s_n$ such that $s_0 = \ddot{s}$, $s_n = s$, and $s_0 -a_1\rightarrow s_1 -a_2\rightarrow \ldots -a_n\rightarrow s_n$. When $n > 0$, we have $s_0 -a_1\rightarrow$, and Ä0 guarantees that there is some a such that $s_0 \ddot{-}a\ddot{\rightarrow}$. If none of $a_1, \ldots, a_n$ belongs to $\ddot{A}(s_0)$, then $s_n -a\rightarrow$ by Ä2, which is a contradiction with $next(s) = \emptyset$. There is thus $1 \leq j \leq n$ such that $a_j \in \ddot{A}(s_0)$. By choosing the smallest such j we obtain $a_i \notin \ddot{A}(s_0)$ for $1 \leq i < j$. Now Ä1 implies the existence of $s'_0, \ldots, s'_{j-1}$ such that $s_0 \ddot{-}a_j\ddot{\rightarrow} s'_0$, $s'_0 -a_1 \ldots a_{j-1}\rightarrow s'_{j-1}$, and $s'_{j-1} = s_j$. We may choose $\ddot{s}' = s'_0$, $a = a_j$, $a'_1 = a_1, \ldots, a'_{j-1} = a_{j-1}$, and $a'_j = a_{j+1}, \ldots, a'_{n-1} = a_n$.

(b) The "if"-part is obvious from $\ddot{\Delta} \subseteq \Delta$. To show the "only if" part we will show that if $\ddot{s} \in \ddot{S}$ and $\ddot{s} -a_1 a_2 \ldots\rightarrow$, then there are $\ddot{s}'$, a, and $a'_1, a'_2, \ldots$ such that $\ddot{s} \ddot{-}a\ddot{\rightarrow} \ddot{s}'$ and $\ddot{s}' -a'_1 a'_2 \ldots\rightarrow$. The claim follows then by induction.

Let $s_0, s_1, \ldots$ be chosen such that $s_0 = \ddot{s}$ and $s_0 -a_1\rightarrow s_1 -a_2\rightarrow \ldots$. If there is a j such that $a_j \in \ddot{A}(s_0)$ and $a_i \notin \ddot{A}(s_0)$ when $1 \leq i < j$, then Ä1 implies the existence of $s'_0, \ldots, s'_{j-1}$ such that $s_0 \ddot{-}a_j\ddot{\rightarrow} s'_0$ and $s'_0 -a_1 \ldots a_{j-1}\rightarrow s'_{j-1} -a_{j+1}a_{j+2}\ldots\rightarrow$, where $s'_{j-1} = s_j$. Otherwise Ä0 and Ä3 ensure the existence of an a and $\ddot{s}'$ such that $s_0 \ddot{-}a\ddot{\rightarrow} \ddot{s}' -a_1 a_2 \ldots\rightarrow$. □

Without additional assumptions about the selection of stubborn sets, the stubborn set method does not guarantee much more than Theorem 3.4. This is because of two reasons.

Firstly, when a transition is "moved to the front" by Ä1, the ordering of actions changes. As a consequence, all possible orderings of visible actions are not necessarily included into the reduced LTS. This may lead to the omission of traces, stable failures, and so on. For instance, if both a and b are visible in Figure 2, then $tr(L_1 \parallel L_2) = \{\varepsilon, a, b, ab, ba\}$. (In all LTS figures in this article, the alphabet of an LTS is exactly the set of labels of its transitions. Furthermore, a, b and c are visible, and u and v are invisible.) It is possible that the stubborn set used in the initial state is $\{a\}$. Then the dashed transitions are left out of the reduced LTS, and its traces are $\{\varepsilon, a, ab\}$.

Secondly, it is even possible that some action is *ignored* in the sense that it does not occur at all in the reduced LTS although it is enabled. Consider the system $L_3 \parallel L_4$ in Figure 2. If $\ddot{A}(is) = \{u\}$, then the stubborn set method investigates only the transition $is -u\rightarrow is$. But this transition takes the system back to a state that has already been investigated, so the method terminates. Intuitively, the justification for not investigating a initially is that a is independent of u, so the occurrence of a may be postponed until u has occurred. But in this example, u can occur an infinite number of times. By postponing the occurrence of a until u is no more enabled, the stubborn set method postpones a forever.

4. Preserving Trace Equivalence

Throughout this and the following two sections, let $L = (S, \Sigma_V, \Sigma_I, \Delta, is)$ be an LTS such that all of its states are reachable from is, $\ddot{A}$ a stubborn set generator for it, and $\ddot{L} = (\ddot{S}, \Sigma_V, \Sigma_I, \ddot{\Delta}, is)$ the resulting reduced LTS.

In order to prevent the stubborn set method from changing the ordering of visible actions, we introduce an additional condition for the selection of stubborn sets. The condition requires that either all enabled actions in the stubborn set are invisible, or the set contains all (both enabled and disabled) visible actions.

($\ddot{A}$4) For every $s \in \ddot{S}$, either $\Sigma_V \cap \ddot{A}(s) \cap next(s) = \emptyset$ or $\Sigma_V \subseteq \ddot{A}(s)$ (or both).

It is clear from $\ddot{\Delta} \subseteq \Delta$ that $tr(\ddot{L}) \subseteq tr(L)$. The system $L_3 \parallel L_4$ in Figure 2 demonstrates that Ä4 is not sufficient for ensuring that $tr(L) \subseteq tr(\ddot{L})$. Ä4 suffices, however, for showing that $sfail(L) \subseteq sfail(\ddot{L})$.

Lemma 4.1 If Ä0, Ä1, Ä2 and Ä4 hold, then $sfail(L) \subseteq sfail(\ddot{L})$.

Proof Let $(\sigma, A) \in sfail(L)$. There are $n \geq 0$, $a_1, \dots, a_n \in \Sigma$ and $s_0, \dots, s_n \in S$ such that $s_0 = is$, $s_0 -a_1\rightarrow \dots -a_n\rightarrow s_n$, $vis(a_1 \dots a_n) = \sigma$, and $next(s_n) \subseteq \Sigma_V - A$. We will show for increasing values of m that there are $s_{0,m}, \dots, s_{n,m} \in S$ and a permutation $a_{1,m}, \dots, a_{n,m}$ of $a_1, \dots, a_n$ such that $s_{0,m} = is$, $s_{0,m} \ddot{-}a_{1,m}\ddot{\rightarrow} \dots \ddot{-}a_{m,m}\ddot{\rightarrow} s_{m,m} -a_{m+1,m}\rightarrow \dots -a_{n,m}\rightarrow s_{n,m}$, $vis(a_{1,m} \cdots a_{n,m}) = \sigma$, and $s_{n,m} = s_n$. The biggest value of m for which this will be shown is at most n, and it has the property that $a_{m+1,m}, \dots, a_{n,m} \in \Sigma_I$, $\ddot{n}ext(s_{m,m}) \subseteq \Sigma_V$, and $\ddot{n}ext(s_{m,m}) \cap A = \emptyset$. This implies that $vis(a_{1,m} \cdots a_{m,m}) = \sigma$ and $(\sigma, A) \in sfail(\ddot{L})$.

The claim becomes valid for $m = 0$ if we choose $s_{0,0} = s_0 = is$, $s_{i,0} = s_i$, and $a_{i,0} = a_i$ for $1 \leq i \leq n$. For the induction step, assume that the claim holds for m. Consider the situation where

(*) $a_{j,m} \in \ddot{A}(s_{m,m})$ for some $m + 1 \leq j \leq n$, and $a_{k,m} \notin \ddot{A}(s_{m,m})$ for $m + 1 \leq k < j$.

If (*) holds, then Ä1 guarantees the existence of $s_{m+1,m+1}, \dots, s_{n,m+1}$ such that $s_{m,m} \ddot{-}a_{j,m}\ddot{\rightarrow} s_{m+1,m+1}$, $s_{n,m+1} = s_{n,m}$, and $s_{m+1,m+1} -a_{m+2,m+1}\rightarrow \dots -a_{n,m+1}\rightarrow s_{n,m+1}$, where the sequence $a_{m+2,m+1} \cdots a_{n,m+1}$ is obtained from $a_{m+1,m} \cdots a_{n,m}$ by removing $a_{j,m}$. We define $a_{m+1,m+1} = a_{j,m}$, $s_{0,m+1} = s_{0,m}$, and $s_{k,m+1} = s_{k,m}$ and $a_{k,m+1} = a_{k,m}$ for $1 \leq k \leq m$. If $a_{j,m} \in \Sigma_I$, then clearly $vis(a_{1,m+1} \cdots a_{n,m+1}) = vis(a_{1,m} \cdots a_{n,m})$. Otherwise $a_{j,m} \in \Sigma_V \cap \ddot{A}(s_{m,m}) \cap next(s_{m,m})$. By Ä4, $\Sigma_V \subseteq \ddot{A}(s_{m,m})$. Thus by (*) $a_{k,m} \notin \Sigma_V$ for $m + 1 \leq k < j$, and $vis(a_{1,m+1} \cdots a_{n,m+1}) = vis(a_{1,m} \cdots a_{n,m})$. Therefore, the induction step follows, if we can show (*).

If $\ddot{A}(s_{m,m})$ contains some enabled invisible action a, then $s_n \not{-}a\not\rightarrow$, because $next(s_n) \subseteq \Sigma_V$. So Ä2 implies (*). If all enabled actions in $\ddot{A}(s_{m,m})$ are visible and at least one of $a_{m+1,m}, \dots, a_{n,m}$ is visible — let it be called $a_{v,m}$ —, then $m < n$. Thus $next(s_{m,m}) \neq \emptyset$ and $\ddot{A}(s_{m,m})$ contains an enabled action by Ä0. Because it is visible, Ä4 implies $\Sigma_V \subseteq \ddot{A}(s_{m,m})$. Therefore, $a_{v,m} \in \ddot{A}(s_{m,m})$, and (*) holds for some $m + 1 \leq j \leq v$.

If all enabled actions in $\ddot{A}(s_{m,m})$ and none of $a_{m+1,m}, \dots, a_{n,m}$ are visible, then m has reached its biggest value. We have all parts of the claim except that $\ddot{n}ext(s_{m,m}) \cap A = \emptyset$. To obtain a contradiction, assume that $a \in \ddot{n}ext(s_{m,m}) \cap A$. Because $next(s_n) \subseteq \Sigma_V - A$, we have $a \notin next(s_n)$, and Ä2 guarantees that at least one of $a_{m+1,m}, \dots, a_{n,m}$ is in $\ddot{A}(s_{m,m})$. Let $a_{k,m}$ be the first of them. Then Ä1 implies that $a_{k,m}$ is an enabled invisible action in $\ddot{A}(s_{m,m})$, a contradiction. Thus $\ddot{n}ext(s_{m,m}) \cap A = \emptyset$ holds. □

To preserve all traces, it is sufficient to add a condition that guarantees that visible actions are not ignored for "too long". It suffices to require that for every state in the reduced LTS and for all actions that are enabled in that state, it is possible to reach a state in the reduced LTS such that the action is in its stubborn set.

($\ddot{A}$5) $\forall\, s \in \ddot{S}: \forall\, a \in next(s): \exists\, s' \in \ddot{S}: s \ddot{\rightarrow}^* s' \wedge a \in \ddot{A}(s')$.

Theorem 4.2 If Ä0, Ä1, Ä2, Ä4 and Ä5 hold, then $tr(L) = tr(\ddot{L})$.

Proof It is clear from $\ddot{\Delta} \subseteq \Delta$ that $tr(\ddot{L}) \subseteq tr(L)$. To prove that $tr(L) \subseteq tr(\ddot{L})$, assume that $\sigma \in tr(L)$. There are $n \geq 0$ and $a_1, \ldots, a_n \in \Sigma$ such that $is -a_1 \ldots a_n\rightarrow$ and $vis(a_1 \ldots a_n) = \sigma$. We will show for increasing values of m the existence of s_m, $\ddot{a}_1, \ldots, \ddot{a}_m$, and $a'_1, \ldots, a'_k$ such that $is \ddot{-}\ddot{a}_1 \ldots \ddot{a}_m \ddot{\rightarrow}\, s_m -a'_1 \ldots a'_k\rightarrow$ and $vis(\ddot{a}_1 \ldots \ddot{a}_m a'_1 \ldots a'_k) = \sigma$. We let m grow until it reaches such a value that $vis(a'_1 \ldots a'_k) = \varepsilon$, implying that $\sigma = vis(\ddot{a}_1 \ldots \ddot{a}_m) \in tr(\ddot{L})$.

The claim becomes valid for $m = 0$ if we choose $s_0 = is$, $k = n$, and $a'_i = a_i$ for $1 \leq i \leq n$. Assume that the claim holds for an m such that $vis(a'_1 \ldots a'_k) \neq \varepsilon$. We consider two cases.

(a) If at least one of $a'_1, \ldots, a'_k$ belongs to $\ddot{A}(s_m)$, then, like before, Ä1 guarantees the existence of a j and s_{m+1} such that $s_m \ddot{-}a'_j\ddot{\rightarrow}\, s_{m+1}$ and $s_{m+1} -a'_1 \ldots a'_{j-1} a'_{j+1} \ldots a'_k\rightarrow$. Furthermore, $vis(a'_j a'_1 \ldots a'_{j-1} a'_{j+1} \ldots a'_k) = vis(a'_1 \ldots a'_k)$ due to Ä4. So the claim is valid for m+1.

(b) Assume that none of $a'_1, \ldots, a'_k$ belongs to $\ddot{A}(s_m)$. At least one of them is visible because $vis(a'_1 \ldots a'_k) \neq \varepsilon$. Since $s_m -a'_1\rightarrow$, Ä0 gives $next(s_m) \cap \ddot{A}(s_m) \neq \emptyset$. Ä4 implies that if $a \in next(s_m) \cap \ddot{A}(s_m)$, then a is invisible, because otherwise the visible one of $a'_1, \ldots, a'_k$ would belong to $\ddot{A}(s_m)$. Furthermore, if s_{m+1} is any state such that $s_m -a\rightarrow s_{m+1}$, then $s_m \ddot{-}a\ddot{\rightarrow}\, s_{m+1}$ because $a \in \ddot{A}(s_m)$, and Ä2 implies that $s_{m+1} -a'_1 \ldots a'_k\rightarrow$. Again, the claim is valid for m+1.

It remains to be proven that m may reach such a value that $vis(a'_1 \ldots a'_k) = \varepsilon$. The case (a) clearly makes progress towards such a value, but the case (b) does not. We will now show that it is possible to ensure that the case (b) occurs at most a finite number of times without an intervening (a). Ä5 guarantees that there is s' such that $s_m \ddot{\rightarrow}^* s'$ and $a'_1 \in \ddot{A}(s')$. Let $\ddot{s}_0 \ddot{-}b_1\ddot{\rightarrow}\, \ddot{s}_1 \ddot{-}b_2\ddot{\rightarrow} \ldots \ddot{-}b_h\ddot{\rightarrow}\, \ddot{s}_h$ be some shortest path from s_m to s' in $\ddot{L}$. No assumptions about the choice of a from $next(s_m) \cap \ddot{A}(s_m)$ were made in the case (b). So we may choose $a = b_1$ in $\ddot{s}_0$, $a = b_2$ in $\ddot{s}_1$, and so on, until a state $\ddot{s}_i$ is reached such that the condition of case (a) holds. This happens after h steps at the latest. □

A practical and reasonably fast implementation of Ä5 for finite reduced LTSs was described in [Val91]. It is based on recognising the *terminal strong components* of $\ddot{L}$. A non-empty set of states $S_T \subseteq \ddot{S}$ is a terminal strong component, if for every $s \in S_T$, $s \ddot{\rightarrow}^* s'$ if and only if $s' \in S_T$. The idea is to choose an arbitrary state from each terminal strong component and ensure that every action that is enabled in it occurs somewhere in the component. The algorithm is built upon Tarjan's strong component algorithm [Tar72, AHU74]. (Tarjan's algorithm suits the task better than the more modern strong component algorithm described in [CLR90], for instance.)

Instead of Ä5, the following condition could be used. It takes into account the fact that only visible actions are important for traces, at the price of slightly more complicated or less efficient implementation. It may thus save states when the occurrence of some invisible enabled action does not lead to occurrences of any visible actions. It is more complicated to implement than Ä5, because it is easy to check whether an action occurs anywhere in a terminal strong component, but somewhat more complicated to ensure that a disabled visible action is taken into account in some state of the component. The main reason for mentioning Ä5′ is that it has an interesting relationship with the condition Ä7 presented in the next section.

(Ä5′) $\forall s \in \ddot{S}: \forall a \in \Sigma_V: \exists s' \in \ddot{S}: s \ddot{\rightarrow}^* s' \wedge a \in \ddot{A}(s')$.

5. Preserving CSP- and CFFD-Equivalence

Consider the system $L_3 \parallel L_4$ in Figure 2. If a is visible and u is not, then its divergence traces are ε and a. The conditions imposed so far allow choosing $\{a\}$ as the stubborn set of the initial state of the system. The resulting reduced LTS does not have ε as a divergence trace. As a consequence, the conditions Ä0 to Ä5 are not sufficient for guaranteeing CSP- or CFFD-equivalence between the full and reduced LTS.

Regarding CSP-equivalence, only the minimal divergence traces are important. In order to preserve them, a condition is formulated that requires the presence of an enabled invisible action in the stubborn set, if such an action exist.

(Ä6) For every $s \in \ddot{S}$, if $\Sigma_I \cap next(s) \neq \emptyset$, then $\ddot{A}(s) \cap \Sigma_I \cap next(s) \neq \emptyset$.

Lemma 5.1 If Ä0, Ä1, Ä3, Ä4 and Ä6 hold, then $mindiv(L) = mindiv(\ddot{L})$.

Proof Obviously $mindiv(\ddot{L}) \subseteq divtr(L)$. The claim follows if we show that also $mindiv(L) \subseteq divtr(\ddot{L})$. If $\sigma \in mindiv(L)$, then there are $a_{1,0}, a_{2,0}, \ldots$ such that $is -a_{1,0}a_{2,0}\cdots\rightarrow$ and $vis(a_{1,0}a_{2,0}\cdots) = \sigma$. Let $s_0 = is$. We will show that for every $m \geq 1$, there are s_m, $\ddot{a}_m$, and $a_{1,m}, a_{2,m}, \ldots$ such that $s_0 \;\text{-}\ddot{a}_1\text{-}\!\!\rightarrow\; s_1 \;\text{-}\ddot{a}_2\text{-}\!\!\rightarrow \;\ldots\; \text{-}\ddot{a}_m\text{-}\!\!\rightarrow\; s_m$, $s_m -a_{1,m}a_{2,m}\cdots\rightarrow$, and $vis(\ddot{a}_1\ddot{a}_2\ldots\ddot{a}_m a_{1,m}a_{2,m}\cdots) = \sigma$. As a consequence, $vis(\ddot{a}_1\ddot{a}_2\ldots) \in divtr(\ddot{L})$. Furthermore, $vis(\ddot{a}_1\ddot{a}_2\ldots) \in divtr(L)$ and $vis(\ddot{a}_1\ddot{a}_2\ldots) \leq \sigma \in mindiv(L)$, so $vis(\ddot{a}_1\ddot{a}_2\ldots) = \sigma$.

Assume that the claim holds for m.

If at least one of $a_{1,m}, a_{2,m}, \ldots \in \ddot{A}(s_m)$, then the existence of s_{m+1}, $\ddot{a}_{m+1}$, and $a_{1,m+1}$, $a_{2,m+1}, \ldots$ follows from Ä1, and Ä4 guarantees that $vis(\ddot{a}_1\ddot{a}_2\ldots\ddot{a}_{m+1}a_{1,m+1}a_{2,m+1}\cdots) = vis(\ddot{a}_1\ddot{a}_2\ldots\ddot{a}_m a_{1,m}a_{2,m}\cdots)$.

Assume now that none of $a_{1,m}, a_{2,m}, \ldots \in \ddot{A}(s_m)$. Ä0 implies that there is some $\ddot{a}_{m+1} \in \ddot{A}(s_m) \cap next(s_m)$. If $a_{1,m} \in \Sigma_V$, then $\ddot{a}_{m+1} \in \Sigma_I$ due to Ä4. If $a_{1,m} \in \Sigma_I$, then Ä6 guarantees that there is some $\ddot{a}_{m+1} \in \ddot{A}(s_m) \cap \Sigma_I \cap next(s_m)$. In both cases, Ä3 gives the required s_{m+1} and $a_{1,m+1}, a_{2,m+1}, \ldots$. □

Lemma 5.2 If Ä0, Ä1, Ä2, Ä4 and Ä6 hold, then $sfail(L) = sfail(\ddot{L})$.

Lemma 4.1 guarantees that $sfail(L) \subseteq sfail(\ddot{L})$. To show $sfail(\ddot{L}) \subseteq sfail(L)$, let $(\sigma, A) \in sfail(\ddot{L})$. There are $s \in \ddot{S}$ and $a_1, \ldots, a_n \in \Sigma$ such that $is -a_1\ldots a_n\rightarrow s$, $vis(a_1\ldots a_n) = \sigma$, and $\ddot{n}ext(s) \subseteq \Sigma_V - A$. Assume that $s -a\rightarrow$. Ä6 and $\ddot{n}ext(s) \subseteq \Sigma_V$ imply that a is visible. Thus $\Sigma_V \subseteq \ddot{A}(s)$ by Ä0 and Ä4. Therefore, $a \in \ddot{A}(s)$ and $a \in \ddot{n}ext(s)$. As a conclusion, $next(s) \subseteq \ddot{n}ext(s)$, and $(\sigma, A) \in sfail(L)$. □

The condition Ä6 allows us to strengthen the proof of Lemma 4.1 a bit. Namely, if it is assumed, then the reduced LTS contains all reachable stable states of the full LTS. That is, if Ä0, Ä1, Ä2, Ä4 and Ä6 hold, $is \rightarrow^* s$, and $next(s) \subseteq \Sigma_V$, then $s \in \ddot{S}$.

It is now straightforward to show that Ä0, …, Ä4 and Ä6 suffice to preserve CSP-equivalence.

Theorem 5.3 If Ä0, Ä1, Ä2, Ä3, Ä4 and Ä6 hold, then $CSPfail(L) = CSPfail(\ddot{L})$ and $CSPdiv(L) = CSPdiv(\ddot{L})$.

Proof Lemmas 5.1 and 5.2 give $mindiv(L) = mindiv(\ddot{L})$ and $sfail(L) = sfail(\ddot{L})$, from which $CSPdiv(L) = CSPdiv(\ddot{L})$ and $CSPfail(L) = CSPfail(\ddot{L})$ follow by Definition 2.6. □

Notice that Ä5 was not needed for preserving CSP-equivalence. This is because an action may be ignored only after a divergence trace, and CSP-equivalence does not need any information about the behaviour after a divergence trace. When implementing a stub-

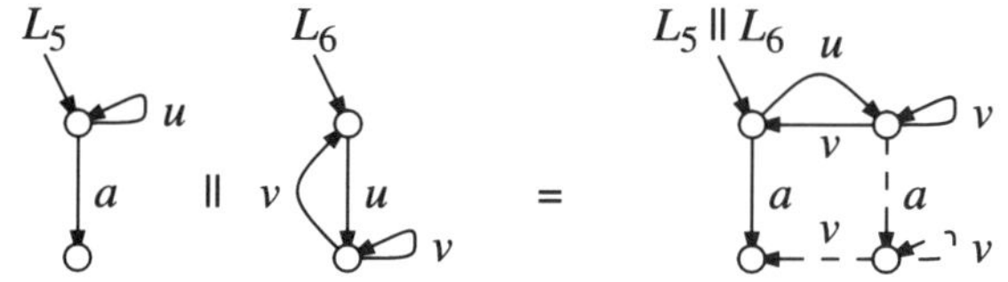

Figure 3 A reduced LTS obeying Ä0 to Ä6

born set method for CSP-equivalence, it is not necessary to continue analysis from states that have proven divergent.

The conditions Ä0 to Ä6 are not sufficient for preserving CFFD-equivalence, not even if Ä5 is included. This can be seen from the system $L_5 \parallel L_6$ in Figure 3. In it, a is visible, and u and v are invisible. The stubborn set used at the right-most state in the top row is $\{v\}$. The full LTS has the infinite path $is -uav^{\omega}\rightarrow$, so $a \in divtr(L_5 \parallel L_6)$. However, $a \notin divtr(\ddot{L})$.

In order to preserve CFFD-equivalence, a new condition is introduced. It requires that every infinite path of the reduced LTS contains at least one state whose stubborn set contains all visible actions. Because the start state of the path needs not be the initial state, the condition may be applied also to any suffix of an infinite path. Thus all infinite paths should have infinitely many states with all visible actions in their stubborn sets.

(Ä7) For every $s_0, s_1, \ldots \in \ddot{S}$ and $a_1, a_2, \ldots \in \Sigma$, if $s_0 \stackrel{..}{-}a_1\stackrel{..}{\rightarrow} s_1 \stackrel{..}{-}a_2\stackrel{..}{\rightarrow} \ldots$, then there is $i \geq 0$ such that $\Sigma_V \subseteq \ddot{A}(s_i)$.

Lemma 5.4 If Ä0, Ä1, Ä3, Ä4 and Ä7 hold, then $inftr(L) = inftr(\ddot{L})$. If, furthermore, Ä6 holds, then $divtr(L) = divtr(\ddot{L})$.

Proof The parts $divtr(\ddot{L}) \subseteq divtr(L)$ and $inftr(\ddot{L}) \subseteq inftr(L)$ are obvious from $\ddot{\Delta} \subseteq \Delta$. To prove $inftr(L) \subseteq inftr(\ddot{L})$ and $divtr(L) \subseteq divtr(\ddot{L})$, let $s_0 = is$ and let $a_{1,0}, a_{2,0}, \ldots$ be such that $s_0 -a_{1,0}a_{2,0}\ldots\rightarrow$ and $vis(a_{1,0}a_{2,0}\ldots) = \sigma \in divtr(L) \cup inftr(L)$. We demonstrate for every $m > 0$ the existence of s_m, $\ddot{a}_m$, and $a_{1,m}, a_{2,m}, \ldots$ such that $s_0 \stackrel{..}{-}\ddot{a}_1\stackrel{..}{\rightarrow} s_1 \stackrel{..}{-}\ddot{a}_2\stackrel{..}{\rightarrow} \ldots \stackrel{..}{-}\ddot{a}_m\stackrel{..}{\rightarrow} s_m$, $s_m -a_{1,m}a_{2,m}\ldots\rightarrow$, and $vis(\ddot{a}_1\ddot{a}_2\ldots\ddot{a}_m a_{1,m}a_{2,m}\ldots) = \sigma$.

Assume that the claim holds for m. If $\Sigma_V \cap \ddot{A}(s_m) \cap next(s_m) = \emptyset$, then Ä0 guarantees that $\ddot{n}ext(s_m) \neq \emptyset$, and, depending on whether any of $a_{1,m}, a_{2,m}, \ldots \in \ddot{A}(s_m)$, either Ä1 or Ä3 yields s_{m+1}, $\ddot{a}_{m+1}$, and $a_{1,m+1}, a_{2,m+1}, \ldots$ with the required properties. If $\Sigma_V \cap \ddot{A}(s_m) \cap next(s_m) \neq \emptyset$ and at least one of $a_{1,m}, a_{2,m}, \ldots \in \Sigma_V$, then Ä4 guarantees that $a_{j,m} \in \ddot{A}(s_m)$ for some $j \geq 0$, and Ä1 yields s_{m+1} and so on. If $\Sigma_V \cap \ddot{A}(s_m) \cap next(s_m) \neq \emptyset$ and none of $a_{1,m}, a_{2,m}, \ldots \in \Sigma_V$, then $\sigma \in divtr(L)$. Ä6 and $s_m -a_{1,m}\rightarrow$ imply that there is $a \in \ddot{A}(s_m) \cap next(s_m) \cap \Sigma_I$. Again, either Ä1 or Ä3 yields s_{m+1} etc.

Because $vis(\ddot{a}_1\ddot{a}_2\ldots\ddot{a}_m a_{1,m}a_{2,m}\ldots) = \sigma$ for every $m \geq 0$, we have $vis(\ddot{a}_1\ddot{a}_2\ldots) \leq \sigma$. Because condition Ä7 guarantees that $\Sigma_V \subseteq \ddot{A}(s_m)$ for infinitely many m, it is not possible that $vis(\ddot{a}_1\ddot{a}_2\ldots) < \sigma$. Therefore, $vis(\ddot{a}_1\ddot{a}_2\ldots) = \sigma$, and the claim has been proven. □

Theorem 5.5 If Ä0 to Ä4 and Ä6 and Ä7 hold, then L and $\ddot{L}$ are CFFD-equivalent.

Proof Lemmas 5.2 and 5.4 give $sfail(L) = sfail(\ddot{L})$, $divtr(L) = divtr(\ddot{L})$ and $inftr(L) = inftr(\ddot{L})$. That $stable(L) = stable(\ddot{L})$ follows directly from $\ddot{\Delta} \subseteq \Delta$ and Ä6. □

Practical implementations of Ä4, Ä6 and Ä7 have been described in [Val92a, Val92b]. In them, Ä4 and Ä6 are taken into account in the construction algorithm for stubborn sets. To obtain best reduction results, the implementation tries first to find a stubborn

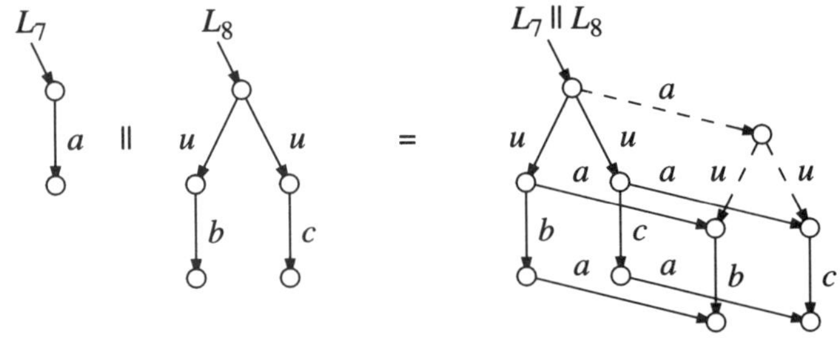

Figure 4 A reduced LTS obeying Ä0 to Ä7

set with no enabled visible actions. If the construction of stubborn sets is based on an independency relation, as is often the case, then Ä4 can be also implemented simply by treating all visible actions as not independent of each other. In the context of Theorem 3.2 this could be done by adding to the parallel composition one more process $L_0 = (S_0, \Sigma_{V0}, \Sigma_{I0}, \Delta_0, is_0)$ such that $S_0 = \{is_0\}$, $\Sigma_{V0} = \Sigma_{V1} \cup \ldots \cup \Sigma_{Vn}$, $\Sigma_{I0} = \emptyset$, and $\Delta_0 = S_0 \times \Sigma_{V0} \times S_0$.

The implementation of Ä7 in [Val92a, Val92b] assumes that the reduced LTS is finite. Under that assumption, Ä7 becomes equivalent to the requirement that every cycle of the reduced LTS contains a state whose stubborn set contains all visible actions. (A cycle of $\ddot{L}$ is a set $\{s_1, \ldots, s_n\}$ of states such that there are actions $a_1, \ldots, a_n$ such that $s_1 -a_2\rightarrow s_2 -a_3\rightarrow \ldots -a_n\rightarrow s_n$ and $s_n -a_1\rightarrow s_1$.) The articles [Val92a, Val92b] describe an efficient technique for detecting and repairing cycles which do not satisfy the above requirement. An alternative, not equivalent, implementation of Ä7 can be found in [GK+95], for instance.

Ä7 has an interesting relationship with Ä5′. A deadlock state can be considered as a state where all actions are in the stubborn set. Therefore, Ä7 claims, in essence, that for any state in the reduced LTS, a state where all visible actions are in the stubborn set is eventually reached. Ä5′ claims that for any state in the reduced LTS and any visible action, it is always possible to go into a state where the action is in the stubborn set. Ä7 is thus strictly stronger than Ä5′. This added strength was needed to guarantee that all infinite executions have a correct representative in the reduced LTS.

6. Preserving Branching Bisimilarity

A method that is close to the stubborn set method was applied in [GK+95] to the verification of formulae in the CTL*-X logic and to constructing reduced state spaces that are branching bisimilar with full state spaces. In this section we translate the method into the framework of this article. We give it a new correctness proof that is simpler than the original one and allows non-deterministic transitions.[2]

We first demonstrate that Ä0 to Ä7 do not guarantee that the reduced LTS is even weakly bisimilar with the full LTS. Figure 4 shows a counter-example. In it, a, b and c are visible and u is invisible. The full LTS contains a state where the next visible action may be b or c but not a, but the reduced LTS does not contain such a state.

It is apparent from the above counter-example that a very strong condition is needed to preserve weak and branching bisimilarity. So we require that if a stubborn set does not

[2]During the POMIV '96 workshop it turned out that [Pel96b] contains a very similar proof to the one presented in this section. The [Pel96b] and [GK+95] proofs cover also the preservation of CTL*-X that the proof in this section lacks, but they assume deterministic structural transitions.

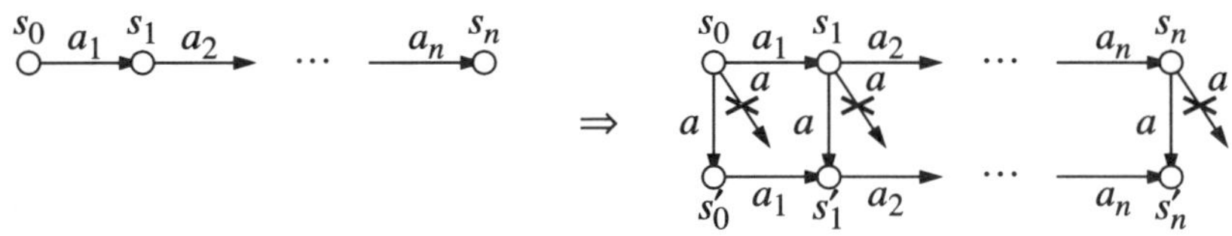

Figure 5 Illustration of super-determinism

contain all actions, then it contains only one enabled action, and (unlike the u-action in Figure 4) an occurrence of that action may have only one outcome. Furthermore, this action should be invisible and commutative with all other enabled actions, and retain its nice properties when other actions occur. Except invisibility, these requirements are formulated in the notion of *super-determinism*.

Definition 6.1 Action a is *super-deterministic* in state s_0, if and only if for every $n \geq 0$, $s_1, \ldots, s_n \in S$, and $a_1, \ldots, a_n \in \Sigma - \{a\}$ such that $s_0 -a_1\rightarrow \ldots -a_n\rightarrow s_n$, there are $s'_0, \ldots, s'_n$ such that

- $s'_0 -a_1\rightarrow \ldots -a_n\rightarrow s'_n$ and
- for every $0 \leq i \leq n$, $s_i -a\rightarrow s'_i$ and $\{ s \in S \mid s_i -a\rightarrow s \} = \{s'_i\}$. □

Super-determinism is illustrated in Figure 5. The following is easy to check from Definition 6.1.

Lemma 6.2 If a is super-deterministic in s and $s -a'\rightarrow s'$ where $a' \neq a$, then a is super-deterministic in s'. □

The branching-bisimilarity-preserving stubborn set method requires that a stubborn set either contains all actions, or contains only one enabled action. In the latter case, the action should be super-deterministic and invisible.

(Ä8) For every $s \in \ddot{S}$, either $\ddot{A}(s) = \Sigma$, or there is $a \in \Sigma_I$ such that $\ddot{A}(s) \cap next(s) = \{a\}$ and a is super-deterministic in s.

Theorem 6.3 If Ä5 and Ä8 hold, then $\ddot{L}$ and L are branching-bisimilar.

Proof We will show that the following relation "$\sim$" is a branching bisimulation between $\ddot{L}$ and L:

$\ddot{s} \sim s$ if and only if there are $n \geq 0$, $s_0, \ldots, s_n \in S$, and $a_1, \ldots, a_n \in \Sigma_I$ such that $s = s_0$, $s_n = \ddot{s}$, $s_0 -a_1\rightarrow \ldots -a_n\rightarrow s_n$, and a_i is super-deterministic in s_{i-1} for $1 \leq i \leq n$.

It is obvious from the definition that $s \sim s$ for every $s \in \ddot{S}$. Therefore, any transition $\ddot{s} \ddot{-}a\ddot{\rightarrow} \ddot{s}'$ of $\ddot{L}$ can be simulated by the sequence $s -a_1 \ldots a_n\rightarrow \ddot{s} -a\rightarrow \ddot{s}'$ of L. It remains to be proven that any transition $s_0 -a\rightarrow s'_0$ of L can be simulated by $\ddot{L}$.

If $a = a_j$ for some $1 \leq j \leq n$ and $a \neq a_i$ for every $1 \leq i < j$, then a is invisible. Because of the super-determinism of $a_1, \ldots, a_{j-1}$ in $s_0, \ldots, s_{j-2}$, there are $s'_1, \ldots, s'_{j-1}$ such that $s'_0 -a_1\rightarrow \ldots -a_{j-1}\rightarrow s'_{j-1}$ and $s_i -a_j\rightarrow s'_i$ for $1 \leq i < j$ and $a_1, \ldots, a_{j-1}$ are super-deterministic in $s'_0, \ldots, s'_{j-2}$. Furthermore, $s'_{j-1} = s_j$ because a_j is super-deterministic in s_{j-1}. As a consequence, $\ddot{s} \sim s'_0$, and $\ddot{L}$ may simulate the transition $s_0 -a\rightarrow s'_0$ by doing nothing.

If $a \neq a_j$ for every $1 \leq j \leq n$, then the super-determinism of $a_1, \ldots, a_n$ in $s_0, \ldots, s_{n-1}$ guarantees the existence of $s'_1, \ldots, s'_n$ such that $s_n -a\rightarrow s'_n$, $s'_0 -a_1\rightarrow \ldots -a_n\rightarrow s'_n$, and $a_1, \ldots, a_n$ are super-deterministic in $s'_0, \ldots, s'_{n-1}$. If $a \notin \ddot{A}(s_n)$, then by Ä8 there are s_{n+1}, s'_{n+1}, and an invisible a_{n+1} such that $s_n \ddot{-}a_{n+1}\ddot{\rightarrow} s_{n+1} -a\rightarrow s'_{n+1}$, $s'_n -a_{n+1}\rightarrow s'_{n+1}$, and a_{n+1} is super-deterministic in s_n and s'_n. Moreover, there are only one a_{n+1} and s_{n+1} such that $s_n \ddot{-}a_{n+1}\ddot{\rightarrow} s_{n+1}$. By induction, if $a \notin \ddot{A}(s_n), \ldots, \ddot{A}(s_{n+k-1})$, then by Ä8 there are $s_{n+1}, \ldots, s_{n+k}, s'_{n+1}, \ldots, s'_{n+k}$, and invisible $a_{n+1}, \ldots, a_{n+k}$ such that $s_n \ddot{-}a_{n+1}\ddot{\rightarrow} \ldots \ddot{-}a_{n+k}\ddot{\rightarrow} s_{n+k}$, $s_{n+k} -a\rightarrow s'_{n+k}$, $s'_n -a_{n+1}\rightarrow \ldots -a_{n+k}\rightarrow s'_{n+k}$, and $a_{n+1}, \ldots, a_{n+k}$ are super-deterministic in $s_n, \ldots, s_{n+k-1}$ and in $s'_n, \ldots, s'_{n+k-1}$. Moreover, s_{n+k} is the only state that can be reached from s_n by k steps in $\ddot{L}$. Ä5 guarantees that $a \in \ddot{A}(s_{n+k})$ for some k. For that k, $s_{n+k} \ddot{-}a\ddot{\rightarrow} s'_{n+k}$, $s_{n+k} \sim s_0$, and $s'_{n+k} \sim s'_0$. As a consequence, $\ddot{L}$ may simulate the transition $s_0 -a\rightarrow s'_0$ by the sequence $s_n \ddot{-}a_{n+1}\ldots a_{n+k}\ddot{\rightarrow} s_{n+k} \ddot{-}a\ddot{\rightarrow} s'_{n+k}$. For future use we point out that $s_{n+i} \sim s_0$ for every $0 \le i \le k$. □

The following fact is worth mentioning here. It guarantees, among other things, that $\ddot{L}$ simulates all divergence traces of L by divergence traces, instead of doing nothing. As a consequence, $\ddot{L}$ preserves certain branching-time liveness properties of L.

Theorem 6.4 Assume that Ä5 and Ä8 hold. If $s_0 -a_1\rightarrow s_1 -a_2\rightarrow \ldots$ and $s'_0 \sim s_0$, where $s'_0 \in \ddot{S}$, then there are $s'_1, s'_2, \ldots$ and $a'_1, a'_2, \ldots$ such that $s'_0 \ddot{-}a'_1\ddot{\rightarrow} s'_1 \ddot{-}a'_2\ddot{\rightarrow} \ldots$ and $vis(a_1a_2\ldots) = vis(a'_1a'_2\ldots)$. Furthermore, for every $i \ge 0$ there is $j \ge 0$ such that $s'_j \sim s_i$, and for every $j \ge 0$ there is $i \ge 0$ such that $s'_j \sim s_i$.

Proof Consider the construction used for showing that $\ddot{L}$ can simulate transitions of L. When it is applied repeatedly to the transitions $s_0 -a_1\rightarrow s_1$, $s_1 -a_2\rightarrow s_2$, and so on starting at $s'_0 \sim s_0$, it finds for each $i \ge 0$ a $k(i) \ge 0$ and states $s'_{k(i)+1}, \ldots, s'_{k(i+1)}$ and actions $a'_{k(i)+1}, \ldots, a'_{k(i+1)}$ such that $k(0) = 0$, $s'_{k(i)} \ddot{-}a'_{k(i)+1}\ddot{\rightarrow} \ldots \ddot{-}a'_{k(i+1)}\ddot{\rightarrow} s'_{k(i+1)}$, and $s'_j \sim s_i$ and $vis(a'_1\ldots a'_j) = vis(a_1\ldots a_i)$ when $j = k(i)$ and when $k(i) < j < k(i+1)$. The definition of "$\sim$" guarantees for each $i \ge 0$ the existence of an action sequence ρ_i such that $s_i -\rho_i\rightarrow s'_{k(i)}$. Let n_i be the length of ρ_i. The construction implies that $n_i = n_0 + k(i) - i$ for every i. Because n_i cannot become negative, $k(i)$ has to grow without limit when i grows without limit. □

The condition Ä8 is not difficult to implement. The following theorem gives a sufficient structural condition for super-determinism in the spirit of Theorem 3.2. It requires that all component LTSs that synchronise on the super-deterministic action can perform next only that action and in only one way. $\ddot{A}(s)$ may be implemented by seeking for a super-deterministic invisible action a and choosing $\ddot{A}(s) = \{a\}$. If that fails, then one should choose $\ddot{A}(s) = \Sigma$, that is, all (enabled) actions should be used for constructing the immediate successors of the state.

Theorem 6.5 Let $L_1 \parallel \ldots \parallel L_n$ be a parallel composition of the LTSs $L_1 = (S_1, \Sigma_{V1}, \Sigma_{I1}, \Delta_1, is_1), \ldots, L_n = (S_n, \Sigma_{Vn}, \Sigma_{In}, \Delta_n, is_n)$, and let $(s_1, \ldots, s_n) -a\rightarrow (s'_1, \ldots, s'_n)$. Assume that for every $1 \le i \le n$ such that $a \in \Sigma_i$, and for every $a' \in \Sigma_i$ and $s' \in S_i$, $s_i -a'\rightarrow_i s'$ implies $a' = a$ and $s' = s'_i$. Then a is super-deterministic in $(s_1, \ldots, s_n)$. □

A "terminal strong component" technique for the implementation of Ä5 when the reduced LTS is finite was mentioned in Section 4. In the case of branching bisimilarity, if $\ddot{A}(s) \ne \Sigma$, then s has only one successor state in the reduced LTS. Therefore, strong components that violate Ä5 collapse to cycles. This simplifies the detection of strong components that violate Ä5. Indeed, they may be detected and repaired efficiently with the techniques in [Val92a, Val92b] that were intended for implementing Ä7. For repair, it is necessary to put all enabled actions to the stubborn set, instead of all visible actions.

7. Conclusions

We described several methods for constructing reduced labelled transition systems that are equivalent with the corresponding full LTSs. We covered "deadlock equivalence" (the reduced LTS has exactly the same deadlock states as the full one), trace equivalence, CSP-equivalence, CFFD-equivalence, and branching bisimilarity. The methods are based on requiring that certain conditions are satisfied by the stubborn sets used in the states of the reduced LTS (Ä0, Ä1, Ä2, Ä3, Ä4, Ä6, Ä8), and by the reduced LTS as a whole (Ä5, Ä7). The condition Ä8 implies Ä0, Ä1, Ä2, Ä3, Ä4, and Ä6; and Ä7 implies a variant of Ä5. Table 1 summarizes the conditions required by each method.

Table 1: Conditions required by the methods in this article

	Ä0	Ä1	Ä2	Ä3	Ä4	Ä5	Ä6	Ä7	Ä8
deadlocks	×	×	×						
trace	×	×	×		×	×			
CSP	×	×	×	×	×		×		
CFFD	×	×	×	×	×		×	×	
branching bisim.						×			×

Hundreds of process equivalences have been described in the literature, and we examined only a small minority of them. Perhaps the most important equivalence that we did not treat separately is the *weak bisimilarity* of the CCS theory [Mil89]. Because branching bisimilarity implies weak bisimilarity, the method for branching bisimilarity preserves also weak bisimilarity. On the other hand, the more a method preserves, the less reduction it gives. A method that preserves weak bisimilarity but not branching bisimilarity might therefore lead to better reduction results than the use of the branching bisimilarity method for weak bisimilarity. Unfortunately, the example in Figure 4 leaves little hope of finding such a method.

Most of the numerous equivalences in the literature are based on a small set of ideas. If the experience with weak bisimilarity will generalise to many other equivalences, then it will not be possible to fine-tune reduced LTS construction methods to each equivalence separately. In such a case the methods presented in this article might be near optimal for many equivalences that we did not discuss. It is, however, impossible to say at the present state of knowledge whether this is really the case.

Most, if not all, of the conditions Ä0 to Ä8 are difficult to implement in their full generality. Therefore, the implementations mentioned in this article give sufficient conditions that are often more stringent than absolutely necessary, and alternative implementations do not necessarily yield equal results. In Theorem 3.2, "dependency" between transitions was analysed at a rather coarse level. It seems possible to devise more and more complicated structural conditions that correspond to more and more careful analysis. It would thus be hopeless to try to find any "best" structural conditions or implementations of Ä0 to Ä8. Furthermore, although we attempted to present Ä0 to Ä8 in as abstract forms as possible, we failed to capture all possibilities. For instance, [Val91] develops a theory of so-called *weak* stubborn sets, where Ä2 does not hold for every enabled action. Again, it seems hopeless to find any "most general" versions of Ä0 to Ä8.

An important topic not covered in this article is *on-the-fly* verification. The goal of an on-the-fly method is to demonstrate already during the construction of the reduced state space the presence or absence of some property. One could, for instance, monitor for illegal traces on-the-fly, and stop the construction of the reduced LTS when an illegal trace is found. "Ordinary" (i.e. based on constructing the full, not a reduced, state space) on-the-fly methods have been developed for several properties. Also the combination of on-the-fly and reduced state space methods has been investigated [Val93, Pel96a]. The method in [Pel96a] is intended for linear time temporal logic properties, and it was presented in a framework with deterministic transitions. [Val93] uses the framework of parallel LTSs and non-deterministic actions, but there is some evidence that the methods suggested in it are not necessarily optimal. Apparently some more research is needed to find the best combination of on-the-fly and stubborn set techniques for process-algebraic verification.

In the process algebra literature, "reduction" sometimes means the transformation of an LTS to a smaller, equivalent LTS. Reduction algorithms in that sense of the word facilitate *compositional LTS construction*: if each component process of a parallel composition is reduced before computing the parallel composition, then a smaller, but equivalent result is obtained. This approach may be applied hierarchically for even better results. It is worth noticing that the stubborn set method and compositional LTS construction take advantage of different aspects of systems, and neither one makes the other unnecessary. That compositional LTS construction does not make the stubborn set method unnecessary was demonstrated in [Val92b] by analysing an example system taken from [GrS91]. The example has $9n \cdot 2^{n-2}$ states, where n is the number of the components of the system. The example had been intentionally constructed to demonstrate that ordinary compositional LTS construction does not always work well. Indeed, it fails totally by yielding intermediate LTSs that are bigger than the full LTS. [GrS91] suggested an advanced compositional LTS construction method that relies on some manual guidance, and requires the construction of several LTSs from the example. Experimental evidence reported in [GrS91] strongly suggests that the biggest of them has $4n+4$ states. The CFFD-preserving stubborn set method is fully automatic and requires the construction of only one LTS, and the LTS has $5n$ states. So at least in this case, the stubborn set method beats compositional LTS construction, and compares favourably with its advanced version in [GrS91].

8. References

[AHU74] Aho, A. V., Hopcroft, J. E. & Ullman, J. D.: *The Design and Analysis of Computer Algorithms*. Addison-Wesley 1974, 470 p.

[BrR85] Brookes, S. D. & Roscoe, A. W.: *An Improved Failures Model for Communicating Sequential Processes*. Proc. NSF-SERC Seminar on Concurrency, Lecture Notes in Computer Science 197, Springer-Verlag 1985, pp. 281–305.

[CLR90] Cormen, T. H., Leiserson, C. E. & Rivest, R. L.: *Introduction to Algorithms*. The MIT Press 1990, 1028 p.

[Esp94] Esparza, J.: *Model Checking Using Net Unfoldings*. Science of Computer Programming (1994) 23: 151–195.

[GK+95] Gerth, R., Kuiper, R., Peled, D. & Penczek, W.: *A Partial Order Approach to Branching Time Logic Model Checking*. Proc. Third Israel Symposium on the Theory of Computing and Systems, IEEE 1995, pp. 130–139.

[God96] Godefroid, P.: *Partial-Order Methods for the Verification of Concurrent Systems, An Approach to the State-Explosion Problem*. Ph.D. Thesis, University of Liège 1994. Lecture Notes in Computer Science 1032, Springer-Verlag 1996, 142 p.

[GrS91] Graf, S. & Steffen, B.: *Compositional Minimization of Finite State Processes.* Proc. Computer-Aided Verification '90, AMS-ACM DIMACS Series in Discrete Mathematics and Theoretical Computer Science, Vol. 3, American Mathematical Society 1991, pp. 57–73.

[Hoa85] Hoare, C. A. R.: *Communicating Sequential Processes.* Prentice-Hall 1985, 256 p.

[McM93] McMillan, K.: *Using Unfoldings to Avoid the State Explosion Problem in the Verification of Asynchronous Circuits.* Proc. CAV '92, 4th Workshop on Computer-Aided Verification, Lecture Notes in Computer Science 663, Springer-Verlag 1993, pp. 164–177.

[Mil89] Milner, R.: *Communication and Concurrency.* Prentice-Hall 1989, 260 p.

[Pel93] Peled, D.: *All from One, One for All: On Model Checking Using Representatives.* Proc. CAV '93, 5th International Conference on Computer-Aided Verification, Elounda, Greece, Lecture Notes in Computer Science 697, Springer-Verlag 1993, pp. 409–423.

[Pel96a] Peled, D.: *Combining Partial Order Reductions with On-the-fly Model-Checking.* Formal Methods in System Design 8 (1) 1996: 39–64.

[Pel96b] Peled, D.: *Partial Order Reduction: Linear and Branching Temporal Logics and Process Algebras.* This volume.

[Tar72] Tarjan, R. E.: *Depth First Search and Linear Graph Algorithms.* SIAM Journal on Computing 1(2) 1972: 146–160.

[Val88] Valmari, A.: *State Space Generation: Efficiency and Practicality.* PhD Thesis, Tampere University of Technology Publications 55, 1988, 169 p.

[Val91] Valmari, A.: *Stubborn Sets for Reduced State Space Generation.* Advances in Petri Nets 1990, Lecture Notes in Computer Science 483, Springer-Verlag 1991, pp. 491–515.

[Val92a] Valmari, A.: *A Stubborn Attack on State Explosion.* Formal Methods in System Design (1992) 1: 297–322. (Earlier version: 2nd International Conference on Computer-Aided Verification, New Brunswick, NJ, USA 1990.)

[Val92b] Valmari, A.: *Alleviating State Explosion during Verification of Behavioural Equivalence.* Department of Computer Science, University of Helsinki, Report A-1992-4, Helsinki, Finland 1992, 57 p.

[Val93] Valmari, A.: *On-the-fly Verification with Stubborn Sets.* Proc. CAV '93, 5th International Conference on Computer-Aided Verification, Elounda, Greece, Lecture Notes in Computer Science 697, Springer-Verlag 1993, pp. 397–408.

[Val94] Valmari, A.: *State of the Art Report: Stubborn Sets.* Petri Net Newsletter 46, April 1994, pp. 6–14.

[VaC91] Valmari, A. & Clegg, M.: *Reduced Labelled Transition Systems Save Verification Effort.* Proc. CONCUR '91, Lecture Notes in Computer Science 527, Springer-Verlag 1991, pp. 526–540.

[VaT91] Valmari, A. & Tienari, M.: *An Improved Failures Equivalence for Finite-State Systems with a Reduction Algorithm.* Proc. Protocol Specification, Testing and Verification XI, North-Holland 1991, pp. 3–18.

[VaT95] Valmari, A. & Tienari, M.: *Compositional Failure-Based Semantic Models for Basic LOTOS.* Formal Aspects of Computing (1995) 7: 440–468.

[vGl90] van Glabbeek, R.: *Comparative Concurrency Semantics and Refinement of Actions.* PhD Thesis, Centrum voor Wiskunde en Informatica, Amsterdam 1990.

[vGW89] van Glabbeek, R. & Weijland, W.: *Branching Time and Abstraction in Bisimulation Semantics (Extended Abstract).* Proc. IFIP International Conference on Information Processing '89, North-Holland 1989, pp. 613–618.

Software Systems Laboratory, Tampere University of Technology, PO Box 553, FIN-33101 Tampere, Finland

E-mail address: Antti.Valmari@cs.tut.fi

DIMACS Series in Discrete Mathematics
and Theoretical Computer Science
Volume **29**, 1997

Partial Order Reduction: Linear and Branching Temporal Logics and Process Algebras

Doron Peled
Bell Laboratories
700 Mountain Avenue
Murray Hill, NJ 07974
doron@research.bell-labs.com

Abstract

Partial order reductions are a family of techniques for diminishing the state-space explosion problem for model-checking concurrent programs. They are based on the observation that execution sequences of a concurrent program can be grouped together into equivalence classes that are indistinguishable by the property to be checked. Applying the reduction to a description of a program results in a reduced state-space that generates at least one representative for each equivalence class. When moving to branching models, e.g., as in branching temporal logics or process algebras, the execution sequences are grouped together into a single tree. In this case, the reduction must also be sensitive to preserving the branching points, where executions with a common prefix depart from each other.

1 Introduction

Total order semantics, also referred to as *interleaving semantics*, are traditionally considered easier to work with, as they lend themselves to simple representations and manipulation, e.g., using finite state machines. Partial order semantics is more recent in modeling concurrent programs. It is argued by its supporters that it can reflect the executions of concurrent systems more accurately, and hence is sometimes called *true concurrency*. In recent years, new research showed several advantages of various partial order specification and verification methods over total order based methods in terms of efficiency and expressiveness.

Partial order reduction techniques were developed to alleviate the state-space explosion in automatically verifying concurrent programs [32, 9, 12, 11, 33, 28, 29, 17, 6]. These techniques were integrated in tools such as SPIN [17] and VFSM-valid [11]. Using the partial order reduction techniques, it has become possible to analyze problems of larger size, which did not lend themselves to automatic

1991 *Mathematics Subject Classification.* Primary 68Q60; Secondary 68Q10, 68Q45, 68Q55.

verification before. The simplicity of the principles behind these methods suggest that they can be integrated into any state-based automatic verification tool.

In this paper we survey a family of partial order reduction methods. We show how equivalence relations can be used to group together sequences that are indistinguishable with respect to the specification. This allows to construct a reduced state-space for the checked system. A reduced state-space for a concurrent system contains only representative sequences from each equivalence class rather than all the sequences in the class. An algorithm for deciding whether a specification cannot distinguish between equivalent sequences for such an equivalence relation is described. We also show how this approach can be extended to deal with branching-time specification.

We concentrate here on the reduction strategy called ample sets method [28, 29, 6]. We will mention, but not survey, related methods for partial order based verification and model-checking, including faithful decompositions [19, 20], stubborn sets [32, 33], persistent and sleep sets [9, 12, 11]. These methods share the idea of selecting only a subset of the successors from a given program state. They differ in the details of selecting these subsets, and the properties preserved by the reduction.

2 Modeling Concurrent Systems

2.1 State Spaces of Concurrent Systems

A *finite state system* $\mathcal{F}$ is a triple $\langle S, T, \iota \rangle$, where

- S is a finite set of *states*,
- T is a finite set of deterministic *transitions*. For each transition $a \in T$ we associate a partial function $S \mapsto S$, with a domain $en_a \subseteq S$.
- $\iota \in S$ is the *initial state*.

The states $en_a \subseteq S$ are those from which a is *executable* or *enabled*. The set of transitions enabled at a state s is denoted by *enabled*(s). When a is enabled from s, executing a from s results in the state $t = a(s)$. We will also denote this by $(s, t) \in a$. Executing the transitions $a_0 a_1 \ldots a_i$ hence obtains the state $a_i(a_{i-1}(\ldots a_1(a_0(\iota)) \ldots))$.

An *interpreted* system is a triple $\mathcal{I} = \langle \mathcal{F}, P, M \rangle$, where

- $\mathcal{F} = \langle S, T, \iota \rangle$ is a finite state system,
- P is a finite set of *propositions*, and
- $M : S \mapsto 2^P$ is the *state labeling* function.

In the sequel we will use the term *system* for interpreted finite state systems.

The *(full) state-space* $SP(\mathcal{I})$ of a system $\mathcal{I} = \langle \mathcal{F}, P, M \rangle$ where $\mathcal{F} = \langle S, T, \iota \rangle$, is a labeled graph $\langle V, E \rangle$ such that

- $V \subseteq S$ is the minimal set of *reachable states* satisfying:
    1. $\iota \in V$,
    2. If $s \in V$ and $(s, t) \in a \in T$, then $t \in V$.
- $E = \{s \xrightarrow{a} t) | (s, t) \in a \in T\}$

Thus, the state-space of $\mathcal{I}$ contains the states reachable from the initial state ι by repeatedly executing the transitions T of $\mathcal{I}$. The *label* of $e = s \xrightarrow{a} t$ is a.

The *transitions sequences* generated by $\mathcal{I}$ correspond to edge labels along the maximal paths of $SP(\mathcal{I})$ that start from the initial state ι. Hence, a transitions sequence is a finite or infinite sequence of transitions $a_0 a_1 a_2 \ldots$ such that there exists a sequence of states $s_0 s_1 s_2 \ldots$ satisfying

- $s_0 = \iota$ [The first state is the initial state.]
- for each $i \geq 0$, $(s_i, s_{i+1}) \in a_i$. [Each adjacent pairs of states correspond to the execution of a transition. We say that s_{i+1} is *reached after executing* a_i.]
- The sequence is maximal, namely it is either infinite, or ends with a state s such that $enabled(s) = \phi$.

The states sequence that correspond to a transitions sequence v is denoted by $states(v)$. For simplicity, it is possible to assume that all transitions sequences are infinite. This can be achieved by adding a new transition a' such that $en_{a'} = S \setminus \cup_{a \in T} en_a$, and $a' = \{(s, s) | s \in en_{a'}\}$. In this case, each state has at least one successor.

Notice that the state-space of a system $\mathcal{I}$ can be considered as a more explicit representation of $\mathcal{I}$; $\mathcal{I}$ contains in S all the *potential* states of $\mathcal{I}$, while $SP(\mathcal{I})$ contains in V only the *actual* states that can be reached. The partial order reduction algorithms are aimed at generating a graph smaller than $SP(\mathcal{I})$ that represents enough information about the property that we want to check.

For each transitions sequence v of $SP(\mathcal{I})$ there is a sequence $prop(v)$ of sets of propositions obtained in the following way: if $states(v) = s_0 s_1 s_2 \ldots$, then $prop(v)$ is the sequence $M(s_0)M(s_1)M(s_2)\ldots$. Thus, there are three languages defined for an interpreted system $\mathcal{I}$:

- The language $\mathcal{L}(\mathcal{I}) \subseteq T^{\omega}$ of transitions sequences.
- The language $\mathcal{L}_{states}(\mathcal{I}) \subseteq S^{\omega}$ of states sequences.
- The language $\mathcal{L}_{prop}(\mathcal{I}) \subseteq 2^{P^{\omega}}$ of propositional sequences.

A *specification* for a system $\mathcal{I}$ can be given as a language over one of the three domains T, S or 2^P. Most specifications use transitions or propositional sequences. In the rest of this section we will usually treat the latter case; the others can be dealt with similarly. In model-checking, the specification is often given using a regular automaton over infinite words, e.g., as a Büchi automaton, or using a logic, such as linear temporal logic (LTL) [31]. A system $\mathcal{I}$ *satisfies* the specification φ, corresponding to the language L_φ, where both are using the same set of propositions P, iff $\mathcal{L}_{prop}(\mathcal{I}) \subseteq L_\varphi$. Graph-theoretical algorithms [23] can then be applied to state space graphs to check that $\mathcal{I}$ satisfies φ.

2.2 Traces and Trace Equivalence

Using interleaving semantics has a lot of advantages for modeling concurrent systems. In particular, its simplicity and use of sequences allows exploiting automata and language theory. On the other hand, interleaving semantics is often criticized for distinguishing between entities that are basically the same. Namely, it can distinguish between executions which differ from each other only by the order of some concurrently executed transitions. This order is largely artificial. Trace semantics groups transitions sequences into equivalence classes, allowing a higher abstraction of the specified system. One can exploits this for model-checking properties that do not distinguish between different sequences that are trace-equivalent.

A *concurrent alphabet* is a pair (T, D), where T is a finite set (representing transitions in our context), and $D \subseteq T \times T$ is a symmetric and reflexive relation called the *dependency relation.*

We define trace equivalence in several steps:

1. Define the relation $\stackrel{1}{\equiv} \subseteq T^* \times T^*$ such that $v \stackrel{1}{\equiv} v'$ iff $v = v'$ or $v = uabw$, $v' = ubaw$ for some $u, w \in T^*$, $(a, b) \notin D$.
2. Define the *trace equivalence* [24] relation for finite sequences as the reflexive and transitive closure of $\stackrel{1}{\equiv}$. Thus, $v \equiv w$ iff one can obtain v from w by repeatedly commuting the order of adjacent independent letters.
3. Define trace preorder relation $\sqsubseteq$ among infinite strings as follows: $v \sqsubseteq v'$ iff for each finite prefix u of v, there exists a finite prefix u' of v' and a finite string w such that $uw \equiv u'$.
4. Define trace equivalence among infinite strings [2] such that $v \equiv v'$ iff $v \sqsubseteq v'$ and $v' \sqsubseteq v$.

Thus, for the concurrent alphabet $(\{a, b\}, \{(a, a), (b, b)\})$ we have $aabb \stackrel{1}{\equiv} abab$, $aabb \equiv bbaa$, $aaab^\omega \sqsubseteq (ab)^\omega$, and $(ab)^\omega \equiv (aab)^\omega$.

Traces are then the equivalence classes of the relation $\equiv$ over finite or infinite strings.

To achieve that if $v \equiv w$, then v is a transitions sequence of $\mathcal{I}$ iff w is a transitions sequence of $\mathcal{I}$, we enforce the following two conditions for independent transitions $(a, b) \notin D$:

D1 if $s \in en_a$, then $s \in en_b$ iff $a(s) \in en_b$. [executing a does not affect the enabledness of b].

D2 If $s \in en_a \cap en_b$ then $a(b(s)) = b(a(s))$. [When both a and b are enabled, executing them in either order results in the same state].

2.3 Stuttering Equivalence

Denote $\Sigma^\infty = \Sigma^* \cup \Sigma^\omega$. The stuttering removal operator $\natural : \Sigma^\infty \mapsto \Sigma^\infty$ applied to a string v replaces every maximal finite subsequence of identical elements by a single copy of this element. For example, $\natural(aabaaacc) = abac$, $\natural(aabaac^\omega) = abac^\omega$.

Two sequences v, w will be considered *stuttering-equivalent* iff $\natural v = \natural w$. We denote this by $v \rightleftharpoons w$. Lamport argued [22] that a specification should not distinguish between two propositional sequences that are stuttering equivalent.

2.4 Fairness Constraints

The *total order semantics* or *interleaving semantics* of a program identifies transitions (or states) sequences as *executions* of a program. Sometimes, the transitions sequences that are considered to be executions are constrained using a *fairness assumption*. Such a constraint can be given as a language **R**. If a fairness assumption **R** is imposed, only sequences that are fair are considered to be execution of a system. Hence, the fair transitions sequences $\mathcal{L}^{\mathbf{R}}(\mathcal{I})$ of a system $\mathcal{I}$ are $\mathcal{L}(\mathcal{I}) \cap R$.

The following fairness assumption is in particular natural when using partial order semantics:

F-fairness. If a transition a is enabled from some state reached in a fair execution sequence, then some transition that is dependent on a must appear later in this sequence.

This fairness assumption was shown in [21, 27] to be equivalent to restricting the set of sequences to those that are maximal with respect to the relation $\sqsubseteq$.

2.5 Syntax and Semantics of CTL*, CTL and LTL

Let P be a finite set of propositions. The set of CTL* state and path formulas are defined inductively:

S1. every member of P is a state formula,

S2. if φ and ψ are state formulas, then so are $\neg\varphi$ and $\varphi \wedge \psi$,

S3. if φ is a path formula, then $\mathsf{A}\varphi$ is a state formula,

P1. any state formula φ is also a path formula,

P2. if φ, ψ are path formulas, then so are $\varphi \wedge \psi$ and $\neg\varphi$,

P3. if φ, ψ are path formulas, then so is $\varphi \mathsf{U} \psi$.

The modal operator A has the intuitive meaning: "for all paths". U denotes the standard strong "until". CTL* consists of the set of all state formulae. The following abbreviations will be used: $\mathsf{E}\varphi = \neg\mathsf{A}\neg\varphi$, $\mathsf{F}\varphi = true\mathsf{U}\varphi$, $\mathsf{G}\varphi = \neg\mathsf{F}\neg\varphi$.

The logic CTL is obtained by restricting the *state* modalities E and A and the *path* modalities U, F and G to appear paired, i.e., in the combinations EU, EF, EG, AU, AF and AG.

The logic LTL is obtained by restricting the set of formulas to the form $\mathsf{A}\varphi$, where φ does not contain A and E. We write φ instead of $\mathsf{A}\varphi$, when confusion is unlikely. We purposely avoided using the nexttime operator X, which can express that a change is made from one specific state to another. (The use of the nexttime operator can defy the ability to exploit partial order reduction.)

A *model* for CTL* is a quadruple $\mathcal{M} = \langle V, E, \iota, M\rangle$, where V are states, E are edges, $\iota \in V$ is a distinguished initial state, and M is an interpretation function, mapping V into subsets of a set of propositions P. The labels on the edges in the definition of the graph are only used for the benefit of the description of the suggested algorithm, but are ignored by the interpretation of the temporal logics.

Denote by $\pi = (s_0, s_1, \ldots)$ a maximal path (i.e., a path that is either infinite or cannot be extended) of $\mathcal{S}$, starting at $s_0 \in V$. Denote the first state of π by $first(\pi)$. The suffix of π, starting from state s_i will be denoted π_i. The satisfaction of a formula φ in a state s of V is written $\mathcal{M}, s \models \varphi$, or just $s \models \varphi$. It is defined inductively as follows:

S1. $s \models q$ iff $q \in M(s)$, for $q \in P$,

S2. $s \models \neg\varphi$ iff not $s \models \varphi$, $s \models \varphi \wedge \psi$ iff $s \models \varphi$ and $s \models \psi$,

S3. $s \models A\varphi$ iff $\pi \models \varphi$ for every maximal path π starting at s,

P1. $\pi \models \varphi$ iff $first(\pi) \models \varphi$ for any state formula φ,

P2. $\pi \models \neg\varphi$ iff not $\pi \models \varphi$, $\pi \models \varphi \wedge \psi$ iff $\pi \models \varphi$ and $\pi \models \psi$,

P3. $\pi \models \varphi\mathsf{U}\psi$ iff there is an $i \geq 0$ such that $\pi_i \models \psi$ and $\pi_j \models \varphi$ for all $0 \leq j < i$.

When using a fairness assumption to limit the execution sequences, we replace "path" by "fair path" in the above definition. (As usual, we require that a fairness assumption satisfies that an infinite sequence is fair iff each suffix of it is fair). We write $\mathcal{M} \models \varphi$ iff $\mathcal{M}, \iota \models \varphi$. Notice that for an LTL specification $\mathsf{A}\varphi$, $\mathcal{M} \models \mathsf{A}\varphi$ iff every (fair) sequence of $\mathcal{M}$ satisfies φ.

3 Verification Using Representatives

We are interested in generating a reduced state-space for a system $\mathcal{I}$ (without having to construct first the full state space). Although we want the reduced state-space to be as small as possible, it must still contain enough information to preserve the checked property. The aim is that the model-checking algorithm would be applicable to the reduced state-space instead of the full one. Besides preserving the truth of the checked specification, the reduced state-space needs also to be able to supply a counter-example in the case that the specification does not hold for the checked system.

3.1 Ample Sub-state-spaces

A *sub-state-space* $\mathcal{S}$ for a system $\mathcal{I} = \langle \mathcal{F}, P, M \rangle$ is a labeled subgraph $\langle V', E' \rangle$ of $SP(\mathcal{I}) = \langle V, E \rangle$ such that

- $\iota \in V'$ [V' includes the initial state],
- $V' \subseteq V$, and
- $E' \subseteq E \cap (V' \times T \times V')$.

Similar to state-spaces, a sub-state-space $\mathcal{S}$ generates a set of transitions sequences $\mathcal{L}(\mathcal{S})$, a set of states sequences $\mathcal{L}_{states}(\mathcal{S})$ and a set of propositional sequences $\mathcal{L}_{prop}(\mathcal{S})$. In fact, we have:

$$\mathcal{L}(\mathcal{S}) \subseteq \mathcal{L}(\mathcal{I}),\ \mathcal{L}_{states}(\mathcal{S}) \subseteq \mathcal{L}_{states}(\mathcal{I}),\ \mathcal{L}_{prop}(\mathcal{S}) \subseteq \mathcal{L}_{prop}(\mathcal{I})$$

Definition 3.1 *A language $\mathcal{L}$ is said to be* closed under an equivalence relation $\sim$, *if for every equivalence class C of $\sim$, either $C \subseteq \mathcal{L}$ or $C \cap \mathcal{L} = \phi$. We also say that* $\sim$ saturates $\mathcal{L}$.

Definition 3.2 *A sub-state-space of a system $\mathcal{I}$ is said to be* ample with respect to the equivalence relation $\sim$ *if it generates at least one transitions (or states, or propositional) sequence for every equivalence class C of $\sim$ such that $C \cap \mathcal{L}(\mathcal{I}) \neq \phi$.*

The following simple observation suggests the use of equivalences in conjunction with sub-state-spaces:

> Let L_φ be the language of a specification φ that is closed under an equivalence relation $\sim$. Let $\mathcal{S}$ be an ample sub-state-space for a system $\mathcal{I}$ with respect to $\sim$. Then, $\mathcal{L}(\mathcal{S}) \subseteq L_\varphi$ ($\mathcal{L}_{prop}(\mathcal{S}) \subseteq L_\varphi$, respectively) iff $\mathcal{L}(\mathcal{I}) \subseteq L_\varphi$ ($\mathcal{L}_{prop}(\mathcal{I}) \subseteq L_\varphi$, resp.).

To exploit the above observation, we need an equivalence relation $\sim$ where the following exist:

1. An effective way to decide whether a given specification φ is closed under $\sim$.
2. An effective way to construct an ample sub-state-space for $\mathcal{I}$ with respect to $\sim$.

3.2 Checking Equivalence Closedness

Section 3.1 motivated the need for checking whether a specification φ is closed under a given equivalence relation $\sim$. In [30], an algorithm is given for deciding the closure of a specification for a given class of equivalence relations, represented as either a non-deterministic automaton (over infinite words) or as linear temporal logic formula. This class includes in particular trace and stuttering equivalence. It is characterized by having a symmetric and reflexive relation $\overset{1}{\sim}$ on finite strings such that

- $\sim^{fin}$ is the transitive closure of $\overset{1}{\sim}$ (hence $\sim^{fin}$ is an equivalence relation).
- $\overset{1}{\sim} \subseteq \Sigma^* \times \Sigma^*$ is a regular language (i.e., recognizable by a finite automaton) over the alphabet $\Sigma \times \Sigma$. Thus, $\overset{1}{\sim}$ is defined between strings of equal lengths.
- $\sim^{fin}$ is a left cancellative relation, i.e., if $vw \sim^{fin} vw'$, then $w \sim^{fin} w'$.
- $\sim$ is defined as the *limit extension* of $\sim^{fin}$, namely $v \sim v'$ iff
  - for each finite prefix u of v, there exists a finite prefix u' of v' and a finite string w such that $uw \sim^{fin} u'$, and
  - for each finite prefix u' of v', there exists a finite prefix u of v and a finite string w' such that $u'w' \sim^{fin} u$.

The definition of trace equivalence $\equiv$ in Section 2.2 already uses the relation $\overset{1}{\equiv}$, which satisfies the above conditions.

For stuttering equivalence, there is a small technical complication in obtaining a relation $\overset{1}{\rightleftharpoons}$, as it needs to be defined between pairs of strings of equal length. We achieve this by extending the alphabet into $\Sigma \cup \{\$\}$, where \$ serves only to force the strings to have the same length. Then, $\overset{1}{\rightleftharpoons}$ can relate u with itself, and $uav\$$ with $uaav$, where $u, v \in \Sigma^*$ and $a \in \Sigma$.

Checking that an ω-regular language L, represented by a Büchi automaton A_L, is closed under an equivalence relation $\sim$ that satisfies the above conditions can be done using the following algorithm, introduced in [30]. The algorithm checks the emptiness of the intersection of the following three languages over the alphabet $\Sigma \times \Sigma$ ($(\Sigma \cup \{\$\}) \times (\Sigma \cup \{\$\})$ for stuttering equivalence, respectively). Hence, each infinite word $\mathbf{w} = (w_1, w_2)$ over this alphabet has a left component w_1 and a right component w_2. The three languages are:

1. The language where the left component w_1 of the input is in L (after removing the \$ symbols, respectively).
2. The language where the right component w_2 of the input is not in L (after removing the \$ symbols, respectively).
3. An automaton that checks that the input can be decomposed into infinitely many factors that are all elements of $\overset{1}{\sim}$.

The naive way to implement the algorithm by constructing the automata for the three languages and then intersecting them can take space exponentially bigger than A_L. However, the algorithm can be implemented in PSPACE [30]. The idea is that there is no need to fully construct the automaton for the complement of the language L; instead, one can use a binary search through the state-space of such a complement automaton [35].

When the specification L is given as a temporal formula φ_L, it is not necessary to translate first the formula into a Büchi automaton. Such a translation requires again in the worse case space exponential in the size of the formula. It is again possible to conduct a binary search through the state-space of the corresponding automata, for φ_L and for $\neg\varphi_L$. This requires space only polynomial in the size of the checked formula. For the stuttering and trace equivalences, checking closeness is in PSPACE-complete, by a reduction from universality of ω-regular automata [30].

4 Partial Order Reduction for Linear Specifications

Partial order reduction methods is a generic name for a family of model-checking methods that avoid constructing the full state-space of the checked program. The family of methods are historically related to partial orders because of the connection between traces and partial order semantics [24]. The basic ideas of the reduction is to generate at least one transitions sequence for each such trace. However, as will be seen later, this is not always the case, i.e., there are cases where there is a single sequence that represents a collection of traces.

4.1 The Ample-Sets Reduction Method

Partial order reduction is based upon modifying the depth first search (DFS) construction of a state-space, depicted in Figure 1. (Alternatively, one can use other search methods, e.g., breadth first search [4].) The DFS creates a node for a global state (starting with the initial state ι), pushes this node into its stack, then recursively creates nodes for all the successors of this node, and pops the node from the stack after all their successors were created. When a new node is generated, the value is hashed using a hashing table (using the procedure create_node at lines 9). Checking if a node is new is facilitated by checking if it already exists in the hashing table (using the function new at line 8). A node that is already discovered during the search is said to be 'open' if it is on the stack (line 2) and 'closed' once it is removed from the stack (line 13). Although the information about whether a node is open or closed is not used here, it will be used in the sequel for detecting cycles. Recall that a cycle is detected exactly when an edge is created (at line 11) pointing to a node that is open (hence not new).

The partial order reduction algorithm modifies the DFS by expanding only a subset of the enabled transitions from each state:

```
3            working_set(s):=ample( s );
```

where $ample(s) \subseteq enabled(s)$. If $ample(s) = enabled(s)$, we say that s is *fully expanded.*

The modified DFS obviously generates a sub-state-space. The problem is how to select these ample sets of successors such that the sub-state-space will be ample with respect to a given effective equivalence relation.

The ample sets method provides a set of constraints for selecting the successors of a state. The set of constraints depends on the effective equivalence relation used.

```
proc DFS(s);
    push s; /* s is becoming open */
    working_set(s):=enabled(s);
    while working_set(s)≠ φ do
      let a ∈working_set(s);
      working_set(s):=working_set(s)\{a};
      t:=a(s);
      if new(t) then
        create_node(t);
        DFS(t) fi;
      create_edge(s, a, t);
    end while;
    pop s; /* s is becoming closed */
end DFS.
```

Figure 1: Using DFS to construct the state-space graph of a program

This in turn can depend on the specification to be checked and whether a fairness constraint is assumed.

In order to present such a set of constraints, define a *visible* transition [33] to be a transition $a \in T$ that can change the propositional interpretation of a state:

Definition 4.1 *Given a system $\langle \mathcal{I}, P, M\rangle$ where $\mathcal{F} = \langle S, T, \iota\rangle$, a transition $a \in T$ is* visible *if there are two states $s, t \in S$ such that $M(s) \neq M(t)$ and $t = a(s)$.*

We will consider the following constraints:

C0 [Non-emptiness condition] *ample*(s) is empty iff *enabled*(s) is empty.

C1 [Faithful decomposition [19, 32, 28, 11]] For every path of $SP(\mathcal{I})$, starting from the state s, a transition that is dependent on some transition in *ample*(s) cannot appear before a transition from *ample*(s).

C2 [Cycle closing condition [28]] If s is not fully expanded then for no transition $a \in$ *ample*(s) it holds that $a(s)$ is on the search stack (i.e., is open).

C3 [Non-visibility condition [29]] If s is not fully expanded then none of the transitions in it is visible.

Condition **C2** can be weaken to require that for every cycle in the reduced state space there is at least one fully expanded node. An algorithm for checking this weaker condition was suggested in [32].

We have the following results concerning sub-states-space constructed using ample sets:

Theorem 4.2 **([28])** *The sub-state-space constructed using conditions* **C0–C2** *is ample with respect to trace equivalence under* **F**-*fairness.*

Hence, if the specification is given as a language that is closed under trace equivalence, and **F**-fairness is assumed, one can use a sub-state-space that is constructed while conditions **C0-C2** are satisfied at each one of its state. Several temporal logics were devised for expressing properties that are closed under trace equivalence, e.g., the logics TrPTL [36] and TLC [1]. Alternatively, one can use the decision procedure of [30], presented in Section 3.2, to check whether a given LTL or Büchi automaton specification is closed under trace equivalence.

If the specification is not closed under trace equivalence, one can keep adding new dependencies, until it becomes closed. Of course, adding dependencies can ultimately completely prohibit the reduction, e.g., when all transitions are made interdependent.

There is a subtle point to notice about adding dependencies: the definition of **F**-fairness is sensitive to the dependency relation used. By adding more dependencies, more sequences would become **F**-fair. Hence, at worst, representatives for sequences that were not originally fair are generated. Since the model-checking algorithm applied to the reduced state-space will ignore unfair (defined w.r.t. the *original* dependence relation) sequences, correctness is preserved.

To understand why Theorem 4.2 holds, observe the following Lemmas, assuming the sub-state-space are constructed under conditions **C0–C2**:

Lemma 4.3 **([29])** *Let s be a state in a sub-state-space $\mathcal{S} = \langle V', E' \rangle$ of an interpreted system $\mathcal{I}$. Let v be a sequence of transitions labeling a path of $SP(\mathcal{I})$, staring at s. Then there exists a transition $a \in ample(s)$ such that $v \equiv aw$, for some $w \in T^\omega$.*

Proof. According to **C1**, only transitions that are independent of those in $ample(s)$ can appear in v before some transition of $ample(s)$ appears. The fairness **F** requires that transitions dependent of those enabled in s, in particular those in $ample(s)$, eventually appear. (Notice that the dependency relation D is always reflexive.) Combining the two, v must contain a transition $a \in ample(s)$ that appears after transitions independent of it. Thus, a can be commuted to the beginning. ∎

We aim at simulating each fair path of $\mathcal{I}$ by a fair path of the reduced sub-state-space $\mathcal{S}$. The basic simulation step is based on the following:

Lemma 4.4 **([29])** *Let s and v be as in Lemma 4.3. Let a be the first transition of v. Then, the reduced sub-state-space $\mathcal{S}$ contains a finite path labeled with $b_1 b_2 \ldots b_n a$, such that each b_i is independent of a, and $a b_1 b_2 \ldots b_n w \equiv v$ for some $w \in T^\omega$.*

Proof. The proof is by induction on the order in which nodes are removed from the stack (at line 13 in Figure 1), i.e., are closed. There are two cases. In the first case,

$a \in ample(s)$, hence the corresponding path has length of one. In the second case, $a \notin ample(s)$. Hence, according to Lemma 4.3, there is a transition $b_0 \in ample(s)$ that is independent of a and appears in v after a sequence of transitions that are independent of b_0. We can look now at the state $s' = b_0(s)$. Since $a \notin ample(s)$, we know from Condition **C2** that the transition b_0 could not close a cycle. Hence, s' is created after s and thus according to the DFS order, will be removed from the stack before s. Therefore, we can assume the induction hypothesis from s', i.e., there exists a sequence $b_1 b_2 \ldots b_n a$ from s' such that each b_i is independent of a. The required sequence is then $b_0 b_1 b_2 \ldots b_n a$. ∎

Lemma 4.4 can be used to show that for each sequence v of $\mathcal{I}$ there exists a sequence w such that $w \equiv v$ in $\mathcal{S}$, proving Theorem 4.2. The proof in [29] constructs the path w: each transition a_i, taken in its turn from $v = a_0 a_1 a_2 \ldots$, either (a) appears in w after some 'deficit' sequence of independent transitions $b_1 b_2 \ldots b_n$, according to Lemma 4.4, or (b) has already appeared as part of the so far accumulated deficit.

Unfortunately, when the fairness condition **F** (or any stronger fairness condition) is not assumed, Lemma 4.3 does not hold. Hence, also Lemma 4.4 and Theorem 4.2 do not hold. To see this, assume there is a transition a which is enabled at a state s, and independently, a loop starts at s, consisting of the transitions b and c, which are independent of a. Thus, $enabled(s) = \{a, b\}$. Then, without assuming **F**-fairness, the transitions sequence $v = (bc)^\omega$, starting at state s is allowed. Choosing $ample(s) = \{a\}$ satisfies the conditions **C0-C2**, hence no sequence equivalent to v starts from s in the constructed sub-state-space.

To recover the situation, observe that although the sequence $w = a(bc)^\omega$ is not trace-equivalent to v, a appears before a sequence of independent transitions. If a is invisible, then no stuttering-closed specification can distinguish between v and w. We have the following:

Theorem 4.5 ([29]) *The sub-state-space constructed using conditions* **C0–C3** *is ample with respect to stuttering equivalence.*

5 Reduction for Branching TL and Process Algebras

Preserving properties based on branching semantics, where execution sequences are embedded in a tree requires an additional constraint. The reason is that with branching properties one can observe the points where execution sequences depart from each other.

The lefthand structure of Figure 2 contains an example of a full state space $\mathcal{M}$ for a system with a set of transitions $T = \{a, b, c, d, e\}$ such that $D = T \times T \setminus \{(a, b), (b, a), (a, c), (c, a)\}$. This structure does not satisfy the CTL formula $\varphi = \mathsf{AG}((p \wedge \neg q) \rightarrow (\mathsf{AF}q \vee \mathsf{AF}\neg q))$. The reduced state space $\mathcal{M}'$ on the lefthand of Figure 2 obtained by preserving conditions **C0–C3**, satisfies φ.

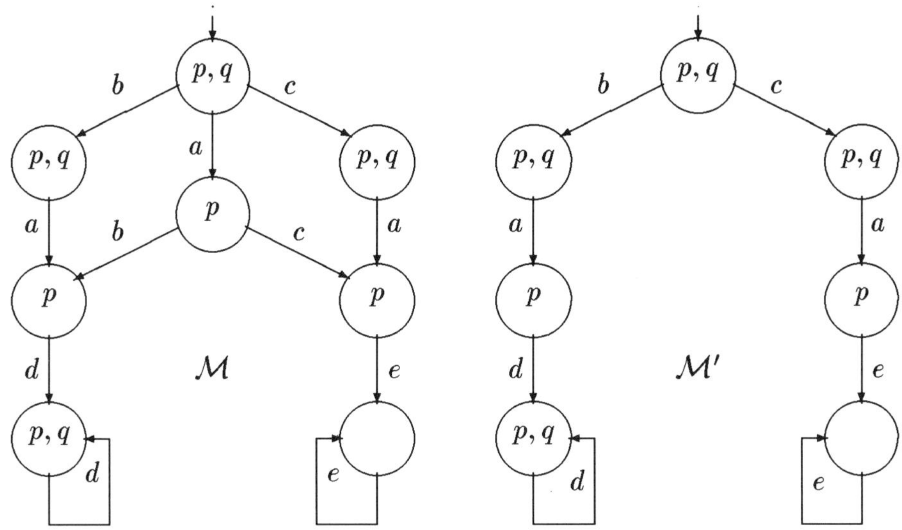

Figure 2: Example where **C0–C3** do not suffice to preserve CTL.

To recover the correctness of the reduction for the branching case, we impose the following constraint:

C4 [Singleton condition [6]] Either s is fully expanded, or *ample*(s) contains exactly one transition.

5.1 Behavioral Equivalences

We consider here several notions of behavioral equivalences that are preserved under our partial order reduction. Some connections between behavioral equivalences and logics allow adopting the reduction for various logical formalisms.

Definition 5.1 ([3]) *A relation* $\cong_{sb} \subseteq V \times V'$ *is a* stuttering simulation *between the states of two structures* $\mathcal{M} = \langle V, E, \iota, M\rangle$ *and* $\mathcal{M}' = \langle V', E', \iota', M'\rangle$ *if the following conditions hold:*

1. $\iota \cong_{sb} \iota'$,
2. *if* $s \cong_{sb} s'$, *then* $M(s) = M'(s')$ *and for every maximal path* π *of* $\mathcal{M}$ *that starts at* s, *there is a maximal path* π' *in* $\mathcal{M}'$ *that starts at* s', *a partition* $B_1, B_2 \ldots$ *of* π, *and a partition* $B'_1, B'_2 \ldots$ *of* π' *such that for each* $j \geq 0$, B_j *and* B'_j *are nonempty and finite, and every state in* B_j *is related by* $\cong_{sb}$ *to every state in* B'_j.

A relation $\cong_{sb}$ *is a* stuttering bisimulation *if both* $\cong_{sb}$ *and* $\cong_{sb}^T$ *(the transpose of* $\cong_{sb}$*) are stuttering simulations.*

The following theorem connects CTL* (as defined without the nexttime operator) and stuttering bisimulation:

Theorem 5.2 (see [3]) *Let φ be a CTL* formula with the set of atomic propositions P. Let $\mathcal{M}$ and $\mathcal{M}'$ be two structures, where the range of the labeling function M_1 and M_2 is the subsets of atomic propositions P. Let the relation $\cong_{sb}$ be a stuttering bisimulation between the states of $\mathcal{M}$ and $\mathcal{M}'$. Then for every pair of stuttering bisimilar states $s \cong_{sb} s'$ it holds that $\mathcal{M}, s \models \varphi$ iff $\mathcal{M}', s' \models \varphi$.*

Definition 5.3 (Branching bisimulation [8, 26]) *A relation $\cong_{bb} \subseteq V \times V'$ is a* branching simulation *between the states of two structures $\mathcal{M} = \langle V, E, \iota, M' \rangle$ and $\mathcal{M}' = \langle V', E', \iota', M' \rangle$ if it satisfies the following conditions:*

1. *$\iota \cong_{bb} \iota'$ and*
2. *if $s \cong_{bb} s'$ and $s \xrightarrow{b} t$, then either $b = \tau$ and $t \cong_{bb} s'$, or there exists a path $s' = s_0 \xrightarrow{\tau} s_1 \xrightarrow{\tau} \dots \xrightarrow{\tau} s_n \xrightarrow{b} t'$ in $\mathcal{M}'$ such that $s \cong_{bb} s_i$ for $0 \leq i \leq n$, and $t \cong_{bb} t'$.*

A relation $\cong_{bb}$ is a branching bisimulation *if both $\cong_{bb}$ and $\cong_{bb}^{T}$ are branching simulations.*

Let $\mathcal{M} = \langle V, E, \iota, M \rangle$ be a structure. Denote $s \stackrel{a}{\Longrightarrow} s'$ if there exists path $s = s_0 \xrightarrow{\tau} s_1 \xrightarrow{\tau} \dots \xrightarrow{\tau} s_i \xrightarrow{a} s_{i+1} \xrightarrow{\tau} \dots \xrightarrow{\tau} s_n = s'$. When a is τ, the path can be empty, whence s equals s'.

Definition 5.4 *A relation $\cong_{wb} \subseteq V \times V'$ is a* weak simulation *[25] between structures $\mathcal{M} = \langle V, E, \iota, M \rangle$ and $\mathcal{M}' = \langle V', E', \iota', M' \rangle$ if it satisfies the following conditions:*

1. *$\iota \cong_{wb} \iota'$ and*
2. *if $s \cong_{wb} s'$ and $s \xrightarrow{b} t$, then there exists t' such that $s' \stackrel{b}{\Longrightarrow} t'$ in $\mathcal{M}'$ such that $t \cong_{wb} t'$.*

A relation $\cong_{wb}$ is a weak bisimulation *if both $\cong_{wb}$ and $\cong_{wb}^{T}$ are weak simulations.*

Notice that the interpretation functions M and M' are irrelevant and hence can be omitted in both branching and weak bisimulation. We define now a behavioral equivalence that includes conditions on both states and edges. To tie together stuttering bisimulation, which observes states but ignores transitions, and branching bisimulation, which observes transitions and ignores states we define the following stronger equivalence relation:

Definition 5.5 *A relation $\cong_{vb} \subseteq V \times V'$ is a visible simulation between the states of two structures $\mathcal{M} = \langle V, E, \iota, M \rangle$ and $\mathcal{M}' = \langle V', E', \iota', M' \rangle$ if $\iota \cong_{vb} \iota'$, and when $s \cong_{vb} s'$, the following conditions hold:*

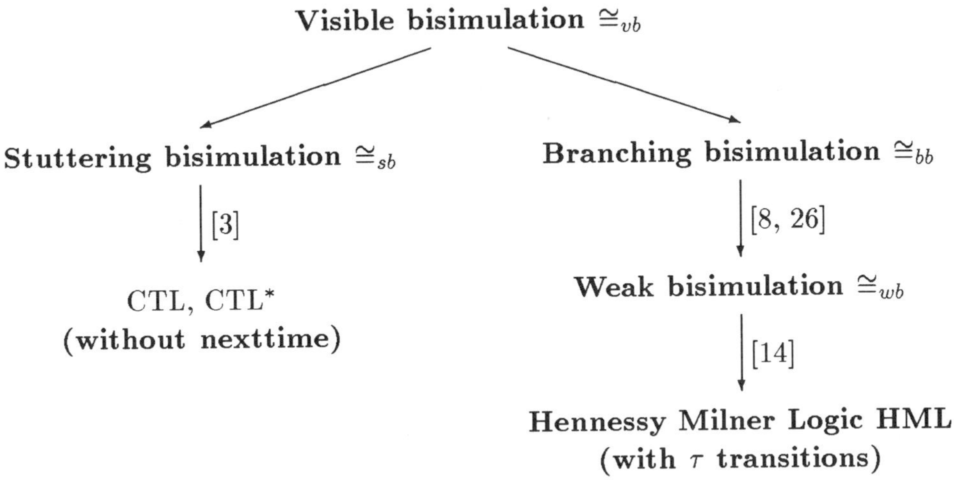

Figure 3: Connections between equivalences and logics

1. $M(s) = M'(s')$.

2. *If* $s \xrightarrow{b} t \in E$, *either* b *is invisible and* $t \cong_{vb} s'$, *or there exists a path* $s' = s_0 \xrightarrow{a_0} s_1 \xrightarrow{a_1} \dots \xrightarrow{a_{n-1}} s_n \xrightarrow{b} t'$ *in* $\mathcal{M}'$ *such that* $s \cong_{vb} s_i$ *for* $0 \leq i \leq n$, a_i *is invisible for* $0 \leq i < n$ *and* $t \cong_{vb} t'$.

3. *If there is an infinite path* $s = t_0 \xrightarrow{b_0} t_1 \xrightarrow{b_1} \dots$, *where* b_i *is invisible and* $t_i \cong_{vb} s'$ *for* $i \geq 0$, *then there exists a path* $s' = r_0 \xrightarrow{c_0} r_1 \xrightarrow{c_1} \dots \xrightarrow{c_{j-1}} r_j \xrightarrow{c_j} r_{j+1}$, *with* $j \geq 0$, *such that* $s \cong_{vb} r_i$ *and* c_i *is invisible for* $0 \leq i \leq j$, *and* $t_1 \cong_{vb} r_{j+1}$.

A relation $\cong_{vb}$ *is a* visible bisimulation *if both* $\cong_{vb}$ *and* $\cong_{vb}^T$ *are visible simulations.*

It is simple to show that visible bisimulation is stronger than stuttering bisimulation. Hence from Theorem 5.2 we conclude that it preserves CTL* properties (without nexttime). When all invisible transitions are labeled as τ, visible bisimulation is stronger than branching bisimulation, which in turn is stronger than weak bisimulation. This interaction between behavioral equivalences and logics is depicted in Figure 3. In the Section 5.2 we show that our reduction (with conditions **C0**–**C4**) preserves visible bisimulation. By the connection between weak bisimulation and Hennessy-Milner logic (HML) with τ transitions [14], the reduction preserves specification expressed in HML.

The paper [34] in this volume relaxes the requirement that the transitions are deterministic. It also studies various other equivalence relations related to Hoare's CSP [15].

5.2 Correctness of the Algorithm

Let $\mathcal{M} = \langle V, E, \iota, M \rangle$ be the full state space of an interpreted system $\mathcal{I}$. In order to obtain a visible bisimulation between the full state space and a reduced sub-state-space, define the following relation:

Definition 5.6 *Define the relation* $\sim \subseteq V \times V$ *such that* $s \sim s'$ *iff there exists a path* $s = s_0 \xrightarrow{a_0} s_1 \xrightarrow{a_1} \ldots \xrightarrow{a_{n-1}} s_n = s'$ *such that* s_i *is invisible and* $\{a_i\}$ *satisfies condition* **C1** *from state* s_i *for* $0 \leq i \leq n-1$.

Such a path will be called a *forming path.* The length of a shortest forming path between s and s' will be called the *distance between* s *and* s'. It is easy to see that the relation $\sim$ is transitive and reflexive (but not necessarily symmetric).

Let $\mathcal{M}' = \langle V', E', \iota', M' \rangle$ be a sub-state-space generated for $\mathcal{F}$ by our partial order reduction algorithm.

Definition 5.7 *Let* $\approx = \sim \cap (V \times V')$.

Notice that by definition, $\approx \subseteq \sim$. Our goal is to show that $\approx$ is a visible bisimulation. We will use a number of simple lemmas:

Lemma 5.8 *Let* $s \xrightarrow{a} t$ *be an edge of* E *such that* $\{a\}$ *satisfies Condition* **C1** *from the state* s. *Let* $s \xrightarrow{b} r$ *be another edge of* E, *with* $a \neq b$. *Then* $\{a\}$ *satisfies Condition* **C1** *from* r.

The following can be proved by a simple induction:

Lemma 5.9 *Let* $s = s_0 \xrightarrow{a_0} s_1 \xrightarrow{a_1} \ldots \xrightarrow{a_{n-1}} s_n = s'$ *be a forming path, and* $s \xrightarrow{b} t \in E$. *Then there are exactly two possibilities (see Figure 4):*

1. *b is independent of a_i for $0 \leq i < n$. There exists a forming path $t = t_0 \xrightarrow{a_0} t_1 \xrightarrow{a_1} \ldots \xrightarrow{a_n} t_n$, with $s_i \xrightarrow{b} t_i$ for $0 \leq j \leq n$.*
2. *There exists $j < n$ such that b is independent of a_i for $0 \leq i < j$, and $b = a_j$. There exists a forming path $t = t_0 \xrightarrow{a_0} t_1 \xrightarrow{a_1} \ldots \xrightarrow{a_{j-1}} t_j$, with $s_i \xrightarrow{b} t_i$ for $0 \leq i \leq j$. In this case, there is a forming path of length $n-1$ from t to s'.*

Corollary 5.10 *Let* $s \sim s'$ *and* $s \xrightarrow{b} t \in E$. *Then there exists an edge* $s' \xrightarrow{b} t' \in E$ *such that* $t \sim t'$ *in each one of the following cases:*

1. *b does not appear on some forming path from s to s' (in particular, when b is visible), or*

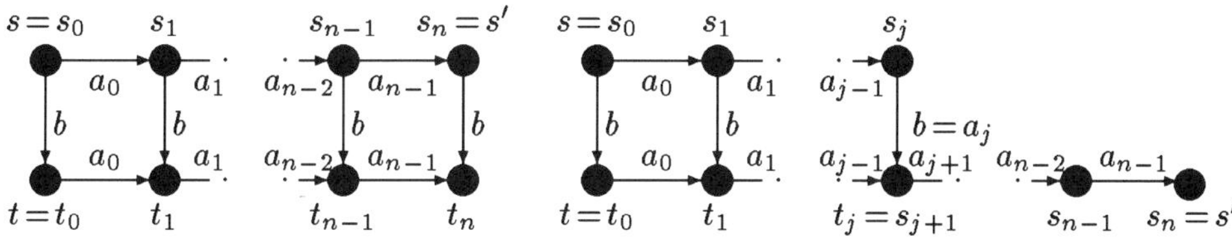

Figure 4: Two cases of Lemma 5.9

2. $t \not\sim s'$.

The reduction algorithm with conditions **C0-C4** guarantees the following:

Lemma 5.11 *Let s be a state in the reduced sub-state-space $\mathcal{M}'$. Then there is a forming path in $\mathcal{M}'$ from s to some fully expanded node s'.*

Theorem 5.12 (See [6]) *The relation $\approx$ is a visible bisimulation.*

Proof. First, observe that $\iota = \iota'$ and $\iota \in V'$. Hence $\iota \approx \iota'$. Let $s \approx s'$. Thus, $s \sim s'$. Condition *1* of Definition 5.5 is satisfied since according to Definition 5.6, there is a path of invisible transitions from s to s'. Hence, by Definition 4.1, $M(s) = M(s')$.

We show that condition *2* of Definition 5.5 holds. Let $s \xrightarrow{b} t \in E$. We argue by cases:

Case 1. $t \sim s'$ and b is invisible. Immediate from the definition.

Case 2. $t \not\sim s'$ or b is visible. According to Corollary 5.10, in both cases there is an edge $s' \xrightarrow{b} t'$ in $\mathcal{M}$ such that $t \sim t'$. Notice that by the definition of $\approx$, $s' \in V'$, but it is not necessary the case that $t' \in V'$. By Lemma 5.11, there is a forming path in $\mathcal{M}'$ from s' to some fully expanded node s''. Hence, $s \sim s' \sim s''$, which implies by transitivity of $\sim$ that $s \sim s''$. Since $s'' \in V'$, also $s \approx s''$. Again there are two cases (see Figure 5):

Case 2.1. $t' \sim s''$ and b is invisible. Then, $t \sim t' \sim s''$, hence $t \sim s''$ and also $t \approx s''$.

Case 2.2. $t' \not\sim s''$ or b is visible. Then, according to Corollary 5.10, there is an edge $s'' \xrightarrow{b} t''$, with $t' \sim t''$. Thus, $t \sim t' \sim t''$, hence $t \sim t''$. Since s'' is fully expanded, $t'' \in V'$, thus $t \approx t''$.

Conversely, let $s' \xrightarrow{b} t' \in E'$. Since $s \sim s'$, there is a forming path $s = s_0 \xrightarrow{a_1} s_1 \xrightarrow{a_2} \ldots \xrightarrow{a_n} s_n = s'$. To satisfy Condition *2* of Definition 5.5, we need only to extend this path with the transition $s_n \xrightarrow{b} t'$.

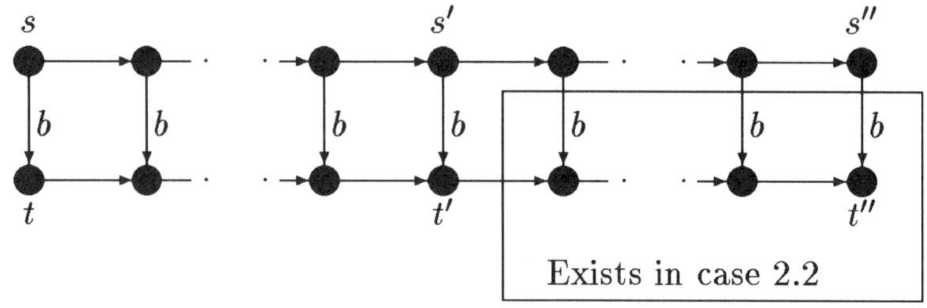

Figure 5: Cases 2.1 and 2.2 of Theorem 5.12

For proving Condition *3* of Definition 5.5, let $s = t_0 \xrightarrow{b_0} t_1 \xrightarrow{b_1} \ldots$ be an infinite path, with b_i invisible and $t_i \approx s'$ for $i \geq 0$. By Lemma 5.11, there is a forming path from s' to s'', with s'' fully expanded. Thus, $t_i \approx s''$ for $i \geq 0$.

We will show that there exists some $j \geq 0$ such that b_j does not occur on some forming path from t_j to s''. The proof will construct a sequence of forming paths l_i from t_i to s'', for $0 \leq i \leq j$, with l_0 a path from s to s'' via s'. Observe that by Lemma 5.9, if b_i appears on l_i, then we can construct a path l_{i+1} that is shorter than l_i. Since there are infinitely many nodes t_i, and l_0 has a finite length, this construction must terminate with some j as above. Now, according to Corollary 5.10, there is an edge $s'' \xrightarrow{b_j} t' \in E$ such that $t_{j+1} \sim t'$. Since s'' is fully expanded, also $t_{j+1} \approx t'$. Appending the edge $s'' \xrightarrow{b_j} t'$ to the forming path from s' to s'', results in a path that satisfies Condition *3*.

The other direction of Condition *3* is similar to the other direction of Condition *2* above. ∎

6 Implementation Issues

Finding ample sets that satisfy condition **C1** is based on analyzing the current global state. We will discuss two types of concurrent systems, with matching algorithms. In both cases, we assume that each system consists of a set of *processes*, with each process containing a (not necessarily disjoint) set of transitions. Each process has a set of local variables that can be changed only by transitions that belong to the process. Transitions whose effect is only to change the process variables are called *local transitions*. The local state of each process includes the values of its local variables. Each (global) system state is a combination of the local states of all the processes.

Synchronous Communication

Synchronous communication systems incorporate CSP or ADA-like communication. Communication is done cooperatively at the same time by the sender and the receiver. Sending and receiving can thus be considered a single transition, shared by two processes. Hence, the communication transition belongs to both the sending and the receiving process. We say that a communication transition a between a pair of processes $\mathcal{P}_i$ and $\mathcal{P}_j$ is *locally enabled* by a process $\mathcal{P}_i$ at state s if it can be executed at the current state s, or any state s' such that the local states of $\mathcal{P}_i$ in s and s' are the same. This means that $\mathcal{P}_i$ is willing to do his part in the communication transition a. We assume that such a system includes only local and synchronous communication transitions.

The dependency relation for synchronous communication systems relates transitions that belong to the same process. Hence, two transitions are interdependent iff they belong to the same process. Notice that a communication transition belongs to and hence is dependent on transitions of two processes. Choosing a subset of the enabled transitions that satisfy condition **C3** can be done as follows:

> Choose all the transitions enabled in the current state s that belong to a subset $\mathcal{P}$ of the processes, such that there is no communication transition between a process $\mathcal{P}_i$ in $\mathcal{P}$ and a process outside $\mathcal{P}$ that is locally enabled by $\mathcal{P}_i$.

The above rule prevents the case where, by executing transitions outside the selected ample set, a communication that is dependent on transitions in the set will become (globally) enabled and will execute before any transition in the ample set, contradicting **C1**. Such a set of transitions can be found by choosing initially the currently enabled transitions that belong to a single process. If the above rule does not hold, repeat adding transitions of additional processes, until the rule holds.

Asynchronous Communication

In this communication model, we have separate sends and receives. In addition to the local variables of each process, pairs of processes that can communicate with each other share fifo queues, through which the communication is handled. The sender does not have to wait for the receiver, unless the message queue it uses is full. Similarly, the receiver does not have to wait for the sender unless there is no message in its input queue. Send and receive transitions are matching if they share the same communication queue. We will assume that for each queue there is only a single (different) process that can send, and a single process that can receive.

It is evident that matching sends and receives do not satisfy the conditions on the dependency relation from Section 2.2. However, one can weaken condition **D1**, allowing transitions a and b to be independent when executing one cannot disable the other (but can enabled the other, as oppose to condition **D1**). Notice that in this case, it is no longer true that when $v \equiv w$ and v is a transitions sequence of a system $\mathcal{I}$, then w is also a transitions sequence of $\mathcal{I}$.

Choosing a subset of the enabled transitions at s that satisfy condition **C3** can be done as follows:

> Choose all the transitions enabled in the current state that belong to a subset $\mathcal{P}$ of the processes, such that

- there is no send transition of a process $\mathcal{P}_i$ in $\mathcal{P}$ that could send a message to a process outside $\mathcal{P}$ if its queue was not full in s.
- there is no receive transition of a process $\mathcal{P}_i$ in $\mathcal{P}$ that could receive a message from a process outside $\mathcal{P}$ if its queue was not empty in s.

Separate Process Analysis

As explained above, additional knowledge about the future enabledness of transitions allows certifying more subsets as ample sets. As an example, in synchronous communication, we can weaken the requirement that the subset of processes $\mathcal{P}$ does not contain a locally enabled communication transition a, communicating with a processes that is outside $\mathcal{P}$; the existence of such a transition a does not prohibits the enabled transitions of $\mathcal{P}$ from being an ample set if the process $\mathcal{P}_j$ can not participate in such a communication in every state that is reachable from the current one. A similar weakening is possible for the asynchronous communication case.

The future disabledness of a transition from a given state is as hard to check as the model-checking problem itself. Thus, we may be satisfied with a solution that would not identify *every* transition that can no longer become enabled from the current state, but would identify at least a subset of such transitions. This can be done using a *separate process reachability.* In the above example for synchronous communication, we will check whether process $\mathcal{P}_j$ could have reached the matching communication from its current *local state.* This search looks at the process $\mathcal{P}_j$ in isolation. It assumes all transitions that are joint with other processes to be locally enabled by the other processes. Furthermore, we may even choose to ignore data values, reverting to static analysis.

Such a search can be done in a preparatory stage, identifying from each local state 'offending' transitions (which can include synchronous communication transitions, asynchronous communication transitions or use of global variables) that are *not* reachable. This information can be used then to improve the reduction by identifying more subsets as ample sets.

On-the-fly Reduction

In previous sections, the model-checking algorithm was explained as a two-phase process, where at the first phase, the (reduced) state-space is constructed, and in the second phase, a graph-theoretic algorithm is applied to it. In practice, many model-checking tools work in a slightly different, more efficient, way. They combine the construction of the state space with checking that it satisfies the specification. Then, it is sometimes possible to identify 'on-the-fly' that the system violates the specification, before completing the construction. We will describe how partial order reduction can be applied while doing on-the-fly model-checking.

Obtaining an on-the-fly model-checking algorithm can be done by using a Büchi automaton $\mathcal{A}$ that corresponds to the complement of the specification φ. Namely,

$\mathcal{A}$ recognizes the sequences that are not allowed by the specification. A translation from LTL formulas to Büchi automata can be found e.g., in [37, 7].

A Büchi automaton is a fivetuple $\langle Q, i, \Sigma, \delta, F \rangle$, where Q is a finite state of *automaton states*, $i \in Q$ is the *initial automaton state*, Σ is a finite set of *input values*, which is in our case 2^P, $\delta \subseteq Q \times \Sigma \times Q$ is a non-deterministic *transition function*, and $F \subseteq Q$ is the set of *accepting states*. A *run* of the automaton $\mathcal{A}$ over an infinite sequence $\sigma \in \Sigma^\omega$, where $\sigma = r_0 r_1 r_2 \ldots$ is an infinite sequence of automaton states $q_0 q_1 \ldots$ such that for each $i \geq 0$, $(q_i, r_i, q_{i+1}) \in \delta$. A run is *accepting* iff at least one automaton state from F appears on it infinitely many times.

Verifying that a system $\mathcal{I}$ satisfies a specification φ is thus done by checking whether there are execution sequences of $\mathcal{I}$ that are accepted by runs of $\mathcal{A}$. If there are such sequences, they correspond to counter-examples (since $\mathcal{A}$ accept the sequences disallowed by the specification). Otherwise, $\mathcal{I}$ satisfies φ.

To carry out the above task, we can generate the *product automaton* $\mathcal{I} \times \mathcal{A}$: the states of the product are pairs from $S \times Q$. We will refer to such pairs simply as *states*. The transitions are pairs from $T \times \delta$. The accepting states are fixed by the automaton state component, i.e., are pairs $\langle s, q \rangle$ such that $q \in F$. The initial state is the pair $\langle \iota, i \rangle$. To make the sequences of $\mathcal{I} \times \mathcal{A}$ correspond to runs of $\mathcal{A}$ over sequences of $\mathcal{I}$, we make the following correspondence: $\langle s, q \rangle \xrightarrow{\langle a,b \rangle} \langle s', q' \rangle$ is a transition of $\mathcal{I} \times \mathcal{A}$ iff (1) $s' = a(s)$, (2) $(q, b, q') \in \delta$, and (3) $M(s) = b$. The last requirement means that the $\mathcal{A}$ transition b agrees with the labeling of the outgoing system state s.

We can now construct $\mathcal{I} \times \mathcal{A}$ on-the-fly: from the current pair $\langle s, q \rangle \in S \times Q$, generate all possible transitions $\langle a, b \rangle$ that satisfy (1), (2) and (3) above. Better yet, we can employ the partial order reduction and restrict the first component such that $a \in ample(s)$.

The only condition that appears to be problematic is the cycle closing condition **C2**: the cycles in the product are not necessarily the same as the ones in the reduced state-space for $\mathcal{I}$. However, in [29] it is shown that it is correct to use the cycles of $\mathcal{I} \times \mathcal{A}$.

Using Tarjan's DFS algorithm, we can find the maximal strongly connected components of $\mathcal{I} \times \mathcal{A}$. A strongly connected component that is reachable from the initial state and contains an accepting state means that the property φ does not hold for $\mathcal{I}$, and can be used to construct a counter-example.

An even more efficient model-checking procedure is obtained by observing that an accepting run exists iff there is a cycle through a reachable accepting state. The procedure [16, 5] applies an interleaved double DFS procedure: when the first DFS retracts to an accepting state, the second DFS starts searching for a cycle through this state. If the second DFS fails to find a cycle, the first DFS resumes from the point it has stopped. We can use the following bits for every state of the product that is put in the hash table:

- The state was found during the first DFS.

- The state was found during the second DFS.
- The state is in the first DFS stack.
- The state is in the second DFS stack.

Notice that these bits allow information about the two different (virtual) copies of the same state in the two searches. Notice further that there is no need to explicitly store the edges.

Applying the partial order reduction to the improved search requires a subtle change in the algorithm: it is important to guarantee that the second DFS uses the states that were already found in the first DFS. Repeating exactly the same reduction from every state is thus important to achieve this goal. However, notice that when the second search reaches a state that is on the stack of the first DFS, it may continue to search new states that were not encountered yet during the first DFS. Notice also that once a state x that is on the stack of the first DFS is reached in the second DFS, the search can terminate: it is guaranteed that there is a path from x to the accepting state from which the second DFS has begun, hence completing a cycle through it. Hence, the algorithm in [16, 5] can be changed as follows [18]:

> Upon reaching during the second DFS a state that is on the stack of the first DFS, terminate the search. Use the concatenation of the states in the first and second DFS as a counter-example.

This early termination of the algorithm can be applied to the full search as well and can result in shorter counter-examples.

Albeit eliminating some incorrect search scenarios, this provision is not sufficient to guarantee that the second DFS will follow the same reduced set of states as the first one. A problem may arise when the first search backtracks from a strongly connected component that does not include an accepting state, hence the second search was not applied to this component. While searching another component, which contains an accepting state, the second DFS can propagate now to the previously abandoned component. This time it starts from a different node in the component, potentially closing cycles in a different order. This might influence the reduction, causing different nodes to be discovered in the second search.

Thus, additional state information is needed in order to make sure that the second DFS will generate the same sets of successors as the first one for every generated state s. This information reflects how the closing cycle condition **C2** was resolved during the first DFS [18]. One possibility is that it identifies the processes whose operations where selected for the ample set from s during the first DFS. Another possibility is that the reduction algorithm checks condition **C2** against the first set that satisfies the other conditions from s. If this set fails to satisfy **C2**, then s is fully expanded. In this case, the information about the success or failure to find a subset can be stored for the use of the second DFS using a single additional bit.

The SPIN Implementation

The model-checking tool SPIN [16] contains an implementation of the ample sets method. SPIN allows a variety of communication mechanisms, including synchronous and asynchronous message communication. It also allows global transitions, which change values of variables that belong to all the processes. Hence, the rules to achieve ample sets that satisfy condition **C1** are more complicated. SPIN includes the on-the-fly partial order reduction [17], with the double DFS described above [18].

Acknowledgement I would like to thank the people that I had the pleasure of working with on various aspects of partial order verification: Rajeev Alur, Ching-Tsun Chou, Rob Gerth, Patrice Godefroid, Gerard Holzmann, Shmuel Katz, Ruurd Kuiper, Wojciech Penczek, Amir Pnueli, Mark Staskauskas, Thomas Wilke, Pierre Wolper and Mihalis Yannakakis. I would like to thank Bob Kurshan for many illuminating discussions. Thanks for Antti Valmari for a his comments and the careful reading of the manuscript.

References

[1] R. Alur, D. Peled, W. Penczek, Model-Checking of Causality Properties, *10th Symposium on Logic in Computer Science*, IEEE, 1995, San Diego, California, USA, 90–100.

[2] E. Best, R. Devillers, Sequential and Concurrent Behaviour in Petri net Theory, *Theoretical Computer Science*, 55 (1987), 87–137.

[3] M.C. Browne, E.M. Clarke, O. Grümberg, Characterizing Finite Kripke Structures in Propositional Temporal Logic, *Theoretical Computer Science* 59 (1988), Elsevier, 115–131.

[4] C.T. Chou, D. Peled, Verifying a Model-Checking Algorithm, *Tools and Algorithms for the Construction and Analysis of Systems*, LNCS 1055, Springer-Verlag, 1996, Passau, Germany, to appear March 1996, 241–257.

[5] C. Courcoubetis, M. Vardi, P. Wolper, M, Yannakakis, Memory-efficient algorithms for the verification of temporal properties, *Formal methods in system design* 1 (1992) 275–288.

[6] R. Gerth, R. Kuiper, W. Penczek, D. Peled, A Partial Order Approach to Branching Time Logic Model Checking, ISTCS'95, *3rd Israel Symposium on Theory on Computing and Systems*, IEEE press, 1995, Tel Aviv, Israel, 130-139.

[7] R. Gerth, D. Peled, M.Y. Vardi, P. Wolper, Simple On-the-fly Automatic Verification of Linear Temporal Logic, *PSTV95, Protocol Specification Testing and Verification*, 3-18, Chapman & Hall, 1995, Warsaw, Poland.

[8] R.J. van Glabbeek, W.P. Weijland, Branching time and abstraction in bisimulation semantics, *Information Processing 89*. Elsevier Science Publishers, 1989, 613–618.

[9] P. Godefroid. Using partial orders to improve automatic verification methods. In Proc. *2nd Workshop on Computer Aided Verification*, LNCS 531, Springer-Verlag, New Brunswick, NJ, 1990, 176–185.

[10] P. Godefroid, D. Pirottin, Refining dependencies improves partial order verification methods, *5th Conference on Computer Aided Verification*, LNCS 697, Elounda, Greece, 1993, 438–449.

[11] P. Godefroid, D. Peled, M. Staskauskas, Using Partial Order Methods in the Formal Validation of Industrial Concurrent Programs, 1996, ISSTA'96, *International Symposium on Software Testing and Analysis*, ACM Press, San Diego, California, USA, 261-269.

[12] P. Godefroid, P. Wolper, A Partial Approach to Model Checking, *6th Annual IEEE Symposium on Logic in Computer Science*, 1991, Amsterdam, 406–415.

[13] M.J.C. Gordon, T.F. Melham, *Introduction to HOL: A Theorem-Proving Environment for Higher-Order Logic*, Cambridge University Press, 1993.

[14] M. Hennessy, R. Milner, Algebraic laws for nondeterminism and concurrency, *Journal of the ACM*, 32, 1985, 23–52.

[15] C.A.R. Hoare, *Communication Sequential Processes*, Prentice Hall, 1995.

[16] G. J. Holzmann, *Design and Validation of Computer Protocols*, Prentice Hall Software Series, 1992.

[17] G.J. Holzmann, D. Peled, An Improvement in Formal Verification, *7th International Conference on Formal Description Techniques*, Berne, Switzerland, 1994, 177–194.

[18] G.J. Holzmann, D. Peled, M. Yannakakis, On Nested Depth First Search, *2nd SPIN workshop*, Rutgers, NJ, August 1996.

[19] S. Katz, D. Peled, Verification of Distributed Programs using Representative Interleaving Sequences, *Distributed Computing* 6 (1992), 107–120. A preliminary version appeared in Temporal Logic in Specification, UK, 1987, LNCS 398, 21–43.

[20] S. Katz, D. Peled, Defining conditional independence using collapses, Theoretical Computer Science 101 (1992), 337-359, a preliminary version appeared in *BCS–FACS Workshop on Semantics for Concurrency*, Leicester, England, July 1990, Springer, 262–280.

[21] M. Z. Kwiatkowska, Event Fairness and Non-Interleaving Concurrency, *Formal Aspects of Computing* 1 (1989), 213–228.

[22] L. Lamport, What good is temporal logic, *Information Processing 83*, Elsevier Science Publishers, 1983, 657-668.

[23] O. Lichtenstein, A. Pnueli, Checking that finite-state concurrent programs satisfy their linear specification, *11th Annual ACM Symposium on Principles of Programming Languages*, 1984, 97–107.

[24] A. Mazurkiewicz, Trace Theory, *Advances in Petri Nets 1986*, Bad Honnef, Germany, LNCS 255, Springer, 1987, 279–324.

[25] R. Milner, *A Calculus of Communicating System*, LNCS, Springer-Verlag, 92.

[26] R. de Nicola, F. Vaandrager, Three Logics for Branching Bisimulation, *Logic in Computer Science '90*, IEEE, 1990, 118–129.

[27] D. Peled, A. Pnueli, Proving Partial Order Properties, *Theoretical Computer Science*, 126(1994), 143–182.

[28] D. Peled, All from one, one for all, on model-checking using representatives, *5th Conference on Computer Aided Verification*, Greece, 1993, LNCS, Springer, 409–423.

[29] D. Peled. Combining partial order reductions with on-the-fly model-checking. *Formal Methods in System Design* 8 (1996), 39–64.

[30] D. Peled, Th. Wilke, P. Wolper, An Algorithmic Approach for Checking Closure Properties of ω-Regular Languages, to appear in *CONCUR'96, 7th International Conference on Concurrency Theory*, Piza, Italy, August 1996.

[31] A. Pnueli, The temporal logic of programs, *18th FOCS, IEEE Symposium on Foundation of Computer Science*, 1977, 46–57.

[32] A. Valmari, Stubborn sets for reduced state space generation, *10th International Conference on Application and Theory of Petri Nets*, Bonn, Germany, 1989, LNCS 483, Springer Verlag, 491–515.

[33] A. Valmari, A stubborn attack on state explosion. *Formal Methods in System Design*, 1 (1992), 297–322.

[34] A. Valmari, Stubborn Set Methods for Process Algebras, *POMIV'96, Partial Orders Methods in Verification*, American Mathematical Society, DIMACS, Princeton, NJ, USA, 1996, this volume.

[35] A.P. Sistla, M.Y. Vardi, P. Wolper, The Complementation Problem for Büchi Automata with Applications to Temporal Logic, *Theoretical Computer Science*, 49 (1987), 217—237.

[36] P.S. Thiagarajan, A Trace Based Extension of Linear Time Temporal Logic. *Proc. 10th IEEE Conference on Logic In Computer Science*, 1994, 438–447.

[37] M.Y. Vardi, P. Wolper, An automata-theoretic approach to automatic program verification, *1st Annual IEEE Symposium on Logic in Computer Science*, 1986, Cambridge, England, 322–331.

DIMACS Series in Discrete Mathematics
and Theoretical Computer Science
Volume **29**, 1997

History Dependent Verification for Partial Order Systems

Ugo Montanari and Marco Pistore

ABSTRACT. In this paper we propose a new approach to check bisimulation-based equivalences for models of concurrency which take into account causal dependencies between the actions a system can perform. The existing approaches are based on special definitions of bisimulation and do not allow for reuse of techniques and tools developed for ordinary labeled transition systems. This is not the case in our approach, since we map causal systems into ordinary transition systems. As a consequence, we obtain minimal realizations and Hennessy-Milner logics also for causal systems. We show how our approach applies to history-preserving bisimulation for Petri nets [**1**] and to location equivalence for CCS [**3, 4**].

1. Introduction

Bisimulation is widely used to equip concurrent systems with an abstract semantics. A well-established theory and efficient algorithms have been developed for it. Automatic checking is successful in practice, since many interesting systems are finite state. One of the most used algorithms is the so-called partition refinement algorithm [**11, 18**]. It is particularly interesting since it allows for minimization, i.e., it can be used to find the minimal transition system in a class of bisimilar transition systems. Minimization is important both from a theoretical point of view — equivalent systems give rise to the same (up to isomorphism) minimal realization — and from a practical point of view — smaller state spaces can be obtained.

However, the standard definition of bisimulation — and most of the results and algorithms which have been developed for it — can be applied only to systems whose operational behavior is modeled by labeled transition systems. In this case computations are simply sequences of atomic actions and hence parallelism of actions is reduced to interleaving.

Many attempts have been made to overcome the limits of this interleaving approach and to allow the observer to discriminate systems via bisimulation also according to the degree of parallelism they exploit in their computations. A possible approach is to modify the operational semantics so that dependencies between

1991 *Mathematics Subject Classification.* Primary 68Q55, 68Q10.
Research supported in part by Progetto Integrato CNR/Università "Metodi e Strumenti per la Progettazione e la Verifica di Sistemi Eterogenei Connessi mediante Reti di Comunicazione".

actions are taken into account. Dependencies may be of different kinds: for instance they can be *causal* dependencies (each action refers to the actions in the past it depends on) or *localities* dependencies (the dependencies are used to describe sublocation relations: each action depends on the actions in the past that generated the location in which the action occurs).

Bisimulation-based abstract semantics can then be used on the richer operational semantics. In these cases, however, particular definitions of bisimulation have to be exploited, since they have to deal with dependencies, and they do not allow for a full reusage of the existing theories and algorithms for standard bisimulation. Moreover, since the past history of the system has to be remembered to define dependencies, the operational models are usually finite only when the system cannot perform infinite computations. Special techniques must be studied to obtain decidability also for some systems with infinite behaviors.

In this paper we describe a possible solution to these problems which has been proposed in [**15, 13**]. We first define *causal automata* as a general model for dealing with dependencies between actions. In this model the dependencies are represented by means of names: each transition generates a new name which is then referenced in the labels of the transitions which depend from it. The names which are relevant for a state of the system are also explicitly remembered in the corresponding state of the causal automaton.

When a system is mapped on causal automata, it is important to discard part of the past events and to remember just those events that can (but not necessarily will) be referenced in the future behavior. This pruning of the past history allows for reusing the same state of the causal automaton to represent different stages of a computation. Moreover, by considering as inessential the syntactical identity of the names, it is possible to identify states whose future behaviors differ just for a renaming. This allows us to represent classes of systems with infinite behavior with finite-state — and possibly very compact — causal automata.

To show that causal automata are a good model for dependencies, we give a hint of how it is possible to translate two classical non-interleaving models of concurrency — Petri nets with process-based semantics [**9, 1**] and CCS with localities [**3, 4**] — into causal automata.

We also equip causal automata with a notion of bisimulation. This bisimulation equivalence correctly deals with dependencies. In fact, two systems described in one of the two formalisms above are equivalent if and only if the corresponding causal automata are equivalent according to the proposed bisimulation.

Finally we show how, starting from causal automata, it is possible to build ordinary transition systems and to reuse ordinary bisimulation on them to decide bisimulation on causal automata. To obtain this, a notion of *active names* is exploited, where a name is active for a state if it appears in the label of a transition reachable from the state. Non-active names can be discarded, thus allowing for a static correspondence of names between bisimilar states.

This translation into ordinary transition systems allows for the reusing of standard techniques and tools. In particular, it is possible to associate to each Petri net a transition system which is minimal w.r.t. those associated to history-preserving bisimilar nets. As far as we know, this is the first approach which leads to minimal realizations for Petri nets up to history-preserving bisimulation and for CCS with localities.

The structure of the paper is as follows. In Section 2 causal automata and bisimulation on causal automata are defined, whereas in Section 3 it is sketched how Petri nets and CCS with localities are mapped into causal automata. In Section 4 ordinary automata are obtained from causal automata and in Section 5 an algorithm and a tool are described which exploit the proposed approach.

2. Causal automata

In this section we define causal automata. They are a model for describing systems whose transitions may refer to previous transitions. Since these references can be used to represent dependencies and, hence, partial orders, it is clear that causal automata are an interesting operational model for partial order semantics. We also equip causal automata with an abstract semantics based on bisimulation.

DEFINITION 2.1 (causal automaton). Let $\mathcal{N}$ be a fixed infinite denumerable set of event names.
A *causal automaton* is a tuple $A = \langle Q, w, \mapsto, q_0 \rangle$ where:

- Q is a set of *states*;
- $w : Q \to \mathcal{P}_f(\mathcal{N})$ associates to each state a finite set of names;
- $\mapsto$ is a set of *transitions*; each transition has the form $q \overset{a}{\underset{M}{\mapsto}}_\sigma q'$, where:
  - $q, q' \in Q$ are the *source* and *target* states;
  - $a \in \mathit{Labels}$ is the *label*;
  - $M \subseteq w(q)$ are the *dependencies* of the transition;
  - $\sigma : w(q') \hookrightarrow w(q) \cup \{\star\}$ is the injective (inverse) *renaming* for the transition; the special mark $\star \notin \mathcal{N}$ is used to recognize in the target state the name corresponding to the current transition;
- $q_0 \in Q$ is the *initial state*; we require that $w(q_0) = \emptyset$.

A causal automaton is hence an automaton particularly suited for dealing with dependencies between transitions. Each state q is labeled by the set $w(q)$ of names, which correspond to the past events that can still (but not necessarily will) be referenced in the future behaviors. These names have a meaning that is local, private to the state. Hence, the particular choice of names cannot by itself make a distinction between two states of the causal automaton.

Each transition $\overset{a}{\underset{M}{\mapsto}}_\sigma$ depends on the past transitions identified by M. Due to the local meaning of names, each transition must also specify the correspondence between the names of the source and those of the target. This correspondence is obtained via the renaming σ, which permits also to deduce which names of the source are forgotten in the target; the name (if any) used in the target state to represent the current transition in mapped into the special mark $\star$.

If there are invisible transitions, as for instance in CCS, we add to the automata a new kind of transitions, which has the form $q \overset{\tau}{\mapsto}_\sigma q'$.

On causal automata a bisimulation cannot simply be a relation on states: also a partial correspondence between the names of the states has to be specified and the same pairs of states can be in relation via more than one correspondence.

DEFINITION 2.2 (bisimulation on causal automata). A *causal bisimulation* for two causal automata A and B is a set $\mathcal{R}$ of triples such that:

- if $(p, \delta, q) \in \mathcal{R}$ then $p \in Q_A$, $q \in Q_B$ and δ is a partial injective function from $w_A(p)$ to $w_B(q)$;

- $(q_{0A}, \emptyset, q_{0B}) \in \mathcal{R}$;
- if $(p, \delta, q) \in \mathcal{R}$ and $p \overset{a}{\underset{M}{\mapsto}}_\sigma p'$ in A then there exist some $q \overset{a}{\underset{\delta(M)}{\mapsto}}_\rho q'$ in B and some δ' such that $\langle p', \delta', q' \rangle \in \mathcal{R}$ and $\delta'(m) = n$ implies $\sigma(m) = \star = \rho(n)$ or $\delta(\sigma(m)) = \rho(n)$;
- if $(p, \delta, q) \in \mathcal{R}$ and $q \overset{a}{\underset{M}{\mapsto}}_\sigma q'$ in B then there exist some $p \overset{a}{\underset{\delta^{-1}(M)}{\mapsto}}_\rho p'$ in A and some δ' such that $\langle p', \delta', q' \rangle \in \mathcal{R}$ and $\delta'(m) = n$ implies $\sigma(m) = \star = \rho(n)$ or $\delta(\sigma(m)) = \rho(n)$.

The causal automata A and B are ***bisimilar***, written $A \sim_{ca} B$, if there is some bisimulation for them.

Notice that if p and q correspond via δ in some bisimulation $\mathcal{R}$, then to each transition of p a transition of q must correspond, such that *i*) the two transitions perform the same action, *ii*) they depend on the same past events (via δ), and *iii*) the reached states correspond in $\mathcal{R}$ via some δ' which relates two names of the target states only if they both are the names corresponding to the current transitions or if they are related by δ in the source states.

The definition of bisimulation can be easily extended to causal automata with $\overset{\tau}{\mapsto}$ transitions. Moreover, it is also possible to define a weak causal bisimulation, which allows each transition $\overset{a}{\underset{M}{\mapsto}}_\sigma$ to be simulated with a suitable sequence of transitions $\overset{\tau}{\mapsto}_{\sigma_1} \cdots \overset{\tau}{\mapsto}_{\sigma_{h-1}} \overset{a}{\underset{M'}{\mapsto}}_{\sigma_h} \overset{\tau}{\mapsto}_{\sigma_{h+1}} \cdots \overset{\tau}{\mapsto}_{\sigma_k}$.

We conclude this section with a remark. The idea of using names to model dependencies is not new. It has been introduced for instance in [**5**] and in [**3, 4, 12**]. There, however, names are global and syntactic (they appear in the terms describing the system). In the case of causal automata, instead, names are local to states and are semantic objects; this has the double advantage of making possible to work directly on names — for instance by discarding some of them from an automaton, as we will do in Definition 4.2 — and of allowing those states to collapse which differ just for the syntactical choice of names. Moreover, we will see in Section 4 that, by fixing a strategy for choosing new names, it is possible to generate ordinary transition systems from causal automata. To have a model which is independent from the allocation strategy of names is interesting in itself, also since different strategies have been actually proposed in the literature.

3. Causal automata for partial order systems

In this section we show how it is possible to translate two classical non-interleaving models of concurrency — Petri nets with process-based semantics [**9, 1**] and CCS with localities [**3, 4**] — into causal automata.

Causal automata can be associated also to other models — as, for instance, CCS with causality [**5**] — using techniques similar to those used in the two cases we consider.

3.1. Causal automata for Petri nets. In the context of Petri nets partial order semantics is obtained via processes. They have been defined in [**9**] to represent concurrent runs of the net. In particular, from processes it is possible to obtain the partial order of the events of the run, which represents the causal dependencies between them (an event directly causes another event if it generates a token which is consumed by the second event). A notion of bisimulation, called *history-preserving* *bisimulation*, which takes into account the partial order behavior has been defined in [**20**] for event structures. The same notion has been introduced in [**7**] using mixed ordering observations. History-preserving bisimulation has been applied to Petri nets in [**1**].

Since processes grow during a computation, infinite-state systems are associated to all nets which allow for infinite computations. Some alternative approaches [**21, 10**] have been proposed so that history-preserving bisimulation can be checked also for classes of nets with infinite behaviors, namely safe nets. Essentially, in those approach it is shown how it is possible to remember just a finite part of the past history of a computation in order to decide equivalence of nets.

In [**13**] decidability of history-preserving bisimulation on Petri nets has been extended to a more general subclass of P/T nets, using causal automata. Now we summarize the approach of [**13**].

Essentially, a P/T net is defined by:

- a set S of *places*; each place is supposed to contain a certain number of tokens; a state of the net is then represented by a function $m : S \to \mathbf{N}$, called a *marking*, which describes the distribution of tokens in the places;
- a set T of transitions; each transition fires erasing a certain number of tokens from some places of the net and adding a certain number of new tokens to some possibly different places; transition t is *enabled* at marking m if m contains enough tokens in the places and in this case we write $m \xrightarrow{t} m'$, where m' is the suitably updated marking;
- a *labeling function* for the transitions $l : T \to \mathit{Labels}$;
- an *initial marking* m_0.

A formal definition of P/T nets and of history-preserving bisimulation on them can be found in the Appendix.

As mentioned above, the classical definition of history-preserving bisimulation is based on processes. Not all the informations carried by processes, however, are used in the bisimulation. Now we define configurations, which contain only the informations of processes which are relevant to bisimulation.

DEFINITION 3.1 (configuration). Let N be a P/T net. A *configuration* for N is a tuple $c = (E, \rho, \leq)$, where:

- E is a set of *events*;
- $\rho : S \times (E \cup \mathtt{init}) \to \mathbf{N}$;
- $\leq$ is a partial ordering for E.

We require that, for each $e \in E$, $\sum_{s \in S} \rho(s, e) > 0$.
The *initial configuration* for N is $c_0(N) = (\emptyset, \rho_0, \emptyset)$, where $\rho_0(s, \mathtt{init}) = m_0(s)$ for all $s \in S$.

In a configuration, the set E represents (part of) the past events. Since we are interested in a partial order semantics, a partial order is defined on E, which represents the causal dependencies between the past events. Function ρ represents the current marking of the net; instead of simply defining how many tokens are in each place of the net, it also remembers which events generated these tokens (`init` is a special mark used for the tokens in the initial marking).

We require that in a configuration only the events are remembered which generated tokens still present in the net. This is important to obtain a finite number of different configurations also for certain classes of nets with infinite behaviors.

It is possible to define transitions on configurations[1]: essentially $c \xrightarrow{t} c'$ if c' is obtained from c by performing transition t of the net. Tokens are discarded and added according to the pre- and post-conditions of the net; events which have no more tokens are discarded, whereas a new event $\bar{e}$ is added and the tokens generated by the transition are associated to $\bar{e}$; suitable dependencies for $\bar{e}$ are added to the partial order, following the rule that $\bar{e}$ directly depends on all the past events which generated tokens consumed by the transitions. These events are called the *immediate causes* of the transition; we denote with $\mathcal{IC}(c \xrightarrow{t} c')$ the set of immediate causes of transition $c \xrightarrow{t} c'$.

When a causal automaton is generated from a net, states of the automaton correspond to configurations of the net. However, to obtain a compact automaton, it is important to identify configurations which are isomorphic. This can be obtained by fixing a representative for each class of isomorphic configurations and by defining a function $\mathtt{norm}$ such that $\mathtt{norm}(c) = \langle c', \sigma \rangle$ where c' is the representative of the class of configurations isomorphic to c and σ is the bijection between $E_{c'}$ and E_c.

Now we are ready to show how, given a net, it is possible to build the causal automaton corresponding to it, by using its behavior on configurations.

DEFINITION 3.2 (from nets to causal automata). The causal automaton corresponding to P/T net N is $\mathtt{aut}(N) = \langle Q, w, \mapsto, c_0 \rangle$, where $c_0 \in Q$ is the initial configuration for N and whenever $c \in Q$ then:

- $w(c) = E_c$;
- if $c \xrightarrow{t} c'$ and $\langle c'', \sigma \rangle = \mathtt{norm}(c')$ then $c'' \in Q$ and $c \overset{a}{\underset{M}{\mapsto}}_{[\star/\bar{e}]\circ\sigma} c''$, where:
  - $a = l(t)$,
  - $\bar{e} = E_{c'} \setminus E_c$ (if $E_{c'} \setminus E_c = \emptyset$ then we can assume $\bar{e} = \star$), and
  - M are the events in $\mathcal{IC}(c \xrightarrow{t} c')$ which are maximal w.r.t. $\leq_{c}$.

Notice that the renaming corresponding to a transition on the causal automaton is obtained from the bijection defined by function $\mathtt{norm}$: it is sufficient to re-direct the new name $\bar{e}$ to $\star$. Moreover, the maximal causes of the transition are used as dependencies in the automaton.

This construction generates finite causal automata for the finite nets which are n-safe for some n, i.e., for the nets whose reachable markings have n or less tokens in each place.

The general definition of bisimulation on causal automata exactly matches the classical definition of history-preserving bisimulation on nets, as it is proved in [**13**].

THEOREM 3.3. *Given two P/T nets N_1 and N_2, $\mathtt{aut}(N_1) \sim_{ca} \mathtt{aut}(N_2)$ iff $N_1 \sim_{hp} N_2$.*

3.2. Causal automata for CCS with locations. The location semantics for CCS we consider has been introduced in [**3, 4**]. It discriminates CCS agents also with respect to how their computations are distributed in space; to each sequential component of the agent a different location is assigned and two agents are equivalent if they can bisimulate by performing the same actions in the same locations.

The syntax of CCS is enriched with a location prefix operator $l :: p$ meaning that $l \in \mathrm{Loc}$ is the location of agent p; the nesting of location prefixes represents

[1] See [**13**] for a formal definition of $c \xrightarrow{t} c'$.

the sublocalities relation for the agent. Whenever an action is performed, a new sublocation is created for the subagent activated by the action; the location in which an action occurs is added to the label, so that transitions have the form $p \xrightarrow[u]{a} p'$, where $u = l_1 l_2 \dots l_n$ is a sequence of locations.

For instance, agent $l :: (a.b.p \mid c.q)$ can perform the following computation:

$$l :: (a.b.p \mid c.q) \xrightarrow[lm]{a} l :: (m :: b.p \mid c.q) \xrightarrow[ln]{c} l :: (m :: b.p \mid n :: q) \xrightarrow[lmo]{b} l :: (m :: o :: p \mid n :: q).$$

We say that two agents p and q are *location equivalent* ($p \sim_{loc} q$) if each transition of one of the agents is matched by a transition of the other agent so that the two transitions correspond to the same action and occur in the same location, and the target agents are still equivalent.

This is the standard approach of [**3, 4**]. The problem is that locations are created but never forgotten, so that location prefixes continue to grow during the computation.

In [**15**] a slightly different approach is followed. Here, we just explain the main ideas and we refer to [**15**] for the formal definitions.

First of all, we can notice that the location relation of a particular state can be deduced also by observing the labels of the past computation: for instance, by just observing the labels, we know that, in the final state of the computation above, n is a sublocation of l and o is a sublocation of m and l. So, instead of representing the sublocation relation directly in the terms, a flat structure can be given to locations: each agent, up to suitable structural axioms, has then the form:

$$(l_1 :: p_1 \mid l_2 :: p_2 \mid \cdots \mid l_n :: p_n) \setminus R$$

where p_i do not contain location prefixes and R is the set of restricted channels.

The previous computation can then be rewritten as follows:

$$l :: (a.b.p \mid c.q) \xrightarrow[lm]{a} m :: b.p \mid l :: c.q \xrightarrow[ln]{c} m :: b.p \mid n :: q \xrightarrow[mo]{b} o :: p \mid n :: q.$$

If we assume that $p = \mathrm{rec}\, x.b.x$ and $q = \mathrm{rec}\, x.c.x$ we see that the second state and the final state of this computation are the same up to the choice of location names; this was not true in the approach of [**3, 4**].

The fact that the location names are different in the two states becomes inessential when we map agents on causal automata; in fact, we define a function `norm` that, given a agent p, returns a pair $\langle p', \sigma \rangle$, where p' is obtained from p by normalizing the location names and σ describes which location of p corresponds to a location of p'. CCS agents can now be mapped on causal automata.

DEFINITION 3.4 (from CCS agents to causal automata). Let $l_{\mathtt{init}}$ be a special location and let p_0 be a CCS agent without location prefixes. The causal automaton $\mathtt{aut}(p_0) = \langle Q, w, \mapsto, q_0 \rangle$ is so defined:

- $q_0 = l_{\mathtt{init}} :: p_0 \in Q$;
- $w(p)$ are those locations appearing in p which are different from $l_{\mathtt{init}}$;
- whenever $p \in Q$, $p \xrightarrow[lm]{a} p'$ and $\langle p'', \sigma \rangle = \mathtt{norm}(p')$ then $p'' \in Q$ and:
  - $p \overset{a}{\underset{\{l\}}{\mapsto}}_{[\star/m]\circ\sigma} p''$ if $l \neq l_{\mathtt{init}}$,
  - $p \overset{a}{\underset{\emptyset}{\mapsto}}_{[\star/m]\circ\sigma} p''$ if $l = l_{\mathtt{init}}$.

Also in this case, the general definition of bisimulation on causal automata exactly matches the ordinary definition of location equivalence, as it is shown in [**15**].

THEOREM 3.5. *Given two CCS agents p and q, $p \sim_{loc} q$ iff* $\mathtt{aut}(p) \sim_{ca} \mathtt{aut}(q)$.

In this case, with some garbage collecting of terminated (i.e., `nil`) subagents, finite causal automata can be obtained for the class of finitary agents. An agent is finitary if all agents which are reachable from it have a bounded number of non-terminated parallel components.

4. From causal automata to ordinary automata

In the construction of the causal automata, we consider only names of past events which are referenced in the present state. In fact, the remaining names cannot for sure be relevant for the future computation. However it can happen that some of the names associated to a state are never referenced in future computations. These names can be safely discarded from the automaton, obtaining a more compact structure.

DEFINITION 4.1 (active names). Given a causal automaton A, the sets of *active names* corresponding to the states of A, denoted by $\mathrm{an}(p)$ with $p \in Q_A$, are the smallest sets such that:

- if $p \underset{M}{\overset{a}{\mapsto}}_\sigma p'$ then $M \subseteq \mathrm{an}(p)$;
- if $p \underset{M}{\overset{a}{\mapsto}}_\sigma p'$, $m \in \mathrm{an}(p')$ and $\sigma(m) \neq \star$ then $\sigma(m) \in \mathrm{an}(p)$.

DEFINITION 4.2 (irredundant reduction). Let $A = \langle Q, w, \mapsto, q_0 \rangle$ be a causal automaton. Its *irredundant reduction* is the causal automaton $\Downarrow A = \langle Q, \mathrm{an}, \mapsto', q_0 \rangle$ where $\mapsto'$ is obtained from $\mapsto$ by restricting the renamings to the active names of the target states.
We say that an automaton A is *irredundant* if $\Downarrow A = A$.

PROPOSITION 4.3. *Let A be a causal automaton. Then $\Downarrow A \sim_{ca} A$.*

A causal automaton A can be visited beginning from the initial state. In this visit, the global meaning of the private names of the reached states is made explicit[2]. If the global meaning corresponding to the names of a reached state p is given by $\sigma : w(p) \hookrightarrow \mathcal{N}$ and transition $p \underset{M}{\overset{a}{\mapsto}}_\rho q$ is followed, the global meaning for q is given essentially by $\sigma \circ \rho$. However, a global meaning has to be associated also to the name created in the transition (the name of the target state mapped in $\star$ by the transition renaming). To this purpose we use a function `new`, which gets a transition $p \underset{M}{\overset{a}{\mapsto}}_\rho p'$ and a global meaning σ for the names of p and returns a new name. A possible definition of `new` is as follows:

$$\mathtt{new}(p \underset{M}{\overset{a}{\mapsto}}_\rho p', \sigma) = \min\{\mathcal{N} \setminus \sigma(\rho(w(p')))\}$$

This means that the first name is chosen, that is not already used in the target state. Other allocation strategies can be adopted by changing function `new`.

To formalize the idea of visiting a causal automaton A, we associate to A a standard labeled transition system (called the *unfolding* of A); each state of the

[2]A state can be visited more than once, with different meanings for its private names.

unfolding is a pair ⟨state of the causal automaton, global meaning of its names⟩ and each transition has the form

$$\langle p, \sigma \rangle \underset{m,M}{\overset{a}{\rightarrow}} \langle p', \sigma' \rangle$$

where a is an action, M are the names the action depends from and m is the newly created name.

DEFINITION 4.4 (unfolding). The *unfolding* corresponding to a causal automaton $A = \langle Q, w, \mapsto, q_0 \rangle$ is the labeled transition system $\mathtt{unf}(A) = \langle Q_u, \rightarrow, q_{0u} \rangle$ defined as follows:

- the initial state is $q_{0u} = \langle q_0, \emptyset \rangle \in Q_u$;
- if $\langle p, \sigma \rangle \in Q_u$ and $p \underset{M}{\overset{a}{\mapsto}}_\rho p'$ then $\langle p', \sigma' \rangle \in Q_u$ and $\langle p, \sigma \rangle \underset{m,M'}{\overset{a}{\rightarrow}} \langle p', \sigma' \rangle$, where $\sigma' = (\sigma \cup (\star, m)) \circ \rho$, $M' = \sigma(M)$ and $m = \mathtt{new}(p \underset{M}{\overset{a}{\mapsto}}_\rho p', \sigma)$.

It is easy to show that there are equivalent causal automata with non-equivalent unfoldings. This happens because two equivalent states of the causal automata can have a different number of names, and in the unfolding this can lead to different choices for the new names.

The following theorem expresses an important result of this paper: given two *irredundant* causal automata, they are equivalent if and only if the corresponding unfoldings are equivalent. This allows us to apply a standard partitioning algorithm for checking the equivalence of two automata and to obtain minimal (standard) automata corresponding to them.

THEOREM 4.5. *If A and B are irredundant causal automata then $A \sim_{ca} B$ iff* $\mathtt{unf}(A) \sim \mathtt{unf}(B)$.

5. A tool for verifying causal automata

Theorem 4.5 suggests an algorithm for checking history-preserving equivalence of two systems based on partial orders:

1. construct (separately) the causal automata corresponding to the systems;
2. discover (separately) the active names of the two automata and get the irredundant reductions: start marking the names that are active due to the first condition of Definition 4.1 and continue marking all the names reachable following the dependencies in the other condition of Definition 4.1; at the end discard the unmarked names;
3. unfold (separately) the obtained irredundant automata;
4. use a standard algorithm for checking the (strong or weak) equivalence of the obtained transition systems (for instance, partition refinement [**11, 18**]).

Notice that, while step 1 depends on the formalism in which the systems are described (CCS, Petri Nets, ...) and on the desired partial order semantics (localities, causality, ...), steps 2–4 work for generic causal automata and are hence common to all these formalisms.

To add a new formalism, moreover, it is sufficient to define a new function which maps systems described in this new formalism into causal automata; obviously, this function must map history-preserving equivalent systems into equivalent causal automata. Moreover, it has to map an interesting set of systems into finite causal automata. As shown in Section 3, this is obtained by having a syntactic notion to decide if a past name can be forgotten in a particular state. Step 2 of the algorithm refines then this notion, discarding all the inactive names that were created during the generation phase.

In the studied cases, the class of systems which are captured is very significant: in the case of CCS with localities, all the finitary agents; in the case of Petri nets, all the n-safe nets.

The proposed algorithm can also be used to generate the minimal transition system corresponding to a system; to obtain this, the same procedure has to be applied by starting with just a net and, at the end, a minimization algorithm has to be applied. As far as we know, this is the first approach which leads to minimal realizations for Petri nets up to history-preserving bisimulation and for CCS with localities.

A verification environment is being developed[3] in Pisa which is based on the above approach. The tool is based ***history-dependent automata*** **[14]**, which are slightly more general than the causal automata presented in this paper. In fact, they model also π-calculus agents. The π-calculus is an extension of CCS in which channel names can be used as values in communications, allowing for dynamic creation of new channels; since channels can be created by some actions and then used in following communications, it is clear that also π-calculus has to deal with dependencies between transitions.

The environment provides a set of tools on history-dependent automata to edit, visualize, make irredundant and unfold them. A number of front ends that translate several formalisms into causal automata are also planed. An existing verification environment for process algebras, the JACK systems **[2]**, is used instead to work on ordinary automata (equivalence checking and minimization). Moreover, a model checker for verifying logical properties of systems has also been implemented. The model checker allows the user to check behavioral properties (expressed in a variant of Hennessy-Milner logic) directly on history-dependent automata. Tools are also under investigation that directly check for bisimulation and minimize history-dependent automata. The logical structure of the verification environment is illustrated in Figure 1.

References

[1] E. Best, R. Devillers, A. Kiehn and L. Pomello. Fully concurrent bisimulation. *Acta Informatica* 28:231–264, 1991.

[2] A. Bouali, S. Gnesi and S. Larosa. The integration project for the JACK environment. In *EATCS Bullettin*, 1994.

[3] G. Boudol, I. Castellani, M. Hennessy and A. Kiehn. A theory of processes with localities. INRIA Report 1632, 1991. Extended abstract in *Proc. CONCUR'92*, LNCS 630, 1992.

[4] G. Boudol, I. Castellani, M. Hennessy and A. Kiehn. Observing localities. *Theoretical Computer Science*, 114:31–61, 1993.

[5] Ph. Darondeau and P. Degano. Causal trees. In *Proc. ICALP'89*, LNCS 372. Springer-Verlag, 1989.

[6] P. Degano, R. De Nicola and U. Montanari. Observational equivalences for concurrency models. In *Proc. Formal Description of Programming Concepts – III*, 1986. North-Holland, 1987.

---

[3]Besides the authors of this paper, the people working on the project are: Gianluigi Ferrari (Dept. of Computer Science, University of Pisa), Giovanni Ferro (IEI-CNR, Pisa), Stefania Gnesi (IEI-CNR, Pisa) and Gioia Ristori (Scuola Superiore di Studi Universitari e di Perfezionamento S. Anna, Pisa).

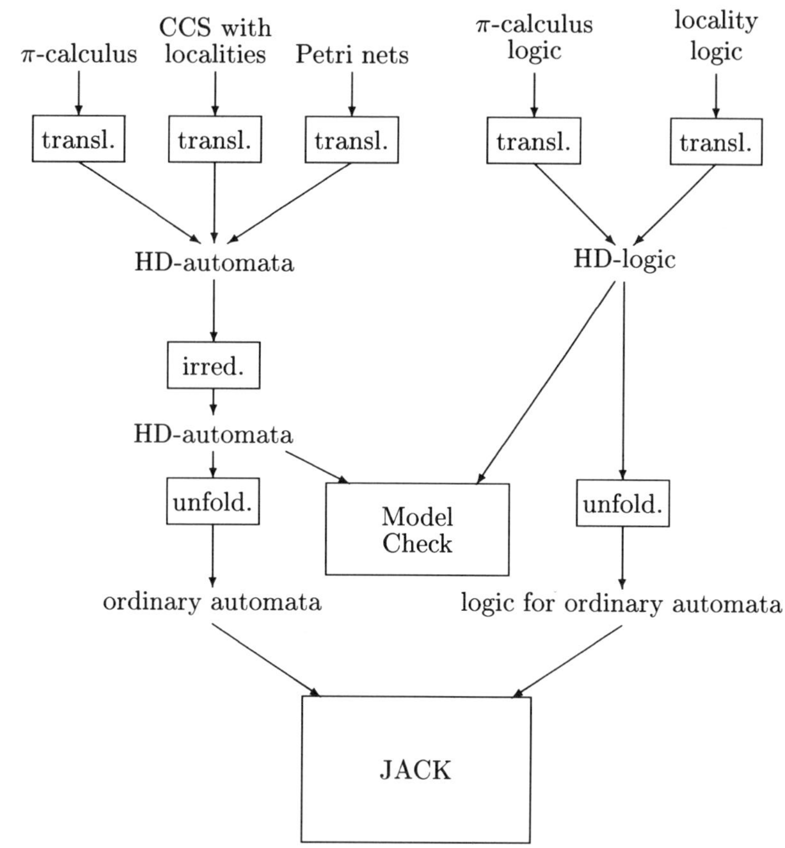

FIGURE 1. Structure of the verification environment.

[7] P. Degano, R. De Nicola and U. Montanari. Partial orderings descriptions and observations of nondeterministic concurrent processes. In *Proc. REX School/Workshop on Linear Time, Branching Time and Partial Orders in Logica and Models for Concurrency*, LNCS 354. Springer Verlag, 1989.

[8] P. Degano, R. De Nicola and U. Montanari. Universal axioms for bisimulation. *Theoretical Computer Science*, 114:63–91, 1993.

[9] U. Goltz and W. Reisig. The non-sequential behaviour of Petri nets. *Information and Control* 57:125–147, 1983.

[10] L. Jategaonkar and A. Meyer. Deciding true concurrency equivalences on finite safe nets. In *Proc. ICALP'93*, LNCS 700. Springer Verlag, 1993.

[11] P. C. Kanellakis and S. A. Smolka. CCS expressions, finite state processes, and three problems of equivalence. *Information and Computation*, 86:43–68, 1990.

[12] A. Kiehn. Local and global causes. Tech. Rep. 42/23/91, Institut für Informatik, TU München, 1991.

[13] U. Montanari and M. Pistore. Minimal transition systems for history-preserving bisimulation. Submitted, 1996. Available as `ftp://ftp.di.unipi.it/pub/Papers/pistore/pnets.ps.gz`.

[14] U. Montanari and M. Pistore. History-dependent automata. Draft, 1996. Available as `ftp://ftp.di.unipi.it/pub/Papers/pistore/HDautomata.ps.gz`. Also: Technical Report, Università di Pisa, to appear.

[15] U. Montanari, M. Pistore and D. Yankelevich. Efficient minimization up to location equivalence. In *Proc. ESOP'96*, LNCS 1058. Springer Verlag, 1996.

[16] U. Montanari and D. Yankelevich. A parametric approach to localities. In *Proc. ICALP'92*, LNCS 623. Springer Verlag, 1992.

[17] U. Montanari and D. Yankelevich. Location Equivalence in a Parametric Setting. *Theoretical Computer Science*, 149:299–332, 1995.

[18] R. Paige and R. E. Tarjan. Three partition refinement algorithms. *SIAM Journal on Computing*, 16(6):973–989, 1987.

[19] D. Yankelevich. *Parametric Views of Process Description Languages.* PhD Thesis. Dipartimento di Informatica, Università di Pisa, 1993. Available as report TD-23/93.

[20] A. Rabinovich and B. A. Trakhtenbrot. Behaviour structures and nets. *Fundamenta Informaticae*, 11:357–404, 1988.

[21] W. Vogler. Deciding history preserving bisimilarity. In *Proc. ICALP'91*, LNCS 510. Springer Verlag, 1991.

Appendix

In this appendix we present the basic definitions on Petri nets we use in the paper. Most of the definitions and of the notations are from **[9]**.

DEFINITION 5.1 (net). A *net* N is a tuple (S, T, F) where:

- S is a set of *places* and T is a set of *transitions*; we assume $S \cap T = \emptyset$;
- $F \subseteq (S \times T) \cup (T \times S)$ is the *flow relation*.

If $x \in S \cup T$ then ${}^\bullet x = \{y \mid (y, x) \in F\}$ and $x^\bullet = \{y \mid (x, y) \in F\}$ are called respectively the *pre-set* and the *post-set* of x.
Let ${}^\circ N = \{x \in S \cup T \mid {}^\bullet x = \emptyset\}$ and $N^\circ = \{x \in S \cup T \mid x^\bullet = \emptyset\}$.
A net N is finite if S and T are finite sets.

Given a net $N = (S, T, F)$, we often write S_N, T_N, F_N for S, T, F. We will apply a similar convention also to the other structures we are going to define.

DEFINITION 5.2 (P/T net). A *(labeled, marked) place/transition net* (or simply *P/T net*) N is a tuple (S, T, F, W, l, m_0), where:

- (S, T, F) is a net;
- $W : F \to \mathbf{N}^+$ assigns a positive *weight* to each arc of the net; we sometimes assume that W is defined on $(S \times T) \cup (T \times S)$ by requiring $W(x, y) = 0$ if $(x, y) \notin F$;
- $l : T \to Labels$ is the *labeling function*, where *Labels* is a fixed set of action labels;
- $m_0 : S \to \mathbf{N}$ is the *initial marking*.

A *marking* is a mapping $m : S \to \mathbf{N}$. It represents a distribution of the *tokens* in the places of the net.
Transition $t \in T$ is *enabled* at marking m if $m(s) \geq W(s, t)$ for all $s \in {}^\bullet t$. In this case, the *firing* of t at m produces the marking m' with $m'(s) = m(s) + W(t, s) - W(s, t)$, and we write $m \xrightarrow{t} m'$.

DEFINITION 5.3 (occurrence net). An occurrence net is a net $K = (C, E, G)$ (in this case, states are also called *conditions* and transitions are also called *events*) such that:

- for all $c \in C$, $|{}^\bullet c| \leq 1$ and $|c^\bullet| \leq 1$ (conditions are not branching), and
- the transitive closure G^+ of G is irreflexive (the net is acyclic).

DEFINITION 5.4 (process). A *process* π of a P/T net $N = (S, T, F, W, l, m_0)$ is a tuple (C, E, G, p), where $K = (C, E, G)$ is a finite occurrence net and $p : (C \cup E) \to (S \cup T)$ is such that:

- $p(C) \subseteq S$ and $p(E) \subseteq T$;
- $m_0(s) = |p^{-1}(s) \cap {}^\circ K|$ for all $s \in S$;
- $W(s, p(e)) = |\{c \in {}^\bullet e \mid p(c) = s\}|$ and $W(p(e), s) = |\{c \in e^\bullet \mid p(c) = s\}|$ for all $e \in E$ and all $s \in S$.

We write ${}^\circ \pi$ for ${}^\circ K$ and π° for K°.
The *initial process* of net N is the[4] process $\pi_0(N)$ with an empty set of events.
Let $\pi = (C, E, G, p)$ and $\pi' = (C', E', G', p')$ be two processes of N. If:

- $E' = E \cup \{\bar{e}\}$ for some $\bar{e} \notin E$;

[4]Notice that the initial process of a net is unique only up to isomorphism of the set of initial conditions.

- $C' \supseteq C$;
- $p'|_{C \cup E} = p$

then we write $\pi \xrightarrow{\bar{t}} \pi'$, where $\bar{t} = p'(\bar{e})$.

Now we define history-preserving bisimulation. We follow a classical characterization, as it appears in [**1**] under the name of *fully concurrent bisimulation.*

DEFINITION 5.5 (event structure). The *(deterministic) event structure* for process $\pi = (C, E, G, p)$ of net N is the tuple $\mathtt{ev}(\pi) = (E, F^+|_E, l_N \circ p|_E)$. An *isomorphism* between two event structures is a bijective function between their events which respects ordering and labels.

DEFINITION 5.6 (history-preserving bisimulation). A set $\mathcal{R}$ of triples is a *history-preserving bisimulation* for nets N_1 and N_2 if:

- if $(\pi_1, f, \pi_2) \in \mathcal{R}$ then π_1 is a process of N_1, π_2 is a process of N_2 and f is an isomorphism between $\mathtt{ev}(\pi_1)$ and $\mathtt{ev}(\pi_2)$;
- $(\pi_0(N_1), \emptyset, \pi_0(N_2)) \in \mathcal{R}$;
- if $(\pi_1, f, \pi_2) \in \mathcal{R}$ and $\pi_1 \xrightarrow{t_1} \pi_1'$ then $\pi_2 \xrightarrow{t_2} \pi_2'$ with $(\pi_1', f', \pi_2') \in \mathcal{R}$ and $f'|_{\mathtt{ev}(\pi_1)} = f$;
- if $(\pi_1, f, \pi_2) \in \mathcal{R}$ and $\pi_2 \xrightarrow{t_2} \pi_2'$ then $\pi_1 \xrightarrow{t_1} \pi_1'$ with $(\pi_1', f', \pi_2') \in \mathcal{R}$ and $f'|_{\mathtt{ev}(\pi_1)} = f$.

Two nets N_1 and N_2 are *history-preserving bisimilar*, written $N_1 \sim_{hp} N_2$, if there is a history-preserving bisimulation for them.

COMPUTER SCIENCE DEPARTMENT, UNIVERSITY OF PISA, CORSO ITALIA 40, 56100 PISA, ITALY
E-mail address: `{ugo,pistore}@di.unipi.it`

DIMACS Series in Discrete Mathematics
and Theoretical Computer Science
Volume **29**, 1997

Transition Systems with Independence and Multi-Arcs

Thomas T. Hildebrandt and Vladimiro Sassone

ABSTRACT. We extend the model of transition systems with independence in order to provide it with a feature relevant in the *noninterleaving* analysis of concurrent systems, namely *multi-arcs*. Moreover, we study the relationships between the category of transition systems with independence and multi-arcs and the category of labeled asynchronous transition systems, extending the results recently obtained by the authors for (simple) transition systems with independence (cf. *Proc. CONCUR'96*), and yielding a precise characterisation of transition systems with independence and multi-arcs in terms of (*event-maximal, diamond-extensional*) labeled asynchronous transition systems.

Introduction

Following the leading idea of CCS **[12]** and related process calculi **[11, 2, 13, 9]**, the behaviour of concurrent systems is often specified *extensionally* by describing their 'state-transitions' and the observable behaviours that such transitions produce. The simplest formal model of computation able to express naturally this idea is that of *labeled transition systems*, where the labels on the transitions are thought of as the actions of the system at its 'external ports', or, more generally, the observable part of its behaviour.

Transition systems are an *interleaving* model of concurrency, which means that they do not allow to draw a natural distinction between interleaved and concurrent execution of actions. More precisely, transition systems do not model the fact that concurrent actions can overlap in time and reduce concurrency to a nondeterministic choice of action interleavings, so loosing track of the casual dependencies between actions and, consequently, of the fact that computations that differ only for the order of independent actions represent, actually, the same behaviour. In other words, interleaving models abstract away from the difference between the factual *temporal* occurrence order and the more conceptual *causal* ordering of actions. The simplest exemplification of this situation is provided by the CCS terms $a \mid b$ and $a.b + b.a$, both described by the following transition system.

(1)

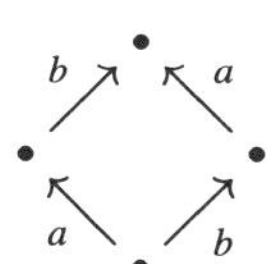

1991 *Mathematics Subject Classification.* Primary 68Q55, 68Q10, 68Q05.

Key words and phrases. Semantics of Concurrency, Noninterleaving, Independence Models.

Second author partly supported by EU **H**uman **C**apital and **M**obility grant ERBCHBGCT920005.

Although for many applications this level of abstraction is appropriate, for several other kinds of analysis a model may be desirable that takes full account of concurrency. For instance, apart from any philosophical consideration about the semantic relevance of cause/effect relationships, knowing that different interleavings represent the same behaviour can reduce considerably the state-space explosion problem when checking system properties such as safety [**8**] and liveness properties [**21, 17**].

Several efforts have been devoted to the search of transition-based *noninterleaving* models, e.g., transition systems enriched with additional features that make expressing concurrency explicitly possible (cf., e.g., [**18, 4, 6, 7, 5, 3**]). The present paper focuses on two such models, namely *asynchronous transition systems*, introduced independently by Bednarczyk [**1**] and Shields [**20**], and *transitions systems with independence*, proposed by Winskel and Nielsen [**22**]. These two competing approaches are, among the others, those building on the simplest idea: endow transition systems with some formal notion of 'similarity' of transitions that enables to distinguish whether or not the opposite edges in diagrams such as (1) represent the same action. Intuitively, this is achieved in both approaches by thinking of transitions as *occurrences* of *events*, two transitions representing the same event if they correspond to the same action. However, the differences induced on the models by the different choices of how to assign events to transitions are definitely not trivial. And so are the relationships that these models bear to each other.

Getting to the details, asynchronous transition systems assign events to transitions explicitly and enrich the structure further by adding an *independence relation* on the events that describes their causal relationships. This clearly makes distinguishing nondeterminism and concurrency possible; $a.b + b.a$ and $a|b$ can be represented respectively by, e.g., the following *labeled* asynchronous transition systems, where $\sim$ indicates whether or not the events e and e' (labeled by a and b) are independent.

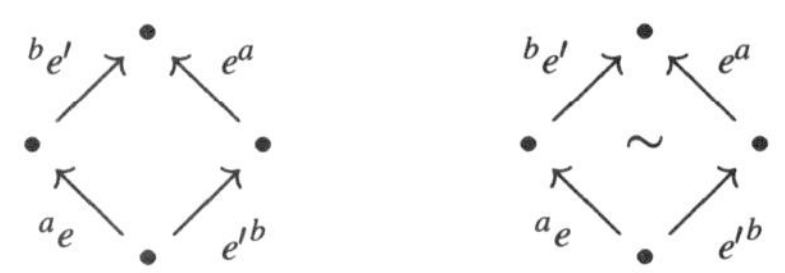

Observe that here and in the rest of the paper we consider *labeled* asynchronous transition systems [**1, 22**], i.e., asynchronous transition systems with a further labeling of events, as the proper extension of labeled transition systems.

The expressive power of asynchronous transition systems is clearly not limited to the example above; for instance, Bednarczyk [**1**] and Mukund and Nielsen [**15**] have shown that noninterleaving related issues for CCS processes — such as *localities* — can be modeled faithfully using this model. However, it can be argued that assigning both the independence relation and the decoration of transitions with events explicitly means assigning too much. In fact, this obviously introduces some *redundancies* in the model: there are, for instance, many non-isomorphic variations of the asynchronous transitions systems above which can still be reasonably thought as models of $a|b$ and $a.b + b.a$. Moreover, although it is usually easy to tell about independence of transitions, in many important cases it is at least *not* immediate to assign events to transitions: it might very well be the goal of the entire semantic analysis to understand what the events of the system and their mutual relationships are. This consideration seems to indicate that asynchronous transitions systems cannot have a significant impact in Plotkin's SOS style semantics, unless the independence relation is promoted to a greater role.

Transition systems with independence are an attempt to answer to the previous observation. Here events are *not* introduced explicitly. They are rather *derived* from the structure of the 'simply-labeled' transitions, upon which the independence relation is directly layered. In such a model, each of the CCS terms discussed above admits only one transition system which can faithfully represent it, viz., respectively,

The implicit information about events can be easily deduced from the presence (or the absence) of $\sim$, making the achieved expressive power comparable to that of asynchronous transition systems. Moreover, avoiding a primitive notion of event makes providing a *'noninterleaving'* operational semantics in the SOS style a relatively simple task (cf. **[22]**).

However, in order to be consistent with the computational intuition, the axiomatics of transition systems with independence involves (apparently necessarily **[19]**) *one* condition expressed 'globally' in terms of all the transitions representing occurrences of the same event. This contrasts with the 'local' conditions defining asynchronous transition systems (due to the globally identified events) and can make hard checking that a given structure is a transitions system with independence. Thus, the differences induced on the two models by the choice of a *primitive* versus a *derived* notion of event are far-reaching and seem to make them suitable for different applications. This indicates that it is not wise to choose *once and for all* between asynchronous transition systems and transition systems with independence, which, in turn, opens the issue of investigating *formally* their analogies and differences.

An exhaustive analysis of this question was carried out by the authors in **[10]**, showing that transition systems with independence, besides being nicely related to a class of asynchronous transition systems called *extensional*, are *equivalent* to the so-called *event-maximal* asynchronous transition systems. The results of *loc. cit.* are summarized by the following diagram, where TSI, LATS, eLATS, and meLATS are, respectively, the categories of transitions systems with independence, labeled, extensional, and event-maximal asynchronous transitions systems, and where $\hookrightarrow$, $\perp$, and $\cong$ stand respectively for embeddings, coreflections, and equivalences.

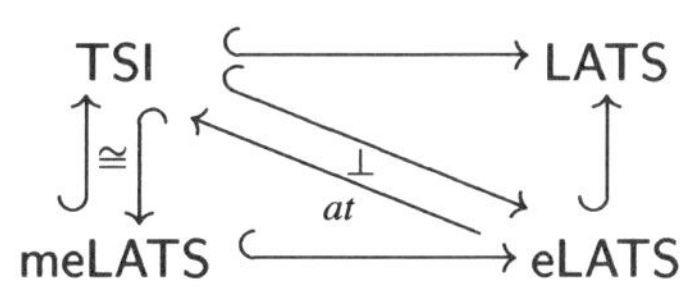

Essentially, the extensionality condition refers to the existence of a *unique* way to 'complete' pairs of independent transitions to *'independence-diamonds'*. Also, it excludes multi-arcs, i.e., multiple transitions with the same label between the same two states. Event-maximality, on the other hand, can be seen at the same time as identifying those transition systems that make as few identifications of transitions as possible, i.e., contain no confusion about event identities, and those in which such identities are derivable from the independence relation, i.e., reduce the redundancy. It is worth noticing here that *at*: eLATS $\to$ TSI, the right adjoint of the coreflection, complements and corrects a non-well-defined construction sketched in **[22]**: as a matter of fact, due to the greater generality of asynchronous transition systems, eLATS happens to be the largest subcategory of LATS on which such a construction makes sense.

A question left open by **[10]** is whether or not the need to restrict to extensional asynchronous transition systems is a consequence of the intrinsic differences between the two notions of events considered, i.e., if in order to be able to model situations ruled out by the extensionality constraints it is necessary to assign events explicitly. This paper addresses such a question; namely, we remove the restriction to transition systems without multi-arcs, relaxing the definition of transition systems with independence, and yielding the new notion of *transition systems with independence and multi-arcs* (*nonextensional transition systems with independence* would probably be a better name, though).

This represents, in our view, an interesting enhancement of the model. In fact, in noninterleaving semantics, to be able to treat multi-arcs is clearly very relevant. In a sense, it can be seen as allowing 'quotienting' of the state-space while retaining full information about events and causality. As an example, consider the CCS term $(a|b)+a.b$, traditionally described by the following transition system.

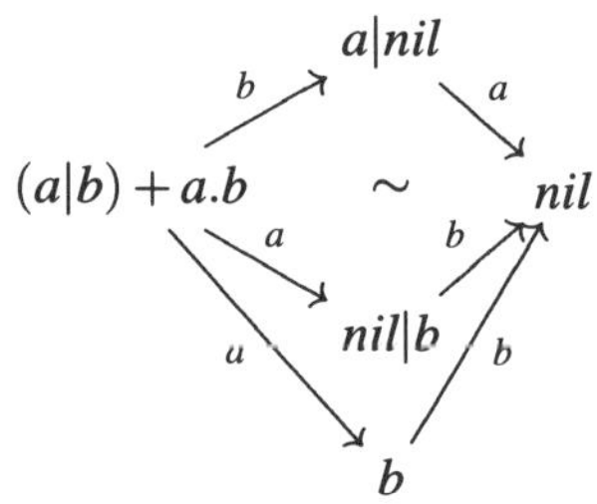

It is common (see e.g. **[13, 15]** among others) to *quotient* the state-space by some structural congruence that, e.g., collapses the states b and $nil|b$, obtaining the more compact representation — with multi-arcs — shown below.

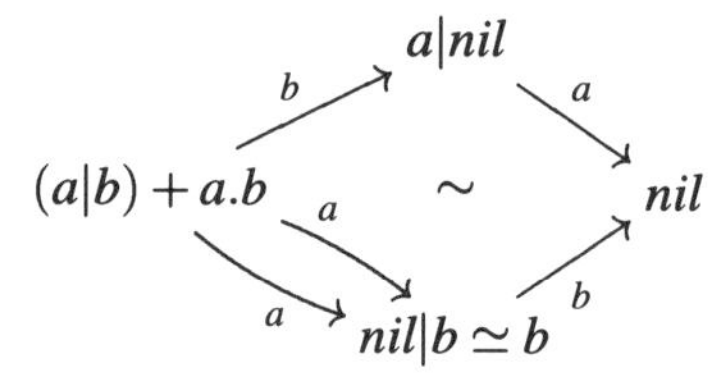

Observe that, contrarily to the interleaving case, it is *vital* here to have *two different a*-transitions, since they rappresent different events: one is part of the independence-diamond and is, therefore, independent of b; the other is not.

In order to justify our definition, we prove that, except for the extensionality condition, the category TSI_m of transition systems with independence and multi-arcs bears exactly the same relationships as TSI to LATS. More precisely, we prove that TSI_m is *coreflective* in the category dLATS of the *diamond-extensional* asynchronous transition systems — intuitively, those transition systems that make no confusion about the identities of the events carried by transitions facing each other in independence-diamonds. Similarly to the case of TSI, dLATS is the largest subcategory of LATS for which such a result holds. Moreover, among the *diamond-extensional*, we identify the *event-maximal* asynchronous transition systems and prove that they induce the largest full subcategory of LATS, mdLATS, for which the coreflection cuts down to an *equivalence*. This yields a precise characterisation of TSI_m in terms of LATS that extends the relationships between TSI and LATS discussed above: in fact, the category of eLATS and its full subcategory meLATS are, respectively, the full subcategories of dLATS and mdLATS consisting of transition systems without multi-arcs.

Summing up, this paper presents the following diagram of formal relationships between the new model of transition systems with independence and multi-arcs and asynchronous transition systems which can be useful in practise to translate back and forth between the two models when the application one has in mind requires it.

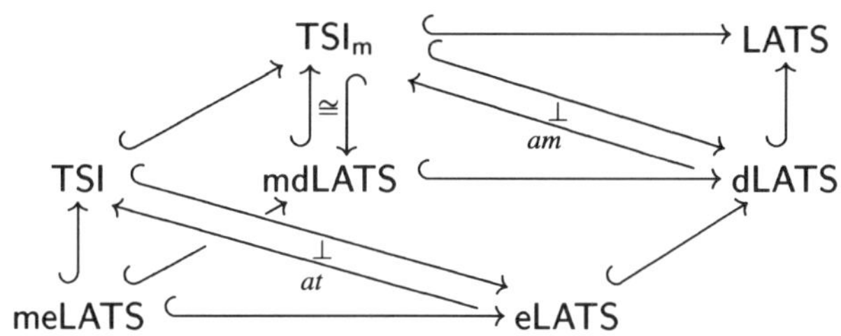

Although the technical development here goes along the lines of **[10]**, and therefore, strictly speaking, this paper is simply an extension of *loc. cit.*, we believe that the definition of $\mathsf{TSI_m}$ is a relevant contribution on its own.

1. Preliminaries

In this section we recall briefly the definitions of asynchronous transition systems, transition systems with independence, and their respective categories **[1, 22]**.

As discussed in the introduction, asynchronous transition systems are simply transition systems whose transitions are decorated by events equipped with an independence relation. Four axioms (A1–A4) are needed to guarantee the intended meaning for the events and the independence relation.

DEFINITION 1.1 (Labeled Asynchronous Transition Systems). A *labeled asynchronous transition* system (lats for short) is a structure

$$A = (S_A, i_A, E_A, Tran_A, I_A, L_A, \ell_A),$$

where $(S_A, i_A, E_A, Tran_A)$ is a transition system with set of *states* S_A, *initial state* $i_A \in S_A$, and *transitions* $Tran_A \subseteq S_A \times E_A \times S_A$, and where E_A is a set of *events*, L_A a set of labels, $\ell_A : E_A \to L_A$ a *labeling* function, and $I_A \subseteq E_A \times E_A$, the *independence relation*, is an irreflexive, symmetric relation such that

A1. $e \in E_A \quad \Rightarrow \quad \exists s_1, s_2 \in S_A.\ (s_1, e, s_2) \in Tran_A$;

A2. $(s, e, s_1), (s, e, s_2) \in Tran_A \quad \Rightarrow \quad s_1 = s_2$;

A3. $e_1\, I_A\, e_2,\ (s, e_1, s_1), (s, e_2, s_2) \in Tran_A \quad \Rightarrow$
$\exists u.\ (s_1, e_2, u), (s_2, e_1, u) \in Tran_A$;

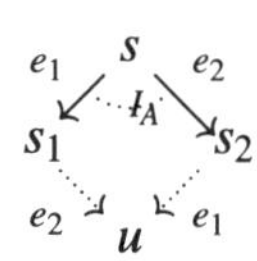

A4. $e_1\, I_A\, e_2,\ (s, e_1, s_1), (s_1, e_2, u) \in Tran_A \quad \Rightarrow$
$\exists s_2.\ (s, e_2, s_2), (s_2, e_1, u) \in Tran_A$.

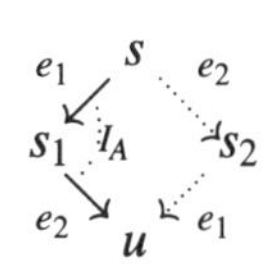

In the rest of the paper we shall let $I(e)$ denote the set $\{e' \mid e\, I_A\, e'\}$ and, for convenience, use (s, e^a, s') as a shorthand for a transition (s, e, s') with $\ell_A(e) = a$.

The following is the standard definition of morphisms for lats, which essentially mimics the idea of *simulation* (cf. **[1, 22]**).

DEFINITION 1.2 (Asynchronous Transition System Morphisms). For A and A' lats, a *morphism* from A to A' is a triple of (partial) functions[1]

$$(\sigma\colon S_A \to S_{A'}, \eta\colon E_A \rightharpoonup E_{A'}, \lambda\colon L_A \rightharpoonup L_{A'}),$$

where (σ,η) is a morphism of labeled transition systems, i.e.,

- $\sigma(i_A) = i_{A'}$;
- $(s_1,e,s_2) \in Tran_A,\ \eta(e)\downarrow \quad\Rightarrow\quad (\sigma(s_1),\eta(e),\sigma(s_2)) \in Tran_{A'}$;
  $(s_1,e,s_2) \in Tran_A,\ \eta(e)\uparrow \quad\Rightarrow\quad \sigma(s_1) = \sigma(s_2)$;

which preserves the labeling, i.e., makes the following diagram commutative

$$\begin{array}{ccc} E_A & \xrightarrow{\ \eta\ } & E_{A'} \\ {\scriptstyle \ell_A}\downarrow & & \downarrow{\scriptstyle \ell_{A'}} \\ L_A & \xrightarrow[\ \lambda\ ]{} & L_{A'}, \end{array}$$

and the independence, i.e.,

$$e_1\, I_A\, e_2,\ \eta(e_1)\downarrow,\ \eta(e_2)\downarrow \quad\Rightarrow\quad \eta(e_1)\, I_{A'}\, \eta(e_2).$$

It is immediate to see that lats and their morphisms form a category, which we shall refer to as LATS.

Starting from Definition 1.1, transition systems with independence attempt to simplify the structure retaining explicitly only the independence, now layered directly on the transitions. As already mentioned, the notion of event becomes implicit, determined by the independence relation through the equivalence-classes of the relation $\sim$.

DEFINITION 1.3 (Transition Systems with Independence). A *transition system with independence* (tsi for short) is a structure

$$T = (S_T, i_T, L_T, Tran_T, I_T),$$

where $(S_T, i_T, L_T, Tran_T)$ is a *transition system* and $I_T \subseteq Tran_T \times Tran_T$, the independence relation, is an irreflexive, symmetric relation, such that, denoting by $\prec$ the binary relation on transitions given as

$$\begin{aligned} (s,a,s_1) \prec (s_2,a,u) \quad & \text{if and only if} \\ & \exists b \in L_T.\ (s,a,s_1)\ I_T\ (s,b,s_2), \\ & \qquad (s,a,s_1)\ I_T\ (s_1,b,u),\ (s,b,s_2)\ I_T\ (s_2,a,u), \end{aligned}$$

and by $\sim$ the least equivalence on transitions which includes it, we have

T1. $(s,a,s_1) \sim (s,a,s_2) \quad\Rightarrow\quad s_1 = s_2$;

T2. $(s,a,s_1)\ I_T\ (s,b,s_2) \quad\Rightarrow\quad \exists u.\ (s,a,s_1)\ I_T\ (s_1,b,u),\ (s,b,s_2)\ I_T\ (s_2,a,u)$;

T3. $(s,a,s_1)\ I_T\ (s_1,b,u) \quad\Rightarrow\quad \exists s_2.\ (s,a,s_1)\ I_T\ (s,b,s_2),\ (s,b,s_2)\ I_T\ (s_2,a,u)$;

T4. $(s,a,s_1) \prec\cup\succ (s_2,a,u)\ I_T\ (w,b,w') \quad\Rightarrow\quad (s,a,s_1)\ I_T\ (w,b,w')$.

The $\sim$-equivalence classes are to be thought of as events, i.e., $t_1 \prec t_2$ means that t_1 and t_2 are part of a 'concurrency diamond', whilst $t_1 \sim t_2$ means that they are occurrences of the same event. Concerning the axioms, notice then that T1 corresponds to A2 and axioms T2 and T3 correspond, respectively, to A3 and A4.

[1]We use, respectively, $f\colon A \to B$ and $f\colon A \rightharpoonup B$ to indicate total and partial functions. For f a partial function, $f(x)\downarrow$ ($f(x)\uparrow$) means that f is (un)defined at x.

The following definition of morphisms for transition systems with independence resembles closely the one given above for lats.

DEFINITION 1.4 (Transition System with Independence Morphisms). For T and T' tsi, a morphism from T to T' consists of a pair of (partial) functions

$$(\sigma\colon S_T \to S_{T'}, \lambda\colon L_T \rightharpoonup L_{T'})$$

which is a morphism of transition systems and, in addition, preserves independence, i.e.,

$$(s_1,a,s_2)\ I_T\ (s_1',b,s_2'),\ \lambda(a)\downarrow, \lambda(b)\downarrow \quad \Rightarrow \\ \big(\sigma(s_1),\lambda(a),\sigma(s_2)\big)\ I_{T'}\ \big(\sigma(s_1'),\lambda(b),\sigma(s_2')\big).$$

We shall use TSI to denote the category of tsi and their morphisms.

The following lemma states that tsi morphisms are well defined as maps of events, an easy consequence of the fact that they preserve independence that we shall use in order to embed TSI into LATS.

LEMMA 1.5 (Morphisms map Events to Events). *For* $(\sigma,\lambda)\colon T \to T'$ *a morphism of tsi,* (s_1,a,s_2) *and* (s_1',a,s_2') *transitions of* T, $\big(\sigma(s_1),\lambda(a),\sigma(s_2)\big) \sim \big(\sigma(s_1'),\lambda(a),\sigma(s_2')\big)$ *whenever* $(s_1,a,s_2) \sim (s_1',a,s_2')$ *and* $\lambda(a)\downarrow$*, i.e., lats morphisms preserve* $\sim$.

2. Comparing LATS with TSI: Considering multi-arcs

In this section we first recall the results of the comparison of TSI and LATS carried out by the authors in **[10]**, and then, reconsidering a restriction used in *loc. cit.*, we introduce the notion of *transition systems with independence and multi-arcs* — i.e., tsi in which multiple transitions carrying the same label are allowed between the same two states. In the next section we shall then perform an analysis matching that of **[10]**, investigating the relationship between such a category and LATS, and showing that, in a precise sense, our definition provides a minimal, conservative way to extend tsi with multi-arcs.

The starting point of the analysis in **[10]** is the obvious inclusion $ta\colon$ TSI $\to$ LATS which acts on objects by decorating each transition with the event identified by the $\sim$-class the transition belongs to, and by inheriting the independence relation directly from the tsi. On the opposite direction, we considered the 'abstraction' *at* from LATS to TSI that forgets the events and brings the independence from the events down to the transitions. However, a simple argument shows that the presence of multi-arcs in LATS makes it impossible for *at* to be well-defined as a map to TSI. Thus, the very first step of **[10]** is to consider only those lats A satisfying

(Ex) $$(s_1,e_1^a,s_2) \neq (s_1,e_2^b,s_2) \in Tran_A \quad \Rightarrow \quad a \neq b,$$

whose purpose is to forbids multi-arcs. This allows to prove that the *diamond-extensional* asynchronous transition systems, whose definition follows, are exactly those lats A such that $at(A)$ belongs to TSI.

DEFINITION 2.1 (Diamond-Extensional lats). A *diamond extensional labeled asynchronous transition* system (dlats for short) is a lats that satisfies

A!3. $e_1\ I_A\ e_2,\ (s,e_1^a,s_1),(s,e_2^b,s_2) \in Tran_A \quad \Rightarrow$
$$\exists!\ \text{pair}\ (s_1,x_2^b,u),(s_2,x_1^a,u) \in Tran_A.\ e_1\ I_A\ x_2,\ e_2\ I_A\ x_1,\ x_1\ I_A\ x_2;$$

A!4. $e_1\ I_A\ e_2,\ (s,e_1^a,s_1),(s_1,e_2^b,u) \in Tran_A \quad \Rightarrow$
$$\exists!\ \text{pair}\ (s,x_2^b,s_2),(s_2,x_1^a,u) \in Tran_A.\ e_1\ I_A\ x_2,\ e_2\ I_A\ x_1,\ x_1\ I_A\ x_2.$$

The category dLATS is the full subcategory of LATS consisting of the *diamond-extensional* lats.

We call *extensional* the diamond-extensional lats that in addition satisfy (Ex), and we denote by eLATS the full subcategory of dLATS that they determine. We can now give the formal definitions of the functors $ta\colon \mathsf{TSI} \to \mathsf{LATS}$ and $at\colon \mathsf{eLATS} \to \mathsf{TSI}$.

DEFINITION 2.2 (TSI $\hookrightarrow$ LATS). For T a tsi, let $ta(T)$ be the structure

$$(S_T, i_T, E, Tran, I, L_T, \ell),$$

where, denoting by $\sim$ the equivalence relation induced by I_T as in Definition 1.3,

- ▶ $E = Tran_T/\!\sim$, the set of $\sim$-classes of $Tran_T$;
- ▶ $Tran = \{ (s_1, [(s_1,a,s_2)]_\sim, s_2) \mid (s_1,a,s_2) \in Tran_T \}$;
- ▶ $[(s_1,a,s_2)]_\sim \; I \; [(s'_1,a,s'_2)]_\sim$ if and only if $(s_1,a,s_2) \; I_T \; (s'_1,a,s'_2)$;
- ▶ $\ell([(s_1,a,s_2)]_\sim) = a$.

For $(\sigma,\lambda)\colon T \to T'$ a morphism of tsi, let $ta((\sigma,\lambda))$ be (σ,η,λ), where

$$\eta([(s,a,s')]_\sim) = \begin{cases} [(\sigma(s),\lambda(a),\sigma(s'))]_\sim & \text{if } \lambda(a)\downarrow, \\ \textit{undefined} & \text{if } \lambda(a)\uparrow. \end{cases}$$

The proof that ta is well defined follows easily from Lemma 1.5. Actually, ta is a *full* and *faithful* functor, i.e., an embedding of TSI in LATS. In the following, when no confusion is possible, we may occasionally omit the index $\sim$ from the notation for $\sim$-classes.

DEFINITION 2.3 (eLATS $\hookrightarrow$ TSI). For A a lats, let $at(A)$ be the structure

$$(S_A, i_A, L_A, Tran, I),$$

where

- ▶ $(s,a,s') \in Tran$ if and only if $(s,e^a,s') \in Tran_A$,
- ▶ $(s,a,s_1) \; I \; (s_2,b,s_3)$ if and only if $(s,e_1^a,s_1),(s_2,e_2^b,s_3) \in Tran_A$, $e_1 \; I_A \; e_2$.

For $(\sigma,\eta,\lambda)\colon A \to A'$ a morphism of lats, let $at((\sigma,\eta,\lambda))$ be (σ,λ).

The result of **[10]** is that ta and at form a *coreflection* of TSI in eLATS.

PROPOSITION 2.4 ($ta \dashv at\colon \mathsf{TSI} \rightharpoonup \mathsf{eLATS}$). TSI *is coreflective in* eLATS.

PROOF. Subsumed by that of the forthcoming Proposition 3.8. □

The lats corresponding to tsi are characterised as the *event-maximal* lats. Intuitively, a lats is *event-maximal* if its events and independence are 'tightly coupled', so that one cannot 'split' events without destroying the global lats structure. In other words, the identity of the events in event-maximal lats is forced by the independence relation. This will provide a direct characterisation of tsi in terms of lats

DEFINITION 2.5 (Event-Maximal lats). For A a lats, $\bar{e} \in E_A$, and $T \subset T_{\bar{e}}$, where $T_{\bar{e}} = \{(s,e,s') \in Tran_A \mid e = \bar{e}\}$, let $A[T]$ denote the replacement of $\bar{e}$ on the transitions in T for a fresh event $\tilde{e} \notin E_A$, i.e.,

$$A[T] = (S_A, i_A, E_A \cup \{\tilde{e}\}, Tran, I, L_A, \ell),$$

where

- ▶ $Tran = (Tran_A \setminus T) \cup \{(s_1,\tilde{e},s_2) \mid (s_1,\bar{e},s_2) \in T\}$;

▶ $I = I_A \cup \{(\tilde{e}, e) \mid \bar{e}\, I_A\, e\}$;

▶ $\ell(e) = \begin{cases} \ell_A(e) & \text{if } e \in E_A, \\ \ell_A(\bar{e}) & \text{if } e = \tilde{e}. \end{cases}$

A lats A is *event-maximal* if for each $\bar{e} \in E_A$ and each nonempty $T \subset T_{\bar{e}}$, the transition systems $A[T]$ is *not* a lats.
The category mdLATS is the full subcategory of LATS consisting of the *diamond-extensional, event-maximal* lats.

The definition above, stating that any structure obtained by 'rearranging' events non-trivially must fail to be a lats, is our way to express that — as remarked before — the identity of the events in event-maximal lats is forced by the independence relation.

Now, if we denote by meLATS the restriction of mdLATS to the full subcategory induced by the objects satisfying (Ex), we can state the final result of **[10]**.

PROPOSITION 2.6 (meLATS $\cong$ TSI). meLATS *is equivalent to* TSI.

PROOF. Subsumed by that of the forthcoming Proposition 3.9. □

Technically, the contribution of this paper is to re-address the choice of condition (Ex) which forbids multiple transitions with the same label between the same two states. Namely, instead of restricting lats in order to get a well-defined functor *at* to TSI, we relax the definition of tsi to allow multi-arcs, proposing below the notion of *transition systems with independence and multi-arcs*. This represents an interesting evolution of tsi, whose relevance goes beyond the comparison of tsi and lats; morally, it constitutes the main contribution of this paper. In other words, we propose here transition systems with independence and multi-arcs and justify their definition by showing how their multi-arcs relates to those of lats.

Formally, we extend tsi in the simplest possible way: transitions are represented by a map assigning to each element of a set *Tran* of transitions a triple consisting of its source, label, and target. This allows to have more transitions between the same two states with the same label simply by having more elements of *Tran* mapped to the same triple. The independence relation and the defining axioms are the obvious translations of those of tsi.

DEFINITION 2.7 (tsi with Multi-Arcs). A *transition system with independence and multi-arcs* (tsi_m for short) is a structure

$$T = (S_T, i_T, L_T, Tran_T, \langle - \rangle_T, I_T),$$

where $\langle - \rangle_T \colon Tran_T \to S_T \times L_T \times S_T$ and $(S_T, i_T, L_T, \langle Tran_T \rangle_T)$ is a *transition system* and $I_T \subseteq Tran_T \times Tran_T$, the independence relation, is an irreflexive, symmetric relation, such that, denoting by $\prec$ the binary relation on transitions given as

$$\begin{aligned} t \prec t' \quad \text{if and only if} \quad & \langle t \rangle_T = (s,a,s_1),\ \langle t' \rangle_T = (s_2,a,u), \\ & \exists t_1,t_2 \in Tran_T.\ \langle t_1 \rangle_T = (s,b,s_2),\ \langle t_2 \rangle_T = (s_1,b,u), \\ & \qquad \text{with } t\, I_T\, t_1,\ t\, I_T\, t_2,\ t_1\, I_T\, t', \end{aligned}$$

and by $\sim$ the least equivalence on transitions that includes $\prec$, we have

$\mathsf{T_m}1.$ $t \sim t',\ \langle t \rangle_T = (s,a,s_1),\ \langle t' \rangle_T = (s,a,s_2) \quad \Rightarrow \quad t = t'$;

$\mathsf{T_m}2.$ $t\, I_T\, t',\ \langle t \rangle_T = (s,a,s_1),\ \langle t' \rangle_T = (s,b,s_2) \quad \Rightarrow$

$$\exists t_1,t_2.\ \langle t_1 \rangle_T = (s_2,a,u),\ \langle t_2 \rangle_T = (s_1,b,u),\ t\, I_T\, t_2,\ t'\, I_T\, t_1;$$

$\mathsf{T_m3}$. $t\, I_T\, t',\ \langle t\rangle_T = (s,a,s_1),\ \langle t'\rangle_T = (s_1,b,u) \quad \Rightarrow$

$$\exists t_1,t_2.\ \langle t_1\rangle_T = (s_2,a,u),\ \langle t_2\rangle_T = (s,b,s_2),\ t\, I_T\, t_2,\ t_1\, I_T\, t_2;$$

$\mathsf{T_m4}$. $t \prec\cup\succ t'\, I_T\, t'' \quad \Rightarrow \quad t\, I_T\, t''$.

As for tsi, the $\sim$-equivalence classes — in the following denoted by $[t]_\sim$, for t a representative of the class — are to be thought of as events. The axioms are recast to fit with the indirect way of assigning source, label, and target to transitions. Notice that a global axiom like $\mathsf{T_m1}$ is still necessary, since the intended notion of events still cannot be determined locally. Axiom $\mathsf{T_m4}$ ensures that the independence relation determines a well-defined relation on events.

In the rest of the paper we shall see that this view of $[t]_\sim$ agrees with the notion of events for lats and that, in fact, $\mathsf{tsi_m}$ relates well to the category of diamond-extensional lats.

Using $I(t)$ to denote the set $\{t' \mid t\, I_T\, t'\}$, we can state the following lemma which will be useful later on. As a matter of notations, we shall use $\langle - \rangle_i$, $i = 1,\dots,3$, to denote the composition of $\langle - \rangle_T$ with the appropriate projection, i.e., if $\langle t\rangle_T = (s,a,s')$, then $\langle t\rangle_1 = s$, $\langle t\rangle_2 = a$, and $\langle t\rangle_3 = s'$.

LEMMA 2.8. *Axiom* $\mathsf{T_m4}$ *is equivalent to*

$$(\mathsf{T^m4'}) \qquad t_1 \sim t_2 \quad \Rightarrow \quad I(t_1) = I(t_2).$$

PROOF. Easy, by induction. □

The definition of morphisms for transition systems with independence and multi-arcs necessarily involves a (partial) function on transitions, which, of course, must respect the mapping of states and labels.

DEFINITION 2.9 ($\mathsf{tsi_m}$ Morphisms). For T and T' $\mathsf{tsi_m}$, a morphism from T to T' consists of a triple of (partial) functions

$$(\sigma\colon S_T \to S_{T'}, \lambda\colon L_T \rightharpoonup L_{T'}, \tau\colon \mathit{Tran}_T \rightharpoonup \mathit{Tran}_{T'})$$

that respects sources, targets, and labels, i.e., that makes the following diagram commute

$$\begin{array}{ccc} \mathit{Tran}_T & \xrightarrow{\quad\tau\quad} & \mathit{Tran}_{T'} \\ {\scriptstyle\langle - \rangle_T}\big\downarrow & & \big\downarrow{\scriptstyle\langle - \rangle_{T'}} \\ S_T \times L_T \times S_T & \xrightarrow[<\sigma,\lambda,\sigma>]{} & S_{T'} \times L_{T'} \times S_{T'}, \end{array}$$

preserves independence, i.e.,

$$t\, I_T\, t',\ \tau(t)\downarrow,\ \tau(t')\downarrow \quad \Rightarrow \quad \tau(t)\, I_{T'}\, \tau(t'),$$

and preserves the 'diamond relation' $\preceq$, i.e.,

$$t \preceq t',\ \tau(t)\downarrow \text{ (or } \tau(t')\downarrow) \quad \Rightarrow \quad \tau(t) \preceq \tau(t').$$

We shall use $\mathsf{TSI_m}$ to denote the category of $\mathsf{tsi_m}$ and their morphisms.

Observe that in the definition above it is necessary to consider the reflexive closure $\preceq$ of the relation $\prec$, since morphisms can be partial and, therefore, collapse diamonds.

Concerning the relationships between TSI and $\mathsf{TSI_m}$, every tsi can be regarded as a $\mathsf{tsi_m}$ simply by defining the map $\langle - \rangle_T$ to act as the 'identity', i.e., interpreting transitions as themselves. Such a mapping extends to an inclusion functor $\mathit{tm}\colon \mathsf{TSI} \hookrightarrow \mathsf{TSI_m}$ by defining $\mathit{tm}((\sigma,\lambda))$ to be (σ,λ,τ), where $\tau((s,a,s')) = (\sigma(s),\lambda(a),\sigma(s'))$. It follows immediately from the last condition in Definition 2.9 that τ is well defined as a map of events, a fact that we shall use in later on to embed $\mathsf{TSI_m}$ into LATS.

LEMMA 2.10 (Morphisms map Events to Events). *For* $(\sigma,\lambda,\tau)\colon T \to T'$ *a morphism of tsi*$_\mathsf{m}$ *and* $t \sim t'$ *equivalent transitions of* T, *if* $\tau(t)\downarrow$, *then* $\tau(t) \sim \tau(t')$, *i.e., tsi*$_\mathsf{m}$ *morphisms preserve* $\sim$.

In general, it is not possible to define a map from $\mathsf{TSI_m}$ to TSI that forgets multi-arcs and preserves independence. This is shown by the following example in which collapsing the a-multi-arcs would make the two a-labeled transitions sticking out of s break axiom T1

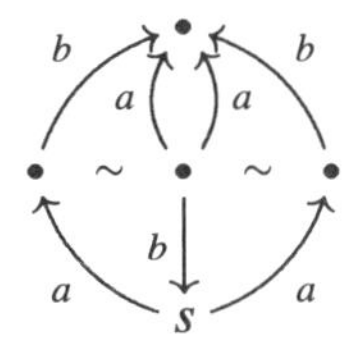

This means that the embedding tm: $\mathsf{TSI} \hookrightarrow \mathsf{TSI_m}$ does not have a right adjoint. Dually, it can be proved that tm cannot have a left adjont either (a proof that we shall omit, though). Thus, TSI is neither *reflective* nor *coreflective* in $\mathsf{TSI_m}$.

3. From LATS to $\mathsf{TSI_m}$: A coreflection

Now that all the bricks are in play, we can complete the picture showing how to extend the functors ta and at to a pair of adjoint functors ma and am forming a coreflection between $\mathsf{TSI_m}$ and dLATS. There is only one reasonable way to define the embedding ma.

DEFINITION 3.1 ($\mathsf{TSI_m} \hookrightarrow \mathsf{dLATS}$). For T a tsi, let $ma(T)$ be the structure

$$(S_T, i_T, E, Tran, I, L_T, \ell),$$

where, denoting by $\sim$ the equivalence relation induced by I_T as in Definition 2.7,

- ▶ $E = Tran_T/\!\sim$, the set of $\sim$-classes of $Tran_T$;
- ▶ $Tran = \big\{ \big(\langle t\rangle_1, [t]_\sim, \langle t\rangle_3\big) \;\big|\; t \in Tran_T \big\}$;
- ▶ $[t]_\sim \, I \, [t']_\sim$ if and only if $t \, I_T \, t'$;
- ▶ $\ell\big([t]_\sim\big) = \langle t\rangle_2$.

It follows from Lemma 2.8 and the definition of $\sim$ that the definition of the independence and labels on the events of $ma(T)$ is well given. It is now easy to verify the following.

PROPOSITION 3.2. *The transition system* $ma(T)$ *is a dlats.*

PROOF. Axiom A1 is trivially satisfied. Axiom A2 is satisfied because of $\mathsf{T_m1}$, for, by definition of ma, two transitions carry the same event if and only if they belong to the same $\sim$-class in T. Concerning A3 and A4, they correspond directly to $\mathsf{T_m2}$ and $\mathsf{T_m3}$, and the uniqueness criteria imposed by A!3 and A!4 are a direct consequence of T1. □

In order to define ma as a functor, we need to define its action on the morphisms of $\mathsf{TSI_m}$.

DEFINITION 3.3 ($\mathsf{TSI_m} \hookrightarrow \mathsf{dLATS}$). For $(\sigma,\lambda,\tau)\colon T \to T'$ a morphism of $\mathsf{tsi_m}$, let $ma\big((\sigma,\lambda,\tau)\big)$ be (σ,η,λ), where

$$\eta([t]_\sim) = \begin{cases} [t']_\sim & \text{if } \tau(t) = t', \\ \textit{undefined} & \text{if } \tau(t)\uparrow. \end{cases}$$

That Definition 3.3 is well given follows from Lemma 2.10; it is also easy to check that ma is a *full* and *faithful* functor, i.e., an embedding of $\mathsf{TSI_m}$ in dLATS.

The obvious way to define the 'abstraction' am to $\mathsf{TSI_m}$ on the objects of LATS is, for a lats A, to make the transitions $Tran_A$ the elements of the transition set $Tran_{am(A)}$ and then interpret them (via $\langle - \rangle_{am(A)}$) simply by replacing the event with its label. We shall prove that this gives a well-defined object-map from the category of diamond-extensional lats to $\mathsf{TSI_m}$, and that dLATS is actually the largest full subcategory of LATS whose every object is mapped by am to a $\mathsf{tsi_m}$.

DEFINITION 3.4 ($\mathsf{dLATS} \hookrightarrow \mathsf{TSI_m}$). For A a lats, let $am(A)$ be the structure

$$(S_A, i_A, L_A, Tran, \langle - \rangle, I),$$

where,

- ▶ $(s,e^a,s') \in Tran$ if and only if $(s,e^a,s') \in Tran_A$,
- ▶ $\langle (s,e^a,s') \rangle = (s,a,s')$,
- ▶ $(s,e_1^a,s_1)\, I\, (s_2,e_2^b,s_3)$ if and only if $e_1\, I_A\, e_2$.

PROPOSITION 3.5. *For A a lats, $am(A)$ belongs to $\mathsf{TSI_m}$ if and only if A belongs to* dLATS.

PROOF. The pairs of transitions in A!3 and A!4 exist because of axioms A3 and A4. If $am(A) \in \mathsf{TSI_m}$, their uniqueness is needed in order for $am(A)$ to satisfy axiom $\mathsf{T_m1}$. Suppose that, on the contrary, in the case of A!3 there are two pairs $(s_1,x_2^b,u),(s_2,x_1^a,u)$ and $(s_1,y_2^b,w),(s_2,y_1^a,w)$ satisfying the condition. Assume, without loss of generality, that $y_2 \neq x_2$. Then we have $(s_1,y_2^b,w) \neq (s_1,x_2^b,u)$, but we also have that $(s,e_2^b,s_2) \prec (s_1,y_2^b,w)$ (as transitions of $am(A)$) and $(s,e_2^b,s_2) \prec (s_1,x_2^b,u)$, i.e., that $(s_1,x_2^b,u) \sim (s_1,y_2^b,w)$, which contradicts $\mathsf{T_m1}$. The case for A!4 can be proved along the same lines, thus showing the necessity of the uniqueness conditions.

Concerning their sufficiency, the property of symmetry and irreflexivity for $I_{am(A)}$ is inherited from I_A. It remains to check that the axioms $\mathsf{T_m1}$–$\mathsf{T_m4}$ defining $\mathsf{tsi_m}$ hold for $am(A)$. Axioms A3, A4 and A!3, A!4 ensure that if $(s,e_1^a,s_1) \prec (s_2,e_2^a,s_3)$, then $e_1 = e_2$. It follows then by induction that $(s,e_1^a,s_1) \sim (s_2,e_2^a,s_3)$ implies $e_1 = e_2$, for all $(s,e_1^a,s_1),(s_2,e_2^a,s_3) \in Tran_{am(A)}$. If in addition $s = s_2$, then axiom A2 implies that $s_1 = s_3$, and so $(s,e_1^a,s_1) = (s_2,e_2^a,s_3)$, i.e., $\mathsf{T_m1}$ is satisfied. Actually, this also implies that $\mathsf{T_m4}$ holds. For, since the independence in $am(A)$ is inherited from that on the events in A, we have that $(s,e_1^a,s_1) \sim (s_2,e_2^a,s_3)$ implies $I\big((s,e_1^a,s_1)\big) = I\big((s_2,e_2^a,s_3)\big)$. This, as proved by Lemma 2.8, is equivalent to $\mathsf{T_m4}$. Finally, $\mathsf{T_m2}$ and $\mathsf{T_m3}$ hold because of the corresponding A3 and A4. □

The definition of am on morphisms depends on the fact that LATS morphisms preserve independence on events.

DEFINITION 3.6 ($\mathsf{dLATS} \hookrightarrow \mathsf{TSI_m}$). For $(\sigma,\eta,\lambda)\colon A \to A'$ a morphism of lats, let $am\big((\sigma,\eta,\lambda)\big)$ be (σ,λ,τ), where

$$\tau((s,e^a,s')) = \begin{cases} (\sigma(s),\eta(e)^{\lambda(a)},\sigma(s')) & \text{if } \eta(e)\downarrow, \\ \textit{undefined} & \text{if } \eta(e)\uparrow. \end{cases}$$

By inspecting Definition 3.4, it is easy to verify that the above definition makes the diagram in Definition 2.9 commute. Moreover, it preserves $\preceq$, since axioms A!3 and A!4 ensure that $e_1 = e_2$, whenever $(s,e_1^a,u) \preceq (s',e_2^a,u')$, i.e., since η preserve independence, $am\big((\sigma,\eta,\lambda)\big)$ is well defined.

In order to prepare for our main proof, we first prove the following lemma.

LEMMA 3.7. *For any T in $\mathsf{TSI_m}$, we have that $am \circ ma(T)$ is isomorphic to T.*

PROOF. (Sketch) We show that there is a bijection θ between $Tran_T$ and $Tran_{am\circ ma(T)}$ such that (id_S,id_L,θ) and (id_S,id_L,θ^{-1}) are morphisms of $\mathsf{TSI_m}$, respectively from T to $am \circ ma(T)$ and vice versa, inverses of each other. The obvious choice for $\theta(t)$ is $(\langle t\rangle_1,[t]^{\langle t\rangle_2},\langle t\rangle_3)$. Observe that this gives an injective map because of axiom $\mathsf{T_m}1$. □

The isomorphisms of 3.7 directly extends to a natural transformation

$$\eta = \big\{(id_S,id_L,\theta)\colon T \to am \circ ma(T)\big\}_{T\in\mathsf{TSI_m}} : \mathbf{1}_{\mathsf{TSI_m}} \Longrightarrow am \circ ma.$$

We shall prove now that such a transformation is the *unit* of an adjunction involving *ma* and *am*, i.e., that *am* is right adjoint to $ma\colon \mathsf{TSI_m} \hookrightarrow \mathsf{dLATS}$.

PROPOSITION 3.8 ($ma \dashv am\colon \mathsf{TSI_m} \rightharpoonup \mathsf{dLATS}$). *For any $A \in \mathsf{dLATS}$ and any morphism $m\colon T \to am(A)$ in $\mathsf{TSI_m}$, there exists a unique morphism $m^T : ma(T) \to A$ in dLATS such that $am(m^T) \circ \eta_T = m$.*

PROOF. Let m be (σ,λ,τ). Clearly, by definition of *am*, m^T must be of the form (σ,γ,λ) for some $\gamma\colon E_{ma(T)} \to E_A$. It is easy to realize that the only possible choice for γ is the following: for $t \in Tran_T$ and $\tau(t)\downarrow$, let $\gamma([t]) = e$, if $\tau(t) = (s,e^a,s')$. This is a well given definition, for Lemma 2.10 ensures that m maps all transitions in $[t]$ to the same $\sim$-class of $Tran_{am(A)}$, and the proof of Proposition 3.5 shows that if two transitions belong to the same $\sim$-class of $Tran_{am(A)}$, they originate from transitions in $Tran_A$ carrying the same event. This proves both existence and uniqueness of m^T. Finally, it immediate to check that $am(m^T) \circ \eta_T = m$. □

Since η is an isomorphism, by standard results in category theory, we have that the adjunction $ma \dashv am\colon \mathsf{TSI_m} \rightharpoonup \mathsf{dLATS}$ is a coreflection, i.e., $\mathsf{TSI_m}$ is *coreflective* in dLATS.

Concerning the coreflection described in the previous section, it is immediate to verify that the functors obtained by composing *ma* and *am* with the inclusion $tm\colon \mathsf{TSI} \hookrightarrow \mathsf{TSI_m}$ and with the obvious inclusion of eLATS into dLATS coincide, respectively, with *ta* followed by $\mathsf{eLATS} \hookrightarrow \mathsf{dLATS}$ and with *at* followed by *tm*, as illustrated in the following diagram.

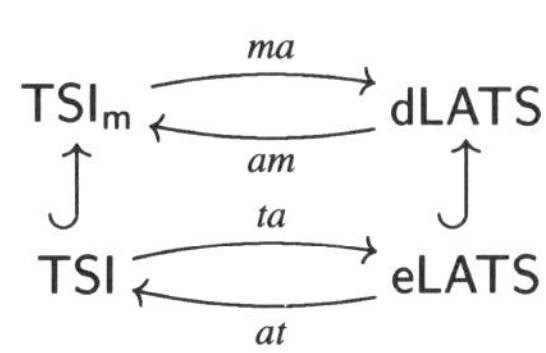

This supports our claim of $\mathsf{TSI_m}$ being a *conservative* and *minimal* extension of TSI, since regarding $\mathsf{tsi_m}$ as lats, the extension corresponds exactly to removing the constraint (Ex).

To complete our analysis, we identify the *replete* image of *ma* in LATS, i.e., the full subcategory mdLATS of dLATS consisting of the objects isomorphic to $ma(T)$, for some $T \in \mathsf{TSI_m}$.

Recall from basic category theory that mdLATS is determined by the coreflection: it consists of those $A \in$ dLATS for which the corresponding component ε_A of the *counit* of $ma \dashv am$ is iso. Applying standard categorical results to derive ε from $(-)^T$ and η, we find that it is the natural transformation

$$\varepsilon = \{(id_{S_A}, \gamma, id_{L_A}) \colon ma \circ am(A) \to A\}_{A \in \mathsf{dLATS}} \colon ma \circ am \Longrightarrow \mathbf{1}_{\mathsf{dLATS}},$$

where, for $(s, e^a, s') \in Tran_{am(A)}$, $\gamma([(s, e^a, s')]) = e$. Clearly, ε_A is iso if and only if γ is such, i.e.,

$$(s, e_1, s_1), (s_2, e_2, s_3) \in Tran_A,\ e_1 = e_2 \quad \Rightarrow \quad (s, e_1, s_1) \sim (s_2, e_2, s_3) \in Tran_{am(A)},$$

which means that two transitions carry the same event if and only if they belong to the same $\sim$-class of A (viewed as a $\mathsf{tsi_m}$). Expressed purely in terms of LATS, this is, as it was the case for TSI, exactly the event-maximal LATS. Observe that in Definition 2.5 the interesting, nontrivial choices for T are those such that $\varnothing \subset T \subset T_{\bar{e}}$, i.e., those in which at least one $\tilde{e}$-transition is added and at least one $\bar{e}$-transition is kept in $A[T]$.

PROPOSITION 3.9 (mdLATS $\cong$ $\mathsf{TSI_m}$). mdLATS *is equivalent to* $\mathsf{TSI_m}$.

PROOF. Let A be a diamond-extensional lats. We prove that the counit ε_A is iso if and only if A belongs to mdLATS. To this purpose, let γ be the event component of ε_A.

If γ is iso, i.e., for all $(s, e_1, s_1), (s_2, e_2, s_3) \in Tran_A$ we have that $e_1 = e_2$ implies $(s, e_1, s_1) \sim (s_2, e_2, s_3)$, for any choice of $\bar{e} \in E_A$ and any $\varnothing \subset T \subset T_{\bar{e}}$, then the condition in Definition 2.5 is satisfied, since, by the diamond-extensionality of A, either A3 or A4 must fail for $A[T]$. In fact, in order for $A[T]$ to be a LATS, diamond-extensionality implies that we must have $(s, e_1, s_1) \in T$ whenever a $(s, e_1, s_1) \sim (s_2, e_2, s_3)$ for some $(s_2, e_2, s_3) \in T$, i.e., by the hypothesis on γ, T should be $T_{\bar{e}}$. So A is event-maximal.

If γ is not iso, i.e., if there exist (s, e, s_1) and (s_2, e, s_3) such that $(s, e, s_1) \not\sim (s_2, e, s_3)$, then $T = \{(s, e', s') \mid (s, e', s') \sim (s, e, s_1)\} \subset T_e$ is a nonempty set for which the 'splitting' of e yields a lats, i.e., A is not event-maximal. □

4. Conclusion

Based on a comparison between the model of asynchronous transition systems (a model with explicitly defined events) and the model of transition systems with independence (a more abstract model, with a derived notion of events) carried out by the authors in [**10**], we have introduced the *transition systems with independence and multi-arcs* — a *conservative* and *minimal* extension of transition systems with independence that features multi-arcs — showing that the ability of asynchronous transition systems to model multi-arcs does not depend inherently on the choice of having explicitly given events.

Adding multi-arcs to transition systems with independence constitutes a valuable enhancement to the model, which allows to model important situations in which multiple transitions between the same states represent different events with different causal histories.

Investigating the relationship between the category of transition systems with independence and multi-arcs and the category of labeled asynchronous transition systems that matches the one in [**10**], we have shown that the former is *coreflective* in the category of *diamond-extensional* labeled asynchronous transition systems, which intuitively are those transition systems that make no confusion about the identities of the events carried by transitions facing each other in independence-diamonds. This coreflection provides a way to translate semantics forth and back between the two models. Finally, we have identified the *event-maximal* labeled asynchronous transition systems as the largest class of asynchronous transition systems for which the coreflection cuts down to an *equivalence*, so providing a precise characterisation of transition systems with independence and multi-arcs in terms of labeled asynchronous transition systems.

The analysis carried out in this paper helps in deciding when it is necessary to move to a more 'intensional' framework (a lower level of abstraction) in which further distinctions of events are introduced by assigning them explicitly. The definition of transition systems with independence and multi-arcs raises the threshold by allowing a derived notion of event also when multi-arcs are required.

References

[1] M.A. BEDNARCZYK, *Categories of Asynchronous Systems*. PhD thesis in Computer Science, University of Sussex (1988), report n. 1/88.

[2] J.M.C. BAETEN AND W.P. WEIJLAND, *Process Algebra*. Cambridge Tracts in Theoretical Computer Science, 18 (1990), Cambridge University Press.

[3] G. CATTANI AND V. SASSONE, Higher Dimensional Transition Systems, *Proceedings of LICS'96*, IEEE Computer Society Press (1996), 55–62.

[4] R. VAN GLABBEEK, *Bisimulations for higher dimensional automata*, email message sent to the *Concurrency* mailing list on July 7, 1991. Available at `http://theory.stanford.edu/people/rvg/hda`.

[5] R. VAN GLABBEEK AND G. PLOTKIN, Configuration Structures, *Proceedings of LICS'95*, IEEE Computer Society Press (1995), 99–109.

[6] E. GOUBAULT, Domains of Higher-Dimensional Automata, *Proceedings of CONCUR'93*, E. Best (Ed.), LNCS 715 (1993), Springer-Verlag, 293–307.

[7] E. GOUBAULT AND T. JENSEN, Homology of Higher-Dimensional Automata, *Proceedings of CONCUR'92*, W.R. Cleaveland (Ed.), LNCS 630 (1992), Springer-Verlag, 254–268.

[8] P. GODEFROID AND P. WOLPER, Using Partial Orders for the Efficient Verification of Deadlock Freedom and Safety Properties, *Proceedings of CAV'91*, K.G. Larsen *et al.* (Eds.), LNCS 575 (1991), Springer-Verlag, 332–342.

[9] M. HENNESSY, *Algebraic Theory of Processes*. Series in the Foundations of Computing (1988), The MIT Press.

[10] T.T. HILDEBRANDT AND V. SASSONE, Comparing Transition Systems with Independence and Asynchronous Transition Systems, *Proceedings of CONCUR'96*, U. Montanari and V. Sassone (Eds.), LNCS 1119 (1996), Springer-Verlag, 84–97.

[11] C.A.R. HOARE, *Communicating Sequential Processes*. Series in Computer Science (1985), Prentice-Hall.

[12] R. MILNER, *Communication and Concurrency*. Series in Computer Science (1989), Prentice Hall.

[13] R. MILNER, *The polyadic π-calculus: a tutorial*. In *Logic and Algebra of Specification*, F.L. Bauer *et al.* (Eds.), Springer-Verlag (1993), 203–246.

[14] M. MUKUND, Petri Nets and Step Transition Systems. *International Journal of Foundations of Computer Science*, vol. 3, n. 4 (1992), 443–478.

[15] M. MUKUND AND M. NIELSEN, CCS, Locations and Asynchronous Transition Systems, *Proceedings of FST & TCS'92*, R. Shyamasundar (Ed.), LNCS n. 652 (1992), Springer-Verlag, 328–341.

[16] M. NIELSEN, V. SASSONE AND G. WINSKEL, Relationships between Models of Concurrency, *Proceedings of REX'93. A Decade of Concurrency: Reflections and Perspectives*, LNCS n. 803 (1994), J.W. de Bakker *et al.* (Eds.), Springer-Verlag, 425–476.

[17] D. PELED, All from One, One for All: On Model Checking Using Representatives, *Proceedings of CAV'93*, C. Courcoubetis (Ed.), LNCS n. 697 (1993), Springer-Verlag, 409–423.

[18] V. PRATT, Modelling Concurrency with Geometry, *Proceedings of 18th ACM Symposium on Principles of Programming Languages*, ACM Press (1991), 311–322.

[19] V. SASSONE, M. NIELSEN, AND G. WINSKEL, Models for Concurrency: Towards a Classification. To appear in *Theoretical Computer Science*. An extended abstract appears as 'A Classification of Models for Concurrency' in *Proceedings of CONCUR'93*, E. Best (Ed.), LNCS 715 (1993), Springer-Verlag, 82–96.

[20] M.W. SHIELDS, Concurrent machines. *Theoretical Computer Science* n. 28 (1985), 449–465.

[21] A. VALMARI, A Stubborn attack on state explosion, *Proceedings of CAV'90*, DIMACS Series n. 3 (1991), 25–42.

[22] G. WINSKEL AND M. NIELSEN, Models for Concurrency. In *Handbook of Logic and the Foundations of Computer Science*, vol. IV, S. Abramsky *et al.* (Eds.), Oxford University Press (1995).

BRICS – BASIC RESEARCH IN COMPUTER SCIENCE, CENTRE OF THE DANISH NATIONAL RESEARCH FOUNDATION, COMPUTER SCIENCE DEPT., UNIVERSITY OF AARHUS, NY MUNKEGADE BLD. 540, DK-8000 AARHUS C, DENMARK

E-mail address: `hilde@brics.dk`

DIPARTIMENTO DI INFORMATICA, UNIVERSITÀ DI PISA, CORSO ITALIA 40, I-56125 PISA, ITALY

E-mail address: `vs@di.unipi.it`

DIMACS Series in Discrete Mathematics
and Theoretical Computer Science
Volume **29**, 1997

On the Costs and Benefits of using Partial-Order Methods for the Verification of Concurrent Systems (Invited Paper)

Patrice Godefroid

ABSTRACT. Verification by state-space exploration is one of the most successful strategies for analyzing the correctness of finite-state concurrent reactive systems. Partial-order methods are algorithms for dynamically pruning the state space of such systems without incurring the risk of any incompleteness in the verification results. This paper presents results of experiments performed with these algorithms on real protocol examples, and discusses the practical significance of partial-order methods.

1. Introduction

State-space exploration is one of the most successful strategies for checking the correctness of finite-state concurrent reactive systems. It consists in exploring a global state graph, called the *state space*, representing the combined behavior of all concurrent components in the system. Many different types of properties of a system can be checked by exploring its state space: deadlocks, dead code, unspecified receptions, violations of user-specified assertions, etc. Moreover, the range of properties that state-space exploration techniques can verify has been substantially broadened during the last decade thanks to the development of model-checking methods for various temporal logics (e.g., [**CES86, LP85, QS81, VW86**]).

The main limit of this approach to verification is the often excessive size of the state space. Owing to simple combinatorics, this size can be exponential in the size of the description of the system being analyzed. This exponential growth is known as the *state-explosion problem.* The state-explosion problem is due, among other causes, to the modeling of concurrency by interleaving, or, more accurately, to the exploration of all possible interleavings of concurrent events. For instance, the execution of n concurrent events is investigated by exploring all $n!$ interleavings of these events.

Recently, a collection of verification techniques, referred to as *"partial-order methods"*, have demonstrated that exploring *all* interleavings of concurrent events is not a priori necessary for verification. Indeed, interleavings corresponding to the same concurrent execution contain related information. The intuition behind partial-order methods is that concurrent executions are really partial orders and that expanding such a partial order into the set of *all* its interleavings is an inefficient

1991 *Mathematics Subject Classification.* Primary 68Q05, 68Q60; Secondary 03B70.

way of analyzing concurrent executions. Instead, concurrent events should be left unordered since the order of their occurrence is irrelevant. Hence the name "partial-order methods". However, rather than choosing to work with direct representations of partial orders, these algorithms keep to an interleaving representation of partial orders, but attempt to limit the expansion of each partial-order computation to just *one* of its interleavings, instead of all of them. Precisely, given a property φ, partial-order methods explore only a reduced part of the global state space that is provably sufficient to check the given property. The difference between the reduced and the global state spaces is that not all interleavings of concurrent events are systematically represented in the reduced one. In what follows, we call "partial-order method" any algorithm for generating such a reduced state space.

Partial-order methods as defined above first appeared independently in [**Val88a, Val88b**] and [**God90, GW91b**], and were developed further in [**Val90, GW91a, GHP92, HGP92, GP93, Pel93, Val93, WG93, GKPP94, HP94, Pel94**]. A detailed comparison of the results published in these papers is available in [**God96**]. Partial-order methods are now used in several existing verification tools, and have been tested on numerous real-protocol examples (e.g., see [**GHP92, HGP92, HP94, GPS96**]).

Of course, it has been recognized for some time before the early 90's that concurrency and nondeterminism are not the same thing. This observation has actually inspired a fairly large body of work on so-called "partial-order models" of concurrency (e.g., [**Lam78, Maz86, Pra86, Win86**]). Work in this area studies various semantics for concurrency, and compares their properties. Also, partial-order temporal logics (e.g., [**PW84, KP86, KP87, Pen88, Pen90**]) have been designed to be semantically more expressive than previously existing (linear-time and branching-time) temporal logics. In contrast, partial-order methods yields results identical to those of verification methods based on classical interleaving semantics, they just make it possible to perform the verification more efficiently.

Several approximate methods based on simple heuristics have been proposed to restrict the number of interleavings that are explored [**GH85, Wes86, Hol87**]. These heuristics carry with them the risk of incomplete verification results, i.e., they can detect errors but cannot prove the absence of errors. In contrast, partial-order methods reduce the number of interleavings that must be inspected in a completely reliable manner, provably without the risk of any incompleteness in the verification results.

Strategies for proving properties of concurrent systems without considering all possible interleavings of their concurrent actions have been proposed in [**AFdR80, EF82, Pnu85, SdR89, KP92b, JZ93**]. These proof methods are applied in the context of an inference system, in which the correctness of a system is established by proving assertions about its components. This approach to verification has the advantage of not being restricted to finite-state systems. On the other hand, it requires proofs that are manual. Even with the help of a theorem prover, carrying out proofs with a theorem prover is far from fully automatic since most steps of the proof require inventive interventions from the user. In contrast, the focus of the partial-order methods we discuss in this paper is purely on algorithmic issues, since we discuss fully-automatic state-space exploration techniques.

The idea that the cost of modeling concurrency by interleaving can be avoided in finite-state verification also appeared in [**JK90, PL90, McM92, Esp94**]. In [**JK90**], the problem of finding an "optimal" reduced state space with just enough transitions and states to preserve Mazurkiewicz's trace semantics is addressed. In [**PL90**], a method that relies on a pomset grammar description of the system is introduced. Also, in [**McM92, Esp94**], one finds a verification method that works by unfolding a Petri net description of a concurrent system into a finite acyclic structure. These methods are quite different from those discussed in this work. Note that so far none of these other methods have been widely experimented on a large set of realistic examples, as it has been the case for the partial-order methods discussed here.

2. Basic Notions

Consider a concurrent system composed of several processes. Let us assume that the system is represented by a set δ of *system transitions*, specified for instance in some guarded-command modeling language. The choice of a particular modeling language and semantics is not essential for the following discussion. What matters is that it is possible to compute from δ a global transition system A_G (or "global state space") representing the joint behavior of all the processes in the system. For the sake of simplicity, we will assume that each transition of A_G corresponds to the execution of one system transition $t \in \delta$.[1] We will write $s \xrightarrow{t} s'$ to mean that the execution of the transition $t \in \delta$ leads the system from the state s of A_G to the state s' of A_G, and $s \stackrel{w}{\Rightarrow} s'$ to mean that the execution of the sequence $w \in \delta^*$ of transitions leads from s to s'.

The basic idea that enables us to check properties of A_G without constructing the whole of A_G is the following: A_G contains many paths that correspond simply to different execution orders of the same system transitions. If these transitions are "independent", for instance because they are executed by noninteracting processes, then changing their order will not modify their combined effect.

This notion of independency between transitions and its complementary notion, the notion of dependency, can be formalized by the following definition (adapted from [**KP92a**]).

DEFINITION 2.1. Let δ be the set of system transitions and $D \subseteq \delta \times \delta$ be a binary, reflexive, and symmetric relation. The relation D is a *valid dependency relation* for the system iff for all $t_1, t_2 \in \delta$, $(t_1, t_2) \notin D$ (t_1 and t_2 are independent) implies that the two following properties hold for all global states s in the global state space A_G of the system:

1. if t_1 is enabled in s and $s \xrightarrow{t_1} s'$, then t_2 is enabled in s iff t_2 is enabled in s' (independent transitions can neither disable nor enable each other); and
2. if t_1 and t_2 are enabled in s, then there is a unique state s' such that $s \stackrel{t_1 t_2}{\Rightarrow} s'$ and $s \stackrel{t_2 t_1}{\Rightarrow} s'$ (commutativity of enabled independent transitions).

This definition characterizes the properties of possible "valid" dependency relations for the transitions of a given system. Note that it is not practical to check the two properties listed above for all pairs of transitions for all states in order to determine which transitions are independent and which are not. Therefore, in practice, one uses easily checkable syntactic conditions that are sufficient for transitions to be independent. See [**God96**] for a detailed presentation of that topic.

[1] Transitions are assumed to be deterministic: the execution of a transition t in a state s leads to a *unique* successor state. This is not a restriction since "nondeterministic transitions" can always be modeled by a set of deterministic transitions with non mutually exclusive guards.

Following the work of Mazurkiewicz [**Maz86**], one can use the notion of independent transitions to define an equivalence relation on sequences of transitions: two sequences of transitions are equivalent if they can be obtained from each other by successively permuting adjacent independent transitions. Thus, given an independency relation, sequences of transitions can be grouped into equivalence classes which Mazurkiewicz calls traces. It is easy to see that sequences of transitions w_1 and w_2 belonging to the same trace lead to the same state of A_G. This property is basically what will allow us to only explore part of the global state space A_G: to determine if a state is reachable by a trace, it is sufficient to explore *one* transition sequence corresponding to that trace.

It might thus appear that we are using Mazurkiewicz's trace semantics. This is not really so. Indeed, to view Mazurkiewicz's theory as a semantics, the independency relation should be considered as part of the semantics: given an independency relation, one can determine the Mazurkiewicz semantics of a system. The criterion for a partial construction of the state-space would then be that the Mazurkiewicz semantics are preserved. Here a less restrictive point of view is taken. The semantic criterion is that the result of checking a property in the class of interest should be the same as if checking the property on A_G. The link with Mazurkiewicz's semantics is only in the fact that the algorithms presented in the next section rely on the concept of independency and on the properties it implies. With some algorithms, it is even possible to use definitions of independence that are weaker than the one of Definition 2.1 (e.g., [**GP93, God96**]).

3. The Algorithms

In this section, we present the basic algorithmic ideas used in the style of partial-order verification methods we are considering. For simplicity, we only consider the problem of detecting terminating (deadlock) states. In order to check for properties more elaborate than deadlocks (such as arbitrary safety properties or linear-time temporal-logic formulas), it is usually necessary to preserve more information in the reduced state space A_R, i.e, to explore more states and transitions. This is done by enforcing additional conditions that have to be satisfied during the generation of A_R. We refer the reader to [**God96**] for a detailed comparison of the various techniques that have been proposed to address this problem.

The specification of the algorithms we discuss here is thus that they should find all states of A_G with no outgoing transitions while exploring as small a fraction as possible of A_G. All the partial-order algorithms follow the same basic pattern: they operate as classical state-space searches except that, at each state s reached during the search, they compute a subset T of the set of transitions enabled at s and explore only the transitions in T, the other enabled transitions are not explored. We call such a search a *selective search*. It is easy to see that a selective search through A_G only reaches a subset (not necessarily proper) of the states and transitions of A_G.

Two main techniques for computing such sets T have been proposed in the literature. The first technique actually corresponds to a whole family of algorithms [**Ove81, Val91, GW91b, GP93**]. It is shown in [**God96**] that all these algorithms (including Valmari's algorithms for computing "strong stubborn sets") compute *persistent sets*. The second type of technique is the sleep set technique (e.g., [**GW93**]). Interestingly, these two techniques are compatible and can be used simultaneously to further improve the selection of the set T. We first describe persistent-set techniques.

Intuitively, a subset T of the set of transitions enabled in a state s of A_G is called *persistent in s* if all transitions not in T that are enabled in s, or in a state reachable from s through transitions not in T, are independent with all transitions in T. In other words, whatever one does from s, while remaining outside of T, does not interact with or affect T. Formally, we have the following [**GP93**].

DEFINITION 3.1. A set T of transitions enabled in a state s is *persistent in s* iff, for all nonempty sequences of transitions

$$s = s_1 \xrightarrow{t_1} s_2 \xrightarrow{t_2} s_3 \ldots \xrightarrow{t_{n-1}} s_n \xrightarrow{t_n} s_{n+1}$$

from s in A_G and including only transitions $t_i \notin T$, $1 \leq i \leq n$, t_n is independent with all transitions in T.

Note that the set of all enabled transitions in a state s is trivially persistent since nothing is reachable from s by transitions that are not in this set. Persistent sets are very similar, although not equivalent, to the "faithful decompositions" introduced (independently) in [**KP92b**] and to the "ample sets" used in [**Pel93**].

Let a *persistent-set selective search* be a selective search through A_G which, in each state s that it reaches, explores only a set T of enabled transitions that is persistent in s, and that is nonempty if there exist transitions enabled in s. It is easy to prove that a persistent-set selective search started from the initial state of A_G will explore all deadlocks of A_G [**God96**].

Of course, the key element required for the implementation of a persistent-set selective search is an algorithm for computing persistent sets. Such algorithms [**Ove81, Val91, GW91b, GP93**] infer the persistent sets from the static structure (code) of the system being verified. They differ by the type of information about the representation of the system that they use (e.g., "distinguishing between internal and global transitions", "which process can access which variable", "which process can access which variable from its current location", etc.). The aim of these algorithms is to obtain the smallest possible persistent sets. Usually, the more information about the program the algorithm uses, the smallest the persistent set it produces are, albeit at the cost of a higher computational complexity. See [**God96**] for a detailed comparison of these algorithms and of their complexity. Note that exploring the smallest number of enabled transitions at each step of the search is only a heuristic: it does not necessary lead to the exploration of the smallest number of states in A_R.

The second technique for computing the set of transitions T to consider in a selective search is the sleep set technique [**GW93**] introduced in [**God90**]. This technique does not exploit information about the static structure (code) of the program, but rather about the past of the search. Used alone it reduces the number of transitions explored, but not the number of states [**God96**], which can still be very useful as we will see in Section 6. Used in conjunction with a persistent set technique it can further reduce the number of states explored. Indeed, when the persistent set technique cannot avoid the selection of *independent* transitions in a state, sleep sets can avoid the exploration of multiple interleavings of these transitions. Again, we refer the reader to [**God96**] for a detailed presentation of the sleep set algorithm and of its complexity.

4. How Can Partial-Order Methods Be Evaluated?

How much can one gain by using these algorithms? It is very difficult to give a general answer. Indeed, one can quite easily construct families of systems for which nothing is gained whatsoever. Examples of such systems are systems where the coupling between the processes is so tight that two independent transitions are never simultaneously enabled. (The system is in fact purely sequential.) In this case, partial-order methods yield no reduction, and the selective search becomes equivalent to a classical exhaustive search.

On the other hand, it is also easy to construct systems for which the growth of the state space when the number of processes in the system increases is reduced from exponential to polynomial by a selective search. This is the case, for instance, for the well-known dining-philosophers example [**Val88a**]. Going one step further, it is also possible to find examples of systems for which the global state space increases in size when the value of some parameter grows, while the reduced state space remains the same. See Chapter 8 of [**God96**] for such an example.

Clearly, by a biased choice of examples, an arbitrarily exaggerated impression of the improvements could thus be suggested. For instance, by setting the number of philosophers to a sufficiently large number, we can claim that we can verify properties of systems with astronomical numbers of states, like 10^{20} states as in [**BCM$^+$90**], or even systems with infinite numbers of states. Of course, this should be taken with a grain of salt since the fact that checking only a small part of such enormous state spaces is sufficient only indicates that most of the states in the global state space are uninteresting. This observation leads us to the following conclusion: the number of states in the global state space of a system does not give a good measure of its "complexity".

Along the same line of thought, the study of the asymptotic behavior of the function giving the number of states for different numbers of processes in a system is only of limited practical interest. Indeed, state-space exploration techniques are rarely used to verify systems composed of tens of identical processes. For such systems, it is preferable to use other verification techniques specially tailored for proving properties of systems with undefined numbers of participants (e.g., [**KM89, WL89**]).

Consequently, experiments with realistic examples, including industrial-size ones, appear to be the most informative approach to evaluating partial-order verification methods.

5. Evaluation

In order to perform experiments on complex concurrent systems, we have implemented a selective search algorithm using persistent sets and sleep sets in an add-on package for the protocol verification system SPIN [**Hol91**]. SPIN is a verification tool for communication protocols described in the Promela language. Promela is a nondeterministic guarded-command language. Promela defines systems of asynchronously executing concurrent processes that can interact via shared variables and message channels. Interaction via message channels can be either synchronous (i.e., by rendez-vous) or asynchronous (buffered) with arbitrary (user-specified) buffer capacities, and arbitrary numbers of message parameters. These different types of communication can be combined. Given a concurrent system described by a Promela program, SPIN can verify properties of the system by performing a depth-first search in the global state space of the system.

The partial-order package for SPIN that we have developed is available free of charge for educational and research purposes by anonymous ftp from ftp.montefiore.ulg.ac.be in the /pub/po-package directory. More information on the partial-order package can be found in the README file in this directory.

The partial-order package has been tested on various examples of protocols. The aim of these experiments was to determine the type of reduction that can be expected on real protocol examples when using the partial-order verification algorithms, and to evaluate the respective impact of these algorithms on the reduction obtained. In this Section, results obtained with four sample protocols are detailed.

- PFTP is a file transfer protocol presented in Chapter 14 of [**Hol91**], modeled in 206 lines of Promela. It consists of three processes communicating via FIFO channels.
- MULOG3 is a model of a mutual exclusion algorithm presented in [**TN87**], for 3 participants, modeled in 97 lines of Promela. It consists of six processes communicating via FIFO channels and shared variables.
- ABRA is a model of the Abracadabra protocol presented in [**Tur93**], modeled in 168 lines of Promela. It consists of four processes communicating via FIFO channels.
- DTP is a data transfer protocol, modeled in 406 lines of Promela. It consists of three processes communicating via FIFO channels.

We report here experiments performed using four different algorithms.

- DFS denotes an exhaustive search performed in a depth-first order.
- SLEEP denotes a selective search using sleep sets.
- PS denotes a selective search using persistent sets.
- PS+SLEEP denotes a selective search using both persistent sets and sleep sets.

Results of these experiments are presented in Table 1. All experiments were performed on a SPARC2 workstation with 64 Megabytes of RAM, using the Partial-Order Package version 3.0. For each run, the numbers of visited states and traversed transitions are given. Time (in seconds) is user time plus system time as reported by the UNIX-system time command. All visited states are stored in a hash table. To avoid significant run-time penalties for disk-access, visited states can only be stored in randomly accessed memory, i.e., in the main memory available in the computer on which the experiments are performed. Consequently, parameter settings in all the protocols considered were chosen to produce global state spaces that can easily be stored in 64 Megabytes of RAM. For each run, the amount of memory used is directly proportional to the number of stored states.

From the numbers given in Table 1, two main observations can be made concerning the respective impact of persistent sets and sleep sets on the reduction obtained.

- *Persistent Sets yield the most important reductions on the number of visited states. They can also yield good reductions on the number of explored transitions.*
- *Sleep sets yield a less impressive reduction on the number of visited states, but yield very good reductions on the number of explored transitions.*

Protocol	Algorithm	Stored States	Transitions	Time
PFTP	DFS	446,982	1,257,317	478.2
	SLEEP	446,982	622,364	639
	PS	276,722	482,722	662.7
	PS+SLEEP	249,994	351,633	684.7
MULOG3	DFS	38,181	111,668	25.3
	SLEEP	38,181	38,241	30.5
	PS	18,537	38,906	25.8
	PS+SLEEP	17,984	18,057	26
ABRA	DFS	149,816	372,010	494.2
	SLEEP	149,816	176,469	546
	PS	32,289	40,931	166.3
	PS+SLEEP	27,781	34,381	155.7
DTP	DFS	251,409	648,467	200.2
	SLEEP	251,409	269,912	189
	PS	9,904	10,351	11.3
	PS+SLEEP	9,904	10,351	11.5

TABLE 1. Evaluation

For all protocols, the best reductions can be obtained with PS+SLEEP, i.e., by using simultaneously persistent sets and sleep sets. Using persistent sets and sleep sets gives better reductions than using persistent sets alone in almost all cases. For DTP, persistent sets are so good in reducing the number of states and transitions that sleep sets are not able to improve this result.

These results show that using the partial-order methods discussed in this work is basically a no-risk improvement. In the worst case, when the reduction is not sufficient to make up the additional run time overhead (PFTP), the selective search can be slightly slower than a classical search, but the overall time complexity remains linear in the number of explored transitions.

Moreover, using partial-order methods can strongly decrease *both* the time and the memory resources needed to verify properties of concurrent systems (DTP). Therefore, they can be used to verify more complex protocols.

6. State-Space Caching

Another observation that can be made from the results given in Table 1 is the following: when using partial-order methods, and especially when using sleep sets, the number of state matchings, i.e., the number of visited transitions minus the number of visited states, strongly decreases. This phenomenon can be explained as follows [**GHP92**].

When performing a classical search (like DFS), almost all states in the state space of a concurrent system are typically visited several times. There are two causes for this:

1. From the initial state, the explorations of all interleavings of a single finite concurrent execution of the system always lead to the same state. This state will thus be visited several times because of all these interleavings.
2. From the initial state, explorations of different finite concurrent executions may lead to the same state.

When using partial-order methods, and especially when using sleep sets, most of the effects of the first cause given above can be avoided, and, in many cases, most of the states are visited *only once* during the selective search.

States that are visited only once do not need to be stored in memory. Indeed, the only reason why visited states are stored in memory is to avoid redundant explorations of parts of the state space: when a state that has already been visited is visited again later during the search, it is not necessary to revisit all its successors. Unfortunately, it is impossible to determine which states are visited only once before the search is completed. However, if most of the states are visited only once, the probability that a state will be visited again later during the search is very small, and the risk of double work when not storing an already visited state becomes very small as well. This enables one not to store most of the states that have already been visited without incurring too much redundant explorations of parts of the state space. The memory requirements can thus strongly decrease without seriously increasing the time requirements.

State-space caching [**Hol85, JJ91**] is a memory management technique for storing the states encountered during a depth-first search that consists in storing all the states of the current explored path (i.e., those in the current depth-first search "stack") plus as many other states as possible given the remaining amount of available memory. It thus creates a restricted *cache* of selected system states that have already been visited. Initially, all states encountered are stored into the cache. When the cache fills up, old states that are not in the stack are removed from the cache to accommodate new ones. This method never tries to store more states than possible in the cache. Thus, if the size of the cache is greater than the maximal size of the stack during the exploration, the search is not truncated, and eventually terminates.

We have implemented such a caching discipline in our partial-order package. The caching discipline can be used with any of the selective-search algorithms that were considered in the previous section. Results of experiments with different cache sizes and the algorithms DFS, PS, and PS+SLEEP for the MULOG3 protocol are presented in Figure 1. For each run, the run time is directly proportional to the number of explored transitions.

With DFS, these results clearly show that the size of the cache, i.e., the number of stored states, can be reduced to approximately the third of the total number of states in A_G without seriously affecting the number of explored transitions and hence the run time. If the cache is further reduced, the run time increases dramatically, due to redundant explorations of large parts of the state space. This run-time explosion makes state-space caching inefficient under a certain threshold.

With PS, this threshold can be reduced to approximately the eighth of the total number of states. This improvement is not very spectacular because the number of matched states, even when using PS, is still too important (see Table 1). The risk of double work when reaching an already visited state that has been removed from the cache is not reduced enough.

With PS+SLEEP, the situation is different: there is no run-time explosion anymore. Indeed, the number of matched states is reduced so much (see Table 1) that the risk of double work becomes very small. When the cache size is reduced up to the maximal depth of the search (this maximal depth is the lower bound for the cache size since all states of the stack are stored to ensure the termination of the search), the increase of the number of explored transitions is still less than 10%

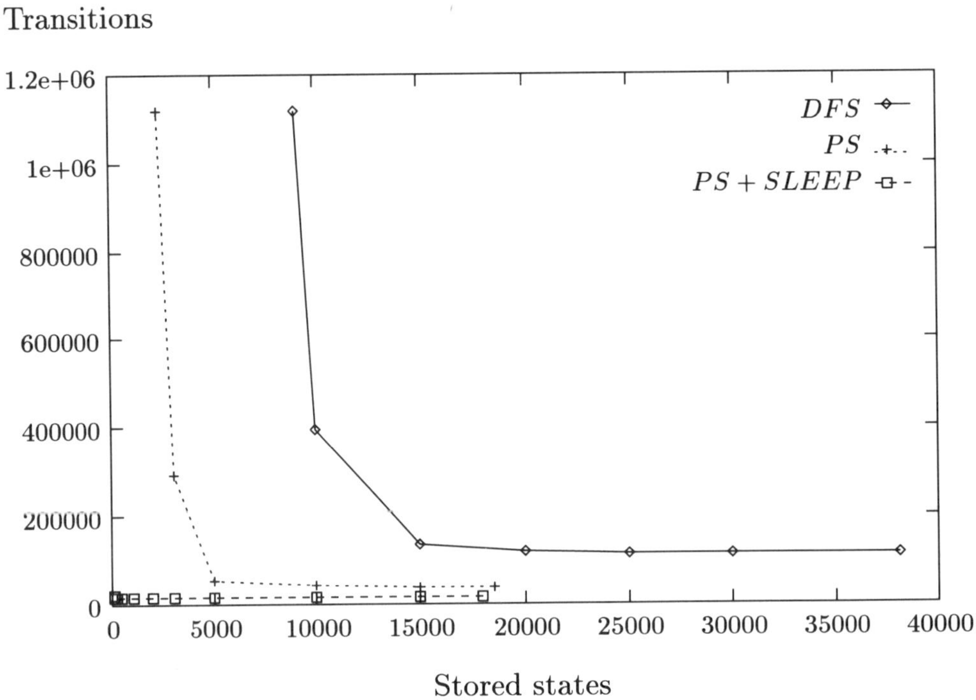

FIGURE 1. Performances of state-space caching for MULOG3

with respect to the number of transitions explored by PS+SLEEP when all visited states are stored in memory, i.e., without using state-space caching.

In other words, the MULOG3 protocol, which has 38,181 reachable states that can be visited by DFS in 25 seconds (see Table 1), can be analyzed with the same run time by using PS+SLEEP and state-space caching while storing no more than 150 states. *The memory requirements are reduced by a factor of 200 while the run time remains the same.*

Of course, the practical interest of this result is that *using partial-order methods and state-space caching together makes possible the complete exploration of very large state spaces*, that could not be explored so far.

For instance, consider two other versions of the MULOG protocol, denoted MULOG4 and MULOG5, with respectively four and five participants. Let PS+SLEEP+Caching denote a selective search using persistent sets, sleep sets, and state-space caching. Tables 2 and 3 present results of experiments performed on MULOG4 and MULOG5 with the algorithms DFS, PS+SLEEP, and PS+SLEEP+Caching. "Stored states" is the number of stored states at the end of the search. When state-space caching is used, the maximum number of stored states, i.e., the size of the cache, is limited to 300,000 states. (This number is approximately the maximum number of states that can be stored in RAM for MULOG4 and MULOG5 while still avoiding any paging.) "Cleared states" is the number of times a state was removed from the cache. "Matched states" is the number of state matchings that occurred during the search.

Algorithm	Stored St.	Cleared St.	Matched St.	Transitions	Time
DFS	–	–	–	–	–
PS+SLEEP	654,600	0	6,189	660,789	986.4 (2516.7)
PS+SLEEP+Caching	300,000	354,676	6,198	660,874	1122.6 (1184.4)

TABLE 2. Verification of MULOG4

Algorithm	Stored St.	Cleared St.	Matched St.	Transitions	Time
DFS	–	–	–	–	–
PS+SLEEP	–	–	–	–	–
PS+SLEEP+Caching	300,000	28,613,162	349,904	29,263,066	60,633.1

TABLE 3. Verification of MULOG5

For MULOG4, DFS was not able to complete its search, since its global state space is too large to be stored in (64 Megabytes of) memory. Using state-space caching with DFS does not help, because of the run time explosion mentioned above. MULOG4 can still be verified using PS+SLEEP, even without state-space caching. Real time as reported by the UNIX-system time command is given between parentheses below the run time (user time plus system time). The important difference between these two numbers for PS+SLEEP is due to paging (storing 654,600 states of MULOG4 requires more than 64 Megabytes of RAM, so some of them had to be stored on disk).

For MULOG5, the only algorithm that is able to completely verify the correctness of this protocol is PS+SLEEP+Caching. The complete selective search takes approximately 17 hours, and explores 29,263,066 transitions. This means that the *reduced* state space A_R explored by PS+SLEEP contains at most 29,263,066 states. The size of the global state space A_G of MULOG5 is not known, but is very likely several orders of magnitude larger than the largest state spaces that can be explored by other existing verification tools.

Note that the efficiency of the state-space caching technique can be dynamically estimated during the search: if the maximum stack size remains acceptable with respect to the cache size and if the proportion of matched states remains small enough, the run-time explosion will likely be avoided. Else one cannot predict if the cache size is large enough to avoid the run-time explosion.

7. Conclusion

Using partial-order methods is basically a no-risk improvement with respect to a classical exhaustive search in the state space of the system being analyzed. Moreover, partial-order methods can yield substantial improvements in the performances of the verification. Therefore, these methods broaden the applicability of state-space exploration techniques to more complex systems.

The reduction obtained depends on the coupling between the processes in the system. When the coupling is very tight, partial-order methods yield no reduction, and the selective search becomes equivalent to a classical exhaustive search. When the coupling between the processes is very loose, the reduction can be very impressive. For most realistic examples, partial-order methods provide a significant reduction of the memory and time requirements needed to verify protocols.

It is worth noticing that partial-order methods can already yield good performance improvements for verifying systems containing only a handful of processes. It is not necessary to consider systems composed of tens of processes to obtain spectacular reductions. To put it in another way, the part of the state explosion due to the exploration of all possible interleavings of independent transitions can already be very important for systems containing only a few processes, and partial-order methods are able to get rid of most of this explosion.

This very important point emphasizes the practical significance of partial-order methods. Indeed, most of the protocol models that are analyzed with state-space exploration techniques typically contain only a handful of processes. The examples we have considered in Section 5 reflect this reality. For instance, a typical protocol example is usually composed of a few processes that communicate asynchronously by exchanging messages through some communication medium, each process being described by a long piece of sequential code, with complex interactions between control and data.

Not only these systems are very frequent, but they are also very hard to verify: they are complex (several hundreds lines of (Promela) code are needed to model these systems), and their state spaces are highly irregular. Specifically, their state spaces seem to be much more irregular than, for instance, those of systems composed of many identical processes (or pieces of hardware), for which symbolic verification techniques are able to capture the regularity of the state space with the guidance of the user (see, e.g., [**BCM$^+$90, McM93**]). In contrast, for examples of the type we are considering here, existing symbolic verification techniques were reported to be inferior to classical state-space exploration algorithms [**HD93**]. Consequently, for this particular, though important, class of systems, partial-order methods are one of the most successful approaches to tackle the state explosion arising during the analysis of such systems.

Finally, we have shown that using partial-order methods, and especially using sleep sets, can substantially improve the state-space caching discipline by getting rid of the main cause of its previous inefficiency, namely prohibitive state matching due to the exploration of all possible interleavings of concurrent executions all leading to the same state. Thanks to sleep sets, the memory requirements needed to verify large *reduced* state spaces can be strongly decreased (several orders of magnitude) without seriously affecting the time requirements. This makes possible the complete exploration of very large reduced state spaces (several tens of million states) in a reasonable time (one night). Used together, partial-order methods and state-space caching significantly push back the limits of verification by state-space exploration.

Note

The results reported in this paper appeared in [**God96**].

References

[AFdR80] K. R. Apt, N. Francez, and W. P. de Roever. A proof system for communicating sequential processes. *ACM Transactions on Programming Languages and Systems*, 2:359–385, 1980.

[BCM+90] J.R. Burch, E.M. Clarke, K.L. McMillan, D.L. Dill, and L.J. Hwang. Symbolic model checking: 10^{20} states and beyond. In *Proceedings of the 5th Symposium on Logic in Computer Science*, pages 428–439, Philadelphia, June 1990.

[CES86] E.M. Clarke, E.A. Emerson, and A.P. Sistla. Automatic verification of finite-state concurrent systems using temporal logic specifications. *ACM Transactions on Programming Languages and Systems*, 8(2):244–263, January 1986.

[EF82] T. Elrad and N. Francez. Decomposition of distributed programs into communication closed layers. *Science of Computer Programming*, 2:155–173, 1982.

[Esp94] J. Esparza. Model checking using net unfoldings. *Science of Computer Programming*, 23:151–195, 1994.

[GH85] M. G. Gouda and J. Y. Han. Protocol validation by fair progress state exploration. *Computer Networks and ISDN systems*, pages 353–361, May 1985.

[GHP92] P. Godefroid, G. J. Holzmann, and D. Pirottin. State space caching revisited. In *Proc. 4th Workshop on Computer Aided Verification*, volume 663 of *Lecture Notes in Computer Science*, pages 178–191, Montreal, June 1992. Springer-Verlag.

[GKPP94] R. Gerth, R. Kuiper, D. Peled, and W. Penczek. A partial order approach to branching time model checking. Proceedings of the Third Israel Symposium on Theory of Computing and Systems, 1994.

[God90] P. Godefroid. Using partial orders to improve automatic verification methods. In *Proc. 2nd Workshop on Computer Aided Verification*, volume 531 of *Lecture Notes in Computer Science*, pages 176–185, Rutgers, June 1990. Springer-Verlag. Extended version in ACM/AMS DIMACS Series, volume 3, pages 321–340, 1991.

[God96] Patrice Godefroid. *Partial-Order Methods for the Verification of Concurrent Systems – An Approach to the State-Explosion Problem*, volume 1032 of *Lecture Notes in Computer Science*. Springer-Verlag, January 1996.

[GP93] P. Godefroid and D. Pirottin. Refining dependencies improves partial-order verification methods. In *Proc. 5th Conference on Computer Aided Verification*, volume 697 of *Lecture Notes in Computer Science*, pages 438–449, Elounda, June 1993. Springer-Verlag.

[GPS96] P. Godefroid, D. Peled, and M. Staskauskas. Using partial-order methods in the formal validation of industrial concurrent programs. In *Proceedings of ISSTA'96 (International Symposium on Software Testing and Analysis)*, pages 261–269, San Diego, January 1996.

[GW91a] P. Godefroid and P. Wolper. A partial approach to model checking. In *Proceedings of the 6th IEEE Symposium on Logic in Computer Science*, pages 406–415, Amsterdam, July 1991.

[GW91b] P. Godefroid and P. Wolper. Using partial orders for the efficient verification of deadlock freedom and safety properties. In *Proc. 3rd Workshop on Computer Aided Verification*, volume 575 of *Lecture Notes in Computer Science*, pages 332–342, Aalborg, July 1991.

[GW93] P. Godefroid and P. Wolper. Using partial orders for the efficient verification of deadlock freedom and safety properties. *Formal Methods in System Design*, 2(2):149–164, April 1993.

[HD93] A. J. Hu and D. L. Dill. Efficient verification with bdds using implicitly conjoined invariants. In *Proc. 5th Conference on Computer Aided Verification*, volume 697 of *Lecture Notes in Computer Science*, pages 3–14, Elounda, June 1993. Springer-Verlag.

[HGP92] G. J. Holzmann, P. Godefroid, and D. Pirottin. Coverage preserving reduction strategies for reachability analysis. In *Proc. 12th IFIP WG 6.1 International Symposium on Protocol Specification, Testing, and Verification*, pages 349–363, Lake Buena Vista, Florida, June 1992. North-Holland.

[Hol85] G. J. Holzmann. Tracing protocols. *AT&T Technical Journal*, 64(12):2413–2434, 1985.

[Hol87] G. J. Holzmann. Automated protocol validation in argos — assertion proving and scatter searching. *IEEE Trans. on Software Engineering*, 13(6):683–696, 1987.

[Hol91] G. J. Holzmann. *Design and Validation of Computer Protocols*. Prentice Hall, 1991.

[HP94] G. J. Holzmann and D. Peled. An improvement in formal verification. In *Proc. FORTE'94*, pages 177–191, Bern, 1994.

[JJ91] C. Jard and Th. Jeron. Bounded-memory algorithms for verification on-the-fly. In *Proc. 3rd Workshop on Computer Aided Verification*, volume 575 of *Lecture Notes in Computer Science*, Aalborg, July 1991. Springer-Verlag.

[JK90] R. Janicki and M. Koutny. On some implementation of optimal simulations. In *Proc. 2nd Workshop on Computer Aided Verification*, volume 531 of *Lecture Notes in Computer Science*, pages 166–175, Rutgers, June 1990. Springer-Verlag.

[JZ93] W. Janssen and J. Zwiers. Specifying and proving communication closedness in protocols. In *Proc. 13th IFIP WG 6.1 International Symposium on Protocol Specification, Testing, and Verification*, pages 323–339, Liège, May 1993. North-Holland.

[KM89] R. P. Kurshan and K. McMillan. A structural induction theorem for processes. In *Proceedings of the Eigth ACM Symposium on Principles of Distributed Computing*, pages 239–248, Edmonton, Alberta, August 1989.

[KP86] Y. Kornatzky and S. S. Pinter. A model checker for partial order temporal logic. EE PUB 597, Department of Electrical Enginering, Technion-Israel Institute of Technology, 1986.

[KP87] S. Katz and D. Peled. Interleaving set temporal logic. In *Proc. 6th ACM Symp. on Principles of Distributed Computing*, pages 178–190, Vancouver, August 1987.

[KP92a] S. Katz and D. Peled. Defining conditional independence using collapses. *Theoretical Computer Science*, 101:337–359, 1992.

[KP92b] S. Katz and D. Peled. Verification of distributed programs using representative interleaving sequences. *Distributed Computing*, 6:107–120, 1992.

[Lam78] L. Lamport. Time, clocks, and the ordering of events in a distributed system. *Communications of the ACM*, 21(7):558–564, 1978.

[LP85] O. Lichtenstein and A. Pnueli. Checking that finite state concurrent programs satisfy their linear specification. In *Proceedings of the Twelfth ACM Symposium on Principles of Programming Languages*, pages 97–107, New Orleans, January 1985.

[Maz86] A. Mazurkiewicz. Trace theory. In *Petri Nets: Applications and Relationships to Other Models of Concurrency, Advances in Petri Nets 1986, Part II; Proceedings of an Advanced Course*, volume 255 of *Lecture Notes in Computer Science*, pages 279–324. Springer-Verlag, 1986.

[McM92] K. McMillan. Using unfolding to avoid the state explosion problem in the verification of asynchronous circuits. In *Proc. 4th Workshop on Computer Aided Verification*, volume 663 of *Lecture Notes in Computer Science*, pages 164–177, Montreal, June 1992. Springer-Verlag.

[McM93] K. L. McMillan. *Symbolic Model Checking.* Kluwer Academic Publishers, 1993.

[Ove81] W. T. Overman. *Verification of Concurrent Systems: Function and Timing.* PhD thesis, University of California Los Angeles, 1981.

[Pel93] D. Peled. All from one, one for all: on model checking using representatives. In *Proc. 5th Conference on Computer Aided Verification*, volume 697 of *Lecture Notes in Computer Science*, pages 409–423, Elounda, June 1993. Springer-Verlag.

[Pel94] D. Peled. Combining partial order reductions with on-the-fly model-checking. In *Proc. 6th Conference on Computer Aided Verification*, volume 818 of *Lecture Notes in Computer Science*, pages 377–390, Stanford, June 1994. Springer-Verlag.

[Pen88] W. Penczek. A temporal logic for event structures. *Fundamenta Informaticae*, 11(3):297–326, 1988.

[Pen90] W. Penczek. Proving partial order properties using CCTL. Proc. Concurrency and Compositionality Workshop, San Miniato, Italy, 1990.

[PL90] D. K. Probst and H. F. Li. Using partial-order semantics to avoid the state explosion problem in asynchronous systems. In *Proc. 2nd Workshop on Computer Aided Verification*, volume 531 of *Lecture Notes in Computer Science*, pages 146–155, Rutgers, June 1990. Springer-Verlag.

[Pnu85] A. Pnueli. Applications of temporal logic to the specification and verification of reactive systems: A survey of current trends. In *Proc. Advanced School on Current Trends in Concurrency*, volume 224 of *Lecture Notes in Computer Science*, pages 510–584, Berlin, 1985. Springer-Verlag.

[Pra86] V. Pratt. Modelling concurrency with partial orders. *International Journal of Parallel Programming*, 15(1):33–71, 1986.

[PW84] S. S. Pinter and P. Wolper. A temporal logic for reasoning about partially ordered computations. In *Proc. 3rd ACM Symposium on Principles of Distributed Computing*, pages 28–37, Vancouver, 1984.

[QS81] J.P. Quielle and J. Sifakis. Specification and verification of concurrent systems in CESAR. In *Proc. 5th Int'l Symp. on Programming*, volume 137 of *Lecture Notes in Computer Science*, pages 337–351. Springer-Verlag, 1981.

[SdR89] F. A. Stomp and W. P. de Roever. Designing distributed algorithms by means of formal sequentially phased reasoning. In *Proc. 3rd International Workshop on Distributed Algorithms*, volume 392 of *Lecture Notes in Computer Science*, pages 242–253, Nice, 1989. Springer-Verlag.

[TN87] M. Trehel and M. Naimi. Un algorithme distribué d'exclusion mutuelle en log(n). *Technique et Science Informatiques*, pages 141–150, 1987.

[Tur93] K. J. Turner et al. *Using Formal Description Techniques – An Introduction to Estelle, Lotos and SDL*. Wiley, 1993.

[Val88a] A. Valmari. Error detection by reduced reachability graph generation. In *Proc. 9th International Conference on Application and Theory of Petri Nets*, pages 95–112, Venice, 1988.

[Val88b] A. Valmari. Heuristics for lazy state generation speeds up analysis of concurrent systems. In *Proc. of the Finnish Artificial Intelligence Symposium STeP-88*, volume 2, pages 640–650, Helsinki, 1988.

[Val90] A. Valmari. A stubborn attack on state explosion. In *Proc. 2nd Workshop on Computer Aided Verification*, volume 531 of *Lecture Notes in Computer Science*, pages 156–165, Rutgers, June 1990. Springer-Verlag.

[Val91] A. Valmari. Stubborn sets for reduced state space generation. In *Advances in Petri Nets 1990*, volume 483 of *Lecture Notes in Computer Science*, pages 491–515. Springer-Verlag, 1991.

[Val93] A. Valmari. On-the-fly verification with stubborn sets. In *Proc. 5th Conference on Computer Aided Verification*, volume 697 of *Lecture Notes in Computer Science*, pages 397–408, Elounda, June 1993. Springer-Verlag.

[VW86] M.Y. Vardi and P. Wolper. An automata-theoretic approach to automatic program verification. In *Proceedings of the First Symposium on Logic in Computer Science*, pages 322–331, Cambridge, June 1986.

[Wes86] C. H. West. Protocol validation by random state exploration. In *Proc. 6th IFIP WG 6.1 International Symposium on Protocol Specification, Testing, and Verification*, pages 233–242. North-Holland, 1986.

[WG93] P. Wolper and P. Godefroid. Partial-order methods for temporal verification (invited paper). In *Proc. CONCUR'93*, volume 715 of *Lecture Notes in Computer Science*, pages 233–246, Hildesheim, August 1993. Springer-Verlag.

[Win86] G. Winskel. Event structures. In *Petri Nets: Applications and Relationships to Other Models of Concurrency, Advances in Petri Nets 1986, Part II; Proceedings of an Advanced Course*, volume 255 of *Lecture Notes in Computer Science*, pages 325–392. Springer-Verlag, 1986.

[WL89] P. Wolper and V. Lovinfosse. Verifying properties of large sets of processes with network invariants. In *Automatic Verification Methods for Finite State Systems, Proc. Int. Workshop, Grenoble*, volume 407 of *Lecture Notes in Computer Science*, pages 68–80, Grenoble, June 1989. Springer-Verlag.

Bell Laboratories, Lucent Technologies, 1000 E. Warrenville Road, Naperville, IL 60566, U.S.A.

E-mail address: god@bell-labs.com

DIMACS Series in Discrete Mathematics
and Theoretical Computer Science
Volume 29, 1997

Partial Order Verification with PEP*

Eike Best

Institut für Informatik, Universität Hildesheim,
Marienburger Platz 22, D-31141 Hildesheim, Germany
Fax: +49 5121 860475, email: e.best@informatik.uni-hildesheim.de

(August 1996)

Abstract

This paper describes the current status of the verification testbed PEP (Programming Environment based on Petri Nets) from a personal perspective of the author. The paper concentrates on what are perceived as the main highlights and the major shortcomings of PEP.

1 Overview of PEP

PEP [8, 48] is a programming and verification environment which is based on Petri nets, but in which nets play a background role. Primarily, the system accepts two types of input: a program π written in a concurrent programming language and a property ϕ expressed in some temporal logic language. The atoms of ϕ can, for instance, refer to variables and/or to control points of π. Through a sequence of compilation and verification steps, PEP allows ϕ to be checked against π, i.e. to determine whether or not ϕ is true for π (in other words, whether or not π is a model of ϕ). Figure 1 describes the core functional dependencies between PEP's implemented modules.

The user may input a parallel program written in a simple language called $B(PN)^2$ (Basic Petri Net Programming Notation) [9]. A program may be edited and compiled either into a process algebraic expression of the PBC (Petri Box Calculus [3], an extension of CCS [50]) or into a high-level Petri net of the M-net variety [6], and, from either, further into a 1-safe low-level net; both routes yield equivalent low-level nets. In addition, the user may input and edit a temporal logic formula which

1991 *Mathematics Subject Classification.* Primary 68N05, 68N15, 68Q10, 68Q22, 68Q55, 68Q60; Secondary 68Q90.

*This work has been supported by the Deutsche Forschungsgemeinschaft (DFG) under grants Be 1267/2-1, Be 1267/2-2, Be 1267/6-1, Fl 207/1-1 and Sta 450/1-1. Cooperation with the Technische Universität München has been supported by project A3 (Spezifikation, Analyse, Modellierung) of the DFG-Sonderforschungsbereich SFB-342 (Methoden und Werkzeuge für die Nutzung paralleler Rechnerarchitekturen).

refers to a program. This formula is compiled into a formula referring to the net associated with the program, if there exists one. It is also possible to edit a net (or a formula referring to it), but then, of course, the connection with any program (formula) it may have come from is destroyed.

Once the system knows of a 1-safe low-level net (which may have been created either directly or through a program by compilation), the computation of its finite prefix [43] may be initiated. This prefix represents the partial order semantics of the net in concise form. When the finite prefix is constructed, the model-checker is ready to be run. It accepts a (net) formula ϕ and the finite prefix, executes Esparza's model checking algorithm [21] and yields a 'yes' or a 'no', depending on whether or not the formula is true of the net (and hence also whether or not the corresponding program formula – if any – is true of the program – if any).

PEP also has various sideline functionalities in addition to the mainstream functionality just described. For example, $B(PN)^2$ programs can be created automatically by input filters, for instance from PFA (Parallel Finite Automata) [29]. There are output filters as well, for example one for transforming a $B(PN)^2$ program into executable C code [46]. Moreover, PEP includes various algorithms to check specific properties of a net, some of them without needing to compute its prefix. Also, an alternative model checker (which does not need the finite prefix) has been implemented for a special class of nets [4, 65]. These additional functionalities are represented by broken lines in figure 1.

Section 2 describes history and the rationale of PEP, section 3 deals with the programming language and its Petri net semantics, and section 4 describes some of the verification techniques implemented in PEP.

2 History and rationale of PEP

The PEP system unites two lines of development: Petri net semantics of concurrent programs and verification algorithms on nets and their partial order semantics.

2.1 Petri net semantics of concurrent programs

For the verification of parallel algorithms expressed in a programming notation, verification techniques such as the Owicki/Gries method [52] are available. For the verification of parallel algorithms expressed by means of Petri nets, other verification techniques such as through S-invariants and traps can be applied [1, 56, 58]. Good programming notations come with an indigenous technique for structuring programs, while Petri nets come with indigenous partial order semantics and analysis methods. Giving a net semantics to a concurrent language may raise the hope that both advantages can be combined, and that verification techniques can be transferred between programming languages and Petri nets.

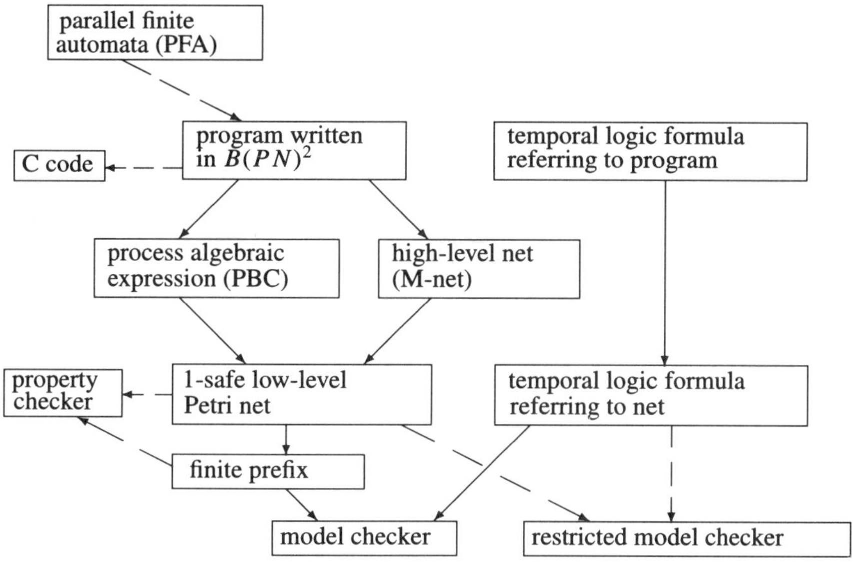

Figure 1: Functionality diagram of the PEP system

It may be hoped of such a combination that its compositionality and its usefulness are in proportion. For instance, if a program is made up of variables, sequential compositions and inner blocks, then it is reasonable to expect its associated Petri net to be made up similarly of smaller nets corresponding to the variables and the inner blocks, and combined via a sequential composition defined on nets. This calls for a special kind of algebra on nets, and the box algebra [3] has been developed with that aim in mind.

2.2 Verification algorithms on nets and their partial order semantics

On Petri nets there is a tradition of relating graph-theoretical properties – as well as linear-algebraic properties based on the net's incidence matrix – to behavioural properties. For instance, if a net is covered by an S-invariant [56], then it follows that its state graph (under any initial marking) is finite. Most conditions of this kind are either sufficient or necessary, but not both. It is reasonable to expect that fast graph-theoretical algorithms – or, for that matter, fast linear-algebraic algorithms such as linear programming – can be exploited to check some of these conditions, and then to exclude or to assert certain behavioural properties. Such an approach may be called *static*, because assertions are deduced about the state graph without ever constructing any part of it. Of course, there are limits to this approach, but nevertheless, these limits are far from being fully explored.

More recently, the static approach has been extended to cover not specific properties but a whole class of properties, i.e. a temporal logic. Starting with an observation by Javier Esparza, we showed that a small branching-time temporal logic that can be characterised as

'propositional logic over places, plus the Diamond operator'

can be model-checked by linear algebra – without constructing the state graph – for safe T-systems [4], which are a class of persistent nets, i.e. nets that are essentially without conflicts and choices [39]. It was already clear at the time of writing of [4] it would be difficult to generalise this result to a larger class of nets. Nevertheless, Javier Esparza found a way of model-checking the entire class of safe Petri nets against the same logic which retains a key characteristic property of [4], namely avoiding the construction of the state graph [21]. He showed that instead of constructing the state graph, McMillan's idea [43] of computing a finite prefix of the occurrence net [20, 51] of a net can be exploited.

2.3 Historical remark and acknowledgments

When the PEP project was conceived by Hans Fleischhack and myself in 1993, we were hoping to create not just a testbed for checking the performance of existing Petri-net-based analysis algorithms and for searching for new algorithms, but also a user-friendly environment in which both programs and nets can harmoniously be input, edited, related to each other, simulated, and verified. At that time, all existing Petri net tools were either oriented towards graphical input and had no or very little analysis support, or were oriented exclusively towards analysis without graphical support (the most advanced system of this kind being Peter Starke's INA [62]). None of the systems had the kind of close connection with a concurrent notation that we had envisaged. Thus, we (which initially meant a group consisting of myself and Bernd Grahlmann – who has since then been the chief project researcher and organiser – in Hildesheim and another group led by Hans Fleischhack in Oldenburg) took the risk of starting an implementation effort from scratch, using only know-how from the MOBY project at Oldenburg [23] and input from several students' projects at both sites. The DFG (Deutsche Forschungsgemeinschaft) supports this project with two persons per year over a period of (so far) 1993–1996. In the second stage of the project, 1995–1996, the Humboldt-Universität zu Berlin (by a group led by Peter Starke) has joined the project.

PEP was lucky in getting quite a number of good students interested in the project and contribute to its realisation – names that come to mind are Burkhard Bieber [13], Matthias Damm [16], Burkhard Graves [30], Tobias Himstedt [34], Lars Jenner [37], Michael Kater, Stephan Melzer [46], Stefan Römer [59], Andree Seidel [61] and Thomas Thielke [65], many of whom are still working on and around the project. PEP was also fortunate to have the strong and continued support by Esparza's research group at the Technische Universität München. By these means, as well as by the fortunate circumstance that the EU (European Union), DAAD (Deutscher Akademischer Austauschdienst) and its French counterpart provided funding for related theoretical work (projects DEMON, CALIBAN and POEM), it was possible to develop PEP to the point it has now reached.

It is the work of the persons mentioned in this subsection (and others), more than my own work, that is described in this paper.

3 PEP's inputs and their semantics

PEP primarily accepts two types of input: a program written in the language $B(PN)^2$ [9] and a property referring to a program or to its associated net. $B(PN)^2$ and its Petri net semantics are discussed in sections 3.1 and 3.2. Ways of inputting properties are described in section 3.3.

3.1 PEP's programming language

Ideally, the notation implemented in PEP was meant to serve a similar purpose for parallel programs as Dijkstra's guarded command notation [19] served for sequential nondeterministic programs, namely to represent algorithms in a 'pure' form while having a simple formal semantics. However, at least two additional questions are raised:

- *Should different hardware topologies be supported?* In $B(PN)^2$, the answer is a restricted 'yes', in the sense that both shared memory and message-based topologies are supported. Message buffers may have arbitrary integer size, ranging from 0 for handshake communication to ∞ for unbounded buffers. This may be contrasted with occam [45] which is limited to handshake communication between processes (other communication methods are possible but have to be implemented explicitly).

- *Should special features such as priorities and interrupts be supported?* After convincing ourselves that at least a restricted (i.e. not optimally concurrent) formal semantics of priorities can be given in terms of ordinary Petri nets [10, 32], we have decided, for the time being, not to include priorities in $B(PN)^2$. This may again be contrasted with occam which contains two constructs for expressing priorities between activities.

In addition, it was decided that $B(PN)^2$ should support the following features:

- *Explicit atomic actions.* $B(PN)^2$ allows angular brackets $\langle \ldots \rangle$ to delineate atomic actions. In the translation, every such construct is translated into one, or a set of alternative, single transitions of a Petri net.

- *Pre- and postvalue programming in predicative style.* For instance, an atomic action $\langle x{:=}y\rangle$ would be written as $\langle x'{=}'y \wedge y'{=}'y\rangle$, where $'v$ and v' denote the prevalue and the postvalue, respectively, of v. The idea is that an action touches only such variables mentioned explicitly in it, and any value change making the predicate **true** is acceptable. Note the difference between the above action and $\langle x'{=}'y\rangle$. For the latter, any value change of y would be acceptable in addition to setting the postvalue of x equal to the prevalue of y.

- *Unification of shared memory and channel communication.* To describe channel communication in predicative style, we introduced $c?$ and $c!$ as primitives denoting the value last read on channel c and the value last output to channel c, respectively. They are analogous to the pre- and postvalues of variables.

- *Unification of choices and loops.* $B(PN)^2$ contains a single **do** . . . **od** clause both for choices and for loops. The symbol $\Box$ separates alternatives, which can be ended either by the keyword **exit** (indicating exit from the loop) or by the keyword **repeat** (indicating a repetition of the loop).

For instance, figure 2 shows a three-component parallel program which exhibits both shared memory and buffered communication. Note that, due to the channel having capacity 2, both values could be deposited in it without any value being read. If its declaration is changed to **var** c : **chan** 1 **of** $\{3, 5\}$, then at most one value could be written before reading, and if it is changed to **var** c : **chan** 0 **of** $\{3, 5\}$, then writing and reading are simultaneous. In either case, any of the states $(y, z){=}(3, 3)$, $(y, z){=}(3, 5)$, $(y, z){=}(5, 3)$ or $(y, z){=}(5, 5)$ could be a result of the program.

```
begin  var x : {3,5};  var c : chan 2 of {3,5};
          ⟨x'=3⟩;  ⟨c!='x ∧ x'='x⟩
       ‖  ⟨x'=5⟩;  ⟨c!='x ∧ x'='x⟩
       ‖  begin var y, z : {3,5};  ⟨y'=c?⟩;  ⟨z'=c?⟩ end
end
```

Figure 2: A $B(PN)^2$ program with three components and an inner block

$B(PN)^2$ has served a useful purpose of representing algorithms (or nets) linearly. However, it has also turned out to have at least two shortcomings. First, for any large-scale applications, it would be indispensable to include recursion, procedures, and other features. Second, the core language is perhaps slightly too liberal.

As to the first problem, work is in progress to extend $B(PN)^2$ by procedures while still retaining its property of having a compositional net semantics [24, 42]. In a further line of development, object-oriented features are being investigated with respect to their compositional net semantics [41]. These investigations are encouraging, in the sense that all extensions seem to be possible without significant extension of the existing Petri net model on which the semantics of $B(PN)^2$ is based (section 3.2).

Secondly, there seem to be some problems – or at least, debatable issues – with the prevalue/postvalue approach to atomic actions and their Petri net semantics. One of these issues is the (Petri net) semantics of actions such as $a_0 = \langle\mathbf{true}\rangle$, $a_1 = \langle x'{=}'x\rangle$ and $a_2 = \langle x'{=}x'\rangle$. At present, a_0 is translated into a single 'silent' transition, a_1 is translated into a choice of transitions which access the variable x but do not change its value, and a_2 is translated into a choice of transitions accessing x and allowing any value change. Operationally, this makes sense: for example, the first action does not interfere with a parallel fourth action accessing x, while the second and third actions do. However, axiomatically, it does not make much sense since the predicate **true** is normally considered equivalent with predicates such as $x'{=}x'$.

Another issue is the syntax of choices and loops. The idea to combine them in a single **do**... **od** originally arose from translating them into a process algebra which contains only recursion but no iteration. For instance, the program fragment **do** a_1; **exit** $\square$ a_2; **repeat od** can be translated into the recursive process algebraic expression $X = (a_1 \square (a_2; X))$ [11]. It turns out that with a well-behaved (in terms of its net semantics) process algebraic iteration construct such as $[E_1 * E_2 * E_3]$, where E_1 is the initialisation, E_2 is the body of the repetition and E_3 is finalisation, the semantics of the general **do**... **od** is awkward because E_1 must be assumed to be a silent action in general. Other iteration constructs such as $[E_2 * E_3]$ (E_2 being the body and E_3 being finalisation) or more simply $[E_2]$ (denoting E_2^* in terms of regular expressions) are more convenient for giving the semantics of the loop construct, but are less well-behaved in terms of their Petri net semantics.

To avoid these problems, at the present time I favour imposing on $B(PN)^2$ the same restriction that is already built in the guarded command notation and that leads to well-formed [1] nets: that every alternative of a loop construct must begin with a plain action which is not itself another loop. In the present version of $B(PN)^2$, this is implemented by the **enter** clause which separates the initialisation of a **do**... **od** construct from its body (see figure 3 below for an example).

Another issue is the semantics of multiple communications such as

$$\langle c!{=}5 \wedge d!{=}3\rangle \,\|\, \langle c?{=}x' \wedge c?{=}y'\rangle,$$

where c and d are channels of capacity 0 and x and y are variables. In the present implementation, this parallel command leads to a deadlock, which is due to the underlying semantic ideas stipulating that a single channel should be sufficient (and necessary) for creating a handshake synchronisation out of two separate atomic actions. This approach has been found too restrictive in some contexts and generalisations have been proposed [18, 25].

3.2 The compositional Petri net model underlying $B(PN)^2$

In our approach, two important ideas in giving Petri net semantics to a language such as $B(PN)^2$ are, firstly, that it should be *compositional* and, secondly, that it should be *transparent*. Transparency means that the translation should introduce neither too many auxiliary places and/or transitions nor additional behaviour. Compositionality means that every program object – a variable declaration, an atomic action or a block, ... – should be describable by a stand-alone Petri net, and that the set of all these Petri net ingredients can be combined at the Petri net level by operations which match the syntactic operators used in the program to combine its ingredients (variable declarations, atomic actions, inner blocks, ...).

Robin Milner has already shown in both his books [49, 50] how such a translation can be achieved compositionally at the process algebra level. His approach is, however, lacking in transparency (in the above sense) because of the way of CCS is constructed. For example, sequential composition has to be implemented in a roundabout way, which is not too complicated conceptually, but adds complexity to the resulting expression. As another example, atomic actions such as $\langle x{:=}y\rangle$, where x and y are declared in different blocks, lead to overhead in the translation and hence also in CCS-based analysis of the properties of programs containing such actions.

The box algebra [3] has been devised as a modification and (partial) extension of CCS in order to avoid such overheads. This algebra has been defined together with a direct translation into a class of labelled 1-safe elementary Petri nets called boxes. PEP originally used this translation in order to create a net from a program: first an expression of the algebra is created from the program, and then a box is created from the expression. In practice, however, this approach is of limited usefulness because the resulting nets are usually very large; they are necessarily so large, of course, because all information contained in the program (in particular, variable types) needs to be stored in Petri net form. Already the expressions, which are used as intermediate translation results between programs and nets, tend to become very large in general. (However, they provide a possible interface to tools such as the Edinburgh Concurrency Work Bench [64].) The advantage of this approach is that the full set of Petri net analysis methods – described below in section 4 – is applicable to the result of the translation.

In practice, it turns out that one would wish to translate a program only partially into a net, or into an abbreviated net from which the full net can be derived in a further step if desired. Net theory provides a class of nets for just such a purpose: so-called *high-level nets* ([26, 38] and others). However, in the PEP project high-level nets could not be used directly, because we required all translations to be compositional. Hence prior to using high-level nets, we needed to impose an algebra to make the box algebra operations available for them.

This line of thought gave rise to the model which is now used in PEP: the M-net (modular net) model [6, 7]. M-nets are high-level nets with an additional algebra containing box algebra operations such as choice composition, parallel composition and synchronisation. It is then possible to create an M-net associated with a $B(PN)^2$ program by first constructing little M-nets corresponding to the ingredients (declarations, atomic actions etc.) of the program and then composing these M-nets in the same way as the ingredients of the program are combined. As a rule, the M-net of a program is not significantly larger than the program itself – but, of course, it has a set of inscriptions so as not to lose information. The disadvantage of this approach is that, even though finding structural analysis methods for high-level nets is presently a vigorous area of research (I mention e.g. [60]), there exist very few general methods for analysing a high-level net short of unfolding it, i.e. creating its associated elementary net (which, of course, beats the idea of saving space).

The existing version of PEP does not exploit the compositionality which is built in the semantics. More pessimistically, while it is clear that compositionality is vital for semantics such as Hoare-style axiomatic semantics [35] or weakest precondition semantics [19], it is not yet clear whether compositionality of Petri net semantics can be exploited in any significant way in proofs of programs. The current version of PEP concentrates much more on what I have called transparency, i.e. on minimising the nets that are created, and on applying analysis algorithms to these objects.

3.3 PEP's (current) ways of specifying properties

PEP supports various ways of specifying properties: directly (see section 4.1); by a simple branching-time logic (on which the analysis algorithms described in sections 4.2 and 4.3 are based); and in a linear-time notation (for the semidecision analysis described in section 4.5). The reader will notice that PEP does not (yet) support a truly strong logic, i.e. that some desirable properties may not be expressible, and hence not checkable (in the present version). This is due to a conscious effort of getting as static (and hence, hopefully, as efficient) as possible algorithms for a small (yet not uninteresting) logic first, before extending them at a later stage. It is understood that in a further development of the system, if PEP's indigenous algorithms turn out to be non-generalisable or not easily generalisable, it will be attempted to complement the existing techniques by more traditional state-graph-based algorithms.

The language of the branching-time logic, call it **BL**, refers to a given 1-safe net N with place set $S=\{s_1, \ldots, s_n\}$. An atomic formula is either the constant **true** or a place name s_i. If ϕ, ϕ_1 and ϕ_2 are formulae, then so are $\neg\phi$, $\phi_1 \vee \phi_2$ and $\Diamond\phi$. The semantics of this logic refers to pairs (N, M) where N is a net as above and M is a marking of N. By definition, (N, M) always satisfies **true**; (N, M) satisfies s_i iff $M(s_i)>0$; (N, M) satisfies $\neg\phi$ iff it does not satisfy ϕ; (N, M) satisfies $\phi_1 \vee \phi_2$ iff it satisfies ϕ_1 or ϕ_2; and (N, M) satisfies $\Diamond\phi$ iff there is a successor marking M' of

M such that (N, M') satisfies ϕ. There are derived operators, such as $\wedge = \neg\vee\neg$, $\Box = \neg\Diamond\neg$, etc.

As usual, this simple definition is computationally uninteresting, because using it, the evaluation of a formula ϕ for any given (N, M) involves the (computation and the) traversal of the state graph, possibly many times, depending on the depth of nesting of the diamond operators $\Diamond$. In section 4, more efficient algorithms are described. Examples of properties that can be expressed are:

$\Box\Diamond(\forall s \in {}^\bullet t : s)$	(liveness of transition t)
$\Diamond\Box s_i$	(token trappable on s_i)
$\Diamond(s_1 \wedge \neg s_2 \wedge \ldots \wedge \neg s_n)$	(reachability of a marking, in this case $(1, 0, \ldots, 0) \in \mathbf{N}^{\|S\|}$).

Eventuality properties cannot, as a rule, be expressed in **BL**.

A slight change in the syntax of the logic makes formulae refer to programs rather than to nets: given a program, we may allow atomic formulae of the form **true** or $x{=}v$ (where x is a variable and v is a value) or **at** p (where p is a control point). When the program is translated into a corresponding 1-safe net, a program formula may automatically be translated into a corresponding formula referring to that net, because every term of the form $x{=}v$ or **at** p refers to a place of the net. Moreover, the formula is true of the program in its initial state if and only if the corresponding formula is true of the net and its corresponding initial marking. For example, in figure 2, the formula $\Diamond\ (y{=}3 \wedge z{=}3)$ is true, because there exists an execution in which both y and z are set to the value 3.

4 PEP's verification components

PEP attempts to do its verification business as statically as possible, e.g. by running algorithms on the structure of a net (or a program) to deduce properties of the net's (or the program's) behaviour. Five classes of verification techniques can be distinguished in PEP: dedicated analysis, restricted static model-checking, model-checking based on occurrence nets, interfacing to other systems such as INA, and analysis based on linear algebra. Sections 4.1 to 4.5 describe these techniques in turn.

4.1 Dedicated analysis algorithms

In its initial phase, PEP was used as a testbed for students to implement static analysis algorithms. For instance, [17] describes a wealth of theorems giving (often exact) structural conditions for a variety of behavioural properties of certain subclasses of Petri nets. In PEP, nets may first be checked as to whether or not they belong to such a subclass, and if so, one of the structural algorithms can be invoked to test a corresponding property. The test of belonging to a subclass is split into several subtests: 'is the net free-choice?', 'is it a T-system?', 'is it n-bounded' (this test can be neglected if the net comes from a program, since it is then 1-bounded by construction), 'is it live if bounded?' and 'is it deadlock-free?' (using McMillan's algorithm).

The boundedness test involves constructing the state graph, and the corresponding algorithm of PEP is therefore (and because it has not been optimised) rather slow. Nets coming from programs are nearly always non-free-choice, and hence the implemented algorithms for free-choice nets are not useful for such nets. In fact, for these reasons, this line of development of PEP has been all but discontinued, but nevertheless, it may still serve a useful purpose as a testbed for new algorithms. The test for boundedness is faster using the optimised algorithms of INA described below in section 4.4.

4.2 Static model-checking for persistent nets

The essential idea of this model-checker [4] can be described as follows. Let a net N with an initial marking M^0 and a formula ϕ of the temporal logic **BL** be given, such that (N, M^0) is a safe T-system; the problem is to decide whether or not (N, M^0) satisfies ϕ. To check this, consider an innermost subformula of the form $\Diamond(l_1 \wedge \ldots \wedge l_m)$ of ϕ, where each l_i is a literal, i.e. either s_i or $\neg s_i$ for some place s_i. Exploiting the persistence of (N, M^0), it can be shown that this subformula can be equivalently replaced by a formula of the form $\forall t_i \in T : t_i \leq k_i$, where T is the set of transitions of N and the k_i arise as solutions of a linear programming problem which encodes the following question:

> 'What is the maximal number of times that t_i can be executed such that the resulting sequence (there is only one up to equivalent permutations by persistence) does not lose the property of being extendable to a sequence leading to a marking such that all of s_1–s_n are marked/unmarked, depending on whether l_i is $s_i/\neg s_i$?'

Replacing $\Diamond(l_1 \wedge \ldots \wedge l_m)$ by $\forall t_i \in T : t_i \leq k_i$ is satisfiability-invariant, i.e. the resulting formula is valid for (N, M^0) if and only if the original formula was. It is now a routine matter to apply this procedure repeatedly until no temporal operator $\Diamond$ (nor $\Box$) are left in the formula, and temporal-operator-free formulae can be evaluated directly on the initial state without computing the state graph. (In order to apply this procedure, the logic has to be extended – temporarily – by atomic formulae of the form $t \leq k$, with k being an element of the set $\{-1\} \cup \mathbf{N} \cup \{+\infty\}$; but this is not a problem [4].)

In PEP, this algorithm has been implemented for safe T-systems [65]. Its performance can be startling for people who are used to check other algorithms on very concurrent systems, such as the CCS expression $a_1 \| \ldots \| a_n$ which generates 2^n reachable states (or, to mention a less trivial example, Milner's well-known scheduler [50], which is also a T-system). PEP checks formulae on such systems rather quickly.

The model-checking algorithm described in this section has an interesting characteristic property: it shifts complexity away from one of its input parameters (the model) towards the other input parameter (the formula). Since our temporal logic includes the propositional calculus, any model checker is bound to be exponential in the size of the net (note: this is the net, not its state graph!) or in the length of the formula. Interleaving-based model-checking algorithms are exponential in the size of the net (because they generate the state graph) and linear in the length of the formula. The algorithm described in this section is exponential in the length of the formula (because it has to compute disjunctive normal forms repeatedly in order to obtain subformulae of the form $\Diamond(l_1 \wedge \ldots \wedge l_m)$), but is provably polynomial in the size of the net. We consider this a desirable property of a model-checking algorithm: the net (and *a fortiori* its state graph) will be very large, in most cases, while the interesting formulae will – in most cases – be of limited size[1] and, in particular, of limited nesting depth.

4.3 Model-checking on finite prefices of occurrence nets

Javier Esparza's model-checking algorithm [21] can be viewed as a generalisation of the algorithm described in section 4.2. The generalisation consists in allowing any safe Petri net, rather than just persistent ones, as input while retaining essentially the same logic, **BL**. The algorithm itself had to be extended and modified considerably, but Esparza did this in such a way that one of its main properties – viz., shifting algorithmic complexity from the size of the net to the size of the formula – remains as much as possible intact.

Some form of representing behaviour turns out to be necessary, and Esparza has shown that it is in essence sufficient to keep knowledge about the maximal nonsequential processes (i.e. the maximal partial order behaviours [5, 28]) of the input net. (If the net is persistent, then there is only one such process.) A succinct way of representing all processes of the net is by its occurrence net [20, 51], which can loosely be described as a branching structure with processes as 'paths'; the occurrence net of a net is to the set of its processes what the execution tree of a net is to the set of its interleavings.

Unfortunately, the occurrence net of a net is, in general, infinite. Fortunately, there is a way (detected by McMillan [43]) of defining a 'sufficiently large' prefix of the occurrence net – where 'sufficiently large' means that it contains implicitly every reachable marking. That prefix is always finite. Esparza has shown that

[1] Although we will consider an exception in section 5.

not only all reachable markings, but also the maximal processes, are recoverable from that finite prefix. Using this finite prefix, model-checking can be done in a similar way as described above, i.e. by replacing innermost subformulae of the form $\Diamond(l_1 \wedge \ldots \wedge l_m)$ by suitable conjunctions not involving $\Diamond$. However, the actual algorithm is significantly more complicated, and it involves the reconstruction of the relevant (maximal) processes from the finite prefix using a continuous 'shift' operator.

Theoretical results about this model-checking algorithm are, (1): that in the special case of safe persistent systems it has polynomial complexity in the size of the prefix, and (2): that for a certain class of safe persistent systems, called safe conflict-free systems, it has polynomial complexity in the size of the net. A corollary of (1) and (2) is that in the special case of safe T-systems, the runtime of this algorithm is provably of the same complexity as that of the previously described algorithm (by orders of magnitude). Moreover, given that there are examples where the finite prefix is an order of magnitude smaller than the state graph, this algorithm performs better than ones based on the latter.

```
begin var h : {1, 2} init 1;  var in₁, in₂ : {false, true} init false;
do   ⟨true⟩  enter  ⟨in₁'=true⟩;
                    do ⟨true⟩  enter  ⟨in₂=false⟩; exit
                                □     ⟨in₂=true⟩;
                                      do ⟨true⟩  enter  ⟨h=2⟩; ⟨in₁'=false⟩;
                                                        ⟨h=1⟩; ⟨in₁'=true⟩;
                                                        exit
                                                    □   ⟨h=1⟩; exit
                                      od; repeat
                    od;
                    % cs₁ : Critical Section 1
                    ⟨h'=2⟩; ⟨in₁'=false⟩; repeat
od
||   do   ... analogous (exchanging 1 and 2) ...           od
end
```

Figure 3: Dekker's algorithm in $B(PN)^2$ notation

As before, the algorithm performs particularly well for systems with lots of concurrency and little choice, such as $a_1 \| \ldots \| a_n$. By contrast, in a typical system without concurrency and with lots of choice, the finite prefix may even be exponential whereas the state graph is only polynomial in size. Consider, for example, the process algebraic term $(a_1+b_1); (a_2+b_2); \ldots; (a_n+b_n)$. The Petri net of this term generates a state graph of size $O(n)$ and a finite prefix of size $O(2^n)$, because after each i'th choice, the rest of the occurrence net gets duplicated. The paper [22], however, describes an improvement of McMillan's unfolding algorithm which allows the calculation of optimised finite prefixes, such that a further result holds, (3): the optimised finite prefix is always of size less or equal to the state graph (in terms of orders of magnitude), and, moreover, the previous results (1) and (2) still hold for the optimised prefix. This optimisation is implemented in the current version of PEP.

After implementing the algorithm in PEP, it was tested on various examples. For instance, at one point of the development, we tested PEP's model-checking algorithm on Dekker's protocol for mutual exclusion (see e.g. [1]). This protocol is reproduced in figure 3 in $B(PN)^2$ notation.[2] At that point in time, we checked the following formulae:

$$\left.\begin{array}{l}
\neg\Diamond(\mathbf{at}\ cs_1 \wedge \mathbf{at}\ cs_2) \\
\Box\ (\mathbf{at}\ cs_1\ \Rightarrow\ (\Diamond\ \mathbf{at}\ cs_2)) \\
\Box\ (\mathbf{at}\ cs_2\ \Rightarrow\ (\Diamond\ \mathbf{at}\ cs_1)) \\
\Diamond\ \mathbf{at}\ cs_1 \\
\Diamond\ \mathbf{at}\ cs_2 \\
\Box\ \Diamond\ (\mathbf{at}\ cs_1) \\
\Box\ \Diamond\ (\mathbf{at}\ cs_2) \\
\Box\ \Diamond\ (\mathbf{at}\ cs_1 \vee \mathbf{at}\ cs_2),
\end{array}\right\}
\quad \text{obtaining, respectively,} \quad
\left\{\begin{array}{l}
\mathbf{true} \\
\mathbf{true} \\
\mathbf{true} \\
\mathbf{true} \\
\mathbf{true} \\
\mathbf{false} \\
\mathbf{false} \\
\mathbf{false}.
\end{array}\right.$$

This result is fine for the first five formulae but not for the last three. Burkhard Graves analysed the problem and traced it back to an error in Javier Esparza's paper. It is not possible to describe the full details in this paper, but the essential point is that the finite prefix as defined by McMillan is 'too small' for the 'shift' operator to function in the way it is supposed to function. It is possible to fix this problem by creating a finite prefix which is sufficiently large. This solution is easy to describe and recovers the theoretical results (1) and (2) of Esparza's paper, but it slows down the entire model-checker very significantly. It is only now (July 1996) that Burkhard Graves hopes to have found a way of enlarging the finite prefix in a minimal way while ensuring that the 'shift' operator works as it should and, at the same time, retaining the efficiency of the algorithm. This work will be reported in [31].

4.4 INA interface

There have been recent efforts to combine PEP with Peter Starke's analysis tool INA (Integrated Net Analyser) [62]. Thanks mainly to work by Lutz Pogrell [55], the present version of PEP contains a user-transparent interface between the two tools that were originally developed independently of each other. INA can now be called from the same graphical interface, and nets that are input by PEP can be analysed by INA. In this paper, I refrain from describing the interface, but I mention the analysis capabilities of INA just in order to indicate the added capabilities of the combined tool, PEP/INA. The following is a sample, insignificantly shortened, output of INA,

[2] We use $\langle h{=}2\rangle$ as an abbreviation of $\langle {}'h{=}2{=}h'\rangle$, and we show this algorithm here explicitly just to give an example for the notation.

referring to a random net (figure 22 of [2]), reproduced here by courtesy of Peter Starke.

> Start of INA output:
>
> *Current net options are: token type – black (for place/transition nets); time option – intervals; elements – transitions; firing rule – safe; priorities – not to be used; strategy – single transitions.*
>
> *Information on elementary structural properties: the net has no bad reachable states; the net is not statically conflict-free; the net is pure; the net has transitions without pre-places; the net is not coverable by state-machines; the net is not strongly connected; the net is not covered by semipositive P-invariants; the net has transitions without post-place; the net is ordinary, homogeneous, not conservative, not subconservative, not a state machine, not free choice, not extended free choice, not extended simple, not marked, not marked with exactly one token, not a marked graph, connected; the net has a non-blocking multiplicity, no nonempty clean trap, no places without pre-transition, no places without post-transition; the maximal in/out-degree is 4.*
>
> *Computation of the reachability graph. Current analysis options are: no depth restriction; do not print all states; print the dead states; do not print the bad states; no reachability / coverability test. Number of states generated: 642.*
>
> *The net has no dead transitions at the initial marking; the net is bounded; the net is safe; the net has no dead reachable states.*
>
> *Current graph analysis options are: no computation of dynamic conflicts; no computation of distances; no computation of circuits; computation of terminal SC-components; resetability; liveness test.*
>
> *Graph analysis: The initial state is reproducible.*
>
> *Computation of the terminal SC-components. The net is reversible (resetable), covered by semipositive T-invariants, live, live if dead transitions are ignored, live and safe, has no time deadlocks.*
>
> End of INA output.

INA's computation of the reachability graph (state graph) is very fast. Moreover, INA has capabilities for exploiting the stubborn-set method by Valmari [67] and for detecting (and exploiting) state graph symmetries [63]. INA has a small in-built expert system which allows the conclusions of some known theorems to be added to the set of analysis results, provided the premises leading to those conclusions have already been verified for the particular net under consideration.

4.5 Linear-algebraic semidecision analysis

PEP offers a semidecision verification method which is based on a linear upper approximation of the state space. The theory of this method is described in [47] and briefly in [48]. The method extracts from the description of the net and its initial marking, in linear time, a set of linear constraints L that every reachable marking must satisfy. Thus, the solutions of L are a superset of the reachable markings. In order to make use of L for verification, a new set L_P of linear constraints is added to it which specify the markings that do not satisfy a desirable property P. Then, linear programming is used to solve the system $L \cup L_P$; if the system has no solution, every reachable marking satisfies P.

The set of constraints L is actually the union of two subsets L_1 and L_2. L_1 comes from the state equation and has been known for many years. The upper approximation of the state space that can be derived from L_1 is often rough and insufficient to prove many properties. The main contribution of [47] is the definition of L_2, a new set of constraints derived from the traps of the net.

Presently there exist semidecision algorithms for deadlock-freenes (yielding either 'deadlock-free' or 'possibly not deadlock-free, with marking ... being potential deadlock marking' as results) and for the reachability of a marking or a partially specified marking.

Semidecision algorithms, in my opinion, provide good compromises between the inherent algorithmic complexity of full automated verification and the desire to have computer-assistance during validation. Even if such an algorithm yields an indecisive answer, this may still help the user. Another role of automatic verification is in prototyping: typically, a program is verified on a small data domain to gain confidence (or not) for the case of arbitrarily large domains, when automatic verification fails and, if any, manual verification prevails.

5 Performance results

PEP is both a general model-checker and a specific Petri net tool. Hence, its performance can be compared with other model-checkers and with other specific net tools. I report on two such comparisons: one done by Stefan Römer using an article by James C. Corbett [14] and one carried out by Monika Heiner and Peter Deussen as described in [33].

Corbett compares existing systems (SPIN [36], SPIN plus Partial Orders [53], SMV [44] and INCA [15]) on a series of examples, using deadlock detection as a common property to be checked on all examples and all systems. Stefan Römer of the Technische Universität München translated the examples into PEP input and measured the times for checking the same property (deadlock detection) using PEP's algorithm. It so happens that deadlock-freeness is one of the properties which can be expressed in **BL**, but lead to very large formulae.[3] Because of the importance

[3]For a net with about 50 transitions, Bernd Grahlmann has estimated that deadlock-freeness would lead to disjunctive normal forms – which arise necessarily as intermediate stages of the verification – that are about 4 GB long.

of deadlock-freeness, therefore, PEP implements a dedicated algorithm (namely, McMillan's) to check this, which uses and exploits the finite (optimised) prefix. Hence this comparison is not really about the general model checking algorithm of PEP but about the dedicated deadlock-detection algorithm.

Table 1 – reproduced here by courtesy of Stefan Römer – gives the preliminary results of the experiment. The 'P(size)' (Problem) column refers to the set of examples given in Corbett's paper. The sets S, T and B, E refer to the places and transitions of the original net and of the finite prefix, respectively.[4] The 'Cuts' column refers to the set of cutoff events (used by the algorithm calculating the finite prefix). The 'F-prefix' and 'Check' columns give the times (in seconds) measured for calculating the finite prefix and for checking the deadlock-freeness property, respectively. The 'C' (Compare) column gives a very crude indication of how PEP's performance relates to the performance of the other systems described in Corbett's paper; $\uparrow$ stands for 'better', $\downarrow$ stands for 'worse' and – stands for 'not applicable' (mainly because the other systems did not give results). The results contained in table 1 have to be read with a pinch of salt, because it was not possible to reproduce exactly the same hardware environment as used by Corbett for his comparison. To compare memory usage, it is necessary to look at the columns 'States' and '$|E|$'. It must be mentioned also that we did not check the examples themselves; Stefan Römer just received files from Corbett which he used as input for PEP.[5] We are presently in the process of repeating the comparisons on a more uniform hardware platform.

The experiment gives a mixed result for PEP: for some examples it performs better than the other model-checkers, for other examples it performs worse. In the light of the theory explained above, PEP is at its best when there is a lot of concurrency but very little choice, and performs comparatively badly in the other extreme, when there is a lot of choice and little concurrency. (In the majority of 'real' cases, there would be a good mix of both concurrency and choice, which PEP, as well as any other automatic model-checker, will have difficulty in coming to grips with.)

The authors of [33] have tested three specifically Petri-net-oriented analysis systems, INA [62], PROD [66] and PEP, on a single common example and a series of properties. The example concerns an industrial production cell with six components: two conveyor belts, a rotatable robot equipped with two extendable arms, an elevating rotatable table, a press and a travelling crane. This case study has recently been used in various (German) projects as a reference example on which various methods, not just Petri nets, can be tested and compared [40].

I will not repeat the experimental results reported in [33], except for mentioning that the speed of checking a property is not unfavourable towards PEP, whenever

[4]Note that the 'transitions' (i.e. $|T|$) column does *not* refer to the transitions of the state graph. Indeed, the number of these transitions has not been counted as they are irrelevant for the algorithms.

[5]This has led to strange effects such as a net with 1047 places and 5633 transitions but only 125 reachable markings.

P(size)	States	$\|S\|$	$\|T\|$	$\|B\|$	$\|E\|$	Cuts	F-prefix	Check	C
CYCL(9)	7423	71	53	172	77	10	0.05	2.18	–
CYCL(12)	74264	95	71	232	104	13	0.13	31.18	–
DAC(12)	14334	84	70	260	146	0	0.12	0.0	↑
DAC(15)	114686	105	88	371	206	0	0.23	0.0	↑
DP(10)	48897	60	40	580	280	90	0.30	0.92	↑
DP(12)	–	72	48	840	408	132	0.62	2.97	↑
DPD(6)	19861	54	54	3786	1892	499	8.92	103.56	↓
DPD(7)	109965	63	63	8630	4314	1129	43.13	1266.08	↓
DPFM(8)	49	87	321	426	209	162	0.08	0.68	–
DPFM(11)	125	1047	5633	2433	1211	1012	1.27	98.30	–
DPH(6)	16897	57	97	14474	7231	3377	85.78	10344.9	–
DPH(7)	79927	66	121	–	–	–	–	–	–
ELEV(3)	7121	327	783	7398	3895	1629	23.75	496.10	↓
ELEV(4)	43440	736	1939	32354	16935	7337	417.32	>13463	↓
FURN(3)	30861	53	99	34505	20770	13837	330.04	>49927	↓
FURN(4)	214757	66	139	–	–	–	–	–	↓
GASN(4)	14847	258	465	15928	7965	2876	115.93	19370.2	↓
GASN(5)	115184	428	841	–	–	–	–	–	↓
GASQ(3)	1705	284	475	2593	1297	490	3.37	102.0	–
GASQ(4)	15431	1428	2705	19864	9933	4060	177.56	35342.2	–
HART(75)	153	377	227	529	302	1	1.13	0.22	↑
HART(100)	203	502	302	704	402	1	2.20	0.32	↑
KEY(4)	44820	164	174	135556	67775	32081	8811.0	–	↓
KEY(5)	–	199	215	–	–	–	–	–	↓
MMGT(3)	7703	122	172	11575	5841	2529	51.56	3166.6	↓
MMGT(4)	66309	158	232	92940	46902	20957	7509.80	–	↓
OVER(4)	4175	71	74	1561	797	240	1.65	7.52	↓
OVER(5)	33460	90	95	7388	3761	1251	30.70	618.39	↓
RING(7)	1700	91	77	813	403	79	0.63	1.20	↑
RING(9)	211528	117	99	1599	795	137	2.20	4.67	↑
RW(9)	523	48	181	9272	4627	4106	5.32	9567.2	↓
RW(12)	4110	63	313	98378	49177	45069	316.84	–	↓
SENT(75)	332	254	105	533	266	40	0.93	1.07	↑
SENT(100)	382	329	130	608	291	40	1.42	1.67	↑
ABP(1)	113	43	95	337	167	56	0.12	0.60	↑
BDS(1)	36097	53	59	12310	6330	3701	44.83	6971.3	↓
DART(1)	–	331	257	–	–	–	–	–	–
FTP(1)	104911	176	529	178077	89042	35247	15645.5	–	↓
FTP(2)	–	229	934	–	–	–	–	–	–
Q(1)	123597	163	194	16090	8402	1173	220.77	1125.12	–
SPD(1)	8690	33	39	5317	3138	1311	15.30	510.7	↓

Table 1: Experimental results by Stefan Römer (cf. [14])

the property can be expressed in the first place. However, it has to be added that every system compared in [33] has its specific strengths and weaknesses. This is also true for the systems compared in the Corbett experiment described earlier. The authors of [33], therefore, conclude that 'the combination of different tools (even if they provide similar features at first glance) seems to be desirable',[6] a view which I can endorse.

6 Conclusion

PEP is still only a testbed comprising several approaches for the (partial order) verification of Petri nets and concurrent algorithms. In order to create 'a user-friendly environment in which both programs and nets can harmoniously be input, edited, related to each other, simulated, and verified' (quote from section 2), I consider several significant developments to be necessary:

- Adding stronger logics while extending the prefix-based model-checking algorithm conservatively, i.e. preserving its efficiency in the restricted cases.
- Adding other (trace-based or interleaving-based) verification algorithms. Possibly, adding interfaces to SPIN [36] and/or the CWB [64].
- Adding high-level-net analysis methods that do not require unfolding, or that require only partial unfolding into low-level nets.
- Extending the versatility of the input language(s) both by adding procedures to $B(PN)^2$ and by adding new input filters.
- Provision for interactive use and for re-use of intermediate analysis results.
- Better exploitation of compositionality and support for user-defined (as opposed to automatic) verification.
- Modularisation of the system with a view to (partially) providing its source code to the public domain.

I hope that the existing PEP system provides a feasible starting point for such developments.

7 Postscript

During POMIV'96 (which was jointly organised by G. Holzmann, D. Peled and V. Pratt), there has been some discussion about 'true' partial order verification.[7] Doron

[6] I changed 'unavoidable' [33] into 'desirable'.

[7] It is slightly ironic that during the last years, 'true concurrency semantics' has often been used as a synonym of 'partial order semantics'.

Peled remarked during his talk that what could perhaps be described collectively as 'the set methods' (stubborn sets, sleep sets, persistent sets, ample sets, ... [27, 54, 68]) are essentially based on the exploitation of the (conditional) commutativity of actions, rather than on partial orders, and thus calling them 'partial order methods' may be partially misleading. This point can be seen on the example

$$\langle x{:=}x+1\rangle \parallel \langle x{:=}x+1\rangle,$$

where the two actions commute and are independent in the sense of [27, 54], but do not yield a true partial order when executed, nor are independent in the sense of [12]. Thus, semantic independence – in the sense of giving rise to partial orders – is only one of the circumstances in which the set methods can model-check efficiently, which may partly explain why they would sometimes perform better than PEP on some examples (cf. section 5). By contrast, Esparza's algorithm presented in section 4.3 is based on the representation of behaviour as partial orders and, more particularly, of global states as cuts in such partial orders. The fact that this algorithm performs better than set methods on other examples, is most likely due to the fact that it completely avoids the construction (and hence also the traversal) of the state graph.

On the occasion of comparing the two classes of approaches, another observation could be mentioned. The computation of the finite prefix is often a bottleneck, but it does not have to be recomputed for different properties; once it has been computed for a system, it can be used to check any of the properties expressible in the logic for that system. This is in contrast to most set approaches, where the transition system has to be recomputed each time a different (or sufficiently different) property is to be checked.

Acknowledgments

It is a pleasure to thank Burkhard Bieber, Javier Esparza, Bernd Grahlmann, Hans Fleischhack, Burkhard Graves, Doron Peled and Tom Thielke for comments.

References

[1] E. Best: *Semantics of Sequential and Parallel Programs*. Prentice Hall (1996).

[2] E. Best: A Memory Module Specification using Composable High-level Petri Nets. To appear in *Formal System Specification: 15 Contributions for the RPC-Memory Specification*. M. Broy, St. Merz and K. Spies (eds). Springer-Verlag, LNCS (1996).

[3] E. Best, R. Devillers and J.G. Hall: The Petri Box Calculus: a New Causal Algebra with Multilabel Communication. *Advances in Petri Nets 1992*, G. Rozenberg (ed.). Springer-Verlag, LNCS Vol. 609, 21–69 (1992).

[4] E. Best and J. Esparza: Model Checking of Persistent Petri Nets. Proc. *5th Workshop Computer Science Logic-91*. Springer-Verlag, LNCS Vol. 626, 35-52 (1992).

[5] E. Best and C. Fernández: *Nonsequential Processes: A Petri Net View*. Springer-Verlag, EATCS Monographs on Theoretical Computer Science 13 (1988).

[6] E. Best, H. Fleischhack, W. Frączak, R.P. Hopkins, H. Klaudel and E. Pelz: A Class of Composable High Level Petri Nets. Proc. *Petri Nets'95*, Torino, G. De Michelis, M. Diaz (eds). Springer-Verlag, LNCS Vol. 935, 103–120 (1995).

[7] E. Best, H. Fleischhack, W. Frączak, R.P. Hopkins, H. Klaudel and E. Pelz: An M-net Semantics of $B(PN)^2$. Proc. *STRICT'95*, Berlin, J. Desel (ed.). Springer-Verlag, Workshops in Computing, 85–100 (1995).

[8] E. Best and B. Grahlmann: PEP - more than a Petri Net Tool. Proc. *Tools and Algorithms for the Construction and Analysis of Systems*, 2nd International Workshop, TACAS'96, Passau, March 1996, T. Margaria, B. Steffen (eds). Springer-Verlag, LNCS Vol. 1055, 397–401 (1996).
The system can be downloaded from ftp.informatik.uni-hildesheim.de.

[9] E. Best and R.P. Hopkins: $B(PN)^2$ – a Basic Petri Net Programming Notation. Proc. *PARLE'93*, A. Bode, M. Reeve, G. Wolf (eds). Springer-Verlag, LNCS Vol. 694, 379–390 (1993).

[10] E. Best and M. Koutny: Petri Net Semantics of Priority Systems. *Theoretical Computer Science* 96, 175-215 (1992).

[11] E. Best and M. Koutny: Solving Recursive Net Equations. Proc. *ICALP'95*, Szeged, F. Gecseg, Z. Fülöp (eds). Springer-Verlag, LNCS Vol.944, 605-623 (1995).

[12] E. Best and Ch. Lengauer: Semantic Independence. *Science of Computer Programming* Vol. 13, 23–50 (1989/90).

[13] B. Bieber: Blockabstraktion in einer Programmiersprache für verteilte Systeme. Diploma Thesis, Universität Hildesheim (1996).

[14] J.C. Corbett: Evaluating Deadlock Detection Methods for Concurrent Software. Technical Report, Dep. of Information and Computer Science, University of Hawaii at Manoa (1995).

[15] J.C. Corbett and G.S. Avrunin: A Practical Method for Bounding the Time between Events in Concurrent Real-time Systems. Proc. *Int. Symp. on Software Testing and Analysis*. New York, 110–116 (1993).

[16] M. Damm: Implementierung der High-Level-Netz-Semantik für $B(PN)^2$. Diploma Thesis, Universität Oldenburg (1995).

[17] J. Desel and J. Esparza: *Free Choice Petri Nets*. Cambridge Tracts in Theoretical Computer Science 40. Cambridge University Press (1995).

[18] R. Devillers: On a more Liberal Synchronisation Operator for the Petri Box Calculus. Technical Report LIT-281, Université Libre de Bruxelles (1993).

[19] E.W. Dijkstra: *A Discipline of Programming*. Prentice Hall (1976).

[20] J. Engelfriet: Branching Processes of Petri Nets. *Acta Informatica* 28, 575–591 (1991).

[21] J. Esparza: Model Checking based on Branching Processes. Habilitation, Hildesheim (1993). Published as: Model Checking Using Net Unfoldings. Proc. *TAPSOFT'93* (1993), M.C. Gaudel, J.P. Jouannaud (eds). Springer-Verlag, LNCS Vol. 668, 613–628 (1993). Full version in *Science of Computer Programming* Vol. 23, 151–195 (1994).

[22] J. Esparza, St. Römer and W. Vogler: An Improvement of McMillan's Unfolding Algorithm. Proc. of *Tools and Algorithms for the Construction and Analysis of Systems*, 2nd International Workshop, TACAS'96, Passau, March 1996, T. Margaria, B. Steffen (eds), LNCS Vol. 1055, Springer-Verlag (1996).

[23] H. Fleischhack: Objektnetze in der Büromodellierung – Probleme und Lösungsmöglichkeiten. Internal Report, Universität Oldenburg (1992).

[24] H. Fleischhack and B. Grahlmann: A Petri Net Semantics for $B(PN)^2$ with Procedures which Allows Verification. Hildesheimer Informatikbericht 21/96 (1996).

[25] W. Frączak: *Composition Parallèle et Synchronisation de Systèmes à Événements Discrets*. PhD Thesis, Université Paris-Sud (1996).

[26] H. Genrich: Predicate-transition Nets. In *Petri Nets: Central Models and their Properties*, Advances in Petri Nets 1986, Part I. Springer-Verlag, LNCS Vol.254, 207-247 (1987).

[27] P. Godefroid: On the Costs and Benefits of using Partial-order Methods for the Verification of Concurrent Systems. Proc. *POMIV'96*.

[28] U. Goltz and W. Reisig: The Non-sequential Behaviour of Petri Nets. *Information and Control* Vol. 57/2–3, 125–147 (1983).

[29] B. Grahlmann, M. Moeller and U. Anhalt: A New Interface for the PEP Tool: Parallel Finite Automata. Proc. 2nd Workshop *Algorithmen und Werkzeuge für Petrinetze 1995*, J. Desel, H. Fleischhack, A. Oberweis, and M. Sonnenschein (eds), Report AIS 22, Universität Oldenburg (1995).

[30] B. Graves: Ein Modelchecker für eine Linear-Time-Logik. Diploma Thesis, Universität Hildesheim (1995).

[31] B. Graves: Identification of Specific Processes Contained in McMillan's Finite Unfolding. Work in progress (1996).

[32] M.H.T. Hack: Petri Net Languages. MIT, Laboratory of Computer Science, TR-159 (1976).

[33] M. Heiner and P. Deussen: Petri Net Based Design and Analysis of Reactive Systems. Proc. *WODES'96, Workshop on Discrete Event Systems*, Edinburgh (1996).

[34] T. Himstedt: Entwurf und Implementierung eines High-level-Petrinetzeditors und -simulators. Diploma Thesis, Universität Hildesheim (1995).

[35] C.A.R. (Tony) Hoare: An Axiomatic Basis for Computer Programming. *Communications of the ACM* Vol. 12, 576–580 (1969).

[36] G. Holzmann: *Design and Validation of Computer Protocols*. Prentice Hall (1990).

[37] L. Jenner: Ein Prozedurkonzept für die parallele Hochsprache $B(PN)^2$. Diploma Thesis, Universität Hildesheim (1994).

[38] K. Jensen: *Coloured Petri Nets. Basic Concepts, Analysis Methods and Practical Use. Volume 1*. EATCS Monographs on Theoretical Computer Science (1992).

[39] L.H. Landweber and E.L. Robertson: Properties of Conflict-free and Persistent Petri Nets. *Journal of the ACM* Vol. 25(3), 352–364 (1978).

[40] C. Lewerentz and T. Lindner: Formal Development of Reactive Systems – Case Study: a Production Cell. Springer-Verlag, LNCS Vol. 891 (1995).

[41] J. Lilius: $OOB(PN)^2$: an Object Oriented Petri Net Programming Notation. Proc. *2nd Workshop on Object-Oriented Programming and Models of Concurrency*, Osaka, Japan, 89–103 (1996).

[42] J. Lilius and E. Pelz: An M-net Semantics for $B(PN)^2$ with Procedures. Draft (1995/1996).

[43] K.L. McMillan: Using Unfoldings to Avoid the State Explosion Problem in the Verification of Asynchronous Circuits. Proc. *4th Workshop on Computer Aided Verification*, 164–174 (1992).

[44] K.L. McMillan: *Symbolic Model Checking*. Kluwer Academic Publishers, Boston (1993).

[45] D. May: Occam. *ACM SIGPLAN Notices* Vol. 18/4, 69–79 (1983).

[46] St. Melzer: Ein C-Codegenerator für $B(PN)^2$. Diploma Thesis, Universität Hildesheim (1995).

[47] St. Melzer and J. Esparza: Checking System Properties via Integer Programming. Proc. *ESOP'96*, Hanne Riis Nielson (ed.). Springer-Verlag, LNCS 1058, 250–264 (1996).

[48] St. Melzer, St. Römer and J. Esparza: Verification using PEP. Proc. *AMAST'96*. Springer-Verlag, LNCS 1101, pp. 591–594. (1996).

[49] A.J.R.G. (Robin) Milner: *A Calculus of Communicating Systems*. Springer-Verlag, LNCS Vol. 92 (1980).

[50] A.J.R.G. (Robin) Milner: *Communication and Concurrency*. Prentice Hall (1989).

[51] M. Nielsen, G.D. Plotkin and G. Winskel: Petri Nets, Event Structures and Domains. *Semantics of Concurrent Computation*, G. Kahn (ed.). Springer-Verlag, LNCS Vol. 70, 266–284 (1979).

[52] S.S. Owicki and D. Gries: An Axiomatic Proof Technique for Parallel Programs. *Acta Informatica* Vol. 6, 319–340 (1976).

[53] Doron Peled: Combining Partial Order Reductions with On-the-fly Model-Checking. *Journal of Formal Methods in Systems Design*, Vol. 8(1), 39–64 (1996).

[54] D. Peled: Partial Order Reduction: Linear and Branching Temporal Logics and Process Algebras. Proc. *POMIV'96*.

[55] L. Pogrell: Inatcl – eine flexible Schnittstelle zu INA. Proc. 2nd Workshop *Algorithmen und Werkzeuge für Petrinetze 1995*, J. Desel, H. Fleischhack, A. Oberweis, and M. Sonnenschein (eds), Report AIS 22, Universität Oldenburg (1995).

[56] W. Reisig: *Petri Nets. An Introduction*. EATCS Monographs on Theoretical Computer Science Vol. 4, Springer-Verlag (1985).

[57] W. Reisig: Petri Nets and Algebraic Specifications. *Theoretical Computer Science* 80, 1-34 (1991).

[58] W. Reisig: Petri Net Models of Distributed Algorithms. Springer-Verlag, LNCS Vol. 1000 (1996).

[59] St. Römer: Implementierung der Branching-Box-Algebra. Diploma Thesis, Universität Hildesheim (1993).

[60] K. Schmidt: *Symbolische Analysealgorithmen für algebraische Petrinetze*. Dissertation (December 1995).

[61] A. Seidel: Entwurf und Implementierung eines Editors für elementare Petriboxen. Diploma Thesis, Universität Oldenburg (1993).

[62] P.H. Starke: *INA – Integrated Net Analyser*. Manual (1992).

[63] P.H. Starke: *Analyse von Petrinetzmodellen*. Verlag B.G. Teubner (1990).

[64] P. Stevens: http://www.dvcs.ed.ac.uk/staff/pxs/index.html

[65] Th. Thielke: Modelchecking als Komponente der Petrinetz-basierten Entwicklungs- und Programmierumgebung PEP. Proc. *Algorithmen und Werkzeuge für Petrinetze*, J. Desel, A. Oberweis, W. Reisig (eds), Berlin (1994).

[66] K. Varpaaniemi, J. Halme, K. Hiekkanen and T. Pyssysalo: PROD reference Manual. Helsinki University of Technology, Digital Systems Laboratory, Series B: Technical Report No.13 (1995).

[67] A. Valmari: Stubborn sets for Reduced State Space Generation. Proc. *10th Int. Conf. on Petri Nets*, Vol. II, Bonn, 1–22 (1989).

[68] A. Valmari: Stubborn Set Methods for Process Algebras. Proc. *POMIV'96*.

DIMACS Series in Discrete Mathematics
and Theoretical Computer Science
Volume **29**, 1997

Rapide: A Language and Toolset for Simulation of Distributed Systems by Partial Orderings of Events *

David C. Luckham †

November 1, 1996

Abstract

This paper describes the RAPIDE concepts of system architecture, causal event simulation, and some of the tools for viewing and analysis of causal event simulations. Illustration of the language and tools is given by a detailed small example.

1 Introduction

RAPIDE-1.0 [LKA+95],[LV95] is a computer language for defining and executing models of system architectures. The result of executing a RAPIDE model is a set of events that occurred during the execution together with *causal* and *timing* relationships between events. The production of *causal history* as a simulation result is, at present, unique to RAPIDE among event-based languages. Sets of events with causal histories are called *posets* (partially ordered event sets). [1] Simulators that produce posets provide many new opportunities for analysis of models of distributed and concurrent systems.

RAPIDE-1.0 is structured as a set of languages consisting of the Types, Patterns, Architecture, Constraint, and Executable Module languages. This set of languages is called the RAPIDE *language framework*.

The purpose of the framework is twofold: *(i)* to encourage multi-language systems, *(ii)* to define language components that may be applied to, or migrated into, other event generating systems. Towards *(i)*, we anticipate that the Executable Module, Constraint or Architecture sublanguages may be changed in fairly substantial ways, and that the Executable Module and Constraint sublanguages may be interchanged with other languages provided certain compatibility requirements are met. Towards *(ii)*, for example, the use of constraints expressed in terms of event patterns will have many applications to systems that generate events, not

1991 *Mathematics Subject Classification.* Primary 68M05, 68M15, 68M20; Secondary 68N05, 68N15.

*This project is funded by DARPA under ONR contract N00014-92-J-1928 and Air Force Rome Labs Grant F30602-96-2-0191, and by AFOSR under Grant AFOSR91-0354.

†Present members of the RAPIDE project team are: David Luckham, Walter Mann, John Kenny, James Vera, Sigurd Meldal, Neel Madhav, Alex Santoro, Francois Guimbretierre, Woosang Park, Marc Abramowitz, Alvin Cham, Claudio Garcia.

[1] Posets differ from Pomsets [Pra86] in that every event in a poset has a unique identifier; but posets produced by RAPIDE can contain equivalence classes of events, as we discuss later.

just the RAPIDE simulator. Such applications could include monitoring distributed object systems based on CORBA (or other commercial middleware) for security, for conformance to standards, and for many other properties.

The Types language provides the basic features for defining interface types and function types, and for deriving new interface type definitions by inheritance from previous ones. Its semantics consists of the general rules defining the subtype (and supertype) relationship between types so as to allow dynamic substitution of modules of a subtype for modules of a supertype. The other sublanguages of the framework are extensions of the Types language. They assume the basic type definition features, and add new features in a way compatible with strong typing (i.e., every expression has a type). The architecture language extends the types language with constructs for building interface connection architectures. The Executable Module language adds modules, control structures, and standard types and functions. Standard types (i.e., data types available in many languages) are specified in a separate document as interface types. The Constraint language provides features for expressing constraints on the poset behaviors of modules and functions. The Event Pattern Language is a fundamental part of all of the executable constructs (reactive processes, behavior rules and connection rules) in the executable module and architecture languages, and also of the constraint language.

This paper is a short introduction to some of the topics and issues surrounding RAPIDE. Specifically, we discuss :

1. interface connection architectures.
2. the RAPIDE concepts of *event*, *cause*, and *causal event history*.
3. tools for depicting and analyzing causal event histories.
4. constructing a small example – a model of the Dining Philosophers – and viewing its behavior.
5. some research and development issues.

We do not have the space to deal with different concepts of *system architecture*, or the design of *constraint languages* that are specially suited to causal event behaviors. More information on RAPIDE can be found in the Internet Web page:

http://anna.stanford.edu/rapide/rapide.html

The treatment of concepts of *architecture* given here is an extremely cursory and incomplete excerpt from one of our publications. It is included here because there is currently so much vagueness about "architecture", and so much use of the term without any attempt to define what it means. People mean many different things by "architecture". It is important that the reader has some understanding of the concepts of architecture that have motivated the design of RAPIDE.

RAPIDE is an event-based language and simulation toolset. We give a short but quite detailed overview of *events*, causal histories of events, and RAPIDE computations. This is followed by a short description of the present tools to support architecture modelling, i.e., building models of system architectures, simulating architectures and analyzing simulation results.

Finally, there is an example illustrating some features of the RAPIDE POV (Point of View Viewer) for browsing causal event histories and constraint violation detection.

2 Interface Connection Architectures

The concept of architecture we shall illustrate here is called *interface connection architecture* [LVM95], so called because all communication between modules is explicitly defined by connections between interfaces — no longer are connections buried in the modules, but instead they are defined between the features in interfaces. Figure 1 depicts this kind of architecture.

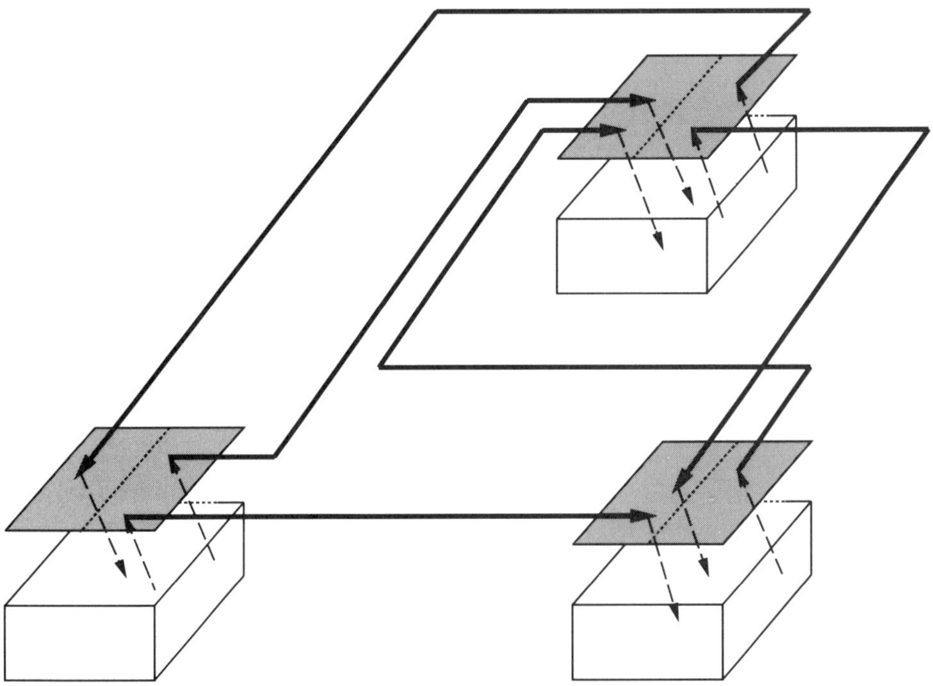

Figure 1: An interface connection architecture and conforming system

An interface connection architecture can be defined *before* the modules of the system are built. It can be used as a plan or early prototype of the system. To define interface connection architectures requires more sophisticated interfaces than are found in programming languages, and a completely new concept to define connections between interfaces. RAPIDE provides new features for representing *interface connection architecture*, not normally found in programming languages or middleware IDLs. In summary, the architecture features are:

- *interfaces* that specify both the features a module provides and, in addition, the features it requires from other modules. Moreover, there are two kinds of features, those implying synchronization (i.e., functions) and those implying asynchronous communication (i.e., actions). RAPIDE interfaces are more complex than, say, package specifications in Ada or classes in C++ which do not specify features required from other objects.

- *behaviors* in interfaces: Behaviors are sets of reactive rules that define abstract, executable specifications of the behavior that is required of modules in order to conform to that interface.

- *connections* between interfaces define relationships between the required features of interfaces and the provided features of the interfaces. The simplest kind of connection is *identification* between a required feature and a provided feature. [2] Identification connections have the effect that whenever a required feature is used then the connection invokes the provided feature in its place. More general kinds of connections allow sets of required features to be connected to sets of provided features.

  Connections are dynamic. A connection can depend upon runtime parameters, or the sets of features that are connected can vary at runtime, or the interfaces that are connected can also vary dynamically.

- *constraints* are declarative statements that restrict the behavior of the interfaces and connections in an architecture. They can be used to explicitly specify requirements on the behavior of an architecture as a whole, or of its individual components. Conformance to constraints can be checked at runtime, or, in some cases, decided by proof methods.

RAPIDE interfaces can contain executable behaviors as illustrated in the example ahead. Connections are also executable in the sense that whenever their required features are invoked, they result in execution of the provided features that they connect to. Consequently, in RAPIDE an interface connection architecture can be executed (or simulated) before modules are programmed for its interfaces.

Example: *An Interface Connection Architecture with asynchronous connections*

```
type Producer(Max : Positive) is interface
    action out Send(N : Integer);
    action in  Reply(N  : Integer);
behavior
     Start => Send (0);
    (?X in Integer) Reply(?X) where ?X < Max => Send(?X + 1);
end Producer;

type Consumer is interface
    action in Receive(N : Integer);
    action out Ack(N : Integer);
behavior
    (?X in Integer) Receive(?X) => Ack(?X);
end Consumer;
```

[2] Also called a *basic* connection.

```
architecture ProdCon() return SomeType is
    Prod : Producer(100);
    Cons : Consumer;
connect
    (?n in Integer)
    Prod.Send(?n) => Cons.Receive(?n);
    Cons.Ack(?n) => Prod.Reply(?n);
end architecture ProdCon;
```

Commentary:

Here is a simple example of an interface connection architecture. There are two interface types, Producer [3] and Consumer. They define the interfaces of producer and consumer objects. These interfaces define asynchronous communication features called *actions*. The Producer interface contains two actions, an **out** action Send and an **in** action, Reply. Objects of this type can generate Send events and can receive Reply events. The Producer interface also contains reactive behavior transition rules. The first one triggers on a Start event (which all objects receive when they are elaborated) and reacts by generating an **out** event, Send(0). The second behavior rule triggers on Reply events containing integer data provided the data is less than Max, and generates a Send event containing the next integer.

The Consumer interface type is similar. It can receive Receive events, and its behavior is to react by generating Ack events containing the same data.

The ProdCon architecture contains two components, Prod and Con, each of an interace type. Connections between these two components are defined by two reactive connection rules. The first triggers whenever Prod generates a Send and reacts by generating a Receive event of Cons with the same data. So it connects the Prod component's **out** action Send and the Cons component's **in** action Receive. The second rule connects the Cons component's **out** action Ack with the Prod component's **in** action Reply.

The architecture defines the communication between the two components in terms of the actions in their interfaces. The architecture can be refined by introducing detailed modules for Prod and Cons. The refined system is called an *instance* of the interface connection architecture. As long as the new modules communicate only by calling the actions in their own interfaces, they will communicate in the instance only as defined by the connections in the architecture. The instance conforms to the architecture if its modules behave consistently with the behavior rules defined in their interfaces, and preserve its communication. Conformance implies that many properties of the system are defined by its

[3] More accurately, Producer is a *type constructor*; when it is applied to a value for its parameter, Max, the result is a type.

architecture. For example, conformance implies that the instance will have the property that an interval of integers, $0, 1, 2, \ldots, Max - 1$ is communicated between the producer and consumer, according to a protocol whereby there is an acknowledgement from the consumer before the next integer is sent by the producer.

□

An interface connection architecture can be used to analyze properties of a system that conforms [4] to that architecture, but we have to omit discussion of this topic here.

Although Figure 1 depicts connections between the interfaces as static wires, interface connection architectures in RAPIDE can be *dynamic* architectures. Typically, a *static* architecture has a fixed number of components and a fixed number of connections, and the properties of the connections do not vary at runtime — hardware architectures that can be modelled in languages like VHDL [VHD87] are a typical example. In a *dynamic* architecture the numbers of (interfaces of) components can vary at runtime, and connections between the interfaces can exist or not, depending upon runtime conditions. An air traffic control system is an example of a dynamic architecture with varying numbers of aircraft and connections that depend upon distance, radio frequency, and other factors.

2.1 Conformance of a System to an Architecture

An interface connection architecture can be built *before* any system of modules that, in some sense, *has* that architecture. How can it be decided if a system has that architecture?

An architecture defines a constraint on all of its instances. That is, an architecture is a formal constraint on the system's behavior. Conversely, a system *has* an architecture if it *conforms* to it. There are three basic conformance criteria:

1. **decomposition** : for each interface in the architecture there should be a unique module corresponding to it in the system (i.e., the component implementing that interface). [5]

2. **interface conformance**: each component in the system must conform (as described below) to its interface. Since RAPIDE behaviors and constraints can be part of interfaces, this conformance criterion is, in general, stronger than the syntactic interface conformance usually required by programming languages.

3. **communication integrity**: All communication between components is constrained by the architecture. Two components cannot communicate with each other directly unless a connection (possibly conditional on runtime parameters) between their interfaces is defined by the architecture.

---

[4] see Section 2.1.

[5] More sophisticated decomposition criteria, such as requiring an abstraction mapping from sets of system components to interfaces in the architecture, are allowed by RAPIDE mapping constructs, but are beyond the scope of this presentation.

Conformance of modules to interfaces in programming languages usually only requires a module to contain features that match names and parameter signatures of features in their interfaces — a simple compiletime check. In RAPIDE conformance of modules to interfaces requires satisfying both behavior and semantic constraints. In general, determining if a module conforms to an interface with semantic constraints is an undecidable problem, although there are many useful cases where it can be decided by practical methods. Developing tools for testing architecture simulations for conformance to constraints, and proving correctness of architectures, is a challenging activity at present. The RAPIDE toolset supports testing for interface conformance by both compiletime and runtime checking (see Section 6). In the future, tools for applying proof techniques to interface conformance may be added.

Although determining interface conformance in the presence of behaviors and constraints is a tougher problem than the usual syntactic signature requirements between interfaces and modules, it allows us to conclude much more about the modules of a system. Interface constraints allow us to specify modules sufficiently to ensure that any two modules conforming to an interface can be interchanged without changing the behavior of the system. Also, if the connections in an architecture are correct — i.e., the constraints on a provided feature logically imply the constraints on a required feature connected to it — then instances of the architecture where interfaces have been assigned modules conforming to those interfaces will also have correct connections.

There are many strategies one may adopt to try to ensure that a system satisfies communication integrity. For example, one may adopt restrictions on the coding of modules (called a *style guides*). A possible style guide could be that a module should be constrained to only communicate with other modules of the system, or its parent architecture (i.e., the architecture of which it is a component), through its own interface, as shown in (Figure 1). This style helps to ensure that only the communication defined in the architecture takes place between modules. [6] Sufficient conditions for communication integrity involve *(i)* restrictions of the RAPIDE visibility rules, and *(ii)* restrictions of the types of parameters of actions and functions so that particular types of objects cannot be passed between components.

2.2 The Role of Constraints in defining architectures

Constraints in RAPIDE are event pattern constraints. That is, they define patterns of events which must, or must not, occur during the execution. Constraints can be part of a RAPIDE interface or an architecture. Generally, constraints in an interface are used to specify restrictions on the behavior of modules with that interface. Constraints in architectures are used to restrict the activity in the architecture. For example, constraints can specify certain sequencing of communication between components, such as might be required by a particular protocol. When a module or architecture executes, its behavior is checked for conformance to the constraints.

[6] This style, although encouraged, is not enforced by RAPIDE for reasons discussed later.

3 Event-based Computation

A *computation* is a set of events together with partial orderings that relate events in the set. The partial orderings in RAPIDE 1.0 computations represent *dependence* between events and the *time* at which events happen with respect to various clocks. The dependence relation is also called the *causal* relation since it models which events caused an event to happen. Computations are also called *executions*.

3.1 Events

An *event* is an object generated by a call to an action. An action declaration defines an associated *event type*; this event type is the type of events generated by calls to that action. Every action call generates new event which is distinct from all previous events.

The constituents of an event are the name of the generating action, parameters, information [7] defining which events caused the event, and timestamps. Thus an event, may be defined as a tuple consisting of these data. Not all of these constituents are visible to the user. Some constituents (such as the dependency information) are useable only through predefined operations.

3.2 Operations on events

An event is *generated* by an action call . The predefined **event** type provides the following operations on events:

1. E.Action_Name — a string naming the action used to generate E,
2. E.From_Module — the object that generated E,
3. E.parameter_name — the value of a component of E corresponding to the parameter_name of the action E.Name,
4. C.Start(E) — the start time of E according to clock C, undefined if E was not generated in the scope of C,
5. C.Finish(E) — the finish time of E according to clock C, undefined if E was not generated in the scope of C.

Timing orderings are imposed by the clocks (if any) in a RAPIDE 1.0 program. Each clock partially orders the events that are generated within its scope.

3.3 Relationships between events

RAPIDE provides facilities for defining and referencing two kinds of relationships between events:

- *dependence*,
- *time* with respect to a clock.

Both relationships are partial orderings of events.

[7] Dependency is captured by means of so-called Fidge-Mattern vectors of counters [Fid91],[Mat88]; we omit discussion of details here.

4 How events are generated in Rapide

Roughly speaking, all active modules [8] in a RAPIDE model execute independently. They observe and generate events, and they do this independently of each other unless their activity depends upon the events they observe. Modules can themselves be multi-threaded, so dependency is not defined at the object level, but rather at the level of *process*, *behavior rule*, *connection rule* and reading/writing *operations* on particular types of object.

Models are *hierarchical*, that is modules can themselves be architectures of modules [9]. Whether or not two modules can communicate at any given point in an execution depends upon a concept of the *context* of a module. Roughly speaking, a module M can observe events resulting from a module invoking M's interface actions and functions, and M can invoke interface features of a module in its context, and can broadcast events to those modules in whose context it is. Context starts out initially corresponding to well known scope rules of algol-like languages, but varies at runtime because modules can be passed as event or function parameters to other modules.

4.1 Generating dependent events

There are three kinds of language features that define dependence between events:

- *reactive* rules and processes. Reactive rules are transition rules in interface behaviors, connection rules in architectures, and mapping rules in maps. Reactive processes are **when** statements in modules. Whenever a set of events with the required relationships is observed (see later) by a reactive rule or process, and *matches* its trigger, then that rule or process executes (i.e., the rule or process *triggers*). The events then generated by the rule or process on that particular execution depend upon those events that triggered it.

- *sequential* code — events generated by sequential executions have a strict linear dependence represented by their order of generation,

- *ref objects* — a **ref** type object defines dependence between the events generated by the processes that share the object. If an event results from a computation that dereferenced a **ref** object, then the event depends on the (unique) event that last changed the contents of that **ref** object — i.e., operations on **ref** objects are linearly ordered.

4.2 Generating timed events

A type or module can be *timed* by having a clock associated with it, or by being placed in the scope of a clock. The type Clock and several subtypes of it are predefined. Events receive start and finish time values for each clock within whose scope they are generated.

Action calls may specify the time taken for actions to be performed with respect to a clock. If action A is defined to take duration d with respect to clock C, then for

[8] We use "Module" and "object" synonomously here.
[9] called their components

an event E generated by A, C.Start(E) + d = C.Finish(E). If no duration is defined, the events are generated infinitely fast with respect to any clock.

4.3 Observation of Events

The events generated by a module of a RAPIDE program are *visible* to, and can be *observed* by, other modules if it is in their context. Conversely, events are made *available* to a particular module for observation when other modules call its interface **provides** functions and **in** actions.

The ability to call the interface functions and actions of a module depends upon visibility rules of the language. For example, a typical way (but not the only way) that a module can communicate with another module is by generating events which trigger connection rules in the architecture in which both modules are components. Both components are visible to the architecture. The connection rules are then executed by the architecture and result in calls to the other module's interface functions or actions.

4.4 Observing events by pattern matching

Features for observing events, and the dependency ordering between events, are provided by the *pattern language*. Briefly, patterns are templates that allow the definition of posets of events. Patterns can specify relationships between events by means of dependence operators. For example, "A depends on B" is written as A → B, and "A is independent of B" is written as A || B.

The timing parameters of events can be accessed by clock operations as described in Section 3.2. The pattern language also defines abstract pattern operations dealing with time and events.

Patterns can be used as the triggers of: *(i)* processes, *(ii)* transition rules in interface behaviors, *(iii)* connections in architectures, and *(iv)* map rules. Events that are made available to a module are observed by *matching* the pattern triggers of the reactive rules or processes in the module.[10] If and when an event contributes to matching the pattern trigger of a rule or process, it can no longer be observed by that rule or process.

Finally, patterns can be used in formal constraints. Events that are available to a module are also observed by matching the constraints of that module. Violations of constraints are reported as they happen.

4.5 Orderly observation

Events are *observed* (that is, considered for matching in patterns) in an order consistent with the causal ordering of the events. That is, an event may only be observed after all events it depends on, and independent events may be observed in any possible order. This principle is known as *orderly observation*.

Orderly observation is important in efficiently matching patterns that refer to dependencies between events.

---

[10] Pattern matching is explained in the RAPIDE LRMs (see http://anna.stanford.edu/rapide/rapide.html).

5 Computations

The events generated by all the modules of a RAPIDE 1.0 program comprise the computation [11] generated by the program. A computation consists of a set of events, S, a dependence partial ordering, $\leq_d$, and timing partial orderings, $\leq_C$, for objects C of type Clock.

$A <_C B$ is defined as $C.Finish(A) < C.Start(B)$.

Posets generated by RAPIDE programs satisfy two invariants.

The dependence *and* time orderings satisfy a consistency invariant:

- **Consistency invariant between dependence and time**
  For all events A, B, and each clock, C,

$$\mathrm{A} \leq_d \mathrm{B} \rightarrow \mathrm{A} \leq_C \mathrm{B}.$$

This means that, with respect to each clock, an event in the past may not depend on an event in the future.

The consistency invariant may be expressed within RAPIDE 1.0 as a constraint:

```
never
    ( ?A in event(), ?B in event(), ?C in Clock )
    ?A -> ?B where not ?C.Finish(?A) ≤ ?C.Start(?B);
```

Similarly, the various time orderings obey a consistency invariant:

- **Consistency invariant between time orderings**
  For all events A, B, and clocks, C, C',

$$\mathrm{A} <_C \mathrm{B} \rightarrow \mathbf{not}\ \mathrm{B} <_{C'} \mathrm{A}.$$

This means that, with respect to any two clocks, an event that precedes any event temporally with respect to one clock may not follow that event temporally with respect to the other clock.

This invariant may be expressed within RAPIDE 1.0 as a constraint:

```
never
    ( ?A in event(), ?B in event(),
      ?C1 in Clock, ?C2 in Clock )
    ?A ~ ?B where ( ?C1.Finish(?A) < ?C1.Start(?B) and
                    not ?C2.Finish(?B) < ?C1.Start(?A) );
```

6 Architecture Simulation and Analysis

When a RAPIDE model is executed a causal event history of its behavior is generated. Each object receives a Start event when it is elaborated. It may react by

[11] Also called an *execution* or *simulation history*.

generating events. Connections between components of the model (i.e., objects it contains) then trigger and generate events at the interfaces of components. Components react to these events, and generate further events, which are communicated by connections to other components, and so on. Models can be organized hierarchically, and connections can also connect actions in the interface of an object with actions in interfaces of its components. A model can also interact with its environment through a predefined I/O module.

The simulation result is a poset showing the causal history of events in the execution, independent activity, timing, dataflow and other properties. This gives us the capability to simulate the behavior of a system architecture very early during the requirements analysis and design phases of the system. [12]

To make maximal use of causal event simulations requires new kinds of analysis tools. RAPIDE is presently supported by three kinds of tools for analyzing simulations:

- *Constraint Checkers.* Constraint checkers automatically detect violations of constraints in the simulations. Whenever a violation is detected, the checker enters an event in the simulation at the causal position where it happened. The causal history of a violation event indicates why the violation happened.
- *Poset Browsers.* It is often necessary to browse a simulation simply to see how a given architectural design behaves. Indeed, one of the most important uses of early lifecycle simulation is experimental. Poset bowsers usually represent causal event simulations in a DAG form, nodes representing events and directed arcs representing causality. They supply a user interface with pattern directed operations to display pieces of large simulations, and to organize a display into a hierachy of sub-simulations.
- *Animation Tools.* The wealth of information in posets together with the somewhat abstract display formats provided by browsers, often results in the human viewer missing important properties. [13] Animation tools give the user a capability to animate in visual forms the event activity in any poset. usually, a picture of the architecture is used as the basis for animation, and both the poset and the animation can be viewed simultaneously. The user is thereby given a human understandable intepretation of a poset simulation — in fact more than one animation view of the same poset can be provided.

6.1 Architecture-Driven System Development

RAPIDE is also intended to allow exploration of new methods of using architectures to build and test systems. In one approach to *architecture driven* system development, a RAPIDE interface connection architecture is used as a framework for building a system. One starts with an architecture consisting of interfaces and connections. The architecture is executed under different input scenarios to simulate the behavior of a system with that architecture. Assuming simulations of the

[12] The RAPIDE tools shown in Figure 2 have been implemented by Walter Mann, James Vera, John Kenney, Alex Santoro, Francois Guimbretierre, Earnest Lam, Alvin Cham, Marc Abramowitz, Wolf Polak, and Doug Bryan.

[13] This happens in all manner of simulations nowadays, whether or not causal information is avialable.

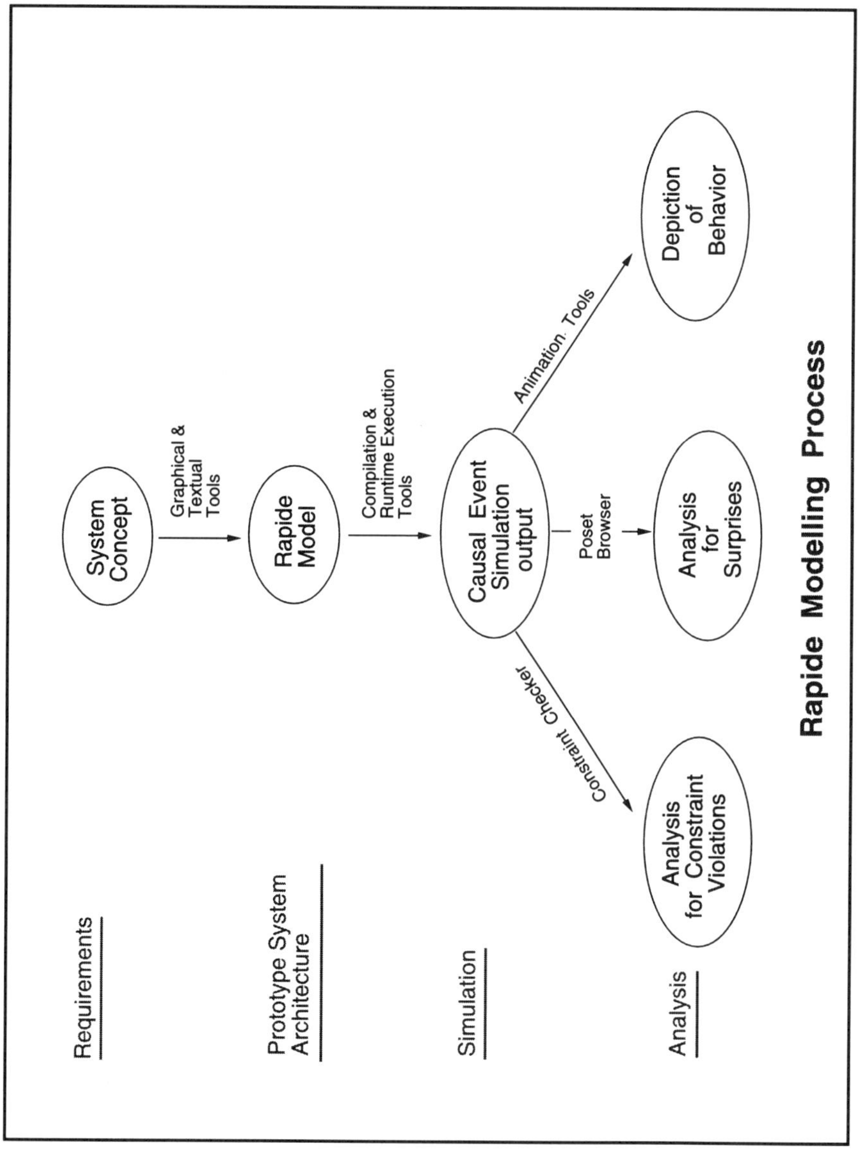

Figure 2: The Rapide simulation and analysis toolset

architecture show behavior that meets the requirements for the system, modules are then assigned to interfaces one at a time. Each module must conform to the interface it is assigned to (RAPIDE type rules help towards this, but as mentioned in Section 2.1, testing satisfaction of semantic constraints is a difficult problem.) When a module is assigned to an interface, the module is executed and the role of the interface behavior is to act as a constraint to which the module's behavior must conform (in addition to the semantic constraints). The result of assigning a module to an interface is called an *instance* of the architecture. Each instance is tested for comformance to the architecture's interface constraints, and also to the constraints on the architecture's connections. The final result should be a system of modules satisfying the architecture's interface and constraints.

This style of architecture-driven system development has an analogy with hardware. Interface connection architectures can be viewed as "architecture boards" in which interfaces play the role of "plugs" and "sockets" into which component modules can be plugged, and connections play the role of "wires" between the sockets.

Methodology surrounding the use of architectures, to prototype behavior and predict system performance early in the life cycle, and to develop finished systems by instantiation (i.e., replacing interfaces by modules, probably in languages other than RAPIDE) is beyond the scope of this overview. There are many outstanding research questions surrounding RAPIDE, both practical (e.g., developing good simulation and analysis tools), and theoretical (e.g., determining if a module conforms to its interface, and if the connections in an architecture satisfy the architecture constraints).

7 Dining Philosophers

The familiar classic example of the dining philosophers due to Dijkstra is a simple distributed system with a resource contention problem. Here is a version of it that serves to illustrate some of the RAPIDE architecture concepts and issues related to designing "user friendly" tools for analyzing posets.

You can see the code for this architecture in the figures ahead. There are two types of component, a type of round table at which a number of philosophers can sit, and a type of philosopher.

To understand the architecture, first scan the interface types, then see how the objects of those types are connected in the architecture.

The Table interface is parameterized by the number of philosophers — it is a type constructor, each instance of which is a type of table object, e.g., the type of tables for one philosopher, two philosophers, etc. A table controls and dispenses the chopsticks by means of its interface actions. Actions specify the events that objects of the interface type can receive or generate. Tables can receive StickRequested and StickRecovered events (mode **in**), and can generate ReleaseStick events (mode **out**).

The behavior of tables is specified by the reactive rules in the behavior part. Essentially, a table will release a chopstick to a requestor when the chopstick becomes free (i.e., is initially free, or is recovered).

The rule,

```
(?a in Chopstick, ?i in PhilosopherId)
StickRequested(?a, ?i) and FreeStick(?a) ||> ReleaseStick(?a, ?i);;
```

will trigger whenever a chopstick ?a is requested by something denoted by ?i (the architecture connections will show that ?a, ?i have to be bound to ids for a Chopstick and a Philosopher) *and* ?a is free. "?a is free" if an event FreeStick(?a) has been generated and not yet used to trigger a rule (the RAPIDE semantics of behavior rules allows an event to be used only once to trigger any given rule, but may contribute to triggering different rules by helping to match their pattern triggers.) When the rule triggers it generates an **out** event, ReleaseStick with the bindings of ?a, ?i.

The ||> operator indicates an *agent* rule. The semantics is that each triggering of an agent rule is executed by a new thread of control. As a result, the event generated by the rule will be causally dependent upon the two triggering events, but will be independent of any events generated by previous triggerings of the rule.

A Chopstick gets to be free again according to this behavior rule:

(?a **in** Chopstick)
StickRecovered(?a) ||> FreeStick(?a);;

Note that FreeStick is an internal event of the Table types (i.e., is declared in the behavior part), which means that it is not visible at the architecture level.

The event behavior of a Table (i.e., the causally related events it will generate in response to the events it receives) can be predicted from the semantics of behavior rules. The three behavior rules of Tables execute independently, so the events they generate are independent – unless the rules are triggered by events that other rules generated, like FreeStick. So a ReleaseStick event will depend upon a FreeStick and a RequestStick event – and by transitivity, the events that caused them. So it will also have a StickRecovered event (with the chopstick in question as argument) in its history.

Each table is a multi-threaded object, executing independently of other objects, unless it communicates with them by means of the architecture's connection rules.

```
---------------- Types --------------------------

    type PhilosopherId is integer;
    type Chopstick is integer;

---------------- Table type. --------------------

type Table(numPhils : integer) is interface
    action in  StickRequested(n : Chopstick; id: PhilosopherId),
                  StickRecovered(n : Chopstick);
    action out ReleaseStick(n : Chopstick; id: PhilosopherId);
behavior
    action  FreeStick(n : Chopstick);
begin
    start =>   for i: integer in 0..(numPhils-1) do        -- table rule 1.
                    FreeStick(i);
                end for;;

    (?a in Chopstick, ?i in PhilosopherId)                   -- table rule 2.
     StickRequested(?a, ?i) and FreeStick(?a) ||> ReleaseStick(?a, ?i);;

    (?a in ChopStick)                                        -- table rule 3.
     StickRecovered(?a) ||>   FreeStick(?a);;
end Table;
```

The philosopher interface type specifies philosopher objects. They can perform two activities: they can generate RequestStick and PutDownStick events (**out** actions), and they can receive StickReceived events (an **in** action). These events carry Ids for a chopstick and a Philosopher. Philosophers are generated by a simple module generator, newPhilosopher, which takes the Id and the number of philosophers as parameters, and generates a module containing instances of the concurrent processes. These processes define the behavior of philosophers: i.e., when a philosopher generates RequestStick and PutDownStick events, and when it generates certain internal events such as thinking and eating.

The semantics of RAPIDE processes allows us to reason about the event behavior of Philosophers. A philosopher must acquire two chopsticks in order to eat rice. The two processes that trigger on a Hungry event will request the two chopsticks independently. Another process triggers when a pattern of two StickReceived events match (each having a correct chopstick for the philosopher), where the events may be either causally dependent or not (the $\sim$ relation). This process then generates an Eat event, which in turn will trigger a process that generates PutDownStick events. Consequently, the StickReceived events will be in the causal history of each of the PutDownStick events.

```
------------------Philosopher type -------------------
type Philosopher is interface

   action out RequestStick(n: Chopstick; id: PhilosopherId),
                 PutDownStick(n : Chopstick);
              in  StickReceived(n : Chopstick; id: PhilosopherId);

end;


------------------module generator for philosophers-----

module  newPhilosopher  (id: PhilosopherId; numPhils:integer)
                        return Philosopher is
    action Hungry(),
           Think(),
           Eat();

parallel
    when Start
    do
        Hungry();
    end;


    ||
    when Hungry
    do
        RequestStick(id, id);                       -- request left chopstick
    end;


    ||
    when Hungry
    do
        RequestStick((id+1) mod numPhils, id);      -- request right chopstick
    end;


    ||
    when
        StickReceived(id, id) ~                     -- received left chopstick
        StickReceived((id+1) mod numPhils, id)      -- received right chopstick
    do
        Eat();
    end;
```

```
    ||
    when
        Eat
    do
        PutDownStick(id);
        PutDownStick((id+1) mod numPhils);
        Think();
    end;
end;
```

NOTE: we could have used behavior rules in the philosopher interface, as we did for Tables, but we would have to introduce the number of philosophers as a parameter, and this is an implementation detail which should not appear in the interface. So we illustrate the use of module generators (which, generally, can contain more complex programs than interface behaviors).

The architecture, diners1(), contains one table and an array of 5 philosophers. Philosophers (i.e., the objects generated by the newPhilosopher module generator) have an Id number which differentiates them from their colleagues. The table associates two chopsticks with each philosopher by means of chopstick Ids (actually all Ids are integers anyway!). The Ids encode the model of a chopstick being placed to the left and to the right of each philosopher, In diners1, philosophers and the table interact through actions defined in their interfaces. These actions are wired together by connection rules in the **connect** section of the architecture.

A connection rule triggers on a pattern of **out** events generated by objects in the arhcitecture (and also **in** events of the architecture's interface received by the architecture itself) and in turn generates a pattern of **in** events which are received by objects (and also **out** events of the architecture's interface). [14] An example connection rule is:

```
(?a in Chopstick, ?i in PhilosopherId) Ta.ReleaseStick(?a, ?i)
  to
  Ph[?i].StickReceived(?a, ?i);
```

which is a point-to-point communication between the Table and each of the requesting Philosophers. It connects the Table's **out** action, ReleaseStick to a unique Pilosopher's **in** action, StickReceived, depending upon the Id of the Philosopher. Here "connect" means that whenever the Table generates a ReleaseStick event the rule will trigger and generate a StickReceived event of the Philosopher whose Id is the binding of ?i. The connection operator, **to** means that the two events are causally equivalent (i.e., indestinguishable by either the cause or time relations).

We use a generate statement to define the connections between the **out** actions of each Philosopher in the array and the **in** actions of the Table — a "fan-in" of 5 rules; the generate is an iterative statement that defines the set of connections that are instances of its connection rules for each value of the iteration parameter, j. [15] There are two sets of 5 rules in the **generate**. The first set of rules defines

[14] Architectures can be nested as components of other architectures through their interface events.

[15] Generate connection rules can be found in hardware description languages like VHDL. In

connections so that whenever a Philosopher generates RequestStick events, the Table will receive StickRequested events with the same parameter bindings. The second set of connections trigger whenever a Philosopher generates a PutDownStick event for a chopstick ?a and then generate a StickRecovered for the same ?a which is received by the Table.

When diners1 is executed, the Philosophers activity is triggered by their Start events, which makes them hungry, then they request chopsticks, etc. Philosophers are active for only one cycle of eating and thinking; it is easy to change this so they continue to cycle, but we don't do it to keep our posets small.

NOTE that different executions of diners1 may produce posets with different causal relationships between events because of the non-deterministic behavior rules (if two rules trigger on the same events, RAPIDE does not define an order in which they execute). Indeed, some posets will show that all philosophers ate while other posets will show the usual deadlock with nobody eating.

---

combination with the RAPIDE pattern-triggered connections, they are a powerful notation for defining large numbers of connections.

```
------------ Dining Room architecture. -----------------

architecture diners1() is

   num_philosophers : integer is 5;

   Ph : array(PhilosopherId, Philosopher) is (
                                      0 is newPhilosopher(0, num_philosophers),
                                      1 is newPhilosopher(1, num_philosophers),
                                      2 is newPhilosopher(2, num_philosophers),
                                      3 is newPhilosopher(3, num_philosophers),
                                      4 is newPhilosopher(4, num_philosophers)
                                                 );
   Ta: Table(num_philosophers);

connect
   (?a in Chopstick, ?i in PhilosopherId) Ta.ReleaseStick(?a, ?i)
    to
    Ph[?i].StickReceived(?a, ?i);

    for j : PhilosopherId in 0..num_philosophers-1   generate

        (?a in Chopstick, ?i in PhilosopherId) Ph[j].RequestStick(?a, ?i)
         to
         Ta.StickRequested(?a, ?i);

        (?a in Chopstick )Ph[j].PutDownStick(?a)
         to
         Ta.StickRecovered(?a);
    end;
end architecture diners1;
```

8 Viewing and Analyzing Posets

Figure 3 is a DAG representation of a poset generated by this model. The POV (Point Of View) viewer displays a poset in this kind of representation, and provides capabilities to explore the poset. [16]

Figure 3 is a very simple example of a poset. The DAG is oriented vertically with the causally earlier events at the top. Here are a few things it tells us at first glance about the execution of our dining philosophers. There are 7 Start events, one for the Diners1 architecture, the Table and the 5 Philosophers. They are all in a causal chain corresponding to the execution of a single thread that elaborated

[16] The POV is being implemented at Stanford by Francois Guimbretierre, Earnest Lam, Alvin Cham and Marc Abramovitz. An earlier prototype viewer was implemented by Doug Bryan.

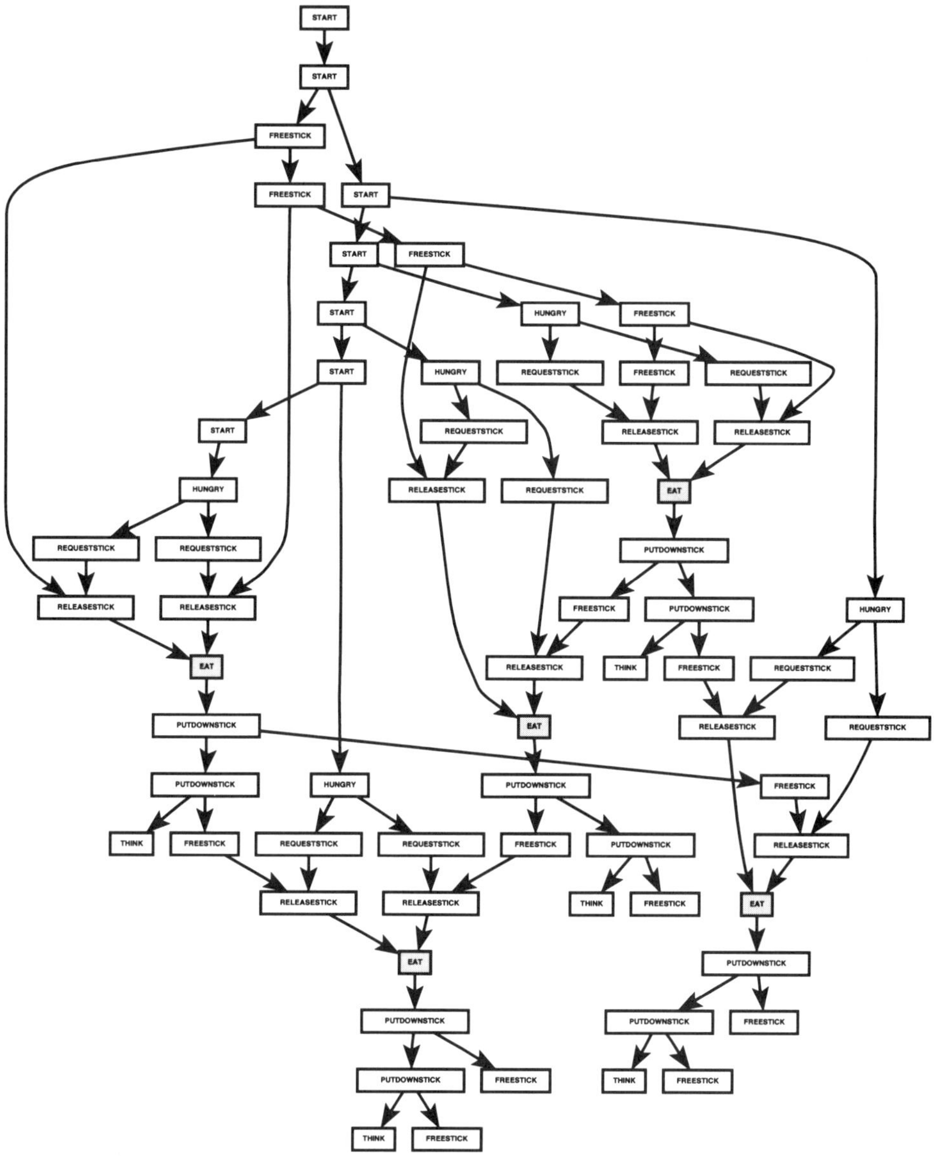

Figure 3: A poset generated by the diners1 system

Diners1. The second start is the Table's because it immediately causes a FreeStick. Each start causes a sub-poset of events, the initial events being all independent of one another — so there are initially 7 threads of control after starting. We can see the Table's first sequential behavior rule results in a single causal chain of FreeStick events. (Using the POV we could trace this chain by placing the cursor on its arcs. An arc "lights up" when the cursor is on it and the thread id and causally related events coresponding to the arc are displayed in the window. So a chain corresponding to a single thread can be easily traced.)

A Philosopher, after starting, immediately generates a Hungry event which then triggers two parallel processes (see the newPhilosopher module). This causes two independent RequestStick events. These are shown as causing ReleaseStick events generated by the Table. How did that happen? Well, a philosopher's RequestStick action is connected to the Table's StickRequested action by a **to** connection rule. This kind of rule implies that the two events, a triggering RequestStick and the event it generates, StickRequested, are *equivalent*. So the node showing "RequestStick" is an equivalence class of two events, but only one of them is displayed. (By clicking with cursor and mouse on an event node, POV will display all events in the equivalence class.)

Tracing a little further, a StickRequested event received by the Table, and a FreeStick event with the same Chopstick Id, will trigger the Table's second behavior rule and generate a ReleaseStick event. So, a ReleaseStick event is caused by two events. Again, due to a **to** connection rule (the first one), a node labelled with "ReleaseStick" represents an equivalence class containing also a StickReceived event received by a Philosopher. When a Philosopher receives two StickReceived events, it eats and then generates PutDownStick events for the two sticks. Notice that the PutDownStick events are causally ordered because they are generated by a single sequential process in a Philosopher, in constrast to the RequestStick events. There is no good reason for this — they could be put down independently.

More importantly, notice that since an Eat event must have two StickReceived events causing it, and it causes the PutdownStick events, then the StickReceived events are in the causal history of both PutDownStick events for the same pair of chopsticks that were used in eating.

The PutdownStick events are connected (and equivalent by the third **to** connection rule) to the Table's StickRecovered events, which cause the Table's behavior to generate FreeStick events. A Philosopher's second PutDownStick event is followed by a Think event, which is the end of its activity.

Figure 4 shows some features of POV. First, the poset in Figure 3 has been filtered down to the poset in Figure 4. This filtering was done by using the POV to select the causal history of the third StickReceived event. Events that are not selected are deleted from the poset. In general one can select a sub-poset matching a given pattern. This feature allows the user to reduce the poset to events "of interest". So, what we are looking at is the causal history of a particular StickReceived event. All StickReceived events in this poset have been "selected" – a facility of the POV which results in selected events being colored. The tearoff windows show the result of querying the selected (colored) events with the POV by clicking on them. Each window shows the data of the event: *(i)* the name of the corresponding action, *(ii)* the Id of the object generating the event (by calling the action), *(iii)* the Id of the object receiving the event, and *(iv)* parameters of the events. Parameter #1 of these events is the chopstick Id. So we see that Philosopher #31 received sticks #1 and #2, which allowed it to eat, and causally afterwards to put down stick #1, which was then freed. Stick #1 was then received by Philosopher #30. [17] It is not hard to see using the POV on the full poset that all StickReceived events with the

[17] Stick #2 was also put down, but does not appear in the causal history of the event whereby Philosopher #30 receives stick #1.

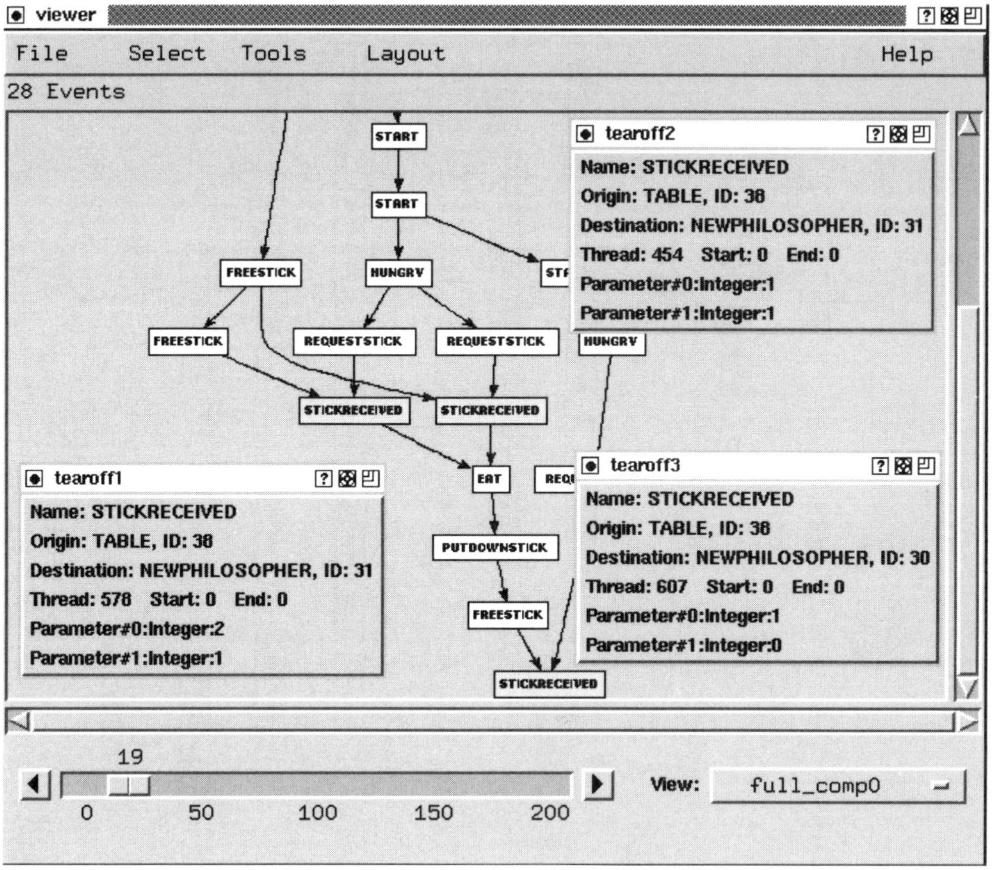

Figure 4: Exploring a poset with the POV

same chopstick as parameter are causally related. This gives us a hypothesis (**H**) that StickReceived events with the same chopstick parameter are always causally related in any poset behavior of this model, which is easily shown to be true.

The poset in Figure 3 has varied during the writing of this paper. Sometimes it shows that all Eat events are causally related. But, the model can also generate posets in which some Eat events are independent because the Philosophers may be scheduled differently on different executions. The DAG layout of the poset makes it hard to see which of these two posets we have in the Figure. This illustrates the need for ways to select events of interest — e.g., we might like to be able to say, "show all the Eat events" and get displayed the subposets containing just those events. More generally, we may want to organize a complex poset into subcomputations corresponding to abstraction levels in the model's architecture and components — e.g., just the top level events in Diners1. POV provides such capabilities, but we cannot describe them here.

Figure 5 shows another behavior of Diners1 — one in which deadlock occurs.

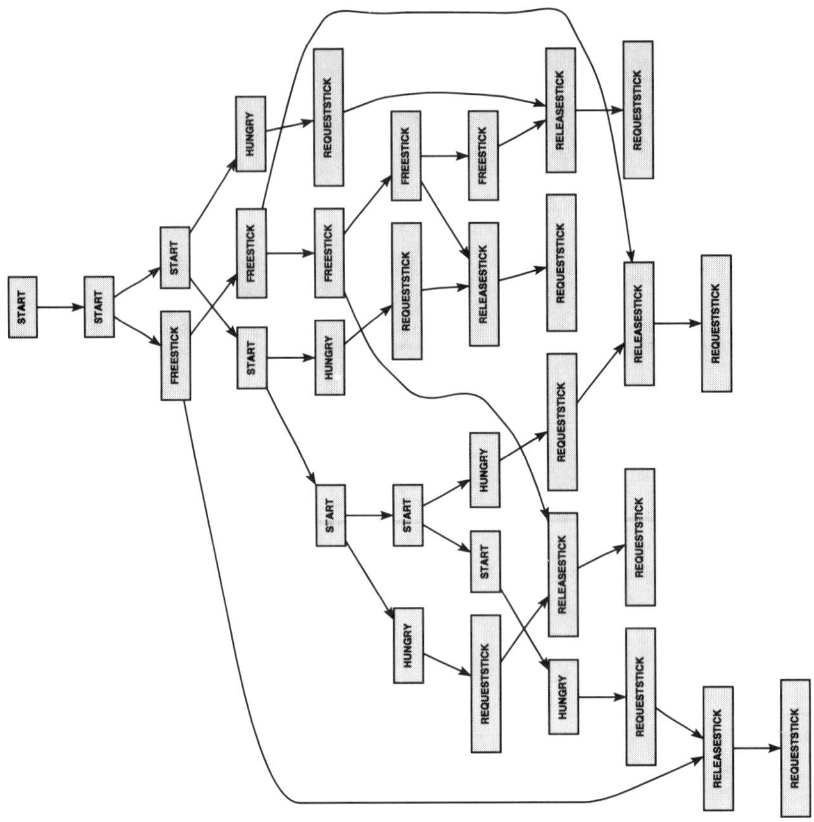

Figure 5: Deadlock in the dining room

9 Constraining poset behaviors

Figure 5 brings up another question. Remembering that RAPIDE is intended as a prototyping language, which means essentially that it can be used to explore properties of a proposed system architecture *before* it is really well understood or "completely decided upon". If the posets produced by a model are large or complex, one may well miss seeing some important aspects of the model's behaviors with the POV. So, RAPIDE provides a formal constraint language which can be used to specify constraints on behaviors. There is a constraint checker which will detect if a poset contains violations of constraints. [18]

Constraints can be used in two ways. First, to automatically analyze posets for particular properties. Secondly, to build a purely constraint-based model of a system architecture — one that has no executable behavior at all, but simply bounds the allowable behaviors by constraints. In the latter case, a constraint-based architecture is one approach to defining a standard for systems to conform to.

We do not have space to go into the details of the RAPIDE constraint language, [19] so we give just a couple of examples of constraints on the dining philosophers.

An example of a constraint in the interface of the Philosopher type, specifying part of the behavior of philosopher objects is:

```
-- Philosopher_Protocol:
match [* rel —→]
  (?id : Integer)
  (RequestStick(?id, ?id) ~ RequestStick(?id, (?id+1) mod numSeats)) —→
  (StickReceived(?id, ?id) ~ StickReceived(?id, (?id+1) mod numSeats)) —→
  (PutDownStick(?id, ?id) ~ PutDownStick(?id, (?id+1) mod numSeats));
```

The poset occuring at the interface of a Philosopher (i.e., those events corresponding to the actions declared in the interface) must match the constraint. The pattern of the constraint is a pair of RequestStick events in any causal relation to one another (i.e., dependent or independent, denoted by the $\sim$ relation), which must both cause two StickReceived events (also this pair may be in any causal relationship to one another), which must cause a pair of PutDownStick events. The iterator preface of the constraint ([* **rel** —→]) specifies arbitrarily many (*) matches of the pattern, and each match must be causally related to the next one (i.e., in the relation, —→). So the interface behavior must be a causal chain of matches of the pattern. Many different modules can satisfy this constraint. Similar constraints can be used to specify essential properties of Tables. Our present constraint checker does not check for violations of constraints like this example.

Note, that since the constraint specifies relationships between both **out** and **in** events of philosophers, it specifies a property of the environment that Philosophers interact with. Namely, whenever a Philosopher generates RequestStick events, the environment shall causally respond with StickReceived events — and only then. Certainly, the environment cannot simply send a Philosopher unsolicited chopsticks, independently of a request for them. This point, that the interfaces of types of objects need to specify something about the environment in which the objects are intended to operate, is an on-going research area in Architecture Definition Lan-

[18] The present constraint checker detects violations of only a subset of the constraint language. It is experimental, and a new constraint checker is planned.

[19] The constraint language is being redesigned by Walter Mann, John Kenny, Sigurd Meldal, Woosang Park and David Luckham.

guages at present. Causal relationships between the environment and the objects are a powerful constraint mechanism.

Now, what about deadlock? This is a constraint on the architecture, but because of the causal relations in our model, it can be expressed as a constraint on the interface events of Tables:

```
never [i:positive 0..4 rel || ] Ta.ReleaseStick(i, i);

never [i:positive 0..4 rel || ]
        Ta.ReleaseStick(i, (i+1) mod 5);
```

These two constraints are placed in the architecture, Diners1. They are violated if a Table ever generates five causally independent ReleaseStick events, one to each Philospher. Because of hypothesis (**H**) about our Diners1 model, one of these two constraints will be violated if and only if deadlock happens. [20] Our present constraint checker detects violations of this kind of "never" constraint — see Figure 6.

10 Research and development Issues

In this final section we mention a few of the research and development issues surrounding RAPIDE and its present toolset. Many open topics, particularly to do with the design of Architecture Definition Languages, and with animation tools, are omitted altogether.

10.1 Tracking Causality

The causal history of an event is a data component of the event itself as described in Section 3. This causal history is computed when an event is generated by the well-known method of vectors of counters associated with threads of control — a method attributed independently to Fidge [Fid91] and Mattern (F-M) [Mat88]. One problem affecting the ability of the RAPIDE simulator to handle large models is the space consumed by the F-M vectors — the worst case upperbound is n^2 where n is the number of threads of control. [21] Making the F-M vector method more efficient, e.g., by taking advantage of the communication structure defined in the model's architecture to reduce the size of the vectors, and garbage collect them at appropriate points in a computation. This is a very important issue for us. [22]

There may be methods of encoding and tracking causal history that are entirely different from F-M vectors. If there are, they need to be investigated and compared for efficiency with F-M.

10.2 Patterns and Constraints

Design of pattern and constraint languages for specifying patterns of posets with timing is very much in its infancy. The RAPIDE constraint language is currently

[20] We leave finding an elegant proof of this to the reader.

[21] A performance anlaysis of F-M vectors is being undertaken by Park and Vera, using the RAPIDE model of the Sparc V9 instruction set.

[22] James Vera is currently working on this issue, and some previous results are given in [MSV91].

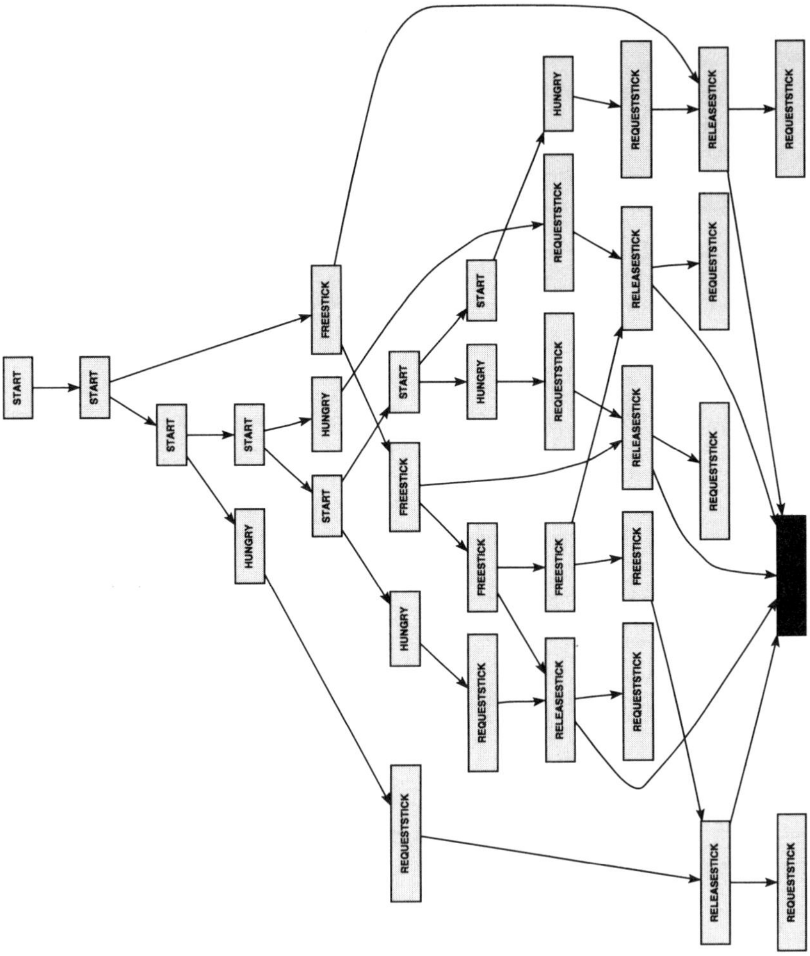

Figure 6: Deadlock with constraint violation history

undergoing a major revision. Although there are close similarities with languages such as regular expressions and various temporal logics, the specification of causal dependence and independence introduces a new dimension.

Perhaps an even more pressing issue is the development of efficient algorithms for matching patterns on posets. [23] Efficiency of pattern matching affects both the execution of reactive rules, and the checking of posets for constraint violations.

10.3 Poset Viewers

Design of poset viewers and their implementation is entirely new ground. I mention two areas: User Interfaces and Graph layout algorithms.

For user interface design there is very little relevent experience with previous tools to draw upon. For example, Netscape Viewers had the previous Macintosh UI as well as various office software UIs to draw ideas and idioms from. But there is not much prior art on which to draw for poset viewer interfaces. We must pretty much experiment on our own with such questions as: [24]

- what common processes of poset viewing and manipulation will users find most natural and useful — those are the ones the UI should make easy to carry out,
- what tools for poset analysis should be provided to support the processes,
- how to organize access to the tools into menus in the Viewer UI.

Our basic premiss that posets are best represented by some kind of DAG format appears quite natural. The visualization tool (called Raptor) which is not discussed here, provides the ability to construct other visualizations of posets. But, in order to persist with DAG formats as our primary visual presentation, we need layout algorithms that are both *(i)* fast, and *(ii)* stable — i.e., the layout does not change radically under small operations on the poset, such as deleting one or two events. Both of two these issues with DAG layout algorithms appear to be interesting research areas at present.

References

[Fid91] Colin J. Fidge. Logical time in distributed systems. *Computer*, 24(8):28–33, August 1991.

[LKA+95] David C. Luckham, John J. Kenney, Larry M. Augustin, James Vera, Doug Bryan, and Walter Mann. Specification and analysis of system architecture using Rapide. *IEEE Transactions on Software Engineering*, 21(4):336–355, April 1995.

[LV95] David C. Luckham and James Vera. An event-based architecture definition language. *IEEE Transactions on Software Engineering*, 21(9):717–734, September 1995.

[LVM95] David C. Luckham, James Vera, and Sigurd Meldal. Three concepts of system architecture. *submitted to the Communications of the ACM*, July 1995.

[23] John Kenney is working on a new RAPIDE pattern matcher.

[24] The new POV is being developed by Francois Guimbretierre and Marc Abramowitz.

[Mat88] F. Mattern. Virtual time and global states of distributed systems. In M. Cosnard, editor, *Proceedings of Parallel and Distributed Algorithms*. Elsevier Science Publishers, 1988. Also in: Report No. SFB124P38/88, Dept. of Computer Science, University of Kaiserslautern.

[MSV91] Sigurd Meldal, Sriram Sankar, and James Vera. Exploiting locality in maintaining potential causality. In *Proceedings of the Tenth Annual ACM Symposium on Principles of Distributed Computing*, pages 231–239, New York, NY, August 1991. ACM Press. Also Stanford University Computer Systems Laboratory Technical Report No. CSL–TR–91–466.

[Pra86] V.R. Pratt. Modeling concurrency with partial orders. *Int. J. of Parallel Programming*, 15(1):33–71, February 1986.

[VHD87] IEEE, Inc., 345 East 47th Street, New York, NY, 10017. *IEEE Standard VHDL Language Reference Manual*, March 1987. IEEE Standard 1076–1987.

DIMACS Series in Discrete Mathematics
and Theoretical Computer Science
Volume **29**, 1997

Debate'90: An Electronic Discussion on True Concurrency

Abstract

The following electronic correspondence was posted to the concurrency mailing list, moderated at the time by Albert Meyer, between October 21 and November 19, 1990. It has been reformatted for publication and edited for spelling but otherwise is largely untouched. —*Vaughan Pratt*

To: pratt@cs.Stanford.EDU
From: dcl@anna.Stanford.EDU
Subject: Partially Ordered Computations
Date: Sun, 21 Oct 90 13:39:23 -0700

Vaughan,

In some recent discussions with people funded by ONR's program on distributed and realtime computing, I have found an attitude that

"sets of linear traces are entirely sufficient for analyzing distributed/concurrent computations, AND Partial Orders are unnecessary".

I also notice that sets of linear traces are the basis for Hoare's PROCOS project.

Questions to you:

1. What is your favorite simple example of a system where a partial order representation of its execution is superior to a set of linear traces of its execution,

2. Would you disagree with the ONR people, and how?

- David

To: dcl@anna.stanford.edu
From: pratt@cs.Stanford.EDU
Subject: Re: Partially Ordered Computations
Date: 21 Oct 90 15:14:37 PDT (Sun)
In-Reply-To: Your message of Sun, 21 Oct 90 13:39:23 -0700.
<9010212039.AA07939@Aphid.Stanford.EDU>

The belief that linear orders capture partial is predicated on several assumptions, most of which have to hold at the same time in order for it to be reliable.

1991 *Mathematics Subject Classification.* Primary 68Q55.

While these assumptions tend to hold in very simple or abstract systems, they all gradually fade away as the systems you look at get larger and more concrete.

Here are seven such assumptions.

1. Fixed granularity.
2. No variability of atomic events.
3. Absence of autocurrence.
4. Single-poset processes.
5. Race-free.
6. Single-observer model.
7. Discrete time.

Here is the meaning of each of these concepts.

1. Variable granularity can arise in various quite different ways. One way is just to look at a supposedly atomic event more closely and resolve substructure. But another is to take a binary program whose *specification* treats it as atomic (on the ground that the vendor doesn't want you to assume anything about the package) and find when you run it that it has a series of side effects on your system, that may interleave with the side effects of other such packages.

You might find it interesting to look at "Teams Can See Pomsets" by Plotkin and myself to see what influence variable granularity can have. It turns out this is not the theoretically worst problem in our paper, #2 below is worse, but it does have some influence.

You can anonymous-ftp a preliminary version of this paper from boole.stanford.edu on pub/pp2.*. [Also in this proceedings. -vp]

2. Variability of atomic events means that although an event stays atomic it might not do identical things each time it happens. Plotkin and I use this phenomenon to show that a sufficiently large team of observers (see item 6) can distinguish *any* two finite pomsets.

3. Autocurrence means two concurrent and identical events. Without the concurrency requirement we find two such repetitions in the word "identity": there are two t's and two i's. An example with concurrence is when you ask the bank teller for two dollars. If dollars always came sequentially there'd be no quarrel about the legitimacy of the string 11 as a specification for two dollars. But what about 1|1 meaning "Give me two dollars please." This phenomenon arises as soon as you distinguish pomsets from posets.

With autocurrence you can get $a|a$, which traces can't distinguish from aa. This can be solved via so-called "action refinement", used in solving 1 above. But action refinement gets you only so far, in particular it can't be used in conjunction with traces to distinguish $TR|TR$ (two parallel sequences each of $T \to R$, e.g. two parallel message streams) from the same thing with the extra requirement that one of the T's precede *both* of the R's. But pomsets can make that distinction, using the N pomset.

4. A single-poset process is one defined by a single poset. This is a key assumption in the theorem coding posets as their linearizations. However this

assumption is rarely achievable in practice. It is false that a set of posets can be encoded with the union of their respective sets of linearizations.

5. When a and b are in a race, the trace model reveals only ab+ba. But race-free nondeterminism, which chooses one of $ab + ba$, has the same trace representation. This matters for example in the glitch problem. You may want to implement $ab + ba$ glitch-freely, but you cannot say it with traces. This is a pretty simple argument, so you might use it first (I suppose I should have).

The same argument applies to distinguishing the mutually exclusive execution of two atomic operations from their concurrent execution. The trace model has built into it the assumption that mutually exclusive execution and concurrent execution are the same thing for atomic events. This interacts with item 1.

6. Most models of concurrency assume that one observer collects all the observations. In practice observers are as distributed as the systems they observe, and can pool their distributed observations in ways entirely unrelated to the computational model used to prove correctness of a particular distributed system. This is a subtle point that Plotkin and I go to pains to explain in detail in our paper. [Shortened for the proceedings version. -vp]

7. Time must be discrete for traces to model interleaving. Just what exactly is the set of all interleavings of two copies of the unit interval [0,1]? Consider a dual beam oscilloscope. Are you going to describe its two beams in terms of their interleavings?

These issues are specific technical problems that arise with traces. But besides any question of what might actually go wrong, there is also the question of the most *natural* model. I feel that models should attempt to be reasonably faithful to what they model, *if* the mathematics supports this. Even if your unnatural model happens to be working today, my feeling is that unnatural models are more likely to break down in the future than natural ones..

When you have a computer in Europe talking via satellite to one in the US, the time between instructions is thousands of times less than that between computers. A natural way to model the instruction streams of the two computers then is with two sequences. The trace model does not accept this, on the ground that a computation consists of one sequence. It says that you must interleave the two sequences in all possible ways before you can reason soundly about the system.

The problem is that the only serious mathematics that many practicing computer scientists get exposed to is computation theory, where they are taught that all computation is sequential. Getting through their computation theory course was one of the bigger struggles of their college education, but mastery of it vindicated the enormous outlay of tuition and board for all those years when they could have been learning on the job.

So then they run into concurrency in the real world and they simply cannot cope with the concept of two parallel streams, because they have never seen any such concept in their textbooks, nor any theorems about such concepts.

Therefore they do the only thing possible: they interleave in order to reduce to a known model with known theorems.

I can say on the basis of having worked with both models for many years that posets are far more flexible and easier to work with than traces. Having to think about systems in terms of traces is like trying to do arithmetic with Roman numerals. Yes, Roman numerals indeed code integers, and furthermore the algorithms for adding and multiplying Roman numerals do work, but that's not a great reason to stick with Roman numerals.

Vaughan Pratt

```
To: concurrency@theory.lcs.mit.edu
From: rance@adm.csc.ncsu.edu (Rance Cleaveland)
Date: Mon, 22 Oct 90 11:29:48 -0400
```

Another reason for using posets crops up when one wishes to reason about the real-time properties of a system. Assuming that one is working in a setting where each atomic action takes 1 time unit, $a|b$ ("a and b truly in parallel") should also take 1 time unit, while ab + ba will take 2. So it seems a bit surprising to me that a group of people interested in real time would find linearizations an adequate model of concurrency.

Rance Cleaveland

```
To: concurrency@theory.lcs.mit.edu
From: Vaughan Pratt <pratt@cs.Stanford.EDU>
Subject: modeling concurrency with partial orders
Date: Mon, 22 Oct 90 12:57:26 PDT
```

Rance's comment on real time reminds me. I neglected to connect up with recent work explaining why true-concurrency hackers seem to prefer the poset side of an otherwise surely symmetric duality between posets as schedules and distributive lattices as automata, a duality generalized by Winskel et recently many al to event structures, dual to families of configurations.

The reason is that automata are 1-dimensional and hence can only exhibit the structure of interleaving concurrency. This is intuitively obvious to true true concurrency hackers, and I can only infer that the proponents of this duality in its published form are false true concurrency hackers.

In order to faithfully and continuously represent, on the automaton side of the duality, the structure of true concurrency that its proponents like myself so vividly imagine to exist on the poset side, automata should be made higher dimensional. This has been done implicitly by van Glabbeek and Vaandrager in PARLE-87 via the notion of ST-bisimulation. I will be momentarily sending off my POPL paper explaining how to make more explicit the geometry implicit in this (if I just can restrain myself long enough from writing these damn messages).

Apropos of real time, the phenomenon by which two pencils can be put into a shirt pocket only high enough to accommodate one, impossible in the interleaving world as Rance points out, translates under this duality to the need for the L_∞ norm (i.e. $\max(x, y)$) in measuring duration of truly concurrent processes in higher-dimensional automata. In contrast the L_1 norm or Manhattan metric $x + y$ measures duration of interleaved processes, that operate the way a New York taxi has to in alternating between going East and North. (So you should have inferred by now that this is the model where one lays out parallel instruction streams orthogonally, as Papadimitriou does in treating deadlock).

If one tries to approach true concurrency by refining the granularity of this interleaving, one arrives in the limit at still the L_1 norm. That is, you may have a perfectly straight line running diagonally across the product square (the product of two transitions, a surface, arising just as in the product construction for automata) but it still represents interleaved concurrency by being its limit. In this extreme case true concurrency can be distinguished from interleaving not by its shape but only its speed.

Vaughan Pratt

```
To: concurrency@theory.lcs.mit.edu
From: infhil!eike@relay.eu.net (Eike Best)
Subject: Re: The discussion on (sometime) superiority of p.orders
Date: Thu, 25 Oct 90 16:08:58 +0100
```

Here are my 2 Pfennige worth of contribution. I claim:

Sometimes partial orders let you define a concept more smoothly than arbitrary interleavings. A case in point is "finite delay". Finite delay is supposed to mean: if an action is continually enabled, then it occurs sometime.

In a sequential system, finite delay can be expressed by the maximality of an execution sequence (you would like to go as far as possible).

Consider $a * || b*$ versus $(a[]b)*$ (where $[]$ is nondet. choice). The sequence *aaaaa...* (infinitely often a but no b) contradicts the finite delay property in $a * || b*$, since the b is not prohibited from occurring and could always occur. However, *aaaaa...* does NOT contradict the finite delay property in $(a[]b)*$, since the occurrence of a is always alternative to b, and so b is continually prohibited from occurring.

The distinction can be captured by noticing that *aaaaa...*, while being maximal as a string, is not maximal as a partial order of $a * || b*$, but IS maximal as a partial order of $(a[]b)*$.

Eike Best

PS I don't claim you NEED partial orders here, but I do claim that it's nice to use them, since the concept of maximality directly generalizes the sequential one.

```
To: pratt@cs.stanford.edu
Cc: concurrency@theory.lcs.mit.edu, dcl@anna.stanford.edu
From: meyer@theory.lcs.mit.edu (Albert R. Meyer)
Subject: modeling concurrency with partial orders
In-Reply-To: pratt@cs.stanford.edu Mon, 22 Oct 90 09:57:06 EDT
Date: Fri, 26 Oct 90 14:01:09 EDT
```

I support most of your remarks, but I don't think we should accept David Luckham's formulation of the issue as

(1) Linear versus Partial Order

but rather emphasize

(2) Interleaving Nondeterminacy versus Concurrency

Formulation (1) highlights the particular detail of whether concurrent processes are abstractly represented by some structure involving linear, rather than partial, orders. This can hardly be crucial, since, as you well know, every partial order is uniquely determined by the set of its linearizations.

Formulation (2) forces us to clarify the limitations of the in many respects successful interleaving-concurrency models of CCS, CSP, MEIJE, ACP, etc. Though the following remarks are well known to you and the Continental research community in concurrency, Luckham's note confirms my impression that the issue is still not well understood elsewhere, so maybe it's worth rehashing the basis of the story another time:

The crux of the criticism of interleaving is captured in the equation

(3) $$a|b = ab + ba.$$

Equation (3) may be read as asserting that the process $a|b$, which can CONCURRENTLY perform actions a and b, may be identified with the process $ab + ba$, which NONDETERMINISTICALLY chooses to do either a-then-b or else b-then-a.

Equation (3) is an axiom in the interleaving-based theories, but maintaining it RULES OUT extensions of the theory to include

(i) observations of simultaneity: a and b can be observed simultaneously in the computation of process $a|b$, but not in $ab + ba$.

(ii) observations of the same computation by two or more sequential observers at distributed locations: under reasonable assumptions about signal propagation over distance, two such observers watching a computation of $a|b$ might see DIFFERENT linear traces (namely one could see 'ab' during the same interval that the other saw 'ba'), but under the same assumptions two observers would always see the SAME trace (namely, exactly one of ab or ba) in any given computation of ab+ba. I was delighted by this remark when I first learned it from you and Plotkin.

(iii) refinement of action atomicity–what you felicitously called "variable granularity": refining a in $a|b$ to be the two step sequential process cd yields a process with the trace cbd, but refining a in $ab + ba$ yields no such trace; I first learned this point from a note in 1987 by Castellano et al in the EATCS Bulletin.

Insofar as these extensions are desirable, one has to retreat from the simple interleaving model. The ideas that actions have duration, and more generally the ideas of critical regions and atomicity, are usually regarded as an important aspect of pragmatic concurrent processing. Because (iii) seems like a plausible theoretical way to model both action duration and relaxing atomicity requirements, extending the theory to cover it does seem desirable.

On the other hand, having agreed that interleaving theories need modification, I don't think we can say that your pomset models or the Mazurkiewicz-trace models have been fully justified as appropriate concurrency theories. For example, multiple observers don't justify distinguishing the pomset processes $P1$ and $P2$ where $P1$ is the singleton pomset $(.a.b)$ and $P2 = P1$ union one of its augmentations, say the singleton

```
.a
|
.b
```

Similarly, the various proposed event/behavior structure models are all based on generalized notions of bisimulation. I have raised my doubts in earlier messages to this forum about how the detailed distinctions between processes made by bisimulation can be justified computationally.

Despite these reservations, let me say that I do believe that the modeling of a concurrent run of a computation with a pomset is pretty natural.

Regards, A. Moderator, concurrency@theory.lcs.mit.edu

```
To: concurrency@THEORY.LCS.MIT.EDU, dcl@anna.stanford.edu
From: pratt@cs.stanford.edu
Subject: Re: modeling concurrency with partial orders
In-Reply-To: Your message of Fri, 26 Oct 90 14:01:09 EDT.
     <9010261801.AA13008@stork>
Date: 26 Oct 90 14:52:07 PDT (Fri)
```

I appreciate your words of support, Albert. Some minor comments on four points.

```
>This can hardly be crucial, since, as you well know, every
>partial order is uniquely determined by the set of its
>linearizations.
```

This is Szpilrajn's theorem [1], a "fragile" theorem in the following sense. A robust theorem about a structure should remain true when one adds further structure. Szpilrajn's theorem holds neither for a set of posets nor for labeled posets. Both these structures must be added to the basic poset structure to make it useful as a model of concurrency. I therefore view David's comparison of linear to partial orders in the context of their application to concurrency as quite appropriate.

```
>(3)        a|b = ab+ba.
>Equation (3) is an axiom in the interleaving-based theories, but
>maintaining it RULES OUT extensions of the theory to include
```

The equational logic of regular expressions has a very interesting property. If you regard its variables as denoting only themselves as symbols of an alphabet, the set of equations valid under that very restricted interpretation turns out to be the same as when you let the variables range over arbitrary languages. That is, the theory does not change when you treat its variables as self-denoting constants.

This interesting property fails as soon as you add almost any other operation, whether or not that operation preserves regularity. Such operations include complement $-a$, intersection $a \cap b$, interleaving $a|b$, quotient $a \backslash b$, and residual $a \rightarrow b = -(ab)$.

Equational theories are closed under substitution. In view of this I would like to discourage extending to other languages the practice in the language of regular expressions of denoting atoms by variables. I would be more comfortable seeing (3) written as a conditional implication:

$$atomic(a) \wedge atomic(b) \rightarrow a|b = ab + ba$$

or more generally:

$$atomic(a) \wedge atomic(b) \rightarrow mutex(a, b)$$

$$mutex(a, b) \rightarrow a|b = ab + ba$$

since $mutex(a, b)$ (I hope the meaning is clear) is at its most useful when it holds of particular nonatomic processes.

```
For example, multiple observers don't justify distinguishing the
pomset processes P1 and P2 where P1 is the singleton pomset
( .a .b ) and P2 = P1 union one of its augmentations, say the
singleton
```

Provably so of course: our multiple observer model can't distinguish a process from its augment closure. Gordon and I now have the converse of this, at least for finite pomsets, that is that distinct augment closed processes of finite pomsets are distinguishable by sufficiently large teams (infinite when the dimension of the pomsets is unbounded).

```
I have raised my doubts in earlier messages to this forum about
how the detailed distinctions between processes made by
bisimulation can be justified computationally.
```

Having written about it you're better qualified than I to express such reservations. However my intuitive feeling is that Hennessy-Milner logic, which justifies all distinctions made by bisimulation, is not an excessively strong language in the context of debugging, where the programmer marches backwards and forwards along a misbehaved nondeterministic computation trying to find what caused the misbehavior and experimenting by making little changes and seeing how they propagate side-effects forward and predicates backwards (through predicate transformers).

[1] E. Szpilrajn, Sur l'extension de l'ordre partiel, Fund. Math. 16, 386-389, 1930.

```
To: sri-unix!theory.lcs.mit.edu!meyer@unix.sri.com,
        sri-unix!theory.lcs.mit.edu!concurrency@unix.sri.com
From: tcipro!ramu@unix.sri.com (Ramu Iyer)
In-Reply-To: Albert R. Meyer Fri, 26 Oct 90 14:01:09 EDT
Subject: modeling concurrency with partial orders
Date: Fri, 26 Oct 90 16:09:54 PDT
```

On Fri, 26 Oct 90 14:01:09 EDT, Albert R. Meyer said:

```
Albert> I support most of your remarks, but I don't think we
Albert> should accept David Luckham's formulation of the issue as
Albert> (1)         Linear versus Partial Order
Albert> but rather emphasize
Albert> (2)        Interleaving Nondeterminacy versus Concurrency
```

Here are three references that discuss these pioneering issues:

L. Castellano, G. De Michelis, L. Pomello. Concurrency vs Interleaving: An Instructive Example. Bulletin of the EATCS, 31, 1987, pp. 12-15.

D.B. Benson, Concurrency and Interleaving are Equally Fundamental. Bulletin of the EATCS, 33, 1987.

W. Reisig, Concurrency is More Fundamental than Interleaving, Bulletin of the EATCS, ??, 1988.

Cheers,

–Ramu Iyer

```
To: concurrency@theory.lcs.mit.edu
From: Vaughan Pratt <pratt@cs.stanford.edu>
Subject: modeling concurrency with partial orders
Date: Sat, 27 Oct 90 00:55:01 PDT
```

```
>>>From: tcipro!ramu@unix.sri.com (Ramu Iyer)
>>>Subject: modeling concurrency with partial orders
>>>Here are three references that discuss these pioneering issues:
>>>  <3 references from 1987-88: Castellano et al, Benson, Reisig>
```

I'd like to suggest some earlier dates than 1987 or 1988 as more suitable candidates for "pioneering."

The earliest proposal I'm aware of to model concurrency with partial orders is Irene Greif's MIT Ph.D. thesis from 1975. Jan Grabowski and Nielsen-Plotkin-Winskel both have 1981 journal papers on partial orders for concurrency, with both parties reporting on work done at the end of the 1970's. C.A. Petri allegedly had advocated partial orders long ago, though not in writing as far as I'm aware.

Unlike these pioneers I did not appreciate the need for partial orders in concurrency myself until 1980. This was not for want of experience with concurrent computing. I had implemented various interrupt-driven packages in 1967-69, and I wrote and thought a fair bit about concurrency during the 1970's (1972: thesis chapter on sorting networks; 1974: showed with Larry Stockmeyer that P=NP on parallel computers; 1974-5: two circuit complexity results; 1976: solved the mutual exclusion problem for unreliable processes with Ron Rivest; 1979: axiomatized process logic).

But I did not appreciate the advantages of partial orders for concurrency until early 1980 when I was trying to understand Brock and Ackerman's paper. My pomset campaign began with my POPL-82 paper on that subject, "On the Composition of Processes" which proposed formalizing Brock and Ackerman's solution to their anomaly in terms of partially ordered multisets. I coined the abbreviation "pomset" a few months later.

I wrote a short paper on applying pomsets to the Two-Way-Channel-With-Disconnect problem for the 1983 concurrency workshop in Cambridge UK, LNCS 207, as well as a statement I circulated at IFIP-83 a week after that conference as part of a concurrency panel session chaired by Robin Milner in which I argued the case for pomsets. I also spoke about pomset semantics at Logics of Programs 1983 (no written paper unfortunately), and again in LOP 85.

This last paper was subsequently published in International Journal of Parallel Programming, 15:1, 33-71, 1986, as "Modeling Concurrency with Partial Orders" (same title as the subject line of the last 10 messages). (If you don't have that journal in your library you can retrieve this paper by anonymous FTP from boole.stanford.edu as /pub/ijjp.{tex,dvi}.)

I reproduce here the arguments I gave in that 1986 paper in support of partial orders. Note particularly item (v), which begins

(v) "A serious difficulty with the interleaving model is that exactly what is interleaved depends on which events of a process one takes to be atomic."

and goes on to explain how refinement (as it is now called) distinguishes

$a|b$ from $ab + ba$ and hence makes the meaning of interleaving dependent on granularity. While I know of no prior reference in the literature to the use of refinement to distinguish $a|b$ from $ab + ba$ I'm sure the idea had occurred to many people before, even if writing it down had not.

See also the postscript-1990 at the end, on the outcome of my long-standing problem of axiomatizing the equational theory of concatenation and interleaving for formal languages. It is noteworthy that the solver independently invented pomsets for the express purpose of solving this purely interleaving question.

Extract from "Modeling Concurrency with Partial Orders, 1986

1.2 Why Partial Orders?

Strings arise naturally in modeling ongoing sequential computation, whether the symbols in the string correspond to states, commands, or messages. Thus the string uvu may model the sequential execution of three commands u, v, u, or a transition from state u to state v followed by a transition back to u, or a sequence of three messages u, v, u transmitted sequentially on some channel.

Strings are linearly ordered sets, or rather linearly ordered multisets (since repetitions are possible), of symbols from some alphabet. In unison with the workers mentioned at the end of this section we advocate partial orders in place of linear orders in modeling concurrent computation. At present however partial orders have nowhere near the popularity of linear orders for modeling concurrent computation. This could be for any of the following reasons.

(i) Languages and their associated operations, particularly union, concatenation, Kleene star, and shuffle, provide a natural model for the corresponding programming language control structures: choice, sequence, iteration, and concurrency. The behavior of languages under these operations has been studied intensively for more than two decades. Thus languages provide a familiar and well-understood model of computation. In this model the linear order on the elements of a string is interpreted as the linear temporal order of events, and the operations on languages may be interpreted as control structures: concatenation as begin-end sequencing, star as iteration, shuffle as concurrency, etc.

(ii) Every poset is representable as the set of its linearizations. This theorem would appear to confer on linear orders the same representational ability as partial orders.

(iii) Linear orders appear to be faithful to physical reality. In the practical engineering world, as opposed say to the physicist's relativistic world, instantaneous events have a well-defined temporal order, justifying the assumption of linearly ordered time. Furthermore, in any rigid system temporal order is well-defined even in a relativistic model. Any departures from rigidity are assumed to be sufficiently minor in practice as to justify adhering to a linear-order model.

Reason (i) would lose most of its force if partial orders were to be equipped with operations analogous to those of formal languages that could be interpreted as programming language control structures. This is just what this paper does; some of the operations on pomsets that we introduce correspond to more or less familiar programming language constructs, others are merely candidates for possible future programming or hardware languages.

Reason (ii) is based on the following well-known theorem, which shows that a partial order can be represented as the set of its linearizations.

Theorem 1. The intersection of the linearizations of a partial order is that partial order.

(For the purposes of defining intersection, a partial order is considered to be its graph, that is, the set of all pairs (a, b) such that $a \leq b$.)

This theorem is easily proved under the (non-obvious) assumption that every partial order has at least one linearization, by showing that any partial order in which a and b are incomparable can be extended to one in which $a < b$ and to another in which $b < a$.

This theorem about posets runs into two difficulties when trying to apply it to processes modeled as sets of pomsets. The theorem generalizes neither to *pomsets* nor to sets of *posets*, and *a fortiori* not to sets of pomsets. We will return to this issue in section 2.6, after the necessary definitions have been given.

Reason (iii), that the engineer's world is linear in time, fails in at least three situations: complex systems, nonatomic events, and relativistic systems. Beyond a certain scale of system complexity it becomes infeasible to keep thinking in terms of a global clock and a linear sequence of events. A cover story in the magazine Electronics(3) describes a growing trend in the design of logic circuits to eliminate global clocks and rely more on self-timed circuits. On a larger scale asynchrony has been with us for a long time. When a large number of computers communicate with each other over channels whose delay is several orders of magnitude greater than the clock time of each computer, the concept of global time provides neither a faithful account of the concurrent computation of all those computers nor even a particularly useful one. There is no reason to suppose that the various instructions streams of these computers are interleaved to form one stream. Indeed it is much more convenient, both conceptually and computationally (e.g. when computing with such streams as part of reasoning about them) just to lay down these streams side by side and call this juxtaposition of streams a model of their concurrent execution. Data flowing between the computers may augment the order implicit in the juxtaposition, but this relatively sparse augmentation of the order is motivated by the actual mechanics of communication, unlike the more stringent and totally artificial ordering requirement of completely interleaving the streams.

A concrete situation that may make this more compelling consists of a ship rolling somewhere in the Pacific, in satellite communication with another ship in the Indian Ocean. The events on the buses of the computers on each ship take place with a precision measured in nanoseconds, but the delay in getting a packet from one computer to another may be on the order of a second or more. The idea that the totality of events in the two computers has a well-defined linear ordering can have no practical status beyond that of a convenient mathematical fiction. Our position is that it is neither convenient nor mathematically useful. It is just as convenient, and more useful, to work with partial orders.

Nonatomic events provide another situation where linear orders break down. An event may be more complex than a moment in time. It may be an interval, in the sense of a convex subset of a linear order. It may be a set of intervals, such as a game punctuated by timeouts or a TV movie punctuated by commercials. More generally still it may be some arbitrary set of moments. However even for such complex events it still makes sense to say that one event may precede or follow another, meaning that every moment of the first event precedes every moment of the second. Yet such events are clearly not linearly ordered.

Relativity provides yet another situation where time is not linearly ordered. In any nonrigid system, that is, one whose components are moving with respect to each other, simultaneity ceases to be well-defined and two moving observers can report contradictory orders of occurrence of a pair of events. Any system nontrivially subject to relativistic effects is a candidate for a partially ordered model of computation. Of course many systems will not be so subject, but we see it as an advantage of the partial-order approach that it applies equally well to relativistic and Newtonian (global-time) situations.

In addition to our responses to (i)-(iii), we have the following additional reasons for preferring partial orders.

(iv) Some concepts are only definable for partial orders, in particular orthocurrence, which amounts to the direct product of pomsets, which we define in full later. The solution given above to the problem of specifying the two-way-channel-with-disconnect contains two essential uses of orthocurrence, along with two less essential uses. The concept is an extremely natural and useful one for partial orders, but it is not at all obvious how one would go about defining it in a linear-order model, or even whether it is definable.

(v) A serious difficulty with the interleaving model is that exactly what is interleaved depends on which events of a process one takes to be atomic. If processes P and Q consist of the single atomic events a and b respectively then their interleaving is $\{ab, ba\}$. However if the same events a and b are perceived by someone else not to be atomic, by virtue of having subevents, then P and Q have a richer interleaving than $ab \cup ba$. It is reasonable to consider instantaneous events as absolutely atomic, but we would like a theory of processes to be just as usable for events having duration or structure, where a single event can be atomic from one point of view and compound from another. In the partial-order model what it means for two events to be concurrent does not depend on the granularity of atomicity.

(vi) In some situations pomsets appear to be easier to reason about than strings. For example it is relatively straightforward to axiomatize the equational theory of pomsets under the operations of concurrence and concatenation (Theorem 5.2[(4)]). The corresponding theory for strings has resisted all attempts at its axiomatization. Gischer and the author have both worked extensively on the problem of whether this simply described theory has a finite axiomatization. The problem has been posed on two occasions at the (San Francisco) Bay Area Theory Symposium, generating interest but no answers in more than eighteen months.

[Postscript 1990: this problem was finally solved in 1988 by Steven Tschantz, an algebraist at Vanderbilt, who settled it in the affirmative by a truly beautiful argument only a week after I posed the problem along with a list of others at the end of an invited lecture at a universal algebra conference in 1988. In doing so he reinvented pomsets quite independently as an essential tool in the proof; I had stated the problem purely for languages with no mention of pomsets at any point in my talk, which was about dynamic logic. -vp]

[Postscript 1996: Tschantz's result was subsequently published in Mathematical Structures in Computer Science 4:4 (December 1994), pp. 505-511. -vp]

Vaughan Pratt

```
To: concurrency@theory.lcs.mit.edu
From: lamport@src.dec.com (Leslie Lamport)
Subject: for the concurrency mailing list
  [Moderator's retitle: Flame re distributed processes and
  granulity]
Date: Tue, 6 Nov 90 17:13:59 -0800
```

I admire philosophers. They have so much to teach us. From Aristotle I learned that heavier bodies fall faster than lighter ones; Kant showed me that nonEuclidean geometry is impossible; and Spinoza proved that there can be at most seven planets. And now, the philosophers on the concurrency mailing list have told me all the things I can't do because I use a logic based on an interleaving model:

I can't reason about distributed systems.

In 1982 I published a proof of the distributed algorithm then used in the Arpanet to maintain its routing tables ["An Assertional Correctness Proof of a Distributed Algorithm", Science of Computer Programming 2, 3 (Dec. 1982), 175-206]. Since then I have written more formal proofs of more complicated distributed algorithms.

I can't deal with changes in the grain of atomicity.

In 1983 I published a paper ["Specifying Concurrent Program Modules", TOPLAS 5, 2 (April 1983) 190-222] containing:

A specification of a queue, in which adding or removing an element is a single atomic operation.

An implementation in which an element is moved into and out of the queue one bit at a time.

A proof that the implementation satisfies the specification.

Nowadays, my standard approach to verification is to start with a high-level program having a coarse grain of atomicity, and to refine the grain of atomicity until I reach the desired program.

I can't reason about (nondiscrete) real time.

At a workshop in 1988, I gave a one-hour lecture in which I:

Specified a distributed spanning-tree algorithm having the requirement that the computation reach and maintain a correct configuration within a fixed length of (real) time.

Gave an implementation using timers. I assumed only that timers ran at a rate of 1 +/- epsilon seconds per second, and that messages were delivered within delta seconds of the time they were sent. (Epsilon is any real number in the range [0, 1) and delta is any positive real number.)

Sketched a proof that the implementation satisfied the specification.

I have since written a detailed formal correctness proof.

I can't reason about programs without assuming a fixed granularity.

A recent paper of mine ["win and sin–Predicate Transformers for Concurrency", TOPLAS 12, 3 (July 1990), 396-428] gave a rigorous correctness proof for the bakery algorithm. This algorithm makes no assumption about the grain of atomicity of its operations. (It was the first algorithm to achieve mutual exclusion without assuming lower-level mutual exclusion.)

I'm sure the philosophers can explain why I haven't really done these things. I'll be happy to listen to their explanations, as soon as they can use their philosophically approved methods to reason formally about something more complicated than a biscuit machine.

```
To: concurrency@theory.lcs.mit.edu
From: pratt@cs.Stanford.EDU
Subject: Re: Flame re distributed processes and granulity
Date: 08 Nov 90 12:58:19 PST (Thu)
```

On p.419 of the proceedings of Logics of Programs 81 (LNCS 131) appears the following extract from the panel discussion that wrapped up that conference. Context: Amir Pnueli had just expressed the wish that every paper on programming logic say something about how this programming logic is to be applied to proving something about programs.

"Nemeti: I'd like to protest a little bit about what you (Pnueli) said about our papers. The structure of our technological society is just not like that. There was a guy called Roentgen. You could have gone to him and said, 'What are you doing playing around with these funny things of yours? Why don't you try to heal people who have colds?' There are theoreticians who are doing basic research, and there are less theoretical theoreticians, and there are technologists, so there is a whole spectrum of research in science. The theoreticians doing the basic research are really needed, because the basic ideas, the fundamental ways we look at things, come from there. Now, if you want to restrict them to report each time how this will be used, then it will result in impotence."

While I have nothing to add to this, I do have a question arising out of it. Who believes that "the basic ideas, the fundamental ways *systems people* look at things" come from the theoreticians? Do systems people believe this? And do theoreticians believe it?

Vaughan Pratt

```
To: concurrency@theory.lcs.mit.edu
From: lamport@src.dec.com (Leslie Lamport)
Subject: [lamport@src.dec.com: for the concurrency mailing list]
Date: 10 Nov 1990 1721-PST (Saturday)
```

Dear Dr. Roentgen,

I am writing to congratulate you on the success of your continuing experiments with X-rays. I can imagine your dismay at the many charlatans who have used your X-rays to justify "invisible ray"" theories based on fancy rather than science. And those silly French physicists with their N-rays! How fortunate that we live in a society where scientific validity is determined by rigorous experiment. I presume you are aware of the disturbing developments in the Soviet Union, where Dr. Lysenko attacks the work of Mendel on ideological grounds. I'm afraid it will be many years before the Soviets permit sound research in genetics, since they value philosophical correctness above empirical observation.

Sincerely yours,

Leslie Lamport

```
To: pratt@cs.stanford.edu, concurrency@theory.lcs.mit.edu
From: Robert J. Hall <RJH@ai.mit.edu>
Subject: re: Re: Flame re distributed processes and granulity
In-Reply-To: <9011082123.AA07740@stork>
Date: Sat, 10 Nov 90 12:58 EST
```

```
From: pratt@cs.stanford
On p.419 of the proceedings of Logics of Programs 81 (LNCS 131)
appears... "Nemeti: ..." (regarding need for theoreticians,
etc)
```

It seems to me this quote does not directly address Lamport's complaint which was, I believe, that the theoreticians on this list seem to be making false claims (as enumerated by Lamport). He seemed to be fraternally suggesting that one way of avoiding such false claims may be to keep a closer contact between theory and practice, if indeed theory is attempting to have some benefits for practice. In particular, if one's claim is to the effect that a technologist "can't do" something using a theory, one must at least be more precise about what it means to do that thing. Obviously, Lamport believes he has successfully used the interleaving-based view to reason about multiple granularities, whereas previous discussions on the list seem to claim he can't have done so (similarly for the other issues raised).

– Bob

```
To: "Robert J. Hall" <RJH@ai.mit.edu>
Cc: concurrency@theory.lcs.mit.edu
From: pratt@cs.Stanford.EDU
Subject: Re: Flame re distributed processes and granulity
Date: 11 Nov 90 20:22:55 PST (Sun)
```

```
It seems to me this quote does not directly address Lamport's
complaint which was, I believe, that the theoreticians on this
list seem to be making false claims (as enumerated by
Lamport).
```

My quote addressed Leslie's complaint in the most direct way possible under the circumstances. Leslie did not identify any particular claim made on the list. Rather he complained generally that certain contributors to the list, whom he did not specify, had claimed there were certain things he couldn't do, which he did specify. There have been various claims on this list about limitations of interleaving, but none that I recall making the claims Leslie was complaining about, nor any that conflicted with the evidence he adduced in support of his complaint.

One claim about interleaving in this forum is in my October 26 message to David Luckham. There I claimed that Szpilrajn's representation theorem for posets, that every poset is representable as the set of its linearizations, depends on several assumptions. For each assumption I showed informally in what way the theorem could fail in the absence of that assumption, in some cases giving pointers to where more detailed proofs of those failure modes could be found.

I see no logical connection between Leslie's complaint and my claim. And even if there were some connection, the existence of failure modes of trace-based logic when certain assumptions are violated in no way implies that every trace-based proof violating those assumptions must be unsound. I do not begrudge Leslie his sound proofs, however obtained.

The failure modes of Szpilrajn's theorem are not just mathematical curiosities but potentially real engineering problems. Perhaps Leslie knows how to take care of these problems using trace-based logic, but I don't see how his cited examples demonstrate this at all. How might a logic based on sets of traces deal with each of the following situations?

1. Distinguish the race implicit in $a|b$ from the race-free situation implied by $ab + ba$.

2. Reason about observations made by a team of distributed observers who agree on what events happened but not in what order.

3. Reason about the possible interleavings of two concurrent sine waves. (Presumably one falls back on some other technique for combining traces than interleaving them.)

He seemed to be fraternally suggesting that one way of avoiding such false claims may be to keep a closer contact between theory and practice

I found no hint of such a suggestion in Leslie's message.

Vaughan Pratt

```
To: concurrency@theory.lcs.mit.edu
From: pratt@cs.Stanford.EDU
Subject: Re: for the concurrency mailing list
Date: 12 Nov 90 13:20:57 PST (Mon)
```

Leslie's "fraternal suggestions" could easily create the impression that he is for interleaving and I am against. This construes my position too narrowly. Let me set this in the historical perspective of a FOCS-76 paper by Ron Rivest and myself that Leslie attacked at that time.

Ron and I had given an interleaving proof of correctness of our solution of the mutual exclusion problem for two unreliable processes. The gist of our proof was that the many paths through our code fell into 6 classes, permitting a straightforward case analysis each case of which had a simple argument. We found this program by making small random perturbations to a tiny but buggy mutual exclusion protocol. Even after looking at the four instructions of our resulting program for a long time we had absolutely no intuitive understanding of why that perturbation was correct and others very like it were not!

Leslie protested to us that such a proof as ours based on classification of interleavings was inappropriate. He showed us a proof of correctness of our procedure based on a theory he had evolved of why it worked.

Had we considered our program to be the final word on this subject we could well have agreed with Leslie that having an "insightful theory" of our code was worthwhile. After all, the method used to find a prime need not be the best method to convince someone of its primality.

However even assuming that Leslie's proof gave us the additional insight into our procedure that he claimed it should, it seemed to us that our procedure was surely just one of more to come, and that the effort of making up such a theory after the fact was therefore wasted. Furthermore our strategy for discovering new such algorithms depended critically on the automatic nature of interleaving analysis; we had no idea how to write a program which given a random algorithm would generate a theory of how it might work, whereas we knew how to enumerate and check all its interleavings mechanically in a short time.

This was borne out by the subsequent extension of our work by Mike Fischer and Gary Peterson, published in STOC-77. Whereas our solution involved I think 7 states for each of two processes they had 3 states each (3+3, and another solution with 4 states at one process and 2 states at the other, 4+2). They found their very economical solutions by trying out various possible programs and checking all interleavings of each until they found one that worked. They used two such checkers, written independently by Mike and Gary.

Gary did come up with a Lamport-style after-the-fact theory of why their 3+3 mutex procedure worked. Mike's comment to me about that proof was that since they'd already mechanically checked correctness simply by running their procedure through all possible interleavings, this more conventional proof, which had to be manually checked, added nothing to Mike's confidence in the correctness of their procedure, and indeed seemed to him more likely to contain lacunae.

Now I can see clearly that such post hoc theories of these procedures might have a certain esthetic attraction, and might even be useful. My point is not to fault Leslie for coming up with such a theory but only to demonstrate that I am not a religious zealot on the use of interleaving analysis in concurrency. Indeed I still know of no simpler proof of our FOCS-76 algorithm than our 6-case interleaving analysis, and if I were writing it up today I would still prove it correct in that way. Moreover I have no problem with the use of interleaving in any situation to which it is applicable. In particular I have no quarrel with Leslie on the applicability of logics based on interleaving to the problems he listed in his flame.

I trust that Leslie uses a different logic to prove the correctness of his algorithms from the one he uses to prove that those of us who have in the course of twenty-five years gradually moved from writing concurrent programs to reasoning abstractly about them have by so doing turned themselves into charlatans. This was the only fraternal suggestion I found in Leslie's two messages. A century ago the same logic would have demonstrated with equal validity that Cantor was a charlatan.

Vaughan Pratt

(In the course of my obtaining publication clearances from the contributors to this debate in July 1996, Leslie Lamport asked that the following response to the above be included. —Vaughan Pratt)

My objection was not that your proof was "inappropriate", but that it wasn't believable. It was a hand proof based on analyzing about 26 cases. Your paper did not mention, and at the time I knew nothing about, your exhaustive computer checking of the algorithm. I would not have objected to your written "proof" had it been called a sketch of a mechanical verification.

Leslie

`To: concurrency@theory.lcs.mit.edu`
`From: mischu@allegra.tempo.nj.att.com (Michael Merritt)`

Subject: Begin-the great debate-End
Date: Mon, 12 Nov 90 15:45:48 EST

While I can't pretend to follow all the subtleties of the ongoing discussion, I do have a fairly specific query for the proponents of partial orders, growing out of my fairly extensive experience in modeling concurrent algorithms using interleaving.

Specifically, I generally model operations as consisting of a sequence of two atomic events, the beginning and ending of the operation. When communication is involved, these are described as requests and replies. (E.g. Request-Read(register-x), Reply-Read(register-x,value).) When operations run concurrently, their begin and end events occur in an interleaved sequence. Using this approach, I would resolve the $a|b$ vs $ab + ba$ debate by denoting a and b by begin-a,end-a and begin-b,end-b, respectively. Then $a|b$ is the set of sequences: (begin-a,end-a,begin-b,end-b), (begin-b,end-b,begin-a,end-a), (begin-a,begin-b,end-a,end-b), (begin-b,begin-a,end-b,end-a)

and $ab + ba$ is the (very different set)

(begin-a,end-a,begin-b,end-b), (begin-b,end-b,begin-a,end-a).

Similar causally distinct processes would seem to be distinguished by such a semantics, as well.

When refining an operation, I never change the symbols denoting the begin and end of the operation. I simply change the (internal) operations that occur between the begin and end actions.

The begin/end distinction is particularly useful at interfaces, where the system issues a request and the environment responds, or vice-versa.

I am interested in reactions to this method of resolving the (over-emphasized, in my mind) debate.

On multiple observers of concurrent systems: it seems to me that an accurate model of such systems should distinguish between the occurrence of an event and its observation. (I think even the physicists do this much.) A run of such a system then consists of an interleaved sequence of events and their observations. The subsequence experienced by a single observer is obviously consistent with a set of runs.

What's missing?

I'll send references and/or papers if anyone is interested in seeing these ideas applied to algorithmic problems. But I should say that I work within the formal framework (I/O automata) devised by Nancy Lynch and Mark Tuttle.

Now, it is true that in reasoning about concurrent systems I often find myself reasoning about partial orders embedded in the language (set of sequences) denoted by the system, and I am interested in tools that would help me do that. But I am also reluctant to give up induction as a proof technique. Why can't I have both?

Michael Merritt

```
To: concurrency@theory.lcs.mit.edu
From: pratt@cs.stanford.edu
Subject: DO the great debate CONTINUE
In-Reply-To: Your message of Tue, 13 Nov 90 08:49:13 EST.
     <9011131349.AA01750@stork>
Date: 13 Nov 90 12:30:27 PST (Tue)

From: mischu@allegra.tempo.nj.att.com (Michael Merritt)
Specifically, I generally model operations as consisting
of a sequence of two atomic events, the beginning and
ending of the operation
...
What's missing?
```

In fact for deterministic parallel constructs this is a provably sound abstraction (or contrapositively, languages are a fully abstract model with respect to the semantics defined by just sets of such begin-end pairs). Theorem 2.3 of Gischer's thesis (Stanford report STAN-CS-84-1033, 1984) is that two pomsets are language equivalent iff they are digram equivalent. (I don't know why Jay omitted this theorem from the journal version, TCS 61:199-224.) That is, take the operations of one's language to be all pomset-definable operations (namely concatenation, concurrence, $N(a, b, c, d)$, etc.), and let the variables range over arbitrary sets of strings. Then the resulting equational theory, consisting of all equations between terms of this language that are universally true in this interpretation, is the same theory as obtained when the strings are restricted to strings of length two.

Perhaps you don't care about *all* pomset definable operations, but presumably you at least care about two of them, namely concatenation and interleaving. This case can be formally defined and treated without mentioning pomsets or true concurrency at all. In this case the theorem is just about how sets of strings combine under concatenation and interleaving. Jay's theorem 2.3 applies equally to this restricted case.

This seems to provide positive support for the two-event interpretation of operations. But in fact there *is* something missing, namely nondeterminism. (Pomset definable operations such as concurrence, although indeed nondeterministic from a false-concurrency perspective, are properly considered deterministic in the true concurrency world.)

In 1988 Van Glabbeek and Vaandrager asked whether digrams sufficed for the richer language obtained by expanding this deterministic language of pomset-definable operations with the nondeterministic choice operator p+q, interpreted simply as language union. Their initial answer was that a gap now appeared between digrams and trigrams, which they showed with an automaton they called the "owl" because of its shape. They have subsequently extended this result to show that (n+1)-grams make finer distinctions than n-grams for all n.

(This incidentally is a *very* nontrivial result, which took them a long time to find. I tried very hard even just to separate 3 from 4 without success, I guess my brain is out to lunch these days.)

So why don't practitioners notice these phenomena in their work? Presumably because they don't leap out at the casual observer. For just this reason 19th century engineers did not notice discrepancies in their day-to-day work due to relativity and quantum mechanics. It is true that any engineer whose measurements depended on the velocity of light not changing between summer and winter by an amount as large as twice the earth's orbital velocity would be grateful for relativity, but how many engineers in those days felt this was a serious problem?

Nowadays surveyors who use $10,000 interferometers routinely in the field to measure hundreds of feet to an accuracy of hundredths of an inch would find these seasonal variations in the velocity of light very distracting if they existed. The earth's orbital velocity is 29.8 km/s and light travels at 299,800 km/s, so according to the ether theory the length of a 500-foot boundary would appear to be gently oscillating at 32 nanohertz with a peak-to-peak amplitude of 1.2 inches.

By the same token Wien's law did have an odd bump, but how many practicing chemical and other engineers of the day had their work thrown off by it?

Nowadays quantum mechanics explains a host of phenomena that would have started accumulating without explanation at an alarming rate during this century had quantum mechanics not been in place to account for them.

But to early 20th century engineers relativity and quantum mechanics were just theoretical curiosities that one would only notice if one looked extremely closely in the neighborhood of where their delicate effects were to be felt. Perhaps more strikingly, it has been said that a common view among late 19th century physicists was that the structural aspects of physics had been fully elucidated, with the bulk of the remaining work being a matter of measuring everything more accurately.

I suggest that we have much the same situation here. Take the largest concurrent algorithm that anyone has ever proved correct. Is the future of concurrency just a matter of extending the proof techniques that worked there to yet larger code fragments? I don't think so, for the various reasons I gave in my message to David Luckham. As we pass to more widely distributed computations, as the ratio of end-to-end time over bit-to-bit time increases, as observations become more complex, and as glitching intrudes itself into yet more situations, the linear-time model will become a Procrustean bed that some may continue to find the equal of a Beautyrest mattress but that many others will find unreasonably painful.

```
Now, it is true that in reasoning about concurrent systems I
often find myself reasoning about partial orders embedded in
```

```
the language (set of sequences) denoted by the system, and I am
interested in tools that would help me do that.  But I am also
reluctant to give up induction as a proof technique.  Why can't
I have both?
```

I could not ask for a better example of reason (i) in my 1986 IJPP paper (obtainable by ftp from boole.stanford.edu as ijpp.tex,dvi, instructions in Boole's /pub/README) for why people prefer interleaving. Over the years people have built up a substantial workshop full of tools for manipulating strings and sets of strings. Put them in a partial order environment and they feel disoriented and deprived of their tools.

My answer to this reason was that we should remove it by building the tools needed for a universe in which time is partially ordered. To this end my IJPP paper developed a number of language constructs some of which like orthocurrence had no analog in the world of linear orders, and some of which like network composition could be defined for linear orders but were then vulnerable to the Brock-Ackerman anomalies in the presence of nondeterminism.

With regard specifically to induction, my recent paper "Action Logic and Pure Induction" (similarly obtainable from Boole as jelia.{tex,dvi}) shows how to do induction in a wide range of situations, going well beyond languages and binary relations. In commutative action logic the "horizontal" operation ab becomes concurrence, $a|b$. Yet one can still perform induction on iterated concurrence. Another interpretation of ab is orthocurrence, as per my IJPP 86 paper. Again one can do induction with iterated orthocurrence. And as always one can do induction on iterated concatenation, i.e. the usual Kleene star but in other settings than languages and relations, e.g. pomsets, where the concatenation of pomsets is only linear when the given pomsets are linear.

If all you want is the ability to reason as you have always done by induction, that is no reason to replace pomsets by strings.

Tony Hoare disagrees with me that unfamiliarity with partially ordered time is a major obstacle to its greater adoption. I confess I don't have any strong evidence (though the above is one data point), but I do have a very strong feeling that if people felt that they could move from linear time to partial without giving up *any* of their tools, and also appreciated the advantages I and others have been pointing out for partial orders, there would be a lot more such migration than at present.

The argument is sometimes made that linear time is fully abstract for concurrent computation and partial time is not (i.e. it makes unobservable distinctions), e.g. Bengt Jonsson in POPL-89, Jim Russell in FOCS-89, and I think others (I recently saw a mention by Tony Hoare of a similar sounding result by Mark Josephs). While this is true in the domain of Szpilrajn's theorem, outside its domain what happens is that partial time becomes fully abstract while linear time becomes unsound (asserts false equalities), see my paper on this with Gordon Plotkin (pp2.tex,dvi obtainable from Boole as above).

Given the choice of two theories such that, as one moves in and out of the domain of Szpilrajn's theorem, one theory varies between being fully abstract and not fully abstract, but always remaining sound, while the other varies between sound and unsound, but always remaining fully abstract, which would *you* choose?

Vaughan Pratt

```
To: concurrency@theory.lcs.mit.edu
From: Rob van Glabbeek <rvg@frege.Stanford.EDU>
Subject: Begin-the great debate-End
In-Reply-To: Michael Merritt Tue, 13 Nov 90 08:49:13 EST
Date: Tue, 13 Nov 90 16:53:13 PST

    From: mischu@allegra.tempo.nj.att.com (Michael Merritt)
    Date: Mon, 12 Nov 90 15:45:48 EST
    I am interested in reactions to this method of
    resolving the (over-emphasized, in my mind) debate.
```

This idea occurs in many texts on interleaving semantics. The following formulation is taken from HOARE 85: 'The actual occurrence of each event in the life of an object should be regarded as an instantaneous or an atomic action without duration. Extended or time-consuming actions should be represented by a pair of events, the first denoting its start and the second denoting its finish.'

The idea of splitting events with a duration is a very powerful one, and makes that many features of concurrent systems can in principle be modeled adequately in interleaving semantics. However, in a lot of cases one can doubt whether it is *natural* to model a concurrent system in interleaving semantics only, even if this can be done theoretically.

Take for instance the extremely useful distinction between functional behaviour and performance. The idea is that for a given (distributed) system one first studies whether it is functionally correct, and only when this has been shown (ideally), one moves to questions concerning its time/space complexity. The problem that we see in the above 'solution' for dealing with actions with duration, is that the issues of functional behaviour and performance get mixed up. The following trivial example to illustrate this point comes from Frits Vaandrager, but is for the opportunity adapted by me to a setting with biscuit machines.

Suppose we are interested in a vending machine which produces two biscuits when a coin is inserted and then returns to its initial state. The machine should satisfy the following trace-specification S:

$$2 \times (coins - 1) \leq biscuits \leq 2 \times coins,$$

i.e. for each sequential trace of the machine we should have that the number of occurrences of the action biscuit in this trace is bounded by 2 times the occurrences of the action coin and 2 times (coins - 1).

A first proposal for a machine with this property is described by the recursion equation

VMS = coin ; bisc ; bisc ; VMS .

An alternative proposal could be

VMS' = coin ; (bisc || bisc) ; VMS' .

In interleaving semantics we of course have: VMS = VMS'. This means that under certain conditions we may infer that VMS and VMS' have the same functional behaviour. So as soon as we have shown in some appropriate calculus that VMS satisfies S, we can conclude that also VMS' satisfies S. We now can make two observations:

1. Especially when dealing with the functional aspects of the system the above choice of actions seems very natural. Working with actions begin-coin, end-coin, etc. gives an overhead which nobody would like to have. The traditional problem of interleaving semantics, namely combinatorial state explosion, will arise even faster in case actions are split. Moreover the functional equivalence of the two machines can not so easily be determined.

2. Intuitively the situation concerning performance is clear: machine VMS' is *faster* than machine VMS because it will work in parallel. So why not build a semantic theory in which this intuition can be formalized?

In the view of Frits and myself the above considerations strongly plead for a semantic theory with at least *two* notions of equivalence: (1) an interleaving equivalence for dealing with functional aspects, and (2) a non-interleaved equivalence for dealing with performance. The idea is then that at the non-interleaved level actions can have duration and structure, whereas at the interleaving level one abstracts from these aspects and imposes a total order on the actions.

One of the options for the non-interleaved equivalence — in the spirit of Hoare and Merritt — is to say that two processes are to be regarded as equivalent iff their split versions have the same interleavings. This non-interleaved semantics lies somewhere between interleaving semantics and partial order semantics.

```
Similar causally distinct processes would
seem to be distinguished by such a semantics, as well.
```

However not *all* causally distinct processes can be distinguished by such a semantics. Especially when permitting autoconcurrency (the independent execution of two events which on the chosen level of abstraction are considered to be occurrences of the same action) the proposed semantics falls short in a number of aspects:

Consider the processes $(abc||b) + (ab||bc)$ and $(ab||bc)$.

Here ab is the sequential composition of actions a and b, $ab||bc$ is the parallel and independent composition of the processes ab and ac, and $P + Q$ denotes a (nondeterministic) process that behaves either like P or like Q. If we don't care for branching time the left hand side process can be represented by the automata:

```
    *-----a---->*-----b---->*
    ^           ^           ^
    |           |           |
    c           c           c
    |           |           |
    |           |           |
    *-----a---->*-----b---->*-----c---->*
    ^           ^           ^           ^
    |           |           |           |
    b           b           b           b
    |           |           |           |
    |           |           |           |
START-----a---->*-----b---->*-----c---->*
```

After splitting al actions in two the automaton looks like:

```
    *-a0->*-a1->*-b0->*-b1->*
    ^     ^     ^     ^     ^
    |     |     |     |     |
    c1    c1    c1    c1    c1
    |     |     |     |     |
    |     |     |     |     |
    *-a0->*-a1->*-b0->*-b1->*
    ^     ^     ^     ^     ^
    |     |     |     |     |
    c0    c0    c0    c0    c0
    |     |     |     |     |
    |     |     |     |     |
    *-a0->*-a1->*-b0->*-b1->*-c0->*-c1->*
    ^     ^     ^     ^    /^     ^     ^
    |     |     |     |   / |     |     |
    b1    b1    b1    b1 /  b1    b1    b1
    |     |     |     | /   |     |     |
    |     |     |     |/    |     |     |
    *-a0->*-a1->*-b0->*-b1->*-c0->*-c1->*
    ^     ^     ^    /^     ^     ^     ^
    |     |     |   / |     |     |     |
    b0    b0    b0 /  b0    b0    b0    b1
    |     |     | /   |     |     |     |
    |     |     |/    |     |     |     |
START-a0->*-a1->*-b0->*-b1->*-c0->*-c1->*
```

By mirroring the right wing of the automaton in the displayed diagonal one easily sees that all interleavings originating from $(abc||b)$ are already present in the big square $(ab||bc)$. Hence the two processes $(abc||b) + (ab||bc)$ and $(ab||bc)$ (if allowed to exist) are equivalent in Merritt's semantics. Nevertheless one can argue that $(ab||bc)$ can be executed *faster* than $(abc||b) + (ab||bc)$. If all actions a, b and c are considered to take one hour each, and the automata don't wait needlessly, the left hand automaton has the possibility to need one hour more than the right hand one.

A slightly more complicated example shows that in fact it makes a difference whether actions are split in two or in three (considering start, end and halfway actions for instance)!

```
When refining an operation, I never change the symbols
denoting the begin and end of the operation.  I simply
change the (internal) operations that occur between
the begin and end actions.
```

In case you don't allow autoconcurrency - as occurs in the example above - that's fine. In order to capture the more general case, where processes like the one above are considered, you have to do some bookkeeping linking end actions explicitly to begin actions. Otherwise the operation of refining an action fails to be a congruence for your semantical equivalence, i.e. cannot be defined consistently. Counterexamples on request.

```
The begin/end distinction is particularly useful at interfaces,
where the system issues a request and the environment responds,
or vice-versa.
```

Don't misunderstand me; I do think the distinction can be applied usefully.

```
On multiple observers of concurrent systems:  it seems to me
that an accurate model of such systems should distinguish
between the occurance of an event and its observation.  (I
think even the physicists do this much.) A run of such a
system then consists of an interleaved sequence of events and
their observations.  The subsequence experienced by a single
observer is obviously consistent with a set of runs.

What's missing?
```

The coordination, at the end of each single run of the investigated system, of the data obtained by different observers. Suppose that the system $(a||b)$, where the occurrences of a and b may even be considered to be instantaneous events, runs only once, and is observed by two experimenters (traveling in different inertial frames for instance). Then it may happen that one of them observes ab

whereas the other observes ba. If they now would simply drop there observations into a big bag of interleavings where also sequences that where observed during other runs of the system are gathered, their work does not provide evidence for the fact that they are observing $(a||b)$ rather than $(ab + ba)$. However, if the two meet after their observations and compare notes, they may realize that they perceived the very same run of the system in a different way. From this they conclude that a and b must have been executed independently.

```
I'll send references and/or papers if anyone is interested
in seeing these ideas applied to algorithmic problems.
```

Send me.

```
But I should say that I work within the formal framework
(I/O automata) devised by Nancy Lynch and Mark Tuttle.
```

Oh... Well, send me anyway.

```
Now, it is true that in reasoning about concurrent systems I
often find myself reasoning about partial orders embedded in
the language (set of sequences) denoted by the system, and I
am interested in tools that would help me do that.  But I am
also reluctant to give up induction as a proof technique.  Why
can't I have both?
```

Yes, why can't you?
Rob van Glabbeek

```
To: concurrency@theory.lcs.mit.edu
From: lamport@src.dec.com (Leslie Lamport)
Subject: Reply to Pratt
Date: Thu, 15 Nov 90 11:43:10 -0800
```

Vaughan asks

How might a logic based on sets of traces deal with each of the following situations?

1. Distinguish the race implicit in $a|b$ from the race-free situation implied by $ab + ba$.

2. Reason about observations made by a team of distributed observers who agree on what events happened but not in what order.

3. Reason about the possible interleavings of two concurrent sine waves. (Presumably one falls back on some other technique for combining traces than interleaving them.)

The answer is that I don't know and I don't care. These questions never arise in my work.

How can it be that I find these issues to be irrelevant when Vaughan, who's an intelligent and (generally :-) reasonable computer scientist, considers them important? To answer this, I must begin with a discussion of the nature of science.

Any science is ultimately concerned with the real world. A scientific theory consists of a mathematical formalism together with a way of relating that formalism to the real world. For example, Newtonian mechanics consists of a mathematical theory of point masses moving along trajectories in mathematical 3-space, together with a way of relating those mathematical objects to the motions of real objects, such as planets. Note that not every concept in the mathematical formalism need correspond to something in the physical reality–for example, the vector potential of classical electromagnetism has no physical counterpart.

Any useful scientific theory has a limited domain of application. A theory-of-everything is generally good for nothing. Newtonian mechanics can't describe the flow of fluids, for which one needs a theory containing mathematical concepts corresponding to friction and viscosity.

For computer science, the real world usually consists of computers (hunks of wire and silicon) executing programs. Theories in computer science are based on such diverse mathematical formalisms as Turing machines, temporal logic, and CCS.

To judge a scientific theory, one must know what its claimed domain of applicability is. The work of mine that I mentioned in an earlier message involves a theory whose domain is the specification and verification of functional properties of concurrent systems. I won't describe this domain here, except to note that "functional properties" include eventual termination and upper and lower time bounds on termination; they exclude probability of termination and expected time to termination.

Computer scientists have tended to be vague about the domain of applicability of their theories. As a result, people who work in one theory often think their theory is good for everything. For example, I have heard people say that the algebraic laws of CCS make it good for verifying distributed algorithms. CCS works fine for verifying biscuit machines. It is hopelessly impractical for verifying even the simplest distributed spanning tree algorithm, let alone the more complex algorithms that system builders use. Robin Milner realizes this (I've discussed it with him), but many of his disciples don't.

This doesn't mean that CCS is worse than my theory; just that it has a different domain of applicability. It is as silly to say that CCS is better or worse than my theory as it is to say that physics is better or worse than biology. Human nature being what it is, almost all physicists believe in their hearts that physics is more important than biology. However, physicists understand that not everyone believes this, so a university will teach biology even if the dean of faculty is a physicist. One wishes that computer scientists were as understanding.

I think there are two general reasons why a concept that's important to theory A may be absent from theory B:

(i) The concept is irrelevant to the domain of applicability of theory B.

(ii) The concept belongs to the mathematical formalism of theory A and, even though the two theories have overlapping domains of applicability, theory B's method of translating reality into mathematical formalism makes the concept irrelevant or meaningless.

Case (ii) is the more insidious cause of misunderstanding. People get so used to their favorite theory that they confuse its mathematical formalism with physical reality. For example, some advocates of CCS will say that my theory is deficient because it doesn't distinguish between internal and external nondeterminism. They don't realize that internal/external nondeterminism is part of the mathematical formalism of CCS, not a property of physical reality, so there is no reason why it should be a meaningful concept in another theory. This error is not confined to one side of any ideological fence. A colleague of mine once asserted that he could prove any kind of property of a program, since he could prove safety and liveness properties and any property is the conjunction of a safety and a liveness property. He was confusing the real-world concept of a property (in "prove any kind of property") with the mathematical concept of a property as a set of behaviors (in "any property is the conjunction ...").

It can be argued that (ii) is an unavoidable source of misunderstanding, since one can discuss physical reality only in terms of mathematical models. I don't think the situation is so hopeless. We can make statements about the physical world like "if you press this key, then the system crashes" that mean approximately the same thing to everyone, regardless of his philosophical persuasion.

I think that Vaughan's question 3 (sine waves) is an example of (i) and his question 2 (teams of observers) is an example of (ii). His question 1 (race conditions) is more interesting and warrants discussion.

A race condition is bad if it makes the circuit behave incorrectly. When verifying circuits, one is interested only in proving that a circuit behaves correctly, not that it behaves incorrectly. So, one never has to prove the existence of a race condition. The specification of the circuit describes its external behavior, and a race condition is something that happens inside the circuit. So, proving the absence of a race condition is never a primary goal. If there is a potential race condition that never actually occurs–for instance, because of the initial conditions–then the proof will contain a lemma (a mathematical formula) whose physical interpretation will be the absence of a race condition.

However, the concept of a race condition is not irrelevant. A race condition on its inputs might cause a circuit component to produce an invalid output voltage–a "1/2" instead of a "0" or a "1". In this case, a mathematical model of the component that allows only the outputs "0" and "1" is inadequate. With such a model, the domain of applicability of the theory would not include the actual circuit. Fortunately, with more sophisticated models (for example, by including a "1/2" output), I believe it is possible to use my theory to reason about real circuits. (I haven't done such reasoning myself, but others have using similar theories.) The concept of a race condition is relevant for modeling the real circuit in the mathematical formalism, but it doesn't appear in the formalism itself.

Scientific theories are useful because the mathematical formalism is simpler than physical reality. Newtonian physics eliminates an awful lot of important details–like you and me–when it represents the earth as a point mass. Those details are irrelevant for computing planetary orbits. They are not irrelevant for studying human history. Science is the art of simplification.

A theory should be as simple as possible, but no simpler. - Albert Einstein

The test of a scientific theory is how well it helps us understand and/or manipulate the real world.

I will close with a word about mathematics. Many computer scientists aren't scientists at all; they're mathematicians. They work in the domain of mathematical formalism, with no concern for its application to the real world. That's fine. The world needs pure mathematicians as well as scientists. But it's important for mathematicians to realize that they're not scientists. Number theorists don't criticize Newtonian mechanics for using real numbers rather than integers. Computer-scientist/mathematicians should be equally sensible.

[Postscript contributed for this proceedings, Sept. 1996.]

I now believe that one can use process algebra (though probably not pure CCS) to write a practical correctness proof of a spanning-tree algorithm—at least of its safety properties. I'm not sure if this is because the process-algebra folks have made progress, or because I now understand better how to write proofs in process algebra. (On the other hand, progress in assertional methods has not stopped either.)

```
To: concurrency@theory.lcs.mit.edu
From: lynch@holmes.lcs.mit.edu (Nancy A. Lynch)
Subject: On Lamport and Milner
Date: Sat, 17 Nov 90 07:03:36 EST
```

I have been following the debate about trace models with interest, and liked Leslie Lamport's most recent comments. They do seem to get at the heart of the differences between the different research communities.

One of the most interesting (and troubling) comments he makes is the remark about CCS not being useful for verifying distributed algorithms of any complexity; supposedly, Robin Milner agrees with this (!). Now, I thought I understood that a major goal of process algebraic research WAS to verify complex concurrent and distributed algorithms. I would like to hear more about this issue from proponents of CCS-like methods. More specifically, can anyone tell me clearly what types of algorithms such methods are suited for verifying, and what are outside their domain of applicability? If the methods so far have really had only limited success, then is this limitation inherent in the methods (or their intended domain of applicability) or just a matter of time?

Nancy Lynch

To: concurrency@theory.lcs.mit.edu
From: pratt@cs.Stanford.EDU
Subject: Reply to Lamport's reply to Pratt
In-Reply-To: Your message of Fri, 16 Nov 90 18:28:10 EST.
<9011162328.AA05325@stork>
Date: 18 Nov 90 00:04:52 PST (Sun)

[The story so far.] On Oct. 21 David Luckham queried me about an attitude to partial orders that he'd run into during discussions with ONR-funded software people. I shared my reply to David with this list, which led to considerable discussion. On Nov. 6 Leslie Lamport entered the discussion with a complaint that certain parties to this discussion whom he did not name were claiming that he couldn't do what he was doing, an assertion that he could indeed do what he was doing, and a deduction that those parties must therefore be charlatans.

I pleaded innocent to the complaint, agreed with the assertion, and, in case Leslie had me in mind as one of the charged parties, attempted to refute the deduction with some situations where partial orders helped.

Leslie's reply of yesterday (Nov. 16) put my situations into three classes: those outside his world, e.g. sine waves, those in his world but independent of his theory of his world, e.g. multiple observers, and those that potentially conflicted with his theory but which he felt confident his theory could be extended gracefully to handle, e.g. race conditions. He concluded by chastising mathematicians who criticize what scientists do. [Now read on.]

This conclusion leaves me puzzled. While Leslie has defended himself admirably, I cannot tell what criticism stung him into defense. Let me repeat what I said on Nov. 12:

There have been various claims on this list about limitations
of interleaving, but none that I recall making the claims
Leslie was complaining about, nor any that conflicted with the
evidence he adduced in support of his complaint.

Leslie's techniques seem to be fine for their purposes. I don't know why this message isn't getting through.

Echoing Sol Feferman's "Bravo," I heartily concur with the rest of Leslie's stimulating essay, to within the following differences.

The answer is that I don't know and I don't care. These
questions never arise in my work.

I know that and I didn't care at first. Robert Hall supplied the necessary existence proof that there were people on the list who did care, or I would have let the matter rest with just the Nemeti quote from LOP-81 (LNCS 131, p.419), my initial response to Leslie's opening message.

Although Leslie's view of concurrency is adequate for him, it is also somewhat of a straitjacket. There are aspects of concurrency that he does not find worth studying but that others do. Perhaps the implications of those aspects will never insinuate themselves into Leslie's world, but who knows? Which residents of Nagasaki and Hiroshima foresaw the abrupt intrusion of the abstract equation $E = mc^2$ into their world?

```
Fortunately, with more sophisticated models (for example, by
including a "1/2" output), I believe it is possible to use my
theory to reason about real circuits.
```

Yes, this is an excellent idea. Its origins are surely shrouded in history, but it can be found recently in van Glabbeek and Vaandrager's PARLE-87 notion of ST-bisimulation, with Leslie's 1/2 represented as marked transitions. It is also the basis for the "prosset" model Gaifman and I described in LICS-87, a model described more elegantly in "Temporal Structures" (in LNCS 389 21-51, also STAN-CS-89-1297, also available by ftp from boole.stanford.edu as man.{tex,dvi}, and to appear in Math. Struct. in CS 1:2), in terms of the "idempotent closed ordinal" 3'. In Leslie's notation 3' = {0,1/2,1}. This important (non-cartesian-closed) ordinal is also the dualizing object 3 in the Stone-Birkhoff duality described in my POPL-91 paper, though space and time have conspired to let me do little more than name 3 in that paper; a proper account of the dualizing role of 3 will appear in a subsequent paper. The essential idea is that {0,1/2,1}, or {0,T,1} as I call it in the POPL paper, refer respectively to before, transition, and after. A race is characterized by the possibility of having two processes both being in state T. The function of mutual exclusion is to rule out that combination. This is the essential distinction between $a|b$ and $ab+ab$: both permit 8 of the $9 = 3^2$ combinations in $\{0, T, 1\} \times \{0, T, 1\}$, but only the former permits the 9th combination (T,T),

I apologize for the large amount of algebraic machinery in which we have embedded Leslie's 1/2 in some of this work, like Sigourney Weaver in her exoskeleton in Aliens. Those wishing to meet 1/2 in a more comfortable outfit will have to await our return to planet Earth, hopefully soon. Meanwhile let me assure you that this unnerving exoskeleton really does amplify power just like the ads promise. I had no idea by how much until my students started using it on big jobs.

```
CCS works fine for verifying biscuit machines.  It is
hopelessly impractical for verifying even the simplest
distributed spanning tree algorithm, let alone the more complex
```

```
algorithms that system builders use.  Robin Milner realizes
this (I've discussed it with him), but many of his disciples
don't.
```

You could get both Robin and me to agree to this, much as perhaps Robin and certainly I would agree that the axiomatic theory of vector spaces is fine for treating sums and scalar multiples of vectors, but is hopelessly impractical for inverting even the most well-conditioned matrices, let alone the ill-conditioned matrices that arise in transcontinental surveys. Surveyors just want their programs to give the right results, their passion for the axiomatic theory of vector spaces rarely exceeds that of Leslie's for CCS.

```
But it's important for mathematicians to realize that they're
not scientists.
```

This is indeed the popular, standard, and authorized view. Nicolas Goodman makes a strong argument for the opposing view in a recent article entitled "Mathematics as Natural Science," JSL 55(1)182-193 (March 1990).

My own view (I do hope no one is actually paying to receive this stuff:-) strays even further from the standard than Goodman's. I think of us as dealing with incoming data from the world mainly by inventing theories through which this data is filtered to yield predictions about the world; that, *mutatis mutandis* (important), natural selection selects for those theories whose predictions are more accurate; and (the most controversial bit) that the theories most successful at predicting are sufficiently like the most successful theories of pure mathematics that the latter should prove to have good survival value while the former could with little violence be turned into respectable mathematics. The controversial bit has the merit that both directions are in principle testable given suitable advances in AI and brain mapping respectively.

```
A theory-of-everything is generally good for nothing...
For computer science, the real world usually consists of
computers (hunks of wire and silicon) executing programs.
```

It has not escaped the attention of some contributors to concurrency theory that it is starting to look like a "theory of everything." This is the result of abstracting away wire, silicon, and programs to leave a set of abstractions that could as readily be applied to the interactions of galaxies of stars, swarms of bees, and rioting soccer fans as to processes communicating via ethernets, IP/TCP, and remote procedure calls.

However concurrency theory is only a "theory of everything" in the same sense that number theory and group theory are "theories of everything." Just as number theory is more than the theory of counting sheep and beans, and group theory more than a means of proving that quintics don't have solutions expressible in radicals, so is concurrency theory more than the theory of what concurrent "hunks of wire and silicon" do.

There are then two roads one may follow here, the conservative and the liberal. The conservative road requires keeping wire and silicon in mind as the ultimate domain of application of concurrency research. The liberal road replaces "computer science" by "information science" and seeks instead a theory of information processing that will turn out to be applicable to information processors in general, whether dumb like galaxies, smart like bees and computers, or brilliant like us (pats all round).

I am most interested in the liberal road because it seems to me that the techniques of both computer science and engineering, provided they are not artificially constrained, should turn out to be broadly applicable.

For example today's factory designers have only relatively primitive tools to help them develop a design on line, test it out to get a better feeling for how well it might work in practice, turn it into a detailed blueprint for a factory, and make it the basis both for the ongoing operation and maintenance of the factory and for future modifications and redesigns.

The analog of this scenario for software systems is much further along, though it too has far to go or software research would have nothing left to do. There is no reason why the foundations of the latter should not also prove to be equally useful foundations for the former. If this is the case then the taxpayers' research dollars are spent more efficiently by working out concurrency theory so as to fully realize its benefits in all domains to which it is applicable.

I want very badly to follow the liberal road. My big problem has always been that I don't know how to write a good program until I understand the theory of what that program is about. Hence my current preoccupation with theory. This is now well along however, and I hope to be able to start designing and implementing soon. I'm hoping that many of Leslie's excellent ideas will prove useful in aspects of this work.

Vaughan Pratt

```
To: concurrency@theory.lcs.mit.edu
From: Luca Aceto <luca@cogs.sussex.ac.uk>
Subject: Two papers on begin-end
Date: Mon, 19 Nov 90 14:20:31 GMT
```

In the debate on "True Concurrency vs. Interleaving" on the concurrency mailing list some of the recent messages have been concerned with the modeling of the behaviour of concurrent systems under the assumption that actions have a beginning and an ending. We have been working on semantic theories for process algebras based on variations on the above idea and our results are reported in a series of papers, which are available to whoever requests them.

L Aceto, M Hennessy

Towards Action Refinement in Process Algebras
Luca Aceto and Matthew Hennessy
ABSTRACT

We present a simple process algebra which supports a form of refinement of an action by a process and address the question of an appropriate equivalence relation for it. The main result of the paper is that an adequate equivalence can be defined in a very intuitive manner. In fact we show that it coincides with the "timed-equivalence" proposed by one of the authors in [H88]. This is a bisimulation-like equivalence based upon the idea of splitting every action into two sub-actions, the beginning and the end. For the language which we consider this equivalence also coincides with a variation, called "refine equivalence", in which the beginnings and endings of actions with the same name must be properly matched.

Reference: [H88] M. Hennessy, Axiomatizing Finite Concurrent Processes, SIAM Journal on Computing 17(5), pp. 997-1017, 1988.

Adding Action Refinement to a Finite Process Algebra
Luca Aceto and Matthew Hennessy
ABSTRACT

In this paper we present a process algebra for the specification of concurrent, communicating processes which incorporates operators for the refinement of actions by processes, in addition to the usual operators for communication, nondeterminism, internal actions and restrictions, and study a suitable notion of semantic equivalence for it. We argue that action-refinements should, in some formal sense, preserve the synchronization structure of processes and their application to processes should consider the restriction operator as a "binder". We show that, under the above assumptions, the weak version of the refine equivalence introduced in [AH89] is preserved by action refinement and, moreover, is the largest such equivalence relation contained in weak bisimulation equivalence. We also discuss an example showing that, contrary to what happens in [AH89], refine equivalence and timed equivalence are different notions of equivalence over the language considered in this paper.

Reference: [AH89] This is the paper mentioned above.

```
To: concurrency@theory.lcs.mit.edu
From: rounds@caen.engin.umich.edu (Prof Rounds)
Subject: can't resist a comment
Date: Mon, 19 Nov 90 12:09:21 EST
```

I'd like to throw two cents' worth into what seems to be one of the best "bulletin board" discussions I've seen in a long time.

I agree with both Leslie Lamport and Vaughan Pratt. A mathematical model is always just that; it represents our cognitive abstraction of what reality we perceive. The theorems true in the model make predictions, which we then reinterpret in the real world, at least that part of the world which interests us. The best models simplify and constrain reality enough so that they make really strong predictions (I would put the finite-state machine in that category.) Of course, in a particular domain, the model may not account for observed phenomena, and may in fact be contradicted. If one wants to predict these new phenomena, one must refine the mathematical model. This process, though painful for those who believe in the old model, is at the heart of scientific progress.

The preceding paragraph talked about science; there is another point to make about engineering. In the field of computers we have the unprecedented opportunity to create real-world systems which conform to our mathematical perceptions. So, machines were designed to mirror our conception of digital computation; programming languages help us express mathematical algorithms, and so forth. The fascinating thing about concurrency theory is that it seems to be on the fence between science and engineering. We can use it to "explain" race conditions, or we can use it to help us design programs (witness CSP, occam, and the transputer.) Of course this was true about computability theory itself in the 30's and 40's. Witness the creation of the stored-program machine to embody the Universal Turing machine.

One other nice thing about mathematical models is that they port themselves into other domains of applicability. About 4 years ago I was working with a graduate student, Bob Kasper, on some problems in natural language processing. The problem involved specifying disjunctive information in record-like structures – more or less like variant record types are specified in Pascal. We saw a simple way to understand and to implement a system, using extremely basic notions from concurrency theory. Essentially one views a complex record as a transition system. The states are the individual nodes, and the transitions are the field designators. Then the simple logic of Hennessy and Milner, or the simplest possible subcase of deterministic PDL, becomes a way of declaring record types. Once this is seen, there are a lot of ways to reinterpret the concepts of concurrency in data types. I've been using the notions of Smyth and Hoare powerdomains, along with Aczel's non-wellfounded set theory, for example, to help understand and design so-called complex objects in object-oriented databases. Notice that Aczel's work came from an attempt to provide a proper mathematical foundation for SCCS!

The point of this last experience is that one should always keep an open mind, especially where mathematical models are concerned.

Bill Rounds

To: concurrency@theory.lcs.mit.edu

From: Haim Gaifman <hg17@cunixd.cc.columbia.edu>
Subject: Lamport on Spinoza, Science and related matters
Date: Mon, 19 Nov 90 19:39:10 EST

This is rather a belated reaction to some of the claims made in the exchange that has started with Leslie Lamport's message of November 7 ("Flame etc.") While Lamport's observations concerning Aristotles, Kant and Spinoza are marginal to the real issues of the debate, at least one point needs correction:

".... and Spinoza proved that there can be at most seven planets."

As a matter of fact, Spinoza never "proved" that there can be at most seven planets. Lamport is probably confusing Spinoza with Hegel (who lived two centuries later). Somewhere in Hegel's dissertation, so the story goes, is buried an argument purporting to show that the number of planets should be seven.

Perhaps the difference between Spinoza and Hegel does not mean much to Lamport. After all, they were both philosophers, that is to say vaporizing theoreticians making ridiculously unfounded claims. But, as a scientist, he should have gotten his facts straight.

As to the debate itself:

If A claims to have done something that B has proved to be impossible, then either

(i) there is an errors in A's construction,

or

(ii) there is an error in B's proof,

or

(iii) they are speaking about different things.

In cases (i) and (ii) the debate can be clearly decided; the errors are found, one of the claims (perhaps both) is withdrawn and there the matter ends. But this happy state of affairs is mostly a privilege of mathematicians. In philosophy it is usually the third case that obtains. When things get clarified, it turns out that the real issue is not the correctness of a certain proof, but the correct way of defining certain notions, or of setting up a framework. The debate is about which setup is more intuitive, illuminating, fruitful, efficient, etc.

It appears that, in this respect, many computer scientists share the fate of philosophers. What has started as a claim for a contradiction ("I have done something that somebody proved cannot be done") turns out to be a claim about the relative merits of trace models versus partial order models.

Lamport is certainly entitled to the view that the methods developed by him are simpler and more efficient, for the purposes of analyzing and proving correctness of distributed algorithms. No doubt, he can produce his own impressive work as an argument for this view. The claim could be evaluated (certainly not by me!) in a matter of fact way. This does not guarantee that the question would be settled, but at least we would have a clearer view of what is involved. Unfortunately, he has got this bad habit of philosophers to start with an imprecise presentation of the problem.

Another bad influence of popularized philosophy is the temptation to anchor one's views, no matter what the subject is, in some major principles; in the present case maxims about what is and what is not good science are mobilized for the sake of the argument:

```
"Any useful scientific theory has a limited domain of
application.  A theory-of-everything is generally good for
nothing."
```

In one sense, this is a sound rule of thumb that one would hardly wish to quarrel with: The more phenomena you try to accommodate the more likely you are to get an impractical system. The rule has, nonetheless, some spectacular exceptions. A higher level description that encompasses a wider range of phenomena might be more efficient then a narrower view. Every mathematician knows cases in which generalizing (hence strengthening) a theorem leads to a conceptually clearer, hence easier, proof of it. From an Aristotelian point of view Newtonian physics would have been a project unlikely to succeed, because it tried to account for the immense variegated domain of movement phenomena by few simple laws.

As a general *prescription* for science, the above quote goes certainly against the grain that is exemplified by great scientists, such as Newton, Maxwell or Einstein. A "theory-of-everything" is the elusive goal that has motivated big scientific enterprises. What else is the point of the reduction of chemistry to physics, or of finding a unified field theory?

All this has no direct bearing on whether an interleaving model, or a partial order model, or some other abstract model, is more suitable for reasoning about concurrent processes. But in trying to drag in general philosophical principles, Leslie Lamport seems to have committed himself to quite a narrow perspective of science, it is rather an engineer's view than anything else.

Haim Gaifman

```
To: concurrency@theory.lcs.mit.edu
From: Vaughan Pratt <pratt@cs.Stanford.EDU>
Subject: Early pomset paper
Date: Sun, 25 Nov 90 12:25:32 PST
```

If there are any historians of concurrency theory subscribing to this forum they might be interested in the origins (as I understand them) of the term "pomset."

The terms "labeled partial order" and "partial word" had been used previously, but the earliest paper I'm aware of that refers explicitly to partially ordered multisets as a synonym for these notions is:

```
@InProceedings(
```

```
Pr82,   Author="Pratt, V.R.",
        Title="On the Composition of Processes",
        Booktitle="Proceedings of the Ninth Annual ACM Symposium
                on Principles of Programming Languages",
        Month=Jan, Year=1982)
```

However I had not at that time come up with the contraction "pomset." This term was first advertised in a talk I gave on Sept. 13, 1983 at a workshop whose proceedings however were not published until 1985:

```
        @InProceedings(
Pr83,   Author="Pratt, V.R.",
        Title="Two-Way Channel with Disconnect",
        Booktitle="The Analysis of Concurrent Systems:
                Proceedings of a Tutorial and Workshop, LNCS 207",
        Publisher="Springer-Verlag", Year=1985)
```

I also used it in a talk I gave the following week at IFIP-83 in Paris. It appears in the position statement I circulated at that panel, a hundred or so copies of which were distributed to the audience:

```
        @Unpublished(
Pr83b,  Author="Pratt, V.R.",
        Title="Position Statement",
        Note="Circulated at the Panel on Mathematics of Parallel
        Processes, chair A.R.G. Milner, IFIP-83",
        Month=Sep, Year=1983)
```

Now that I look at it again it seems to me that this position statement is quite clear about my motivation in those days for pomsets and how I thought they should be used. Since it's reasonably short and can't be found elsewhere I've appended it below. (My apologies for it's being in Scribe, this was what many of us at MIT and Stanford used back then. Just read the raw Scribe, the only obscurity should be x@-[y], the Scribe for x_y. [Fixed for this proceedings -vp])

The cryptic allusion therein to $ab|ab$ and $N(a, a, b, b)$ refers to the fact, found by my student Jay Gischer, that these two pomsets are language-equivalent. That is, regarded as language operations applied to languages a and b under the evident interpretation, they denote the same language. In 1982 Jay independently came up with the partially ordered multiset concept, though not by that name, while investigating the problem of completely axiomatizing the equational theory of concatenation and shuffle of languages which I had posed to him. Jay reduced my axiomatization problem to the question of whether for any two N-free pomsets, language-equivalence implied isomorphism. I was quite surprised to find the partially ordered multisets of my POPL-82 paper arising so naturally in connection with this question about pure interleaving semantics. Neither Jay nor I found an answer to this question, which I publicized (as an axiomatization question) on various occasions during 1986-1988. It was eventually solved in 1988 by Steve Tschantz, an algebraist at Vanderbilt, in

```
@Unpublished(
Tsch, Author="Tschantz, S.T.",
Title="Languages under concatenation and shuffling (preliminary)",
Note="Manuscript, Department of Mathematics, Vanderbilt
University",
Month=Jun, Year=1988)
```

Steve independently discovered the same reduction of the axiomatization problem to the question about language-equivalence of N-free pomsets, which he answered affirmatively by an ingenious argument. Luca Aceto subsequently applied Tschantz's theorem to infer the surprising result [correspondence, Apr. 1989] that timed-equivalence coincides with trace-equivalence for the language $p ::= 0 \mid a \mid p;p \mid p|p$.

Since 1983, starting with my LOP-85 paper

```
        @InProceedings(
Pr85,   Author="Pratt, V.R.",
        Title="Some Constructions for Order-Theoretic Models of
Concurrency", Booktitle="Proc. Conf. on Logics of Programs,
LNCS 193", Address="Brooklyn", Publisher="Springer-Verlag",
Pages="269-283", Year=1985),
```

which turned into

```
        @Article(
Pr86,   Author="Pratt, V.R.",
        Title="Modeling Concurrency with Partial Orders",
        Journal="International Journal of Parallel Programming",
        Volume=15, Number=1, Pages="33-71", Month=Feb, Year=1986),
```

my thoughts on the appropriate combinators for pomsets have shifted from the network emphasis in my POPL-82 paper and IFIP-83 statement to a more arithmetic kind of language in which pomsets are added and multiplied (and these days exponentiated, whose relevance to concurrency I did not appreciate in 1985). Nowadays, at my student Roger Crew's prodding, I regard network combination as merely one of several variants of addition.

Vaughan Pratt
Nov. 25, 1990

APPENDIX—IFIP-83 STATEMENT

IFIP-83 - Panel on Mathematics of Parallel Processes
Position Statement

V. R. Pratt
Stanford University

September, 1983

Abstract. The notion of function as a set of ordered pairs is mathematically appealing but not quite rich enough for modeling processes. Our position is that it suffices to generalize ordered pairs to pomsets (partially ordered multisets) to obtain a satisfactory notion of process.

Functions. A function abstracts the essence of stimulus-response: it collects all possible stimuli and pairs each with a corresponding response. Furthermore functions obey the principle of behavioral extensionality: two functions with the same set of stimulus-response pairs are considered not merely behaviorally equivalent functions but in fact the same function. These two attributes are captured simultaneously in defining a function from A to B to be a subset of $A \times B$ (with additional conditions when being single-valued and total matters).

Processes. Processes are like functions in some respects. Processes accept stimuli and emit responses. And behavioral extensionality is just as natural for processes as for functions.

A process is not however an ordinary function. It may for example respond to each of a series of numeric inputs with the sum of all inputs to date; this is the behavior of a cumulative "function," which is not really a function since it takes memory to keep a running sum.

Functions on Histories. A process can be made a function if the domain is taken to be sequences of stimuli instead of individual stimuli. That is, a process may be defined to be a function from histories. It is natural to then take the codomain to be histories as well, i.e. a process is a function on histories.

This definition is the basis for the semantics of parallel processes given at IFIP 74 by G. Kahn [K], and elaborated on at IFIP 77 by Kahn and D. MacQueen [KM]. This definition works well for deterministic processes.

The Nondeterminism Anomaly. In 1978 D. Brock and W. Ackerman exhibited an anomaly demonstrating that the straightforward extension of Kahn-MacQueen semantics to nondeterministic processes, namely relations on histories, did not yield sensible behaviors [BA]. They identified the problem as a lack of information about the relative timing of individual input and output events. The Kahn-MacQueen model did not specify any interleaving information between input and output histories. Brock and Ackerman noted that a little additional information of this sort sufficed to dispose of the anomaly at hand.

Our Position. We consider the Brock-Ackerman fix, appropriately formalized [Pr], to provide a very attractive model of processes. Before defining this model we introduce the notion of partially ordered multiset or pomset.

Pomsets. A *pomset* on a set A is, up to isomorphism, a structure $(U, L, \leq)$

consisting of an underlying set U, a labelling function $L : U \to A$, and a partial order $\leq$ on U.

The labels supply the elements of the pomset. The same label can be reused, hence multiset rather than set. Pomsets are defined only up to isomorphism (of structures) because the identity of the underlying set is unimportant; only the labels (the *real* multiset elements) and the order matter.

Main definition. *A process on a set E is a set of pomsets on E.*

Intended Interpretation. E is a set of events. Each pomset of events is one of the possible computations of the process. The order on each pomset is that of necessary temporal precedence; the order of the events in a computation need not be completely specified.

Contrast with Functions. A function is a set of totally ordered doubletons. This definition exposes three differences between functions and processes: the dropping of the cardinality requirement that each element of a function have two elements, the switch from sets to multisets, and the switch from a total order to a partial order.

The cardinality change is motivated by the ongoing nature of a process: many events may need to be considered as part of a single computation. Multisets are needed because an event may be repeated, e.g. the arrival of the number 3. Partial orders are preferred over total because it is not always natural to totally order events - consider for example two communicating processes on Earth and Saturn respectively, each running at nanosecond speeds.

Inadequacy of Total Orders. The use of total rather than partial orders enjoys some currency in modeling parallel processes [H][Pn]. However there does not appear to be a natural way of using total orders to distinguish the following two ways in which two a's might precede two b's.

```
a   a a   a
|   | |\  |
|   | | \ |
|   | |  \|
b   b b   b
```

Thus not only are total orders unnatural, they are not an expressively adequate substitute for pomsets.

Examples. The above-drawn pomsets together form a two-element process. Any n-ary relation (hence binary relation, and hence function) is a process if each n-tuple in the relation is regarded as a totally ordered set. A power set is a process if each element is regarded as a set with the empty partial order. The power set C of a power set B is a process if each element of C is regarded as ordered by inclusion on B: event e necessarily follows event d just when e is d with some additional elements - the process makes progress by accumulating elements and distinct accumulations leading to the same subset are (in this case) considered the same event.

Spatial Localization. In order to put processes in communication with each other it is helpful to know where their events are taking place (cf. [W], p.64). We define an *event space* to be a Cartesian product $C \times D$, consisting of *spatial events*. The intended interpretation is that C is a set of *channels* or *places* (cf. [B]) where the events may be found and D the set of *data* that may be sent over the channels of C. A *spatial process* is a process on an event space.

Nets. A *net* is a process P on $C \times D$ having constituent processes $P_1, \ldots, P_n$ on $C_1 \times D, \ldots, C_n \times D$ respectively. Process P_i is a *constituent* of P just when there exists a function $a_i : C_i \to C$ determining a projection $A_i : P \to P_i$. (a_i gives the attachment of the channels (i.e. ports) of P_i to the channels of the net.) The projection A_i is determined from a_i by taking $A_i(p)$ to be the multiset $\{(c,d)|(a_i(c),d) \in p\}$. Order is preserved, that is, $(c,d) < (c',d')$ in $A_i(p)$ iff $(a_i(c),d) < (a_i(c'),d')$ in p. (Note that A_i need not be onto, i.e. it is not required that P_i equal $A_i(P)$, only that it include it.)

Process Composition. Processes are composed to form a new process in two steps: given the processes P_i with corresponding attachments $a_i : C_i \to C$ for i from 1 to $n-1$, the maximum (under set inclusion) net P having those processes as constituents is formed, and then an additional attachment $a_n : C_n \to C$ is used to determine the projection $A_n : P \to P_n$. The result is $A_n(P)$. The n attachments themselves can thus be seen to determine an $(n-1)$-ary operation on processes.

Example. Ordinary composition of binary relations on D is determined by $C_1 = C_2 = C_3 = \{0,1\}$, $C = \{0,1,2\}$ with $a_1(c) = c$, $a_2(c) = c+1$, and $a_3(c) = 2c$. In this net P_1 and P_2 are composed to yield P_3. This is of course a particularly simple example.

Bibliography

[B] Brauer, W., Net Theory and Applications, Springer-Verlag LNCS 84, 1980.

[BA]Brock, J.D. and W.B. Ackerman, Scenarios: A Model of Non-Determinate Computation. In LNCS 107: Formalization of Programming Concepts, J. Diaz and I. Ramos, Eds., Springer-Verlag, New York, 1981, 252-259.

[H] Hoare, C.A.R., Communicating Sequential Processes, CACM, 21, 8, 666-672, August, 1978,

[K] Kahn, G., The Semantics of a Simple Language for Parallel Programming, IFIP 74, North-Holland, Amsterdam, 1974.

[KM] Kahn, G. and D.B. MacQueen, Coroutines and Networks of Parallel Processes, IFIP 77, 993-998, North-Holland, Amsterdam, 1977.

[M] Milner, R., A Calculus of Communicating Systems, Springer-Verlag LNCS 92, 1980.

[Pn] Pnueli, A., The Temporal Logic of Programs, 18th IEEE Symposium on Foundations of Computer Science, 46-57. Oct. 1977.

[Pr] Pratt, V.R., On the Composition of Processes, Proceedings of the Ninth Annual ACM Symposium on Principles of Programming Languages, Jan. 1982.

[W] Winskel, G., Events in Computation, Ph.D. Th., Dept. Comp. Sci, U. of Edinburgh, Dec. 1980.

```
To: concurrency@theory.lcs.mit.edu
From: Eike Best <gmdzi!eike@relay.eu.net>
Subject: Re: Zeno machines
Date: Wed, 2 Jan 91 16:07:24 -0100
```

In a message shortly before Christmas, Vaughan Pratt writes:

```
>>"Probably the earliest mention of partial orders
>>in respect to concurrency is in Irene Greif's Thesis of 1975..."
```

(quote from memory).

Claim:

Partial ordering ideas have been around at least since the mid–sixties.

A fairly extensive formal discussion of "occurrence graphs" (special partial orders of the type I will describe below) and "occurrence systems" (sets of occurrence graphs) is in:

A.W.Holt: Final Report of the Information System Theory Project. Technical Report RADC-TR-68-305, Rome Air Development Center, Grifiss Air Force Base, New York (1968).

Or compare A.W.Holt: Events and Conditions, Project MAC Conference (1970):

"Two ... occurrences are ordered if they are connected by a directed path. They are then ordered in the sense of the path. ... ... if (two events) are not ordered with respect to one another, (then they are) *concurrent.*"

Or from Suhas Patil's PhD Thesis (Coordination of Asynchronous Events, MIT, June 1970):

"...The events corresponding to the nodes which are ordered must occur in that order but the events corresponding to nodes which are not ordered may occur concurrently."

REPORT DOCUMENTATION PAGE	Form Approved OMB No. 0704-0188

1. AGENCY USE ONLY (Leave blank)	2. REPORT DATE	3. REPORT TYPE AND DATES COVERED
	9/30/96	Final: 4/15/96 - 08/30/96

4. TITLE AND SUBTITLE	5. FUNDING NUMBERS
Workshop on Partial Order Methods in Verification	Grant No: N00014-96-1-0892 PR No.: 96PRO5310-00 P.O. Code: 311 Disbursing Code: N68892 AGO Code: N66018 CAGE Code: 2B898
6. AUTHOR(S) Doron Peled Vaughan Pratt Gerard Holzmann	

7. PERFORMING ORGANIZATION NAME(S) AND ADDRESS(ES)	8. PERFORMING ORGANIZATION REPORT NUMBER
DIMACS, Rutgers University Piscataway, NJ 08855-1179 Stanford University Stanford, CA 94305	

9. SPONSORING/MONITORING AGENCY NAME(S) AND ADDRESS(ES)	10. SPONSORING/MONITORING AGENCY REPORT NUMBER
Office of Naval Research Ballston Tower 800 North Quincy Street Arlington, VA 22217-5660	

11. SUPPLEMENTARY NOTES

12a. DISTRIBUTION/AVAILABILITY STATEMENT	12b. DISTRIBUTION CODE
Approved for public release: distribution unlimited.	

13. ABSTRACT (Maximum 200 words)

This report consists of the written papers presented at POMIV, the Workshop on Partial Order Methods in Verification held at Princeton July 24-26. POMIV is one of the workshops participating in the DIMACS Special Year in Logic, 1995-1996, and also immediately preceded the Federated Logic Conference (FLoC) held at Rutgers July 27-August 3. The theme of the workshop was the transition from the traditional interleaving model of concurrent computation to the "true concurrency" model based on computations as partially ordered sets of events.

14. SUBJECT TERMS	15. NUMBER OF PAGES
Parallel computation, distributed computation, concurrency modeling, true concurrency, partial orders, events, event structures.	16. PRICE CODE

17. SECURITY CLASSIFICATION OF REPORT	18. SECURITY CLASSIFICATION OF THIS PAGE	19. SECURITY CLASSIFICATION OF ABSTRACT	20. LIMITATION OF ABSTRACT
unclassified	unclassified	unclassified	unlimited